John Willis

Screen World

Volume 53
2002

Associate Editor
Barry Monush

APPLAUSE
THEATRE & CINEMA BOOKS

Screen World
Volume 53

Printed in Canada

Library of Congress Card No. 50-3023

ISBN: 1-55783-598-5 (hardcover)
ISBN: 1-55783-599-3 (paperback)

Applause Theatre & Cinema Books
151 West 46th Street, 8th Floor
New York, NY 10036
Phone: (212) 575-9265
Fax: (646) 562-5852
Email: info@applausepub.com
Internet: www.applausepub.com

SALES & DISTRIBUTION

North America:
HAL LEONARD CORP.
7777 West Bluemound Road
P. O. Box 13819
Milwaukee, WI 53213
Phone: (414) 774-3630
Fax: (414) 774-3259
Email: halinfo@halleonard.com
Internet: www.halleonard.com

UK:
COMBINED BOOK SERVICES LTD.
Units I/K, Paddock Wood Distribution Centre
Paddock Wood, Tonbridge, Kent TN12 6UU
Phone: (44) 01892 837171
Fax: (44) 01892 837272
United Kingdom

Table of Contents

EDITOR: JOHN WILLIS

ASSOCIATE EDITOR: BARRY MONUSH

Acknowledgements: Anthology Film Archives, Artistic License, Jenna Bagnini, Castle Hill, Samantha Dean, DreamWorks, Brian Durnin, The Film Forum, First Look, First Run Features, Fox Searchlight, Kino International, Leisure Time Features, Tom Lynch, Mike Maggiore, Miramax Films, New Line Cinema/Fine Line Features, New Yorker Films, October Films, Paramount Pictures, Kristen Schilo, 7th Art Releasing, Sony Pictures Entertainment, Sheldon Stone, Strand Releasing, Twentieth Century Fox, Universal Pictures, Walt Disney Pictures, Zeitgeist Films

Walk on the Wild Side

Period of Adjustment

Barefoot in the Park

They Shoot Horses, Don't They?

Klute

Steelyard Blues

Fun with Dick and Jane

Julia

Coming Home

TO
JANE FONDA

A magnetic and influential talent whose impact reached beyond motion pictures to make her one of the most thought-provoking, outspoken, and unforgettable figures of our time.

FILMS: *Tall Story* (1960); *Walk on the Wild Side* (1962), *The Chapman Report* (1962), *Period of Adjustment* (1962); *In the Cool of the Day* (1963); *Sunday in New York* (1964), *Joy House* (1964); *Cat Ballou* (1965), *Circle of Love* (1965); *The Chase* (1966), *The Game Is Over* (1967), *Hurry Sundown* (1967), *Barefoot in the Park* (1967); *Barbarella* (1968); *Spirits of the Dead* (1969), *They Shoot Horses, Don't They?* (Academy Award nomination, 1969); *Klute* (Academy Award for Best Actress, 1971); *F.T.A.* (also producer, 1972); *Steelyard Blues* (1973), *Tout va Bien* (1973), *A Doll's House* (1973); *Introduction to the Enemy* (1974); *The Blue Bird* (1976); *Fun With Dick and Jane* (1977), *Julia* (Academy Award nomination, 1977); *Coming Home* (Academy Award for Best Actress, 1978), *Comes a Horseman* (1978), *California Suite* (1978); *The China Syndrome* (Academy Award nomination, 1979), *An Almost Perfect Affair* (1979), *The Electric Horseman* (1979); *No Nukes* (1980), *Nine to Five* (1980); *On Golden Pond* (Academy Award nomination, 1981), *Rollover* (1981); *Agnes of God* (1985); *The Morning After* (Academy Award nomination, 1986); *Leonard Part 6* (1987); *Old Gringo* (1989); *Stanley & Iris* (1990).

The China Syndrome

Nine to Five

The Morning After

TOP BOX OFFICE STARS
OF 2001

1. Tom Cruise

2. George Clooney

3. Julia Roberts

4. Russell Crowe

5. Nicole Kidman

6. Denzel Washington

7. Will Smith

8. Brad Pitt

9. Ben Affleck

10. Jackie Chan

2001
Releases

Russell Crowe in
A Beautiful Mind

Julia Stiles, Sean Patrick Thomas

Kerry Washington, Sean Patrick Thomas

Julia Stiles

SAVE THE LAST DANCE

(PARAMOUNT) Producers, Robert W. Cort, David Madden; Director, Thomas Carter; Screenplay, Duane Adler, Cheryl Edwards; Story, Duane Adler; Photography, Robbie Greenberg; Designer, Paul Eads; Editor, Peter E. Berger; Costumes, Sandra Hernandez; Co-Producer, Marie Cantin; Music, Mark Isham; Music Supervisor, Michael McQuarn; Choreographer, Fatima; Ballet Choreographer, Randy Duncan; Casting, Avy Kaufman; a Cort/Madden production, presented in association with MTV Films; Dolby; Deluxe color; Rated PG-13; 105 minutes; Release date: January 12, 2001

CAST

Sara ....Julia Stiles
Derek ....Sean Patrick Thomas
Chenille ....Kerry Washington
Malakai ....Fredro Starr
Roy ....Terry Kinney
Nikki ....Bianca Lawson
Snookie ....Vince Green
Kenny ....Garland Whitt
Diggy ....Elisabeth Oas
Arvel ....Artel Jarod Walker
Lip ....Cory Stewart
Glynn ....Jennifer Anglin
Momma Dean ....Dorothy Martin
Lindsay ....Kim Tlusty
Woman on Train ....Felicia Fields
Mrs. Gwynn ....Ora Jones
Mr. Campbell ....Tab Baker
and Kevin Reid (Wonk), Andrew Rothenberg (Stern Judge), Mekdes Bruk (Lakisha), Ronald Ray (Stepps Slacker), Tai'isha Davis (Tiffnee), Karimah Westbrook (Alyssa), Eric Hubbard (Jasmine), Richmond Talauega (Stepps Dancer), Whitney Powell (Toni), Brenda Pickleman (Older Disgusted Woman), Julie Greenberg (Gymnastics Teacher); Anna Paskeveska (Ballet Instructor), Malaika Paul (Basketball Player), Jennifer Echols (Lavatory Girl), Ellie Weingardt (Ballet Judge's Assistant), Earl Manning, Latisha Oliver, Nefertiti Robinson, Roland "Ro Ro" Tabor, Anthony Talauega, Richard Whitebear, Earl Wright (Hip-Hop Dancers), Ariane Dolan, Chryssie Whitehead, Sarita Smith Childs, Trinity Hamilton, Randy Herrera, Audrey Leung, Katrina Oeffling, Joanna Wozniak (Ballet Dancers), Maia Wilkins, Davis C. Robertson (Sea Shadow Dancers), Michael Anderson, Deanne Brown, Deborah Dawn, Nicole Marie Duffy, Sam Franke, Jennifer Goodman, Taryn Kaschock, Stacy Joy Keller, Calvin Kitten, Michael Levine, Pierre Lockett, Suzanne Lopez, Brian McSween, Jeremiah O'Connor, Emily Patterson, Domingo Rubio, Tracy Shields, Patrick Simonello, Guoping Wang, Teanna Zarro (Les Presages Dancers)

Having given up her dreams of training for ballet at Juilliard, Sara moves in with her father in Chicago's South Side, where she finds romance with hip-hop dancer Derek.

© Paramount Pictures

Julia Stiles, Terry Kinney

Claire Forlani, Ryan Phillippe

ANTITRUST

(MGM) Producers, Nick Wechsler, Keith Addis, David Nicksay; Executive Producers, David Hoberman, Ashok Amritraj, C. E. Erickson, Julia Chasman; Director, Peter Howitt; Screenplay, Howard Franklin; Photography, John Bailey; Designer, Catherine Hardwicke; Editor, Zach Staenberg; Costumes, Maya Mani; Music, Don Davis; Casting, Amanda Mackey Johnson, Cathy Sandrich; an Industry Entertainment production, presented in association with Hyde Park Entertainment; Dolby; Panavision; Color; Rated PG-13; 108 minutes; Release date: January 12, 2001

CAST

Milo Hoffman	Ryan Phillipe
Lisa Calighan	Rachael Leigh Cook
Alice Poulson	Claire Forlani
Gary Winston	Tim Robbins
Bob Shrot	Douglas McFerran
Lyle Barton	Richard Roundtree
Larry Banks	Tygh Runyan
Teddy Chin	Yee Jee Tso
Brian Bissel	Nate Dushku
Phil Grimes	Ned Bellamy

and Tyler Labine (Redmond), Scott Bellis (Randy), David Lovgren (Danny), Zahf Hajee (Desi), Jonathon Young (Stinky), Rick Worthy (Shrot's Assistant), Nathaniel Deveaux (Lawyers), Ian Robison (Lawyers), Linda Ko (Gary's Secretary), Ed Beechner (Ken Cosgrove), Bobby Stewart, Eric Breker, Colin Cunningham (Building 20 Guards), J. R. Bourne (Building 21 Guard), Eric Keenleyside (Coffee Guard), Dayna Devon (TV Interviewer), Ron Halder (Houseman), Sarah Deakins (DOJ Receptionist), Daniel McKellar (Co-Worker), Howard Storey (Rent-a-Guard), Elizabeth Carol Savenkoff (Clarissa Winston), Ingelise Nherlan (Yoga Woman), Peter New, Blaine Perrin (Skinheads), Colin Foo (Grocer), Helena Yea (Grocer's Wife), Kevin Hayes (News Anchor), Claire Riley, Patti Vieta, Rob Court, Scott Fee, Norma Wick, Tamara Taggart, Linden Banks (Reporters), Benita Ha (Party Reporter), Justin Sain, Ricardo Scarabelli, Ian Bliss (Reporters), Peter Goudie, Anees Peterman (Senators), Gregor Trpin (Computer Guy), Peter Howitt (Homeless Man), Julie McDowell (Concerned Guest), Miguel de Icaza, Scott McNealy (Themselves), Brian Walley (Press Photographer), Robert J. Halas (Cameraman), Daniel Cruz, Dino Pallome, Tyson Holmes, Paresh Ramji, Rachel McGinnis, Jason Singer, Francisco Ortiz, Simon Wong, Greg Armstrong-Morris (Geeks), David Clennon (Barry Linder)

Computer genius Milo Hoffman is recruited to join software millionaire Gary Winston's corporation, N.U.R.V., where he begins to suspect illegal and dangerous motives behind his boss's pet project, Synapse, a digital convergence system.

© Metro-Goldwyn-Mayer Pictures, Inc.

DOUBLE TAKE

(TOUCHSTONE) Producers, David Permut, Brett Ratner; Executive Producers, Barry Bernardi, Michael Rotenberg; Director/Screenplay, George Gallo; Photography, Theo Van De Sande; Designer, Stephen Lineweaver; Editor, Malcolm Campbell; Costumes, Sharen Davis; Co-Producers, Steven A. Longi, Frank Pesce; Music, Graeme Revell; Music Supervisors, Gary Jones, Happy Walters; Casting, Marcia Ross, Donna Morong, Gail Goldberg; a Permut Presentations/Rat Entertainment production; Dolby; Panavision; Technicolor; Rated PG-13; 88 minutes; Release date: January 12, 2001

CAST

Daryl Chase	Orlando Jones
Freddy Tiffany	Eddie Griffin
Timothy Jarrett McCready	Gary Grubbs
Agent Norville	Daniel Roebuck
Agent Gradney	Sterling Macer
Agent Martinez	Benny Nieves
Chloe	Garcelle Beauvais
Maque Sanchez	Andrea Navedo
Charles Allsworth	Edward Herrmann
Thomas Chela/Minty Gutierrez	Shawn Elliot
Junior Barnes	Brent Briscoe

and Donna Eskra (Kiki Barnes), Carlos Carrasco (Captain Garcia), Frank Pesce (Vito), Julie Lott (Julie), Robby Robinson (Man in Suit), John M. Seiber (Security Guard), Jeff Griggs (Fashion Show Security Guard), James Gregory, Ted White (Troopers), Tony Genaro (Governor Quintana), Martin Morales (Border Guard), Jimmy Evangelatos (Border Patrol Agent), Raul Julia-Levy (Quintana Driver), George Sharperson (Thug), Joe Gironda (Doorman Joe), Joe Basile, Mark Chalant Phifer (Cops), Brent Sexton, Kevin Will (NYPD Cops), Richard Miro (Federale), Alexander Folk (Amtrak Waiter), Annie O'Donnell, Pamela Kosh (Nuns), Frank Gallegos (Shoeshine Guy), Tom Adams (FBI Agent), Johanna Cypis (Screaming Woman), Shirley Thomas (Lady by Phone), Norm Compton (Mexican Thug), George Czarnecki (Bar Patron #1), Xanthia Decaux (Fiona), Robert Harvey (McCready's Agent), Ana Bianco (Latino Crying Woman), Juan Soto, Jr. (Grieving Boy), Loran Taylor (Charles Allsworth's Wife), Chelsea Bond (Waitress at Malibu), Lisa Zee (Flight Attendant), Willow (Delores), Vivica A. Fox

A New York investment banker, fleeing from the FBI because he's been framed for laundering money for a Mexican drug cartel, switches identity with a petty thief.

© Touchstone Pictures

Orlando Jones, Eddie Griffin

Robin Wright Penn, Jack Nicholson

THE PLEDGE

(**WARNER BROS.**) Producers, Michael Fitzgerald, Sean Penn, Elie Samaha; Executive Producer, Andrew Stevens; Director, Sean Penn; Screenplay, Jerzy Kromolowski, Mary Olson-Kromolowski; Based on the novel *Versprechen* by Friedrich Dürrenmatt; Photography, Chris Menges; Designer, Bill Groom; Editor, Jay Cassidy; Music, Hans Zimmer, Klaus Badelt; Costumes, Jill Ohanneson; Casting, Don Phillips; a Morgan Creek Productions, Inc. and Franchise Pictures presentation of a Clyde Is Hungry Films production; Dolby; Panavision; Color; Rated R; 124 minutes; Release date: January 19, 2001

CAST

Jerry Black	Jack Nicholson
Lori	Robin Wright Penn
Erick Pollack	Sam Shepard
Stan Krolak	Aaron Eckhart
Annalise Hansen	Vanessa Redgrave
Duane Larsen	Michael O'Keefe
Toby Jay Wadenah	Benicio Del Toro
Jim Olstand	Mickey Rourke
Floyd Cage	Harry Dean Stanton
Doctor	Helen Mirren
Gary Jackson	Tom Noonan
Helen Jackson	Lois Smith
Chrissy	Pauline Roberts
Margaret Larsen	Patricia Clarkson
Strom	Dale Dickey
Monash Deputy	Costas Mandylor
Rudy	Beau Daniels
Resort Owner	Wendy Morrow Donaldson
Sheriff	P. Adrien Dorval
Bus Driver	Shawn Henter

and Kathy Jensen (Store Clerk), Taryn Knowles (Ginny Larsen), Nels Lennarson (Hank), J. J. McColl (Real Estate Agent), Gordon May (Criminologist #1), Adam Nelson, Gardinar Millar (Deputies), Tony Parsons (TV Anchorman), Robert Popoff (Prisoner), Nicole Robert (Flea Market Saleslady), Eileen Ryan (Jean), Lucy Schmidt (Alma Cage), John R. Taylor (Grey-Haired Man), Theodore Thomas (Rest Home Resident), Brittany Tiplady (Becky Fiske), Mavourneen Varcoe-Ryan (Crime Scene Reporter), Françoise Yip (Bartender at Airport)

Jerry Black, a recently retired homicide detective, refuses to believe that a case involving the rape and murder of several little girls has been solved and settles down with a young single mother and her daughter with the intention of continuing his quest for the real criminal.

© Franchise Pictures, LLC

Jack Nicholson

Jack Nicholson, Aaron Eckhart, Sam Shepard

Patricia Clarkson, Michael O'Keefe, Jack Nicholson

THE WEDDING PLANNER

(COLUMBIA) Producers, Peter Abrams, Robert L. Levy, Gigi Pritzker, Deborah Del Prete, Jennifer Gibgot; Executive Producers, Nina R. Sadowsky, Moritz Borman, Chris Sievernich, Guy East, Nigel Sinclair; Director, Adam Shankman; Screenplay, Pamela Falk, Michael Ellis; Photography, Julio Macat; Designer, Bob Ziembicki; Costumes, Pamela Withers; Editor, Lisa Zeno Churgin; Co-Producer, Carrie Morrow; Music, Mervyn Warren; Music Supervisors, Mary Ramos, Michelle Kuznetsky; Casting, Mary Gail Artz, Barbara Cohen; an Intermedia Films presentation of a Tapestry Films/Dee Gee Entertainment/IMF Production in association with Prufrock Pictures; Dolby; Panavision; Deluxe color; Rated PG-13; 102 minutes; Release date: January 26, 2001

CAST

Mary Fiore	Jennifer Lopez
Steve Edison	Matthew McConaughey
Fran Donolly	Bridgette Wilson-Sampras
Massimo	Justin Chambers
Penny	Judy Greer
Salvatore	Alex Rocco
Mrs. Donolly	Joanna Gleason
Mr. Donolly	Charles Kimbrough
Dr. John Dojny	Kevin Pollak
Basil St. Mosely	Fred Willard
Burt Weinberg	Lou Myers
Dottie	Frances Bay
Geri	Kathy Najimy
Mary Fiore (7 years old)	Cortney Shounia
Benton	Philip Pavel
Crying Bride	Natalie Jaroszyk

and F. William Parker (Father of the Bride, Mr. Bartlett), Caisha Williams (Self-Conscious Bridesmaid), Dan Finnerty (Best Man), Fabiana Udenio (Anna Bosco), Bree Turner (Tracy, Bride), Don West (Bernard), Susan Mosher (Frieda), Peter Brown (Justice), Adam Loeffler (Boy in Hospital), Chelsea Hollingsworth, Bianca Brockl (Girls in Hospital), Karon Bihari, Nikki Arlyn (Guests), Seth Howard (Bellhop), Greg Lauren (Keith), Magali Amadei (Wendy), Phil Chong (Taxi Driver), Lydell Cheshier (Guard in Statue Park), Dee Dee Weathers (Bride, Copeland Wedding), Harry Danner (Wedding Minister), Anthony Katala (Wedding Photographer), Betsy Brockhurst (Sister Elizabeth Scrabble), Huntley Ritter (Groom), Joan Del Mar (Renee), Raphaela Kleiman (Flower Girl), Rocco Vienhage (Man)

After a chance encounter with Dr. Steve Edison, wedding planner Mary Fiore finds herself falling in love, only to discover that Steve is the groom-to-be of her newest and most lucrative account.

© Columbia Pictures Industries Inc.

Matthew McConaughey, Jennifer Lopez, Bridgette Wilson-Sampras

Jennifer Lopez, Matthew McConaughey

Matthew McConaughey, Jennifer Lopez

Justin Chambers, Matthew McConaughey

Marley Shelton, Melissa George, Mena Suvari,
Sara Marsh, Rachel Blanchard, Alexandra Holden

James Marsden

SUGAR AND SPICE

(NEW LINE CINEMA) Producer, Wendy Finerman; Executive Producers, Claire Rudnick Polstein, Matt Moore, Greg Mooradian; Director, Francine McDougall; Screenplay, Mandy Nelson; Co-Producer, Michael Nelson; Photography, Robert Brinkmann; Designer, Jeff Knipp; Editor, Sloane Klevin; Music, Mark Mothersbaugh; Costumes, Wendy Chuck; Cheerleading Consultant, Beth Knutson; Choreographer, Amber Struzyk; Casting, Juel Bestrop, Jeanne McCarthy; a Wendy Finermann production; Dolby; Super 35 Widescreen; Color; Rated PG-13; 81 minutes; Release date: January 26, 2001

CAST

Lisa	Marla Sokoloff
Diane	Marley Shelton
Cleo	Melissa George
Kansas	Mena Suvari
Hannah	Rachel Blanchard
Fern	Alexandra Holden
Lucy	Sara Marsh
Jack	James Marsden
Mrs. Hill	Sean Young
Hank	W. Earl Brown
Geeky Guy	Adam Busch
Ted	Jake Hoffman
Chris	Nate Maher
Bruce	David Belenky
Factory Worker	Kevin Kling
Apartment Manager	Dave Quimby
Food Valley Cashier	Jacy Dumermuth
Principal Smith	Wiley Harker

and Stevie Ray Rentfrow (Diane's Dad—Dennis), Kirsten Frantzich (Diane's Mom—DeeDee), Christopher Denton (Jack's Dad—Ed), Jan Puffer (Jack's Mom—Edna), Claudia Wilkens (Grandmother), Jeff Hopkins (Police Officer), Kevin Joseph Klein (FBI Agent), Jeremy Kent Jackson, Jamison Haase (Football Players), Jessie Schoen (Butch Girl), Susan Fuller (Bank Loan Officer), Andy Hubbell (Husband), Katie Kelly (Nurse), Ann Kellog (Mink), Isabell Monk, Miriam Must, Jenner Snell (Inmates), Andrea Guilford (Lamaze Instructor)

When pregnant teenager Diane finds herself in deep financial trouble, she convinces her fellow cheerleaders to help her rob a bank.

© New Line Cinema Inc.

Amanda Peet, Jack Black, Steve Zahn

Jack Black, Steve Zahn

Neil Diamond, Jason Biggs, Jack Black, Steve Zahn

Jason Biggs, Amanda Detmer

SAVING SILVERMAN

(COLUMBIA) Producer, Neal H. Moritz; Executive Producers, Bruce Berman, Bernie Goldmann, Brad Luff, Peter Ziegler; Director, Dennis Dugan; Screenplay, Greg DePaul, Hank Nelken; Photography, Arthur Albert; Designer, Michael Bolton; Editor, Debra Neil-Fisher; Music, Mike Simpson; Music Supervisors, Michelle Silverman, Mary Ramos; Co-Producer, Warren Carr; Costumes, Melissa Toth; Casting, Mary Vernieu, Anne McCarthy, Felicia Fasano; a Village Roadshow Pictures presentation in association with NPV Entertainment, of an Original Film production; Dolby; Super 35 Widescreen; Deluxe color; Rated PG-13; 91 minutes; Release date: February 9, 2001

CAST

Wayne Le Fessier	Steve Zahn
J. D. McNugent	Jack Black
Darren Silverman	Jason Biggs
Judith	Amanda Peet
Sandy	Amanda Detmer
Coach	R. Lee Ermey
Himself	Neil Diamond
Bar Dude	Kyle Gass
Minister	Norman Armour
Old Man	Colin Foo
Vageet	Chris Logan

and Esme Lambert (Raccoon Woman), Max Fomitchev (Mime), Tony Parsons (Newscaster), Brett Armstrong (Brett), Patrick Pfrimmer (Clayton), Frank Frazier (Bouncer), Andrew McIlroy (Waiter), Oscar Goncalves (Man), Lillian Carlson (Mother Superior), Eli Ranger (Young Darren), Ivan Jurcev (Young J. D.), Devin Douglas Drewitz (Young Wayne), Carly McKillip (Cute Girl), Carla Boudreau (Beautiful Woman), Phil Trasolini (Referee on Sideline), David Neale, Mary Ann Skoll (Cops at Police Station), Biski Gugushe (Cop at Darren's House), Gus Lynch (Security Guard), Mark Wagner (Luigi), Steven McMichael (Josh), Larry Lam (Thai Kickboxer), Stephen Chang (Thai Referee), Eliza Murbach (Wayne's Mom), Blake Stovin (Wayne's Dad), Brittany Moldowan, Katlyn Ducharme (Little Girls), Michael Roberts (Doctor), Frank Hache (Abe), Odessa Munroe, Tracy Trueman (Hookers), Nicole Robert (Nun), Nancy J. Lilley (Bearded Lady), David Mylrea (Dogfaced Boy), Dario De Iaco (Strong Man), Eleana Johnson, Margaret Ryan (Old Ladies), Lowela Jotie, Shannon Bennett, Theresa Coombe, Leigh Hilary-Lakin, Jennifer Armstrong, Linda Bernath (Cheerleaders), Dennis Dugan (Ref)

After their best friend Darren takes up with a pretentious woman who forbids him to see his pals, Wayne and J. D. formulate a plan to reunite Darren with his high-school sweetheart.

13

Anthony Hopkins, Julianne Moore

Francesca Neri, Giancarlo Giannini

Anthony Hopkins (in hospital)

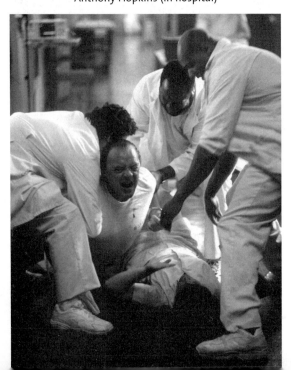

HANNIBAL

(**MGM/UNIVERSAL**) Producers, Dino De Laurentiis, Martha De Laurentiis, Ridley Scott; Executive Producer, Branko Lustig; Director, Ridley Scott; Screenplay, David Mamet, Steven Zaillian; Based upon the novel by Thomas Harris; Photography, John Mathieson; Designer, Norris Spencer; Editor, Pietro Scalia; Music, Hans Zimmer; Costumes, Janty Yates; Casting, Louis DiGiaimo; a Scott Free production, presented in association with Dino De Laurentiis; Dolby; Technicolor; Rated R; 131 minutes; Release date: February 9, 2001

CAST

Hannibal Lecter	Anthony Hopkins
Clarice Starling	Julianne Moore
Mason Verger	Gary Oldman
Paul Krendler	Ray Liotta
Barney	Frankie R. Faison
Pazzi	Giancarlo Giannini
Allegra Pazzi	Francesca Neri
Dr. Cordell Doemling	Zeljko Ivanek
Evelda Drumgo	Hazelle Goodman
FBI Agent Pearsall	David Andrews
FBI Director Noonan	Francis Guinan
DEA Agent Eldridge	James Opher
Gnocco	Enrico Lo Verso
Carlo	Ivano Marescotti
Matteo	Fabrizio Gifuni
Piero	Alex Corrado
Tommaso	Marco Greco
Sogliato	Robert Rietti
Officer Bolton	Terry Serpico
Special Agent Burke	Boyd Kestner
Special Agent Brigham	Peter Shaw
FBI Mail Boy	Kent Linville
Asst. Mayor Benny Holcombe	Don McManus
Larkin Wayne	Harold Ginn
BATF Agent Sneed	Ted Koch
FBI Agent	Wm. Powell Blair II
"Il Mostro" Detective	Aaron Craig
Agent Benetti	Andrea Piedimonte
Ricci	Ennio Coltorti
Young Boy in Plane	Ian Iwataki
Perfume Experts	Mark Margolis, Ajay Naidu, Kelly Piper
FBI Tech (Lecter's Letter)	Bruce MacVittie
Verger's Fingerprint Technician	Giannina Facio
Police Officer	Andrew C. Boothby
Police Sergeant	Kenneth W. Smith
Theatergoer	Roberta Armani
Mr. Konie	Johannes Kiebranz
Dante	Bruno Lazzaretti
Beatrice	Danielle de Niese

and Judie Aronson, Tom Trigo, Sam Wells, Ric Young, Joseph M. West, Jr. (News Reporters)

A millionaire who was hideously deformed during an encounter with Dr. Hannibal Lecter, swears revenge on his assailant, who has managed to elude the FBI for ten years by living undercover in Venice. This is the third film to feature the character of Dr. Hannibal Lecter, who was first played by Brian Cox in the 1986 DeLaurentiis Films release Manhunter *and then by Anthony Hopkins in the 1991 Orion release* The Silence of the Lambs. *Hopkins and Frankie Faison repeat their roles from the latter film.*

Julianne Moore,
Anthony Hopkins

(Below) Anthony Hopkins, Giancarlo Giannini

(Below) Anthony Hopkins, Julianne Moore

(Below) Ray Liotta, Julianne Moore

(Below) Anthony Hopkins, Ray Liotta

RECESS: SCHOOL'S OUT

(WALT DISNEY PICTURES) Producers, Paul Germain, Joe Ansolabehere, Stephen Swofford; Director, Chuck Sheetz; Creators, Paul Germain, Joe Ansolabehere; Story, Joe Ansolabehere, Paul Germain, Jonathan Greenberg; Screenplay, Jonathan Greenberg; Music Score, Denis M. Hannigan; Dialogue Director, Paul Germain; Voice Casting, Allyson Bosch; Supervising Film Editor, Nancy Frazen; Art Director/Lead Character Designer, Eric Keyes; Original Character Design, David Shannon; Visual Development, Plamen Christov, Bob Schaefer, Jose Zelaya; Technical Director, Glo Minaya; Storyboard Supervisors, David Knott, Brad Vandergrift; Associate Producer, Michael Tyau; Song: "Green Tambourine" by Shelley Pinz and Paul Leka/Performed by Robert Goulet; Dolby; Color; Rated G; 84 minutes; Release date: February 16, 2001

Vince, T.J., Spinelli, Gretchen, Gus, Mike

VOICE CAST

Vince	Rickey D'Shon Collins
Mikey	Jason Davis
Gretchen	Ashley Johnson
T. J	Andy Lawrence
Gus	Courtland Mead
Spinelli	Pamela Segall
Principal Peter Prickly	Dabney Coleman
Mikey's Singing Voice	Robert Goulet
Becky	Melissa Joan Hart
Fenwick	Peter MacNicol
Ms. Finster/Mrs. Detweiler	April Winchell
Benedict	James Woods

and Dan Castellaneta, Diedrich Bader (Guards), Allyce Beasley (Miss Grotke), Gregg Berger (Tech #1), Klee Bragger (Digger Sam), Clancy Brown (Bald Guy), Toran Caudell (King Bob), Rachel Crane (Ashley Q), E. G. Daily (Cap'n Sticky), R. Lee Ermey (Colonel O'Malley), Ron Glass (Dr. Lazenby/Tech #2), Tony Jay (Dr. Rosenthal), Clyde Kusatsu (Mr. Yamashiro), Charles Kimbrough (Mort Chalk), Tress MacNeille (Lunch Lady #2/Opera Director/Dr. Steinheimer), Andrea Martin (Lunch Lady #1), Anndi McAfee (Ashley A), Mark Robert Myers (Technician), Ryan O'Donohue (Digger Dave/Randall), Phil Proctor (Golfer #2/Scientist #2), Patrick Renna (Jordan), Nick Turturro, Kevin Michael Richardson (Cops), Jack Riley (Golfer #1), Justin Shenkarow (Soldier Kid/Wrestler Kid), Michael Shulman (Hustler Kid), Francesca Marie Smith (Ashley B/Swinger Girl/Upside-Down Girl), Kath Soucie (Counselor), Robert Stack (Superintendent), Ken Swofford (Coach), Erik Von Detten (Captain Brad/Lawson), Paul Willson (Coach Kloogie/Mr. Detweiler)

T. J. Detweiler summons his friends back from summer camp when he suspects mysterious doings at their supposedly empty school. Based on the ABC series Recess that debuted in 1997.

© Disney Enterprises, Inc.

(Below) Charlize Theron, Keanu Reeves

SWEET NOVEMBER

(WARNER BROS.) Producers, Erwin Stoff, Deborah Aal, Steven Reuther, Elliott Kastner; Executive Producer, Wendy Wanderman; Co-Producer, Marty Ewing; Director, Pat O'Connor; Screenplay, Kurt Voelker; Story, Paul Yurick, Kurt Voelker; Based on a screenplay by Herman Raucher; Photography, Edward Lachman; Editor, Anne V. Coates; Music, Christopher Young; Music Supervisor, G. Marq Roswell; Designer, Naomi Shohan; Costumes, Shay Cunliffe; Associate Producer, Jodi Ehrlich; Casting, Risa Bramon Garcia, Randi Hiller; a 3 Arts Entertainment production, presented in association with Bel-Air Entertainment; Dolby; Technicolor; Rated PG-13; 119 minutes; Release date: February 16, 2001

CAST

Nelson Moss	Keanu Reeves
Sara Deever	Charlize Theron
Chaz	Jason Isaacs
Vince	Greg Germann
Abner	Liam Aiken
Raeford Dunne	Robert Joy
Angelica	Lauren Graham
Brandon	Michael Rosenbaum
Edgar Price	Frank Langella
Manny	Jason Kravits
Buddy Leach	Ray Baker
Al	Tom Bullock
Osiris	Adele Proom
DMV Doctor	L. Peter Callender
Beatrice	June Lomena
Burly Man	Kelvin Han Yee
Homeless Man	David Fine
Lexy	Elizabeth Weber
Chinese Woman	Doreen Croft
Waitress	Susan Zelinsky

and Kathy Garver (Nurse), Chuck Isen (Bald Man), Igor Hiller, Chase Oliver, Nathan McAlone (Kids), Garth Kravits (Techie Nerd), Karina Andrews (Office Manager), Sanford Marshall (Clown on Train), Tessa Koning-Martinez (Marie), Diane Amos (Coffee Shop Waitress), Jeffrey Patrick Dean, Diana C. Weng, Milo Young, Meghan Marx, Reuben Grundy (Art Department Coordinators), Raquel Aurillia (Cute Cashier), Kaliopi Eleni (Woman on Train), Eric Kouba (Big Brother Organizer), Kathy McGraw (Billy Boy's Mother), Tyler Bell (Billy Boy), Ann W. Leon (Hospital Administrator), John Lewis (Jack the Barman)

Sara Deever invites uptight advertising executive Nelson Moss to move in with her for the month of November, intending to make him into a more caring individual. Remake of the 1968 Warner Bros. film that starred Sandy Dennis and Anthony Newley.

© Warner Bros. Pictures and Bel-Air Pictures, LLC.

Eugene Levy, Chris Rock, Chazz Palminteri

Chris Rock, Regina King

Chris Rock, Greg Germann, Jennifer Coolidge

DOWN TO EARTH

(PARAMOUNT) Producers, Sean Daniel, Michael Rotenberg, James Jacks; Executive Producers, Chris Rock, Barry Berg; Directors, Chris Weitz, Paul Weitz; Screenplay, Chris Rock, Lance Crouther, Ali LeRoi, Louis CK; Based on the film *Heaven Can Wait*, screenplay by Elaine May and Warren Beatty, from the film *Here Comes Mr. Jordan*, screenplay by Sidney Buchman and Seton I. Miller, from the play *Heaven Can Wait* by Harry Segall; Photography, Richard Crudo; Designer, Paul Peters; Editor, Priscilla Nedd Friendly; Music, Jamshied Sharifi; Executive Music Producers, Ken Kushnick, Bill Stephney, Matt Walden; Costumes, Debrae Little; a Village Roadshow Pictures presentation in association with NPV Entertainment of an Alphaville 3 Arts Entertainment production; Dolby; Deluxe color; Rated PG-13; 87 minutes; Release date: February 16, 2001

CAST

Lance Barton	Chris Rock
Sontee	Regina King
King	Chazz Palminteri
Keyes	Eugene Levy
Whitney Daniels	Frankie Faison
Cisco	Mark Addy
Sklar	Greg Germann
Mrs. Wellington	Jennifer Coolidge
Wanda	Wanda Sykes
Phil Quon	John Cho
Apollo MC	Mario Joyner
Gospel Singer	Bryetta Calloway
Rosa	Martha Chaves
Charles Wellington	Brian Rhodes
Trashman	Herb Lovelle
Heckler	Kedar
Doorman	Adam Dannheiser
Singers	Malcolm Devine, Colette Wilson, Maiesha McQueen
Women in Balcony	Robin Montague, Hollie Harper
Bouncer	Scott Wickware
Middle-Aged Guy (Bob Krantz)	Jack Newman
Elderly Man	William Lynn
Party Girl (Tina Lovette)	Leah Miller

and David Huband (Maitre D' Serge), Woodrow W. Asai (Asian Man), Laz Alonzo (BET Announcer), Dennis Pressey (MC at Comedy Shack), Arnold Pinnock (Joe Guy), David M. Rodriguez (Flower Delivery Man), Linda Sithole, Gwen Stewart, Chris Ausnit (Protesters), Mary Burton (Reporter Outside Hospital), Jernard Burks (Man in Wheelchair), Clement Moorman (Patient), Hollis Granville (Sick Person), Mung Ling Tsui (Reporter Inside Hospital), Paulette Sinclair (Blanche), Ali LeRoi (Crazy Hostile Dreadlock Guy), Reginald Footman (Dreadlock's Buddy), Michael Port (Mugger), Colin Fox, Paul Hecht, Jack Jessop (Directors), Kenny Robinson (Club MC), Mary Kate Law (Fur Protester), Roger Kugler (Hit Man), Roma Torre (Portraying Herself), Harlin Kearsley (Mike Green), Dan Duran (Reporter)

After comedian Lance Barton is prematurely sent to heaven, he is allowed to return to earth where he is given a new body, that of a millionaire who has just been bumped off by his scheming wife. Remake of Heaven Can Wait *(Paramount, 1978), which starred Warren Beatty, and of* Here Comes Mr. Jordan *(Columbia, 1941), which starred Robert Montgomery.*

© Paramount Pictures

Monkeybone, Brendan Fraser

Chris Kattan

(Below) Citizens of Downtown

(Below) Bridget Fonda, Brendan Fraser

MONKEYBONE

(20TH CENTURY FOX) Producers, Michael Barnathan, Mark Radcliffe; Executive Producers, Lata Ryan, Henry Selick, Sam Hamm, Chris Columbus; Director, Henry Selick; Screenplay, Sam Hamm; Based on the graphic novel *Dark Town* by Kaja Blackley; Photography, Andrew Dunn; Designer, Bill Boes; Editors, Mark Warner, Jon Poll, Nicholas C. Smith; Costumes, Beatrix Aruna Pasztor; Music, Anne Dudley; Music Supervisor, Dawn Solér; Visual Effects Producer, Terry Clotiaux; a 1492 Production; Dolby; Deluxe color; Rated PG-13; 92 minutes; Release date: February 23, 2001

CAST

Stu Miley ....Brendan Fraser
Julie McElroy ....Bridget Fonda
Organ Donor Stu..Chris Kattan
Voice of Monkeybone ....John Turturro
Hypnos ....Giancarlo Esposito
Kitty ....Rose McGowan
Herb..Dave Foley
Kimmy ....Megan Mullally
Head Surgeon ....Bob Odenkirk
Burger God Representative ....Pat Kilbane
Medusa..Lisa Zane
Death..Whoopi Goldberg
Alice..Sandra Thigpen
Hutch..Wayne Wilderson
Clarissa ....Amy Higgins
Dr. Edelstein..Alan Gelfant
Nurse ....Kristin Norton
Bazoom Toy Representative ....Chris Hogan
Beautiful Fan ....Wendy Fowler
and Jamie Donovan, Paul Guiles (Reporters), Skyler Marshall (Janitor), Brendan Burns (Detective #1), Jason Kravitz, Lucy Butler (Guests), John Sylvain (Driver), Lou Romano (Cop), Leon Laderach (Surgeon in Nightmare), Scott Rogers, Chris Thomas Palomino, Tony Pantera (Surgeons), Ted Rooney (Grim Reaper), Christopher Franciosa (Reaper Who Takes Lulu), Mary Stein (Lulu), Randall Bosley (Fred), Fred Pierce (Reaper in Death's Office), Harper Roisman (Earl Biegler), Kristopher Logan (Patron), Scott Workman (Arnold the Super Reaper), Shawnee Free Jones (Lizzie Borden), Ilia Volok (Rasputin), Edgar Allan Poe IV (Edgar Allan Poe), Claudette Mink (Typhoid Mary), Jon Bruno (Man in the Dungeon), Owen Masterson (Jack the Ripper), Jen Sung Outerbridge (Attila the Hun), Mike Mitchell (George), Tracy Zahoryn, Sunshine Deia Tutt, Jo Haugen Gash, Lindsay Bryan, Brooke Boisse, Meron Abebe, Mie Kringelbach (Models), Sybil Azur, Anne Fletcher, Diane Mizota (Museum Dancers), Etty Lau (Sax—All-Girl Band), Latonya Holmes (Percussion—All-Girl Band), Leslee Jean Matta (Drummer—All-Girl Band), Rachen Assapimonwait (Korean Father), Veena Bishasha (Statue Woman), M. Anthony Jackson (Bug Man), Doug Jones (Yeti), Arturo Gil (Rat Guard), Jody St. Michael (Centaur), Frit Fuller, Frat Fuller (3-Headed Devil), Brian Steele (Elephant God), Leif Tilden (Cyclops), Tom Fisher (Community Service Cigarette Sweeper), Joseph Griffo (BBQ Pig), Kim Timbers Patteri (Wasp Woman), Lisa Ebeyer (Betty the Bovine), Wayne D. Doba (Scorpion), Mark Viniello (Ass Backward), Nathan Stein (Sea Monster), Ed Holmes (Buffalo Kachina), Erica Gudis, Melinda Milton., Caroline A. Rice (Party-Babe Hybrids), Michael MacFarlane (Bull Double), Michael Hammond (Reaper Performer); Character Voices: Joe Ranft (Streetsquash Rabbit), Bruce Lanoil (Streetsquash Racoon), Debi Durst (Streetsquash Snake), Phil Brotherton (Subramansa), Roger Jackson (Arnold the Super Reaper), Jym Dingler (Community-Service Cigarette Sweeper), Toby Gleason (Buffalo Kachina)

After an accident puts him in a coma, Stu Miley, creator of a popular comic strip called Monkeybone, finds his conscious spirit transported to a carnival-like purgatory called Downtown, while his simian creation takes over his earthly form.

© Twentieth Century Fox

Arquette, Russell, Costner, Slater, Woodbine

Kurt Russell, Courteney Cox

Kurt Russell, Kevin Costner

Kevin Costner, Courteney Cox

3000 MILES TO GRACELAND

(WARNER BROS.) Producers, Demian Lichtenstein, Richard Spero, Eric Manes, Elie Samaha, Andrew Stevens; Executive Producers, Don Carmody, Tracee Stanley; Director, Demian Lichtenstein; Screenplay, Richard Recco, Demian Lichtenstein; Photography, David Franco; Designer, Robert DeVico; Costumes, Mary McLeod; Editors, Michael Duthie, Miklos Wright; Music, George S. Clinton; Casting, Pam Dixon Mickelson; a Morgan Creek and Franchise Pictures production in association with Lightstone Entertainment; Dolby; Super 35 Widescreen; Color; Rated R; 125 minutes; Release date: February 23, 20001

CAST

Michael Zane.	Kurt Russell
Murphy	Kevin Costner
Cybil Waingrow	Courteney Cox
Hanson	Christian Slater
Damitry	Kevin Pollak
Gus	David Arquette
Jay Peterson	Jon Lovitz
Jack.	Howie Long
Quigley	Thomas Haden Church
Franklin	Bokeem Woodbine
Hamilton	Ice-T
Jesse Waingrow	David Kaye
Otto Sinclair	Louis Lombardi

and Shawn Michael Howard (Roller Elvis), Michael Kopsa (Jefferson), Daisy McCrackin (Megan), Sharron Leigh (Naomi), J. W. Carroll (Captain Vanucci), Paul Anka, Eric James, Tim Misney (Pitt Bosses), Kim Hawthorne (Panel Operator), Craig March (Supervisor), Rod Lake (Mack), Norma Campbell (Elevator Old Lady), Gianni Russo (Money Cart Guard), John Casino (Federal Marshal), Hamilton von Watts (Announcer), Lorraine Cote (Slot Old Woman), David Meeker (Security Guard), Kenneth Anderson (Old Indian), Morgan H. Margolis, Aubrey Jordan, Terry Chen (Policemen), 'r' Nelson Brown (Motor Inn Clerk), Luis Moro (FBI Man), Ross Haines (Gas Station Dad), Christine Chatelain (Sexy Waitress), Michael Busswood (Tourist), Charles Andre (Big Trucker), Campbell Lane (Billy), Raoul Ganeev (Taxi Driver), Mark Acheson (Dockmaster), Peter Bryant (Tom Matthews), John Destrey (Marcus Tittlebaum), Mike St. John Smith (Eugene Gribbs), Scott Swanson (Greg Forester), Doug Abrahams (Det. Steve Finn), Mary Ann Skoll (Paramedic), Dave Babych (Mt. Vernon Cop), Mark Gibbon (Boise Cop), Frank C. Turner (Impound Shop Man), Don MacKay (Judge Carmody), Demian Lichtenstein (Shoplifter), Susse Budde (News Reporter), Colm O'Faolain, Max Goldblatt (Impersonators), Tom Heaton (Captain Elden), Ralph Alderman (Holding Tank Officer), Brian Drummond (Washington State Trooper), Larry Holdridge, Robert "Bobby Z" Zajonc (Helicopter Pilots), Peter Kent (Swat Leader), Greg Miller, Michael Conti, Eddie Powers, Steve Connolly, Jesse Garon, Tim Welch, Jim Leboeuf, Lawrence McMurray, Johnny Edwards (Dancing Elvises), Jennifer Gagliano, Yvonne Grace, Jill Landess, Georgie Bernasek, Angelina McCoy, Laura Lago, Jamie Preston, Melinda Harambasic, Daniella Murray, Terri Gomez (Viva Las Vegas Showgirls), Rice Honeywell (Swat Member), Kevin Mundy (Station Clerk), Renee Cherrier (Cashier), Shelly Lien (Vegas Babe), Marci Lake, Kelly Carlson, Rob Lake, Dante D'Ambruoso, Tim Hoctor, Kerry Puccio, Eric Arlt, Robert Martin, Tony Alves, Jeanette Lee, Bart Dorsa, Stephanie Swinney, Dave Dunlap, Alberto Mastrangelo, Wayne Harter, "J. G." Jim Grant, Duncan Keller, Skylark, Staz (Motocycle Gang)

A group of criminals arrives in Las Vegas during an Elvis Presley impersonation convention to rob a casino.

© 3000 Miles Productions, Inc.

Aunjanue Ellis, Samuel L. Jackson

THE CAVEMAN'S VALENTINE

(UNIVERSAL FOCUS) Producers, Danny DeVito, Michael Shamberg, Stacey Sher, Scott Frank, Elie Samaha, Andrew Stevens; Executive Producers, Samuel L. Jackson, Julie Yorn, Eli Selden, Nicolas Clermont; Co-Producers, Michael Bennett, James Holt, Pamela Abdy; Director, Kasi Lemmons; Screenplay, George Dawes Green, based on his novel; Photography, Amelia Vincent; Designer, Robin Standefer; Editor, Terilyn A. Shropshire; Co-Executive Producers, Stephanie Davis, Jonathan Weisgal; Associate Producers, Michael Drake, Tracee Stanley; Music, Terence Blanchard; a Franchise Pictures presentation of a Jersey Shore production in association with Arroyo Pictures; Dolby; Color; Rated R; 105 minutes; Release date: March 2, 2001

Samuel L. Jackson

CAST

Romulus Ledbetter	Samuel L. Jackson
David Leppenraub	Colm Feore
Moira Leppenraub	Ann Magnuson
Arnold	Damir Andrei
Lulu	Aunjanue Ellis
Sheila	Tamara Tunie
Cork	Peter MacNeill
Joey/No Face	Jay Rodan
Matthew	Rodney Eastman
Bob	Anthony Michael Hall
Betty	Kate McNeil
Shake/Greater No Face	Leonard Thomas
Boy Toy/Andy	Joris Jorsky
Toupee	Pierre Alcide
Walter	Richard Fitzpatrick
Scotty Gates	Sean MacMahon
Penny	Vija Brigita Grosgalvis
Chore	Phillip Jarrett
Manuel	Cecil Phillips

and Henry Stram (Social Worker), Carla Collins (First Reporter), Deborah Lobban (Librarian), Erik Laray Harvey (Young Rom), Mica Le John (Young Lulu), Joanne Jang (Beauty/Cassandra), Alex Karzis (Byzantine Emperor/Dan), Val Boyle (Lucinda); Andre Matthews, Horace Abel, Phillip Harding, Dave Smith, Warren Belle, Lyriq Bent, Robert Warner, Richard Fagon, Julian Adigun, Ken Sylvan, Chad Keens-Douglas, Barrington Bignall, Blair Liburd, Glen Miller, Junior Brown (Seraph Dancers), John Strong, Lowell Hall, Nicholas Shand, Fern Bellavance (Seraph Musicians)

Samuel L. Jackson, Anthony Michael Hall

A former classical musician, now living as a vagrant in Manhattan, begins to snap out of his mentally unhinged state after he discovers the corpse of a young drifter outside of his cave-like dwelling.

Ann Magnuson, Samuel L. Jackson

Julia Roberts, Brad Pitt

Brad Pitt

James Gandolfini, Julia Roberts

Brad Pitt, Julia Roberts

THE MEXICAN

(DREAMWORKS) Producers, Lawrence Bender, John Baldecchi; Executive Producers, William Tyrer, Chris J. Ball, Aaron Ryder, J. H. Wyman; Director, Gore Verbinski; Screenplay, J. H. Wyman; Photography, Dariusz Wolski; Designer, Cecilia Montiel; Editor, Craig Wood; Costumes, Colleen Atwood; Co-Producer, William S. Beasley; Music, Alan Silvestri; Casting, Denise Chamian; Presented in association with Newmarket; Dolby; Panavision; Technicolor; Rated R; 123 minutes; Release date: March 2, 2001

CAST

Jerry Welbach	Brad Pitt
Samantha Barzell	Julia Roberts
Leroy	James Gandolfini
Ted	J. K. Simmons
Nayman	Bob Balaban
Well-Dressed Black Man	Sherman Augustus
Frank	Michael Cerveris
Car Thief	Richard Coca
Beck	David Krumholtz
Joe the Pawnshop Owner	Castulo Guerra
Arnold Margolese	Gene Hackman
Emanuelle	Maira Serbulo
Gunsmith	Salvador Sanchez
Gunsmith's Assistant	Alan Cianguerotti
Gunsmith's Daughter	Melisa Romero
Tropillo	Ernesto Gomez Cruz
Raoul	Daniel Escobar
Estelle	Dale Raoul
Bobby Victory	Jeremy Roberts

and Jorge Malpica (Mexican Gas Station Clerk), Pedro Armendariz (Mexican Policeman), Steve Rossi (Vegas M.C.), Clint Curtis (Vegas Busboy), Lawrence Bender (Vegas Onlooker), Ariane Pellicer (Mexican Ticket Agent), Carlos LaCamara (Car Rental Rep), Daniel Zacapa (Bartender), Alfredo Escobar, Luis Artagnan (Car Thieves), Fermin Martinez (Chicken Farmer), Jose Carlos Rodriguez (Hotel Clark), Gustavo Aguilar (Junk Yard Proprietor), Lucia Pailles (Mexican Woman—Phone), Gilberto Barraza (2nd Man with Gun), Humberto Fernandez Tristan (Nobleman), Luis Felipe Tovar (Nobleman's Son), Fausta Torres (Elderly Mexican Lady), Lolo Navarro (Chosen Grandmother), Emiliano Guerra (Small Boy with Flashlight), Miguel Angel Fuentes (Big Thief #4), Angelina Pelaez (Mother), Harrison Fuller (Big Tom), Gerardo Taracena (Reveler to Fire Gun), John Pisci, Rudy Aikels, Ronald Simone (Musicians)

Despite his promise to girlfriend Samantha that he will sever his ties with the mob, two-bit bagman Jerry Welbach agrees to one last job, to drive down to Mexico to retrieve a priceless antique pistol.

© DreamWorks LLC and Pistolero Productions LLC

SERIES 7: THE CONTENDERS

(USA FILMS) Producers, Jason Kliot, Joana Vicente, Christine Vachon, Katie Roumel; Executive Producer, Charles J. Rusbasan; Director/Screenplay, Daniel Minahan; Co-Executive Producers, Judith Zarin, Tom Brown, Mike Escott; Co-Producers, Evan T. Cohen, Gretchen McGowan; Associate Producer, Pamela Koffler; Line Producer, Libby Richman; Photography, Randy Drummond; Designer, Gideon Ponte; Editor, Malcolm Jamieson; Music, Girls Against Boys; Music Supervisor, Julie Panebianco; Costumes, Christine Bieselin; Casting, Susan Shopmaker; a Blow Up Pictures presentation of a Killer Films/Open City Films production; Dolby; DuArt color; Rated R; 88 minutes; Release date: March 2, 2001

CAST

Dawn	Brooke Smith
Connie	Marylouise Burke
Jeff	Glenn Fitzgerald
Tony	Michael Kaycheck
Franklin	Richard Venture
Lindsay	Merritt Wever
Sheila	Donna Hanover
Doria	Angelina Phillips

and Mark Woodbury (Dairy Mart Clerk), Tom Gilroy (Dawn's Cameraman), Nada Despotovich (Michelle), Stephen Michael Rinaldi (Craig), Alex Yershov (Nathan), Danton Stone (Bob), Joseph Barrett (Doctor), Shawna Moore (Nurse), Jennifer Van Dyck (Laura), Tanny McDonald (Dawn's Mother), Caitlin Bateman (Colby), Robin Borden, Lauren Ward (Doria Look-Alikes), Aydin Bengisu, Josh Mosby (Jeff Look-Alikes), Babo Harrison (Dawn Look-Alike), Will Arnett (Narrator), Adena Shea Loomis (Ultra Sound Baby), Pamela Wehner (Dispatch Operator), Kirsten Krohn, William Graves (Promo Voices)

Dawn, the reigning champion of The Contenders, *a reality television show in which six random people are selected to kill one another, hopes to win the final round and end her obligation to the series.*

Brooke Smith

(Below) Glenn Fitzgerald, Brooke Smith

Bob, Michael Clarke Duncan

SEE SPOT RUN

(WARNER BROS.) Producers, Robert Simonds, Tracey Trench, Andrew Deane; Executive Producers, Michael Alexander Miller, Bruce Berman; Co-Producers, John Peters Kousakis, Ira Shuman; Director, John Whitesell; Screenplay, George Gallo, Gregory Poirier, Danny Baron, Chris Faber; Story, Andrew Deane, Michael Alexander Miller, George Gallo; Adaptation, Stuart Gibbs, Craig Titley; Photography, John Bartley; Editor, Cara Silverman; Designer, Mark Freeborn; Costumes, Diane M. Widas; Music, John Debney; Visual Effects, Perpetual Motion Pictures; Casting, Roger Mussenden; a Village Roadshow Pictures and NPV Entertainment presentation of a Roger Simonds production; Dolby; Technicolor; Rated PG; 94 minutes; Release date: March 2, 2001

CAST

Gordon Smith	David Arquette
Agent Murdoch	Michael Clarke Duncan
Stephanie	Leslie Bibb
Gino Valente	Joe Viterelli
James	Angus T. Jones
Benny	Anthony Anderson
Sonny Talia	Paul Sorvino
Arliss Santino	Steven R. Schirripa
Agent Cassavettes	Kim Hawthorne
Ricky	Kavan Smith

and Peter Bryant, Fiona Hogan (Cops), Roger Haskett (Michaels), Fulvio Cecere (Lawyer), Stephen E. Miller (Danvers), Darcy Laurie (Perierra), Sara-Jane Redmond (Agent Sharp), Rachel McGinnis (Starchild), J. B. Bivens (Desk Sgt.), Tom Shorthouse (Elderly Van Driver), Jason Low (FBI Agent), Farrell Spence (Petting Zoo Driver), Irene Karas (Neighbor), Brena James (Woman at Park), Colin Foo (Shuttler Van Driver), Michael Stunczyk (Tommy), Bill Dow (Doctor), Marcus Hondro (Inmate), Pat Waldron, Rick Tae (Dog Owners), Sadie Lawrence, Lisa Benner (Signing Women), Maria J. Cruz (Woman Watching), Kandyse McClure (Attractive Woman), Dan O'Connell (Voice of Spot)

Stephanie, desperate for a baby-sitter, leaves her six-year-old son with Gordon, an inept mailman in whose van an FBI bull mastiff, wanted by the Mafia, has taken refuge.

15 MINUTES

(NEW LINE CINEMA) Producers, David Blocker, John Herzfeld, Keith Addis, Nick Wechsler; Executive Producer, Claire Rudnick Polstein; Director/Screenplay, John Herzfeld; Photography, Jean Yves Escoffier; Designer, Mayne Berke; Editor, Steve Cohen; Music, Anthony Marinelli, J. Peter Robinson; Costumes, April Ferry; Associate Producers, David Gaines, James M. Freitag; Casting, Mindy Marin; an Industry Entertainment/Tribeca production; Dolby; Super 35 Widescreen; Deluxe color; Rated R; 120 minutes; Release date: March 9, 2001

CAST

Eddie Flemming	Robert De Niro
Jordy Warsaw	Edward Burns
Robert Hawkins	Kelsey Grammer
Leon Jackson	Avery Brooks
Nicolette Karas	Melina Kanakaredes
Emil Slovak	Karel Roden
Oleg Razgul	Oleg Taktarov
Daphne Handlova	Vera Farmiga
Bobby Korfin	John DiResta
Captain Duffy	James Handy
Tommy Cullen	Darius McCrary
Himself	Bruce Cutler
Rose Hearn	Charlize Theron
Cassandra	Kim Cattrall
Mugger	David Alan Grier
Milos	Vladimir Mashkov

and Arina Gasanova (Tamina), Noelle Evans (Honey), Mindy Marin (Maggie), Christine Claibourne (Maggie's Assistant), Paul Herman (Paulie), Gabriel Casseus (Unique), Joe Lisi (Police Captain), Stephen Davis (Murphy), Bill Stanton (Garcia), Louis F. Garcia (Fire Chief), Mike Camello (Fireman Camello), Tygh Runyan (Stephen Geller), Barry Bluejan (Immigration Supervisor), Ritchie Coster (News Stand Vendor), Roseanne, Peter Arnett (Themselves), Ashton Dane (Talk Show Father), Gail Greaves (Talk Show Wife), Bobby Fields (Talk Show Son), Anton Yelchin (Boy in Burning Building), Lynette Ruiz (Sketch Artist), Kurt Andon (Pizza Man), Rikki J. Klieman (Daphne's Lawyer), Sebastian Roche (Ludwig), Kata Dobo (Red Head at Ludwig's), Elma Vann (Linda), Olga Morgounova, Dorit Sauer (Escort Service Women), Haik Garibyan, Marco Kahn (Emigrants), Toni Kalem (Woman at Planet Hollywood), Jorge H. Guzman (Bouncer), Lennox Brown (Lookout Guy), George Poulos (Greek Waiter), Sylvia Lopez Ferullo, Jane Velez Mitchell (Newscasters), Bryan Foster (Hawkins' Cameraman), Alan Cohen (Hawkins' Sound Man), Spiros Stamboulis (Nicolette's Cameraman), Joseph Alfieri (Reporter), Barry Primus (Cab Driver), Julieta Espinoza (Unique's Girlfriend), Brantley Bush (Fireman), Macy Merced, Tracey Mulqueen (Paramedics), Scotty Dillin (Battery Park Policeman), Dominic Maylione, Ron Wall (Police Officers)

An arson investigator and a media-hungry homicide detective team up to stop a pair of killers who have been videotaping their crimes.

© New Line Cinema Inc.

Oleg Taktarov

Edward Burns

Kelsey Grammer

(Below) Melina Kanakaredes, Robert De Niro

Ben Foster, Colin Hanks, Sisqó

Shane West, Melissa Sagemiller, Ben Foster

Kirsten Dunst, Mila Kunis

GET OVER IT

(MIRAMAX) Producers, Michael Burns, Marc Butan, Paul Feldsher; Executive Producers, Jill Sobel Messick, Jeremy Kramer; Director, Tommy O'Haver; Screenplay, R. Lee Fleming, Jr.; Co-Producer, Louise Rosner, Richard Hull, Leanna Creel; Photography, Maryse Alberti; Designer, Robin Standefer; Editor, Jeff Betancourt; Music, Steve Bartek; Music Supervisors, Elliot Lurie, Randy Spendlove; Songs, Marc Shaiman, Scott Wittman; Costumes, Mary Jane Fort; Casting, Kim Davis-Wagner, Justine Baddeley; an Ignite Entertainment and a Morpheus production; Dolby; Super 35 Widescreen; Color; Rated PG-13; 86 minutes; Release date: March 9, 2001

CAST

Kelly	Kirsten Dunst
Berke Landers	Ben Foster
Allison	Melissa Sagemiller
Dennis	Sisqó
Striker	Shane West
Felix	Colin Hanks
Maggie	Zoë Saldana
Basin	Mila Kunis
Beverly Landers	Swoosie Kurtz
Frank Landers	Ed Begley, Jr.
Dr. Desmond Forrest Oates	Martin Short
Mistress Moira	Carmen Electra
Themselves	Vitamin C, Coolio
Peter Wong	Christopher Jacot
Dora Lynn	Kylie Bax
Little Steve	Dov Tiefenbach
Jessica	Jeanie Calleja
Chook	Park Bench
Grendan	Daniel Enright
Hugh	Andrew McGillivray
Shirin	Megan Fahlenboch
Coach Hibble	Jonathan Whittaker

and Shawn Roberts (Colin), Sadie LaBlanc (Jamilla), Jodan Madley (Corrine), Ravi Steve Khajuria (Del Molden, Jr.), Tommy O'Haver ("Love Matters" Director), Reuben Thompson (EMT), Roger McKeen, Chris Benson (Cops), Albert Chung (Trombonist), Antoinette Delond, Krista Leis, Judy Stoimenov, Larissa Gomes (Strippers), Jeffrey Wong, Shawn Fernandez, Catherine Hernandez (Attendants/Fairies), Lindsay Cole (Hippolyta), Dolores Ettienne (Sweet Old Lady), Michael Kremko (Guy in Restaurant), Danny Truelove (Little Boy in Restaurant), Jack Babock, Michael Coristine (Boy Band Members), Christine Nowland, Brent Bushnell, Amy Todd, Troy P. Liddell, Joshua Feldman, Louis Paquette, Jesse Robb, Jenn Butler, Mario Castillo, Michael Boisvert, Krista Martins, Patrick Patterson, Chloe Randel Reis, Diane Fabian, Bradley Garrick, Jamie Holmes (Dancers)

Dumped by the girl he's dated for years, Berke Landers turns to his best friend's sister, Kelly, for love advice.

© Miramax Films

(Below) Kirsten Dunst, Martin Short

Anthony LaPaglia, Douglas McGrath

COMPANY MAN

(PARAMOUNT CLASSICS) Producers, John Penotti, James W. Scotchdopole, Rick Leed, Guy East; Co-Executive Producers, Nigel Sinclair, Matt Williams, Susan Cartsonis, Jon Ein, Robert Greenhut; Directors/Screenplay, Douglas McGrath, Peter Askin; Photography, Russell Boyd; Designer, Jane Musky; Costumes, Ruth Myers; Editor, Camilla Toniolo; Music, David Nessim Lawrence; Casting, Ellen Lewis; an Intermedia Films presentation in association with Foundry Film Partners of a Wind Dancer Films/GreeneStreet Films production; Dolby; Color; Rated PG-13; 86 minutes; Release date: March 9, 2001

Alan Cumming

CAST

Allen Quimp	Douglas McGrath
Daisy Quimp	Sigourney Weaver
Crocker Johnson	John Turturro
General Batista	Alan Cumming
Fidel Castro	Anthony LaPaglia
Rudolph Petrov	Ryan Phillippe
Nora	Heather Matarazzo
Officer Fry	Denis Leary
Ms. Judge	Terry Beaver
Mother Quimp	Kathleen Chalfant
Officer Hickle	Paul Guilfoyle
Senator Biggs	Jeffrey Jones
Danny	Matt Ross
Lowther	Woody Allen

and Reathel Bean (Senator Farwood), Harriet Koppel (Stenographer), Sean Dugan (Skull and Bones Waiter), Grant Walden (Older Man), Nathan Dean (Younger Man), John Randolph Jones (Fobbs), Kim Merrill (Woman in Line), Merwin Goldsmith (Mr. Brisk), Larry Clarke (Fred Quimp), Sandy McGrath (Tom Quimp), Frank Brosens (Chuck Quimp), Luis Placer (Man on the Beach), Norberto Kerner (Cuban Waiter), Jane Reed Martin (Betty Crichton), Liz Welch Tirrell (Sally Smith), Octavio Gómez (Field Worker), Darlene Tejeiro (Rosa), Raul Aranas (Guard #1), José Ramón Rosario (Audience Member), Andrew Driscoll, Bill Greenlee, David McKinley, Brian Nelson (The Lifeguards), Matteo Gómez (Aide), John McDonnell (Emissary), Pablo Cunquiero (Cuban Man), Tuck Milligan (President Kennedy), Susanna Hobrath, Lisa Ganz, Susan Stout (JFK Women), Steven Banks (Officer Emmons)

John Turturro, Sigourney Weaver

In order to impress his social-climbing wife, mild-mannered grammar teacher Allen Quimp pretends to be a CIA agent, a fib that ultimately gets him mixed up in real spy work in Cuba, where he is asked to depose Fidel Castro.

Ryan Phillippe

Guy Pearce

Carrie-Anne Moss

Guy Pearce

MEMENTO

(NEWMARKET) Producers, Jennifer Todd, Suzanne Todd; Executive Producer, Aaron Ryder; Co-Executive Producers, William Tyrer, Chris Ball; Co-Producer, Elaine Dysinger; Director/Screenplay, Christopher Nolan; Based on the short story by Jonathan Nolan; Photography, Wally Pfister; Designer, Patti Podesta; Costumes, Cindy Evans; Editor, Dody Dorn; Music, David Julyan; Casting, John Papsidera; a Team Todd production, presented in association with Summit Entertainment; Dolby; Panavision; Fotokem color; Rated R; 116 minutes; Release date: March 16, 2001

CAST

Leonard Shelby	Guy Pearce
Natalie	Carrie-Anne Moss
Teddy	Joe Pantoliano
Burt	Mark Boone Junior
Waiter	Russ Fega
Leonard's Wife	Jorja Fox
Sammy	Stephen Tobolowsky
Mrs. Jankis	Harriet Sansom Harris
Doctor	Thomas Lennon
Dodd	Callum Keith Rennie
Blonde	Kimberly Campbell
Tattooist	Marianne Muellerleile
Jimmy	Larry Holden

Leonard Shelby, suffering from the inability to form any new memories, chases after the murderer of his wife, a person whose identity he cannot possibly know for sure.

This film received Oscar nominations for original screenplay and editing.

© Newmarket

Joe Pantoliano, Guy Pearce

Guy Pearce,
Carrie-Anne Moss

EXIT WOUNDS

(WARNER BROS.) Producers, Joel Silver, Dan Cracchiolo; Executive Producer, Bruce Berman; Co-Producer, John M. Eckert; Director, Andrzej Bartkowiak; Screenplay, Ed Horowitz, Richard D'Ovidio; Based on the novel by John Westermann; Photography, Glen MacPherson; Designers, Paul Denham Austerberry; Editor, Derek G. Brechin; Music, Jeff Rona, Damon "Grease" Blackman; Costumes, Jennifer Bryan; Casting, Rick Pagano, Diane Kerbel; a Silver Pictures production, presented in association with Village Roadshow Pictures and NPV Entertainment; Dolby; Super 35 Widescreen; Technicolor; Rated R; 117 minutes; Release date: March 16, 2001

Anthony Anderson, Steven Seagal

DMX

CAST

Orin Boyd	Steven Seagal
Latrell Walker	DMX
George Clark	Isaiah Washington
T. K.	Anthony Anderson
Strutt	Michael Jai White
Hinges	Bill Duke
Annette Mulcahy	Jill Hennessy
Henry Wayne	Tom Arnold
Daniels	Bruce McGill
Montini	David Vadim
Trish	Eva Mendes
Useldinger	Matthew G. Taylor
Parker	Paolo Mastropietro
Fitz	Shane Daly
Shaun	Drago-On
Linda	Jennifer Irwin
Rory	Daniel Kash
Housewife	Quancetia Hamilton
Jail Guard	Rick Dennis

and Jason Stephens, Peter Kosaka (Lab Technicians), Chris Lawford (Vice President), Noah Danby (Terrorist Leader), Shakira Harper (Static Waitress), Eduardo Gómez (Father), Yanina Contreras (Mother), Mario Torres (José), Jenny Celly (Maria), Rothaford Gray (Norris), Dean Monroe McKenzie (Carlson), Tom Seniuk, Bobby Johnston, Neville Edwards (Secret Service Agents), Arnold Pinnock (Morris), Gregory Vitale (Car Salesman), Shawn Lawrence (O'Malley), John Ralston (Mulcahy's Date), Simon "Tiger Twins" Kim, James "Tiger Twins" Kim, Shekib Ahmad Foroughi, Ekundayo Odesanyo, Christopher Oster (Thugs), Naomi Gaskin (George's Wife), Phillip Jarrett, Michael Boisvert, John McConnach, Moses Nyarko, Eldridge Hyndman (SWAT Guys), Elio Campbell, Mark Williams (Cops), Stromm Bradshaw (Stormy), Shannon Jobe, Kym Krystalie (Strippers), Peter Walsh (Ducati Guy), Gary Johnston, Joe Alberico, Stone Conway, Barrington Bignall, Greg Zajac, Ed Semenuk, David Boyce, Jaime Estrada (Anger Management Group)

A Detroit police officer is transferred to the tough 15th District where he investigates Latrell Walker, a mysterious drug dealer, whose actions are not what they seem.

© Warner Bros.

Morris Chestnut, D.L. Hughley, Bill Bellamy, Shemar Moore

THE BROTHERS

(SCREEN GEMS) Producers, Darin Scott, Paddy Cullen; Executive Producer, Doug McHenry; Director/Screenplay, Gary Hardwick; Photography, Alexander Gruszynski; Designer, Amy Ancona; Editor, Earl Watson; Costumes, Debraé Little; Music Supervisor, Melodee Sutton; Casting, Reuben Cannon; Dolby; Deluxe color; Rated R; 106 minutes; Release date: March 23, 2001

CAST

Jackson Smith	Morris Chestnut
Brian Palmer	Bill Bellamy
Derrick West	D. L. Hughley
Terry White	Shemar Moore
Denise Johnson	Gabrielle Union
Louise Smith	Jenifer Lewis
Cheré Smith	Tatyana Ali
Sheila West	Tamala Jones
Fred Smith	Clifton Powell
Ursula	Nadege Auguste
Jesse Caldwell	Julie Benz
Spurned Woman	Redena Bivins
Judge Carla Williams	Angelle Brooks
Dr. Thelma Woolridge	Vanessa Bell Calloway
Bailiff	Nicole Cummins
BeBe Fales	Susan Dalian
Sista at Wedding	Marie Frazier
Mary West	Marla Gibbs
T-Boy	Gary Hardwick
Ceyno, the Multi-Ethnic Lover	Henry Kingi, Jr.
Steve on the Strip	Roland "Buddy" Lewis
Sandra the Temp	Kim Porter

and Darin Scott (Derrick's Attorney), Nikki Thompson (Bartender), Nayo Wallace (Red the Stripper), Aloma Wright (Helen Palmer), Tanya Wright (LaMuzindah), Sean P. Young (Tyrel Palmer)

A group of friends are shocked to find out that one of their own is getting married, a decision that causes each of them to try to work out their own romantic problems.

© Screen Gems

HEARTBREAKERS

(MGM) Producers, John Davis, Irving Ong; Executive Producers, Clayton Townsend, Gary Smith, Hadeel Reda; Director, David Mirkin; Screenplay, Robert Dunn, Paul Guay, Stephen Mazur; Photography, Dean Semler; Designer, Lilly Kilvert; Editor, William Steinkamp; Costumes, Gary Jones, Ann Roth; Music, John Debney; Heartbreakers Theme, Danny Elfman; Music Supervisor, Maureen Crowe; Casting, Juel Bestrop, Jeanne McCarthy; a Davis Entertainment Company/Irving Ong production; Dolby; Panavision; Deluxe color; Rated PG-13; 123 minutes; Release date: March 23, 2001

Gene Hackman, Sigourney Weaver

CAST

Max Conners (Angela Nardino/Ulga Yevanova) ....Sigourney Weaver
Page Conners (Wendy/Jane Helstrom) ....Jennifer Love Hewitt
Dean Cumanno (Vinny Staggliano) ....Ray Liotta
Jack Withrowe ....Jason Lee
Gloria Vogal (Barbara)...Anne Bancroft
Mr. Appel ....Jeffrey Jones
William B. Tensy..Gene Hackman
Miss Madress ....Nora Dunn
Leo...Julio Oscar Mechoso
Dawson's Auctioneer..Ricky Jay
Linda ....Sarah Silverman
Bill ....Zach Galifianakis
Davis ....Michael Hitchcock
Priest at First Wedding ....Pierre Gonneau
Minister at Second Wedding ....Shawn Colvin
Wedding Band Singer ....Michael Andrew
Busboy..Andy Brewster
Ray ....Gonzo Raymond
Ms. Surpin ....Carrie Fisher
Mr. Gruber ....Jack Shearer
Man in Gas Station ....Alan Blumenfeld
Waiter...Adam Novicki
Maitre D'..Robert Alan Beuth
Philip Tinker..Steve Mellor
Davis Mom..Janni Brenn
and Jackie O'Brien (Woman at Dawson's), Denalda Williams (David Maid), Haresh Raval (Man in Auction), Jack Douglas Cooper (Other Man at Auction), Peter Spellos (Dawson's Workman), Elya Baskin (Vladimir), Oleg Stefan (Kremlin Band Leader), Ken Magee (Police Sergeant), Geremy Dingle (Breakers Waiter), Patricia Belcher (Hotel Housekeeping Maid), Moné Walton (Bank Teller), Bernadette Birkett (Jack's Mother), David Mirkin (Jack's Lawyer), Catherine Butterfield (Bridal Shop Saleslady), Lawrence Sacco (Man at Banquet), Jennifer Genco (Waitress)

A mother-daughter con artist team sets out to swindle cigarette tycoon William B. Tensy.

© Metro-Goldwyn-Mayer Pictures, Inc.

Jason Lee, Jennifer Love Hewitt

Ray Liotta, Jennifer Love Hewitt, Jason Lee

Anne Bancroft, Sigourney Weaver

Carla Gugino, Daryl
Sabara, Antonio
Banderas, Alexa Vega

Alan Cumming

Daryl Sabara, Alexa Vega

Teri Hatcher,
Alexa Vega

SPY KIDS

(DIMENSION) Producers, Elizabeth Avellan, Robert Rodriguez; Executive Producers, Bob Weinstein, Harvey Weinstein, Cary Granat; Director/Screenplay/Editor, Robert Rodriguez; Photography, Guillermo Navarro; Designer, Cary White; Floop's Song and Spy Kids Theme, Danny Elfman; Costumes, Deborah Everton; Line Producer, Bill Scott; Co-Producer, Tamee Smith-Zimmerman; Special Makeup Effects, Robert Kurtzman, Gregory Nicotero, Howard Berger; Stunts, Jeff Dashnaw; Digital Visual Effects, Hyrbride Technologies, Digital.Art.Media; Casting, Mary Vernieu, Anne McCarthy; a Troublemaker Studios production ; Distributed by Miramax Films; Dolby; Color; Rated PG; 86 minutes; Release date: March 30, 2001

CAST

Gregorio Cortez ....Antonio Banderas
Ingrid Cortez ....Carla Gugino
Carmen Cortez...Alexa Vega
Juni Cortez...Daryl Sabara
Fegan Floop ....Alan Cumming
Alexander Minion ....Tony Shalhoub
Ms. Gradenko ....Teri Hatcher
Felix Gumm ....Cheech Marin
Mr. Lisp ....Robert Patrick
Machete ....Danny Trejo
Donnagon/Donnamight ....Mike Judge
Cool Spy ....Richard Linklater
Pastor...Guillermo Navarro
Agent Johnny...Johnny Reno
FoOglie #1/Flower ....Shannon Shea
FoOglie #2/Tall & Skinny ....Norman Cabrera
FoOglie #3/Too Too..Trant Batey
Brat ....Andy W. Bossley
Brat's Dad ....Jeff Dashnaw
Carmen's Friend ....Kara Slack
Cab Driver ....Ermahn Ospina
and Emilio Navarro Mackissack (Excited Kid at Playground), Evan Sabara ("Intruder" Spy Kid), Rachel Duhame (President's Robot Daughter), Houston Hooker (Lisp's Robot Son), Louis Black, Charles Ramirez-Berg, Dick Clark, Steve Havens, Roberto Santibanez (Financiers), Julio Villarreal (Spy Driver), Becca Rodriguez, Patricia Vonne (Spy Bridesmaids), Angela Lanza (Newscaster), George Clooney (Devlin)

Young Carmen and Juni Cortez find out that their parents are former international spies after the two adults are kidnapped, prompting the kids to spring into action to save them from an evil mastermind determined to take over the world. This film was also reissued in August of 2001 with an additional three minutes of footage.

© Dimension Films

(Below) Daryl Sabara, Alexa Vega

Carla Gugino, Antonio Banderas

Daryl Sabara, Alan Cumming, Alexa Vega

Daryl Sabara, Alexa Vega

Ashley Judd, Greg Kinnear

SOMEONE LIKE YOU

(20TH CENTURY FOX) Producer, Lynda Obst; Executive Producer, Jim Chory; Director, Tony Goldwyn; Screenplay, Elizabeth Chandler; Based upon the novel *Animal Husbandry* by Laura Zigman; Photography, Anthony B. Richmond; Designer, Dan Leigh; Editor, Dana Congdon; Costumes, Ann Roth, Michelle Maitlin; Music, Rolfe Kent; Music Supervisor, Dana Millman-DuFine; Casting, Billy Hopkins, Suzanne Smith, Kerry Barden; a Fox 2000 Pictures presentation of a Lynda Obst production; Dolby; Deluxe color; Rated PG-13; 97 minutes; Release date: March 30, 2001

CAST

Jane Goodale	Ashley Judd
Ray Brown	Greg Kinnear
Eddie Alden	Hugh Jackman
Liz	Marisa Tomei
Diane Roberts	Ellen Barkin
Evelyn	Laura Regan
Alice	Catherine Dent
Stephen	Peter Friedman
Mary Lou Corkle	Donna Hanover
Staff Member	Matthew Coyle
Chinese Vendor	Pon Yang
Realtor	Colleen Camp
Girl in Bar	Sabine Singh
Young Intern	Nicole Leach
Isabel	Murielle Arden

and Jess Platt (Dr. Krane), Shuler Hensley (Hick Farmer), Joe J. Mosso (Technician), AJ Ekoku (Jane's Assistant), Sue Jin Song, Keith Reddin (Scientists), Derick Karlton Grant (Flower Delivery Man), Bear Jackson (Street Vendor), David Kener (Stage Manager), Leanna Croom (Rebecca), Mireille Enos, Adrienne Burke (Instructors), Veronica Webb (Herself), Naomi Judd (Makeup Artist)

Recently dumped by her boyfriend, Jane Goodale reluctantly moves in with her womanizing co-worker, Eddie Alden, and begins formulating a theory that the behavior of men is akin to that of animals, an idea that spins into an anonymous sex column.

© Twentieth Century Fox

Marissa Tomei

Ellen Barkin

Ashley Judd, Hugh Jackman

Jamie Lee Curtis, Pierce Brosnan

THE TAILOR OF PANAMA

(COLUMBIA) Producer/Director, John Boorman; Executive Producer, John Le Carré; Screenplay, Andrew Davies, John Le Carré, based on the novel by John Le Carré; Photography, Philippe Rousselot; Designer, Derek Wallace; Editor, Ron Davis; Costumes, Maeve Paterson; Music, Shaun Davey; Co-Producer, Kevan Barker; Casting, Mary Gail Artz, Barbara Cohen, Jina Jay; a Merlin Films production; U.S.-Irish; Dolby; Panavision; Color; Rated R; 109 minutes; Release date: March 30, 2001

Pierce Brosnan, Geoffrey Rush

CAST

Andy Osnard..Pierce Brosnan
Harry Pendel..Geoffrey Rush
Louisa Pendel ....Jamie Lee Curtis
Marta...Leonor Varela
Mickie Abraxas..Brendan Gleeson
Uncle Benny...Harold Pinter
Francesca...Catherine McCormack
Mark Pendel...Daniel Radcliffe
Sarah Pendel ....Lola Boorman
Luxmore...David Hayman
Rafi Domingo...Mark Margolis
Teddy ....Martin Ferrero
Maltby...John Fortune
Stormont..Martin Savage
Juan-David ....Edgardo Molino
Ramon Rudd..Jon Polito
Cavendish..Jonathan Hyde
Dusenbaker..Dylan Baker
Joe ....Paul Birchard
Elliot...Harry Ditson
Morecombe...Ken Jenkins
President ....Adolfo Arias Espinosa
Marco ....Juan Carlos Adames
Ernesto Delgado ....Luis A. Goti
Customer ....Vladimir Vega
Palace Secretary...Cesar Sanjur
and Heather Emmanuel (Angelo the Manager), Diomara De Ruiz (Mrs. Delgado), Doug Cockle (Pentagon Aide), Patrick Poletti, Andrew French (Officers), Frank Melia, Siraj Zaidi (Officials), Lisa Dwan (Stewardess), Paolo Tulio (Panamanian Businessman)

Lola Boorman, Daniel Radcliffe

A ruthless spy, banished to Panama for his sexual indiscretions, blackmails ex-con-turned-tailor Harry Pendel into finding information about the future ownership of the Panama Canal.

© Columbia Pictures Industries Inc.

Pierce Brosnan, Martin Savage, Catherine McCormack, John Fortune

33

Johnny Depp

BLOW

(NEW LINE CINEMA) Producers, Ted Demme, Joel Stillerman, Denis Leary; Executive Producers, Georgia Kacandes, Michael De Luca; Director, Ted Demme; Screenplay, David McKenna, Nick Cassavetes; Photography, Ellen Kuras; Designer, Michael Hanan; Editor, Kevin Tent; Music, Graeme Revell; Music Supervisor, Amanda Scheer Demme; Costumes, Mark Bridges; Casting, Avy Kaufman; a Spanky Pictures/Apostle production; Dolby; Panavision; Deluxe color; Rated R; 124 minutes; Release date: April 6, 2001

CAST

George Jung	Johnny Depp
Mirtha Jung	Penélope Cruz
Barbara Buckley	Franka Potente
Ermine Jung	Rachel Griffiths
Derek Foreal	Paul Reubens
Diego Delgado	Jordi Mollà
Escobar	Cliff Curtis
Augusto Oliveras	Miguel Sandoval
Tuna	Ethan Suplee
Fred Jung	Ray Liotta
Leon Minghella	Kevin Gage
Kevin Dulli	Max Perlich
Young Georg	Jesse James
Alessandro	Miguel Perez
Cesar Toban	Dan Ferro
Sanchez	Tony Amendola
Mr. T	Bobcat Goldthwait
Dr. Bay	Michael Tucci
Maria	Monet Mazur
Rada	Lola Glaudini
Inez	Jennifer Gimenez
Young Kristina Jung	Emma Roberts
Jack Stevens	Charles Noland

and Genevieve Maylem, Tracy Falco, Pamela Abdy, Sophie Tsimel, Kathleen Mullan (Beach Women), John Harrington Bland, Dale Snowberger, Brantley Bush, Jimmy Burke, Pamela Walker (FBI Waiters), Kevin H. Chapman (DEA Eastham), The Dawk (Guard, Visit Area #2), Edward Demme (Archie Zigmond), Crystal Erickson, Elif Guertin, Vanessa Greyson, Meriah Nelson, Leslie Schirrmacher, Faith Hoover (Stewardesses), Daniel Escobar (Emilio Ochoa), Jean-Carlos Felix (Prison Guard—Warden's Office), Lazaro Galarraga (Band Singer), Brian Goodman (Guard Gus), Josh Herman, Richard LaGravenese (Detectives), Brad Hunt (GG), Patrick Husted (Bank Manager—Mass.), Kristina Jung (Clerk), Ralph Kampshoff (Guard—Visit Area #1), Ajgie Kirkland (James Trout), Skip O'Brien (Customs Agent), Roberto Lopez (Guard—Danbury), Matt Robinson, Raoul Rizik, Lydell M. Cheshier (Inmates), Dorothy Lyman (Judge—Chicago), Jodie Mann (Nurse—Cape Cod), Charles Martinez (Bank Employee), Gonzalo Mendoza (Ramon Ochoa), Alan James Morgan (Young Tuna), Randy Mulkey (Employee #1), Tony Perez (Bank President), Jack Polick (Ben), Elizabeth Rodriguez (Martha Oliveras), Bert Rosario (Bank President—Panama), Julia Vera (Clara Blanca), Santiago Verdu (Juan Carlos)

The true story of how George Jung became one of the top cocaine dealers in the country during the 1970s.

© New Line Cinema Inc.

Penélope Cruz, Johnny Depp

Franka Potente, Rachel Griffiths

(Below) Johnny Depp

Franka Potente, Johnny Depp

Johnny Depp, Ray Liotta

Paul Reubens

Johnny Depp, Jordi Mollà

Morgan Freeman

Morgan Freeman

Morgan Freeman, Monica Potter

ALONG CAME A SPIDER

(PARAMOUNT) Producers, David Brown, Joe Wizan; Executive Producers, Morgan Freeman, Marty Hornstein; Director, Lee Tamahori; Screenplay, Marc Moss; Based on the novel by James Patterson; Photography, Matthew F. Leonetti; Designer, Ida Random; Editor, Neil Travis; Music, Jerry Goldsmith; Costumes, Sanja Milkovic Hays; Casting, Denise Chamian, Stuart Aikins; a David Brown/Phase 1 production in association with Revelations Entertainment in association with MFP Munich Film Partners GmbH & Co., AZL Productions KG; U.S.-German; Dolby; Panavision; Deluxe color; Rated R; 104 minutes; Release date: April 6, 2001

CAST

Alex Cross	Morgan Freeman
Jezzie Flannigan	Monica Potter
Gary Soneji/Jonathan Mercurio	Michael Wincott
Elizabeth Rose	Penelope Ann Miller
Senator Hank Rose	Michael Moriarty
Special Agent Oliver "Ollie" McArthur	Dylan Baker
Megan Rose	Mika Boorem
Dimitri Starodubov	Anton Yelchin
Agent Hickley	Kim Hawthorne
FBI Special Agent Kyle Craig	Jay O. Sanders
Secret Service Agent Ben Devine	Billy Burke
Floyd the Fisherman	Scott Heindl
Jim	Christopher Shyer
Tracie	Jill Teed
Sam	Ian Marsh
Bodyguard	Raoul Ganeev
Mrs. Hume	Samantha Ferris
Amy Masterson	Ocean Hellman
County Chief Cabell	Tom McBeath

and Tamara Taggart, Suzette Meyers, Brian Arnold, Chris Robson, Jonathan Walker, Debra Donahue (Reporters), Mila Dobrozdravich (Hannah), Aaron Joseph (Kennedy), Ravil Isyanov (Leromontov), Ronin Wong (Medical Examiner), Campbell Lane (Mathias), Charles André (Diplomatic Patrol Officer), Claire Riley, Paul Carson, Donna Lysell (News Anchors), Kevin Hayes, Steve Makaj (News Co-Anchors), Anna Maria Horsford (Vickie), Nathaniel Deveuax (Coast Guard Captain), Nguyen Hall (Watergate Employee), Charles Andison, Tarie Tennessey, Darryl Scheelar, Craig March (McArthur Entourages), Darryl Dillard (D.C. Policeman), Carter Jahncke (Man Who Can't Answer Phone), Jim Hild (Potentially Evil Guy on Train)

Detective Alex Cross teams with Secret Service Agent Jezzie Flannigan to save a senator's daughter, who has been kidnapped by the psychopathic Gary Soneji. Morgan Freeman returns as Alex Cross, the character he played in the 1997 film Kiss the Girls.

Craig March, Kim Hawthorne, Charles Andison,
Morgan Freeman, Dylan Baker, Monica Potter

(Clockwise from bottom center): Alan Cumming, Seth Green, Donald Faison, Alex Martin, Breckin Meyer

JOSIE AND THE PUSSYCATS

(UNIVERSAL/MGM) Producers, Marc Platt, Tracey E. Edmonds, Chuck Grimes, Tony DeRosa-Grund; Executive Producers, Kenneth Edmonds, Michael Silberkleit, Richard Goldwater; Directors/Screenplay, Deborah Kaplan, Harry Elfont; Based on characters appearing in Archie comics and the Hanna-Barbera cartoon series; Photography, Matthew Libatique; Designer, Jasna Stefanovich; Editor, Peter Teschner; Co-Producer, Grace Gilroy; Music, John Frizzell; Music Supervisors, Tracey E. Edmonds, Michael McQuarn; Choreographer, Viktoria Langton; a Marc Platt/Riverdale production; Dolby; Color; Rated PG-13; 95 minutes; Release date: April 11, 2001

Rosario Dawson, Tara Reid, Rachael Leigh Cook, Parker Posey

CAST

Josie McCoy	Rachael Leigh Cook
Melody Valentine	Tara Reid
Valerie Brown	Rosario Dawson
Wyatt Frame	Alan Cumming
Fiona	Parker Posey
Alan M	Gabriel Mann
Alexander Cabot	Paulo Costanzo
Alexandra Cabot	Missi Pyle
Agent Kelly	Tom Butler
Les	Alex Martin
Teenage Fans	Faedragh Carpenter, Justin Chatwin, Marites Pineda
Wedding Dress Girl	Kimberly Rimer
Aquarium Tour Guide	Corinne Reilly

and Marnie Alton, Katharine Isabelle, Aeja Goldsmith (Laughing Girls), Nicole Fraissinet, Jessica Murdoch, Juliana Wimbles (Megastore Girls), Zak Alam (Megastore DJ), David Kopp, Sean J. Dory (College Dudes), Heather Robertson (Unstylish Girl), Hiro Kanagawa (Japanese Delegate), Kurt Max Runte (German Delegate), Claude De Martino (French Delegate), Colin Foo (Chinese Delegate), Balinder Johal (Sri-Lankan Delegate), Enuka Okuma, Clay St. Thomas (Fashion Team), Erin Fitzgerald, Linda Ko (Slang Team), Serena Altschul, Mark Seliger, Sally Hershberger, Jann T. Carl, Carson Daly (Themselves), Stuart Lilley, Chris Lovick, Natalye Vivian (New Josie Fans), Karalee Paterson (Pointing Fan), Aries Spears (The Other Carson Daly), Dion Johnstone (Federal Agent), Harry Elfont (Pilot), Tamara Taggart (TV Repoerter), Anthony Creery (Incompetent Techie), JR Bourne (Shop Owner), Shayn Solberg (Geek Guy), Harmoni Everett (Josie's Manicurist), Kris Pope (Gregor), Kevin Bergsman, Todd Talbot, Craig Taylor, Paul Becker, Jay Williams (Fiona's Dancers), Russ Leatherman (Mr. Moviefone). Breckin Meyer, Seth Green, Donald Faison, Eugene Levy

Rosario Dawson, Tara Reid, Gabrielle Mann, Rachael Leigh Cook

Aspiring rock musicians Josie and the Pussycats get their big break when they are signed up by MegaRecords, only to find out that their manager is plotting to control the youth of America through subliminal messages contained in the Pussycats' songs. Based on the Hanna-Barbera animated series, which ran on CBS from 1970–1972.

Tara Reid, Rachael Leigh Cook, Rosario Dawson

KINGDOM COME

(FOX SEARCHLIGHT) Producers, John Morrissey, Edward Bates; Executive Producers, Rochelle Bates, Lawrence Turman; Director, Doug McHenry; Screenplay, David Dean Bottrell, Jessie Jones, based on their play *Dearly Departed*; Photography, Francis Kenny; Designer, Simon Dobbin; Costumes, Francine Jamison-Tanchuck; Editor, Richard Halsey; Co-Producer, Hester Hargett; Music, Tyler Bates; Original Songs, Kirk Franklin; Music Supervisor, Derrick L. Wade; Casting, Robi Reed-Humes; a Bates Entertainment/The Turman-Morrissey Company production; Dolby; Super 35 Widescreen; Color; Rated PG; 92 minutes; Release date: April 11, 2001

CAST

Ray Bud Slocumb	LL Cool J
Charisse Slocumb	Jada Pinkett Smith
Lucille Slocumb	Vivica A. Fox
Marguerite	Loretta Devine
Junior Slocumb	Anthony Anderson
Juanita Slocumb	Toni Braxton
Reverend Hooker	Cedric the Entertainer
Royce	Darius McCrary
Clyde	Richard Gant
Raynelle Slocumb	Whoopi Goldberg
Delightful	Masasa
Antoine Depew	Dominic Hoffman
Merline Depew	Patrice Moncell
Charles Winslow	Clifton Davis
Bernice	Kellita Smith
Veda	Aloma Wright
Nadine	Tamala Jones

and Ellen L. Cleghorne, Tamela J. Mann, Natalie D. Wilson, Sandrina Nicole Shepherd (Ladies), Tony Paul (Tiny), Chuck Campbell (Pedal Steel Player)

Members of the dysfunctional Slocumb family come together for the funeral of patriarch Bud Slocumb, bringing forth a great deal of tension and squabbling.

Whoopi Goldberg, Cedric the Entertainer

Jada Pinkett Smith

Darius McCrary, Loretta Devine

LL Cool J

JOE DIRT

(COLUMBIA) Producer, Robert Simonds; Executive Producers, Adam Sandler, Jack Giarraputo; Director, Dennie Gordon; Screenplay, David Spade, Fred Wolf; Co-Producer, Ira Shuman; Photography, John R. Leonetti; Designer, Perry Andelin Blake; Editor, Peck Prior; Music, Waddy Wachtel; Music Supervisor, Michael Dilbeck; Costumes, Alexandra Welker; Casting, Roger Mussenden; a Happy Madison/Robert Simonds production; Dolby; Deluxe color; Rated PG-13; 91 minutes; Release date: April 11, 2001

CAST

Joe Dirt	David Spade
Brandy	Brittany Daniel
Zander Kelly	Dennis Miller
Kicking Wing	Adam Beach
Clem	Christopher Walken
Jill	Jaime Pressly
Robby	Kid Rock
Little Joe Dirt	Erik Per Sullivan
Joe's Little Sister	Megan Taylor Harvey
Joe's Mom	Caroline Aaron
Joe's Dad	Fred Ward

and John Farley (Security Guard), Bob Zany, Bean Miller (Men), Fred Wolf (Producer Fred), Lee Walker (Zeke), Que Kelly, Kathleen Lambert, Liz Torres, Elisa Leonetti (Beauty College Women), Chris Wylde, Justin Staffer, Justin Kupanoff (Railroad Boys), Hamilton Camp (Meteor Bert), Tom McGillen, John Kirk, Anthony Mastrimauro (Painters), Greg M. Martin (Dude), Angela Paton (Woman with Roadrunner), Robb Skyler (Man at Dental Clinic), Tyler Mane (Bondi), Gordon Michaels (Oil Rig Boss), Lenny Schmidt (Bill/Co-Worker), Rance Howard (Bomb Squad Cop), Erin Murphy, Bree Turner, Natalia Cigliuti (Sorority Girls), Avery Rosin (Kid at Carnival), Brian Thompson (Buffalo Bob), Steven Brill (Cop at Crime Scene), Mitzi Martin (Miss Clipper), Mark Abney, Ian Falk, Matthew Siemonsma, Joshua Farrell, Alexandra Amoscato, Brian Chiesa (Cafeteria Kids), Eric Marquette (Chemistry Student), Fred Stoller (Chemistry Teacher), Steven Schirripa (Hood), Kevin Farley (Cop at Clem's), Richard Riehle (Car Dealer), Blake Clark (Old Cajun Man), Hal Fishman (Newscaster), Eddie Money (Himself), David Garry (Joe's Fan), Jourdan Fremin (Reporter at Parent's House), Kristina Simonds (Newswoman on the Bridge), Karl Makinen, James Tupper (Cops at Bridge), Jana Sandler (Woman on Bridge), Joe Don Baker, Rosanna Arquette, Kevin Nealon, Carson Daly

A grubby, white-trash janitor, abandoned by his family when he was a child, hits the road in hopes of finding his parents.

David Spade, Jaime Pressly

David Spade, Kid Rock

Peter Falk, Charles Durning

George Wendt, Robert Forster

LAKEBOAT

(PANORAMA) Producers, Eric R. Epperson, Tony Mamet, Morris Ruskin; Executive Producer, Alan James; Director/Producer, Joe Mantegna; Screenplay, David Mamet, based on his play; Photography, Paul Sarossy; Designer, Thomas Carnegie; Editor, Christopher Cibelli; Music, Bob Mamet; Co-Producers, Stacia Sekuler Miehe, Andrea Hecht Endewardt; Costumes, Margaret Mohr; Presented in association with Oregon Trail Films and One Vibe Entertainment; Color; Rated R; 98 minutes; Release date: April 13, 2001

CAST

Skippy	Charles Durning
Pierman	Peter Falk
Joe	Robert Forster
Stan	J. J. Johnston
Fireman	Denis Leary
Dale Katzman	Tony Mamet
Fred	Jack Wallace
Collins	George Wendt
Cuthman	Saul Rubinek
Guigliani	Andy Garcia

and Roberta Angelica (Prostitute), Diane Fabian (Janice, 50 years old), Lori Gordon (Janice), Steven Grayhm (Fred, 18 years old), Jason Jazrawy (Joe Litko, 20 years old), Patrick Patterson (Janice's Husband), Charles Seixas (Fred's Uncle)

A young man looking to pick up a few bucks joins the crew of a steel freighter where he becomes engrossed in the lives of the ship's tough-talking but unfulfilled crew members.

Renée Zellweger, Colin Firth

Hugh Grant

Renée Zellweger

Shirley Henderson, Sally Phillips, James Callis

BRIDGET JONES'S DIARY

(MIRAMAX/UNIVERSAL) Producers, Tim Bevan, Eric Fellner, Jonathan Cavendish; Director, Sharon Maguire; Screenplay, Helen Fielding, Andrew Davies, Richard Curtis; Based on the novel by Helen Fielding; Executive Producer, Helen Fielding; Photography, Stuart Dryburgh; Designer, Gemma Jackson; Editor, Martin Walsh; Line Producer, Peter McAleese; Costumes, Rachael Fleming; Music, Patrick Doyle; Music Supervisor, Nick Angel; Co-Producers, Debra Hayward, Liza Chasin; Casting, Michelle Guish; a Working Title production; Dolby; Technicolor; Rated R; 97 minutes; Release date: April 13, 2001

Colin Firth, Embeth Davidtz

CAST

Bridget Jones	Renée Zellweger
Mark Darcy	Colin Firth
Daniel Cleaver	Hugh Grant
Bridget's Dad	Jim Broadbent
Mother	Gemma Jones
Shazza	Sally Phillips
Jude	Shirley Henderson
Tom	James Callis
Natasha	Embeth Davidtz
Una Alconbury	Celia Imrie
Penny Bosworth-Husbands	Honor Blackman
Uncle Geoffrey	James Faulkner
Mrs. Darcy	Charmian May
Mr. Fitzherbert	Paul Brooke
Perpetua	Felicity Montague
Handsome Stranger	Charlie Caine
Simon in Marketing	Gareth Marks
Elderly Man	John Clegg
Themselves	Salman Rushdie, Jeffrey Archer
Kafka Author	Matthew Bates
Julian	Patrick Barlow
Receptionist	Rebecca Charles
Bernard	Dominic McHale
Shirley	Joan Blackman
Lara	Lisa Barbuscia
Interviewers	Joseph Alessi, Rhydian Jai-Persad
Richard Finch	Neil Pearson
Mr. Sit Up Britain	Paul Ross
Stage Manager	Stewart Wright
Magda	Claire Skinner
Woney	Dolly Wells
Cosmo	Mark Lingwood
Alastair	Toby Whithouse
Cameraman	David Cann
Eleanor Ross Heaney	Lisa Kay
Kafit Aghani	Sulayman Al-Bassam
The Musicians	Millennia Strings
Mr. Darcy	Donald Douglas
Mr. Ramdas	Renu Setna
Pauline	Emma Amos
Melinda	Sarah Stockbridge

Renée Zellweger

Renée Zellweger, Hugh Grant

Thirty-two years old and single, Bridget Jones finds herself indulging in an affair with her self-centered boss, all the while finding herself being drawn back into the orbit of family friend Mark Darcy, whom she believes she despises.

This film received an Oscar nomination for actress (Renée Zellweger).

© Miramax Films

Colin Firth, Hugh Grant

THE CENTER OF THE WORLD

(ARTISAN) Producers, Peter Newman, Wayne Wang; Director, Wayne Wang; Screenplay, Ellen Benjamin Wong; Story, Wayne Wang, Miranda July, Paul Auster, Siri Hustvedt; Photography, Mauro Fiore; Designer, Donald Graham Burt; Line Producer, Andrew Loo; Co-Producer, Francey Grace; Editor, Lee Percy; Costumes, Sophie de Rakoff Carbonell; Music Supervisor, Deva Anderson; Casting, Heidi Levitt; a Redeemable Features production; Dolby; Color; Not rated; 86 minutes; Release date: April 18, 2001

CAST

Florence	Molly Parker
Richard Longman	Peter Sarsgaard
Jerri	Carla Gugino
Brian Pivano	Balthazar Getty
Porter	Shane Edelman
Lap Dancer	Karry Brown
Pandora Stripper	Alisha Klass
Roxanne	Mel Gorham
Porn Site Woman	Lisa Newlan
Pete	Jason McCabe Calacanis
Dog Owner	Travis Miljan

and Jerry Sherman (Old Man), Pat Morita (Taxi Driver), Robert Lefkowitz (Motel Manager), John Lombardo (Gondolier), Kathy Florez (Maid), Barbara Ann (Flo's Band), Ian Gomez (Delivery Man)

Richard, a wealthy computer engineer who longs to make human contact, meets Florence, an aspiring musician who moonlights as a stripper. She agrees to accompany him in Las Vegas but only on the condition that the two do not engage in any sexual activity.

Peter Sarsgaard, Molly Parker

Molly Parker, Carla Gugino

Michael Douglas, Matt Dillon

John Goodman, Liv Tyler

ONE NIGHT AT McCOOL'S

(USA FILMS) Producers, Michael Douglas, Allison Lyon Segan; Executive Producer, Whitney Green; Director, Harald Zwart; Screenplay, Stan Seidel; Photography, Karl Walter Lindenlaub; Designer, Jon Gary Steele; Editor, Bruce Cannon; Costumes, Ellen Mirojnick; Music, Marc Shaiman; Music Supervisor, Peter Afterman; Casting, Juel Bestrop, Jeanne McCarthy; an October Films presentation of a Furthur Films production; Dolby; Deluxe color; Rated R; 100 minutes; Release date: April 27, 2001

CAST

Jewel	Liv Tyler
Randy	Matt Dillon
Detective Dehling	John Goodman
Carl	Paul Reiser
Mr. Burmeister	Michael Douglas
Dr. Green	Reba McEntire
Utah/Elmo	Andrew Silverstein
Father Jimmy	Richard Jenkins
Bingo Caller	Mary Jo Smith
Uniformed Cop at Bar	Ric Sarabia
Detective Ertagian	Tim DeZarn
Joey Dinardo	Leo Rossi

and Rob Neukirch (Deliveryman), Andrea Bendewald (Karen), Anthony Winsick (Ethan), David Kronenberg, Michael Kronenberg (Baby Tom), Roscoe DeSpain, Earl Carroll (Bingo Player), Eric Schaeffer (Greg Spalding), Eric Ware, Gary Brussell (Uniformed Cops at House), Donielle Artese (Carl's Assistant), Rad Milo (State Trooper), Veslemoey Ruud Zwart (Clinique Counter Saleswoman), Harry Van Gorkum (Psychic Guru), Jeanne McCarthy (Psychic), Kelly Slater (Jeep Owner)

Three different men take up with a callous, hell-raising woman, prompting one of them to hire a hit man to do away with her.

TOWN & COUNTRY

(NEW LINE CINEMA) Producers, Andrew Karsch, Fred Roos, Simon Fields; Executive Producers, Sidney Kimmel, Michael DeLuca, Lynn Harris; Director, Peter Chelsom; Screenplay, Michael Laughlin, Buck Henry; Co-Producer, Cyrus Yavneh; Photography, William A. Fraker; Designer, Caroline Hanania; Editors, David Moritz, Claire Simpson; Music, Rolfe Kent; Costumes, Molly Maginnis; Casting, Barbara Cohen, Mary Gail Artz; an FR Production/Longfellow Pictures Production in association with Simon Fields production, presented in association with Sidney Kimmel Entertainment; Dolby; Deluxe color; Rated R; 104 minutes; Release date: April 27, 2001

Diane Keaton, Goldie Hawn

CAST

Porter Stoddard .... Warren Beatty
Ellie Stoddard .... Diane Keaton
Mona .... Goldie Hawn
Griffin .... Garry Shandling
Eugenie .... Andie MacDowell
Alex .... Nastassja Kinski
Auburn .... Jenna Elfman
Tom Stoddard .... Josh Hartnett
Alice Stoddard .... Tricia Vessey
Mr. Claybourne .... Charlton Heston
Mrs. Claybourne .... Marian Seldes
Suttler .... Buck Henry
Waiter .... Vincent Lascoumes
Barney .... Bill Hootkins
Yolanda .... Terri Hoyos
Omar .... Marc Casabani
Alejandro .... Del Zamora
Holly .... Katharine Towne
and Tony Abatemarco (McKlellen), Eve Crawford (Margaret), Faith Geer (Mrs. Hadley), Stephen Fischer (Tour Guide), Ken Kensei (Translator), Masayasu Nakanishi, Akira Takayama (Japanese Guests), Stephen Singer, Lois Robbins, David Lindstedt (Party Guests), Morag Dickson (Griffin's Redhead), Carlos K. McAfee (Golf Caddie), Ian McNeice (Peter Principle), Lisa Ekdahl (Herself), Johnny Brown (Chauffeur), Mark Matheisen (Juke Joint Guy), Harry Boykoff (Henry), Azura Skye (Spider), Chris Tuttle (Quasimodo), Christopher Kubasik (Dinnerware Man), Holland Taylor (Mistress of Ceremonies), Scott Adsit (Cab Driver), Angelo Tiffe (Man at Table), Tom Billett, Michael Bailey Smith (Guards), Bonnie Ellen Miller (Lady on Stairs)

Porter Stoddard, a successful and long-married New York architect, finds himself being attracted to several other women, including his friend Mona, whose husband she suspects is having his own affair.

Nastassja Kinski

Garry Shandling, Jenna Elfman, Warren Beatty

Garry Shandling, Warren Beatty

Til Schweiger, Kip Pardue

Sylvester Stallone, Cristián de la Fuente

Kip Pardue, Gina Gershon, Cristián de la Fuente

Sylvester Stallone, Burt Reynolds

DRIVEN

(**WARNER BROS.**) Producers, Elie Samaha, Sylvester Stallone, Renny Harlin; Executive Producers, Andrew Stevens, Don Carmody, Kevin King; Director, Renny Harlin; Screenplay, Sylvester Stallone; Story, Jan Skrentny, Neal Tabachnick; Photography, Mauro Fiore; Designer, Charles Wood; Editors, Stuart Levy, Steve Gilson; Co-Executive Producers, Rebecca Spikings, Tracee Stanley; Costumes, Mary McLeod; Line Producer, Mike Drake; Music, BT; Visual Effects Supervisor, Brian M. Jennings; Race Sequences Coordinators, Andy Gill, Steve Kelso; Stunts, Steve Lucescu; Casting, Heidi Levitt, Monika Mikkelsen; a Franchise Pictures presentation; Dolby; Panavision; Deluxe color; Rated PG-13; 117 minutes; Release date: April 27, 2001

CAST

Joe Tanto	Sylvester Stallone
Carl Henry	Burt Reynolds
Jimmy Bly	Kip Pardue
Beau Brandenburg	Til Schweiger
Cathy	Gina Gershon
Sophia Simone	Estella Warren
Memo Heguy	Cristian de la Fuente
DeMille Bly	Robert Sean Leonard
Lucreatia Jones	Stacy Edwards
Crusher	Brent Briscoe
Nina	Verona Feldbusch
Ingrid	Jasmin Wagner
Team Owner	Chip Ganassi
Team Manager	John Della Penna

and Dan Duran, Rob Smith (Commentators), Richard Zeppieri, Tino Monte (Toronto Reporters), Brian Heighton (Toronto Photographer), Renny Harlin (Replacement Driver), Lukas Harlin (Driver's Son), Peter Kosaka (Japanese Tourist), Frank Blanch (Bill), Barry Stillwell (Bob), Brett Heard (Mechanic), Phillip MacKenzie (Dealership Reporter), Liz West (Radio Reporter), Michael Boisvert (Japan Reporter), Jeffrey Knight (Party Reporter), Wayne Best (Target Manager), Jane Moffat (Nurse), Jake Simons (Carl's Assistant), Jean Alesi, Michael Andretti, Kenny Brack, Patrick Carpentier, Cristiano Da Maata, Adrian Fernandez, Christian Fittipaldi, Dario Franchitti, Luiz Garcia, Jr., Mauricio Gugelmin, Michel Jourdain, Jr., Tony Kanaan, Juan Pablo Montoya, Roberto Moreno, Max Papis, Oriol Servia, Alex Tagliani, Paul Tracy, Jimmy Vasser, Jacques Villeneuve (Race Car Drivers)

Worried that rookie Jimmy Bly is losing focus on the track, car owner Carl Henry asks former race champion Joe Tanto to help train the younger driver.

© Champs Productions, Inc.

Brendan Fraser, Arnold Vosloo

THE MUMMY RETURNS

(UNIVERSAL) Producers, James Jacks, Sean Daniel; Executive Producers, Bob Ducsay, Don Zepfel; Director/Screenplay, Stephen Sommers; Photography, Adrian Biddle; Designer, Allan Cameron; Editors, Bob Ducsay, Kelly Matsumoto; Music, Alan Silvestri; Costumes, John Bloomfield; Animation Supervisor, Daniel Jeannette; Visual Effects Supervisor, John Berton; Visual Effects Producer, Jennifer Bell; Creature & Makeup Effects, Nick Dudman; Casting, Joanna Colbert, Kate Dowd; Stunts, Steve Dent; an Alphaville production; Dolby; Panavision; Color; Rated PG-13; 129 minutes; Release date: May 4, 2001

CAST

Rick O'Connell	Brendan Fraser
Evelyn O'Connell/Nefertiti	Rachel Weisz
Jonathan	John Hannah
Imhotep	Arnold Vosloo
Ardeth Bay	Oded Fehr
Meela/Anck-Su-Namun	Patricia Velasquez
Alex O'Connell	Freddie Boath
Curator	Alun Armstrong
The Scorpion King	The Rock
Lock-Nah	Adewale Akinnuoye-Agbaje
Izzy	Shaun Parkes
Red	Bruce Byron
Jacques	Joe Dixon
Spivey	Tom Fisher
The Pharaoh	Aharon Ipalé
Shafek	Quill Roberts

and Donna Air (Show Girl), Trevor Lovell (Mountain of Flesh)

When mummy Imhotep is once again awoken from his resting place, Rick O'Connell attempts to stop him before the evil spirit can unleash an ancient warrior known as the Scorpion King and absorb his mystical powers. Sequel to the 1999 Universal film The Mummy, *with Fraser, Weisz, Hannah, Vosloo, Fehr, Ipalé, and Velasquez repeating their roles.*

© Universal Studios

John Hannah, Rachel Weisz, Brendan Fraser, Freddie Boath

Brendan Fraser

The Rock

Heath Ledger, Paul Bettany

Heath Ledger

Shannyn Sossamon, Heath Ledger

Mark Addy, Laura Fraser, Alan Tudyk

A KNIGHT'S TALE

(**COLUMBIA**) Producers, Brian Helgeland, Tim Van Rellim, Todd Black; Director/Screenplay, Brian Helgeland; Photography, Richard Greatrex; Designer, Tony Burrough; Costumes/Armor Design, Caroline Harris; Editor, Kevin Stitt; Music, Carter Burwell; 2nd Unit/Stunts, Allan Graf; Sword Fight Choreographer, Paul Weston; Casting, Francine Maisler; an Escape Artists/Finestkind production; Dolby; Super 35 Widescreen; Deluxe color; Rated PG-13; 132 minutes; Release date: May 11, 2001

CAST

William (Sir Ulrich)..Heath Ledger
Count Adhemar ....Rufus Sewell
Jocelyn ....Shannyn Sossamon
Chaucer ....Paul Bettany
Kate ....Laura Fraser
Roland..Mark Addy
Wat ....Alan Tudyk
Christiana..Berenice Bejo
Germaine..Scott Handy
Colville ....James Purefoy
Young William..Leagh Conwell
John Thatcher ....Christopher Cazenove
Simon the Summoner...Steve O'Donnell
Peter the Pardoner ....Jonathan Slinger
Sir Ector ....Nick Brimble
Flanders King of Arms...Karel Dobry
Rouen King of Arms...Philip Lenkowsky
Old Bishop..Roger Ashton-Griffiths
and Petr Meissel (Sword Official), Mathew Mills (Colville's Herald), Daniel Rous (Local Earl Lagny), Vladimir Kulhavy (Fence), Miroslav Mokos, Noel Le Bon, Scott Bellefeuille (French Squires), David Schneider (Relic Seller), Rudolf Kubik (Paris Master of Arms), David Fisher (London King of Arms), David Sterne (Retired Knight), Alice Connor (Lone Girl), Alice Vese (Spy), Berwick Kaler (Man in Stocks), Howie Lotker (Lagny Master at Arms), Jan Kuzelka, Vaclav Krejci, Jan Nemejovsky (Smithees)

The lowborn William unexpectedly fulfills his lifelong dream of becoming a knight when fate allows him to become a jousting champion.

Kaleil Isaza Tuzman

Kaleil Isaza Tuzman

Tom Herman

Kaleil Isaza Tuzman (middle)

STARTUP.COM

(ARTISAN) Producer, D. A. Pennebaker; Executive Producers, Frazer Pennebaker, Jehane Noujaim, Chris Hegedus; Directors, Jehane Noujaim, Chris Hegedus; Photography, Jehane Noujaim; Editors, Chris Hegedus, Erez Laufer, Jehane Noujaim; Music Consultants, Sherief El Katsha, Kit Pennebaker; Associate Producers, Rebecca Marshall, Ed Rogoff; a D. A. Pennebaker presentation; Dolby; Color; Rated R; 103 minutes; Release date: May 11, 2001; Documentary on how two friends joined forces to begin an online service.

FEATURING

Kaleil Isaza Tuzman, Tom Herman, Kenneth Austin, Tricia Burke, Roy Burston, David Camp, Jose Feliciano, Dora Glottman, Julian Herbstein, Christina Ortez, Jonathan Angus, Chieh Cheung, Sean Coar, Ambika Conroy, Patrick Cromer, Jerry Greenberg, Richard Herman, Susan Herman, Tia Herman, Bob Higgins, Maynard Jackson, Brian Locke, Brian Lundy, Spyros Poulios, Marvin Pritchett, Robert Tisch, Ani Tuzman, Kathy Wylde, Kristen Kimball

Office

Princess Fiona, Shrek

Donkey

Shrek

Lord Farquaad, Magic Mirror

SHREK

(DREAMWORKS) Producers, Aron Warner, John H. Williams, Jeffrey Katzenberg; Executive Producers, Penney Finkelman Cox, Sandra Rabins; Co-Executive Producer, David Lipman; Directors, Andrew Adamson, Vicky Jenson; Screenplay, Ted Elliott, Terry Rossio, Joe Stillman, Roger S. H. Schulman; Based upon the book by William Steig; Co-Producers, Ted Elliott, Terry Rossio; Music, Harry Gregson-Williams; Editor, Sim Evan-Jones; Designer, James Hegedus; Visual Effects Supervisor, Ken Bielenberg; Supervising Animator, Raman Hui; Associate Producer, Jane Hartwell; Casting, Leslee Feldman; a PDI/Dreamworks production; Dolby; Technicolor; Rated PG; 88 minutes; Release date: May 16, 2001

VOICE CAST

Shrek/Blind Mouse..Mike Myers
Donkey...Eddie Murphy
Princess Fiona..Cameron Diaz
Lord Farquaad..John Lithgow
Monsieur Hood ....Vincent Cassel
Ogre Hunters ....Peter Dennis, Clive Pearse
Captain of Guards...Jim Cummings
Baby Bear..Bobby Block
Geppetto/Magic Mirror ....Chris Miller
Pinocchio/Three Pigs..Cody Cameron
Old Woman..Kathleen Freeman
Peter Pan ....Michael Galasso
Blind Mouse/Thelonius ....Christopher Knights
Blind Mouse...Simon J. Smith
Gingerbread Man ....Conrad Vernon
Wrestling Fan ....Jacquie Barnbrook
Merry Men..................Guillaume Aretos, John Bisom, Matthew Gonder,
                                       Calvin Remsberg, Jean-Paul Vignon
Bishop...Val Bettin

After the evil Lord Farquaad banishes all fairy tale characters from the kingdom, they take up residence in the swamp of an ornery ogre named Shrek. In order to get back his solitude, Shrek cuts a deal with Farquaad to rescue Princess Fiona from a fire-breathing dragon so that she can be the Lord's bride.

2001 Academy Award-winner for Best Animated Feature (the first winner in this newly established category). This film received an additional Oscar nomination for adapted screenplay.

Donkey, Shrek, Princess Fiona, Lord Farquaad

Shrek

Big Bad Wolf, Shrek

Princess Fiona, Shrek

Princess Fiona, Shrek

Nicole Kidman, Ewan McGregor

Nicole Kidman

Nicole Kidman

Nicole Kidman, Ewan McGregor

Lara Mulcahy, Caroline O'Connor, Natalie Mendoza,
Christine Anu

Ewan McGregor

50

MOULIN ROUGE!

(20TH CENTURY FOX) Producers, Martin Brown, Baz Luhrmann, Fred Baron; Director, Baz Luhrmann; Screenplay, Baz Luhrmann, Craig Pearce; Photography, Donald M. McAlpine; Designer, Catherine Martin; Costumes, Catherine Martin, Angus Strathie; Editor, Jill Bilcock; Co-Producer, Catherine Knapman; Choreographer, John O'Connell; Music, Craig Armstrong; Music Director, Marius DeVries; Song: "Come What May" by David Baerwald; Visual Effects Supervisor, Chris Godfrey; Casting, Ronna Kress, Chris King; a Bazmark production; U.S.-Australian; Dolby; Panavision; Deluxe color; Rated PG-13; 126 minutes; Release date: May 18, 2001

CAST

Satine	Nicole Kidman
Christian	Ewan McGregor
Toulouse Lautrec	John Leguizamo
Zidler	Jim Broadbent
Duke of Worcester	Richard Roxburgh
The Doctor	Garry McDonald
The Unconscious Argentinean	Jacek Koman
Satie	Matthew Whittet
Marie	Kerry Walker
Nini Legs in the Air	Caroline O'Connor
Audrey	David Wenham
Arabia	Christine Anu
China Doll	Natalie Mendoza
Môme Fromage	Lara Mulcahy
Green Fairy	Kylie Minogue
Le Chocolat	Deobia Oparei

and Linal Haft (Warner), Keith Robinson (Le Petomane), Peter Whitford (Stage Manager), Norman Kaye (Doctor), Arthur Dignam (The Father), Carole Skinner (Landlady), Jonathan Hardy (Man in the Moon), Kiruna Stamell (La Petite Princess), Laszlo Lukas (Conductor), Anthony Young (Orchestra Member), Wilson Alcorn, Kerry Casey, Peter Collingwood, Tim Eliott, Nicole Fantl, Judy Howard, Harold Kissin, Paul Maybury, Caroline Nahlous, Scott Peters, David Whitford (Audience Members), Judi Eldred (Patron), Ray Chambers, Darrell Dixon, Otto Luppo, Billy Pat, Adrian Sicari (Fan Bearers), Alexander Houle, Geoffrey Kiem, Peter Muirhead (Stagehands), Pat Evans (Seamstress), Tara Morice (Prostitute), Daniel Scott (Absinthe Drinker/Guitarist), Angus Martin (Pawnbroker), Byron Barriga, Waldo Garrido, Reginald Larner (Musicians), Coralie Eichholtz, Jabe Bromhall (Moulin Rouge Girls), Robert Yearley (Coach), John Pagan (Old Crone), Patrick Hardin-Irmer, Albin Pahernik, Aurel Verne (Waiters), Dee Donavan, Johnny Lockwood, Don Reid (Characer Rakes), Greg Poppleton (Nervous Nellie), Matt Wilson (Slave Trader), Trent Harlow, Troy Harrison, Simon Kriszyk, Chris Pickard, Thern

Ewan McGregor, Nicole Kidman

Reynolds, David Scotchford, Daniel Slater (Dancers), Veronica Beattie, Lisa Callingham, Rosetta Cook, Fleur Denny, Kelly Grauer, Jaclyn Hanson, Michelle Hopper, Fallon King, Wendy McMahon, Tracie Morley, Sue-Ellen Shook, Jenny Wilson, Luke Alleva, Andrew Aroustian, Stephen Colyer, Steven Grace, Mark Hodge, Cameron Mitchell, Deon Nuku, Shaun Parker, Troy Phillips, Rodney Syaranamual, Ashley Wallen, Nathan Wright (Montmartre Dance Team), Susan Black, Nicole Brooks, Danielle Brown, Anastacia Flewin, Fiona Cage, Alex Harrington, Camilla Jakimowicz, Rochelle Jones, Caroline Kaspar, Mandy Liddell, Melanie Mackay, Elise Mann, Charmaine Martin, Michelle Wriggles, Michael Boyd, Lorry D'Ercole, Michael Edge, Glyn Gray, Craig Haines, Stephen Holford, Jamie Jewell, Jason King, Ryan Males, Harlin Martin, Andrew Micallef, Jonathan Schmolzer, Bradley Spargo (Paris Dance Team), Kip Gamblin (Latin Dancer), Dennis Dowlut, Darren Dowlut (Cocoliscious Brothers), Nandy McClean, Maya McClean (Twins), Pina Conti (La Ko Ka Chau), Joseph "Pepe" Ashton, Jordan Ashton, Marcos Falagan, Mitchel Falagan, Chris Mayhew, Hamish Mccann, Adrien Janssen, Shaun Holloway (Tobasco Brothers)

In the middle of decadent, turn-of-the-century Paris, Christian falls hopelessly in love with Satine, a famous entertainer-courtesan at the city's decadent night-club Moulin Rouge. 2001 Academy Award-winner for Best Costume Design and Art Direction. This film received additional Oscar nominations for picture, actress (Nicole Kidman), cinematography, editing, sound, and makeup.

Nicole Kidman, Ewan McGregor

Nicole Kidman

Jim Caviezel, Jennifer Lopez

Jim Caviezel

ANGEL EYES

(**WARNER BROS.**) Producers, Mark Canton, Elie Samaha; Executive Producers, Andrew Stevens, Neil Canton, Don Carmody; Director, Luis Mandoki; Screenplay, Gerald DiPego; Photography, Piotr Sobocinski; Designer, Dean Tavoularis; Co-Producer, Dawn Miller; Costumes, Marie-Sylvie Deveau; Editor, Jerry Greenberg; Music, Marco Beltrami; Music Supervisors, Manish Raval, Tom Wolfe; Casting, Amanda Mackey Johnson, Cathy Sandrich; a Morgan Creek and Franchise Pictures presentation of a Franchise Pictures and Canton Company production; Dolby; Color; Rated R; 103 minutes; Release date: May 18, 2001

CAST

Sharon Pogue..Jennifer Lopez
Catch..Jim Caviezel
Josephine Pogue...Sonia Braga
Robby...Terrence Howard
Larry Pogue...Jeremy Sisto
Carl Pogue..Victor Argo
Kathy Pogue..Monet Mazur
Elanora Davis...Shirley Knight
Larry Jr...Daniel Magder
Annie..Guylaine St. Onge
and Connor McAuley (Max Pogue), Jeremy Ratchford (Ray Micigliano), Peter MacNeill (Lt. Dennis Sanderman), Eldridge Hyndman (Jamal), Karl Matchett (Candace), Michael Cameron (Charlie), Marchello Thadford (Peebo), David Cox (K-Dog), Ron Payne (Priest), Paul A. MacFarlane (Photographer), Daniel Petronijevic (Fighting Kid), Stephen Thomas Kay (Tony Pindella), Grant Nickalls (Joe), Jim Feather, John Shepard (Old Men), Matt Birman (Driver), Eric Coates (Car Man), Chuck Campbell, JJ Authors (Young Men), Stephanie Moore (Officer Vanessa), Ron Johnstone (Bass Player), Nick Ali (Trumpeter), Brian Dickinson (Piano Player), Barry Romberg (Drummer), Neil Brathwaite (Flautist), Kathy Carter (Cop), Darren Marsman (Suspect #2), Brian Jagersky, Chris Lamon (Police Officers), Brenda Adams, Donny Stockford (ND Pedestrians), Matthew Van Hart (Fighting Street Kid #2)

Chicago policewoman Sharon Pogue is saved by a mysterious man named Catch, with whom she begins an affair, all the while hoping to help him confront his troubled past about which he is so vague.

© Seraph Productions, Inc.

Jennifer Lopez

Daniel Petronijevic, Jennifer Lopez

Kerry Washington, Anna Simpson, Melissa Martinez

Melissa Martinez

Anna Simpson, Kerry Washington, Melissa Martinez

D'Monroe, Melissa Martinez

Ray Anthony Thomas,
Kerry Washington

OUR SONG

(IFC FILMS) Producers, Jim McKay, Paul Mezey, Diana E. Williams; Executive Producers, Caroline Kaplan, Jonathan Sehring, Michael Stipe; Director/Screenplay, Jim McKay; Photography, Jim Denault; Costumes, Tiel Roman; Editor, Alex Hall; Music Supervisor, Julie Panebianco; Co-Producers, Alexa L. Fogel, Joseph Infantolino; Associate Producers, Tyrone Brown, Ashaki "Saki" Fenderson, Susannah Ludwig; a C-Hundred Film Corp. movie, presented in association with Beech Hill Films and Journeyman Pictures; Dolby; Color; Rated R; 96 minutes; Release date: May 23, 2001

CAST

Lanisha Brown..Kerry Washington
Joycelyn Clifton ....Anna Simpson
Maria Hernandez..Melissa Martinez
Pilar Brown ....Marlene Forte
Carl Brown...Ray Anthony Thomas
Dawn Clifton ....Rosalyn Coleman
Rita Hernandez...Carmen Lopez
Mr. Miller ....Tyrone Brown
Kim ....Lorraine Berry
Keisha..Natasha Frith
Benjamin..Chuck Cooper
and Iris Little Thomas (Clinc Counselor), Kim Howard (Eleanor), Juan Romero, Jr. (Sampson), D'Monroe (Terell), Reginald Washington (Alex), Tommy Axson (Cam), Tyrus Cox (Anthony, The Playa), Taheim Washington (Troy Harper), Starla Benford (Woman with Flowers), Lisa Collins (School Registrar), Greg Haberny (Cute "Guapo" Guy), Eric Byrd (Malik, the Party Kisser), Sidney O'Loughlin (Rasheed), Shannon Phillips (Party DJ), Madeleine T. Gamble (Steppers Booster), Devin Gray (Natasha Up in the Window), Derrick Williams (Rodney), Syron Martin (Ice Cream Scooper), Jan McLaughlin (E.R. Doctor), The Jackie Robinson Steppers Marching Band (Themselves)

At the end of a hot summer in Crown Heights, Brooklyn, three teenage girl-friends confront the rising tensions in their friendships while rehearsing for marching band.

© IFC Films

PEARL HARBOR

(TOUCHSTONE) Producers, Jerry Bruckheimer, Michael Bay; Executive Producers, Mike Stenson, Barry Waldman, Randall Wallace, Chad Oman, Bruce Hendricks; Director, Michael Bay; Screenplay, Randall Wallace; Photography, John Schwartzman; Designer, Nigel Phelps; Editors, Chris Lebenzon, Steven Rosenblum, Mark Goldblatt, Roger Barton; Costumes, Michael Kaplan; Music, Hans Zimmer; Song: "There You'll Be," music and lyrics by Diane Warren/performed by Faith Hill; Visual Effects Supervisor, Eric Brevig; Aerial Coordinator, Alan Purwin; Aerial Unit Director, David B. Nowell; Casting, Bonnie Timmermann; a Jerry Bruckheimer Films presentation; Dolby; Panavision; Technicolor; Rated PG-13; 189 minutes; Release date: May 25, 2001

CAST

Rafe McCawley	Ben Affleck
Danny Walker	Josh Hartnett
Evelyn Johnson	Kate Beckinsale
Billy	William Lee Scott
Anthony R. Fusco	Greg Zola
Red	Ewen Bremner
Col. James H. Doolittle	Alec Baldwin
Betty	Catherine Kellner
Sandra	Jennifer Garner
President Roosevelt	Jon Voight
Doris "Dorie" Miller	Cuba Gooding, Jr.
Gooz	Michael Shannon
Joe	Matt Davis
Admiral Yamamoto	Mako
Nishikura	John Fujioka
Genda	Cary-Hiroyuki Tagawa
Admiral Kimmel	Colm Feore
Captain Thurman	Dan Aykroyd

and Reiley McClendon (Young Danny), Jesse James (Young Rafe), William Fichtner (Danny's Father), Steve Rankin (Rafe's Father), Brian Haley (Training Captain), David Hornsby (Training Captain), Scott Wilson (Gen. Marshall), Graham Beckel (Admiral), Howard Mungo (George), Randy Oglesby (Strategic Analyst), Ping Wu (Japanese Officer), Stan Cahill (Pentagon Lt.), Kevin Wensing (XO U.S.S. West Virginia), Tom Everett (Presidential Aide), Tomas Arana (Vice Admiral), Beth Grant (Motherly Secretary), Sara Rue (Martha), Sung Kang (Listener), Raphael Sbarge (Kimmel's Aide), Marty Belafsky (Louie the Sailor), Yuji Okumoto (Japanese Shy Bomber), Josh Green (Radar Pvt. Ellis), Ian Bohen (Radar Pvt. #2), Michael Milhoan (Army Cmmdr.), Peter Firth (Capt. of West Virginia), Tom Sizemore (Earl), Marco Gould (Pop-Up Sailor), Andrew Bryniarski (Joe the Boxer), Nicholas Downs (Terrified Sailor), Tim Choate (Navy Doctor), John Diehl (Sr. Doctor), Joe Kelly (Medic), Ron Harper (Minister), Ted McGinley (Army Corps Maj.), Madison Mason (Adm. on the Hornet), Kim Coates (Jack Richards), Andrew Baley (Hornet Radio Op), Glenn Morshower (Adm. Halsey), Paul Francis (Doolittle Co-Pilot), Scott Wiper, Eric Christian Olsen (Gunners), Rod Biermann (Navigator), Noriaki Kamata, Garret T. Sato, Eiji Inoue (Japanese Soldiers), Precious Chong (Nursing Supervisor), Jeff Wadlow (Next Guy in Line), Will Gill, Jr. (Train Conductor), Seth Sakai (Japanese Tourist), Curtis Anderson (18-year-old Typist), Blaine Pate (Orderly in Aftermath), John Pyper-Ferguson (Naval Officer in Hospital), Michael Shamus Wiles (Captain of the Hornet), Brett Pedigo (Next Guy in Line #2), Toru M. Tanaka, Jr. (Samoan Bouncer), Sean Gunn (Traction Sailor), Joshua Ackerman, Matt Casper, Fred Koehler (Wounded Sailors), David Kaufman (Young Nervous Doctor), L. L. Ginter (Captain Low), Joshua Aaron Gulledge (Buster), Guy Torry (Teeny Mayfield), Leland Orser (Maj. Jackson), Peter James Smith (Mission Listener), Mark Noon (Medic), Pat Healy (News Reel Guy), Thomas Wilson Brown (Young Flier), Chad Morgan (Pearl Habor Nurse), James Saito, Angel Sing, Tak Kubota (Japanese Aides), Robert Jayne (Sunburnt Sailor), Vic Chao (Japanese Doctor), Michael Gradilone (Screaming Sailor), John Padget

(Hospital Chaplain), Ben Easter, Cory Tucker, Abe Sylvia, Jason Liggett, Mark Panasuk, Bret Roberts (Baja Sailors), John Howry (Lieutenant in Boat), Rufus Dorsey (Dorie's Friend), Patrice Martinez (French Fisherman), Rodney Bursiel (Sailor with Dog), Rob McCabe (Rescue Sailor), Brandon Lozano (Baby Danny), Seiki Moriguchi (Agaki Communication Officer), Brian D. Falk, Christopher Stroop (Helmsmen), Estevan Gonzalo (Bombing Sailor), Sean Faris (Danny's Gunner), Vincent J. Inghilterra (Preacher), Nicholas Farrell (RAF Squadron Leader), Tony Curran (Ian), Viv Weatherall, Benjamin Farry, Daniel Mays (Pilots)

Two childhood friends, who grow up to become Air Force pilots, both fall in love with the same woman on the eve of the Japanese attack on Pearl Harbor. 2001 Academy Award-winner for Best Sound Effects Editing. This film received additional Oscar nominations for visual effects, sound, and original song ("There You'll Be").

(Above) Ben Affleck, Josh Hartnett

(Below) Cuba Gooding, Jr.

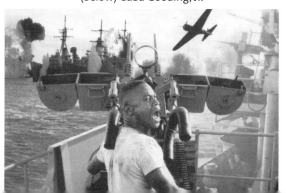

Ben Affleck,
Josh Hartnett

(Above) Catherine Kellner, James King, Kate Beckinsale,
Jennifer Garner, Sara Rue. (Below) Dan Aykroyd

(Above) Alec Baldwin
(Below) Jon Voight, Scott Wilson, Ben Affleck

Michael Caton, Rob Schneider

Colleen Haskell, Rob Schneider

THE ANIMAL

(COLUMBIA) Producers, Barry Bernardi, Carr D'Angelo, Todd Garner; Executive Producers, Adam Sandler, Jack Giarraputo; Director, Luke Greenfield; Screenplay, Tom Brady, Rob Schneider; Story, Tom Brady; Photography, Peter Lyons Collister; Designer, Alan Au; Editors, Jeff Gourson, Peck Prior; Costumes, Jim Lapidus; Co-Producers, Tom Brady, John Schneider; Music, Teddy Castellucci; Music Supervision, Michael Dilbeck; Casting, Roger Mussenden, Tracy Kaplan, Elizabeth Boykewich; Stunts, Gregg Smrz; a Revolution Studios presentation of a Happy Madison production; Dolby; Color; Rated PG-13; 83 minutes; Release date: June 1, 2001

CAST

Marvin Mange	Rob Schneider
Rianna	Colleen Haskell
Sgt. Sisk	John C. McGinley
Chief Wilson	Edward Asner
Dr. Wilder	Michael Caton
Fatty	Louis Lombardi
Miles	Guy Torry
Bob Harris	Bob Rubin
Mrs. De La Rosa	Pilar Schneider
Mayor	Scott Wilson

and Raymond Ma (Mr. Tam), Michael Papajohn (Patrolman Brady), Ron Rogge (Patrolman Jaworski), Holly Maples, Henriette Mantel, Jeremy Kramer, Robb Skyler, Nicko Mariolis (Elkerton Police Officers), Philip Daniel Bolden, Decker Daily, Timmy Deters, Hannah K. Flood, Megan Taylor Harvey, Mitch Holleman, Mollie Rea Patton, Charlie Stewart (Evidence Room Kids), Elizabeth Branson (Heavy-Set Cadet), Sandy Gimpel (Obstacle Course Lady), Paul Short (Burning Man), Arthur Bernard (Elderly Jogger), Tim Herzog (Badger Milk Host), Berglind Olafsdottir (Yolanda), Steven Kravitz (Airport Businessman), Shane Holden, Tom McNulty (Airline Stewards), James Bates (Airport Police), Morisa Taylor Kaplan (Mailbox Girl), Jack Rubens (Old Man Holden), Susan Corwin (TV Anchorwoman), Tom Keische (Bar Patron), Karlee Holden (Waitress), Clare Calvo, Michelle Celestino (Hula Dancers), Luigi Amodeo (Italian Waiter), Wes Takahashi, Fred Stoller (Reporters), Jake Iannarino (Free Press Reporter), John Kirk (Waiter at Party), Brett Smrz (Mayor's Son), Noel Guglielmi (Gang Leader), Adam Sandler (Townie), Norm MacDonald (Mob Member), Brianna Lynn Brown, Amber Collins, John Farley (Other Mob), Pete (Dimples the Dog), Bliss (Nelly the Goat), Kanoozi (Mr. Giggles), Louey (Henry the Orangutan)

Marvin Mange, a police file clerk, survives a near-fatal car accident only to have an eccentric doctor repair his damaged body using animal organs.

WHAT'S THE WORST THAT COULD HAPPEN?

(MGM) Producers, Lawrence Turman, David Hoberman, Ashok Armitraj, Wendy Dytman; Executive Producers, John Morrissey, Martin Lawrence, David Nicksay; Director, Sam Weisman; Screenplay, Matthew Chapman; Based upon the novel by Donald E. Westlake; Photography, Anastas Michos; Designer, Howard Cummings; Editors, Garth Craven, Nick Moore; Costumes, Jeffrey Kurland; Music, Tyler Bates, Marc Shaiman; Music Supervisor, Anita Camarata; Co-Producer, Peaches Davis; Casting, John Papsidera; a Turman-Morrissey Company/Hyde Park Entertainment production; Dolby; Deluxe color; Rated PG-13; 95 minutes; Release date: June 1, 2001

CAST

Kevin Caffery	Martin Lawrence
Max Fairbanks	Danny DeVito
Berger	John Leguizamo
Gloria	Glenne Headly
Amber Belhaven	Carmen Ejogo
Uncle Jack	Bernie Mac
Earl Radburn	Larry Miller
Lutetia Fairbanks	Nora Dunn
Walter Greenbaum	Richard Schiff
Det. Alex Tardio	William Fitchner
Ann Marie	Ana Gasteyer
Tracey Kimberly	Sascha Knopf
Edwina	Siobhan Fallon
Shelly Nix	GQ

and Lenny Clarke (Windham), Robin Brown (Auctioneer), Mike Moyer (Large Man at Auction), Darra Herman, Julie Jirousek (Auction Bidders), Kevin H. Chapman (Bartender), Devon Jencks (Officer Keeble), Paul O'Brien (Officer Overkraut), James Baldwin (Older Tennis Player), Jay Carney (Gentleman at Club), Matt Seigel (Banquet Host), Michael Mulheren (Judge Callahan), Michael Jessel, Ryan Hull, Eddie McCabe (Windham Boys), Karen MacDonald (Washington Real Estate Agent), Lonnie Farmer (Washington Condo Doorman), Michelle Youell (Pepper Spray Lady), Tim Gallin, Paul Marini (Washington Cops), Tracy Oliverio (Junior Detective), Cam Neely (Jerry), Elliot Cuker (Senator Richards), George Blumenthal (Senator Engel), Richard McElvain (Senator Schutt), Stephanie Clayman (Sign Language Interpreter), Christy Scott-Cashman (Roxanne), Dan Weisman (Eagle One), Rick Calnan (Cop at Auction), Jimmy Flynn (Fire Captain), Russell Curry, Susie Spear, Richard Saxton (Reporters), Kerry Kilbride (TV Anchor)

After being captured by the police for breaking into the home of unscrupulous businessman Max Fairbanks, professional thief Kevin Caffrey has his lucky ring taken from him by Fairbanks in retaliation for the intended theft, an act that causes Caffrey to swear revenge.

Danny Devito, Martin Lawrence

John Travolta, Hugh Jackman, Halle Berry

Vinnie Jones, John Travolta

SWORDFISH

(WARNER BROS.) Producers, Joel Silver, Jonathan D. Krane; Executive Producers, Jim Van Wyck, Bruce Berman; Director, Dominic Sena; Screenplay, Skip Woods; Photography, Paul Cameron; Designer, Jeff Mann; Co-Producers, Dan Cracchiolo, Skip Woods; Music, Christopher Young, Paul Oakenfold; Editor, Stephen Rivkin; Costumes, Ha Nguyen; Visual Effects Supervisor, Boyd Shermis; Stunts, Dan Bradley; Casting, Lora Kennedy; a Silver Pictures/Jonathan D. Krane production, presented in association with Village Roadshow Pictures and NPV Entertainment; Dolby; Panavision; Technicolor; Rated R; 100 minutes; Release date: June 8, 2001

CAST

Halle Berry, Hugh Jackman

Gabriel Shear	John Travolta
Stanley Jobson	Hugh Jackman
Ginger	Halle Berry
Agent Roberts	Don Cheadle
Marco	Vinnie Jones
Senator Reisman	Sam Shepard
Melissa	Drea de Matteo
Axl Torvalds	Rudolf Martin
A. D. Joy	Zach Grenier
Holly	Camryn Grimes
Torres	Angelo Pagán
SWAT Leader	Chic Daniel
Lawyer	Kirk B. B. Woller
Agents	Carmen Argenziano, Tim DeKay
Helga	Laura Lane
Ad Agency Executive	Tait Ruppert
Coroner	Craig Braun

and William Mapother, Ilia Volok, Jonathan Fraser, Shawn Woods, Leo Lee (Gabriel's Crew), Marina Black, Kerry Kletter, Ryan Wulff, Ann Travolta, Margaret Travolta, Dana Hee, Denney Pierce, Jeff Ramsey, Joey Box, Debbie Evans, Samuel S. Travolta, Tim Storms (Hostages), Jason Christopher, Jonathan Pessin (Club Kids), Scott Burkholder, Mark Soper (FBI Geeks), Craig Lally, Rusty McClennon, Mark Riccardi (Customs Agents), Debbie Entin, Natalia Sokolova, Anika Poitier (Helga's Friends), Nick Loren (Dark Suit), Tom Morris, Richard Householder, Michael Arias (Policemen), Brenda Eimers (Holly's Teacher), Timothy Omundson (Agent Thomas), Astrid Veillon (Bank Executive), Dean Rader Duval (Security Guard)

Convicted computer hacker Stanley Jacobson agrees to assist Gabriel Shear in electronically diverting billions of dollars in laundered funds for his terrorist activities, so that Stanley can get back his daughter whom Gabriel has kidnapped to ensure his participation in the crime.

© Warner Bros.

John Travolta, Hugh Jackman

Alan Cumming, Jennifer Jason Leigh

THE ANNIVERSARY PARTY

(FINE LINE) Producers, Joanne Sellar, Alan Cumming, Jennifer Jason Leigh; Executive Producer, Andrew Hurwitz; Directors/Screenplay, Jennifer Jason Leigh, Alan Cumming; Photography, John Bailey; Editors, Carol Littleton, Suzanne Spangler; Music, Michael Penn; Co-Producer, Mike Nelson; Associate Producer, Lila Yacoub; Costumes, Christopher Lawrence; Music Supervisor, Robin Urdang; a Joanne Sellar/Pas de Quoi production; Dolby; Color; Rated R; 115 minutes; Release date: June 8, 2001

CAST

Joe Therrian	Alan Cumming
Sally Therrian	Jennifer Jason Leigh
Clair Forsyth	Jane Adams
Monica Rose	Mina Badie
Gina Taylor	Jennifer Beals
Sophia Gold	Phoebe Cates
Jerry Adams	John Benjamin Hickey
Cal Gold	Kevin Kline
Jeffrey	Matt McGrath
Ryan Rose	Denis O'Hare
Syke Davidson	Gwyneth Paltrow
Levi Panes	Michael Panes
Mac Forsyth	John C. Reilly
Himself	Otis the Dog
Yoga Instructor	Steven Freedman
America	Norizzela Monterroso
Rosa	Clara Demedrano
Jack Gold	Owen Kline
Evie Gold	Greta Kline
Sanford Jewison	Matt Malloy
Mary-Lynn	Mary-Lynn Rajskub
Astrid	Blair Tefkin
Herself	Anouk the Dog
Karen	Karen Kilgariff

and Molly Bryant, Michael G. Carroll, Craig Chester, Christopher Lawrence, Jessica Queller Jr., W. Reed (Party Guests)

After a period of estrangement, Joe and Sally Therrian host a sixth-year anniversary party, during which they begin to question their marriage and their relationships to their friends and colleagues. Actors Alan Cumming and Jennifer Jason Leigh make their debuts as motion picture directors.

© Fine Line Features

Gwyneth Paltrow, Michael Panes

Greta Kline, Phoebe Cates, Owen Kline, Kevin Kline

Gwyneth Paltrow, Jennifer Jason Leigh

Jennifer Beals, Alan Cumming, Jennifer Jason Leigh

John Benjamin Hickey, Parker Posey

John C. Reilly, Jane Adams

Mina Badie, Dennis O'Hare

Helga Sinclair, Princess Kida,
Milo Thatch, Commander Rourke

The Ulysses

The Ulysses

Milo Thatch

Milo Thatch

ATLANTIS: THE LOST EMPIRE

(WALT DISNEY PICTURES) Producer, Don Hahn; Directors, Gary Trousdale, Kirk Wise; Screenplay, Tab Murphy; Story, Kirk Wise, Gary Trousdale, Joss Whedon, Bryce Zabel, Jackie Zabel, Tab Murphy; Original Score, James Newton Howard; Song: "Where the Dream Takes You" by Diane Warren (lyrics), Diane Warren, James Newton Howard (music)/Performed by MYA; Associate Producer, Kendra Haaland; Art Director, David Goetz; Artistic Coordinator, Christopher Jenkins; Editor, Ellen Keneshea; Artistic Supervisors: Story, John Sanford; Layout, Ed Ghertner; Background, Lisa Keene; Cleanup, Marshall Toomey; Visual Effects, Marlon West; Computer Graphics Imagery, Kiran Bhakta Joshi; Distributed by Buena Vista Pictures; Dolby; Widescreen; Technicolor; Rated PG; 95 minutes; Release date: June 8, 2001

VOICE CAST

Milo Thatch	Michael J. Fox
Commander Rourke	James Garner
Princess Kida	Cree Summer
The King of Atlantis	Leonard Nimoy
Vinny Santorini	Don Novello
Helga	Claudia Christian
Audrey	Jacqueline Obrados
Preston B. Whitmore	John Mahoney
Mole	Corey Burton
Fenton Q. Harcourt	David Ogden Stiers
Cookie	Jim Varney
Mrs. Packard	Florence Stanley
Dr. Swee	Phil Morris
Young Kida	Natalie Strom

and Jim Cummings, Pat Pinney, Steve Barr (Additional Voices)

Milo Thatch, a linguistics expert and cartographer, is given his grandfather's ancient journal, which may provide the key to finding the lost empire of Atlantis.

© Disney Enterprises, Inc.

Milo Thatch, Princess Kida

King of Atlantis, Milo Thatch

Cookie, Milo Thatch, Vinny, Audrey, Dr. Sweet

Milo Thatch, Preston B. Whitmore, Commander Rourke

David Duchovny, Orlando Jones

EVOLUTION

(DREAMWORKS/COLUMBIA) Producers, Ivan Reitman, Daniel Goldberg, Joe Medjuck; Executive Producers, Tom Pollock, Jeff Apple, David Rodgers; Director, Ivan Reitman; Screenplay, David Diamond, David Weissman, Don Jakoby; Story, Don Jakoby; Photography, Michael Chapman; Designer, J. Michael Riva; Editors, Sheldon Kahn, Wendy Greene Bricmont; Visual Effects Supervisor, Phil Tippett; Costumes, Aggie Guerard Rodgers; Co-Producer, Paul Deason; Music, John Powell; Casting, Margery Simkin; Stunts, Thomas Robinson Harper; a Montecito Picture Company production; Dolby; Technicolor; Rated PG-13; 103 minutes; Release date: June 8, 2001

David Duchovny, Orlando Jones, Seann William Scott

CAST

Dr. Ira Kane	David Duchovny
Allison	Julianne Moore
Prof. Harry Block	Orlando Jones
Wayne	Seann William Scott
Gen. Woodman	Ted Levine
Deke	Ethan Suplee
Danny	Michael Ray Bower
Officer Johnson	Pat Kilbane
Flemming	Ty Burrell
Governor Lewis	Dan Aykroyd
Nadine	Katharine Towne
Cartwright	Gregory Itzin
Lt. Cryer	Ashley Clark
Carla	Michelle Wolff
Denise	Sarah Silverman
Fire Training Inspector	Richard Moll
Fireman	Michael McGrady
Judge Guilder	Steven Gilborn
Dr. Paulson	Wayne Duvall
Sheriff Long	Michael Chapman
Officer Drake	Kyle Gass

David Duchovny, Julianne Moore

and Lucas Dudley (Sgt. Toms), Steven Pierce (Sgt. Larson), Wendy Braun (Nurse Tate), Jennifer Savidge (Claire), Jerry Trainor (Tommy), Stephanie Hodge (Jill Mason), Kristen Meadows (Patty), Winifred Freeman (Debbi), Miriam Flynn (Grace), Mary Pat Gleason (Customer), Tony Mirzoian (Husband), Morgan Nagler (Dressing Room Girl), Andrew Bowen (Road Worker), Steve Kehela, Lee Garlington (Reporters), Joshua Ackerman, Kenny Blank, John Cho, Tressa Pope, Adrienne Smith, Chris Wylde (Students), Marty Belafsky, Lee Weaver (Military Police), Tom Davis, Gary Kent (Governor's Aides), Timothy R. Layton (Guard Gate Soldier), Angelo Vacco (Officer Thompson)

After a meteor crashes in the Arizona desert, two college professors investigate the matter and discover a rapidly evolving species of alien.

Seann William Scott

LARA CROFT: TOMB RAIDER

(PARAMOUNT) Producers, Lawrence Gordon, Lloyd Levin, Colin Wilson; Executive Producers, Jeremy Heath-Smith, Stuart Baird; Director/Adaptation, Simon West; Screenplay, Patrick Massett, John Zinman; Story, Sara B. Cooper, Mike Werb, Michael Colleary; Based on the Eidos Interactive game series developed by Core Design; Photography, Peter Menzies; Designer, Kirk M. Petruccelli; Editors, Dallas S. Puett, Glen Scantlebury; Costumes, Lindy Hemming; Co-Producer, Bobby Klein; Music, Graeme Revell; Music Supervsior, Peter Afterman; Special Effects Supervisor, Chris Corbould; 2nd Unit Director/Stunts, Simon Crane; Casting, John Hubbard, Ros Hubbard, Dan Hubbard; a Mutual Film Company presentation of a Lawrence Gordon production in association with Eidos Interactive Limited; Dolby; Panavision; Deluxe color; Rated PG-13; 100 minutes; Release date: June 15, 2001

CAST

Lara Croft	Angelina Jolie
Lord Croft	Jon Voight
Manfred Powell	Iain Glen
Bryce	Noah Taylor
Alex West	Daniel Craig
Distinguished Gentleman	Richard Johnson
Hillary	Christopher Barrie
Mr. Pimms	Julian Rhind-Tutt
Wilson	Leslie Phillips
Assault Team Leader	Robert Phillips
Young Lara	Rachel Appleton
Boothby's Auctioneer	Henry Wyndham
Head Laborers	David Y. Cheung, David K. S. Tse
Little Cambodian Girl	Ayla Amiral
Young Buddhist Monk	Wai-Keat Lau
Aged Buddhist Monk	Ozzie Yue
Little Inuit Girl	Stephanie Burns
Ancient High Priest	Carl Chase
Imperious Woman	Richenda Carey
UPS Guy	Sylvano Clarke
Russian Commander	Olegar Fedoro
Maid	Anna Maria Everett

Adventurer Lara Croft takes on a dangerous secret society in order to locate two halves of an ancient artifact that can grant its possessor great powers.

© Paramount Pictures Corp.

Angelina Jolie

Jon Voight

Iain Glen

Angelina Jolie, Chris Barrie, Noah Taylor

SONGCATCHER

(LIONS GATE) Producers, Richard Miller, Ellen Rigas-Venetis; Executive Producers, Caroline Kaplan, Jonathan Sehring; Director/Screenplay, Maggie Greenwald; Photography, Enrique Chediak; Designer, Ginger Tougas; Costumes, Kasia Walicka-Maimone; Editor, Keith Reamer; Music, David Mansfield; Casting, Vivian Hasbrouk, Tracy Kilpatrick, Ellen Parks; a Rigas Entertainment in association with the Independent Film Channel Productions presentation of an Ergoarts production; Dolby; Color; Rated PG-13; 105 minutes; Release date: June 22, 2001

CAST

Dr. Lily Penleric	Janet McTeer
Tom Bledsoe	Aidan Quinn
Viney Butler	Pat Carroll
Elna Penleric	Jane Adams
Fate Honeycutt	Gregory Cook
Rose Gentry	Iris DeMent
Alice Kincaid	Stephanie Roth Haberle
Earl Giddens	David Patrick Kelly

and E. Katherine Kerr (Harriet Tolliver), Taj Mahal (Dexter Speaks), Muse Watson (Parley Gentry), Emmy Rossum (Deladis Slocumb), Michael Davis (Dean Arthur Pembroke), Michael Goodwin (Prof. Wallace Aldrich), Bart Hansard (Hilliard), Erin Blake Clanton (Polly), Kristin Hall (Isabel), Mike Harding (Reese Kincaid), Rhoda Griffis (Clementine McFarland), Steve Boles (Ambrose McFarland), Taylor Hayes (Rev. Merriweather), Josh Goforth (Will), Don Pedi (Barn Band, Dulcimer), Sheila Kay Adams (Sheila K. Adams), Bobby McMillon, Hazel Dickens (Singers at Barn Dance), Andrea Powell (Josie Moore), Danny Nelson (Uncle Cratis), David Ducey (Postman Johnson), Steven Sutherland (Cyrus Whittle)

In the early 1900s, Dr. Lily Penleric, a professor of musicology, arrives in a small Appalachian village to study bluegrass music.

Aidan Quinn, Janet McTeer

Janet McTeer

Eddie Murply, Tank the Bear

DR. DOLITTLE 2

(20TH CENTURY FOX) Producer, John Davis; Executive Producers, Neil Machlis, Joe Singer; Director, Steve Carr; Screenplay, Larry Levin; Based on the Doctor Dolittle stories by Hugh Lofting; Photography, Daryn Okada; Designer, William Sandell; Editor, Craig P. Herring; Co-Producers, Michele Imperator Stabile, Heidi Santelli; Visual Effects, Rhythm & Hues, Inc.; Costumes, Ruth Carter; Music, David Newman; Music Supervisor, Spring Aspers; Associate Producer, Aldric La'Auli Porter; Casting, Juel Bestrop, Jeanne McCarthy; a Davis Entertainment Company production; Dolby; Super 35 Widescreen; Deluxe color; Rated PG; 87 minutes; Release date: June 22, 2001

CAST

Dr. John Dolittle	Eddie Murphy
Lisa Dolittle	Kristen Wilson
Charisse Dolittle	Raven-Symoné
Maya Dolittle	Kyla Pratt
Eric	Lil'Zane
Secretary	Denise Dowse
The Crocodile Hunter	Steve Irwin
Eldon	James L. Avery
Eldon's Wife	Elayn J. Taylor
Eugene Wilson	Andy Richter
Jack Riley/Voice of Crocodile	Kevin Pollak
Judge	Victor Raider-Wexler
Joseph Potter	Jeffrey Jones

and Ken Campbell (Animal Control Officer), Mark Griffin (Logger), Tommy Bush (Farmer), Adam Vernier (Worker), Shaun Robinson (Newscaster), R. Doug Seus (Klondike Brown's Delivery Man), Googy Gress (Bear Announcer), Louise Lennon (Waitress), Lisa Marie Huguely (Shamu's Trainer), Tank the Bear (Archie); VOICE TALENT: Steve Zahn (Archie), Jacob Vargas (Pepito), Lisa Kudrow (Ava), Mike Epps (Sonny), Jamie Kennedy, Bob Odenkirk, Kenny Campbell, David Cross (Dogs/Animal Groupies), Renee Taylor (Tortoise), Phil Proctor (Drunk Monkey), Michael Rapaport (Joey the Raccoon), Isaac Hayes (Possum), Richard C. Sarafian (God Beaver), Reni Santoni (Rat #20), Andy Dick (Lennie the Weasel), Cedric the Entertainer, John Witherspoon (Zoo Bears), Joey Lauren Adams (Squirrel), Mandy Moore, Frankie Muniz (Bear Cubs), John DiMaggio (Seeing-Eye Dog), Georgia Engel (Giraffe), Clyde Kusatsu, Keone Young (Bees), David L. Lander, Michael McKean (Birds), Tara Mercurio (Deer), David DeLuise, Hal Sparks (School Fish), Norm Macdonald (Lucky), Arnold Schwarzenegger (White Wolf)

Hoping to help his animal friends save their forest from developers, veterinarian John Dolittle concocts a plan to find an endangered species protected by the law living in the condemned area. Sequel to the 1998 Fox film Dr. Dolittle, *with Murphy, Wilson, Raven-Symoné, and Pratt repeating their roles.*

THE FAST AND THE FURIOUS

(UNIVERSAL) Producer, Neal H. Moritz; Executive Producers, Doug Claybourne, John Pogue; Director, Rob Cohen; Screenplay, Gary Scott Thompson, Erik Bergquist, David Ayer; Screen Story, Gary Scott Thompson; Photography, Ericson Core; Designer, Waldemar Kalinowski; Editor, Peter Honess; Music, BT; Music Supervisors, Gary Jones, Happy Walters; Costumes, Sanja Milkovic Hays; Stunts/Second Unit Director, Mic Rodgers; Visual Effects Supervisor, Michael J. Wassel; a Neal H. Moritz production, presented in association with Mediastream Film; Dolby; Super 35 Widescreen; Deluxe color; Rated PG-13; 108 minutes; Release date: June 22, 2001

Vin Diesel, Paul Walker

CAST

Brian O'Conner ....Paul Walker
Dominic Toretto ....Vin Diesel
Letty ....Michelle Rodriguez
Mia Toretto ....Jordana Brewster
Johnny Tran..Rick Yune
Jesse ....Chad Lindberg
Leon ....Johnny Strong
Vince...Matt Schulze
Sgt. Tanner ....Ted Levine
Edwin ....Ja Rule
Harry ....Vyto Ruginis
Agent Bilkins ....Thom Barry
Muse ....Stanton Rutledge
Hector...Noel Guglielmi
Danny Yamato...RJ De Vera
Ted Gassner ....Beau Holden
Lance Nguyen ....Reggie Lee
Rasta Racer ....David Douglas
Samoan Guard...Peter Navy Tuiasosopo
Ferrari Driver ....Neal H. Moritz
and Doria Clare Anselmo (Ferrari Passenger), Glenn K. Ota (Johnny's Father), F. Valentino Morales (Dispatcher), Mike White (Night Truck Driver), Delphine Pacific (Racer's Edge Clerk), Monica Tamayo (Monica), Megan Baker (Gimel), Tammy Monica Gegamian (Edwin's Babe)

High-octane driver Dominic Toretto welcomes Brian O'Conner into the world of L.A. outlaw racing, not realizing that the new guy is, in fact, an undercover cop investigating a series of big-rig hijackings.

© Universal Studios

Paul Walker, Vin Diesel

(Clockwise from top left) Matt Schulze, Michelle Rodriguez, Vin Diesel, Paul Walker, Jordana Brewster, Rick Yune, Johnny Strong, Chad Lindberg

Ving Rhames, Tyrese Gibson

BABY BOY

(COLUMBIA) Producer/Director/Screenplay, John Singleton; Executive Producer, Dwight Williams; Photography, Charles E. Mills; Designer, Keith Brian Burns; Editor, Bruce Cannon; Costumes, Ruth Carter; Music, David Arnold; Casting, Kimberly R. Hardin; a New Deal Production; Dolby; Deluxe color; Rated R; 129 minutes; Release date: June 27, 2001

CAST

Jody	Tyrese Gibson
Yvette	Taraji P. Henson
Sweetpea	Omar Gooding
Peanut	Tamara Bass
Ms. Herron	Candy Brown Houston
Juanita	A. J. Johnson
Melvin	Ving Rhames
Kim	Angell Conwell
Do Dirty	Kareem Grimes
Sharika	Tracey Cherelle Jones
Joe Joe	Kaylan Bolton
Cake Man	Freez Luv
Patrice	Mo'Nique Imes-Jackson
Rachel	Juanita Jennings
Receptionist	Liris Crosse
Little Boys	Sylvester Robinson, Maasai Singleton
Roger	Mario William Jackson
Sneed	Keith Diamond
Winston	Frederick Ricks
Rodney	Snoop Dogg
Ms. Daniels	Selma McPherson
Woman	Asondra Hunter
Pandora	Tawny Dahl
Woman Inside	Alex Wright
Sheryl	Serese Teate
Chris	Olan Thompson

and Ephraim Benton, Java Benson (Young Thugs), Dejuan Guy (Looney Toon), Deon Gregory (Tony), Tracey L. Davis, Keiwan Spillman (Knuckleheads), Diamond Dawn Cook, Charlee Miyohshi (Women), Roma Alvarez (Mexican Neighbor), Limary Agosto (Lucy Girl), Amentha Dymally (Elderly Woman), Kym Whitley (Host), Hope Flood, Dannon Green (Guests), Cleopatra Singleton (Lil' Nut), Sheila L. Ward (Mourner), Jamaica Carter (Já Toi), Delores Gilbeaux, Yolanda Jones (Co-Workers), Terrance Holloway, Sir Hondes D. Williams, Sr., Calvin L. Valrie, Jr. (Dice Players), Eddie Clark (Street Vendor)

Jody, a 20-year-old African-American still living at his mother's house in South Central Los Angeles, realizes he must grow up and face life's responsibilities, including giving attention to the two women by whom he has fathered children.

© Columbia Pictures Industries Inc.

Snoop Dogg

Tyrese Gibson, Taraji P. Henson

A. J. Johnson, Tyrese Gibson

Jay Hernandez, Kirsten Dunst

Kirsten Dunst, Bruce Davison

Taryn Manning, Kirsten Dunst

Richard Steinmetz, Jay Hernandez

CRAZY/BEAUTIFUL

(TOUCHSTONE) Producers, Mary Jane Ufland, Harry J. Ufland, Rachel Pfeffer; Executive Producer, Guy Riedel; Director, John Stockwell; Screenplay, Phil Hay, Matt Manfredi; Co-Producer, Rick Dallago; Photography, Shane Hurlbut; Designer, Maia Javan; Editor, Melissa Kent; Costumes, Susan Matheson; Music, Paul Haslinger, Music Supervisors, Evyen Klean, P. J. Bloom; Casting, Randi Hiller, Sarah Halley Finn; an Ufland production; Dolby; Technicolor; Rated PG-13; 99 minutes; Release date: June 29, 2001

CAST

Nicole Oakley	Kirsten Dunst
Carlos Nuñez	Jay Hernandez
Tom Oakley	Bruce Davison
Luis	Herman Osorio
Eddie	Miguel Castro
Victor	Tommy De La Cruz
Hector	Rolando Molina
Mrs. Nuñez	Soledad St. Hilaire
Courtney	Lucinda Jenney
Maddy	Taryn Manning
Coach Bauer	Richard Steinmetz
Rosa	Ana Argueta
Jimmy, The Pilot	Neil Looy
Morgan	Marion Moseley
Dr. Linehan	Mike Jones
Mrs. Ellis	Carolyn McKnight
Assistant Football Coach Stover	Michael J. Fisher
Wilcox	Cory Hardrict
Foster	Keram Malicki-Sanchez
Lainie	Kimi Reichenberg
Davis	Matthew McKane

and Jim Jackman (Detail Supervisor), Kevin Kane (Mr. Kane), Griselda Diaz (Taco Vendor), Claudia Soundy (Spandexed Latina Girl), Rick Dallago (Photo Teacher), Berenice Ayala (Blanca), Virginia Sanchez (Aunt Eva), Hank Mendoza (Guy on Street), Maria Diaz (Oakley's Receptionist), Louie Liberti (Casey), Bob Sattler, John Marrott (Police Officers), Josh Vaughn (Curtis), Devon Williams, David Benitez (Band Singers), Tracy Claustro (Luz), Jackie Napal (Jackie), Gary Cruz, Magdaleno Robles, Jr. (Dealers), Matt Hobbie (Quarterback), John Pemberton (Football Official)

Carlos, a straight-A high-school student from East L.A., falls in love with Nicole, the troubled, rebellious daughter of a wealthy congressman.

Jude Law, Haley Joel Osment

Jude Law, Haley Joel Osment

A.I.: ARTIFICIAL INTELLIGENCE

(WARNER BROS./DREAMWORKS) Producers, Kathleen Kennedy, Steven Spielberg, Bonnie Curtis; Executive Producers, Jan Harlan, Walter F. Parkes; Director/Screenplay, Steven Spielberg; Based on a screenplay story by Ian Watson; Based on the short story *Super Toys Last All Summer* by Brian Aldiss; Photography, Janusz Kaminski; Designer, Rick Carter; Costumes, Bob Ringwood; Editor, Michael Kahn; Music, John Williams; Robot Characters Designed by Stan Winston Studio; Special Visual Effects & Animation, Industrial Light & Magic; Casting, Avy Kaufman; an Amblin/Stanley Kubrick production; Dolby; Technicolor; Rated PG-13; 146 minutes; Release date: June 29, 2001

CAST

David	Haley Joel Osment
Gigolo Joe	Jude Law
Monica Swinton	Frances O'Connor
Henry Swinton	Sam Robards
Martin Swinton	Jake Thomas
Lord Johnson-Johnson	Brendan Gleeson
Professor Hobby	William Hurt
Voice of Teddy	Jack Angel

Cybertronics

Syatyoo Sama	Ken Leung
Colleague	April Grace
Executive	Matt Winston
Secretary	Sabrina Grdevich

and Clark Gregg, Kevin Sussman, Tom Gallop, Eugene Osment (Supernerds)

The Birthday Party

Todd	Theo Greenly

and Jeremy James Kisner, Dillon McEwin, Andy Morrow, Curt Youngberg (Kids)

Shangri-La Hotel

Gigolo Jane	Ashley Scott
Mr. Williamson, The Bellman	John Prosky
The Murderer	Enrico Colantoni
Patricia in the Mirrored Room	Paula Malcomson

Flesh Fair

Stage Manager	Michael Berresse
Amanda	Haley King
Teenage Honey	Kathryn Morris
Child Singer	Daveigh Chase
Backstage Bull	Brian Turk

and Justina Machado (Assistant), Tim Rigby (Yeoman), Lily Knight (Voice in the Crowd), Vito Carenzo (Big Man), Rena Owen (Ticket Taker), J. Alan Scott (Worker), Adam Alexi-Malle (Crowd Member), Laurence Mason (Tech Director), Brent Sexton (Russell), Ken Palmer, Jason Sutter (Percussionists)

Jude Law (center)

Haley Joel Osment, Jude Law

Rogue City

Cop	Michael Shamus Wiles
Kate, The Holographic Girl	Kelly McCool

Mechas

Fern Mecha Nanny	Clara Bellar
Roadworker	Keith Campbell
Laboratory Technician	Tim Edward Rhoze
Chef	Jim Jansen
General Circuita	Eliza Coleman
Welder	R. David Smith

and Wayne Wilderson (Comedian), Bobby Harwell (TV Face), Billy Scudder (Mechanic)

Voices

Doctor Know	Robin Williams
Specialist/Narrator	Ben Kingsley
Blue Mecha	Meryl Streep
Comedian	Chris Rock
Gardener	Erik Bauersfeld

and Michael Mantell (Doctor Frasier at Cyrogenic Institute), Miguel Perez, Matt Malloy (Robot Repairmen), Adrian Grenier, Mark Staubach, Michael Fishman (Teens in Van), Jeanine Salla (Sentient Machine Therapist), Laia Salla (Mr. Chan's Assistant), Diane Fletcher (Sentient Machine Security), Kate Nei (Toe Bell Ringing), Red King (Covert Information Retrieval), Al Jourgensen, Paul Barker, Max Brody, Duane Buford, Adam Grossman, Ty Coon (Flesh Fair Band)

In the distant future, a cybertronic robot boy, David, becomes the surrogate child for a couple whose real son is facing a terminal illness. After David accidentally harms the real child, he is cast out into the world where he finds himself being hunted along with other rejected robots.

This film received Oscar nominations for visual effects and original score.

© Warner Bros. and DreamWorks, LLC

CATS & DOGS

(WARNER BROS.) Producers, Andrew Lazar, Chris Defaria, Warren Zide, Craig Perry; Executive Producers, Bruce Berman, Chris Bender, J. C. Spink; Director, Lawrence Guterman; Screenplay, John Requa, Glenn Ficarra; Photography, Julio Macat; Designer, James Bissell; Editors, Michael Stevenson, Rick W. Finney; Music, John Debney; Costumes, Tish Monaghan; Visual Effects Supervisor/Associate Producer, Ed Jones; Animatronic Effects, David Barclay; Creature Effects, Jim Henson's Creature Shop; Visual Effects, Rhythm & Hues; Casting, Marci Liroff; a Mad Chance/Zide/Perry production, presented in association with Village Roadshow Pictures and NPV Entertainment; Dolby; Technicolor; Rated PG; 87 minutes; Release date: July 4, 2001

CAST

Professor Brody	Jeff Goldblum
Carolyn Brody	Elizabeth Perkins
Sophie	Miriam Margolyes
Scott Brody	Alexander Pollock

VOICE CAST

Lou	Tobey Maguire
Butch	Alec Baldwin
Mr. Tinkles	Sean Hayes
Ivy	Susan Sarandon
Peek	Joe Pantoliano
Sam	Michael Clarke Duncan
Calico	Jon Lovitz
Doberman Drill Sergeant	Victor Wilson
Collie at HQ	Salome Jens
The Mastiff	Charlton Heston
Russian Itty	Glenn Ficarra
Ninjas	Danny Mann, Billy West
Wolf Blitzer	Paul Pape

and additional CAST: Myron Natwick (Mr. Mason), Doris Chillcott (Mrs. Calvert), Kirsten Robek (Pie Mom), Frank C. Turner (The Farmer), Mar Andersons (Guard at Gate), Gillian Barber (Factory Receptionist), Carol Ann Susi, Randi Kaplan, Mary Bogue (Sisters), lvin Sanders, Mark Schooley (Employees), Lou Bollo, Scott Nicholson, Trish Schill (Workers), Babe Dolan (Wife Passenger), Reg Glass, Charles André (Truck Drivers), Peggy Logan (Nurse), Alicia Michelle (Jogger)

Mr. Tinkles, a Persian cat bent on world domination, plots to alter a vaccine being developed by Professor Brody, so that it will make all humans allergic to dogs.

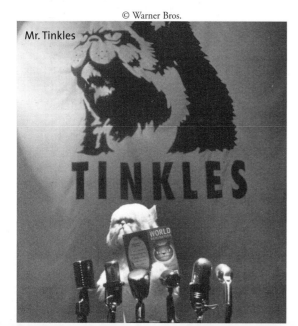

Mr. Tinkles

Dr. Aki Ross

FINAL FANTASY: THE SPIRITS WITHIN

(COLUMBIA) Producers, Hironobu Sakaguchi, Jun Aida, Chris Lee; Director/Story, Hironobu Sakaguchi; Co-Director, Moto Sakakibara; Screenplay, Al Reinert, Jeff Vintar; Music, Elliot Goldenthal; Music Supervisor, Richard Rudolph; Associate Producer, Katsuhiko Toyota; Casting/Voice Director, Jack Fletcher; Conceptual Design Artist, Kazunori Nakazawa; Animation Director, Andy Jones; Computer Graphics Supervisor, Gary Mundell; Original Character Designer, Shuko Murase; Editor, Christopher S. Capp; a Square Pictures presentation; U.S.-Japanese; Dolby; Deluxe color; Rated PG-13; 106 minutes; Release date: July 11, 2001

VOICE CAST

Doctor Aki Ross	Ming-Na
Captain Gray Edwards	Alec Baldwin
Ryan	Ving Rhames
Neil	Steve Buscemi
Jane	Peri Gilpin
Doctor Sid	Donald Sutherland
General Hein	James Woods
Council Members	Keith David, Jean Simmons
Major Elliot	Matt McKenzie

In the distant future, when Earth has been taken over by aliens, Aki Ross and her mentor, Dr. Sid, work to develop an antidote to counteract the alien force.

MADE

(ARTISAN) Producers, Vince Vaughn, Jon Favreau; Executive Producer, John Starke; Director/Screenplay, Jon Favreau; Photography, Chris Doyle; Designer, Anne Stuhler; Costumes, Laura Jean Shannon; Co-Producer, Peter Billingsley; Editor, Curtiss Clayton; Music, John O'Brien, Lyle Workman; Music Supervisors, Damon Booth, Pete Giberga, Sean Riciglaino, Tim Riley; Dolby; Color; Rated R; 94 minutes; Release date: July 13, 2001

CAST

Bobby...Jon Favreau
Ricky..Vince Vaughn
Jessica...Famke Janssen
Max..Peter Falk
Ruiz...Sean "Puffy" Combs
Horrace...Faizon Love
Welshman...David O'Hara
Jimmy...Vincent Pastore
Chloe...Mackenzie Vega
Wendy...Jenteal
and Tom Morello (Best Man), Joe Goossen (Referee), Jonathan Silverman (Bachelor), Kimberley Davies (Bartender), Elizabeth Barondes (Wife), Gary Auerbach (Husband), Bill Capizzi (Arthur), Vernon Vaughn (Coach), Esta-Joy Peters (Salesperson), Jennifer Bransford (Flight Attendant), Jason Delgado (Man on Phone), Leonardo Cimino (Leo), Federico Castelluccio, Matt O'Dwyer, Jason Fabrini (Doormen), Joan Favreau (Zoo Lady), Jamie Harris (Rogue), Tim Gallin (Thug), Dustin Diamond (Himself), Brian Donahue (Westie), Sam Rockwell (Hotel Clerk), Drea de Matteo (Prostitute)

Bobby and his co-worker Ricky decide that the best way to dig themselves out of their dead-end lives is to take a job with mobster Max, who sends the two men to New York to hook up with money-launderer Ruiz.

Vince Vaughn, Jon Favreau

Peter Falk

Vince Vaughn, Faizon Love, Sean "Puffy" Combs,
Jon Favreau

Vince Vaughn

Edward Norton, Robert De Niro

THE SCORE

(PARAMOUNT) Producers, Gary Foster, Lee Rich; Executive Producers, Bernie Williams, Adam Platnick; Director, Frank Oz; Screenplay, Kario Salem, Lem Dobbs, Scott Marshall Smith; Story, Daniel E. Taylor, Kario Salem; Photography, Rob Hahn; Designer, Jackson De Govia; Music, Howard Shore; Executive Music Producer, Budd Carr; Editor, Richard Pearson; Costumes, Aude Bronson-Howard; Casting, Margery Simkin; a Mandalay Pictures presentation of a Horseshoe Bay/Lee Rich production; Dolby; Panavision; Deluxe color; Rated R; 120 minutes; Release date: July 13, 2001

CAST

Nick Wells	Robert De Niro
Jack Teller (Brian)	Edward Norton
Max	Marlon Brando
Diane	Angela Bassett
Burt	Gary Farmer
Danny	Paul Soles
Steven	Jamie Harrold
Laurent	Serge Houde
André	Jean Rene Ouellet
Jean-Claude	Martin Drainville
Albert	Claude Despins
Sapperstein	Richard Waugh
Sapperstein's Cousin	Mark Camacho
Woman in Study	Marie-Josee D'Amours
Man in Study	Gavin Svensson
Tuan	Thinh Truong Nguyen
Cop	Carlo Essagian
Drunk	Christian Tessier
Storekeeper	Lenie Scoffie

and Bobby Brown (Tony), Maurice Demers (Philippe), Christian Jacques, Henry Farmer, Dacky Thermidor, Gerard Blouin (Guards), Charles V. Doucet (Old Engineer), Pierre Drolet (Worker), Norman Mikeal Berketa (Bureaucrat Official), Eric Hoziel (Ironclad Tech), John Talbot (Janitor), Richard Zeman, Nick Carasoulis (Thugs), Cassandra Wilson, Mose Allison (Themselves)

Against his better judgment, master safecracker Nick Wells agrees to team with young thief Jack Teller to steal a valuable item from the Montreal Customs House.

© Paramount Pictures and MP Film Management TS Productions. GmbH & Co. KG

Robert De Niro

Robert De Niro, Edward Norton, Marlon Brando

Robert De Niro, Angela Bassett

BULLY

(LIONS GATE) Producers, Chris Hanley, Don Murphy, Fernando Sulichin; Executive Producers, Jordan Gertner, Mark Mower, Manuel Chiche, Arnaud Duteil, Vincent Maraval; Director, Larry Clark; Screenplay, Zachary Long, Roger Pullis; Based on the novel *Bully: A True Story of High School Revenge* by Jim Schutze; Photography, Steve Gainer; Designer, Linda Burton; Costumes, Carleen Ileana Rosado; Editor, Andrew Hafitz; Co-Producers, Guy Stodel, Peter Block, Robert Pfeffer; Associate Producer, Brad Renfro; Casting, Carmen Cuba; a Studio Canal presentation of a Muse/Blacklist Production in association with Gravity Entertainment; Dolby; Color; Rated R; 106 minutes; Release date: July 13, 2001

CAST

Marty Puccio	Brad Renfro
Lisa Connelly	Rachel Miner
Bobby Kent	Nick Stahl
Ali Willis	Bijou Phillips
Donny Semenec	Michael Pitt
Heather Swallers	Kelli Garner
Derek Dzvirko	Daniel Franzese
Derek Kaufman, The Hitman	Leo Fitzpatrick
Claudia	Nathalie Paulding
Blonde	Jessica Sutta
Mr. Kent	Edward Amatrudo
Mr. Willis	Steven Raulerson
Mrs. Willis	Judith Clayton
Mr. Puccio	Alan Lilly
Mrs. Connelly	Elizabeth Dimon
Mr. Kaufman	Larry Clark

and Jo-Aynne von Born (Claudia's Mother), Marc Pearson (Marty's Brother), Joseph Shrouder (Terry), Scott McHugh (Boy at Beach), John Parker, Phillip Ortiz (Video Game Boys), Lindzee Warren, Alexandra Steele (Girls at Mall), Sam Steele, Anthony Barrineau, Derek Oliveira (Hitman Gang Boy), Rick Amicucci (Hitman's Brother), Rick Seguso (Gay Man), Jesse Dechant (Dildo Man), Det. Frank Ilarraza (Himself), Carlos Hernandez, Danny Norton (Club Dancers on Stage)

The true story of how a Florida teen's bullying behavior toward his friend led to his murder.

Bijou Phillips, Rachel Miner, Brad Renfro

Brad Renfro, Nick Stahl

Bijou Phillips, Kelli Garner, Daniel Franzese

Jennifer Coolidge, Reese Witherspoon

LEGALLY BLONDE

(MGM) Producers, Marc Platt, Ric Kidney; Director, Robert Luketic; Screenplay, Karen McCullah Lutz, Kirsten Smith; Based on the book by Amanda Brown; Photography, Anthony B. Richmond; Designer, Melissa Stewart; Costumes, Sophie de Rakoff Carbonell; Editors, Anita Brandt Burgoyne, Garth Craven; Music, Rolfe Kent; Music Supervisor, Anita Camarata; Co-Producers, David Nicksay, Christian McLaughlin; Casting, Joseph Middleton; a Marc Platt production; Dolby; Super 35 Widescreen; Color; Rated PG-13; 96 minutes; Release date: July 13, 2001

CAST

Elle Woods	Reese Witherspoon
Emmett Richmond	Luke Wilson
Vivian Kensington	Selma Blair
Warner	Matthew Davis
Professor Callahan	Victor Garber
Paulette	Jennifer Coolidge
Professor Stromwell	Holland Taylor
Brooke Taylor Windham	Ali Larter
Margot	Jessica Cauffiel
Serena	Alanna Ubach
Dorky David	Oz Perkins
Chutney	Linda Cardellini
UPS Guy	Bruce Thomas
Enid	Meredith Scott Lynn
Mrs. Windham Vandermark	Raquel Welch
Claire	Samantha Lemole

and Kelly Nyks (Arrogant Aaron), Ted Kairys (Gerard), Michael B. Silver (Bobby), Kimberly McCullough (Amy), Shannon O'Hurley (DA Joyce Rafferty), Greg Serano (Enrique), Francesca P. Roberts (Marina R. Bickford), Lisa Kushell (Boutique Saleswoman), Natalie Barish (Old Lady at Manicurist), Cici Lau (LA Nail Technician), Allyce Beasley (CULA Advisor), Kevin Cooney (Head of Admissions), Ted Rooney, David Moreland, Wayne Federman (Admissions Guys), James Read (Elle's Father), Tane McClure (Elle's Mother), Niklaus Lange (Annoyed 2L), Doug Spinuzza (Intense Ivan Berliner), Lisa K. Wyatt (Jail House Guard), Jason Christopher (Chuck), Corinne Reilly, Victoria Mahoney (Reporters), Lacey Beeman (Nervous 1L Girl), Melissa Young (Blonde Cheerleader), Brody Hutzler (Grant), Chaney Kley (Brandon), John Cantwell (Maurice), Ondrea De Vincentis (Callahan's Assistant), Terrence Michael (Desk Clerk), Nectar Rose (Freshman Girl), Jodi Harris (Another Sister), Patricia Kimes (Blonde Biker), Sasha Barrese (Another Girl), Kelly Driscoll (Blonde Card Carrier), Elizabeth Matthews, Kennedy Stone (Sorority Girls), Moonie (Bruiser), Lily (Rufus)

Dumped by her politically ambitious boyfriend for not being suitably "serious" enough to further his career, Elle Woods makes it her goal to overcome her "dumb blonde" image by getting into Harvard Law School.

© Metro-Goldwyn-Mayer Pictures, Inc.

Selma Blair, Matthew Davis

Linda Cardellini, Reese Witherspoon

Shannon O'Hurley, Victor Garber,
Luke Wilson, Reese Witherspoon

JURASSIC PARK III

(UNIVERSAL) Producers, Kathleen Kennedy, Larry Franco; Executive Producer, Steven Spielberg; Director, Joe Johnston; Screenplay, Peter Buchman, Alexander Payne, Jim Taylor; Based on characters created by Michael Crichton; Photography, Shelly Johnson; Designer, Ed Verreaux; Editor, Robert Dalva; Music, Don Davis, John Williams; Costumes, Betsy Cox; Animation & Special Visual Effects, Industrial Light & Magic; Visual Effects Supervisor, Jim Mitchell; Visual Effects Producer, Mark S. Miller; Live Action Dinosaurs, Stan Winston; Casting, Nancy Foy; Stunts, Pat Romano; an Amblin Entertainment production; Dolby; Color; Rated PG-13; 91 minutes; Release date: July 18, 2001

Sam Neill

CAST

Dr. Alan Grant..Sam Neill
Paul Kirby ....William H. Macy
Amanda Kirby ....Téa Leoni
Billy Brennan ....Alessandro Nivola
Eric Kirby ....Trevor Morgan
Udesky..Michael Jeter
Cooper..John Diehl
Nash..Bruce A. Young
Ellie ....Laura Dern
Mark..Taylor Nichols
Ben Hildebrand ....Mark Harelik
Enrique Cardoso ....Julio Oscar Mechoso
Charlie..Blake Bryan
Cheryl..Sarah Danielle Madison
Hannah ....Linda Park
Symposium Leader ....Sonia Jackson
Science Reporter..Bruce French
Students....................................Bernard Zilinskas, Rona Benson
Man in Suit ....Frank Clem

Two wealthy adventurers agree to fund Dr. Alan Grant's research project if he will accompany them to Isla Sorna, where genetically engineered prehistoric creatures roam and they hope to locate their missing son. Third in the Universal series following Jurassic Park *(1993) and* The Lost World: Jurassic Park *(1997); Sam Neill and Laura Dern repeat their roles from the first film.*

Téa Leoni, William H. Macy, Michael Jeter

Michael Jeter, Alessandro Nivola, Téa Leoni,
Sam Neill, William H. Macy

John Cameron Mitchell

(Clockwise from center): John Cameron Mitchell, Rob Campbell, Stephen Trask, Miriam Shor, Michael Aronov, Theodore Liscinski

Andrea Martin, John Cameron Mitchell

John Cameron Mitchell

Theodore Liscinski, Stephen Trask, Michael Aronov, John Cameron Mitchell, Miriam Shor, Rob Campbell

John Cameron Mitchell, Miriam Shor

John Cameron Mitchell, Michael Pitt

HEDWIG AND THE ANGRY INCH

(FINE LINE FEATURES) Producers, Christine Vachon, Katie Roumel, Pamela Koffler; Executive Producers, Michael De Luca, Amy Henkels, Mark Tusk; Director/Screenplay, John Cameron Mitchell; Photography, Frank G. DeMarco; Designer, Thérèse Deprez; Costumes, Arianne Phillips; Music/Lyrics/Original Score, Stephen Trask; Editor, Andrew Marcus; Hedwig's Hair and Makeup, Mike Potter; Animated Sequences and Artwork, Emily Hubley; Executive Music Producer, Alex Steyermark; Line Producer, Colin Brunton; Casting, Susan Shopmaker; a New Line Cinema presentation of a Killer Films production; Dolby; Color; Rated R; 91 minutes; Release date: July 20, 2001

John Cameron Mitchell

CAST

Hedwig/Hansel Schmidt	John Cameron Mitchell
Yitzhak	Miriam Shor
Skszp	Stephen Trask
Jacek	Theodore Liscinski
Krzysztof	Rob Campbell
Schlatko	Michael Aronov
Phyllis Stein	Andrea Martin
Hansel (6 years old)	Ben Mayer-Goodman
Hansel's Mom	Alberta Watson
Hansel's Dad	Gene Pyrz
Tommy Gnosis	Michael Pitt
Tommy's Publicist	Karen Hines
Goth Menses Boy	Max Toulch
Sgt. Luther Robinson	Maurice Dean Wint
Fat Man	Ermes Blarasin
Kwahg-Yi	Sook-Yin Lee

and Maggie Moore (Trailer Park Neighbor), Renate Options (Tranny Hooker)

Having gone through a botched sex-change operation in an effort to get out of East Berlin, Hedwig makes a living as a second-rate singer, trying to capitalize on her celebrity as the supposed ex-lover of noted rock star Tommy Gnosis. John Cameron Mitchell, Miriam Shor, and Stephen Trask repeat their roles from the original 1998 Off-Broadway production.

John Cameron Mitchell, Michael Pitt

Scarlett Johansson, Thora Birch

Thora Birch, Steve Buscemi

Thora Birch

GHOST WORLD

(UNITED ARTISTS) Producers, Lianne Halfon, John Malkovich, Russell Smith; Executive Producers, Pippa Cross, Janette Day; Director, Terry Zwigoff; Screenplay, Daniel Clowes, Terry Zwigoff; Based on the comic book by Daniel Clowes; Photography, Affonso Beato; Designer, Edward T. McAvoy; Costumes, Mary Zophres; Line Producer, Barbara A. Hall; Editors, Carole Kravetz-Aykanian, Michael R. Miller; Music, David Kitay; Casting, Cassandra Kulukundis; a Granada Film in association with Jersey Shore and Advanced Medien presentation of a Mr. Mudd production; Distributed by MGM Distribution Co.; Dolby; Color; Rated R; 111 minutes; Release date: July 20, 2001

CAST

Enid	Thora Birch
Rebecca	Scarlett Johansson
Seymour	Steve Buscemi
Josh	Brad Renfro
Roberta	Illeana Douglas
Enid's Dad	Bob Balaban
Dana	Stacey Travis
Norman	Charles C. Stevenson, Jr.
Doug	Dave Sheridan
Joe	Tom McGowan
Melorra	Debra Azar
Sidewinder Boss	Brian George
John Ellis	Pat Healy
Graduation Speaker	Rini Bell
Todd	T. J. Thyne
Weird Al	Ezra Buzzington
Maxine	Teri Garr
Vanilla	Lindsey Girardot
Jade	Joy Bisco
Ebony	Venus DeMilo Thomas
Margaret	Ashley Peldon
Phillip	Chachi Pittman
Black Girl	Janece Jordan
Snotty Girl	Kaileigh Martin
Hippy Boy	Alexander Fors
Angry Guy (Jerome)	Marc Vann
Asian Guy (Steven)	James Sie
Fussy Guy (Paul)	Paul Keith
Pushy Guy (Gerrold)	David Cross
Fred Chatman	J. J. Bad Boy Jones
Red-Haired Girl	Dylan Jones
MC	Martin Grey

Blueshammer..........Steve Pierson, Jake LaBotz, Johnny Irion, Nate Wood and Charles Schneider (Joey McCobb), Edward T. McAvoy (Mr. Satanist), Sid Garza-Hillman, Joshua Wheeler (Zine-O-Phobia Creeps), Patrick Fishler (Masterpiece Video Clerk), Daniel Graves (Masterpiece Video Customer), Matt Doherty (Masterpiece Video Employee), Joel Michaely (Porno Cashier), Debi Derryberry (Rude Coffee Customer), Joe Sikora (Regga Fan), Brett Gilbert (Alien Autopsy Guy), Alex Solowitz (Cineplex Manager), Tony Ketcham (Alcoholic Customer), Mary Bogue (Popcorn Customer), Brian Jacobs (Soda Customer), Patrick Yonally (Garage Sale Hipster), Lauren Bowles (Angry Garage Sale Woman), Lorna Scott (Art Show Curator), Jeff Murray (Roberta's Colleague), Jerry Rector (Dana's Co-Worker), Sheriff John Bunnell (Seymour's Boss), Diane Salinger (Psychiatrist), Anna Berger (Seymour's Mother), Bruce Glover (Feldman, Wheelchair Guy)

Two teenage girls, Enid and Rebecca, disillusioned with the phony world they live in, play a practical joke on a lonely older man, Seymour, only to have Enid realize that she has found a soul mate in the alienated malcontent.

This film received an Oscar nomination for adapted screenplay.

Thora Birch, Steve Buscemi

Brad Renfro

Scarlett Johansson, Charles C. Stevenson, Jr., Thora Birch

Bob Balaban, Teri Garr

Illeana Douglas

AMERICA'S SWEETHEARTS

(COLUMBIA) Producers, Susan Arnold, Donna Arkoff Roth, Billy Crystal; Executive Producers, Charles Newirth, Peter Tolan; Director, Joe Roth; Screenplay, Billy Crystal, Peter Tolan; Photography, Phedon Papamichael; Designer, Garreth Stover; Editor, Stephen A. Rotter; Music, James Newton Howard; Music Supervisor, Kathy Nelson; Costumes, Ellen Mirojnick, Jeffrey Kurland; Casting, Junie Lowry-Johnson, Libby Goldstein; a Roth/Arnold Production, a Face Production; Dolby; Panavision; Deluxe color; Rated PG-13; 102 minutes; Release date: July 20, 2001

John Cusack, Catherine Zeta-Jones

CAST

Kiki Harrison ....Julia Roberts
Lee Phillips...Billy Crystal
Gwen Harrison ....Catherine Zeta-Jones
Eddie Thomas ....John Cusack
Hector...Hank Azaria
Dave Kingman...Stanley Tucci
Hal Weidmann...Christopher Walken
Wellness Guide ....Alan Arkin
Danny Wax ....Seth Green
Davis...Scot Zeller
Themselves..Larry King, Byron Allen
Limo Driver ....Steve Pink
Dave O'Hanlon..Rainn Wilson
Security Guards ....Eric Balfour, Marty Belafsky
Leaf ....Keri Lynn Pratt
Adinah ....Maria Canals
and Charley Steiner (Nevada Anchorman), Shaun Robinson (Nevada Anchorwoman), Jeff Michael (Network Anchor), Sibila Vargas (Reporter), Jane Yamamoto (Reporter on Patio), Wendy Schenker (Maura Klein), Jim Ferguson (Mort Josephson), Lisa Joyner (Laura Messinger), Patrick Stoner (Bob), Sam Rubin (Ken), Susan Katz (Interviewer), Maree Cheatham (Matronly Interviewer), Amber Barretto (Alison), Alex Enberg, Sarah Loew (Larry King Producers), Joseph Feingold (Judge), Sherry Jennings (Bar Hostess), Julie Sorrels (Mother), Austin L. Sorrels (Little Boy), Julie Wagner, Leilani Muenter (Callers), Dimitri Moraitis (Agent), Shawn Driscoll (Sean), Misti See (Misti), Gail Laskowski (Gail)

John Cusack, Julia Roberts

In order to save his career, press agent Lee Phillips coaxes estranged movie-star couple Gwen Harrison and Eddie Thomas to appear together at a press junket for their newest film.

© Revolution Studios

Seth Green   Alan Arkin

Julia Roberts, Billy Crystal

Stanley Tucci, Billy Crystal

WET HOT AMERICAN SUMMER

(USA FILMS) Producer, Howard Bernstein; Director, David Wain; Screenplay/Co-Producers, Michael Showalter, David Wain; Photography, Ben Weinstein; Designer, Mark White; Costumes, Jill Kliber; Editor, Meg Reticker; Line Producer, Jill Rubin; Music, Theodore Shapiro, Craig Wedren; Casting, Susie Farris; a Eureka Pictures production in association with North Coast Group of a Showalter/Wain Movie; Dolby; DuArt color; Rated R; 97 minutes; Release date: July 27, 2001

CAST

Beth	Janeane Garofalo
Henry	David Hyde Pierce
Coop/Alan Shemper	Michael Showalter
Katie	Marguerite Moreau
Andy	Paul Rudd
J. J.	Zak Orth
Gene	Christopher Meloni
Gary	A. D. Miles
Gail	Molly Shannon
Aaron	Gideon Jacobs
Victor	Ken Marino
Neil	Joe Lo Truglio
McKinley	Michael Ian Black
Arty	Liam Norton
Susie	Amy Poehler
Ben	Bradley Cooper
Abby	Marisa Ryan
Lindsay	Elizabeth Banks

and Gabriel Millman (Caped Boy), Kevin Sussman (Steve), Kevin Thomas Conroy (Mork Guy), Christopher Cusamano (Medieval Kid), Madeline Blue (Cure Girl), Cassidy Ladden (Mallrat Girl), Nina Hellman (Nancy), Peter Salett (Guitar Dude), Judah Friedlander (Ron), Jacob Shoesmith Fox (Moose), Whitney Vance (Valerie), Benjamin Coppola (Bobby), Jon Benjamin (Can of Vegetables), Jake Fogelnest (Silas), Ian Helfer (Bear Claw Coach), Jordan Maclean (Alexa), Avi Setton (Standup Comic), Kyle Gallner (Bobby's Buddy), Kathleen Pandolfo (Godspell Girl), Zachary Montgomery-Wicks (Gail's Boy Camper), Danny Hopkins, Christopher Connors (Raft Campers), Matt Carmeci (Bunk Boy), Stephen O'Brien, Timothy Gasiewski (Juke Box Kids), Angel Berlane, Christi Berlane (Friends Girls), Bob Walz (Drug Dealer), Joseph Kariuki (Kenyan Runner), Donna Mitchell (Gene's Wife), Joe Bryan, Christine Loebsack, Sandra Kennedy, Keith Oney (Counselors)

A group of counselors and campers spend a day of wacky high jinks on the final day of summer camp in 1981.

© USA Films

Bradley Cooper, Janeane Garofalo, Michael Ian Black

Paul Rudd, Marguerite Moreau

Michael Showalter, Christopher Meloni, A.D. Miles

Gideon Jacobs, Molly Shannon

Tim Roth, Mark Wahlberg

Michael Clarke Duncan

Helena Bonham Carter, Erick Avari, Evan Dexter Parke

Paul Giamatti (Left)

PLANET OF THE APES

(20TH CENTURY FOX) Producer, Richard D. Zanuck; Executive Producer, Ralph Winter; Director, Tim Burton; Screenplay, William Broyles, Jr., Lawrence Konner, Mark Rosenthal; Based on the novel *La Planète des singes (Monkey Planet)* by Pierre Boulle; Photography, Philippe Rousselot; Designer, Rick Heinrichs; Costumes, Colleen Atwood; Editor, Chris Lebenzon; Music, Danny Elfman; Visual Effects Supervisor, Bill George; Special Makeup Effects Designer and Creator, Rick Baker; Casting, Denise Chamian; Stunts, Charles Croughwell; a Zanuck Company production; Dolby; Panavision; Deluxe color; Rated PG-13; 120 minutes; Release date: July 27, 2001

CAST

Captain Leo Davidson	Mark Wahlberg
Thade	Tim Roth
Ari	Helena Bonham Carter
Attar	Michael Clarke Duncan
Limbo	Paul Giamatti
Daena	Estella Warren
Krull	Cary-Hiroyuki Tagawa
Sandar	David Warner
Karubi	Kris Kristofferson
Tival	Erick Avari
Birn	Luke Eberl
Gunnar	Evan Dexter Parke
Senator Nado	Glenn Shadix
Bon	Freda Foh Shen
Commander Karl Vasich	Chris Ellis
Lt. Col. Grace Alexander	Anne Ramsay
Major Maria Cooper	Andrea Grano
Major Frank Santos	Michael Jace
Specialist Hansen	Michael Wiseman
Nova	Lisa Marie
Leeta	Eileen Weisinger
Thade's Father	Charlton Heston
Gorilla Kid/Thade's Niece	Deep Roy
Red Ape Soldier/Man Hunt Ape	Chad Bannon
Limbo's 1st Handler/Ape Commande/2nd Ape Soldier	Kevin Grevioux
Limbo's 2nd Handler/1st Ape Soldier	Issac C. Singleton, Jr.
Ape Soldier	Quincy Taylor
Ape Dinner Guest/Old Man Servant/Old Ape #1	John Alexander
1st Ape Teenager/2nd Ape Soldier	Jay Caputo
2nd Ape Teenager/Gossiping Male Ape	Philip Tan
Little Human Girl	Callie Croughwell
Girl Pet	Allie Habberstad
Human Kid #1	Brett Smrz
Gorilla	Howard Berger
Old Ape #2	Rick Baker
Fruit Vendor	Chet Zar
Woman in Cart	Linda Harrison

and Cameron Croughwell, Joshua Croughwell, Hannah Peitzman, Molly Peitzman, Jesse Tipton, Shane Habberstad (Ape Soccer Kids), Eddie Adams, Todd Babcock, Lorenzo Callender, Shonda Farr, Kam Heskin, Jim Holmes, Todd Kimsey, Candace Kroslak, Joanna Krupa, Elizabeth Lackey, Mark Christopher Lawrence, Melody Perkins, Tate Taylor, Jonna Thompson (Friends at Leo's Party)

Astronaut Leo Davidson goes through a time warp and crash-lands on a planet where apes rule over humans. Remake of the 1968 20th Century Fox film Planet of the Apes; *two of the stars of that movie, Charlton Heston and Linda Harrison, make brief appearances here.*

THE PRINCESS DIARIES

(WALT DISNEY PICTURES) Producers, Whitney Houston, Debra Martin Chase, Mario Iscovich; Director, Garry Marshall; Screenplay, Gina Wendkos; Based on the novel by Meg Cabot; Photography, Karl Walter Lindenlaub; Designer, Mayne Berke; Costumes, Gary Jones; Editor, Bruce Green; Music, John Debney; Music Supervisor, Dawn Solér; Co-Producer, Ellen H. Schwartz; Casting, Marcia Ross, Donna Morong, Gail Goldberg; a Brownhouse production; Distributed by Buena Vista Pictures; Dolby; Technicolor; Rated G; 114 minutes; Release date: August 3, 2001

CAST

Queen Clarisse Renaldi ....Julie Andrews
Mia Thermopolis...Anne Hathaway
Joe ....Hector Elizondo
Lilly Moscovitz...Heather Matarazzo
Lana Thomas..Mandy Moore
Mia's Mom, Helen ....Caroline Goodall
Michael Moscovitz...Robert Schwartzman
Student Josh Bryant ....Erik Von Detten
Student Jeremiah Hart...Patrick Flueger
Teacher Mr. O'Connell ....Sean O'Bryan
Vice Principal Gupta...Sandra Oh
Charlotte Kutaway ....Kathleen Marshall
Paolo..Larry Miller
and Grove High School: Mindy Burbano (Gym Teacher Harbula), Kim Leigh (Music Teacher Wells), Beth Anne Garrison (Cheerleader Anna), Bianca Lopez (Cheerleader Fontana), Tamara Levinson (Cheerleader Lupe), Lenore Thomas (Cable Show Student Melissa), Erik Bragg (Student Bobby Bad), Abigail Green-Dove (Student Linda Green), Meredith Shevory (Student Meredith), Anita Marie Curran (Newspaper Student Anita), Korry Cannon (Newspaper Student Korry), Cassie Rowell (Singing Student Alice), Chrissy Gilman (Beach Student), Todd Lowe (Lana's Date Eric), Joe Unitas (Coach Joe Ewe), Reggie Stanton (Coach Dave Adams) The State Dinner: Joel McCrary (Prime Minister Motaz), Clare Sera (Mrs. Motaz), Juliet Elizondo (Daughter Marissa Motaz), Greg Lewis (Baron Siegfried von Troken), Bonnie Aarons (Baroness Joy von Troken), Darwood Chung (Emperor Sakamoto), Julie Paris (Princess Palisades), Jeff Michalski (Scottish Duke), Erin O'Reilly (Scottish Duchess), Steve Restivo (Count Vitello), Brigitta Lauren (Lady Lindenlaub), Jane Morris (Lady Evergreen), Gary Combs (Lord Fricker), Adam Williams (Dinner Guest Adam), Marvin Braverman, Alan Kent (State Dinner Waiters)

The Genovian Consulate:

Bob Glaudini (Consulate Valet Adolpho), Bill Ferrell (Consulate Guard Darrell), Joe Ross (Consulate Maitre D'), Steve Totland (Consulate Waiter), Charles Guardino (Limo Driver Mel), Sparrow Heatley, Gwenda Perez (Gretchen & Helga), Barbara Marshall (Lady Jerome), Sam Denoff (Lord Jerome), Tracy Reiner (Press Secretary Spencer), Dale Hikawa (Band Leader Dawn Kawa), Daru Kawalkowski (Countess Puck), Diane Frazen (Ball Guest Diane), Stanley Frazen (Ball Guest Stanley), Barbara J. Nabozny (Ball Guest Barbara), Ira Glick (Ball Guest Dr. Glunk), Sol Rosenthal (Lawyer Ball Guest), Hope Alexander-Willis (Lady Caroline), Joe Allen Price (Father Joseph), Garry Marshall (Ball Guest), Major Willie L. Brown, Jr. (Himself)

The San Franciscans:

Patrick Richwood (Neighbor Mr. Robutusen), John McGivern (Cable Car Conductor Macintosh), Terry Brown (Policeman Washington), James Brown Orleans (Doctor Motors), Rob Zylowski (Pizza Delivery Man), Karl Makinen (Climbing Manager Schiavone), Sunny Hawks (Climbing Instructor Vivian), Kathy Garver (Cable Tourist), Mary Knoll, Jason Ashland (Trolley Tourists), Erika Young (Umbrella Lady), Ethan Sandler (Tour Bus Driver), Bill Fricker (Autograph Father), Shan Elliot, Harold Carter (Michael's Band Flypaper), Bud Markowitz (Pear Juggler), Michelle Yerger, Wendy Hallin (911 Nuns), Mark Thompson, Brian W. Phelps (DJ's Mark & Brian), Lily Marshall-Fricker, Charlotte Marshall-Fricker (Kid Autograph Seekers)

Reporters:

Sandra Taylor (Suki Sanchez), Tom Hines (Nelson Davenport), Nicholle Tom (Teen Repoter Cassie), Patrick Noonan (Suki's Cameraman), Ali Gage (Beach Reporter Ali), John Moran (Beach Photographer), Tanya DiFrancesco (Beach Reporter Tanya), Shannon Wilcox, Niloufar Safaie, Tonje Larsgard (Ball Reporters), Flora Chong, Reuben Grundy, Gwen Holloway (Street Reporters), Lori Sigrist, Terri Sigrist (Twin Reporters), Fat Louie (Himself)

Mia Thermopolis, a drab, unpopular San Francisco high school girl, is stunned to find out that her grandmother is the queen of a small European principality, making Mia the rightful heiress to the throne.

© Disney Enterprises, Inc.

Julie Andrews, Anne Hathaway

Anne Hathaway, Erik von Detten

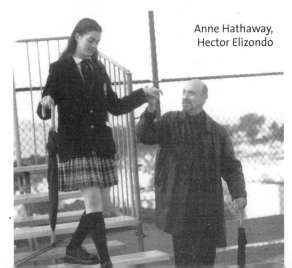

Anne Hathaway, Hector Elizondo

Chris Tucker, Jackie Chan

Chris Tucker

RUSH HOUR 2

(NEW LINE CINEMA) Producers, Arthur Sarkissian, Roger Birnbaum, Jay Stern, Jonathan Glickman; Executive Producers, Andrew Z. Davis, Michael De Luca, Toby Emmerich; Director, Brett Ratner; Screenplay, Jeff Nathanson; Based on character created by Ross La Manna; Co-Executive Producer, Leon Dudevoir; Photography, Matthew F. Leonetti; Designer, Terence Marsh; Editor, Mark Helfrich; Costumes, Rita Ryack; Music, Lalo Schifrin; Stunts/2nd Unit Director, Conrad E. Palmisano; Casting, Matthew Barry, Nancy Green-Keyes; an Arthur Sarkissian and Roger Birnbaum production; Dolby; Panavision; Deluxe color; Rated PG-13; 90 minutes; Release date: August 3, 2001

CAST

Chief Inspector Lee	Jackie Chan
Det. James Carter	Chris Tucker
Ricky Tan	John Lone
Hu Li	Zhang Ziyi
Isabella	Roselyn Sanchez
Agent Sterling	Harris Yulin
Steven Reign	Alan King
Captain Chin	Kenneth Tsang
Receptionist	Lisa Lo Cicero
Girls in Car	Meiling Melancon, Maggie Q.
Club Hostess	Patricia Chan
Karaoke Singer	Gelbert Coloma
Message Parlor Hostess	Lucy Lin
Hostess #2	Cindy Lu
Suit Salesman	Pang Wing Sang
Chicken Lady	Mei Ling Wong
Cab Driver	William Tuen

and Shawn Peretz (Flight Attendant), Audrey Quock (Kenny's Wife), Ernie Reyes, Jr. (Zing), Jeremy Piven (Versace Salesman), Verena Mei (Casino Waitress), Joel McKinnon Miller (Tex), Angela Little, Julia Schultz (Tex's Girlfriends), Saul Rubinek (Box Man), Gianni Russo (Pit Boss), James J. Ghang (Stickman), Michael Chow, Teresa Lin, Tanya Newbould, Matt Barry, James Duke (Gamblers), Don Cheadle (Kenny)

Detectives Lee and Carter, on vacation in Hong Kong, find themselves investigating the bombing of the American Embassy, their trail of clues leading them to the head of the Fu-Cang-Long Triad, the deadliest gang in China. Sequel to the 1998 New Line Cinema release Rush Hour *that also starred Jackie Chan and Chris Tucker.*

© New Line Cinema

Zhang Ziyi

Jackie Chan, Chris Tucker

Angelina Jolie, Thomas Jane

Angelina Jolie, Antonio Banderas

ORIGINAL SIN

(MGM) Producers, Denise Di Novi, Kate Guinzburg, Carol Lees; Executive Producers, Sheldon Abend, Ashok Amritraj, David Hoberman; Director/Screenplay, Michael Cristofer; Based on the novel *Waltz Into Darkness* by Cornell Woolrich; Photography, Rodrigo Prieto; Designer, David J. Bomba; Costumes, Donna Zakowska; Music, Terence Blanchard; Song: "You Can't Walk Away From Me" by Gloria Estefan and Emilo Estefan, Jr./performed by Gloria Estefan; Co-Producer, Edward L. McDonnell; Line Producer, Michael S. Glick; Editor, Eric Sears; Casting, Junie Lowry Johnson, Libby Goldstein; a Via Rosa/Di Novi Pictures production in association with Intermedia/UGC International, presented in association with Hyde Park Entertainment; U.S.-French; Dolby; Panavision; Deluxe color; Rated R; 112 minutes; Release date: August 3, 2001

Angelina Jolie, Antonio Banderas

CAST

Luis Antonio Vargas	Antonio Banderas
Julia Russell/Bonny Castle	Angelina Jolie
Billy/Walter Downs/Mephisto	Thomas Jane
Alan Jordan	Jack Thompson
Colonel Worth	Gregory Itzin
Augusta Jordan	Allison Mackie
Sara	Joan Pringle
Emily Russell	Cordelia Richards
Faust (Stage)	James Haven
Jorge Cortés	Pedro Armendáriz
Cuban Priest	Mario Iván Martinez
Stage Manager	Harry Porter
Wedding Priest	Fernando Torre Lapham
Dressmaker Girl	Shaula Vega
Margareta (Stage)	Lisa Owen

and Daniel Martinez (Rafael), Farnesio de Bernal (Bank Clerk), Nitzi Arellano (Prostitute), Roger Cudney (Ship's Captain), Adrián Makala (Ship's Waiter), Francis Laboriel (Ship's Stewardess), Patricio Castillo (French Dining Steward), Derek Rojo (Bell Boy), Abraham Stavans (Mr. Gutiérrez), Roberto Medina, Julian Sedgwick, Alejandro Corp (Card Players), Alejandro Reza (Train Station Man), Guy de Saint Cyr (Chief Jailer), Julio Bracho (Guard), George Belanger, Osami Kawano (Gentlemen in Morocco)

Luis Vargas marries beautiful Julia Russell only to have her run off with his money, prompting him to look into her past and discover that she is a murderer.

© Metro-Goldwyn-Mayer Pictures, Inc.

Angelina Jolie

Antonio Banderas, Angelina Jolie

Tilda Swinton

Goran Visnjic, Tilda Swinton

Tilda Swinton

THE DEEP END

(FOX SEARCHLIGHT) Producers/Director/Screenplay, Scott McGehee, David Siegel; Based on the novel *The Blank Wall* by Elisabeth Sanxay Holding; Executive Producer, Robert H. Nathan; Photography, Giles Nuttgens; Editor, Lauren Zuckerman; Designers, Kelly McGehee, Christopher Tandon; Music, Peter Nashel; Associate Producers, Eileen Jones, Mindy Marin; Co-Producer, Laura Greenlee; Casting, Mindy Marin; an I5 Picture; Dolby; Panavision; FotoKem color; Rated R; 99 minutes; Release date: August 8, 2001

CAST

Margaret Hall...Tilda Swinton
Alex Spera...Goran Visnjic
Beau Hall...Jonathan Tucker
Jack Hall...Peter Donat
Darby Reese ....Josh Lucas
Carlie Nagle ....Raymond Barry
Paige Hall...Tamara Hope
Dylan Hall ....Jordan Dorrance
Sue Lloyd ....Heather Mathieson
Loan Officer...Holmes Osborne
Deputy Sheriff...Richard Gross
BVD ....Kip Martin
Barrish Brother..Franco Delgado
Male Nurse ....Kip Ellwood
Jackie...Margot Krindel
Heavy-Set Officer...Michael Pizzuto
and Tajma Soleil (Nurse), F. W. McGehee (Music Teacher)

When Margaret Hall discovers the corpse of the man with whom her son has been having an affair, she disposes of the body, only to be blackmailed by a mysterious stranger. Remake of the 1949 Columbia film The Reckless Moment *that starred Joan Bennett and James Mason.*

© Twentieth Century Fox

Goran Visnjic, Tilda Swinton

SESSION 9

(USA FILMS) Producers, David Collins, Dorothy Aufiero, Michael Williams; Executive Producer, John Sloss; Director/Editor, Brad Anderson; Screenplay, Brad Anderson, Stephen Gevedon; Photography, Uta Briesewitz; Designer, Sophie Carlhian; Costumes, Aimee McCue; Music, Climax Golden Twins; Executive Music Producer, Carson Daly; Casting, Sheila Jaffe, Georgianne Walken; a Scout production; Dolby; HD 24P Widescreen; Color; Rated R; 100 minutes; Release date: August 10, 2001

CAST

Phil...David Caruso
Mike..Stephen Gevedon
Bill Griggs...Paul Guilfoyle
Hank...Josh Lucas
Gordon Fleming ....Peter Mullan
Jeff...Brendan Sexton III
and Charles Broderick (Security Guard), Lonnie Farmer (Voice of Doctor), Larry Fessenden (Craig McManus), Jurian Hughes (Voice of Mary Hobbes), Sheila Stasack (Voice of Wendy)

A group of workmen employed to remove dangerous asbestos from the long-shuttered Danvers State Mental Hospital find themselves becoming unnerved by the mysteries that surround the asylum.

David Caruso

Brendan Sexton III

Nastassja Kinski, Mae Whitman, Troy Goldwyn

Scarlett Johansson

AN AMERICAN RHAPSODY

(PARAMOUNT CLASSICS) Producers, Colleen Camp, Bonnie Timmermann; Executive Producers, Jay Firestone, Adam Haight, Andrew G. Vajna; Co-Executive Producers, Tony Thatcher, Eric Sandys; Director/Screenplay, Éva Gardos; Co-Producer, Patricia Foulkrod; Associate Producers, Stephanie Poole, Teri Fettis D'Ovidio; Photography, Elemér Rágalyi; Designer, Alex Tavoularis; Costumes, Beatrix Aruna Pasztor, Vanessa Vogel; Editor, Margie Goodspeed; Music, Cliff Eidelman; Casting, Liz Lang Fedrick; a Fireworks Pictures and Peter Hoffman presentation of a Fireworks Entertainment/Seven Arts Pictures production in association with Colleen Camp and Bonnie Timmermann; Dolby; Color; Rated PG-13; 106 minutes; Release date: August 10, 2001

CAST

Margit ....Nastassja Kinski
Suzanne (15 years old) ....Scarlett Johansson
Peter...Tony Goldwyn
Maria (10 years old) ....Mae Whitman
Jeno ....Balazs Galko
Teri ....Zsuzsa Czinkoczi
Suzanne (6 years old) ....Kelly Endresz Banlaki
Pattie..Lisa Jane Persky
Dottie ....Colleen Camp
Maria (18 years old) ....Larisa Oleynik
and Raffaella Bánsági (Suzanne, infant), Ági Bánfalvy (Helen), Zoltán Seress (George), Klaudia Szabó (Maria—4 years old), Zsolt Zágoni (Russian Soldier), András Szöke (István), Erzi Pásztor (Ilus), Carlos Laszlo Weiner (Boy on Train), Bori Keresztúri (Suzanne—3 years old), Péter Kállóy Molnár (AVO Officer), Zsuzsa Czinóczi (Teri), Balázs Galkó (Jeno), Kata Dobó (Claire), Éva Soreny (Eva), Don Pugsley (Cafe Supervisor), Vladimir Mashkov (Frank), Imola Gáspár (Stewardess), Tatyana Kanavka (Girl in Airport), Lorna Scott (Neighbor with Poodle), Sandra Staggs (Saleswoman), Jacqueline Steiger (Betty), Robert Lesser (Harold), Lou Beach (Partygoer), Marlee Jackson (Sheila—7 years old), Emmy Rossum (Sheila—15 years old), Timothy Everett Moore (Paul), Joshua Dov (Richard), Kati Bács, Zsuzsa Száger (Women at Market)

Suzanne, left behind in Budapest while her parents settle in Los Angeles, is raised by an elderly couple. Her mother and father send for her years later, causing her great difficulty in adjusting to her new lifestyle.

AMERICAN PIE 2

(UNIVERSAL) Producers, Warren Zide, Craig Perry, Chris Moore; Executive Producers, Adam Herz, Paul Weitz, Chris Weitz; Director, J. B. Rogers; Screenplay, Adam Herz; Story, David H. Steinberg, Adam Herz; Photography, Mark Irwin; Designer, Richard Toyon; Editors, Larry Madaras, Stuart Pappé; Co-Producers, Jane Bartelme, Chris Bender; Associate Producer, Stefan Frank; Music, David Lawrence; Music Supervisors, Gary Jones, Dave Jordan; Costumes, Alexandra Welker; Casting, Joseph Middleton, Michelle Morris Gertz; a Zide/Perry-Liveplanet production; Dolby; Panavision; Deluxe color; Rated R; 105 minutes; Release date: August 10, 2001

CAST

Jim	Jason Biggs
Nadia	Shannon Elizabeth
Michelle	Alyson Hannigan
Oz	Chris Klein
Jessica	Natasha Lyonne
Kevin	Thomas Ian Nicholas
Vicky	Tara Reid
Stifler	Seann William Scott
Heather	Mena Suvari
Finch	Eddie Kaye Thomas
Jim's Dad	Eugene Levy
Sherman	Chris Owen
Jim's Mom	Molly Cheek

and Denise Faye (Danielle), Lisa Arturo (Amber), John Cho (John), Justin Isfeld (Justin), Eli Marienthal (Stifler's Brother), Casey Affleck (Kevin's Brother), George Wyner (Camp Director), Steven Shenbaum (Counselor), Matthew Peters (Trumpet Kid), Joelle Carter (Natalie), Matthew Frauman (R.A.), Larry Drake (Natalie's Dad), Lee Garlington (Natalie's Mom), Tsianina Joelson (Amy), Bree Turner, Lacey Beeman (Amy's Friends), Lisa Gould (Woman in Bed), Brian Lester (Grand Harbor Sheriff), Nigel Gibbs (Cop), Ernie Lively (Sergeant), Kevin Cooney (Doctor), Marilyn Brett (Bus Driver), Morgan Nagler (Michelle's Friend), Jack Wallace (Enthusiastic Guy), Jesse Heiman (Petey), Joanna Garcia (Christy), Sarah Laine, Nora Zehetner (Girls at Party), David Smigelski, Luke Edwards, Adam Brody (High-School Guys), Amanda Armato (Cowboy Hat Girl), Nancy Stone (Mom), Kevin Kilner (Dad), Cole Petersen (Kid), Paityn James, Joseph D. Reitman (EMTs), Brian Turk (Trucker), Mike Erwin (Cashier), Robert Peters (Grill Guy), Amara Balthrop-Lewis, Jay Rossi (Deputies), Adam Herz (Younger Business Suit), J. B. Rogers (Older Business Suit), Brett Shuttleworth (Abercrombie & Fitch Guy), Amanda Wilmshurst, Devon Jackson (Finch Girls), Daniel Spink (Boy with Monkey), Tamia Richmond (Party Girl), Rachel Blasko (Amy's Friend), Laurie Ellan Reeves (College Party Girl), Derrick Harper (Counselor), Kelley Schneider (Deputy), Jennifer Coolidge

After spending their first year apart at college, four friends rent a house together and spend a wild summer of partying and looking for the girls of their dreams. Sequel to the 1999 Universal film with most of the cast repeating their roles.

© Universal Studios

Thomas Ian Nicholas, Jason Biggs,
Seann William Scott, Chris Klein

Alyson Hannigan

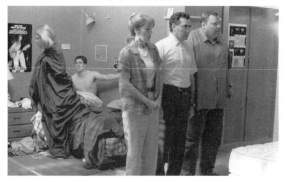

Joelle Carter, Jason Biggs, Molly Cheek,
Eugene Levy, Larry Drake

Shannon Elizabeth,
Jason Biggs

OSMOSIS JONES

(WARNER BROS.) Producers, Bradley Thomas, Peter Farrelly, Bobby Farrelly, Zak Penn, Dennis Edwards; Directors, Peter Farrelly, Bobby Farrelly; Animation Directors, Piet Kroon, Tom Sito; Screenplay, Marc Hyman; Photography, Mark Irwin; Designers, Sidney Jackson Bartholomew, Jr.; Costumes, Pamela Ball Withers; Editors, Lois Freeman-Fox, Stephen R. Schaffer, Sam Seig; Music, Randy Edelman; Animation Production Designer, Steve Pilchar; Supervising Animators, Richard Bazley, Dave Brewster, Ricardo Curtis, Tony Fucile, Wendy Perdue, Dean Wellins; Digital and CGI EFX Designer, Allen Foster; 2-D Effects Designer, Caroline Hu; Casting, Rick Montgomery; a Conundrum Entertainment production; Dolby; Clairmont-Scope; Technicolor; Rated PG; 95 minutes; Release date: August 10, 2001

CAST

Frank	Bill Murray
Mrs. Boyd	Molly Shannon
Bob	Chris Elliott
Shane	Elena Franklin

and Danny Murphy (Zookeeper Superintendent), Jack McCullough (Zookeeper), Kathy Wege (Volcano Lady), Will Dunn (Oyster Boy), Jackie Flynn (School Janitor), Kelsey Jordan, Anna Byers (Bus Girls), Jesse Peter (Laughing Boy), John Jordan (Pea Soup Manager), Nancy Byers (Pea Soup Supervisor), Kevin Flynn (Docky's Clamshack Waiter), Sean Gildea (Dreamy Photographer), Kathryn Frick, Nikki Tyler-Flynn, Elizabeth Jordan (Nurses), Zen Gesner, Marc Hyman, Zak Penn (Emergency Room Doctors), Nicole Brathwaite, Brianna Cabral, Chandler Vuilleumier, Emily O'Day, Catherine Dunphy (The Volcano Gals), Bill Wade, Bruce McIntyre, Bo Cleary (Pea Soup Staff), Brian Mone, Sean Fitzgerald (Police Officers), Beth Jordan, Mattie Ostiguy, Grace Costa, Maura O'Brien (Emergency Room Nurses)

VOICE CAST

Osmosis Jones	Chris Rock
Thrax	Laurence Fishburne
Drix	David Hyde Pierce
Leah	Brandy Norwood
The Mayor	William Shatner
Tom Colonic	Ron Howard

and Robert "Kid Rock" Tichie, Joe C, Uncle Kracker, Kenny Olson, Stefanie Eulenberg, Jason Krause, Jimmie Bones (Kidney Rocks), Jonathan Adams, Carlos Alazraqui, Keith Anthony, Eddie Barth, Sally Ann Brooks, Rodger Bumpass, Michael Carven, Paul Christie, Janis Dardaris, Wendy Dillon, Antonio Fargas, Eddie Frierson, Don Fullilove, Jackie Gonneau, Rif Hutton, Richard Horvitz, Art Kimbro, Joyce Kurtz, Anne Lockhart, Sherry Lynn, Danny Mann, Mickie McGowan, "Stuttering" John Melendez, Hector Mercado, Paul Pape, Marilyn Pasekoff, Chris Phillips, Lynne Redding, Al Rodrigo, Herschel Sparber, Doug Stone, Steve Susskind, Keri Tombazian, Paul Tuerpé, Robert Wisdom (Additional Character Voices)

A zookeeper in poor health eats a tainted hard-boiled egg prompting the white blood cell police within his body to try to track down the viruses.

© Warner Bros.

Osmosis Jones

The Chief, Osmosis Jones

Elena Franklin, Bill Murray

Thrax

Bill Murray, Chris Elliott

Penélope Cruz, Nicholas Cage

Christian Bale

John Hurt, Penélope Cruz

CAPTAIN CORELLI'S MANDOLIN

(UNIVERSAL/MIRAMAX) Producers, Tim Bevan, Eric Fellner, Kevin Loader, Mark Huffam; Director, John Madden; Screenplay, Shawn Slovo; Based on the novel by Louis De Bernieres; Photography, John Toll; Designer, Jim Clay; Costumes, Alexandra Byrne; Editor, Mick Audsley; Music, Stephen Warbeck; Co-Producers, Jane Frazer, Debra Hayward, Liza Chasin; Casting, Mary Selway; a Universal Pictures/Studio Canal/Miramax presentation of a Working Title production; U.S.-British; Dolby; Panavision; Deluxe color; Rated R; 127 minutes; Release date: August 17, 2001

CAST

Captain Antonio Corelli	Nicolas Cage
Pelagia	Penélope Cruz
Dr. Iannis	John Hurt
Mandras	Christian Bale
Weber	David Morrissey
Drosoula	Irene Papas
Carlo	Piero Maggió
Stamatis	Gerasimos Skiadaresis

The Greeks:

Aspasia Kralli (Mrs. Stamatis), Michalis Giannatos (Kokolios), Dimitris Kamperidis (Father Arsenios), Pedro Sarubbi (Velisarios—The Strongman), Viki Maragaki (Eleni, Pelagia's Friend), Joanna-Daria Adraktas (Lemoni—Younger), Ira Tavlaridis (Lemoni—Older), Katerina Didaskalou (Lemoni's Mother), Emilios Chilakis (Dimitris), Nikos Karathanos (Spiros), Antonis Antoniou (Recruiting Officer), George Kotanidis (Mayor), Tasos Palantzidis (Town Clerk), Kostas Philippoglou (Trembling Man), Froso Korrou (Nun), Maria-Louisa Papadopoulou, Dina Kaferani, Vlassis Zotis, Panagiotis Thanassoulis, Alexia Bouloukou (The Mad People), Babis Artelaris, Gerasimos Iakovatos, Nikos Kalogiratos, Dionysis Karlis, Pavlos Lalis, Angelos Liberatos, Panagis Polichronatos, Christos Rangas, Dimitris Vandoros, Gerasimos Xidias (The Partisans), Dimitris Dimoulas, Pantelis Filipatos, Ilias Theofilatos, Makis Filipatos (Musicians)

The Italians:

Vincenzo Ricotta (Quartermaster), Roberto Citran (General Ganadin), Federico Fioresi, Sandro Stefanini, Francesco Guzzo, Germano Di Mattia, Simone Spinazzé, Sergio Albelli, Davide Quatraro, Paco Reconti, Nuccio Siano, Salvatore Lazzaro, Alessandro Repossi (The Soldiers of La Scal), Massimiliano Pazzaglia (Captain), Tim Hardy (Colonel), Francesco Cabras (Soldier with Cigarette), Nunzio Lombardo (Soldier at Dance), Irini Eleftheriou, Sofia Yannioti, Marina Corelli, Evi Tzortzi, Leticia Moustaki, Angelica Lambri, Maria Philipakopoulou, Irene Christidi (Prostitutes), Giovanni Parricelli, Martin Robertson, Ben Gant, Paul Spong, Eddie Hession, Mike Pickering, Oren Marshall (Waterfront Band)

The Germans:

Patrick Malahide (Colonel Barge), Martin Glyn Murray, Till Bahlmann, Renny Krupinski (Officers), Peter Stark (Soldier)

During World War II, Captain Corelli and his troops arrive on the isolated Greek Island of Cephallonia, prompting initial resentment from the inhabitants, including Pelagia, who ultimately finds herself falling for the charming captain.

Wayne Knight,
Rowan Atkinson

RAT RACE

(PARAMOUNT) Producers, Jerry Zucker, Janet Zucker, Sean Daniel; Executive Producers, James Jacks, Richard Vane; Director, Jerry Zucker; Screenplay, Andy Breckman; Photography, Thomas Ackerman; Designer, Gary Frutkoff; Costumes, Ellen Mirojnick; Editor, Tom Lewis; Music, John Powell; Music Supervisor, Bonnie Greenberg-Goldman; Stunts, Tim Gilbert, John Scott; Casting, Jane Jenkins, Janet Hirshenson; an Alphaville/Zucker production, presented in association with Fireworks Pictures; Dolby; Panavision; Deluxe color; Rated PG-13; 112 minutes; Release date: August 17, 2001

CAST

Enrico Pollini	Rowan Atkinson
Donald Sinclair	John Cleese
Vera Baker	Whoopi Goldberg
Owen Templeton	Cuba Gooding, Jr.
Duane Cody	Seth Green
Randy Pear	Jon Lovitz
Nick Shaffer	Breckin Meyer
Beverly Bear	Kathy Najimy
Tracy Faucet	Amy Smart

and Wayne Knight (Zack), Paul Rodriguez (Gus), Vince Vieluf (Blaine Cody), Lanai Chapman (Merrill Jennings), Dean Cain (Shawn), Dave Thomas (Mr. Grisham), Kathy Bates (Squirrel Lady), Jenica Bergere (Hotel Clerk), Carrie Diamond (Casino Bartender), Douglas Haase (Guy at Bar), Chris Myers, Kevin Frazier (Fox Sportscasters), Gloria Allred (Herself), Renee Lee (Witness in Crowd), Corinna Harney Jones, Jane C. Walsh (Cocktail Waitresses), Jillian Marie Hubert (Kimberly Pear), Brody Smith (Jason Pear), Andrew Kavovit (Richie), Mallory Sandler (Guest Services Clerk), Gerard Plunkett, Martin Evans, L. Harvey Gold, David Lereaney, Andy Maton, Manoj Sood, Philip Tsui, Allan Lysell (High Rollers), Marcos Menendez (Other Cabby), Catherine Schreiber (Ticket Agent), Joel Hurt Jones (Charter Pilot), Daryl Sullivan (Man in Line), Kevin Rothery (Air Traffic Controller), Jake Bendel (U Rent It Clerk), Guy Cohen (Rental Car Trainee), Susan Breslau (Rental Car Manager), Steven Tingle, Jared Van Snellenberg (Skinhead Tour Guides), Paul Hayes (Lucy Bus Driver), Anaya Farrell, Peggy Jo Jacobs, Linda Kerns, Christine MacInnis, Christopher Peterson, Deborah Theaker, Roxanne Wong, Charlotte Zucker (Lucys), Kate Zucker (Girl in Lobby), Bob Zucker (Boy in Lobby), Silas Weir Mitchell (Lloyd), Deryl Hayes (Sleeping Trooper), Joanne Resnick (Biker Woman), Gene LeBell (Veteran with Gun), Brandy Ledford (Vicky), John Duerler (Caterer), Rick Cramer (Test Driver), Mike Garibaldi (Press Spokesman), Kathleen Marshall (Reporter), Vic Chao (Engineer), Colleen Camp (Rainbow House Nurse), Junior Ray (Truck Driver), Tristin Leffler (Pierced Girl), Marty Antonini (Monster Truck Driver), Tyler Gauthier, Matthew Gauthier (Baby on Train), Shannon Anderson (Mother), Brian Stollery (Father), Gillian Skupa (Stewardess), Greg Camp, Paul De Lisle, Steve Harwell, Marc Cervantes, Michael Klooster, Michael Urbano (Smash Mouth), Rance Howard (Feed the Earth Spokesman), Lucy Lee Flippin (Feed the Earth Spokeswoman), Jennifer Rugamas (Feed the Earth Girl), Mason Jones (Feed the Earth Boy)

Las Vegas casino tycoon Donald Sinclair invites six random people to participate in a treasure hunt, giving each of them the key to a locker in Silver City, New Mexico, in which two million dollars in cash is stashed.

Christopher Peterson, Cuba Gooding, Jr.

Whoopi Goldberg, John Cleese, Breckin Meyer, Cuba Gooding, Jr., Rowan Atkinson

Jon Lovitz, Seth Green, Amy Smart, Vince Vieluf, Whoopi Goldberg, Rowan Atkinson, Cuba Gooding, Jr., Breckin Meyer, Lanai Chapman

AMERICAN OUTLAWS

(WARNER BROS.) Producer, James G. Robinson; Executive Producer, Jonathan A. Zimbert; Director, Les Mayfield; Screenplay, Roderick Taylor, John Rogers; Story, Roderick Taylor; Photography, Russell Boyd; Designers, Cary White, John Frick; Costumes, Luke Reichle; Editor, Michael Tronick; Music, Trevor Rabin; Music Supervisor, Maureen Crowe; Casting, Pam Dixon Mickelson; a James G. Robinson presentation of a Morgan Creek production; Dolby; FotoKem color; Rated PG-13; 93 minutes; Release date: August 17, 2001

CAST

Jesse James	Colin Farrell
Cole Younger	Scott Caan
Zee Mimms	Ali Larter
Frank James	Gabriel Macht
Jim Younger	Gregory Smith
Thaddeus Rains	Harris Yulin
Ma James	Kathy Bates
Allan Pinkerton	Timothy Dalton
Bob Younger	Will McCormack
Doc Mimms	Ronny Cox
Rollin Parker	Terry O'Quinn

and Nathaniel Arcand (Comanche Tom), Ty O'Neal (Clell Miller), Joe Stevens (Loni Packwood), Barry Tubb (Capt. Malcolm), Jack Watkins (Detective), Tom Schuster (Union Officer), Lee Ritchey (Bank Manager), Robin Christian (Woman), Ed Geldart (Old Man Tucker), Brad Leland (Sheriff), Craig Erickson (Deputy), Mark Walters (Engineer), Michael Costello (Senator), Jack Gould (Head Teller), Morgana Shaw (Lyla), Brady Coleman (Driver), Richard Jones (Pastor), Steven "Dooky" Bland (Man), Jerry Cotton (Teller), Muse Watson (Burly Detective), Lane Thomas Wilson (Boy Soldier), Rony Hayden (Union Lieutenant), Darryl Cox (Jenkins), Riley Flynn (Union Commander), Joe Brown (Pinkerton Commander), Shawn Patrick Nash (Hangman), Jessica Nitsch (Loni's Girl)

The story of how Jesse James and the Younger brothers formed a gang and became the most notorious outlaws in the Old West. Previous films on the Jesse James saga include Jesse James *(20th, 1939; with Tyrone Power),* Bad Men of Missouri *(WB, 1941; Alan Baxter),* Kansas Raiders *(Univ, 1950; Audie Murphy),* The Great Missouri Raid *(Par, 1950; Macdonald Carey),* The True Story of Jesse James *(20th, 1956; Robert Wagner),* Young Jesse James *(20th, 1960; Ray Stricklyn), and* The Great Northfield Minnesota Raid *(Univ, 1972; Robert Duvall).*

© Morgan Creek Productions, Inc.

(Top) Colin Farrell, Ali Larter. (Bottom) Will McCormack, Gregory Smith, Colin Farrell, Scott Caan, Gabriel Macht

Laura Kirk, Nat DeWolf, Daniel London

Laura Kirk, Nat DeWolf

LISA PICARD IS FAMOUS

(FIRST LOOK) Producers, Mira Sorvino, Dolly Hall; Executive Producers, Sidney Kimmel, John Penotti, Fisher Stevens, Bradley Yonover, Andrew S. Karsch; Director, Griffin Dunne; Screenplay, Nat DeWolf, Laura Kirk; Photography, William Rexer II; Designer, Mark Ricker; Costumes, Denise Walch; Editor, Nancy Baker; Music, Evan Lurie; Music Supervisor, Barry Cole; Line Producer, Exile Ramirez; Co-Producer, Celeste Peterka; a Stella Maris Films and Dolly Hall production in association with Sidney Kimmel Entertainment/GreeneStreet Films/Longfellow Pictures; Color; Not rated; 87 minutes; Release date: August 22, 2001

CAST

Lisa Picard	Laura Kirk
Tate Kelley	Nat DeWolf
Boyfriend	Daniel London
Andrew	Griffin Dunne
Leslie Fitzgerald	Leslie Lyles
David Holzman	L. M. Kit Carson
Anna Chenier	Sharon Washington
Brenda	Joelle Carter
Caroline Huff	Karen Kayser

and Jack Howard (Commercial Stud), Rosanna Scotto (TV Reporter), Neil Butterfield, Robert Rodriguez (Punks), Daniella Rich (Sandy's Assistant), Jeff Whitty (Greg), James Yaegashi (Alex), Sam Catlin (Michael), Tony Rigo (Bartender), Zofia Borucka (Soap Actress), Mark Mortimer (Paul), Sarah Jones (Kirsta), Judie Aronson (Liz), Michael Malone (Jeff), Virginia Louise Smith (Amanda), Quentin Mare (Ken), Gregory Arata (Tate's Boyfriend), Carrie Fisher, Buck Henry, Spike Lee, Charlie Sheen, Mira Sorvino, Fisher Stevens (Themselves)

Lisa Picard, a struggling, hopelessly self-deluded actress, searches for fame in this mock documentary.

© First Look Pictures

Woody Allen, David Ogden Stiers, Helen Hunt

Woody Allen

Dan Aykroyd, Helen Hunt

Charlize Theron, Woody Allen

THE CURSE OF THE JADE SCORPION

(DREAMWORKS) Producer, Letty Aronson; Executive Producer, Stephen Tenenbaum; Co-Producer, Helen Robin; Co-Executive Producers, Datty Ruth, Jack Rollins, Charles H. Joffe; Director/Screenplay, Woody Allen; Photography, Zhao Fei; Designer, Santo Loquasto; Costumes, Suzanne McCabe; Editor, Alisa Lepselter; Casting, Juliet Taylor, Laura Rosenthal; a Gravier production, presented in association with VCL Licensing GmbH; Dolby; Technicolor; Rated PG-13; 103 minutes; Release date: August 24, 2001

CAST

CW Briggs	Woody Allen
Chris Magruder	Dan Aykroyd
Jill	Elizabeth Berkley
Betty Ann Fitzgerald	Helen Hunt
Al	Brian Markinson
George Bond	Wallace Shawn
Voltan	David Ogden Stiers
Laura Kensington	Charlize Theron
Sam	John Tormey
Mize	John Schuck
Rosie	Kaili Vernoff
Office Workers	Maurice Sonnenberg, John Doumanian
Ned	Peter Gerety
Lunch Delivery Man	Kevin Cahoon
Rocky's Waiter	Phil Levy

and Vince Giordano, Howard Alden, Ted Sommer, Randy Sandke, Peter Ecklund, Joel Helleny, Chuck Wilson, Ray Beckenstein, Lawrence Feldman, Ken Peplowski (Rainbow Room All Stars), Dick Hyman (Band Leader), Carole Bayeux (Voltan's Assistant), Kenneth Edelson, Brian McConnachie, Judy Gold (Voltan's Participants), Herb Lovelle (Night Guard), Carmen (Rose Kensington), Patrick Horgan, Howard Erskine, Ira Wheeler, Tina Sloan (Kensington Guests), Ramsey Faragallah (Fingerprint Detective), Bob Dorian (Mike), Arthur Nascarella (Tom), Trude Klein (Kensington Maid), Professor Irwin Corey (Charlie), Michael Mulheren (Herb Coopersmith), Peter Linari (Joe Coopersmith), Ray Garvey (Police Station Cop), Bruce Brown (Radio Announcer), Dan Moran (Street Contact)

CW Briggs, a top insurance investigator, is unwittingly hypnotized into committing robberies that he, in his conscious state, tries to solve.

© DreamWorks LLC

Jason Mewes, Kevin Smith, Ben Affleck

Chris Rock

Will Ferrell, Kevin Smith, Jason Mewes, Jennifer
Schwalbach, Eliza Dushku, Ali Larter

Kevin Smith,
Jason Mewes

JAY AND SILENT BOB STRIKE BACK

(DIMENSION) Producer, Scott Mosier; Executive Producers, Bob Weinstein, Harvey Weinstein, Jonathan Gordon; Director/Screenplay, Kevin Smith; Co-Producer, Laura Greenlee; Photography, Jamie Anderson; Designer, Robert "Ratface" Holtzman; Editors, Kevin Smith, Scott Mosier; Music, James L. Venable; Costumes, Isis Mussenden; Visual Effects Supervisor, Joseph Grossberg; Casting, Christine Sheaks; a View Askew production; Distributed by Miramax Films; Dolby; Super 35 Widescreen; Deluxe color; Rated R; 104 minutes; Release date: August 24, 2001

CAST

Jay	Jason Mewes
Silent Bob	Kevin Smith
Holden/Chuckie/Himself	Ben Affleck
Sissy	Eliza Dushku
Justice	Shannon Elizabeth
Willenholly	Will Ferrell
Chrissy	Ali Larter
Brodie/Banky	Jason Lee
Chaka	Chris Rock
Hitchhiker	George Carlin
Cock-Knocker	Mark Hamill
Nun	Carrie Fisher
Dante	Brian O'Halloran
Randal	Jeff Anderson
Brent	Seann William Scott
Alyssa	Joey Lauren Adams
Reg Hartner	Jon Stewart
Sheriff	Judd Nelson
Dealer	Tracy Morgan
Missy	Jennifer Schwalbach

and Amy Noble (Baby Bob's Mother), Harley Quinn Smith (Baby Silent Bob), Ever Carradine (Baby Jay's Mother), Brian Andrew Saible (Baby Jay), Gavin Brooks (Baby Jay Voice), John Willyung (Passerby), Jake Richardson, Nick Fellinger (Teens), Vincent Pereira (Customer), Ernest O'Donnell (Cop), Marc Blucas (Guy), Matthew James (Dude), Jane Silvia (Bookish Girl), Carmen Llywellyn (Beauty), Dan Etheridge (Deputy), Eric Winzenried, Jonathan Gordon, John Maynard, Robert H. Holtzman, Tom Dorfmeister (Cops), Tango (Suzanne), Joe Quesada (Pizza Delivery Guy), Michelle Anne Johnson, Merritt Hicks (Hookers), Steve Kmetko, Jules Asner, Gus Van Sant, Shannen Doherty, Wes Craven, Jason Biggs, James Van Der Beek, Matt Damon (Themselves), Diedrich Bader (Security Guard), Scott Mosier (AD "GWH2" William/Guy), James J. McLauchlin (Clapper/Loader "GWH2"), Scott Winters (Clark), Joseph D. Reitman (AD "Bluntman & Chronic"), Jamie Kennedy (PA), Paul Dini (Clapper/Loader "Bluntman & Chronic"), Quentin Wright (William Dusky), Gregory Owen (Suburban Kid), Ralph Meyer (Receptionist), Bryan Johnson (Steve-Dave), Walter Flannigan (Walt), Renee Humphrey (Trish), Dwight Ewell (Hooper), Alanis Morrissette (God), Morris E. Day, Jerome Benton, Stanley Howard, Gary Johnson, Monte Moir, Torrell Ruffin, Ricky Smith (Morris Day and the Time)

New Jersey slackers Jay and Silent Bob head for Hollywood to stop an unauthorized movie about their alter egos, Bluntman & Chronic.

© Dimension Films

TORTILLA SOUP

(SAMUEL GOLDWYN FILMS) Producer, John Bard Manulis; Executive Producer, Samuel Goldwyn, Jr.; Director, Maria Ripoll; Screenplay, Ramón Menéndez, Tom Musca, Vera Blasi; Based on the screenplay *Eat Drink Man Woman* by Hui-Ling Wang, Ang Lee, James Schamus; Co-Producer, Lulu Zezza; Associate Producer, Meyer Gottlieb; Photography, Xavier Perez Grobet; Designer, Alicia Maccarone; Costumes, Ileane Meltzer; Music, Bill Conti; Music Supervisor, Julianne Jordan; Editor, Andy Blumenthal; Food and Menus Created and Designed by Mary Sue Milliken, Susan Feniger; Casting, Junie Lowry Johnson, Libby Goldstein, Claudia Becker; a Samuel Goldwyn production, presented in association with Starz/Encore Entertainment; Dolby; Color; Rated PG-13; 110 minutes; Release date: August 24, 2001

CAST

Martin Naranjo	Hector Elizondo
Carmen Naranjo	Jacqueline Obradors
Leticia Naranjo	Elizabeth Peña
Maribel Naranjo	Tamara Mello
Andy	Nikolai Kinski
Orlando	Paul Rodriguez
Hortensia	Raquel Welch
Yolanda	Constance Marie
Antonio Urgell	Joel Joan

and Jade Herrera (Eden), Troy Ruptash (Hairdresser), Ken Marino (Jeff), Marisabel Garcia (April), Julio Oscar Mechoso (Gomez), Louis Crugnali (Catering Assistant), Ulysses Cuadra (Snide Student), Mark de la Cruz, Eli Russell Linnetz (April's Classmates), Stoney Westmoreland (Baseball Umpire), Karen Dyer (Jeff's Girlfriend)

The three Naranjo sisters, who have been devoted to their master-chef father, find their destinies taking them in directions that threaten family tradition.

© Samuel Goldwyn Films

(Top) Tamara Mello, Jacqueline Obradors, Elizabeth Peña
(Bottom) Hector Elizondo, Raquel Welch

Jason Statham, Natasha Henstridge, Ice Cube

John Carpenter's GHOSTS OF MARS

(SCREEN GEMS) Producer, Sandy King; Director/Music, John Carpenter; Screenplay, Larry Sulkis, John Carpenter; Photography, Gary B. Kibbe; Designer, William Elliott; Costumes, Robin Michel Bush; Special Makeup Effects, Robert Kurtzman, Greg Nicotero, Howard Berger; Editor, Paul Warschilka; Visual Effects Supervisor, Lance Wilhoite; Casting, Reuben Cannon; a Storm King production; Dolby; Panavision; Deluxe color; Rated R; 97 minutes; Release date: August 24, 2001

CAST

James "Desolation" Williams	Ice Cube
Lt. Melanie Ballard	Natasha Henstridge
Jericho Butler	Jason Statham
Helena Braddock	Pam Grier
Bashira Kincaid	Clea Duvall
Whitlock	Joanna Cassidy
Michael Descanso	Liam Waite
Akooshay	Wanda DeJesus
Uno	Duane Davis
Dos	Lobo Sebastian
Tres	Rodney A. Grant
Rodale	Robert Carradine
McSimms	Peter Jason

and Danielle Burgio (Local Cop), Damon Caro (Shape—Male Intern), Richard Cetrone (Big Daddy Mars), Charlotte Cornwell (Narrator), Rick Edelstein (Zimmerman), Rosemary Forsyth (Inquisitor), Marjean Holden (Young Woman), Michael Krawic (Man in Rover), Rex Linn (Yared), Doug McRath (Benchley), Matt Nolan (Miner), Chad Randall (Big Warrior), Eileen Weisinger (Warrior)

The Martian Police Force arrives at one of the planet's mining colonies to track down an escaped con, only to find themselves facing former miners who have been infected and driven crazy by a deadly force.

© Screen Gems, a Sony Pictures Entertainment Company

HAPPY ACCIDENTS

(IFC FILMS) Producer, Susan A. Stover; Executive Producers, Jonathan Sehring, Caroline Kaplan, John Sloss; Director/Screenplay/Editor, Brad Anderson; Photography, Terry Stacey; Designer, Susan Block; Costumes, Victoria Farrell; Line Producer, Derrick Tseng; Music, Evan Lurie; Music Supervisor, Linda Cohen; Executive Music Producer, Alex Steyermark; Casting, Sheila Jaffe, Georgianne Walken; an Accidental production; Color; Rated R; 110 minutes; Release date: August 24, 2001

CAST

Ruby Weaver	Marisa Tomei
Sam Deed	Vincent D'Onofrio
Gretchen	Nadia Dajani
Therapist	Holland Taylor
Lillian	Tovah Feldshuh
Mark	Sean Gullette
Victor	Bronson Dudley
Jose	Jose Zuniga
Sunil	Jason Chandani
Bette	Cara Buono

and Liana Pai (Claire), Tamara Jenkins (Robin), Richard Portnow (Trip), Saidah Arrika Ekulona (Nurse), Mick Weber (Floor Supervisor), Sam Seder (Ned), Lyn Vaus (Pharmacist), Anthony Michael Hall (Famous Actor), Jon Benjamin, Kathryn Tucker (Revelers), Mike McGlone (Tab), Dan Frazer (Voice of Tom Deed), Michael Buscemi (Pedestrian), Joreen Baquilod (Korean Girl), Elizabeth Gajadharsingh (Sunil's Young Daughter), Steve Gevodan (Frenchman), Larry Fessenden (Junkie), Robert Stanton (Fetishist), Neal Huff (Artist)

Ruby Weaver, a woman who has pretty much given up on relationships, meets Sam Deed and falls in love with him, only to have him claim that he is a time traveler from the year 2470.

© IFC Films

Vincent D'Onofrio, Marisa Tomei

Holland Taylor

Jessica Biel, Freddie Prinze, Jr.

Marc Blucas, Matthew Lillard, Freddie Prinze, Jr.

SUMMER CATCH

(WARNER BROS.) Producers, Mike Tollin, Brian Robbins, Sam Weisman; Executive Producer, Herb Gains; Director, Mike Tollin; Screenplay, Kevin Falls, John Gatins; Story, Kevin Falls; Photography, Tim Suhrstedt; Designer, John D. Kretschmer; Costumes, Juliet Polsca; Editor, Harvey Rosenstock; Music, George Fenton; Baseball Coordinator, Mark Ellis; Casting, Marci Liroff; a Tollin/Robbins production; Dolby; Technicolor; Rated PG-13; 104 minutes; Release date: August 24, 2001

CAST

Ryan Dunne	Freddie Prinze, Jr.
Tenley Parrish	Jessica Biel
Billy Brubaker	Matthew Lillard
John Schiffner	Brian Dennehy
Sean Dunne	Fred Ward
Mike Dunne	Jason Gedrick
Dede Mulligan	Brittany Murphy
Rand Parrish	Bruce Davison
Miles Dalrymple	Marc Blucas
Mickey Dominguez	Wilmer Valderrama

and Corey Pearson (Eric Van Leemer), Christian Kane (Dale Robin), Cedric Pendleton (Calvin Knight), Gabriel Mann (Auggie), Jed Robert Rhein (Pete), Zena Grey (Katie Parrish), Beverly D'Angelo (House Mother), John C. McGinley (Phillies' Scout), Curt Gowdy, Pat Burrell, Dave Collins, Doug Glanville, Ken Griffey, Jr., Jeff Kellogg, Mike Lieberthal, Hank Aaron (Themselves), Dick Allen (Scout in Black Hat), Randi Layne (Vivi Parrish), Traci Dinwiddie (Lauren), Susan Gardner (Marjorie), Jack Baun (Chris Hunt), Tammy Christine Arnold (Vassar Graduate), Tim Lucason (Hyannis Batter), Kenny Gasperson (Statistician), Mark Robert Ellis (Umpire), Herbert W. Gains (Angry Fan), Thaddeus Hill (Coach Sully), Brock Kenne (Chatham Pitcher), Mike Ribaudo, Matt Hobbie (Chatham A's)

Ryan Dunne, a young man hoping to make it into the major leagues, gets his big chance to impress the talent scouts, but he must overcome his low self-esteem and habit of choking under pressure.

© Warner Bros.

Mekhi Phifer

Rain Phoenix, Julia Stiles

O

(LIONS GATE) Producers, Eric Gitter, Anthony Rhulen, Daniel L. Fried; Executive Producers, Michael I. Levy, William Shively; Director, Tim Blake Nelson; Screenplay, Brad Kaaya; Photography, Russell Lee Fine; Designer, Dina Goldman; Costumes, Jill Ohanneson; Co-Executive Producers, Fredrick B. Goodman, Stephen A. Kepniss; Associate Producers, Brad Kaaya, Zack Estrin; Co-Producers, Betsey Danbury, Lisa Gitter; Music, Jeff Danna; Music Supervisor, Barry Cole; Editor, Kate Sanford; Casting, Avy Kaufman; a Chickie the Cop production in association with Filmengine and Daniel Fried productions; Dolby; Deluxe color; Rated R; 95 minutes; Release date: August 31, 2001

CAST

Odin James ....Mekhi Phifer
Hugo Goulding ....Josh Hartnett
Desi Brable ....Julia Stiles
Coach Duke Goulding ....Martin Sheen
Roger ....Elden Henson
Michael Casio...Andrew Keegan
Emily..Rain Phoenix
Dell...Anthony "A. J." Johnson
Dean Brable ....John Heard
Assistant Coach ....Chris Freihofer
Dutchman Player ....Christopher Dong
Brandy ....Rachel Schumate
Radio Announcer ....Marshall Gitter
Ms. Serney...Lisa Benavides
Scout #1 ....Ken French
and Dana Ratliff (TV Announcer), Christopher Jones (Jason), Ronalda Stover (Score Keeper), Kelvin O'Bryant (Ball Boy), Jack "Jay" Munn (Lanny), Mike Flippo (Mr. Bradley), James Middleton (Cop), Julie Fishell (Newscaster), Wally Welch (Mr. Kirby)

In this contemporary take on Shakespeare's Othello, *jealous high-schooler Hugo Goulding sets out to destroy the relationship between popular basketball star Odin James and his girlfriend Desi Brable.*

© Lions Gate Films

Mekhi Phifer, Julia Stiles, Andrew Keegan

Mekhi Phifer, Josh Hartnett

Gina Phillips, Justin Long

Jonathan Breck, Justin Long

JEEPERS CREEPERS

(UNITED ARTISTS) Producers, Barry Opper, Tom Luse; Executive Producers, Francis Ford Coppola, Linda Reisman, Willi Baer, Mario Ohoven, Eberhard Kayser; Director/Screenplay, Victor Salva; Photography, Don E. FauntLeRoy; Designer, Steven Legler; Costumes, Emae Villalobos; Editor, Ed Marx; Music, Bennet Salvay, Randy Kerber; Co-Producer, J. Todd Harris; Makeup & Creature Effects, Make-up & Monsters Studios; Visual Effects Supervisor, Bob Morgenroth, E+MC2 Digital; Casting, Kimberly Mullen; an American Zoetrope/Cinerenta-Cinebeta production in association with Cinerenta Medienbeteiligungs KG; U.S.-German; Dolby; FotoKem color; Rated R; 89 minutes; Release date: August 31, 2001

Jonathan Breck

CAST

Trish	Gina Phillips
Darry	Justin Long
The Creeper	Jonathan Breck
Jezelle Gay Hartman	Patricia Belcher
Sergeant David Tubbs	Brandon Smith
The Cat Lady	Eileen Brennan
Waitress Beverly	Peggy Sheffield
Manager	Jeffrey William Evans
Man at Jukebox	Patrick Cherry
Trooper Gideon	Jon Beshara
Trooper Weston	Avis-Marie Barnes
Cellblock Officer	Steven Raulerson
Roach	Tom Tarantini
Officer with Hole in Chest	Will Hasenzahl
Camper Driver	Kim Kahana
Dying Boy	Chris Shephardson

While driving home for spring break, siblings Darry and Trish chance upon a mysterious cloaked figure that appears to be collecting bodies.

Justin Long, Eileen Brennan, Gina Phillips

© United Artists Films Inc.

THE MUSKETEER

(UNIVERSAL/MIRAMAX) Producer, Moshe Diamant; Director/Photography, Peter Hyams; Screenplay, Gene Quintano; based on the novel *The Three Musketeers* by Alexandre Dumas; Executive Producers, Mark Damon, Steven Paul, Rudy Cohen, Frank Hübner, Romain Schroeder; Co-Producer, Jan Fantl; Line Producer, Tom Reeve; Designer, Philip Harrison; Editor, Terry Rawlings; Music, David Arnold; Costumes, Raymond Hughes, Cynthia Dumont; Stunt Choreographer, Xin-Xin Xiong; Casting, Penny Perry, Celestia Fox; a D'Artagnan Productions, Ltd., Apollomedia, Q&Q Media, and Carousel Picture Company production with the support of Film Fund Luxembourg; U.S.-Luxembourg; Dolby; Super 35 Widescreen; Technicolor; Rated PG-13; 105 minutes; Release date: September 7, 2001

CAST

The Queen	Catherine Deneuve
Francesca	Mena Suvari
Cardinal Richelieu	Stephen Rea
Febre	Tim Roth
D'Artagnan	Justin Chambers
Bonacieux	Bill Treacher
King Louis	Daniel Mesguich
Rochefort	David Schofield
Aramis	Nick Moran
Porthos	Steve Speirs
Athos	Jan Gregor Kremp
Lord Buckingham	Jeremy Clyde

and Michael Byrne (Treville), Jean-Pierre Castaldi (Planchet), Tsilla Chelton (Madam Lacross), Luc Gentile (D'Artagnan's Father), Catherine Erhardy (D'Artagnan's Mother), Max Dolbey (Young D'Artagnan), Florent Bigot de Nesle (Deleon), Stefan Jürgens (Darcy), Ann Marie Pisani (Buxom Woman), Carrie Mullan (Mathilde), Joachim Paul Assböck (Hessian), Oscar Ortega Sanchez (Marquis de Spota), Sven Walser (Man #1 at Bar), Marco Lorenzini (Inn Keeper), Jean-Francois Wolff (Cardinal's Guard #1), Bertrand Witt (Dumas), Stefan Weinert (Mercenary #2), Patrick Dean (Febre Messenger), Christian Bergmann (Last Febre Man), Sascha Schiffbauer, Frank Ferner (Jail Guards), Sven Nichulski (Guard at Door), Jean-Luc Ristic (Pastry Chef), Roland Stemmer, Dean Gregory, Ciaran Mulhern (Musketeers), Jo Stock (Another Musketeer), Gilles Soeder (Cook), Sigal Diamant (Josephine)

Swordsman D'Artagnan sets out to join the king's elite guard, the Royal Musketeers, and to find the man who killed his parents when he was a child.

© Universal Studios

Justin Chambers

Stephen Rea, Tim Roth

Morris Chestnut, Vivica A. Fox

Anthony Anderson, Morris Chestnut

TWO CAN PLAY THAT GAME

(SCREEN GEMS) Producers, Doug McHenry, Mark Brown, Paddy Cullen; Executive Producers, Larry Kennar, Robert N. Fried, Scott Wynne; Director/Screenplay, Mark Brown; Photography, Alexander Gruszynski; Designer, Amy Ancona; Editor, Earl Watson; Music, Marcus Miller; Music Supervisor, Rashad Liston; Casting, Robi Reed-Humes; a Doug McHenry production in association with C4 Pictures; Dolby; Deluxe color; Rated R; 90 minutes; Release date: September 7, 2001

CAST

Shanté Smith	Vivica A. Fox
Keith Fenton	Morris Chestnut
Diedre	Mo'Nique
Tracye	Tamala Jones
Karen	Wendy Raquel Robinson
Conny Spalding	Gabrielle Union
Michael	Bobby Brown
Tony	Anthony Anderson
Bill Parker	Ray Wise
Dwain	Donré T. Whitfield
Jason	David Krumholtz

and Lee Anthony (Attorney in Elevator), Kristen Herold, Cherise Leana Bangs, Libby Genaro (Miller Girls), Zatella Beatty (Cynthia) Mark Brown, Chris Spencer, Pierre Burgess, Mark Christopher Lawrence (Lying Men), Darrel Heath, Wesley Thompson, Caleb LeConte, Michael Massengale, Mark Taborn, Kelvin Brown (Dinner Guys), Darrell "Silver" Hughes (Patrick), Amy Hunter (Nita), Colby Kane (Calvin), Ian "Blaze" Kelly (Diedre's Man), Jeff Markey (Phil the Attorney), Brian Nakauchi (Delivery Man), A. Doran Reed, Mark Swenson (Help Guys), Jason Singleton (Waiter), Yul L. Spencer (Trent), Alex Thomas (Eddie), La La Vazquez (Bobby the DJ), Natashia Williams (Sexy Young Girl)

After Shanté discovers that her boyfriend Keith has been cheating on her, she institutes her "Ten Day Plan" to exact revenge and get him to come crawling back to her, only to find out that Keith has a strategy of his own.

© Screen Gems, a Sony Pictures Entertainment Company

99

Nick Catanese, Jennifer Aniston, Brian Vander Ark,
Mark Wahlberg, Kara Zediker, Blas Elias

ROCK STAR

(WARNER BROS.) Producers, Robert Lawrence, Toby Jaffe; Executive Producers, Steven Reuther, George Clooney, Mike Ockrent; Director, Stephen Herek; Screenplay, John Stockwell; Photography, Ueli Steiger; Designer, Mayne Berke; Costumes, Auggie Guerard-Rodgers; Music, Trevor Rabin; Co-Producer, Michael Fottrell; Editor, Trudy Ship; Concert Supervisors, Nick Jen, Stephen Nimmer; Casting, Sharon Bialy; a Maysville Pictures/Robert Lawrence production, presented in association with Bel Air Pictures LLC; Dolby; Super 35 Widescreen; Technicolor; Rated R; 106 minutes; Release date: September 7, 2001

Mark Wahlberg

CAST

Chris Cole	Mark Wahlberg
Emily Poule	Jennifer Aniston
Bobby Beers	Jason Flemyng
Rob Malcolm	Timothy Olyphant
Mats	Timothy Spall
Kirk Cuddy	Dominic West
A. C.	Jason Bonham
Jorgen	Jeff Pilson
Ghode	Zakk Wylde
Donny Johnson	Blas Elias
Xander Cummins	Nick Catanese
Ricki Bell	Brian Vander Ark
Tania Asher	Dagmara Dominczyk
Joe Jr.	Matthew Glave
Mr. Cole	Michael Shamus Wiles
Mrs. Cole	Beth Grant
Nina	Carey Lessard
Samantha	Kristin Willits

and Jamie Williams (Mason Bell), Keith Loneker, Eric Weinstein (Roadies), Sami Reed (Amber), Kara Zediker (Marci), Stephen Jenkins (Bradley), Colleen Ann Fitzpatrick, Kirk Enochs (Fans), Kevin Ryder (Cream Reporter), Gene Baxter (Melody Maker Reporter), Gregory Hinton (Bouncer), Sonya Stephens (Nurse), Neil Zlozower (Photographer), Miles Kennedy (Thor), Rachle Hunter (A. C.'s Wife), Heidi Mark (Kirk's Wife), Carrie Stevens (Ghode's Wife), Amy Rolle (Jorgen's Wife), William Martin Brennan (Office Worker), Lorna Scott (Mrs. Andrews), Ralph Saenz (Auditioning Singer), Jennifer Rovero, Natalie Raynes (Topless Cuties), Jamal Weathers (Scalper), Hallie Brennand (2-year-old Girl), Jamie White (MTV Veejay), Jeffrey Wetzel (Metal Head), Frederick E. Kowalo (Guitar Tech), Jennifer Uilani Warren (Girl with P Pass), Chad Azadan, Linda Cevallos, Jennifer Edmond, Brian Friedman, Cynthia Fuhrer, Cati Jean, Edward Jenkins, Kelly Knox, Tabbtah Mays, Udee McGreoy, Ted Napolitano, Tomasian Parrott, Gabriel Ramirez, Ursula Whitaker, Zachary Woodlee (Roxy Dancers)

Mark Wahlberg, Jason Flemyng

Aspiring singer and heavy metal fan Chris Cole is given the chance of a lifetime when he becomes lead singer for his favorite group, Steel Dragon.

Mark Wahlberg, Jennifer Aniston, Dagmara Dominczyk

L.I.E.

(LOT 47) Producers, Linda Moran, Rene Bastian, Michael Cuesta; Director, Michael Cuesta; Screenplay, Stephen M. Ryder, Michael Cuesta, Gerald Cuesta; Photography, Romeo Tirone; Designer, Elise Bennett; Costumes, Daniel Glicker; Editors, Eric Carlson, Kane Platt; Music, Pierre Foldes; Co-Producers, Jose Gilberto Molinari-Rosaly, Valerie Romer; Line Producer, Valerie Romer; Associate Producer, Urs Hirschbiegel; Casting, Judy Henderson; an Alter Ego/Belladonna production; Dolby; Color; Rated NC-17; 108 minutes; Release date: September 7, 2001

Billy Kay, Paul Franklin Dano

CAST

Big John Harrigan	Brian Cox
Howie Blitzer	Paul Franklin Dano
Gary Terrio	Billy Kay
Marty Blitzer	Bruce Altman
Kevin Cole	James Costa
Brian	Tony Donnelly
Scott	Walter Masterson
Guidance Counselor	Marcia DeBonis
Elliot, Marty's Lawyer	Adam LeFevre
Newscaster	Michelle Carano
Marty's Girlfriend	Tatiana Burgos
Anne Harrigan	B. Constance Barry
Henry	Brad Silnutzer
Clifford	Bob Gerardi
Man with Pizza	Frank G. Rivers
Tough Kids	Anthony F. Peragine, Jude LoBasso
Sylvia Blitzer	Gladys Dano
Howie (5 years old)	Emilio Cuesta
F.B.I. Woman	Christine Toy Johnson
Police Officer	Francis J. Leik
Desk Sergeant	Chuck Ardezzone
Cop	Risa Ziegler
Brian's Father	Ray Garvey
Mrs. Cole	Angela Pietropinto
Prison Guard	Chance Kelly

Brian Cox, Paul Franklin Dano

Howie, a troubled 15-year-old confused about his own sexuality, befriends a middle-aged man whose sexual preferences run towards teenage boys.

© Lot 47 Films

Tony Donnelly, James Costa, Paul Franklin Dano

Paul Franklin Dano

Leelee Sobieski, Stellan Skarsgård

Trevor Morgan, Leelee Sobieski

Leelee Sobieski

THE GLASS HOUSE

(COLUMBIA) Producer, Neal H. Moritz; Executive Producer, Michael Rachmil; Director, Daniel Sackheim; Screenplay, Wesley Strick; Photography, Alar Kivilo; Designer, Jon Gary Steele; Editor, Howard E. Smith; Music, Christopher Young; Costumes, Chrisi Karvonides-Dushenko; Casting, Mary Vernieu, Anne McCarthy, Felicia Fasano; an Original Film production; Dolby; Panavision; Deluxe color; Rated PG-13; 106 minutes; Release date: September 14, 2001

CAST

Ruby Baker ....Leelee Sobieski
Erin Glass ....Diane Lane
Terry Glass ....Stellan Skarsgård
Alvin Begleiter..Bruce Dern
Nancy Ryan ....Kathy Baker
Rhett Baker...Trevor Morgan
Uncle Jack ....Chris Noth
Dave Baker ....Michael O'Keefe
Grace Baker ....Rita Wilson
and Gavin O'Connor (Don), Vyto Ruginis (Whitey), Carly Pope (Tasha), China Shavers (E. B.), Agnes Bruckner (Zoe), Michael Paul Chan (Mr. Kim), Rachel Wilson (Hannah), Rutanya Alda (Vice Principal), Erick Avari (Ted Ross), Mia Barrentine (Ruby—5 years old), John Billingsley (Driving Instructor), Richard Anthony Crenna, D. Elliot Woods (Cops), Maya Danziger (Deirdre), Leslie Sackheim (Waitress), Stephanie Ittleson (Officer), Harry Johnson (Minister), January Jones (Girl), Kirk Kinder (Sheriff), Maya McGlaughlin (Receptionist), Wayne Morse (Psycho Killer), Michelle Nordin (Teen Queen), Brent Sexton (Mechanic), Paul Tuerpe (Traffic Cop), Julia Vera (Vicki), Kim Webster (Miss Drake), Alice Hirson (Mrs. Morgan), Drew Snyder (Mr. Morgan)

Following the death of their parents in an automobile accident, young Ruby Baker and her brother are taken in by friends of their parents, Erin and Terry Glass, a couple Ruby suspects are less benign than they first appear.

Brian Reed, Keanu Reeves, DeWayne Warren

Keanu Reeves, Julian Griffith

HARDBALL

(PARAMOUNT) Producers, Tina Nides, Mike Tollin, Brian Robbins; Executive Producers, Kevin McCormick, Herbert W. Gains, Erwin Stoff; Director, Brian Robbins; Screenplay, John Gatins; Based on the book *Hardball: A Season in the Projects* by Daniel Coyle; Photography, Tom Richmond; Designer, Jaymes Hinkle; Costumes, Francine Jamison-Tanchuck; Editor, Ned Bastille; Music, Mark Isham; Music Supervisor, Michael McQuarn; Casting, Marci Liorr; a Tollins/Robbins production, presented in association with Fireworks Pictures of a Nides/McCormick Production; Dolby; Deluxe color; Rated PG-13; 106 minutes; Release date: September 14, 2001

CAST

Conor O'Neill	Keanu Reeves
Elizabeth Wilkes	Diane Lane
Ticky Tobin	John Hawkes
Matt Hyland	D. B. Sweeney
Jimmy Fleming	Mike McGlone
Sterling	Sterling Elijah Brim
Miles Pennfield II	A. Delon Ellis, Jr.
Jefferson Albert Tibbs	Julian Griffith
Andre Ray Peetes	Bryan Hearne
Jamal	Michael B. Jordan
Clarence	Kristopher Lofton
Kofi Evans	Michael Perkins
Ray-Ray	Brian Reed
Alex	Alexander Telles
G-Baby	DeWayne Warren

and Michael B. Chait (Straight-Laced Kid), Carol E. Hall (Pearia Evans), Jacqueline Williams (Lenora Tibbs), Freeman Coffey (Darryl Mackey), Mark Robert Ellis (Waatas Coach), Paul Turner (Bartender), Dawn Lewis (Ellen), Kwame Amoaku, Vince Green (Pizza Guys), Mark Margolis (Fink), Tom Milanovich (Ed), Greg Sandquist (Barber's Son), Stephen Cinabro (Gino), Adam Tomei (Barfly), Father Donald M. Siple (Priest), Sammy Sosa (Himself), Aaron Evans (Aaron), Ronnel Taylor (Gang Member), Alexander Telles (Alex), Andre Morgan, Reginal McKinley (Umpires), Josefus Duanah, Jeffrey Oatlin (Tough Kids), James Currie (Check Cashing Station Cashier)

In order to pay off his bookies, Conor O'Neill reluctantly agrees to coach a corporate-sponsored little league team consisting of underprivileged kids.

© Paramount Pictures

Diane Lane, Keanu Reeves

Keanu Reeves, DeWayne Warren

HEARTS IN ATLANTIS

(WARNER BROS.) Producer, Kerry Heysen; Executive Producers, Bruce Berman, Michael Flynn; Director, Scott Hicks; Screenplay, William Goldman; Based on the novel by Stephen King; Photography, Piotr Sobocinski; Designer, Barbara C. Ling; Costumes, Julie Weiss; Editor, Pip Karmel; Music, Mychael Danna; Music Supervisor, John Bissell; a Castle Rock Entertainment presentation in association with Village Roadshow Pictures and NPV Entertainment; Dolby; Panavision; Technicolor; Rated PG-13; 101 minutes; Release date: September 28, 2001

CAST

Ted Brautigan ....Anthony Hopkins
Bobby Garfield ....Anton Yelchin
Liz Garfield...Hope Davis
Carol Gerber ....Mika Boorem
Bobby Garfield (Adult)...David Morse
Monte Man...Alan Tudyk
Len Files...Tom Bower
Alanna Files ....Celia Weston
Don Biderman...Adam LeFevre
Sully-John ....Will Rothhaar
Harry Doolin...Timmy Reifsnyder
Mrs. Gerber...Deirdre O'Connell
Mr. Oliver..Terry Beaver
Richie O'Rourke...Joe T. Blankenship
Willie Shearman ....Brett Fleisher
Sully's Dad ....Joel F. Haberli
Sully's Little Brother...Evan Moses
and Joshua Billings (Cabbie), Valerie Karasek (Sully's Widow), Graham Bardsley (Minister), Keith H. Beyer, Sean Edwards, Robert V. Maine, Mickey Leon McBride (Soldiers at Funeral), Wes Johnson (Sports Announcer)

Bobby Garfield looks back on the summer of 1960, when a mysterious stranger took a room in his Connecticut home and changed the boy's life.

Anthony Hopkins, Anton Yelchin

Anton Yelchin

Hope Davis, Anthony Hopkins

Mika Boorem

DINNER RUSH

(ACCESS MOTION PICTURE GROUP) Producers, Louis DiGiaimo, Patti Greaney; Executive Producers, Phil Suarez, Robert Cheren, Robert Steuer, Michael Baumohl; Director, Bob Giraldi; Screenplay, Rick Shaughnessy, Brian Kalata; Photography, Tim Ives; Designer, Andrew Bernard; Editor, Allyson C. Johnson; Music, Alexander Lasarenko; Music Supervisor, Alex Steyermark; Casting, Stephanie Corsalini; a Giraldi Suarez DiGiaimo Productions presentation of an Entertainment Capital Group Company production; Dolby; Technicolor; Rated R; 100 minutes; Release date: September 28, 2001

Danny Aiello, Kirk Acevedo

CAST

Louis Cropa	Danny Aiello
Udo Cropa	Edoardo Ballerini
Nicole	Vivian Wu
Carmen	Mike McGlone
Duncan	Kirk Acevedo
Jennifer Freeley	Sandra Bernhard
Marti	Summer Phoenix
Natalie	Polly Draper
Sean	Jamie Harris
Fitzgerald	Mark Margolis
Ken	John Corbett
Paolo	Alex Corrado

and Frank Bongiorno (Enrico), Sophie Comet (Food Nymph), Tessa Ghylin (Piper), Andre DeLeon (Nino), Walt MacPherson (Det. Drurry), Ajay Naidu (Ademir), Manny Perez (Gabriel), Andre Haynes Richardson (Machine), John Rothman (Gary), Lexie Sperduto (Lucy Clemente), Marita Stavrou (Kisha), Roma Torre, David Diaz (Themselves), Ellen McElduff (Ellen Drury), Zainab Jah (Adrian), Jimmy Shelgin, Nural Raque (Servers), John Patrick Walker (Waiter), Gabriel Jiminez (Pasta Chef), Joe Gatti, Jr. (Harold), Annika Peterson (Bettina), Juan Hernandez (Joseph), Luigi Celentano (Line Chief), Jonathen Chodash (Black-Out Customer), Ted Koch, Doreen Dunlap (Bar Patrons), Julie Zeger (Baby's Mother), David Phillips (Baby's Father), Marcus Schenkenberg, Jennifer Chambers (Customers)

Gigino's, a fashionable New York restaurant, experiences an especially hectic and crowded evening as various characters converge on the eatery.

© Access Motion Picture Group

John Corbett, Marita Stavrou

Edoardo Ballerini, Sandra Bernhard

Summer Phoenix, Mike McGlone, Alex Corrado

Michael Douglas, Famke Janssen

Victor Argo, Jennifer Esposito

Brittany Murphy, Michael Douglas

Sean Bean, Shawn Doyle

DON'T SAY A WORD

(20TH CENTURY FOX) Producers, Arnon Milchan, Arnold Kopelson, Anne Kopelson; Director, Gary Fleder; Screenplay, Anthony Peckham, Patrick Smith Kelly; Based on the novel by Andrew Klavan; Executive Procucers, Jeffrey Downer, Bruce Berman; Photography, Amir Mokri; Designer, Nelson Coates; Costumes, Ellen Mirojnick; Editors, William Steinkamp, Armen Minasian; Co-Producers, Andrew Klavan, Nana Greenwald; Music, Mark Isham; Music Supervisor, Peter Afterman; Casting, Avy Kaufman; a Regency Enterprises and Village Roadshow Pictures presentation in association with NPV Entertainment of a Kopelson Entertainment/New Regency/Furthur Films production; Dolby; Panavision; Deluxe color; Rated R; 112 minutes; Release date: September 28, 2001

CAST

Dr. Nathan Conrad	Michael Douglas
Patrick B. Koster	Sean Bean
Elisabeth Burrows	Brittany Murphy
Jessie Conrad	Skye McCole Bartusiak
Martin J. Dolen	Guy Torry
Detective Sandra Cassidy	Jennifer Esposito
Russel Maddox	Shawn Doyle
Sydney Simon	Victor Argo
Max J. Dunlevy	Conrad Goode
Jake	Paul Schulze
Arnie Carter	Lance Reddick
Aggie Conrad	Famke Janssen
Dr. Louis Sachs	Oliver Platt
Leon E. Croft	Aidan Devine
Jonathan	Alex Campbell
Intern	Philip DeWilde
Frankie Spaducci	Sam Montesano

and Arlene Duncan (Aide), Judy Sinclair (Zelda Sinclair), Larry Block (Doorman), David Warshofsky (Ryan), Darren Frost (Janitor), Philip Williams (Large Cop), Louis Vanaria (Cop), Daniel Kash (Detective Garcia), Lucie Laurier (Roommate Vanessa), Isabella Fink (Elisabeth—8 years old), Ray Iannicelli (Man at Marina), Colm Magner (Cop #1), Cyrus Farmer (Officer #1), Martin Roach (Transit Cop), Patricia Mauceri (Sofia)

In order to retrieve a stolen diamond, a gang of ruthless thieves kidnaps the daughter of Manhattan psychiatrist Nathan Conrad, whose institutionalized patient, Elisabeth Burrows, is the only one who knows the six-digit figure they need to accomplish their task.

ZOOLANDER

(PARAMOUNT) Producers, Scott Rudin, Ben Stiller, Stuart Cornfeld; Executive Producers, Joel Gallen, Adam Schroeder, Lauren Zalaznick; Director, Ben Stiller; Screenplay, Drake Sather, Ben Stiller, John Hamburg; Story, Drake Sather, Ben Stiller; Photography, Barry Peterson; Designer, Robin Standefer; Costumes, David C. Robinson; Editor, Greg Hayden; Co-Producer, Celia Costas; Music, David Arnold; Music Supervisors, Casting, Juel Bestrop, Jeanne McCarthy, Kathleen Chopin; a Village Roadshow Pictures presentation in association with VH1 and NPV Entertainment; Dolby; Super 35 Widescreen; Deluxe color; Rated PG-13; 89 minutes; Release date: September 28, 2001

CAST

Derek Zoolander	Ben Stiller
Hansel	Owen Wilson
Matilda Jeffries	Christine Taylor
Mugatu	Will Ferrell
Katinka	Milla Jovovich
Maury Ballstein	Jerry Stiller
J. P. Prewitt	David Duchovny
Larry Zoolander	Jon Voight
Scrappy Zoolander	Judah Friedlander
Todd	Nathan Lee Graham
Brint	Alexander Manning
Rufus	Asio Highsmith
Meekus	Alexander Skarsgård
Archie	Matt Levin
Evil DJ	Justin Theroux
Olga the Masseuse	Andy Dick
Prime Minister of Malaysia	Woodrow Asai
Hansel's Corner Guy	Andrew Wilson
Italian Designer	John Vargas
American Designer	Jennifer Coolidge
French Designer	Tony Kanal
German Designer	Endre Hules
British Designer	Nora Dunn
Mugatu's Dog	Kiva
Coal Mine Tavern Dog	Kahlua
Derek's Interview Hairstylist	Ric Pipino
VH1 Reporter	Jerry Stahl
Mugatu Model	Jennifer McComb
Mugatu Bodyguards	Johann Urb, Luc Commeret
Tim Magazine Reader	Herb Lieberz
Night Club Door Person	Zoya
Night Club Security	Colin McNish, Darren Copeland
Night Club Bouncer (Biff)	Richard Stanley
Night Club Bouncer (Maurice)	Shabazz Richardson
Night Club Bouncer	Rohan Quine
Billy Zane's Date	Svetlana
Rico	Eric Winzenried
Abraham Lincoln	Charles Brame
John Wilkes Booth	James Marsden
JFK Assassins	Rudy Segura, Randall Slavin
Monkey Photographer	Patton Oswalt

and Donald Trump, Christian Slater, Tom Ford, Cuba Gooding, Jr., Steve Kmetko, Tommy Hilfiger, Natalie Portman, Fabio, Lenny Kravitz, Gwen Stefani, Heidi Klum, DJ Mark Ronson, Paris Hilton, David Bowie, Tyson Beckford, Fred Durst, Lance Bass, Li'l Kim, Garry Shandling, Stephen Dorff, Sandra Bernhard, Claudia Schiffer, Veronica Webb, Lukas Haas, Carmen Kass, Frankie Rayder, Little Kingz, Winona Ryder, Laura Salem, Billy Zane (Themselves), Vikram Kashana, Jonah Luber, Michael McAlpin, Eve Salvail, Shavo Odadjian, Eliot Johnson, Richard Gladys, Amy Stiller (Hansel's Posse), Irina Pantaeva (Irina), Stan Chu (Sherpa), Kum Ming Ho (Climber), Theo Kogan (Cool Tattoo Girl), Lam Bor (Dalai Lama Guy), Angel 11:11, Luther Creek, Dechen Thurman, Kenny Max (Funky Loft Guests), Kina (Ennui), David Pressman (Maori Tribesman), Godfrey Danchimah (Janitor Derek), Taj Crown (Janitor Hansel), Richie Rich (Derelicte Doorman), King (Derelicte Bouncer), Frederic Fekkai (Derek's Derelicte Hairstylist), Kevyn Aucoin (Derek's Derelicte Makeup Artist), Boris Kachscovsky (Zoolander Center Student), Mitch Winston (Informercial Director), Mason Webb (Derek, Jr.), Alexa Nikolas (Story Hour Girl), Vince Vaughn (Luke Zoolander), Anne Meara (Protester)

Looking for meaning in his life after being dethroned as Male Model of the Year, clueless Derek Zoolander gets a comeback assignment from top fashion designer Mugatu, little realizing that he is being used as part of a nefarious assassination plot.

© Paramount Pictures

Ben Stiller, David Bowie, Owen Wilson

Owen Wilson, Ben Stiller

Ben Stiller, Jerry Stiller

Milla Jovovich, Ben Stiller, Will Ferrell

Denzel Washington, Ethan Hawke

Denzel Washington

TRAINING DAY

(WARNER BROS.) Producers, Jeffrey Silver, Bobby Newmyer; Executive Producers, Bruce Berman, Davis Guggenheim; Director, Antoine Fuqua; Screenplay, David Ayer; Photography, Mauro Fiore; Designer, Naomi Shohan; Costumes, Michele Michel; Editor, Conrad Buff; Music, Mark Mancina; Music Supervisor, John Houlihan; Casting, Mary Vernieu; an Outlaw Production, presented in association with Village Roadshow Pictures and NPV Entertainment; Dolby; Panavision; Technicolor; Rated R; 120 minutes; Release date: October 5, 2001

CAST

Alonzo Harris	Denzel Washington
Jake Hoyt	Ethan Hawke
Roger	Scott Glenn
Stan Gursky	Tom Berenger
Doug Rosselli	Harris Yulin
Lou Jacobs	Raymond J. Barry
Smiley	Cliff Curtis
Paul	Dr. Dre
Blue	Snoop Dogg
Sandman's Wife	Macy Gray
Lisa	Charlotte Ayanna
Sara	Eva Mendes
Tim	Nick Chinlund
Mark	Jaime P. Gomez
Sniper	Raymond Cruz
Moreno	Noel Guglielmi
Letty	Samantha Becker
Waiter, Dining Car	Richard Browner
Gangster	Ronald Ellis
Alonzo's Son	Kyjel N. Jolly
College Driver	Fran Kranz
Waitress, Diner	Janeen Krikorian
Wig Store Owner	Princera Lee
Veterano	Robert Leon
Dreamer	Seidy Lopez
College Passengers	Sarah Danielle Madison, Brett Sorenson
Pee Wee	Rudy Perez
LAPD Pilot	Ben Skorstad
Bone	Cle "Shiheed" Sloan
Neto	Abel Soto
Crackheads	Garland Whitt, Will Foster Stewart
Dimitri	Denzel Whitaker

and Kenneth Allen Madden, Chris Patterson, Darrel Sellers, William English (Dice Players)

Rookie cop Jake Hoyt goes through a day of training under the wing of veteran narcotics officer Alonzo Harris, whose way of dealing with L.A.'s criminal underworld is no less corrupt than those on the opposite side of the law.

2001 Academy Award-winner for Best Actor (Denzel Washington). This film received an additional nomination for supporting actor (Ethan Hawke).

© Warner Bros.

Denzel Washington, Ethan Hawke

Ethan Hawke, Denzel Washington

Denzel Washington

Macy Gray

Snoop Dogg

Ethan Hawke

Brett Sorenson, Denzel Washington

Kate Beckinsale, John Cusack

SERENDIPITY

(MIRAMAX) Producers, Simon Fields, Peter Abrams, Robert L. Levy; Executive Producers, Bob Osher, Julie Goldstein, Amy Slotnick; Director, Peter Chelsom; Screenplay, Marc Klein; Co-Producers, Amy Kaufman, Andrew Panay; Co-Executive Producer, Robbie Brenner; Photography, John De Borman; Designer, Caroline Hanania; Costumes, Marie-Sylvie Deveau, Mary Claire Hannon; Editor, Christopher Greenbury; Music, Alan Silvestri; Music Supervisor, Laura Ziffren; Casting, Mary Gail Artz, Barbara Cohen, Billy Hopkins, Suzanne Smith, Kerry Barden; a Tapestry Films production in association with Simon Fields Productions; Dolby; Color; Rated PG-13; 91 minutes; Release date: October 5, 2001

Molly Shannon, Kate Beckinsale, Ajay Mehta

CAST

Jonathan Tager	John Cusack
Sara Thomas	Kate Beckinsale
Dean Kansky	Jeremy Piven
Eve	Molly Shannon
Halley Buchanan	Bridget Moynahan
Lars Hammond	John Corbett
Bloomingsdale Salesman	Eugene Levy
Caroline Mitchell	Lucy Gordon
Courtney	Kate Blumberg
Superintendent	Mike Benitez
Flight Attendant	Pamela Redfern
Hair Stylist	Brenda Logan
Hippie Woman	Colleen Williams
Host at Serendipity	Stephen Bruce
Janitor	Aron Tager
Priest	Murray McRae
Kenny	Evan Neuman
Kip	Kevin Rice

Jeremy Piven, Eugene Levy, John Cusack

and Christopher Baker, Neil Claxton (Lars's Band), Leo Fitzpatrick (Leasing Office Temp), Ron Payne (Louis Trager), John Ellison Conlee (Artie), Victor Young (Mr. Buchanan), Eve Crawford (Mrs. Buchanan), Marcia Bennett (Mrs. Trager), Jamie Goodwin (Nick Roberts), Ajay Mehta (Pakistani Driver), Sandra Caldwell (PR Woman), Reggi Wyns (Rastafarian), T. Scott Cunningham (Ryan), Jessica Kelly (Sara Lawson), Simon Jutras (Sebastian), Marquis Bobesich (Street Vendor), Catherine Hernandez (Waitress at Serendipity), Catherine Kuhn (Wedding Coordinator), Clark Middleton (Aiport Cab Driver), David Sparrow (Josh's Dad), Gary Gerbrandt (Josh), Conrad Bergschneider (Check-in Clerk), Lilli Lavine (Bloomingdale's Stock Girl), Buck Henry (Glove Man)

In 1990 Manhattan, two people, Jonathan Trager and Sara Thomas, meet and become smitten with each other only to separate accidentally. Leaving their second meeting up to fate, ten years pass, finding them ready to marry others despite the yearning that still exists within them both.

© Miramax Films

Kate Beckinsale, John Corbett

JOY RIDE

(20TH CENTURY FOX) formerly *Squelch*; Producers, J. J. Abrams, Chris Moore; Executive Producers, Arnon Milchan, Patrick Markey, Bridget Johnson; Director, John Dahl; Screenplay, Clay Tarver, J. J. Abrams; Photography, Jeffrey Jur; Designer, Rob Pearson; Costumes, Terry Dresbach; Editors, Eric L. Beason, Scott Chestnut, Todd E. Miller, Glen Scantlebury; Music, Marco Beltrami; Casting, Mali Finn, Emily Schweber; Stunts, Terry Leonard; a Regency Enterprises presentation of a New Regency/Bad Robot/Liveplanet production; Dolby; Panavision; Deluxe color; Rated R; 96 minutes; Release date: October 5, 2001

CAST

Fuller Thomas	Steve Zahn
Lewis Thomas	Paul Walker
Venna Wilcox	Leelee Sobieski
Charlotte Campbell	Jessica Bowman
Danny Rosado (Lewis's Roommate)	Stuart Stone
Car Salesman	Basil Wallace
Officer Keeney	Brian Leckner
Salt Lake City Police Desk Clerk	Mary Wickliffe
Asst. Salt Lake City Police Desk Clerk	McKenzie Satterthwaite
Gas Station Mechanic	Dell Yount
Ronald Ellinghouse	Kenneth White
Night Manager	Luis Cortes
Officer Akins	Michael McCleery
Sheriff Ritter	Jim Beaver
Gas Station Manager	Rachel Singer
Ice Truck Man	Satch Huizenga
Bartender	Terry Leonard

and James MacDonald (Local in Nebraska Bar), Gwenda Deacon (Truck Stop Waitress), Robert Winley (Truck Stop Manager), Ali Gage (Waitress), Jack Moore (Hotwire Consultant), Hugh Dane (Man at Door), Lee Stepp (Traveling Salesman), Jay Hernandez (Marine), Huey Redwine, John Maynard, Peter Weireter (Policemen), Tim Cooney, Sheryl Giffis, Pamela Senatore (Voice Actors), Matthew Kimbrough (Rusty Nail), Ted Levine (Voice of Rusty Nail)

During a cross-country drive, irresponsible Fuller Thomas's insistence on playing a hoax on a trucker backfires and he and his brother find themselves being terrorized by the vengeful driver.

© Monarchy Enterprises S.a.r.l. and Regency Entertainment (USA), Inc.

Paul Walker, Leelee Sobieski, Steve Zahn

Steve Zahn

Leelee Sobieski

Paul Walker, Steve Zahn

111

Vinessa Shaw, Chris Kattan

Chris Penn, Peter Falk, Peter Berg

CORKY ROMANO

(TOUCHSTONE) Producer, Robert Simonds; Executive Producer, Tracey Trench; Director, Rob Pritts; Screenplay, David Garrett, Jason Ward; Co-Producer, Ira Shuman; Photography, Steven Bernstein; Designer, Peter Politanoff; Costumes, Tom Bronson; Editor, Alan Cody; Music, Randy Edelman; Music Supervisor, Lisa Brown; Casting, Roger Mussenden; a Robert Simonds production; Dolby; Panavision; Technicolor; Rated PG-13; 85 minutes; Release date: October 12, 2001

CAST

Corky Romano	Chris Kattan
Agent Kate Russo	Vinessa Shaw
Pops	Peter Falk
Paulie	Peter Berg
Peter	Chris Penn
Leo Corrigan	Fred Ward
Howard Shuster	Richard Roundtree
Agent Brick Davis	Matthew Glave
Agent Bob Cox	Roger Fan
Agent Terrence Darnell	Dave Sheridan

and Michael Massee (Angry Gunman), Vincent Pastore (Tony), Fiona Hale (Florence), Al Eben (Dale), Kip King (Dr. Kipper), Adele Craig (Connie), Irene Olga Lopez (Mrs. Hernandez), Sylvester Jenkins (Mr. Langford—Old Man), Jeanette Miller (Phyllis—Old Woman with Cat), Blake Clark (Security Guard), Zach Galifianakis (Dexter—Hacker), April Tran (Vietnamese Man), Eck Stone (Thai Man), Kevin Indio Copeland, Dennis Keiffer, Justin Riemer, Tim Sitarz (Skinheads), Kristina Simonds (Woman in Classroom), Rena Mero (Bouncer), John Farley (Ice Cream Vendor), Howard Weitzman (Attorney), Dilva Henry, Patrick Stinson, James Hill (Reporters), Steven Wilde (Chaz, Bouncer), James Tupper (FBI Agent), Sean Greenhut (Coughing Kid), Flora Burke (Woman with Dog), Grant Silver (Boy with Mouse), Robin Borovic (Secretary), Gary C. Smith (Hank), Ashton Dane, Joseph Dubow (SWAT Team), Gary C. Smith (Precision Driver)

Corky Romano, a good-natured veterinarian, is ordered by his Mafia-king-pin dad to infiltrate the FBI and steal some important evidence against the old man.

© Touchstone Pictures

Chris Kattan, Fred Ward

Chris Kattan, Matthew Glave, Richard Roundtree

Billy Bob Thornton, Cate Blanchett, Bruce Willis

Cate Blanchett

BANDITS

(MGM) Producers, Ashok Amritraj, David Hoberman, Arnold Rifkin, Barry Levinson, Paula Weinstein, Michael Birnbaum, Michele Berk; Executive Producers, Patrick McCormick, Harley Peyton, David Willis; Director, Barry Levinson; Screenplay, Harley Peyton; Photography, Dante Spinotti; Designer, Victor Kempster; Editor, Stu Linder; Costumes, Gloria Gresham; Music, Christopher Young; Executive Music Producers, Joel Sill, Allan Mason; Casting, Ellen Chenoweth; an Empire Pictures, Lotus Pictures, Baltimore/Spring Creek Pictures, Cheyenne Enterprises production, presented in association with Hyde Park Entertainment; Dolby; Super 35 Widescreen; Deluxe color; Rated PG-13; 123 minutes; Release date: October 12, 2001

CAST

Joe Blake	Bruce Willis
Terry Collins	Billy Bob Thornton
Kate Wheeler	Cate Blanchett
Harvey Pollard	Troy Garity
Darill Miller	Brian F. O'Byrne
Cloe Miller	Stacey Travis
Darren Head	Bobby Slayton
Claire	January Jones
Cheri	Azura Skye
Mildred Kronenberg	Peggy Miley
Charles Wheeler	William Converse-Roberts
Lawrence Fife	Richard Riehle
Sarah Fife	Micole Mercurio
Wildwood Policeman	Scott Burkholder
Phil	Anthony Burch
Billy Saunders	Sam Levinson
Monica Miller	Scout LaRue Willis
Erika Miller	Tallulah Belle Willis

and John Evans (Ralph), John Harrington Bland (Flamingo Clerk), Cindy Goldfield, Heather Matheson, Erin-Kate Whitcomb (Debbie Days), Kim Bogus (Bend Bank Teller), Michael X. Sommers, Rich Sickler (Policemen), Michael Birnbaum (Desk Sergeant), Joe Unitas (Detective), Richard Shuster (LA Chopper Pilot), Jennifer York (LA Reporter), José Guillermo Garcia (Local Youth), Alfred De Contreras (Mexican Priest), Peter Weireter (SWAT Commander), Kerry Kilbride, Jane Velez-Mitchell (Debaters), Mia Lee (Los Angeles Anchor), Louis LeRay, Peter Hutchison, Maya Rossi (Band Members), Joan Palmateer (Bank Teller), Giulio Magnolia (Butler), Rose Aispuro (Bank Hostage), Carrie Casano (Bank Manager), Jaye K. Danford (Alamo Bank Manager), Darryl D. Stewart (Detective), Greg Wilmarth (U.S. Marshal)

Two escaped cons, making a name for themselves as bank robbers known as "the sleepover bandits," find their lives complicated by a runaway housewife who comes between them.

© Metro-Goldwyn-Mayer Pictures, Inc.

Troy Garity, January Jones

Cate Blanchett, Troy Garity, Bruce Willis

Albert Brooks, Leelee Sobieski

Leelee Sobieski

MY FIRST MISTER

(PARAMOUNT CLASSICS) Producers, Carol Baum, Jane Goldenring, Mitchell Solomon, Sukee Chew, Anne Kurtzman; Executive Producers, Frank Hübner, Gerald Green; Director, Christine Lahti; Screenplay, Jill Franklyn; Co-Executive Producers, Jon F. Vein, Howard Rosenman, Robert Kurtzman; Photography, Jeffrey Jur; Designer, Dan Bishop; Costumes, Kimberly A. Tillman; Music, Steve Porcaro; Music Supervisor, Andy Hill; Editor, Wendy Greene Bricmont; Casting, Amanda Mackey Johnson, Cathy Sandrich; a Total Film Group presentation in association with Film Roman, Inc. of a Firelight/Apollomedia co-production; Dolby; Panavision; Deluxe color; Rated R; 109 minutes; Release date: October 12, 2001

CAST

Randall ("R")..Albert Brooks
Jennifer ("J")..Leelee Sobieski
Randy..Desmond Harrington
Bob..Michael McKean
Mrs. Benson..Carol Kane
Patty..Mary Kay Place
Benjamin..John Goodman
Woman in Apartment..Rutanya Alda
Girl in Vintage..Natasha Braisewell
Jack Taylor (Salesman)..Henry Brown
Mr. Smithman..Gary Bullock
Doctor..Kevin Cooney
Blaine (Surfer Boy)..Nic Costa
Customer..William Forward
Woman at R's Store..Shawn Huff
Manager..Chadwick Palmatier
Bebe..Pauley Perrette
Sheila..Lisa Jane Persky
Ashley..Katee Sackhoff
and Lorna Scott (Woman in Store), Matthew St. Clair (Kevin), Chris Wylde (Waiter—Coffee House)

Jennifer, an angry, cynical teenager, gets a job at a clothing store where she forms an unlikely friendship with the manager, Randall, a well-ordered older man who couldn't be less like her.

© Paramount Classics

Desmond Harrington

Carol Kane

Julie Delpy, Ethan Hawke

WAKING LIFE

(FOX SEARCHLIGHT) Producers, Palmer West, Jonah Smith, Tommy Pallotta, Anne Walker-McBay; Executive Producers, Jonathan Sehring, Caroline Kaplan, John Sloss; Director/Screenplay, Richard Linklater; Art Director, Bob Sabiston; Editor, Sandra Adair; Music, Glover Gill, Tosca Tango Orchestra; Animators, Jason Archer, Paul Beck, John Bruch, Jean Caffeine, Zoë Charlton, Randy Cole, Kate Dollenmayer, Jennifer Drummond, Rahab El Ewaly, Pat Falconer, Holly Louise Fisher, Dan Gillotte, Nathan Jensen, Matthew Langland, Michael Layne, Travis C. Lindquist, Chris Minley, Katy O'Connor, John Paul, Shannon Pearson, Eric Power, Bob Sabiston, Susan Sabiston, Katie Salen, Divya Srinivasan, Patrick Thornton, Penny Van Horn, Mary Varn, Rosie Q. Weaver, Wiley Wiggins, Constance Wood; Casting, Lizzie Martinez; a Detour Film production, presented by The Independent Film Channel Productions and Thousand Words; Dolby; Color; Rated R; 97 minutes; Release date: October 17, 2001

CAST

Trevor Jack Brooks, Lorelei Linklater, Wiley Wiggins, Glover Gill, Lara Hicks, Ames Asbell, Leigh Mahoney, Sara Nelson, Jeanine Attaway, Erik Grostic, Bill Wise, Robert C. Solomon, Kim Krizan, Eamonn Healy, J. C. Shakespeare, Ethan Hawke, Julie Delpy, Charles Gunning, David Sosa, Alex Jones, Otto Hofmann, Aklilu Gebrewold, Carol Dawson, Lisa Moore, Steve Fitch, Louis Mackey, Alex Nixon, Violet Nichols, Steven Prince, Ken Webster, Mary McBay, Kregg A. Foote, Jason T. Hodge, Guy Forsyth, John Christensen, Caveh Zahedi, David Jewell, Adam Goldberg, Nicky Katt, E. Jason Liebricht, Brent Green, RC Whittaker, Hymie Samuelson, David Martinez, Ryan Power, Tiana Hux, Speed Levitch, Steve Brudniak, Marta Banda, Steven Soderbergh, Charles Murdock, Mona Lee, Edith Mannix, Bess Cox, Louis Black, Richard Linklater

In this live-action feature on which the footage was afterward graphically "painted" frame by frame by computer, a young man travels through a surreal series of encounters with various people offering him their philosophies on life.

© Twentieth Century Fox

Speed Levitch

Brent Green

David Jewell, Caveh Zahedi

Marta Banda, Wiley Wiggins

Meat Loaf Aday

FOCUS

(PARAMOUNT CLASSICS) Producers, Neal Slavin, Michael R. Bloomberg, Robert A. Miller; Executive Producers, Martin Geller, Neil O'Connor, Jamie Rizzo, Anita Slavin; Co-Producers, Thomas D. Adelman, Kip Konwiser; Director, Neal Slavin; Screenplay, Kendrew Lascelles; Based on the novel by Arthur Miller; Line Producer, Thomas D. Adelman; Photography, Juan Ruiz-Anchia; Designer, Vlasta Svoboda; Editor, Tariq Anwar; Music, Mark Adler; Casting, Mary Vernieu, Anne Mcarthy, Felicia Fasano; a Michael R. Bloomberg and Focus Productions presentation of a Robert A. Miller production in association with Carros Pictures; Dolby; Color; Rated PG-13; 104 minutes; Release date: October 19, 2001

Laura Dern, William H. Macy

CAST

Lawrence Newman	William H. Macy
Gertrude Hart	Laura Dern
Finkelstein	David Paymer
Fred	Meat Loaf Aday
Mrs. Newman	Kay Hewtrey
Carlson	Michael Copeman
Father Crighton	Kenneth Welsh
Gargan	Joseph Ziegler
Mrs. Dewitt	Arlene Meadows
Willy Doyle	Peter Oldring
Meeting Hall Man	Robert McCarrol
Sullivan	Shaunn Austin-Olsen
Cole Stevens	Kevin Jubinville
Mel	B. J. McQueen

and Conrad Bergschneider (Tough's Leader), Brad Austin (1st Tough), David Blacker (Petey), Betariz Pizano (Rape Victim), Rick Braggins (Mr. Lorring), Rodger Barton (Sergeant), Andrew Massingham (Policeman), Bryon Billy (Billy), Anita Burkhart (Speaking Woman on Subway), Olivia Slavin (Mrs. Dewitt's Granddaughter), Wendy Lyon (Elsie), Angela Fusco (2nd Woman on Subway), Barbara Barnes-Hopkins (Maid), Stephan Brogren (Bodyguard), Paulette Sinclair (MP Receptionist), Pat Patterson (Green Grocer), Julia Paton (Waitress), Leo Petrus (Truck Driver), Durward Allen (Photographer), Peter Evans (Man in Theater), Tedde Moore, Anna-Louise Richardson (Women in Theater)

Mild-mannered Lawrence Newman finds himself unexpectedly facing anti-Semitism when his new pair of glasses leads people to believe that he is Jewish.

David Paymer

William H. Macy, Laura Dern

Mark Ruffalo, Robert Redford

James Gandolfini, Robert Redford

THE LAST CASTLE

(DREAMWORKS) Producer, Robert Lawrence; Executive Producer, Don Zepfel; Director, Rod Lurie; Screenplay, David Scarpa, Graham Yost; Story, David Scarpa; Photography, Shelly Johnson; Designer, Kirk M. Petruccelli; Costumes, Ha Nguyen; Editors, Michael Jablow, Kevin Stitt; Music, Jerry Goldsmith; 2nd Unit Director/Stunts, Mic Rodgers; Casting, Deborah Aquila, Mary Jo Slater; a Robert Lawrence production; Dolby; Panavision; Technicolor; Rated R; 131 minutes; Release date: October 19, 2001

Clifton Collins, Jr.

Steve Burton

CAST

General Irwin ....Robert Redford
Colonel Winter ....James Gandolfini
Yates ....Mark Ruffalo
Captain Peretz ....Steve Burton
General Wheeler ....Delroy Lindo
Dellwo...Paul Calderon
Duffy..Samuel Ball
Cutbush..Jeremy Childs
Aguilar...Clifton Collins, Jr.
Thumper ....George W. Scott
Beaupre..Brian Goodman
Enriquez ....Michael Irby
Doc..Frank Military
Rosalie Irwin ....Robin Wright Penn
Sgt. McLaren ....Maurice Bullard
Pvt. Niebolt ....Nick Kokich
Corporal Zamorro ....David Alford
and Dean Hall (Harris), Peg Allen (Secretary, Kelly), Rick Vito (Red Team Leader), Forrest D. Bradford (Simmons), Scott Michael (Gunton), Dean Miller (Carvelli), Kristen Shaw (Clerk, Staff Sgt.), Michael Davis (Honor Guard), Joe Keenan (Trustee, Lester), David Chattam (Wheeler's Aide), Dan Cole (Trustee #2), Hans Mooy (Sgt. Moore), James Jerome Thomas (Rapper), Stephen Sandfort, Jamie Roberto Mantecon, Jeffrey G. Fagan, Lyon Fleming, Darius Willis, Rico Moody, Rocky Abou-Sakher (Inmates), Sean Cameron (Guard), Mary Jean McAdams (Visitor)

Frank Military, Robert Redford

A noted general, court-martialed and stripped of his rank, is sent to a military prison where he clashes with its iron-fisted warden.

Steve Zahn, Drew Barrymore

Adam Garcia

Sara Gilbert, David Moscow, Celine Marget, Lorraine Bracco, Drew Barrymore, James Woods, Steve Zahn, Brittany Murphy, Desmond Harrington

RIDING IN CARS WITH BOYS

(COLUMBIA) Producers, James L. Brooks, Julie Ansell, Richard Sakai, Sara Colleton, Laurence Mark; Executive Producers, Morgan Upton Ward, Bridget Johnson; Director, Penny Marshall; Screenplay, Morgan Upton Ward; Based on the book by Beverly D'Onofrio; Photography, Miroslav Ondricek; Designer, Bill Groom; Costumes, Cynthia Flynt; Editors, Richard Marks, Lawrence Jordan; Music, Hans Zimmer, Heitor Pereira; Co-Producers, Timothy M. Bourne, Amy Lemisch, Beverly Donofrio; Casting, Sheila Jaffe, Georgianne Walken; a Gracie Films production; Dolby; Deluxe color; Rated PG-13; 122 minutes; Release date: October 19, 2001

CAST

Beverly Donofrio	Drew Barrymore
Ray Hasek	Steve Zahn
Fay Forrester	Brittany Murphy
Jason (20 years old)	Adam Garcia
Mrs. Donofrio	Lorraine Bracco
Mr. Donofrio	James Woods
Tina	Sara Gilbert
Bobby	Desmond Harrington
Lizard	David Moscow
Amelia (20 years old)	Maggie Gyllenhaal
Tommy Butcher	Peter Facinelli
Janet (19 years old)	Marisa Ryan
Beverly (11 years old)	Mika Boorem
Amelia (8 years old)	Skye McCole Bartusiak
Jason (8 years old)	Logan Lerman
Jason (6 years old)	Cody Arens
Jason (3 years old)	Logan Arens
Shirley	Rosie Perez
Janet (8 years old)	Celine Marget
Uncle Lou	Vincent Pastore
Aunt Ann	Maryann Urbano
Jenny	Aleksia Landeau
Cindy	Kristin Proctor
Karen	Temple Brooks
Karen's Friend	Lauren Lake
Kevin	Jordan Gelber
Sky Barrister	Gabriel Carpenter
Mark	Kevin Thoms
Jail Ward	Kevin O'Rourke
Mrs. Forrester	Susan Forristal
Mr. Forrester	John Bedford Lloyd
1st Phone Call Flirt	Paz De La Huerta
Janet (12 years old)	Olivia Morgan Scheck
Wedding Singer Tony	Dusty Rizzo
Pete	Gene Canfield
Donofrio Cousin	Heather Hodder
Zippy	Sean Liotine
Nurse	Tracy Reiner
Jason (newborn)	Joseph M. Cannizaro, Noah Hartwick
Jason (baby)	Briana Tilden
Jason (1 year old)	Skye Arens

and Patrick Salerno, Robert Salerno (Jason—2 years old), Samantha Reale (Amelia—3 years old), Wade Mylius (Al), Jon Korkes (Counselor), Samantha Lucier (Amelia—6 years old), Gaetano Lisi (Sweeny's Owner), Michael Linstroth (Dennis Forrester)

Beverly Donofrio looks back on how her life was derailed when she got pregnant at age 15 and ended up married to a man with no ambitions and a drug dependency.

FROM HELL

(20TH CENTURY FOX) Producers, Don Murphy, Jane Hamsher; Executive Producers, Amy Robinson, Thomas M. Hammel, Allen Hughes, Albert Hughes; Director, The Hughes Brothers (Allen Hughes, Albert Hughes); Screenplay, Terry Hayes, Rafael Yglegias; Based on the graphic novel by Alan Moore, Eddie Campbell; Photography, Peter Deming; Designer, Martin Childs; Costumes, Kym Barrett; Editors, Dan Lebental, George Bowers; Music, Trevor Jones; Casting, Joyce Gallie, Sally Osoba; an Underworld Pictures/Don Murphy and Jane Hamsher/Amy Robinson production; Dolby; Panavision; Deluxe color; Rated R; 121 minutes; Release date: October 19, 2001

Johnny Depp

CAST

Fred Abberline	Johnny Depp
Mary Kelly	Heather Graham
Sir William Gull	Ian Holm
Netley	Jason Flemyng
Peter Godley	Robbie Coltrane
Kate Eddowes	Lesley Sharp
Liz Stride	Susan Lynch
Ben Kidney	Terence Harvey
Dark Annie Chapman	Katrin Cartlidge
Ada	Estelle Skornik
Dr. Ferral	Paul Rhys
Officer Bolt	Nicholas McGaughey
Sir Charles Warren	Ian Richardson
Polly	Annabelle Apsion
Ann Crook	Joanna Page
Albert Sickert (Prince Edward)	Mark Dexter
Constable Withers	Danny Midwinter
Martha Tabram	Samantha Spiro
Mcqueen	David Schofield
Robert Best	Bryon Fear
Lord Hallsham	Peter Eyre
Mac (Bartender)	Cliff Parisi
Victoria Abberline	Sophia Myles
Gordie	Ralph Ineson
Gull's Maid	Amy Huck
Doss Landlord	Rupert Farley
Hospital Director	Donald Douglas
Marylebone Governor	John Owens
Opium Den Owner	Tony Tang
Queen Victoria	Liz Moscrop
Sidewalk Preacher	Roger Frost
Robert Drudge	Ian McNeice
Special Branch Constable	Steve John Shepherd
Stonecutter	Al Hunter Ashton
Alice Crook	Poppy Rogers
Ann Crook's Father	Bruce Byron
Ann Crook's Mother	Melanie Hill

and Andy Linden (Carpenter), David Fisher (Carpenter, Letter Writer), Gary Powell, Steve Chaplin, Dominic Cooper (Constables), Vincent Franklin (George Lusk), Louise Atkins (Bold Hooker), Anthony Parker (John Merrick), James Greene (Masonic Governor), Carey Thring (Police Photographer), Vladimir Kulhavy (Rag & Bone Man), Graham Kent (Records Clerk), Ruper Holliday Evans (Sailor), Simon Harrison (Thomas Bond), Paul Moody (Young Doctor), Glen Berry (Young Labourer), Charlie Parish (Labourer #2), Gerry Grennell (Funeral Minister, Ltr. Writer), Pavel Vokoun, John Dent (Horse Masters)

In 1888 London, Fred Abberline, a brilliant police inspector, is called on by Scotland Yard to help solve the murders of several prostitutes.

© Twentieth Century Fox

Robbie Coltrane

Heather Graham

BONES

(NEW LINE CINEMA) Producers, Lloyd Segan, Peter Heller, Rupert Harvey; Executive Producer, Carolyn Manetti; Director, Ernest Dickerson; Screenplay, Adam Simon, Tim Metcalfe; Co-Producer, Leon Dudevoir, Stephen Hollocker; Photography, Flavio Labiano; Designer, Douglas Higgins; Editors, Michael N. Knue, Stephen Lovejoy; Visual Effects Supervisor, Ariel Shaw; Costumes, Dana Campbell; Music, Elia Cmiral; Casting, Susan Taylor Brouse, Anya Colloff, Jennifer Fishman, Amy McIntyre Britt; a Lloyd Segan Company production in association with Heller Highwater Productions; Dolby; Super 35 Widescreen; Deluxe color; Rated R; 96 minutes; Release date: October 24, 2001

CAST

Jimmy Bones	Snoop Dogg
Pearl	Pam Grier
Lupovich	Michael T. Weiss
Jeremiah Peet	Clifton Powell
Eddie Mack	Ricky Harris
Cynthia	Bianca Lawson
Patrick	Khalil Kain
Bill	Merwin Mondesir
Maurice	Sean Amsing

and Katharine Isabelle (Tia), Ronald Selmour (Shotgun), Deezer D (Stank), Garikayi Mutambirwa (Weaze), Erin Wright (Snowflake), Josh Byer (Jason), Kirby Morrow (Palmer), Ellen Ewusie (The Death Lady), Lynda Boyd (Nancy), Boyan Vukelic (Young Cop), Marcus Moldowan (Young Patrick), Mavis D'Andrade (Old Woman, Street), Colin Foo (Elderly Seance Man), Emy Aneke (Clubber), Randy Schooley (Investigator), Tracey Classen (Bones Shadow), Donny Lucas (Crackhead), Shanel Nelson-Murray, Chaynade Knowles, Brittany Moldowan (Skipping Girls), Helena Yea, D. Harland Cutshall, Carlos Joe Costa, Gladys Phillip (Seance People), Jeni Legon (Window Granny), Chaka White (Foxy Lady), Keith Provost, Brantley Bush (Cops), Linda Chow (Jeremiah's 1st Wife), Charles Jones, Jr. (Elderly Man)

Two men purchase a rundown brownstone in a devastated, drug-ridden area, hoping to turn the place into a nightclub, little realizing that the tormented soul of murdered anti-drug crusader, Jimmy Bones, dwells in the building.

© New Line Cinema

(Below) Snoop Dogg, Pam Grier

Shannon Elizabeth, Tony Shalhoub

F. Murray Abraham

THIR13EN GHOSTS

(WARNER BROS./COLUMBIA) Producers, Gilbert Adler, Joel Silver, Robert Zemeckis; Executive Producers, Dan Cracchiolo, Steve Richards; Director, Steve Beck; Screenplay, Neal Marshall Stevens, Richard D'Ovidio; Story, Robb White; Co-Producers, Terry Castle, Richard Mirisch; Photography, Gale Tattersall; Designer, Sean Hargreaves; Editors, Derek G. Brechin, Edward A. Warschilka; Visual Effects Supervisor, Dan Glass; Music, John Frizzell; Special Makeup Effects, Howard Berger, Gregory Nicotero, Robert Kurtzman; Casting, Christine Sheaks; a Dark Castle Entertainment production; Dolby; Technicolor; Rated R; 91 minutes; Release date: October 26, 2001

CAST

Arthur Kriticos	Tony Shalhoub
Kalina	Embeth Davidtz
Rafkin	Matthew Lillard
Kathy Kriticos	Shannon Elizabeth
Bobby Kriticos	Alec Roberts
Ben Moss	JR Bourne
Maggie	Rah Diga
Cyrus	F. Murray Abraham
Damon	Matthew Harrison

and Jacob Rupp (Cyrus's Assistant), Mike Crestejo, Aubrey Lee Culp, Charles Andre (Team Members), Mikhael Speidel (The First Born Son), Daniel Wesley (The Torso), Laura Mennell (The Bound Woman), Kathryn Anderson (Jean Kriticos), Craig Olejnik (The Torn Prince), Shawna Loyer (The Angry Princess), Xantha Radley (The Pilgrimess), C. Ernst Harth (The Great Child), Laurie Soper (The Dire Mother), Herbert Duncanson (The Hammer), Shayne Wyler (The Jackal), John De Santis (The Juggernaut)

Widower Arthur Kriticos inherits a magnificent glass home from his estranged Uncle Cyrus, only to find out that it houses twelve spirits in search of a thirteenth ghost. Remake of the 1960 Columbia film 13 Ghosts *that starred Donald Woods, Charles Herbert, Martin Milner, and Rosemary DeCamp.*

© Warner Bros. and Columbia Pictures

Kevin Spacey, Jeff Bridges

Kevin Spacey

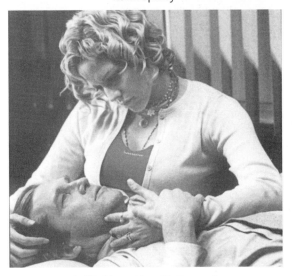

Jeff Bridges, Mary McCormack

K-PAX

(UNIVERSAL) Producers, Lawrence Gordon, Lloyd Levin, Robert F. Colesberry; Executive Producer, Susan G. Pollock; Director, Iain Softley; Screenplay, Charles Leavitt; Based on the novel by Gene Brewer; Photography, John Mathieson; Designer, John Beard; Costumes, Louise Mingenbach; Editor, Craig McKay; Music, Edward Shearmur; Co-Producer, Michael Levy; Casting, Debra Zane; an Intermedia Films presentation of a Lawrence Gordon production; Dolby; Panavision; Technicolor; Rated PG-13; 120 minutes; Release date: October 26, 2001

CAST

Prot	Kevin Spacey
Dr. Mark Powell	Jeff Bridges
Rachel Powell	Mary McCormack
Claudia Villars	Alfre Woodard
Howie	David Patrick Kelly
Ernie	Saul Williams
Sal	Peter Gerety
Mrs. Archer	Celia Weston
Dr. Chakraborty	Ajay Naidu
Maria	Tracy Vilar
Bess	Melanee Murray
Russell	John Toles-Bey
Joyce Trexler	Kimberly Scott
Betty McAllister	Conchata Ferrell
Navarro	Vincent Laresca
Simms	Mark Christopher Lawrence
Steve	Brian Howe
Abby	Mary Mara

and Tess McCarthy (Natalie Powell), Natasha Dorfhuber (Gabby Powell), Brandon Michael DePaul (Josh), Aaron Paul (Michael Powell), William Lucking (Sheriff), Kelly Connell (Walter Fleen), Peter Maloney (Duncan Flynn), Lance Nichols (David Patel), Paul Linke (Stuart Hessler), Christopher Jason Brown (Danny Trexler), Greg Lewis (Dominic McAllister), Clarke Peters (Homeless Veteran), Olga Merediz, Joe Holt (Transit Officers), Lola Pashalinski (Russian Woman), Kateri Walker (Sara Porter), Katya Abelsky (Rebecca Porter), Scott Lincoln (Walker), Clebert Ford (Homeless Man), Norman Alden (Babbling Man), Rawle D. Lewis, Erik Laray Harvey (Security Guards), Zofia Borucka (Woman on Train), Tony Rhune, Vincent Capone (Thugs)

Psychiatrist Mark Powell tries to find the truth behind Prot, an odd man brought into the mental ward who claims to be a visitor from a distant planet called K-PAX.

© Universal Studios

Jeff Bridges

LIFE AS A HOUSE

(NEW LINE CINEMA) Producers, Irwin Winkler, Rob Cowan; Executive Producers, Lynn Harris, Michael DeLuca, Brian Frankish; Director, Irwin Winkler; Screenplay, Mark Andrus; Photography, Vilmos Zsigmond; Designer, Dennis Washington; Costumes, Molly Maginnis; Editor, Julie Monroe; Music, Mark Isham; Casting, Sarah Halley Finn, Randi Hiller; Dolby; Panavision; Deluxe color; Rated R; 124 minutes; Release date: October 26, 2001

Kevin Kline

CAST

George Monroe ....Kevin Kline
Robin Kimball...Kristin Scott Thomas
Sam ....Hayden Christensen
Alyssa Beck ....Jena Malone
Colleen Beck ....Mary Steenburgen
Adam Kimball ....Mike Weinberg
Ryan Kimball ....Scotty Leavenworth
Josh...Ian Somerhalder
Peter Kimball ....Jamey Sheridan
Kurt Walker ....Scott Bakula
Nurses ....Sandra Nelson, Gwen McGee
David Dokos ....Sam Robards
Bryan Burke ....John Pankow
Bob Larson..Kim Delgado
Tom ....Barry Primus
Barbara...Margo Winkler
Marek...Brandon Kessel
Corey...Jon Foster
Steven Gardner ....Art Chudabula
and Claire Yarlitt (Receptionist), Mike O'Guinne (Dale), Tannis Benedict (Secretary), Anne Betancourt (Officer), Lisa Lovett-Mann (Young Woman), Hillary Tuck (Alyssa's Friend), Steven Artenian (Contractor), J. J. (Guster the Dog)

Sacked from his job and aware that he is dying, George Monroe insists that his estranged son Sam spend the summer with him, helping rebuild his house.

Kristin Scott Thomas

© New Line Cinema

Mary Steenburgen

Jena Malone, Hayden Christensen

Noah Wyle, Drew Barrymore

Jake Gyllenhaal, Jena Malone, James Duval

Patrick Swayze

Mary McDonnell, Holmes Osborne

DONNIE DARKO

(NEWMARKET) Producers, Sean McKittrick, Nancy Juvonen, Adam Fields; Executive Producers, Drew Barrymore, Hunt Lowry, Casey La Scala, William Tyrer, Chris J. Ball, Aaron Ryder; Director/Screenplay, Richard Kelly; Photography, Steven Poster; Designer, Alexander Hammond; Costumes, April Ferry; Editors, Sam Bauer, Eric Strand; Line Producer, Tom Hayslip; Music, Michael Andrews; Music Supervisors, Manish Raval, Tom Wolfe; Casting, Joseph Middleton, Michelle Morris Gertz; a Flower Films production presented in association with Pandora; Dolby; Panavision; Color; Rated R; 122 minutes; Release date: October 26, 2001

CAST

Donnie Darko ....Jake Gyllenhaal
Gretchen Ross ....Jena Malone
Ms. Karen Pomeroy ....Drew Barrymore
Frank ....James Duval
Kittie Farmer ....Beth Grant
Elizabeth Darko ....Maggie Gyllenhaal
Rose Darko...Mary McDonnell
Eddie Darko...Holmes Osborne
Dr. Lilian Thurman ....Katharine Ross
Jim Cunningham ....Patrick Swayze
Dr. Monnitoff...Noah Wyle
Seth Devlin ....Alex Greenwald
Sean Smith ....Gary Lundy
Ricky Danforth ....Seth Rogen
Ronald Fisher ....Stuart Stone
and Daveigh Chase (Samantha Darko), Patience Cleveland (Roberta Sparrow/Grandma Death), David Moreland (Principal Cole), Jolene Purdy (Cherita Chen), Arthur Taxier (Dr. Fisher), Mark Hoffman (Police Officer), David St. James (Bob Garland), Tom Tangen (Man in Red Jogging Suit), Jazzie Mahannah (Joanie James), Kristina Malota (Susie Bates), Marina Malota (Emily Bates), Carly Naples (Suzy Bailey), Tiler Peck (Beth Farmer), Lisa K. Wyatt (Linda Connie), Rachel Winfree (Shanda Riesman), Jack Salvatore, Jr. (Larry Riesman), Lee Weaver (Leroy), Phyllis Lyons (Anne Fisher), Ashley Tisdale (Dorky Girl), Alison Jones (Dorky Sister), Jerry Trainor (Lanky Kid), Joan Blair (Mystery Woman), Sarah Hudson (Friend), Fran Kranz (Passenger), Scotty Leavenworth (David)

When teenager Donnie Darko has a near-death experience, he begins to question his existence, ultimately uncovering a power that could allow him to alter time and destiny.

© Newmarket Films

123

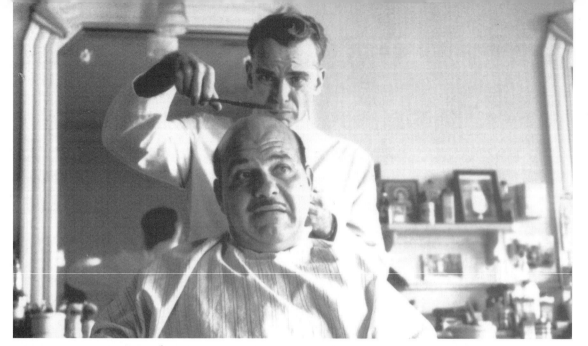

Jon Polito, Billy Bob Thornton

Michael Badalucco

Katherine Borowitz

Scarlett Johannson

James Gandolfini

Billy Bob Thornton, James Gandolfini

THE MAN WHO WASN'T THERE

(USA FILMS) Producer, Ethan Coen; Executive Producers, Tim Bevan, Eric Fellner; Director, Joel Coen; Screenplay, Joel Coen, Ethan Coen; Co-Producer, John Cameron; Photography, Roger Deakins; Designer, Dennis Gassner; Costumes, Mary Zophres; Music, Carter Burwell; Editors, Roderick Jaynes, Tricia Cooke; Casting, Ellen Chenoweth; a Working Title production; Dolby; Black and white; Rated R; 116 minutes; Release date: October 31, 2001

Jon Polito

CAST

Ed Crane	Billy Bob Thornton
Doris Crane	Frances McDormand
Frank	Michael Badalucco
Big Dave Nirdlinger	James Gandolfini
Ann Nirdlinger	Katherine Borowitz
Creighton Tolliver	Jon Polito
Birdy Abundas	Scarlett Johansson
Walter Abundas	Richard Jenkins
Freddy Riedenschneider	Tony Shalhoub
Persky	Christopher Kriesa
Krebs	Brian Haley
Burns	Jack McGee
The New Man	Gregg Binkley
Diedrickson	Alan Fudge
Medium	Lilyan Chauvin
Carcanogues	Adam Alexi-Malle
Bingo Caller	Ted Rooney
Young Man	Abraham Benrubi
Child	Christian Ferratti
Costanza	Rhoda Gemignani
Customer	E. J. Callahan
Sobbing Prisoner	Brooke Smith
Banker	Ron Ross
Waitress	Hallie Singleton
Gatto Eater	Jon Donnelly
Bailiff	Dan Martin
Tony	Nicholas Lanier
Judges	Tom Dahlgren, Booth Colman
New Man's Customer	Stanley DeSantis
Bartender	Peter Siragusa
Macadam Salesman	Christopher McDonald
Doctor	John Michael Higgins
District Attorney	Rick Scarry
Lloyd Garroway	Georges Ives
Swimming Boy	Devin Cole Borisoff
Prisoner Visitor	Mary Bogue
Pie Contest Timer	Don Donati
Flophouse Clerk	Arthur Reeves

Tony Shalhoub, Frances McDormand

Billy Bob Thornton

In a small northern California town in the late 1940s, Ed Crane, a passive barber, tries to better his lot by investing in a new technique for dry cleaning clothing, a scheme that leads him into blackmail and murder. This film received an Oscar nomination for cinematography.

Mike Wazowski, Sulley

Sulley, Henry J. Waternoose

MONSTERS, INC.

(WALT DISNEY PICTURES) Producer, Darla K. Anderson; Executive Producers, John Lasseter, Andrew Stanton; Director, Pete Docter; Co-Directors, Lee Unkrich, David Silverman; Associate Producer, Kori Rae; Screenplay, Andrew Stanton, Daniel Gerson; Original Story, Pete Docter, Jill Culton, Jeff Pidgeon, Ralph Eggleston; Music, Randy Newman; Song: "If I Didn't Have You" by Randy Newman/performed by Billy Crystal and John Goodman; Editor, Jim Stewart; Supervising Technical Director, Thomas Porter; Designers, Harley Jessup, Bob Pauley; Art Directors, Tia W. Kratter, Dominique Louis; Supervising Animators, Glenn McQueen, Rich Quade; Layout Supervisor, Ewan Johnson; Modeling Supervisor, Eben Ostby; Simulation & Effects Supervisors, Galyn Susman, Michael Fong; Casting, Ruth Lambert, Mary Hidalgo; a Pixar Animation Studios Film; Dolby; Technicolor; Rated G; 92 minutes; Release date: November 2, 2001

CAST

James P. "Sulley" Sullivan	John Goodman
Mike Wazowski	Billy Crystal
Boo	Mary Gibbs
Randall Boggs	Steve Buscemi
Henry J. Waternoose	James Coburn
Celia	Jennifer Tilly
Roz	Bob Peterson
Yeti	John Ratzenberger
Fungus	Frank Oz
Needleman/Smitty	Daniel Gerson
Floor Manager	Steve Susskind
Flint	Bonnie Hunt
Bile	Jeff Pidgeon
George	Sam Black

Sulley and Mike, two employees of Monsters, Inc., a corporation dedicated to scaring children in order to capture their screams for power, find themselves in trouble when a little girl from the human universe accidentally crosses over into their world. 2001 Academy Award-winner for Best Original Song ("If I Didn't Have You"). This film received Oscar nominations for animated feature, sound effects editing, and original score.

Mike Wazowski, Sulley

© Disney/Pixar

Mike Wazowski, Sulley

Roz

Mike Wazowski, Celia

Randall Boggs, Mike Wazowski, Sulley

Boo, Sulley

Ethan Hawke

Robert Sean Leonard

Uma Thurman

TAPE

(LIONS GATE) Producers, Gary Winick, Alexis Alexanian, Anne Walker-McBay, John Sloss; Executive Producers, Jonathan Sehring, Caroline Kaplan; Director, Richard Linklater; Screenplay, Stephen Belber, based on his play; Co-Producers, Robert Cole, David Richenthal; Photography, Maryse Alberti; Designer, Stephen J. Beatrice; Editor, Sandra Adair; Costumes, Catherine Thomas; The Independent Film Channel Productions presentation of an InDigEnt Production in association with Detour Filmproduction; Dolby; Color; Rated R; 86 minutes; Release date: November 2, 2001

CAST

Vince...Ethan Hawke
John..Robert Sean Leonard
Amy...Uma Thurman

John meets up with his one-time high-school friend Vince, whose resentment toward John for dating his ex-girlfriend results in an ugly accusation.

128

© Lions Gate Films

THE ONE

(COLUMBIA) Producers, Glen Morgan, Steven Chasman; Executive Producers, Todd Garner, Charles Newirth, Lata Ryan, Greg Silverman; Director, James Wong; Screenplay, Glen Morgan, James Wong; Photography, Robert McLachlan; Designer, David L. Snyder; Editor, James Coblentz; Music, Trevor Rabin; Music Supervisor, Happy Walters; Costumes, Chrisi Karvonides-Dushenko; Visual Effects Supervisor, Eric Durst; Effects Animation Supervisor, Daniel Roizman; Special Effects Supervisor, Terry Frazee; Martial Arts Choreographer, Cory Yuen; Casting, John Papsidera; Stunts, Gary Hymes; a Revolution Studios presentation of a Hard Eight Pictures production; Dolby; Super 35 Widescreen; Deluxe color; Rated PG-13; 87 minutes; Release date: November 2, 2001

CAST

Gabe/Yulaw/Lawless..Jet Li
T. K./Massie Walsh ....Carla Gugino
Roedecker/Attendant ....Delroy Lindo
Funsch..Jason Statham
Aldrich/"A" World Inmate #1 ....James Morrison
Yates...Dylan Bruno
D'Antoni...Richard Steinmetz
MVA Supervisor ....Steve Rankin
Prison Warden...Tucker Smallwood
Nurse Besson ....Harriet Sansom Harris
MRI Technician ....David Keats
Sgt. Siegel..Dean Norris
Rotten Ronnie ....Ron Zimmerman
Hugo..Darin Morgan
Cesar ....Mark Borchardt
Dr. Franklin...Joel Stoffer
Dr. Hamilton ....Kimberly Patton
and Denney Pierce, Boots Southerland (ER Security Guards), Archie Kao (Woo), Ken Kerman, Kevin Indio Copeland ("A" World Inmates), Marco Verdier, Teddy Lane, Jr. ("C" World Inmates), Narinder Samra (Dr. Hackler), Clement E. Blake, Bill Dunnam (Penal Colony Inmates), Edward James Gage (Factory Worker), B. T. Taylor (Orderly), Thanh T. Tran (Sleeping Boy)

In the future, when parallel universes exist, a renegade Multiverse agent sets out to destroy his alternate selves, knowing that eradicating each one will give him greater power toward his goal to become the only version of himself.

© Revolution Studios

(Above) Jet Li. (Below) Jason Statham, Jet Li

Matt O'Leary, John Travolta

John Travolta

Vince Vaughn, Teri Polo

John Travolta, Vince Vaughn

DOMESTIC DISTURBANCE

(PARAMOUNT) Producers, Donald De Line, Jonathan D. Krane; Director, Harold Becker; Screenplay, Lewis Colick; Story, Lewis Colick, William S. Comanor, Gary Drucker; Photography, Michael Seresin; Designer, Clay A. Griffith; Costumes, Bobbie Read; Editor, Peter Honess; Co-Producer, James R. Dyer; Music, Mark Mancina; Casting, Gretchen Rennell Court; a De Line Pictures and Jonathan D. Krane production; Dolby; J-D-C Scope; Deluxe color; Rated PG-13; 91 minutes; Release date: November 2, 2001

CAST

Frank Morrison	John Travolta
Rick Barnes	Vince Vaughn
Susan	Teri Polo
Danny Morrison	Matt O'Leary
Diane	Susan Floyd
Ray Coleman	Steve Buscemi
Sgt. Edgar Stevens	Ruben Santiago-Hudson
Jason	James Lashly
Laurie	Rebecca Tilney
Theresa	Debra Mooney
Coach Mark	Leland L. Jones
Don Patterson	William Parry
Wedding Coordinator	Suzanne Nystrom
Wedding Photographer	George Christy
Priest	David Bridgewater
Walter Ward	Darryl Warren
Patty	Angelica Torn
Shady Tree Motel Clerk	Holmes Osborne
Detective Warren	Chris Ellis

and Zach Hanner (Police Technician), Paul Ligotino (Mike), Nick Loren (Cop), Michael Tomlinson (Berman), Terry Loughlin (Judge), Jim Meskimen (Bob Lerner), Steve Roberts (Bartender), Sara Graves (Conroy's Waitress), Dianne Catterton (Waitress), Vipin Patel (Crestview Motel Manger), Patt Noday (TV Reporter), Benton Hill, Jr. (Wedding Band Leader), Vince Beard, Leroy Harper, Brad Lloyd, Brad Merritt, Marc Siegel, Vince Stout, Lee Venters (Wedding Band)

Young Danny Morrison's dislike of his mother's fiancé, Rick Barnes, proves to be more than justified when he witnesses Barnes murdering a man and disposing of the body.

© Paramount Pictures

Gene Hackman, Danny DeVito

Gene Hackman, Rebecca Pidgeon

HEIST

(WARNER BROS.) Producers, Art Linson, Elie Samaha, Andrew Stevens; Executive Producers, Don Carmody, Tracee Stanley, James Holt; Director/Screenplay, David Mamet; Photography, Robert Elswit; Designer, David Wasco; Costumes, Renée April; Editor, Barbara Tulliver; Music, Theodore Shapiro; Co-Producers, Cas Donovan, Scott Ferguson; Line Producer, Josette Perrotta; Casting, Avy Kaufman; a Morgan Creek Productions Inc. and Franchise Pictures presentation in association with Indelible Pictures; Dolby; Deluxe color; Rated R; 109 minutes; Release date: November 9, 2001

CAST

Joe Moore	Gene Hackman
Mickey Bergman	Danny DeVito
Bobby Blane	Delroy Lindo
Jimmy Silk	Sam Rockwell
Fran	Rebecca Pidgeon
Don "Pinky" Pincus	Ricky Jay
Betty Croft	Patti LuPone
Fast Food Customer	Alan Bilzerian
Counterman	Richard L. Friedman
Fast Food Cook	Robert Lussier
Jewelry Store Guard	Mark Camacho
Coffee Cart Man	Mike Tsarouchas
D. A. Freccia	Jim Frangione
Laszlo	Christopher R. Kaldor
Bartender	Danny Blanco Hall
Pool Player at Bar	Zodia McLean
State Trooper	Andreas Apergis
Coffee Man	Tony Calabretta
Customs Officer	Ted Whittal

and Guy Sprung (Pilot), Richard Zeman (Co-Pilot), Don Jordan (Supervisor in Tower), Pierre LeBlanc (Controller in Tower), Richard Robitaille, Gregory Bryant Goossen (Officers), Charles Doucet (Mechanic), Bill Rowat (Official at Cargo Hangar), Benz Antoine (Trooper at Cargo Hangar), Emillie Cassini (Pincus's Niece), Jennifer Moorehouse (Cashier), Marlyne Affleck (Young Woman with Blane)

Needing money to fund his retirement, thief Joe Moore and his gang agree to one last job to satisfy Joe's fence, Mickey Bergman, who insists his nephew participate in the heist.

© Heightened Productions, Inc.

Gene Hackman, Sam Rockwell

Gene Hackman, Sam Rockwell, Danny DeVito

SHALLOW HAL

(20TH CENTURY FOX) Producers, Bradley Thomas, Charles B. Wessler, Bobby Farrelly, Peter Farrelly; Directors, Bobby Farrelly, Peter Farrelly; Screenplay, Sean Moynihan, Peter Farrelly, Bobby Farrelly; Photography, Russell Carpenter; Designer, Sidney J. Bartholomew, Jr.; Costumes, Pamela Withers; Editor, Christopher Greenbury; Co-Producers, Marc S. Fischer, Mark Charpentier; Music, Ivy; Music Supervisors, Tom Wolfe, Manish Raval; Makeup Effects Designers and Creators, Tony Gardner & Artists' Asylum; Casting, Rick Montgomery; a Condundrum Entertainment production; Dolby; Deluxe color; Rated PG-13; 113 minutes; Release date: November 9, 2001

CAST

Rosemary	Gwyneth Paltrow
Hal Larsen	Jack Black
Mauricio	Jason Alexander
Steve Shanahan	Joe Viterelli
Walt	Rene Kirby
Reverend Larsen	Bruce McGill
Himself	Tony Robbins
Jill	Susan Ward
Ralph	Zen Gesner
Katrina	Brooke Burns
Other Hostess	Rob Moran
Li'iBoy	Joshua "Li'iBoy" Shintani

and Kyle Glass (Artie), Laura Kightlinger (Jen), Nan Martin (Nurse Tanya Peeler), Sasha Joseph Neulinger (Young Hal), John E. Jordan (Waiter), Jill Christine Fitzgerald (Mrs. Shanahan), Fawn Irish (Spastic Bella), Erinn Bartlett (Bella), Daniel Greene (Doctor), Danny Murphy (Cabbie), Brian Mone, Bob Mone (Board Members), Don Gavin (David Bouley), Leslie DeAntonio (Maid), Libby Langdon (Waitress), Gigi Moran, Caryl West (Nurses), Brianna Gardner (Sick Kid #1, Cadence), Mariann Neary, Christal Handy (Information Attendants), Jackie Flynn (Manager), Sascha Knopf (Gorgeous Tanya), Mary Wigmore (Cute Hostess), Heather Ann Rosbeck (Doorperson), Steve Tyler (Bocce Club Waiter), Darius Rucker (Maitre D'), Will Coogan, Lyndon Byers (Punks), Sara Stout (Babe on Dance Floor), Allison Anderson, Molly Bergman, Adriana Biega, Keri Bruno, Morgan Clements, Brittney Leigh daCosta, Jessica Nicole Fife, Stacy Fuson, Zoë Graham, Amanda Tascher Harmon, Nichole Hiltz, Katie Holliday, Ashley B. Howard, T Jamison, Mary Lajoinie, Chelsea Marguerite, Danae Miller, Jennifer Pentecost, Jennifer Sky, Christina Della Rose, Amanda Santos, Dana Zimmer (Sorority Girls), Bonnie Aarons, Lisa Brounstein (Spastic Friends), Herb Flynn, Michael Corrente (Homeless Men), Ron Darling (Other Li'iBoy), Anne E. Hodgson, Kelly McRorie (Bar Girls), John Dennis (Guy in Bar), Dean R. Palozej (Bartender), Dede Kinerk (Party Friend), David Kipper (Department Store Clerk), Sayed Badreya (Pediatric Doctor), David Getz (Dr. James Uler), Tom Hohman, James Badstibner (Frat Boys), Jesse Peter, Anna Byers (Sick Kids), Sean P. Gildea (Pool Dad), Robby Johns (Kid in Tree), Tiffany Anne Marie Lucich (Soda Shop Waitress), Hillary Matthews Thomas (Pretty Girl)

Hal Larsen, a superficial man who judges women strictly on their looks, is put under a spell that forces him to see only a person's inner beauty, thereby allowing him to fall madly in love with a kindly, overweight woman.

© Twentieth Century Fox

(Below) Jason Alexander, Jack Black

Gwyneth Paltrow, Jack Black

Gwyneth Paltrow

Tony Robbins, Jack Black

HARRY POTTER AND THE SORCERER'S STONE

(WARNER BROS.) a.k.a. *Harry Potter and the Philosopher's Stone*; Producer, David Heyman; Executive Producers, Chris Columbus, Mark Radcliffe, Michael Barnathan, Duncan Henderson; Director, Chris Columbus; Screenplay, Steve Kloves; Based on the novel *Harry Potter and the Philosopher's Stone* by J. K. Rowling; Photography, John Seale; Designer, Stuart Craig; Costumes, Judianna Makovsky; Editor, Richard Francis-Bruce; Music, John Williams; Visual Effects Supervisor, Robert Legato; Creature & Makeup Effects, Nick Dudman; Casting, Susie Figgis; a Heyday Films/1492 Pictures/Duncan Henderson production; Dolby; Panavision; Technicolor; Rated PG; 152 minutes; Release date: November 16, 2001

Daniel Radcliffe

CAST

Harry Potter	Daniel Radcliffe
Ron Weasley	Rupert Grint
Hermione Granger	Emma Watson
Nearly Headless Nick	John Cleese
Rubeus Hagrid	Robbie Coltrane
Professor Flitwick/Goblin Bank Teller	Warwick Davis
Uncle Vernon Dursley	Richard Griffiths
Professor Albus Dumbledore	Richard Harris
Professor Quirrell	Ian Hart
Mr. Ollivander	John Hurt
Professor Snape	Alan Rickman
Aunt Petunia Dursley	Fiona Shaw
Professor Minerva McGonagall	Maggie Smith
Mrs. Weasley	Julie Walters
Madame Hooch	Zoë Wanamaker
Draco Malfoy	Tom Felton
Dudley Dursley	Harry Melling
Mr. Filch	David Bradley
Oliver Wood	Sean Biggerstaff
Baby Harry Potter	Saunders Triplets
Bartender in Leaky Cauldron	Derek Deadman
Diagon Alley Boy	Ben Borowiecki
Griphook	Vern Troyer
"He Who Must Not Be Named"	Richard Bremmer
Lily Potter	Geraldine Somerville
Station Guard	Harry Taylor
Ginny Weasley	Bonnie Wright
Percy Weasley	Chris Rankin
Fred Weasely	James Phelps
George Weasley	Oliver Phelps
Dimpled Woman on Train	Jean Southern
Neville Longbottom	Matthew Lewis
Crabbe	Jamie Waylett
Goyle	Josh Herdman
Seamus Finnegan	Devon Murray
Dean Thomas	Alfred Enoch
The Sorting Hat	Leslie Phillips
Susan Bones	Eleanor Columbus

Maggie Smith

and Terence Bayler (The Bloody Barron), Simon Fisher Becker (Fat Friar), Nina Young (The Grey Lady), Luke Youngblood (Lee Jordan), Elizabeth Spriggs (Fat Lady), Danielle Taylor (Angelina Johnson), Leilah Sutherland (Alicia Spinnet), Emily Dale (Katie Bell), David Holmes (Adrian Pucey), Will Theakston (Marcus Flint), Scott Fern (Terrence Higgs), Adrian Rawlins (James Potter), Ray Fearon (Firenze)

(Above) Oliiver Phelps, Daniel Radcliffe, Sean Biggerstaff, James Phelps. (Below) Ian Hart

A young boy, raised by cruel relatives, is startled to discover that he is a wizard and a candidate for Hogwarts School of Witchcraft and Wizardry. This film became the highest-grossing picture to be released in 2001.

This film received Oscar nominations for original score, costume design, and art direction.

© Warner Bros.

Daniel Radcliffe, Rupert Grint, Emma Watson

Matthew Lewis, Rupert Grint, Daniel Radcliffe, Emma
Watson, Zoë Wanamaker

Richard Harris

Alan Rickman

Richard Griffiths, Daniel Radcliffe, Fiona Shaw,
Harry Melling

Robbie Coltrane

Laura Dern

Laura Dern, Steve Martin

NOVOCAINE

(ARTISAN) Producers, Paul Mones, Daniel M. Rosenberg; Executive Producer, Michele Weisler; Director/Screenplay, David Atkins; Story, Paul Felopulos; Photography, Vilko Filac; Designer, Sharon Seymour; Costumes, Denise Wingate; Editor, Melody London; Music, Steve Bartek; Casting, Mary Colquhoun; a Paul Mones/Daniel M. Rosenberg production; Dolby; Deluxe color; Rated R; 94 minutes; Release date: November 16, 2001

CAST

Dr. Frank Sangster	Steve Martin
Susan Ivey	Helena Bonham Carter
Jean Noble	Laura Dern
Harlan Sangster	Elias Koteas
Duane	Scott Caan
Detective Lunt	Keith David
Pat	Lynne Thigpen
Mike	Chelcie Ross
Sally	Polly Noonan
Wayne Ponze	JoBe Cerny
Sunshine Lounge Bartender	Yasen Peyankov
Attractive Complaining Patient	Teri Cotruzzola
Mrs. Langston	Lucina Paquet
Gelding	Preston Maybank
Chinese Wife	Sally Kao
Chinese Husband	Quincy Wong
Lance Phelps	Kevin Bacon

and George Lugg (Liquor Store Owner), Tyler Rostenkowski (Billy), Tom Milanovich (Blue Sands Bartender), Karol Kent (Det. Lily Pons), Eddie Bo Smith (Motel Security Guard), Mary Ann Childers (Anchorwoman), Rich Komenich (Detective), James Chisem (Harris), Joe Kosala (Officer Peter Reilly), Roy Hytower (Skinny Sheriff), Kwame Amoaku (Visiting Room Guard), Christian Stolte (Court Guard), Len Bajenski (Trooper Jarvis), Mindy Bell (Trooper Bunch), Roderick Peeples (Storch)

A dentist finds himself involved in murder after falling for an unorthodox, mysterious patient who seems to be using him for selfish motives.

Steve Martin, Helena Bonham Carter

Steve Martin

Catherine McCormack   Stephen Dillane

Robert Redford, Brad Pitt

SPY GAME

(UNIVERSAL) Producers, Douglas Wick, Marc Abraham; Executive Producers, Armyan Bernstein, Iain Smith, Thomas A. Bliss, James W. Skotchdopole; Director, Tony Scott; Screenplay, Michael Frost Beckner, David Arata; Story, Michael Frost Beckner; Photography, Dan Mindel; Designer, Norris Spencer; Costumes, Louise Frogley; Editor, Christian Wagner; Music, Harry Gregson-Williams; Casting, Bonnie Timmermann, Lucinda Syson; a Beacon Pictures presentation of a Douglas Wick production; Dolby; Panavision; Deluxe color; Rated R; 127 minutes; Release date: November 21, 2001

CAST

Nathan Muir	Robert Redford
Tom Bishop	Brad Pitt
Elizabeth Hadley	Catherine McCormack
Charles Harker	Stephen Dillane
Troy Folger	Larry Bryggman
Gladys Jennip	Marianne Jean-Baptiste
Dr. Byars	Matthew Marsh
Robert Aiken	Todd Boyce
Vincent Vy Ngo	Michael Paul Chan
Cy Wilson	Garrick Hagon
Andrew Unger	Andrew Grainger
Fred Kappler	Bill Buell
Henry Pollard	Colin Stinton
CIA Administrator	Ted Maynard
CIA Lobby Guard	Tom Hodgkins
Folger's Secretary	Rufus Wright
Billy Hyland	Demetri Goritsas
OPS Center Security Officer	Quinn Collins
CIA Back Bencher	Yann Johnson
Back Bencher	Sam Scudder
Cleaner	Pat McGrath
Estate Agent	Shane Rimmer

Hong Kong: David Hemmings (Harry Duncan), James Aubrey (Mitch Alford), In Sook Chappell (Receptionist); Chinese Prison: Benedict Wong (Tran), Ken Leung (Li), Adrian Pang (Jiang), Ho-Yi (Prison Warden), David Y. Cheung (Down's Prisoner), Tony Xu (Interrogator), Mark Sung (Ambulance Driver), David K. S. Tse (Prison Doctor), Logan Wong, Hon Ping Tang (Prison Guards), Daniel Tse (Warden's Lieutenant), Vincent Wang (Outer Gate Guard), Mark Chui (Cell Block Guard); Vietnam: Stuart Milligan (Captain), Joseph Chanet (VC General), Eddie Yeoh (General Hun Chea), Freddie Joe Farnsworth (Radioman); Berlin: Joerg Stadler (Schmidt), Zsolt Zágoni (West German Businessman), Balázs Tardy, Pál Oberfrank (Vopos), Géza Schramek (East German Refugee), Imre Csuja (Bar Owner), Melinda Völgyi (Bar Owner's Wife), Károly Rékasi (East German Border Guard), Kimberly Tufo (Sandy), Iain Smith (Ambassador Cathcart), Gregory Groth (CIA Training Instructor), Peter Linka (CIA Polygraph); Beirut: Omid Djalili (Doumet), Amidou (The Sheik's Doctor), Nabil Massad (Sheik Salameh), Mohamed Picasso (Colonel Ajami), Aziz Ait Essahmi (Checkpoint Guard), Moustapha Moulay (Arab Businessman), Mohamed Quatib (Motorcyclist/Decoy Man), Farid Regragui (Suicide Van Driver); Rescue Sequence: Dale Dye (Commander Wiley), Tim Briggs (Heli Pilot); Reporters: Frank Nall (CNN Reporter), Ian Porter (US-China Reporter), Charlotte Rampling (Anne Cathcart)

Nathan Muir, a veteran CIA officer on the verge of retirement, discovers that his protégé, Tom Bishop, is detained in a foreign prison and scheduled to die, prompting Muir to plan a rescue.

© Universal Studios

Robert Redford

BLACK KNIGHT

(20TH CENTURY FOX) Producers, Arnon Milchan, Darryl J. Quarles, Michael Green, Paul Schiff; Executive Producers, Martin Lawrence, Jeffrey Kwatinetz, Peaches Davis, Jack Brodsky; Director, Gil Junger; Screenplay, Darryl J. Quarles, Peter Gaulke, Gerry Swallow; Photography, Ueli Steiger; Designer, Leslie Dilley; Costumes, Marie France; Editor, Michael R. Miller; Co-Producer, Aaron Ray; Music, Randy Edelman; Casting, Sheila Jaffe, Georgianne Walken; a Regency Enterprises presentation of a New Regency/Runteldat Entertainment/The Firm production; Dolby; Panavision; Deluxe color; Rated PG-13; 95 minutes; Release date: November 21, 2001

CAST

Jamal Walker	Martin Lawrence
Victoria	Marsha Thomason
Knolte	Tom Wilkinson
Percival	Vincent Regan
Steve	Daryl Mitchell
Ernie	Michael Burgess
Mrs. Bostick	Isabell Monk
Knight #1	Kevin Stillwell
Young Man	Michael Post
Puppeteer	Tim Parati
Guards	Mark Joy, Joe Inscoe, Zach Hanner
Man #2	Leslie Dilley
Vindy	Angel Desai
Ling	Elizabeth A. Roberts
Phillip	Michael Countryman
King Leo	Kevin Conway
Princess Regina	Jeannette Weegar

and Erik Jensen (Derek), Dikran Tulaine (Dennis), Graham F. Smith (Royal Messenger), Mark Jeffrey Miller, Tammy Christine Arnold (Peasants), Helen Carey (The Queen), Richard Fullerton (Will), Jayce Tromsness (Thug), Greg Cooper (Rebel Leader), Mark Pitt (Crowd Member), Miki Shelton (Woman), Jason Chimonides (Soldier #2), Robert Leddy, Jr., Denise S. Bass, Eric Paisley (Rebels), William Boyer (Rebel #2/Guard Captain), Melissa Bolden, Harry D. Campbell, John Cronin, Marty Dew, Traci Dinwiddie, Bonnie Dixon, Mark Evans, Kelly Foxworth, Linda K. Huffman, Krystal Jefferson, Chris Madray, Babs McCullen, Jaime Moffett, Dustin Phillips, Dena Rizzo, Monica Semon, Lara Anne Smith, Veronica Sterling, D'Juan Watts (Dancers)

Jamal Walker, an employee at Medieval World theme park, finds himself magically transported through time back to the Middle Ages.

© Twentieth Century Fox and Regency Enterprises

Marsha Thomason, Martin Lawrence

Martin Lawrence, Tom Wilkinson

Martin Lawrence, Kevin Conway

Martin Lawrence (center)

Edward Burns, Heather Graham

SIDEWALKS OF NEW YORK

(PARAMOUNT CLASSICS) Producers, Margot Bridger, Edward Burns, Cathy Schulman, Rick Yorn; Director/Screenplay, Edward Burns; Photography, Frank Prinzi; Costumes, Catherine Thomas; Editor, David Greenwald; Co-Producers, Richard Patrick, Frank Prinzi; Associate Producers, Brian Burns, Aaron Lubin; Music Consultant, Laura Ziffren; Casting, Laura Rosenthal, Ali Farrell; a Marlboro Road Gang Production in association with Artists Production Group; Dolby; Color; Rated R; 107 minutes; Release date: November 21, 2001

CAST

Tommy	Edward Burns
Maria	Rosario Dawson
Carpo	Dennis Farina
Annie	Heather Graham
Ben	David Krumholtz
Ashley	Brittany Murphy
Griffin	Stanley Tucci
Gio/Harry	Michael Leydon Campbell
Hilary	Nadia Dajani
Sue	Callie Thorne
Shari	Aida Turturro
Young Hooker	Penny Balfour
Katy	Kathleen Doyle
Dental Hygenist	Leah Gray
Dr. Lance	Tim Jerome
Makeup Girl	Libby Langdon
Elevator Girl	Alicia Meer
Doctor	Ted Neustadt

A group of diverse New Yorkers seeks love while attempting to sort out their various romantic problems.

© Paramount Classics

Heather Graham, Stanley Tucci

Brittany Murphy, David Krumholtz

Rosario Dawson, Edward Burns

Marisa Tomei, Sissy Spacek, Christopher Adams

Tom Wilkinson, Marisa Tomei

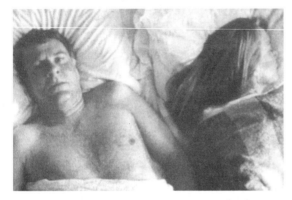

Tom Wilkinson, Sissy Spacek

Sissy Spacek

Marisa Tomei, Nick Stahl

IN THE BEDROOM

Tom Wilkinson, Sissy Spacek

(MIRAMAX) Producers, Graham Leader, Ross Katz, Todd Field; Executive Producers, Ted Hope, John Penotti; Director, Todd Field; Screenplay, Rob Festinger, Todd Field; Based on the story Killings by Andre Dubus; Co-Producer, Tim Williams; Co-Executive Producers, Stephen Dembitzer, Penn Sicre; Photography, Antonio Calvache; Designer, Shannon Hart; Editor, Frank Reynolds; Music, Thomas Newman; Costumes, Melissa Economy; Casting, Randi Hiller, Belinda Monte; a GreeneStreet Films presentation of a Good Machine production; Dolby; Super 35 Widescreen; Color; Rated R; 138 minutes; Release date: November 23, 2001

CAST

Matt Fowler	Tom Wilkinson
Ruth Fowler	Sissy Spacek
Frank Fowler	Nick Stahl
Natalie Strout	Marisa Tomei
Richard Strout	William Mapother
Willis Grinnel	William Wise
Katie Grinnel	Celia Weston
Marla Keyes	Karen Allen
Henry	Frank T. Wells
Carl	W. Clapham Murray
Tim	Justin Ashforth
District Attorney	Terry A. Burgess
Father McCasslin	Jonathan Walsh
Davis's Assistant	Diane E. Hamlin
Jason Strout	Camden Munson
Duncan Strout	Christopher Adams
Young Frank	Henry Field
Janelle	Deborah Derecktor
Alma Adamson	Harriet Dawkins
Elwyn Adamson	Bill Dawkins
Tim's Friend	Kevin Chapman
Judge	The Honorable Joseph Field
Grocery Clerk	Harold Withee
Marlboro Man	David Blair
Elderly Woman	Elisabeth McClure
Young Gymnast	Alida P. Field
Waitress	Andrea Walker
Reporters	John Campanello, Robert Demkowicz
Minister on Television	Veronica Cartwright
Red Sox Replay	Daran Norris
Bridge Operator	Don Lewis
Fork Lift Operator	Doug Rich

Nick Stahl, Sissy Spacek

and Sara Armstrong, Elly Barksdale, Erin Barksdale, Adah Holman, Gwendolyn Gilchrist, Shauneen Grou, Jessie Lanoue, Alicia Laplant, Iris Leslie, Erica Towle-Powers, Nichols Wimbiscus, Anna Winsor (Chorus), Lisa Carlton, Rebecca Benner, Francis Mazzeo, Tyler Shane Smith-Campbell, Brian Hagley, Sam Cousins, Jackie Hagley, Comenic Cuccinello III, Ronald Russell, Rachel Freeman, Dale Johnson, Daniel Hendricks, Parker Spear, Sam Johnson, Henry Field, Matthew Maxwell, Shyann Gauthier, Joshua Mills, Bethany Berry, Eric Rahkonen, Hope Berry, Natalie Russell, Chelsea Peasley, Misty Seekins, Daniel Baxter-Leahy, Philip Spearing, Brandon Carleton, Mackenzie Tucker, Owen Thompson, Ben Staples, Ryan Ecker, Jared Mekin (Rockland T-Ball)

(Above) Tom Wilkinson. (Below) Nick Stahl, Sissy Spacek, Tom Wilkinson

Matt and Ruth Fowler's discomfort over their son Frank's relationship with an older single mother is justified when a tragedy results.

This film received Oscar nominations for picture, actress (Sissy Spacek), supporting actress (Marisa Tomei), and adapted screenplay.

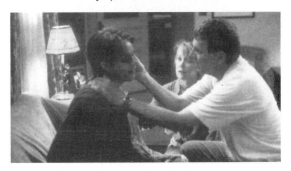

Gene Hackman

Owen Wilson

Owen Wilson (right)

Owen Wilson

BEHIND ENEMY LINES

(20TH CENTURY FOX) Producer, John Davis; Executive Producers, Stephanie Austin, Wyck Godfrey; Director, John Moore; Screenplay, David Veloz, Zak Penn; Story, James Thomas, John Thomas; Photography, Brendan Galvin; Designer, Nathan Crowley; Editor, Paul Martin Smith; Co-Producer, T. Alex Blum; Music, Don Davis; Visual Effects, Reality Check Studios, Pixel Magic, Riot Pictures, Asylum Visual Effects; Stunts, Steve M. Davison; Casting, Sheila Trezise, Eyde Belasco; a Davis Entertainment Company production; Dolby; Panavision; Deluxe color; Rated PG-13; 106 minutes; Release date: November 30, 2001

CAST

Lieutenant Chris Burnett ....Owen Wilson
Admiral Reigart ....Gene Hackman
Stackhouse...Gabriel Macht
Rodway ....Charles Malik Whitfield
Piquet..Joaquim de Almeida
O'Malley ....David Keith
Lokar..Olek Krupa
Tracker ....Vladimir Mashkov
Bazda ....Marko Igonda
Petty Officer Kennedy..Eyal Podell
Admiral Donnelly ....Geoff Pierson
Himself...Aernout Van Lynden
Serb Soldiers ....Igor Hajdarhodzic, Tarik Filipovic and Sam Jaeger, Shane Mikael Johnson, Don Winston, Elizabeth Perry (Red Crown Operators), Peter Palka (Serb Soldier at Lokar's Mansion), Todd Boyce (Junior Officer), Kamil Kollárik (Babic), Saladin Bilal (Ejup), Laurence Mason (Brandon), Leon Russom (Ed Burnett), Goran Grgic (Technician), Ivan Urbánek (Father in Minefield), Ismet Bagtasevic (Muslim Passenger), Dragan Marinkovic (Damir), Kamil Mikulčík, Róbert Franko, Lukas Hoffmann (Tigers), Vedrana Seksan (Serb Anchor), Vladimír Oktavec (Petrovic), Dorothy Lucey (Herself), Gregory B. Goossen (CIA Spook), Filip Nola (Serb Solder at Mass Grave), Bumper Robinson (SCIF Technicain), Ann Sorum (Mom Burnett), George Davis (Sky News Cameraman), Tom Mooney (Carrier Commanding Officer), Mark Bocchetti (Navy Rep), Lucia Srncova (Muslim Girl), Daniel Margolius (Muslim Teenager), Jared Chandler (Piquet's Aide)

After accidentally snapping photographs of a forbidden area while on a routine reconnaissance mission, naval aviator Chris Burnett finds his plane being shot down by the Bosnian military, which is bent on finding the grounded flyer and executing him.

© Twentieth Century Fox

THE AFFAIR OF THE NECKLACE

(WARNER BROS.) Producers, Andrew A. Kosove, Broderick Johnson, Charles Shyer, Redmond Morris; Director, Charles Shyer; Screenplay, John Sweet; Co-Producers, Kira Davis, Stacey Attanasio; Photography, Ashley Rowe; Designer, Alex McDowell; Costumes, Milena Canónero; Editor, David Moritz; Music, David Newman; Casting, Gail Stevens, Billy Hopkins, Suzanne Smith, Kerry Barden, Mark Bennett; an Alcon Entertainment presentation; Dolby; Super 35 Widescreen; Technicolor; Rated R; 120 minutes; Release date: November 30, 2001

CAST

Jeanne St. Remy de Valois	Hilary Swank
Cardinal Louis de Rohan	Jonathan Pryce
Retaux de Vilette	Simon Baker
Nicolas De La Motte	Adrien Brody
Minister Breteuil	Brian Cox
Marie-Antoinette	Joely Richardson
Cagliostro	Christopher Walken
Young Jeanne	Hayden Panettiere
Minister of Titles	Simon Kunz
Monsieur Böhmer	Paul Brooke
Monsieur Bassenge	Peter Eyre
Abel Duphot	Frank McCusker
Louis XVI	Simon Shackleton
Nicole Leguay d'Oliva	Hermione Gulliford
President D'Aligre	Geoffrey Hutchings
Maigstrate Titon	James Vaughan
Magistrate de Marce	Jonathan Newth
Irène de Valois	Kristina Bill

and James Larkin (Darnell de Valois), Diana Quick (Madame Pomfré), Helen Masters (Madame Campan), Victoria Shalet (Colleen), Christophe Paon (Pierre Charron), Michel D'Oz (Marquis de Favras), Donna Flandrin, Liz Baker (Dowagers in Boat), Dick Brannick (Gamekeeper), Daisy Bevan (The Princess Royal), Thomas Dodgson-Gates (The Dauphin), Caroline Lonco (Madame de Largo), Miranda Pleasence (Rosalie), John Grillo (Dr. Legear), Melodie Berenfeld (Mademoiselle Subur), Ben Miles (Baron Courchamps), Niky Wardley (Madame de Neiss), Bill Thomas (Tailor), Emma Wride (Tailor's Daughter), Stephen Noonan (Camille Desmoulins), Emma Pike (Mademoiselle in Pink), William Chubb (Gendarme), Hallie Meyers-Shyer (Demonstrating Girl), Jocelyn Linder, John Commer (Angry Demonstrators), Angus Wright (Sanson), Christopher Logue (Sir Hargrave), Cate Fowler (Lady Standish)

A young woman whose family became disenfranchised and fell out of favor with the royal court of France, makes it her life goal to properly regain her place of honor.

This film received an Oscar nomination for costume design.

Hilary Swank, Jonathan Pryce

Joely Richardson

Simon Baker, Hilary Swank, Adrien Brody

Christopher Walken

George Clooney, Brad Pitt, Matt Damon, Elliott Gould, Don Cheadle

Carl Reiner, Brad Pitt

Julia Roberts, George Clooney

Scott Caan, Casey Affleck

Don Cheadle, George Clooney, Shaobo Qin, Casey Affleck

OCEAN'S ELEVEN

(WARNER BROS.) Producer, Jerry Weintraub; Executive Producers, John Hardy, Susan Ekins, Bruce Berman; Director, Steven Soderbergh; Screenplay, Ted Griffin; Based on a screenplay by Harry Brown and Charles Lederer, and based on a story by George Clayton Johnson and Jack Golden Russell; Photography, Peter Andrews; Designer, Philip Messina; Costumes, Jeffrey Kurland; Editor, Stephen Mirrione; Music, David Holmes; Co-Producer, R. J. Louis; Casting, Debra Zane; a Jerry Weintraub/Section Eight production, presented in association with Village Roadshow Pictures and NPV Entertainment; Dolby; Panavision; CFI color; Rated PG-13; 119 minutes; Release date: December 7, 2001

George Clooney, Brad Pitt

CAST

Danny Ocean	George Clooney
Linus Caldwell	Matt Damon
Terry Benedict	Andy Garcia
Rusty Ryan	Brad Pitt
Tess Ocean	Julia Roberts
Virgil Malloy	Casey Affleck
Turk Malloy	Scott Caan
Basher Tarr	Don Cheadle
Reuben Tishkoff	Elliott Gould
Frank Catton	Bernie Mac
Saul Bloom	Carl Reiner
Livingston Dell	Eddie Jemison
Yen	Shaobo Qin
Blackjack Dealer	Lori Galinski
Bartender	Mark Gantt
Security Guard (Oscar)	Timothy Paul Perez
Lockbox Carrier	Frank Patton
FBI Men	Jorge R. Hernandez, Tim Snay
Explosives Cop	Miguel Perez
Technicians	Barry Brandt, William Patrick Johnson
Eye-in-the-Sky Technicians	Robert Peters, David Jensen
Dancer	Kelly Adkins
Sentry	George Stenson
Billy Tim Denham	Joe Ladue
Hotel Security	John C. Fiore
Hotel Bellman	Tommy Kordick
Casino Manager (Walsh)	Michael Delano
Italian High Roller	Charles La Russa
French High Roller	Anthony Allison
Japanese High Roller	Ronn Soeda
Seller	Robin Sachs
Aide-de-Camp	J. P. Manoux
High Roller	Jerry Weintraub
High Roller Pit Boss (Eddie)	Frankie Jay Allison
Baccarat Dealer	James Curatola
Bucky Buchanan	Richard Reed
Plainclothes Goons	David Sontag, Larry Sontag
Guard	William Allison
Security Officers	Rusty Meyers, Joe Coyle
Bruiser	Scott L. Schwartz

and John Robotham, Vincent M. Ward (Uzi-Carrying Guards), Scott Clark Beringer (Head Goon), James Alfonso (Police Officer), Cecelia Birt, Paul L. Nolan, Carol Florence (Board Members), Lennox Lewis, Vladimir Klitschko, Topher Grace, Joshua Jackson, Barry Watson, Shane West, Holly Marie Combs, Henry Silva, Eydie Gorme, Angie Dickinson, Steve Lawrence, Wayne Newton, Siegfried Fischbacher, Roy Horn, Jim Lampley, Larry Merchant, Richard Steele (Themselves)

Matt Damon, George Clooney

(Above) Andy Garcia, Carl Reiner. (Below) Andy Garcia, George Clooney, Julia Roberts

Fresh out of prison, criminal Danny Ocean gathers together a group of expert thieves to help him pull off an outrageous and seemingly impossible job, robbing three of the top casinos in Las Vegas. Remake of the 1960 Warner Bros. movie that starred Frank Sinatra, Dean Martin, and Sammy Davis, Jr. Angie Dickinson and Henry Silva, who appeared in the earlier film, make cameo appearances here.

© Warner Bros.

Stockard Channing

Julia Stiles

Julia Stiles, Fred Weller, Stockard Channing

Julia Stiles, Stockard Channing

THE BUSINESS OF STRANGERS

(IFC FILMS) Producers, Susan A. Stover, Robert H. Nathan; Executive Producers, Scott McGehee, David Siegel; Director/Screenplay, Patrick Stettner; Photography, Teodoro Maniaci; Designer, Dina Goldman; Costumes, Kasia Walicka Maimone, Dawn Weisberg; Editor, Keiko Deguchi; Music, Alexander Lasarenko; Line Producer, Derrick Tseng; Associate Producer, Ramsey Fong; Casting, Nicole Arbusto, Joy Dickson; an I5 Picture in association with HeadQuarters; Dolby; Color; Rated R; 84 minutes; Release date: December 7, 2001

CAST

Julie Styron	Stockard Channing
Paula Murphy	Julia Stiles
Nick Harris	Fred Weller
Receptionist	Mary Testa
Mr. Fostwick	Jack Hallett
Robert	Marcus Giamatti
Waiter	Buddy Fitzpatrick
Man at Pool	Salem Ludwig
Airport Announcer	Shelagh Ratner

Julie Styron, a high-powered business executive, fires her new personal assistant for failing to show up on time to an important presentation, only to find herself forming a strange bond with the young woman at an airport hotel.

Stockard Channing, Julia Stiles

Benjamin Bratt

Talisa Soto, Benjamin Bratt

PIÑERO

(MIRAMAX) Producers, John Penotti, Fisher Stevens, Tim Williams; Co-Executive Producers, John Leguizamo, Kathy Demarco; Director/Screenplay, Leon Ichaso; Co-Producer, Jamie Gordon; Photography, Claudio Chea; Designer, Sharon Lomofsky; Costumes, Sandra Hernandez; Editor, David Tedeschi; Line Producer, Caroline Jaczko; Casting, Ellyn Marshall, Maria Nelson; Produced by GreeneStreet Films and Lower East Side Films; Dolby; Color; Rated R; 103 minutes; Release date: December 13, 2001

CAST

Miguel Piñero ....Benjamin Bratt
Miguel Algarin...Giancarlo Esposito
Sugar..Talisa Soto
Tito...Nelson Vasquez
Reinaldo Povod ....Michael Irby
Edgar ....Michael Wright
Miguel's Mother..Rita Moreno
Miguel's Father...Jaime Sanchez
Jake ....Rome Neal
Joseph Papp ....Mandy Patinkin
Bodega Man ....Oscar Colon
Bodega Woman ....Miriam Cruz
Shooting Gallery Man ....Lois Caballero
Shooting Gallery Woman ....Sophia Domoulin
Doctor..Robert Klein
Miguel (as teen)..Gilbert Callazo
and Samuel Bruce Campbell (Short Eyes Cop), Loraine Velez (Tutu), Eric Nieves (Nuyorican), Antonia Rey (Señora), Griffin Dunne (Agent), Lisa Rhoden (P.A. Woman), Valentina Quinn (Interviewer), Al D. Rodriguez (Cuqui), Bruno Iannone (Port Authority Cop), Fisher Stevens (Public Theatre Cashier), Jack O'Connell (Chauffeur), Ray Santiago (Willie), Charles Santy (Lincoln), Vanessa Del Sol (Heist Woman), Jamie Tirelli (Marty), O. L. Duke (Paul), Edward Vassallo (Tito Arrest Cop), Amanda KC (Barrio Bar Woman), Bill Boggs (Lennon Anchorman), Tony Vazzo (Auditorium Man 2), Charles Sammarco (Stranger Shower Guy), Lydia Trueheart (Woman with Baby), John Ortiz (Gang Member), Panchito Gomez (Acting Inmate), Amiri Baraka, Pedro Pietri, Jamal Joseph, Miguel Algarin (Themselves), Tara Wilson (Tito's Girlfriend), Joanne Newborn, Francine Berman (Fur Women)

The true story of explosive playwright/poet Miguel Piñero, who became a temporary sensation on the New York scene before his self-destructive behavior got the best of him.

Giancarlo Esposito, Benjamin Bratt

Benjamin Bratt

Penélope Cruz, Tom Cruise

Tom Cruise, Noah Taylor

VANILLA SKY

(PARAMOUNT) Producers, Tom Cruise, Paula Wagner, Cameron Crowe; Executive Producers, Jonathan Sanger, Danny Bramson; Director/Screenplay, Cameron Crowe; Based on the film *Abre los Ojos (Open Your Eyes)* written by Alejandro Amenábar and Mateo Gil; Photography, John Toll; Designer, Catherine Hardwicke; Costumes, Betsy Heimann; Co-Producer, Donald J. Lee, Jr.; Editors, Joe Hutshing, Mark Livolsi; Music Supervisor, Danny Bramson; Music, Nancy Wilson; Song: "Vanilla Sky," written and performed by Paul McCartney; Associate Producer, Michael Doven; Casting, Gail Levin; a Cruise/Wagner-Vinyl Films production; Dolby; Deluxe color; Rated R; 134 minutes; Release date: December 14, 2001

CAST

David Aames...Tom Cruise
Sofia Serrano...Penélope Cruz
Julie Gianni ....Cameron Diaz
McCabe...Kurt Russell
Brian Shelby ....Jason Lee
Edmund Ventura ....Noah Taylor
Thomas Tipp ....Timothy Spall
Rebecca Dearborn..Tilda Swinton
Aaron...Michael Shannon
David's Assistant ....Delaina Mitchell
Colleen ....Shalom Harlow
Lynette ....Oona Hart
Emma ....Ivana Milicevic
Peter Brown..Johnny Galecki
Jamie Berliner..Jhaemi Willens
and Armand Schultz (Dr. Pomeranz), Cameron Watson (Other Doctor), Robertson Dean (Third Doctor), W. Earl Brown (Barman), Ray Proscia (Doctor from Berlin), Tim Hopper (Man in Blue Coat), Alicia Witt (Libby), Ken Leung (Art Editor), Carolyn Byrne (Beatrice), Mark Pinter (Carlton Keller), Jeff Weiss (Raymond Tooley), Conan O'Brien, Jane Pratt, Patrick McMullen, Steven Colvin, Cindy Crowe, The Great John Sypolt, Steven Spielberg (Themselves), Jim Murtaugh (Benny's Owner), Mark Kozelek (Dude, Fix Your Face Guy), John Fedevich (Silent Ed Vallencourt), Bobby Walsh (Young David), Stacey Sher (Rayna), Fred Shruers (Cryo Man), Jessica Siemens, Julia Carothers Hughes (Sofia's Friends), Holly Raye (Dancer), Marty Collins (Martini Waiter), Mark Bramhall (Sneezy), Jack Hall (Bashful), David Lewison (Sleepy), Jennifer Griffin (Happy), Adam LeGrant (Doc), John Kepley (Dopey), Robin Van Sharner (Grumpy), Laurel Wiley (Dr. Jennifer Ash), Nicole Taylor Hart (Party Videographer), Julia Anne Schuler, Jennifer Marie Kelley, Erin McElmurry (Models), Alice Crowe (Lucid Dreamer), Mel Thompson (Life Extension Man), Jonathan Sanger (Frozen Pediatric Cardiologist), Tommy Lee (Frozen Vintage Car Man), Ana Maria Quintana (Frozen Theologist), Paul Haggar (Frozen Risktaker), Randy Woodside (Frozen Dad), Robert F. Harrison (Laughing Guy), Carly Starr Brullo Niles (Carly), Michael Kehoe (Chef), Danielle R. Wolf (Coat Check Girl), Scotch Ellis Loring (L.E. Building Guard), Brent Sexton, Curt Skaggs (Security Guards), Jennifer Gimenez (Lola), Lori Lezama (Skyscraper Girl), Todd Harrison (Skyscraper Guy), Blossom (Benny the Dog), Laura Fraser (The Future)

David Aames, a callous and enormously wealthy New York City publisher, falls in love with Sofia Serrano only to have his face hideously damaged in a car accident caused by a jealous girlfriend. Remake of the 1997 Spanish film Abre los Ojos (Open Your Eyes) that was released in the U.S. in 1999 by Artisan Entertainment. Penélope Cruz repeats her role from that film.

This film received an Oscar nomination for original song ("Vanilla Sky").

© Paramount Pictures

146

Tom Cruise, Jason Lee

NOT ANOTHER TEEN MOVIE

(COLUMBIA) Producer, Neal H. Moritz; Executive Producers, Brad Luff, Michael Rachmil; Director, Joel Gallen; Screenplay, Michael G. Bender, Adam Jay Epstein, Andrew Jacobson, Phil Beauman, Buddy Johnson; Photography, Reynaldo Villalobos; Designer, Joseph T. Garrity; Costumes, Florence-Isabelle Megginson; Editor, Steven Welch; Co-Producers, Phil Beauman, Buddy Johnson, Michael G. Bender; Music, Theodore Shapiro; Casting, Joseph Middleton; a Neal H. Moritz production; Dolby; Deluxe color; Rated R; 89 minutes; Release date: December 14, 2001

Paul Gleason, Cody McMains

CAST

Janey Briggs	Chyler Leigh
Jake Wyler	Chris Evans
Priscilla	Jaime Pressly
Austin	Eric Christian Olsen
Catherine	Mia Kirshner
Malik	Deon Richmond
Ricky	Eric Jungmann
Reggie Ray	Ron Lester
Mitch Briggs	Cody McMains
Ox	Sam Huntington
Sandy Sue	Joanna Garcia
Amanda Becker	Lacey Chabert

and Samm Levine (Bruce), Cerina Vincent (Areola), Beverly Polcyn (Sadie), Nectar Rose (Sara Fratelli), Samaire Armstrong (Kara Fratelli), Ed Lauter (The Coach), Paul Gleason (Richard Vernon), Mr. T (Wise Janitor), Molly Ringwald (Flight Attendant), Randy Quaid (Mr. Briggs), Nathan West (Actor), Michelle Holgate (Actress), Jeanette Miller (Grandma Briggs), Michael Ensign (Father O'Flannagan), Benjamin Waldow (Kid), Josh Radnor (Tour Guide), Ross Mulholland, Dean Sheremet, Becca Sweitzer, Hayley Zelniker (Cheerleaders in Front of School), Lukas Behnken, Josh Jacobson (White Guys), Amber Marie Goetz (Window Girl), Joy Bisco (Ashley), Morisa Taylor Kaplan (Heather), Riley Smith (Les), George Wyner (Mr. Cornish), Ned Brower, Peter Simon (Dudes), Joy Gohring (Albino Folk Singer), Tracy Wolfe (Hottie), Jessica Asher (Naked Girl in Locker Room), Sean Smith (Mr. Keller), Heather Brown (Dainty Girl), Ean Mering (Marty), Lyman Ward (Mr. Wyler), Julie Welch (Mrs. Wyler), Daniel Bess (Panicked Student), Jackie Harris (Preston's Mother), James Read (Preston's Father), Robert Patrick Benedict (Preston), Banks McClintock (Keg Guy), Jay Johnston (Roadie), Jennifer Leone (Naked Girl at Party), Daniel Spink (Curious Guy), Oz Perkins (Uninterested Guy), Kyle Cease (Slow Clapper), Jim Wise (Football Announcer), Kimi Bateman, Staci B. Flood, Sarah Christine Smith (Cheerleaders on Football Field), China Shavers (North Compton Cheerleader), Jon Benjamin (Trainer), Paul Goebel (Fat Short-Order Cook), Good Charlotte (Prom Band), Marissa Fedele, Sam Givens, Kimberly Lyon, Zachary Woodlee (Dancers), Alec Murdoch (Man in Line), Cynthena Sanders (Woman in Line), Will Gill, Jr. (Security Guard), Nicholas Z. Cohen (Little Boy)

Chyler Leigh, Eric Jungmann

The high-school football star makes a bet to turn an outcast girl into the prom queen in this send-up of teen movies.

Dean Richmond, Chris Evans

Beverly Polcyn, Mia Kirshner

Chyler Leigh, Chris Evans

Gwyneth Paltrow, Luke Wilson

Gene Hackman

Danny Glover, Anjelica Huston

THE ROYAL TENENBAUMS

(TOUCHSTONE) Producers, Wes Anderson, Barry Mendel, Scott Rudin; Executive Producers, Rudd Simmons, Owen Wilson; Director, Wes Anderson; Screenplay, Wes Anderson, Owen Wilson; Photography, Robert Yeoman; Designer, David Wasco; Costumes, Karen Patch; Music, Mark Mothersbaugh; Music Supervisor, Randall Poster; Editor, Dylan Tichenor; Casting, Douglas Aibel; an American Empirical Picture; Dolby; Panavision; Technicolor; Rated R; 108 minutes; Release date: December 14, 2001

CAST

Royal Tenenbaum	Gene Hackman
Etheline Tenenbaum	Anjelica Huston
Chas Tenenbaum	Ben Stiller
Margot Tenenbaum	Gwyneth Paltrow
Richie Tenenbaum	Luke Wilson
Eli Cash	Owen Wilson
Raleigh St. Clair	Bill Murray
Henry Sherman	Danny Glover
Dusty	Seymour Cassel
Pagoda	Kumar Pallana
Narrator	Alec Baldwin
Ari Tenenbaum	Grant Rosenmeyer
Uzi Tenebaum	Jonah Meyerson
Young Chas Tenenbaum	Aram Aslanian-Persico
Young Margot Tenenbaum	Irene Gorovaia
Young Richie Tenenbaum	Amedeo Turturro
Dudley Heinsbergen	Stephen Lea Sheppard
Young Eli Cash	James Fitzgerald
Peter Bradley	Larry Pine
Detective	Don McKinnon
Hotel Manager	Frank Wood
Walter Sherman	Al Thompson
Rachael Tenenbaum	Jennifer Wachtell
Hotel Clerk	Donal Ward
Farmer Father/Tex Hayward	Andrew Wilson
Doctor	Dipak Pallana
Sanjay Gandhi	Sanjay Mathew
Chas's Secretary	Mary Wigmore
Sing-Sang	Sonam Wangmo
Neville Smythe-Dorleac	Pawel Wdowczak
Yasuo Oshima	Peter Leung
Franklin Benedict	William Sturgis
Reporter in Blue Cardigan	Liam Craig
Eli's Aunt	Sheelagh Tellerday
Cote d'Ivoire Attendant	Max Faugno
Cote d'Ivoire Radio Operator	Guido Venitucci
Frederick (Bellboy)	Ebon Moss-Bacharach
Elderly "Baumer" Fans	Brian Smiar, Jan V. E. Austell
Cemetery Maintenance Man	Rony Clanton
Anwar	Salim Malik
Judge	Tom Lacy
Royal's Lawyer	Keith Charles
Gypsy Cab Driver	Greg Goossen
Nurse	Sadiah Arrika Ekulona
Sanchez	Vic Mata

and Michael Conti (Irish Longshoreman), Tatiana Abbey (Parisian Girl), Kalani Queypo (New Guinea Tribesman), Mel Cannon (Punk Rocker), Leo Manuelian, Amir Raissi, Roger Shamas (Eli's Egyptian Friends), Philip Denning (Father Petersen), Gary Evans (Police Officer), Rex Robbins (Mr. Levinson), Nova Landaeus-Skinnar (Elaine Levinson), Sam Hoffman, Brian Tenenbaum, Stephan Dignan (Paramedics), Eric Chase Anderson (Medical Student)

Royal Tenenbaum shows up after years away from his estranged family, claiming to be terminally ill and in need of a reconciliation with his children, all of whom feel that their early promise was destroyed by their father's behavior. This film received an Oscar nomination for original screenplay.

Luke Wilson, Gwyneth Paltrow,
Ben Stiller, Gene Hackman

Jonah Mayerson, Gene Hackman

Stephen Lea Sheppard, Bill Murray

Owen Wilson

(Below) Luke Wilson, Gwyneth Paltrow, Gene Hackman, Grant Rosenmeyer, Ben Stiller, Jonah Meyerson, Anjelica Huston, Danny Glover, Kumar Pallana

Cate Blanchett, Elijah Wood

Ian Holm

Christopher Lee

(Above) Dominic Monaghan, Billy Boyd
(Below) Viggo Mortensen

Liv Tyler

Orlando Bloom

THE LORD OF THE RINGS: THE FELLOWSHIP OF THE RING

(NEW LINE CINEMA) Producers, Barrie M. Osborne, Peter Jackson, Fran Walsh, Tim Sanders; Executive Producers, Mark Ordesky, Bob Weinstein, Harvey Weinstein, Robert Shaye, Michael Lynne; Director, Peter Jackson; Screenplay, Fran Walsh, Philippa Boyens, Peter Jackson; Based on the novel by J. R. R. Tolkien; Co-Producers, Rick Porras, Jamie Selkirk; Photography, Andrew Lesnie; Designer, Grant Major; Costumes, Ngila Dickson, Richard Taylor; Editor, John Gilbert; Music, Howard Shore; Song: "May It Be," music and lyrics by Enya, Nicky Ryan, Roma Ryan/performed by Enya; Special Makeup, Creatures, Armor & Miniatures, Taylor/WETA Workshop Ltd.; Visual Effects Supervisor, Jim Rygiel; Digital Visual Effects, WETA Digital; Stunts, George Marshall Ruge; Casting, John Hubbard, Amy MacLean, Victoria Burrows, Liz Mullane, Ann Robinson; a Wingnut Films production; Dolby; Super 35 Widescreen; Deluxe color; Rated PG-13; 178 minutes; Release date: December 19, 2001

Dominic Monaghan

CAST

Frodo Baggins	Elijah Wood
Gandalf	Ian McKellen
Arwen Undomiel	Liv Tyler
Aragorn (Strider)	Viggo Mortensen
Samwise "Sam" Gamgee	Sean Astin
Galadriel	Cate Blanchett
Gimli	John Rhys-Davies
Peregrin "Pippin" Took	Billy Boyd
Meriadoc "Merry" Brandybuck	Dominic Monaghan
Legolas	Orlando Bloom
Saruman	Christopher Lee
Elrond	Hugo Weaving
Boromir	Sean Bean
Bilbo Baggins	Ian Holm
Gollum	Andy Serkis
Celeborn	Marton Csokas
Haldir	Craig Parker
Lurtz	Lawrence Makoare
Voice of the Ring	Alan Howard
Everard Proudfoot	Noel Appleby
Sauron	Sala Baker
Mrs. Proudfoot	Megan Edwards
Gondorian Archivist	Michael Elsworth
Gil-Galad	Mark Ferguson
Witch King	Brent McIntyre
Elendil	Peter Mackenzie
Rosie Cotton	Sarah McLeod
Bounder	Ian Mune
Farmer Maggot	Cameron Rhodes
Gate Keeper	Martyn Sanderson
Isildur	Harry Sinclair
Barliman Butterbur	David Weatherley
Cute Hobbit Children	Billy Jackson, Katie Jackson

and Victoria Beynon-Cole, Les Hartley, Sam La Hood, Chris Streeter, Jonathan Hordan, Semi Kuresa, Clinton Ulyatt, Paul Bryson, Lance Fabian Kemp, Jono Manks, Ben Price, Phillip Grieve (Hero Orcs/Goblins/Uruks/Ringwraiths)

Sean Astin, Elijah Wood

Hobbit Frodo Baggins and his companions venture forth to return a mystical ring to Mount Doom, in hopes of destroying it and saving civilization from its deadly powers. The first of a three-part trilogy to be followed by The Lord of the Rings: The Two Towers *(2002) and* The Lord of the Rings: The Return of the King *(2003).*

2001 Academy Award-winner for Best Cinematography, Visual Effects, Original Score, and Makeup. This film received additional Oscar nominations for picture, director, supporting actor (Ian McKellen), editing, sound, adapted screenplay, costume design, art direction, and original song ("May It Be").

(Above) Hugo Weaving
(Below) Ian McKellen, Elijah Wood

JIMMY NEUTRON: BOY GENIUS

(PARAMOUNT) Producers, Steve Oedekerk, John A. Davis, Albie Hecht; Executive Producers, Julia Pistor, Keith Alcorn; Director, John A. Davis; Screenplay, John A. Davis, David N. Weiss, J. David Stem, Steve Oedekerk; Story, John A. Davis, Steve Oedekerk; Co-Producer, Paul Marshal, Gina Shay; Music, John Debney; Music Supervisors, Jeff Carson, Frankie Pine; Jimmy Neutron Theme by Brian Causey and Jaret Reddick/performed by Bowling for Soup; Designer, Fred Cline; Editors, Jon Michael Price, Gregory Perler; Animation Production, DNA Productions, Inc.; Art Director/Storyboard Supervisor, James Beihold; Character Designer, Keith Alcorn; Director of Modeling, Sean Jensen; Directors of Animation, Keith Alcorn, John A. Davis; Director of Lighting and Effects, Connon "Corndog" Carey; Casting, Paula Kaplan, Ginny McSwain; a Nickelodeon Movies presentation of an O Entertainment and Nickelodeon production; Dolby; Deluxe color; Rated G; 84 minutes; Release date: December 21, 2001.

VOICE CAST

Jimmy Neutron...Debi Derryberry
Mom/VOX...Megan Cavanagh
Dad/Pilot/Arena Guard ....Mark DeCarlo
Sheen..Jeff Garcia
Newscasters..Bob Goen, Mary Hart
Cindy Vortex ....Carolyn Lawrence
Miss Fowl...Andrea Martin
Nick/Brittany/PJ..Candi Milo
Carl/Carl's Mom and Dad/Kid in Classroom/Kid ....Rob Paulsen
Libby...Crystal Scales
Ooblar ....Martin Short
King Goobot...Patrick Stewart
Ultra Lord/Mission Control/General................................Jim Cummings
Yokian Guard/Gus...David L. Lander
Zachery/Reporter/Angie ....Kimberly Brooks
Guard ....Paul Greenberg
Hostess ....Laraine Newman
and Jeannie Elias (Little Girl/Camera Person), Michael Hagiwara (Chris), John A. Davis (Octapuke Kid/Guard/Bennie), Keith Alcorn (Bobby/Kid/Control Yokian), Richard Allen (Digital Voice), Brian Capshaw, Cheryl Ray (Screamers), Mark Menza (Yokian Incubator Operator), Frank Welker (Orthgot/Worm/Demon/Poultra/Girl-Eating Plant/Oyster), Billy West (Yokian Officer/Jailbreak Cop/Guard/Robobearer/Anchor Boy/Old Man Johnson/Flurp Announcer/Bobby's Twin Brother/Butch), Matthew Russell (Hyperactive Kid/Arena Yokian), Carlos Alazraqui (Sheen's Dad), Dee Bradley Baker (Norad Officer)

A young scientific whiz kid gets a chance to put his genius to work and save the day when all of the parents from the town of Retroville are abducted by aliens.

This film received an Oscar nomination for animated feature.

Jimmy Neutron, Goddard

Ooblar, King Goobot

(Above) Cindy Vortex, Jimmy Neutron, Goddard
(Below) Cindy Vortex, Goddard, Libby, Jimmy Neutron, Sheen, Carl Wheezer

Carl Wheezer, Goddard, Jimmy Neutron

HOW HIGH

(UNIVERSAL) Producers, Danny DeVito, Michael Shamberg, Stacey Sher, Shauna Garr, James Ellis; Executive Producers, Pamela Abdy, Louis G. Friedman, Jonathan Weisgal; Director, Jesse Dylan; Screenplay, Dustin Lee Abraham; Photography, Francis Kenny; Designer, Clark Hunter; Costumes, Cindy Evans; Editor, Larry Bock; Music, Rockwilder; Casting, Matthew Berry, Nancy Green-Keyes; a Jersey Films/Native Pictures production; Dolby; Color; Rated R; 93 minutes; Release date: December 21, 2001

CAST

Silas P. Silas	Method Man
Jamal King	Redman
Dean Cain	Obba Babatundé
Baby Powder	Mike Epps
Mrs. King	Anna Maria Horsford
Huntley	Fred Willard
Vice President	Jeffrey Jones
Crew Coach	Hector Elizondo
Lauren	Lark Voorhees

and Al Shearer (I Need Money), Chuck Davis (Ivory), Essence Atkins (Jamie), Chris Elwood (Bart), T. J. Thyne (Gerald), Justin Urich (Jeffrey), Trieu Tran (Tuan), Dennison Samaroo (Amir), Tracey Walter (Prof. Wood), Spalding Gray (Prof. Jackson), Amber Smith (Prof. Garr), Kathy Wagner, Alicia Willis (Intellects), Patrice Fisher (End Table Ass), Sacha Kemp (Hella Back), Scruncho (Baby Wipe), Garrett Morris (PCC Agent), Scott Lincoln (Crackhead), Alem Brhan (Jamaican), Erica Vittina Phillips (Internet Date), Irene Roseen (THC Woman), Dwayne Kennedy, Jimmy Judah (Israelites), Pat Finn (Army Recruiter), Michael Coleman (Priest), James Reese, Rob Nagle (Agents), Judah Friedlander (Student), Joe Ochman (Ben Franklin), Leontine Guilliard, Roz Browne (Mamma's Friends), B-Real, Sen Dog, Bobo (Cypress Hill), Chuck Liddel, Alfonso Alcarez (Tough Guys), Dublin James (Sidekick), Melissa Peterman (Mrs. Cain), David Stebbins (V.P. Aide), Anthony DeSantis (Satanist)

In an effort to diversify the student body, the Harvard chancellor decides to welcome to the university a pair of stoners who passed the entrance exams with the help of a ghost.

Method Man, Redman

Lark Voorhees, Method Man, Redman

Method Man, Redman, Chris Elwood, Lark Voorhees

Tim Allen, Jim Belushi

Kelly Lynch, Hayden Panettiere

JOE SOMEBODY

(20TH CENTURY FOX) Producers, Arnold Kopelson, Anne Kopelson, Matthew Gross, Ken Atchity, Brian Reilly; Executive Producers, Arnon Milchan, Chi-Li Wong, William Wilson III; Director, John Pasquin; Screenplay, John Scott Shepherd; Photography, Daryn Okada; Designer, Jackson De Govia; Costumes, Lou Eyrich, Kathy O'Rear; Editor, David Finfer; Music, George S. Clinton; Music Supervisor, Frankie Pine; Casting, Risa Bramon Garcia; Fight Coordinator, Damon Caro; a Fox 2000 Pictures and Regency Enterprises presentation of a Kopelson Entertainment production; Dolby; Deluxe color; Rated PG; 98 minutes; Release date: December 21, 2001.

CAST

Joe Scheffer	Tim Allen
Meg Harper	Julie Bowen
Callie Scheffer	Kelly Lynch
Natalie Scheffer	Hayden Panettiere
Chuck Scarett	Jim Belushi
Jeremy	Greg Germann
Pat Chilcutt	Robert Joy
Mark McKinney	Patrick Warburton
Rick Raglow	Ken Marino

and James Cada (Yoga Exec. Bill), Tawnja Zahradka (Waver "Tawnja"), Tina Lifford (Cassandra Taylor), Anha Brandvik (Neva), Wolfgang Bodison (Cade Raymond), John Riedlinger, Bill McCallum, Gavin Lawrence (In Crowd Guys), Amy Janette McDonald (Reporter), Emil Herrera (Singing Exec.), Cristi L. Conaway (Abby Manheim), Michelle Barnes (Sharone), Michael Haley (Bartender), Peter Eric Syvertsen, Peter Gregory Thomson (Squash Execs), Claudia Wilkens (Deidre), Jim Labriola, Lowell Sanders, Rob Cowin (Guys at Fight), Ross Turner (Basketball Boy), Bob Aden (Old Man), Rod Johnson (Timberwolves Announcer), Shawn Judge (Woman #1), Marquetta Senters (Linda), Jeff Hopkins (First Man), Jane Hajduk (Receptionist), Sean Grande (Play-by-Play Announcer), Jesse Ventura (Himself), Sarah Agnew (Well Wisher), Patrick Coyle (Man in Parking Lot), Cean Okada (Young Woman), William T. Leaf, Frank E. Adams, Kathleen Winter (Fruit Catchers), Kurt David Anderson (Target Employee), William Borea (Muscle Masseur), Brent Seltzer (Starke Commerical Voiceover)

After being bullied by another employee at his workplace, Joe Scheffer decides to turn his dull existence around and become somebody of value.

© Twentieth Century Fox and Regency Enterprises

Tim Allen, Julie Bowen

Greg Germann

Laurie Holden, Jim Carrey

THE MAJESTIC

(WARNER BROS.) Producer/Director, Frank Darabont; Executive Producer, Jim Behnke; Screenplay, Michael Sloane; Photography, David Tattersall; Designer, Gregory Melton; Costumes, Karyn Wagner; Music, Mark Isham; Editor, Jim Page; Associate Producers, Linda Fields Hill, Michael Sloane, Anna Garduño; Casting, Deborah Aquila; a Castle Rock Entertainment presentation in association with Village Roadshow Pictures and NPV Entertainment of a Darkwoods Production; Dolby; Technicolor; Rated PG; 149 minutes; Release date: December 21, 2001

Jim Carrey, Martin Landau, Jeffrey DeMunn

CAST

Peter Appleton (Luke Trimble)..Jim Carrey
Harry Trimble ....Martin Landau
Adele Stanton ....Laurie Holden
Doc Stanton...David Ogden Stiers
Stan Keller...James Whitmore
Ernie Cole..Jeffrey DeMunn
Kevin Bannerman...Ron Rifkin
Congressman Doyle...Hal Holbrook
Majority Counsel Elvin Clyde ....Bob Balaban
Sandra Sinclair ....Amanda Detmer
Sheriff Cecil Coleman ....Brent Briscoe
Emmett Smith...Gerry Black
Irene Terwilliger ....Susan Willis
Mabel...Catherine Dent
Bob Leffert...Karl Bury
Carl Leffert/Voice of Studio Boss...Brian Howe
Avery Wyatt..Chelcie Ross
Spencer Wyatt ....Matt G. Wiens
Leo Kubelsky...Allen Garfield
Federal Agent Ellerby ....Daniel Von Bargen
and Shawn Doyle (Federal Agent Saunders), Mario Roccuzzo (Jerry the Bartender), Frank Collison (Subpoena Server), Bill Gratton (Daley), Ginger Williams (Louise), Ken Magee (Coastal Engineer), Csilla Horvath (Nurse Muriel), April Ortiz (Vera), Larry Cox (Grauman's Usher), Julie Richardson (Grauman's Bon-Bon Girl), Scotty Leavenworth, Grant Vaught (Boys on Beach), Bob Wells (Reverend), Kevin DeMunn (Western Union Man), Earl Boen (Newsreel Announcer); Sand Pirates of the Sahara: Bruce Campbell (Roland the Intrepid Explorer), Cliff Curtis (The Evil But Handsome Prince Khalid), Michael Sloane (Kindly Old Professor Meredith); Vocal Cameos: Garry Marshall, Paul Mazursky, Sydney Pollack, Carl Reiner, Rob Reiner (Studio Executives), Matt Damon (Luke's Letter)

Jim Carrey

A Hollywood screenwriter, subpoenaed to appear before the House Un-American Activities Committee, has an accident that causes him to lose his memory. He arrives in a small northern California town where he is mistaken for a presumed-dead war hero.

Jeffrey DeMunn, Jim Carrey

Mario Van Peebles, Will Smith

ALI

(COLUMBIA) Producers, Jon Peters, James Lassiter, Paul Ardaji, Michael Mann, A. Kitman Ho; Executive Producers, Howard Bingham, Graham King; Director, Michael Mann; Screenplay, Stephen J. Rivele, Christopher Wilkinson, Eric Roth, Michael Mann; Story, Gregory Allen Howard; Photography, Emmanuel Lubezki; Designer, John Myhre; Costumes, Marlene Stewart; Editors, William Goldenberg, Stephen Rivkin, Lynzee Klingman; Music, Lisa Gerrard, Pieter Bourke; Special Makeup Effects, Greg Cannom; Associate Producers, Gusamano Cesaretti, Kathleen M. Shea; Casting, Victoria Thomas; Presented in association with Initial Entertainment Group; a Peters Entertainment/Forward Pass production in association with Lee Caplin/Picture Entertainment Corp. and Overbrook Films; Dolby; Panavision; Deluxe color; Rated R; 158 minutes; Release date: December 25, 2001

CAST

Cassius Clay/Muhammad Ali ....Will Smith
Drew "Bundini" Brown ....Jamie Foxx
Howard Cosell...Jon Voight
Malcolm X ....Mario Van Peebles
Angelo Dundee..Ron Silver
Howard Bingham ....Jeffrey Wright
Don King...Mykelti Williamson
Sonji Roi...Jada Pinkett Smith
Belinda Boyd ....Nona Gaye
Veronica Porsche...Michael Michele
Chauncy Eskridge ....Joe Morton
Dr. Ferdie Pacheco...Paul Rodriguez
Bradley ....Bruce McGill
Herbert Muhammad....................................Barry Shabaka Henley
Cassius Clay, Sr...Giancarlo Esposito
Elijah Muhammad...Albert Hall
Robert Lipsyte ....David Cubitt
Joe Smiley...Ted Levine
Odessa Clay ....Candy Brown Houston
and David Elliott (Sam Cooke), Shari Watson (Singer), Malick Bowens (Joseph Mobutu), Michael Bentt (Sonny Liston), James N. Toney (Joe Frazier), Alfred Cole (Ernie Terrell), Charles Shufford (George Foreman), Rufus Dorsey (Floyd Paterson), Robert Sale (Jerry Quarry), Vincent Cook (Jimmy Ellis), Damien "Bolo" Wills (Ken Norton), David Haines (Rudy Clay/Rahaman Ali), Victoria Dillard (Betty Shabaz), Brad Greenquist (Marlin Thomas), Morgana Van Peebles, Maya Van Peebles (Malcolm X's Daughters), Maestro Harrell (Young Cassius Clay), William Utay (The Doctor), Kim Robillard (Jimmy Cannon), David Purdham (Madison Square Garden Announcer), Gailard Sartain (Gordon Davidson), Wade Andrew Williams (Lt. Jerome Claridge), Guy Van Swearingen (Induction FBI Man), Doug Hale (Judge Ingraham), LaDonna Tittle (Bundini's Landlady), Marc Grapey (Bob Arum), Herb Mitchell (Boxing Commissioner), Eddie Bo Smith, Jr. (Malcolm's Bodyguard), Bob Stuart (Thomas 15x Johnson), Patrick New (Room Service Guy), Ron OJ Parson (Death Newsman), Ellis E. Williams (Family Photo Man), Bokyun Chun (Asian Cosmetologist), John G. Connolly (Assistant Director), Warner

Saunders (Customer), Jack Reiss (Referee Arthur Mercante), Marty Denkin (Frazier Fight 2 Announcer), Tamara Lynch (Flight Attendant), Theron Benymon (Hampton House Announcer), Bill Plaschke (Miami Weigh-In Reporter), Patrick M. Connolly (Referee), Robert Byrd (Willie Reddick), Ronald A. Dinicola (Prosecutor), Moses Hollins (Man on Train), Danaiel E. Gurevitz (Boxing Commission Reporter), Steven Randazzo, Ray Bokhour (Reporters), Leonard Termo, Johnny Ortiz (Madison Square Garden Reporters), Mark Salem, Sheldon Fogel, Jim Gray (New York Reporters), Melvin Brown, Natalie Carter, Reginald Rootman (Harlem Neighbors), Poe Poe (Harlem Reporter), Mel Dick (Louisville Sponsoring Group), Kim Taylor Coleman (Lana Shabazz), Christian Stolte (Miami Cop), Steve Springer (Miami Weigh-In Reporter), Victor Manni (Dressing Weigh-In Guy), Will Gill, Jr. (Dick Sadler), Sylvaine Struck (ORTF Interviewer), Dennis Luposo (Kinshasa Reporter), Sharon Wilkinson (Rose Jennings), Carol Hatchett, Judith Mwale, Keabetowe Notsilanyane (Pointer Sisters), Richard Katanga (Mobutu Aide/Military Aide), Thomas Kariuki (Lt. Nsakala), Larry Hazzard, Sr. (Zack Clayton), Dereck Brown (Larry Holmes), Rommel Hyacinth (The Pilot), Graham Hopkins (London Banker), Daniel Janks (Other CIA Man), Bradford E. Lang, Michael Dorn (Pilots), Dan Robberse, Graham Clarke, Dimitri Caesar, Frank Notaro, Mark Mulder, David Hess (Mozambique Reporters), Henrikennyo Mukenyi Babibingo (Bula), Nathaniel Malekane (Archie Moore), Millard Arnold (Doc Broadus), Edda Collier (Blonde French Reporter), Wei Yi Lu (Chinese Delegate), Lee Cummings (Hunter Thompson), Zaa Nkweta (Foreman Fight Announcer), Themba Gasa (Idi Amin), Andrew P. Jones (Don King's Aide), Marc Kulazite Mboli, Cimanga Kalambay, Jean Bikoi (Additional Aides to Mobutu), James Gilbert (Sparring Partner in Africa)

The story of boxer Muhammad Ali, from his 1964 defeat of Sonny Liston—which earned him the heavyweight championship title—to his 1974 comeback bout against George Foreman. Previous bio film on Ali was The Greatest *(Columbia, 1977) in which Ali played himself.*

This film received Oscar nominations for actor (Will Smith) and supporting actor (Jon Voight).

© Columbia Pictures

(Above) Jada Pinkett Smith, Will Smith
(Below) Jamie Foxx, Jon Voight, Mykelti Williamson

Will Smith, David Haines, Ron Silver

Will Smith, Michael Michele

Jon Voight, Will Smith

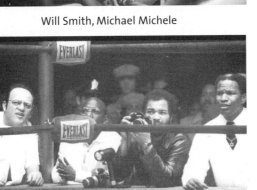

Ron Silver, Paul Rodriguez, Laurence Mason,
Jeffrey Wright, Jamie Foxx

Will Smith, Nona Gaye

Hugh Jackman, Meg Ryan

Bradley Whitford

KATE & LEOPOLD

(MIRAMAX) Producer, Cathy Konrad; Executive Producers, Kerry Orent, Bob Weinstein, Harvey Weinstein, Meryl Poster; Director, James Mangold; Screenplay, James Mangold, Steven Rogers; Story, Steven Rogers; Photography, Stuart Dryburgh; Designer, Mark Friedberg; Costumes, Donna Zakowska; Co-Producer, Christopher Goode; Editor, David Brenner; Music, Rolfe Kent; Song: "Until . . .," written and performed by Sting; Casting, Billy Hopkins, Suzanne Smith, Kerry Barden; a Konrad Pictures production; Dolby; Color; Rated PG-13; 121 minutes; Release date: December 25, 2001

CAST

Kate McKay	Meg Ryan
Leopold	Hugh Jackman
Stuart Besser	Liev Schreiber
Charlie McKay	Breckin Meyer
Darci	Natasha Lyonne
J. J. Camden	Bradley Whitford
Uncle Millard	Paxton Whitehead
Dr. Geisler	Spalding Gray
Colleague Bob	Josh Stamberg
Ad Executive Phil	Matthew Sussman
Patrice	Charlotte Ayanna
Otis	Philip Bosco
Roebling	Andrew Jack
Photographer	Stan Tracy
Miss Tree	Kristen Schaal
Clara	Andrea Barnes

and James Mangold (Movie Director), William Sanford (Barry), David Aaron Baker (Studio Executive), Arthur Nascarella (Gracy), Robert Manning (Passerby), Roma Torre (TV Newscaster), Viola Davis (Policewoman), Ray Seiden (Sanitation Worker), Jonathan Fried (Faux Wolfgang), Francis Dumaurier (Faux Emeril), Cole Hawkins (Hector), Stephanie Montalvo (CRG Intern), Ebony Jo-Ann (Nurse Ester), George Hahn (Assistant Director), Joe Mosso (Cameraman), Cornelius Byrne (Carriage Driver), Chazz Menendez (Purse Thief), Brandon Parrish (Dennis), Brittney Startzman (Monica), Martha Madison (Office Woman), Stephanie Sanditz (Gretchen), Nai Yuan Hu (Rooftop Violinist), Michael Shelle (Distinguished Actor), Matthew Beisner (Commercial Director), Bill Corsair (Limo Driver), John Rothman, Dennis Rees, Michael Cassady (Executives), Brian Letscher (Ad Executive), Meg Gibson (Executive's Wife), Kevin Daniels (Doorman at Party), Henry Boyle (Cab Driver), Russell Di Perna (Bridge Cop), Frank Arcuri (1876 Doorman)

Leopold, an English Duke from the 19th century, finds himself transported to modern-day Manhattan where he falls in love with career woman Kate McKay.

This film received an Oscar nomination for original song ("Until . . .").

© Miramax Films

Meg Ryan, Hugh Jackman

Breckin Meyer, Liev Schreiber

Kevin Spacey, Judi Dench

Julianne Moore

THE SHIPPING NEWS

(MIRAMAX) Producers, Irwin Winkler, Linda Goldstein Knowlton, Leslie Holleran; Executive Producers, Bob Weinstein, Harvey Weinstein, Meryl Poster; Director, Lasse Hallström; Screenplay, Robert Nelson Jacobs; Based on the novel by E. Annie Proulx; Co-Producer, Diana Pokorny; Photography, Oliver Stapleton; Designer, David Gropman; Costumes, Renée Ehrlich Kalfus; Editor, Andrew Mondshein; Music, Christopher Young; Casting, Billy Hopkins, Suzanne Smith, Kerry Barden; an Irwin Winkler production; Dolby; Super 35 Widescreen; Color; Rated R; 111 minutes; Release date: December 25, 2001

CAST

Quoyle	Kevin Spacey
Wavey Prowse	Julianne Moore
Agnis Hamm	Judi Dench
Petal Bear	Cate Blanchett
Tert X. Card	Pete Postlethwaite
Jack Buggit	Scott Glenn
B. Beaufield Nutbeem	Rhys Ifans
Billy Pretty	Gordon Pinsett
Dennis Buggit	Jason Behr
Bayonet Melville	Larry Pine
Silver Melville	Jeanetta Arnette
EMS Officer	Robert Joy
Bunny	Alyssa Gainer, Kaitlyn Gainer, Lauren Gainer
Guy Quoyle	John Dunsworth
Young Quoyle (7 years old)	Anthony Cipriano
Young Quoyle (12 years old)	Kyle Smith
Newspaper Boss	Ken James
Muscular Man	Roman Podhora
Barfly	Luke Fisher

and Terry Daly (Hunky Guy), Gary Levert (Newspaper Employee), Stephen Morgan (Bartender Dave), Katherine Moennig (Grace Moosup), Daniel Kash (Detective Danzig), Will McAllister (Herry Prowse), Marc Lawrence (Cousin Nolan), Kathryn Fraser (Daycare Mom), Nancy Beatty (Mavis Bangs), R. D. Reid (Alvin York), Deborah Grover (Edna Buggit), Jon Whalen (Big Guy), Nicole Underhay (Betty Buggit), Emma Taylor-Isherwood (Young Agnis), Andrew Fowler (Guy Quoyle—15 years old), John MacEachern (Drunken Guy), Jonathan Creaser (Paramedic)

Quoyle, a lonely man who has lost his estranged wife in a car accident, moves with his daughter to his ancestors' home in Newfoundland, where he becomes a reporter on the local paper.

Scott Glenn, Kevin Spacey

Cate Blanchett

Michael Gambon, Emily Watson, Richard E. Grant

Ryan Phillippe, Emily Watson

Clive Owen, Kelly Macdonald

GOSFORD PARK

(USA FILMS) Producers, Robert Altman, Bob Balaban, David Levy; Executive Producers, Jane Barclay, Sharon Harel, Robert Jones, Hannah Leader; Director, Robert Altman; Screenplay, Julian Fellowes; Based on an idea by Robert Altman, Bob Balaban; Photography, Andrew Dunn; Designer, Stephen Altman; Costumes, Jenny Beavan; Editor, Tim Squyres; Music, Patrick Doyle; Co-Producers, Jane Frazer, Joshua Astrachan; Casting, Mary Selway; a Sandcastle 5 production in association with Chicagofilms, presented in association with Capitol Films and the Film Council; U.S.-British; Dolby; Panavision; Technicolor; Rated R; 137 minutes; Release date: December 26, 2001

CAST
Above Stairs

Sir William McCordle ....Michael Gambon
Lady Sylvia McCordle ....Kristin Scott Thomas
Isobel McCordle ....Camilla Rutherford
Constance, Countess of Trentham ....Maggie Smith
Raymond, Lord Stockbridge ....Charles Dance
Louisa, Lady Stockbridge ....Geraldine Somerville
Lieutenant Commander Anthony Meredith ....Tom Hollander
Lady Lavinia Meredith ....Natasha Wightman
The Hon. Freddie Nesbitt ....James Wilby
Mabel Nesbitt ....Claudie Blakley
Lord Rupert Standish ....Laurence Fox
Jeremy Blond ....Trent Ford
Ivor Novello ....Jeremy Northam
Morris Weissman ....Bob Balaban

Below Stairs

Jennings ....Alan Bates
Mrs. Wilson ....Helen Mirren
Mrs. Croft ....Eileen Atkins
Probert ....Derek Jacobi
Elsie ....Emily Watson
George ....Richard E. Grant
Arthur ....Jeremy Swift
Lewis ....Meg Wynn Owen
Dorothy ....Sophie Thompson
Bertha ....Teresa Chucher
Ellen ....Sarah Flind
Lottie ....Lucy Cohu
Janet ....Finty Williams
May ....Emma Buckley
Ethel ....Laura Harling
Maud ....Tilly Gerrard
Albert ....Will Beer
Fred ....Greg Henderson Begg
Jim ....Leo Bill
Strutt ....Ron Puttock
McCordle's Loader ....Adrian Preater

Visiting Servants

Mary Maceachran ....Kelly Macdonald
Robert Parks ....Clive Owen
Henry Denton ....Ryan Phillippe
Renee ....Joanna Maude
Barnes ....Adrian Scarborough
Sarah ....Frances Low
Merriman..John Atterbury
Burkett ....Frank Thornton

Outsiders

Inspector Thompson ....Stephen Fry
Constable Dexter ....Ron Webster

A gathering at the posh English estate of Sir William McCordle ends in murder. 2001 Academy Award-winner for Best Original Screenplay. This film received additional Oscar nominations for picture, director, supporting actresses (Helen Mirren, Maggie Smith), costume design, and art direction.

Kelly Macdonald, Maggie Smith

Ryan Phillippe, Kristin Scott Thomas

Helen Mirren, Stephen Fry

Natasha Wightman, Bob Balaban, Tom Hollander,
Jeremy Northam

Meg Wynn Owen, Richard E. Grant,
Natasha Wightman, Tom Hollander,
Jeremy Swift, Camilla Rutherford,
Maggie Smith, Kristin Scott Thomas

Billy Bob Thornton, Peter Boyle, Heath Ledger

Sean Combs

MONSTER'S BALL

(LIONS GATE) Producer, Lee Daniels; Executive Producers, Michael Paseornek, Michael Burns, Mark Urman; Director, Marc Foster; Screenplay, Milo Addica, Will Rokos; Photography, Roberto Schaefer; Designer, Monroe Kelly; Costumes, Frank Fleming; Editor, Matt Chesse; Music, Asche and Spencer; Music Supervisor, Joel High; Casting, Billy Hopkins, Suzanne Smith, Kerry Barden, Mark Bennett; a Lee Daniels Entertainment production; Dolby; Panavision; Deluxe color; Rated R; 111 minutes; Release date: December 26, 2001

CAST

Hank Grotowski ....Billy Bob Thornton
Sonny Grotowski ....Heath Ledger
Leticia Musgrove ....Halle Berry
Buck Grotowski ....Peter Boyle
Lawrence Musgrove ....Sean Combs
Ryrus Cooper ....Mos Def
Warden Velasco...Will Rokos
Tommy Roulaine ....Milo Addica
Willie Cooper ....Charles Cowan, Jr.
Darryl Cooper...Taylor Lagrange
Tyrell Musgrove...Coronji Calhoun
Lucille ....Taylor Simpson
Betty ....Gabrielle Witcher
Vera ....Amber Rules
Dappa Smith ....Anthony Bean
Georgia Ann Paynes...Francine Segal
Harvey Shoonmaker ....John McConnell
Phil Higgins...Marcus Lyle Brown
Booter ....Leah Loftin
Correction Officer...Marshall Cain
Billy..Anthony Michael Frederick
Minister ....John Wilmot
Clement..Dennis Clement
Nurse ....Stephanie Claire
Hospital Guard ....Jamie Haven
Detective ....Ritchie Montgomery
Maggie Cooper ....Clara Daniels
Mrs. Guillermo ....Carol Sutton
Deputy Jones ....Bernard Johnson
Cos ....Paul Smith

A prison guard, whose personal life is rapidly falling apart, finds himself unexpectedly befriending the lonely widow of a man whose execution he participated in.

2001 Academy Award-winner for Best Actress (Halle Berry). This film received an additional Oscar nomination for original screenplay.

© Lions Gate Films

162

Halle Berry, Coronji Calhoun

Halle Berry, Billy Bob Thornton

Heath Ledger, Sean Combs, Billy Bob Thornton

Gregory Sporleder, Josh Hartnett

Sam Shepard

(Above) Orlando Bloom, Josh Hartnett

Ewan McGregor

BLACK HAWK DOWN

(COLUMBIA) Producers, Jerry Bruckheimer, Ridley Scott; Executive Producers, Simon West, Mike Stenson, Chad Oman, Branko Lustig; Director, Ridley Scott; Screenplay, Ken Nolan; Based on the book by Mark Bowden; Photography, Slawomir Idziak; Designer, Arthur Max; Costumes, Sammy Howarth-Sheldon, David Murphy; Editor, Pietro Scalia; Music, Hans Zimmer; Music Supervisors, Kathy Nelson, Bob Badami; Associate Producers, Terry Needham, Harry Humphries, Pat Sandston; Special Effects Supervisor, Neil Corbould; Casting, Bonnie Timmermann; Stunts, Phil Nielson; a Revolution Studios and Jerry Bruckheimer Films presentation of a Jerry Bruckheimer production in association with Scott Free productions; Dolby; Super 35 Widescreen; Technicolor; Rated R; 147 minutes; Release date: December 28, 2001

Thomas Guiry

CAST

Ranger Staff Sgt. Matt Eversmann	Josh Hartnett
Ranger Spec. Grimes	Ewan McGregor
Ranger Lt. Col. Danny McKnight	Tom Sizemore
Delta Sgt. First Class "Hoot" Gibson	Eric Bana
Delta Sgt. First Class Jeff Sanderson	William Fichtner
Ranger Spec. Shawn Nelson	Ewen Bremner
Maj. Gen. William F. Garrison	Sam Shepard
Ranger Spec. Mike Kurth	Gabriel Casseus
Delta Master Sgt. Chris "Wex" Wexler	Kim Coates
Ranger Sgt. First Class Kurt Schmid	Hugh Dancy
Chief Warrant Officer Mike Durant	Ron Eldard
Ranger Beales	Ioan Gruffudd
Ranger Staff Sgt. Ed Yurek	Thomas Guiry
Ranger Cpl. Jamie Smith	Charlie Hofheimer
Ranger Sgt. Dominick Pilla	Danny Hoch
Captain Mike Steele	Jason Isaacs
Delta Lt. Col. Gary Harrell	Zeljko Ivanek
Lt. Col. Tom Matthews	Glenn Morshower
Chief Warrant Officer Cliff Wolcott	Jeremy Piven
Ranger Pfc. Richard Kowalewski	Brendan Sexton III
Delta Sgt. First Class Randy Shughart	Johnny Strong
Delta Staff Sgt. Dan Busch	Richard Tyson
Ranger Staff Sgt. Jeff Struecker	Brian Van Holt
Delta Master Sgt. Gary Gordon	Nikolaj Coster-Waldau
Lt. Col. Joe Cribbs	Steven Ford
Ranger Pvt. John Waddell	Ian Virgo
Ranger Spec. Lance Twombly	Thomas Hardy
Ranger Sgt. Scott Galentine	Gregory Sporleder
Ranger Sgt. Mike Goodale	Carmine Giovinazzo
Ranger Sgt. James "Casey" Joyce	Chris Beetem
Ranger Spec. Brad Thomas	Tac Fitzgerald
Ranger Spec. Dale Sizemore	Matthew Marsden
Ranger Pvt. First Class Todd Blackburn	Orlando Bloom
Ranger Pfc. Clay Othic	Kent Linville
Ruiz	Enrique Murciano
Ranger Pvt. Maddox	Michael Roof
Osman Atto	George Harris
Mo'alim	Razaaq Adoti
Firimbi	Treva Etienne
Somali Spy	Abdibashir Mohamed Hersi
Briley	Pavel Vokoun
Fales	Dan Woods
Air Force Tech. Sgt. Tim Wilkinson	Ty Burrell
Chief Warrant Officer Mike Goffena	Boyd Kestner
Chief Warrant Officer Dan Jollata	Jason Hildebrandt

and Kofi Amankwah, Joshua Quarcoo (Somali Kids), Johann Myers (Somali Father), Lee Geohagen (Somali Son with Gun)

Josh Hartnett

A group of American soldiers arrives in Mogadishu, Somalia, with the intention of abducting two enemy lieutenants as a peacekeeping strategy, resulting in the biggest military fire fight since Vietnam. 2001 Academy Award-winner for Best Editing and Sound. This film received additional Oscar nominations for director and cinematography.

Ty Burrell, Jeremy Piven (on stretcher)

Michelle Pfeiffer, Sean Penn

I AM SAM

(NEW LINE CINEMA) Producers, Edward Zwick, Marshall Herskovitz; Executive Producers, Claire Rudnick Polstein, Michael De Luca, David Scott Rubin; Director, Jessie Nelson; Screenplay, Kristine Johnson, Jessie Nelson; Co-Producer, Barbara A. Hall; Photography, Elliot Davis; Designer, Aaron Osborne; Costumes, Susie DeSanto; Editor, Richard Chew; Music, John Powell; Casting, Mary Gail Artz, Barbara Cohen; a Bedford Falls Company/Red Fish, Blue Fish Films production; Dolby; Fotokem color; Rated PG-13; 132 minutes; Release date: December 28, 2001

CAST

Sam Dawson	Sean Penn
Rita Harrison	Michelle Pfeiffer
Lucy Diamond Dawson	Dakota Fanning
Annie	Dianne Wiest
Margaret Calgrove	Loretta Devine
Turner	Richard Schiff
Randy Carpenter	Laura Dern
Brad	Brad Allan Silverman
Joe	Joseph Rosenberg
Robert	Stanley DeSantis
Ifty	Doug Hutchison
Lily	Rosalind Chao
Judge McNeily	Ken Jenkins
Miss Wright	Wendy Phillips
Conner Rhodes	Mason Lucero
Duncan Rhodes	Scott Paulin
George	Bobby Cooper
Ms. Davis	Kit McDonough
Gertie	Kimberly Scott

and Michael B. Silver (Dr. Jaslow), Caroline Keenan (Rebecca), Eileen Ryan (Estelle), Mary Steenburgen (Dr. Blake), Marin Hinkle (Patricia), Chase Mackenzie Bebak (Willy), Rafer Weigel (Bruce), Emiko Parise (Nurse), Pamela Dunlap (Grace), Brent Spiner (Shoe Salesman), David Nathan Schwartz (Principal), Kathleen Robertson (Big Boy Waitress), Karen Bankhead (Rita's Colleague), Janet Adderley (Obnoxious Mom), Katie McGloin (Cristina), Steven Maines (Collin), Dennis Fanning (Vice Cop), David Poynter (Cafeteria Worker), R. D. Call (Cop at Park), John Paizis (Starbuck's Father), Russ Fega (Starbuck's Angry Man), Erinn Seaghda Rice Goletz (Starbuck's Barista), Julie Claire (Starbuck's Customer), Marnie Martin (Starbuck's Woman), Tony Abatemarco (Court Clerk), Will Wallace (Bill Carpenter), Scott Weintraub (Scarecrow), Nicholas Mele (Booking Cop), Brian Bialick (Brian), Molly Gordon (Callie), Nora Kroopf (Sara), Allison and Jillian Thormahlen (Lucy, Infant), Ryan Williams (Lucy—6 months old), Felicity Ann and Makindra Sherry Forbes (Lucy—18 months old), Ellie Fanning(Lucy—2 years 10 months old), Amanda Lehaf (Lucy—4 years old)

A mentally handicapped father enlists a self-absorbed attorney to help him fight a social worker who insists that his young daughter be placed in a foster home.

This film received an Oscar nomination for actor (Sean Penn).

© New Line Cinema

Sean Penn, Dakota Fanning

Loretta Devine

Dianne Wiest

Laura Dern, Sean Penn

Paul Bowles in *NightWaltz* © Owsley Brown

NIGHT WALTZ: THE MUSIC OF PAUL BOWLES

(OWSLEY BROWN PRESENTS) Producers, Owsley Brown III, Robin Burke; Director/Screenplay, Owsley Brown III; Photography, David Golia, Gene Salvitore, Rudy Burckhardt, Nathaniel Dorsky; Editor, Nathaniel Dorsky; Music, Paul Bowles; Produced with support from Telefilm Canada; U.S.-Canadian, 1999; Color/black and white; Not rated; 76 minutes; Release date: January 3, 2001. Documentary on author Paul Bowles's work as a composer, featuring Paul Bowles, Allen Ginsberg, William S. Burroughs.

WADD: THE LIFE & TIMES OF JOHN C. HOLMES

(VCA PICTURES) Producer/Director, Cass Paley; Executive Producer, Russ Hampshire; Co-Producer/Editor, Christopher Rowland; Photography, Willie Boudevin; Music, Brad Raylius Daniel, Tad Dery; Color; Not rated; 110 minutes; Release date: January 12, 2001. Documentary on porno star John C. Holmes, featuring Linda Adrain, Bill Amerson, Denise Amerson, Sean "Duke" Amerson, P. T. Anderson, Det. Tom Blake, Bunny Blue, Paul Cambria, Bob Chinn, Cicciolina, David Clark, Hon. Ron Coen, "Dawn," Mitchell Egers, Don Fernando, Larry Flint, Al Goldstein, Annette Haven, Bobby Hollander, Jim Holliday, Laurie "Misty Dawn" Holmes, Sharon Holmes, Mike Horner, Ron Jeremy, Det. Tom Lange, Gloria Leonard, John Leslie, Vonda Lia, Jon Martin, Sharon Mitchell, Kitten Natividad, Richard Pachaco, "Aunt Peg," Ann Perry, Ernie Robuck, Candida Royale, Mike Sager, Sheri St. Clair, Det. Bob Souza, "Reb" Sawitz, Joel Sussman, Ken Turan, Bob Vossee

John C. Holmes in *Wadd: The Life and Times of John C. Holmes* © VCA Pictures

EXTREME FORCE

(PHAEDRA CINEMA) Executive Producers, Michael Belfonti, Paul Raucci; Director, Michel Qissi; Screenplay, Jonathan Davenport, Michel Qissi; Music, Kays Al-Atrakchi; Editor, Tim Gregoire; Casting, Tracy Frenkel; Stunts, Dale Cannon; from Creative Light Entertainment; Dolby; Color; Rated R; 90 minutes; Release date: January 12, 2001. CAST: Hector Echavarria (Marcos DeSantos), Fitz (Pearl), Tracy Frenkel (Mob Boss), Louis Iocaviello (President Khan), Adam Leadbeater (Vat Kallac), Nikki Lemke (Bianca), Myriam Mesdagh (Sharka), Phi-Long Nguyen (Sniper), Michel Qissi (Kong Li), Youssef Qissi (Cole)

THE AMATI GIRLS

(PROVIDENCE) Producers, James Alex, Steve C. Johnson, Michael I. Levy, Henry M. Shea, Jr.; Executive Producers, Howard Kazanjian, Craig C. Darian; Director/Screenplay, Anne DeSalvo; Co-Producers, Melanie Backer, Dan Stone; Photography, Frank Byers; Designer, Jane Stewart; Music, Conrad Pope; Costumes, Amy Stofsky; Editor, C. Timothy O'Meara; Casting, Mary Jo Slater; a Fox Family-Providence Entertainment & Tricor Entertainment presentation of a Triple Axel & Heritage Film Group production; Deluxe color; Rated PG; 91 minutes; Release date: January 19, 2001. CAST: Mercedes Ruehl

Lily Knight, Sean Young, Mercedes Ruehl, Dinah Manoff in *The Amati Girls* © Providence Entertainment

Scottsboro: An American Tragedy © Cowboy

SCOTTSBORO: AN AMERICAN TRAGEDY

(COWBOY BOOKING) Producers/Directors, Daniel Anker, Barak Goodman; Screenplay, Barak Goodman; Photography, Buddy Squires, Tom Hurwitz; Music, Edward Bilous; Editor, Jean Tsien; Narrator, Andre Braugher; a Social Media Prods. production in association with the American Experience; Color; Not rated; 90 minutes; Release date: January 19, 2001. Documentary on how nine black males were accused of the rape of two white women near Scottsboro, AL, in 1931. VOICES: Frances McDormand, Stanley Tucci, Harris Yulin, Jeffrey DeMunn, Daver Morrison.

A FIGHT TO THE FINISH: STORIES OF POLIO

(KEN MANDEL FILMS) Producers, Ken Mandel, Tony Herring; Executive Producer, J.C. Montgomery Jr.; Director/Photography, Ken Mandel; Screenplay, Ralph Meyers; Editors, Ken Mandel, Ralph Meyers; Music, John Bryant, Frank Hames, Tony Herring; Produced by the Texas Scottish Rite Hospital for Children, Mandel/Herring Productions; Color; Not rated; 90 minutes; Release date: January 19, 2001. A documentary chronicling the fight against polio in the United States.

TWO NINAS

(CASTLE HILL) Producers, Denise Doyle, Greg Scheinman; Co-Executive Producers, Seth Kanegis, Adam Sender; Director/Screenplay, Neil Turitz; Photography, Joaquin Baca-Asay; Designer, Tony Gasparro; Editor, Jay Chandrasekhar; Music, Joseph Saba; Dolby; Color; Rated R; 89 minutes; Release date: January 26, 2001. CAST: Amanda Peet (Nina Harris), Ron Livingston (Marty Sachs), Cara Buono (Nina Cohen), Bray Poor (Dave Trout), Linda Larkin (Carrie Boxer), John Rothman (Barry Litzer), Jill Hennessy (Mike the Bartender), Leigh Whitney, Denise Doyle, Brooke Leslie, Meredith Lieber, Amy Veltman, Linette Strauss (Blow-off Girls), Mauro Maccione (Nightmare Date Guy), Fred Norris (Eurotrash), Allison Furman (Waitress), Neil Turitz (Guy at Bar), Dave McGuire, Keith Young (Muggers)

(Grace), Paul Sorvino (Joe), Cloris Leachman (Dolly), Sean Young (Christine), Dinah Manoff (Denise), Lily Knight (Dolores), Lee Grant (Aunt Splendora), Mark Harmon (Lawrence), Jamey Sheridan (Paul), Marissa Leigh (Laura), Doug Spinuzza (Armand), Sam McMurray (Brian), Edith Fields (Aunt Loretta), Joe Greco (Uncle Frankie), Cassie Cole (Carla), Kyle Sabihy (Joey), Asher Gold (Peter), Matt Winston (Johnny Barlotta), Garrison Hershberger (Kevin), Anne DeSalvo (Cathy), Sal Viscuso (Father Dedice), Anna Berger (Stella), Don Marino (Sam), Kivi Rogers (Mike), John Capodice (Danny), Robert Picardo (Grace's Doctor), Fred Tucker (Stage Manager), Carol Ann Susi (Ticket Seller), Nikki Harris (Flight Attendant), Maria Cina (Rockie's Girl), Larrisa Joy (Italian Class Student), Jay Acovone (Mr. Moltianni), Michelle Joyner (Moviegoer), Anthony Pontrello (Nick the Bartender)

Ron Livingston, Amanda Peet in *Two Ninas* © Castle Hill Productions

R2PC: THE ROAD TO PARK CITY

(PHAEDRA CINEMA) Producer, Carolyn Grassl; Director/Screenplay/Photography, Bret Stern; Editor, Peter Vitale; Music, Daniel Gold; Line Producers, Scott Rosenstein, Barbara Steel; Associate Producer, Karl Kempter; a Road to Nowhere Production; Color; Not rated; 83 minutes; Release date: January 26, 2001. CAST: John Viener, Paige Turco, John Mese, Christopher Lawford, Bobby Kennedy Jr., Syd Field, Jed Alpert, Jeannie Macintosh, Allegra Kent, Brody Stevens, Tonia Lynn, Chef Tell (Themselves)

FORGIVE ME, FATHER

(MYRIAD ENTERTAINMENT) Producer/Director, Ivan Rogers; Screenplay, Blair Latta, Thomas Hartigan Fenton, Marisa Caldero; Executive Producers, Bruce Furr, Paul Baugh, Thomas Balsiger, Jim Payton; Photography, Michael D. Off; Editor, Nate Thompson; Designer, Troy Longest; Music, Gary Koftinoff; CFI color; Rated R; 139 minutes; Release date: January 26, 2001. CAST: Ivan Rogers (Virgil Garrett), Rich Komenich (Izzy Goldman), Charles Napier (Frank Ransom), Chris Elbert (Tony Ransom), Alexander Hill (Clarence Garrett), Jeff Bass (Mike Ransom), Jack Rooney (George Haney), Rebecca O'Gorman (Lt. Lena Sohms), Stephen Jon Cohen (Det. Gil Lansing), John E. Blazier (Father Allston), Brad Griffiths (Det. Jacobs), Derrick Perkins (Nigerian Leader), K.A. Killebrew, Guy Camara, James Penn (Nigerians), Amy Ballard, Rebecca Nelly, Erika Szostak (Topless Dancer), Jon Bond (Neil Marshall), Paul Crump (Lionel Pax), Paul Gillard (Bill Riley), Richard Alan Payne (Tom Paltrow)

HEAD OVER HEELS

(UNIVERSAL) Producer, Robert Simonds; Executive Producers, Tracey Trench, Julia Dray, Ed Decter, John J. Strauss; Director, Mark Waters; Screenplay, Ron Burch, David Kidd; Story, John J. Strauss, Ed Decter, David Kidd, Ron Burch; Photography, Mark Plummer; Designer, Perry Andelin Blake; Editor, Cara Silverman; Co-Producer, Ira Shuman; Music, Randy Edelman, Steve Porcaro; a Robert Simonds production; Dolby; Panavision; Color; Rated PG-13; 91 minutes; Release date: February 2, 2001. CAST: Monica Potter (Amanda Pierce), Freddie Prinze, Jr. (Jim Winston/Bob), Shalom Harlow (Jade), Ivana Milicevic (Roxana), Sarah O'Hare (Candi), Tomiko Fraser (Holly), China Chow (Lisa), Jay Brazeau (Halloran/Strukov), Stanley DeSantis (Alfredo), Erin-Marie Dykeman (Amanda—10 years old), James Kirk (Tommy), Elysa Hogg (Tommy's Girlfriend), Kristina Lewis (Amanda—17 years old), Ben Silverman (Charlie), Sam MacMillan (Charlie's Date), Betty Linde (Polly), Norma McMillan (Gladys), Bethoe Shirkoff (Noreen), Tom Shorthouse (Mr. Rankin), Timothy Olyphant (Michael), Brenda Schad (Michael's Lover), Theodore Thomas (Doorman), Alex Doduk (Boy with Crutches), Jill Daum (Boy's Mother), Robert Musnicki (Lobby Guy), Russell Porter (Restaurant Guy), Noot Seear (CK Girl), Jonathon Young (Agent Guy), Maria Luisa Cianni, Katie Lee, Katrina Matthews, Jody Thompson (Party Girls), Raoul Ganeev (Harold), Brendan Beiser (Ellis), Alexander Pervakov (Ivan), Gary Jones (Bernie), Tanya Reichert (Megan O'Brien), Joe Pascual (Officer Rodriguez), Colin Lawrence (Officer Jones), J.B. Bivens (Jim's Building Super), Louis Klimam (Newsstand Guy), Andy Whyte, John Bivens (Plumbers), Jan Owen (Hamlet's Owner), John MacDonald (Limo Driver), Jerry Wasserman (FBI Captain Vince), Matthew Moreau (Aquarium Guy)

Charles Napier in *Forgive Me Father*
© Myriad Entertainment

Monica Potter, Freddie Prinze, Jr. in *Head Over Heels*
© Universal Pictures

Henry Thomas, Teri Hatcher in *Fever* © Lions Gate Films

FEVER

(LIONS GATE) Producer, Christian Martin; Executive Producers, Graham Bradstreet, Ali Lou Mitchell, Connie Tavel; Director/Screenplay, Alex Winter; Photography, Joe DeSalvo; Designer, Mark Ricker; Costumes, Azan Kung; Music, Joe Delia; Editor, Thom Zimny; Casting, Todd M. Thaler; from Fever Productions Inc., ICE Media, Sunlight Pictures, Tavel Productions, Unknown Productions; Dolby; Color; Not rated; 93 minutes; Release date: February 2, 2001.CAST: Henry Thomas (Nick Parker), David O'Hara (Will), Teri Hatcher (Charlotte Parker), Bill Duke (Det. Glass), Sándor Técsy (Sidney Miskowitz), Irma St. Paule (Mrs. Miskowitz), Marisol Padilla Sanchez (Soledad), Patricia Dunnock (Sophie Parker), Helen Hanft (Louisa), Remak Ramsey (Richard Parker), Lisby Larson (Eleanor Parker), Jon Tracy (Leonard Wooley), Charles E. Gerber (Bob), Ken Comer (Det. Comer), William Henry Burns (Det. Burns), Alex Kilgore (Adam), Guy Griffis (Jimmy), Nan Wilson (Bea), Yeluda Duenyas (Erle), Tom Rainone (Officer Field), Larry Fishman (Young Nick Parker), Nina Polan (Polish Woman Witness), Tom Stern (Angry Drunk), Jilly Crook (Voice of Luisa), Alex Halpern, Noah Hunter (Art Movers), Donnel Rawlings, Steve Rannell (Cops), Alex Winter (Subway Passenger)

LEFT BEHIND: THE MOVIE

(CLOUD TEN PICTURES) Producers, Peter Lalonde, Paul Lalonde, Joe Goodman, Ralph Winter; Executive Producers, Peter Lalonde, Paul Lalonde, Bobby Neutz, Ron Booth; Director, Vic Sarin; Screenplay, Allan McElroy, Paul Lalonde, Joe Goodman, Andre van Heerden; Line Producer, Nicholas Tabarrok; Photography, George Jiri Tirl; Designer, Arthur W. Herriot; Editor, Michael Pacek; Music, Jim Covell; Casting, Cathy Henderson, Dori Zukerman; Presented in association with Namesake Entertainment; Color; Not rated; 100 minutes; Release date: February 2, 2001. CAST: Kirk Cameron (Buck Williams), Brad Johnson (Rayford Steele), Janaya Stephens (Chloe Steele), Clarence Gilyard (Bruce Barnes), Colin Fox (Chaim Rosenzweig), Gordon Currie (Nicolae Carpathia), Chelsea Noble (Hattie Durham), Daniel Pilon (Jonathan Stonagal), Tony De Santis (Joshua Cothran), Jack Langedijk (Dirk Burton), Krista Bridges (Ivy Gold), Thomas Hauff (Steve Plank), Neil Crone (Ken Ritz), Sten Eirik (Flattop/Carl), Raven Dauda (Gloria), Marvin Ishmael (Fitzhugh), Philip Akin (Alan Tompkins), Christine MacFadyen (Irene), Jack Manchester (Raymie), Bishop T.D. Jakes (Pastor Billings), Marion Bennett (Young Girl on Plane), David MacNiven (Chris), Thea Andrews (Media Relations Officer), Terry Samuels (General), Robert Levine (Old Man), Alan Rosenthal (Soldier #1), Tufford Kennedy (Husband on Plane), Christine Donato (Wife/Mother), Fran Elliot (Elderly Woman), Lillian Lewis (Old Drunk Lady), David Blacker (Big Man on Plane), Steve Behal (Zombie Man), Stacie Fox (Young Mother on Road), Peter Loung (Washroom Attendant), Chris Gillett (Eric Miller), Richard Hardacre (Tall Man), Katherine Trowell (Woman, Green Blouse), Rufus Crawford, Tony Curtis Bondell (Security Guards), Sherry Hilliard (News Anchor), Regan Moore (Passenger), Rebecca St. James (Buck's Assistant), Bob Carlisle (GNN Reporter), Clay Crosse, Josh Penner, Marty Penner, Toby Penner (U.N. Security Guards), Ava van Heerden (Very Attractive Baby) (This movie had its premiere on video in October of 2000.)

Colin Fox, Kirk Cameron in *Left Behind* © Cloud Ten Pictures

THE INVISIBLE CIRCUS

(FINE LINE FEATURES) Producers, Julia Chasman, Nick Wechsler; Executive Producer, Tim van Rellim; Director/Screenplay, Adam Brooks; Based on the novel by Jennifer Egan; Photography, Henry Braham; Designer, Robin Standefer; Costumes, Donna Zakowska; Editor, Elizabeth Kling; Music, Nick Laird-Clowes; Casting, Laura Rosenthal; an Industry Entertainment production; Dolby; Color; Rated R; 92 minutes; Release date: February 2, 2001. CAST: Jordana Brewster (Phoebe O'Connor), Christopher Eccleston (Wolf), Cameron Diaz (Faith), Blythe Danner (Gail), Patrick Bergin (Gene), Camilla Belle (Young Phoebe), Isabelle Pasco (Claire), Moritz Bleibtreu (Eric), Ricky Koole (Nikki), Nicola Obermann (Hannah), Philipp Weissert (Safehouse Leader), Robert Getter (American Statesman)

VALENTINE

(WARNER BROS.) Producer, Dylan Sellers; Executive Producers, Grant Rosenberg, Bruce Berman; Director, Jamie Blanks; Screenplay, Donna Powers, Wayne Powers, Gretchen J. Berg, Aaron Harberts; Based on the novel by Tom Savage; Photography, Rick Bota; Designer, Stephen Geaghan; Editor, Steve Mirkovich; Music, Don Davis; Presented in association with Village Roadshow Pictures and NPV Entertainment; Dolby; Super 35 Widescreen; Technicolor; Rated R; 96 minutes; Release date: February 2, 2001. CAST: David Boreanaz (Adam Carr), Denise Richards (Paige Prescott), Marley Shelton (Kate Davies), Katherine Heigl (Shelley), Jessica Capshaw (Dorothy Wheeler), Jessica Cauffiel (Lily), Hedy Burress (Ruthie), Fulvio Cecere (Det. Vaughn), Daniel Cosgrove (Campbell), Johnny Whitworth (Max Raimi), Woody Jeffreys (Brian), Adam Harrington (Jason), Claude Duhamel (Gary), Wyatt Page (Evan Wheeler), Benita Ha (Kim Wheeler), Paul Magel (Lance), Haig Sutherland (Bookish Guy), Adrian Holmes (Banker), Ty Olsson (Jock), Daniel Boileau (Shy Guy), G. Patrick Currie (Religious Guy), Jo-Ann Fernandes (Maid), Alex Diakun (Pastor), Karina Carreck (Gallery Employee), Aaron Dudley, Dallas Blake, Chris Webb (Video Men), Basia Antos, Carla Boudreau, Vanessa Volker (Video Women), Joel Palmer (Jeremy Melton), Sarah Mjanes (Young Shelley), Brittany Mayers (Young Kate), Kate Logie (Young Dorothy), Chelcie Bugart (Young Paige), Chelsea Florko (Young Lily), Sterling McKay (Joe Tulga), Kendall Saunders (Waitress), Chad Barager (Chad), Noel Fisher, Cody Serpa, Mark Mullan (Tulga Gang Members), Tammy Pentecost (Waitress), Tyler Vradenburg (Med Student)

Jordana Brewster, Christopher Eccleston in *The Invisible Circus* © Fine Line Features

NEW YORK IN THE FIFTIES

(AVATAR FILMS) Producers, Betsy Blankenbaker, Dorka Keehn; Director, Betsy Blankenbaker; Based on the book by Dan Wakefield; Photography, Bobby Shepard, Dustin Teel, Jeff Watt; Music, Steve Allee; Editor, Steve Marra; Color/black and white; Not rated; 72 minutes; Release date: February 9, 2001. Documentary on the many writers, actors, musicians, artists, and poets who came to Manhattan in the 1950s to flourish in their fields; featuring Dan Wakefield, Gay Talese, Nan Talese, Brock Bower, Ted Steeg, Robert Redford, Mark Van Doren, Joan Didion, John Gregory Dunne, Ed Fancher, Mary Ann DeWees McCoy, Rev. Norm Eddy, Calvin Trillin, Jane Wylie Genth, Nat Hentoff, David Amran, William F. Buckley Jr., James Baldwin, C. Wright Mills, Ned Polsky, Sam Astrachan, Ivan Gold, Ray Grist, Lynn Sharon Schwartz, Knox Burger, J. D. Salinger, Norman Podhoretz, Harvey Shapiro, Bruce Jay Friedman, Art D'Lugoff, Helen Weaver, Ann Brower, Norman Mailer.

Marley Shelton, David Boreanaz in *Valentine*
© Village Roadshow/Warner Bros.

Jesus Chavez in *Split Decision* © First Run Features

SPLIT DECISION

(FIRST RUN FEATURES) Producer/Director/Editor, Marcy Garriott; Associate Producer, Roman Morales; Photography, Marcy Garriott, Robert Garriott; Color; Not rated; 75 minutes; Release date: February 9, 2001. Documentary on Jesus Gabriel Sandoval Chavez, a boxing hopeful who was deported back to Mexico after serving time in prison for robbery, featuring Jesus Gabriel Sandoval Chavez, Rosario Sandoval, Lidia Sandoval, Jimmy Sandoval, Jesus Sandoval, Hermila Sandoval, Sean Curtin, Marc Kadish, Richard Lord, Lou Duva, Nacho Beristain, Richard Gonzalez, Barbara Hines, Nancy Morawetz.

RHYTHM 'N' BAYOUS

(COWBOY BOOKING) Producer/Director/Editor, Robert Mugge; Co-Producer, Tim Healey; Executive Producer, Denise Gutnisky; Photography, David Sperling; a Mug-Shot Production in association with Have a Heart Thru Art; Color; Not rated; 107 minutes; Release date: February 16, 2001. Documentary on Louisiana's musical backwater bayous, featuring Frankie Floyd, Kenny Bill Stinson, Felton Pruit, Claude King, Tillman Franks, Dale Hawkins, Ever Ready Gospel Singers, Buddy Flett, Po' Henry & Tookie, Sister Pearlee Tolliver, Rev. Gerald Lewis, Easter Rock Church, Henry Gray & the Hurricanes, Henry Butler, Kermit Ruffins & His Barbecue Swingers, Alida & Moise Viator, La Famille

Alida Viator, Rosie Ledet in *Rhythm 'n' Bayous* © Cowboy

Julie Condra, Pat Hingle in *Road to Redemption*
© World Wide Pictures

Viator, Hackberry Ramblers, Jambalaya Cajun Band, Warren Storm, Rod Bernard, Dale & Grace, Lil' Alfred, Nathan & the Zydeco Cha Chas, Rosie Ledet & the Zydeco Playboys, Bill Best, Dr. Michael Luster, Rev. Lionel D. Wilson, Rev. Jimmie Lee Jones, Ben Sandmel, Terry Stewart, Etienne Viator, Deborah-Helen Viator, Floyd Soileau, Shane Bernard, Sid Williams.

ROAD TO REDEMPTION

(WORLD WIDE PICTURES) Producer, John Shepherd; Co-Producer, John Schmidt; Executive in Charge of Production, Barry Werner; Co-Executive Producers, Dave Ross, Gordon Druvenga; Director/Screenplay, Robert Vernon; Photography, Michael Balog; Editors, John Schmidt, John Pipes; Music, John Campbell, River; Designer, Dave Avanzino; Casting, Beverly Holloway; Presented in association with Dean River Productions; Dolby; Color; Rated PG; 89 minutes; Release date: February 16, 2001. CAST: Pat Hingle (Nathan Tucker), Julie Condra (Amanda Tucker), Leo Rossi (Sully Santoro), Jay Underwood (Alan Fischer), Tony Longo (Vincent), Wes Studi (Frank Lightfoot), Barry Sigismondi (Sheriff), Dennis Agajanian (Biker Leader), Jack Axelrod (Arnold), Gary Bayer (ER Doctor), Noah Poletiek (Paperboy), Leslie David Baker (Tow Truck Driver), Drinda La Lumia (Race Track Teller), Eddie Matthews (Fireman), Peter Moore (Arson Investigator), Susan Fukuda (VA Nurse), Paul Kiernan (Gas Station Attendant), Joan Johnson (Tourist Woman), Joyce Cohen (Marilyn), Christian Stevens (Gas Station Mechanic), Shauna Parsons (TV Reporter), Mathea Lynne Doyle (Cashier), Lauree Melograno (ER Nurse), Brent Smith (Prison Chaplain)

SOUTHERN COMFORT

(HBO THEATRICAL) Producer/Director/Photography/Editor, Kate Davis; Co-Producer, Elizabeth Adams; Music, Joel Harrison; Songs, The DCvers; Supervising Producer for HBO, Nancy Abraham; Executive Producer for HBO, Sheila Nevins; Color; Not rated; 90 minutes; Release date: February 21, 2001. Documentary on Robert Eads, a 52-year-old female-to-male transsexual living in the back hills of Georgia.

THE FIRST OF MAY

(CONSTELLATION) Producers, Gary Rogers, Paul Simons; Supervising Producer, Sandy Watterson; Executive Producers, Reza Badyi, John B. Goodman; Director, Paul Simons; Screenplay, Gary Rogers; Photography, Stephen Campbell; Designer, Orvis Rigsby; Costumes, Beverly Safer; Editor, Oliver Peters; a SHO Entertainment production; Color; Rated G; 11 minutes; Release date: February 23, 2001. CAST: Julie Harris (Carlotta), Charles Nelson Reilly (Dinghy), Robin O'Dell (Michelle), Tom Nowicki (Dan), Joe DiMaggio (Himself), Dan Byrd (Cory), Mickey Rooney (Boss Ed), Gerard Christopher (Zack), Laurie Coleman (Waitress), David E. Conley (Sgt. David Conley), Patricia Clay (Social Worker), Alan Lilly (Bus Driver)

THE GOSPEL ACCORDING TO PHILIP K. DICK

(FIRST RUN FEATURES) Producers, Mark Steensland, Andy Massagli; Director, Mark Steensland; Color; Not rated; 80 minutes; Release date: March 2, 2001. Documentary on science fiction author Philip K. Dick, featuring Ray Nelson, Robert Anton Wilson, Paul Williams, D. Scott Apel.

CARMAN: THE CHAMPION

(8XENTERTAINMENT) Producers, Matthew Crouch, Gary M. Bettman, Lawrence Mortorff; Executive Producer, Paul Crouch; Director, Lee Stanley; Screenplay, Lee Stanley, Carman, Tony Cinciripini, Tadd Callies; Photography, Steve Adcock; Editor, Shane Stanley; Music, Harry Manfredini; Designer, Nanci B. Roberts; Costumes, Jyl Moder; Casting, Jean Scoccimarro; a TBN Films presentation; Dolby; Color; Rated PG-13; 82 minutes; Release date: March 2, 2001. CAST: Carman (Orlando Leone), Michael Nouri (Freddie), Patricia Manterola (Allia), Jeremy Williams (Keshon Banks), Jed Allan (Laracco), Romeo Fabian (Cesar), Betty Carvalho (Geneva), Jay Arlen Jones (Johnny), Bill Boggs, Steve Albert (Themselves), Robert Catrini (Lawrence), Doc Duhame (Doc), Quinn Gonzalez (Party Girl), PaSean Wilson (Teresa), Cory Hodges (Li'l Drac), Jared Huckaby (Bob Jackal), Lori New (Anna)

Lola Cola, Robert Eads in *Southern Comfort* © HBO

HIT AND RUNWAY

(LOT 47 FILMS) Producers, Andrew Charas, Chris D'Annibale, Christopher Livingston; Director, Christopher Livingston; Screenplay, Jaffe Cohen, Christopher Livingston; Photography, David Tumblety; Designer, Mark Helmuth; Editors, Rhonda L. Mitrani, Christopher Livingston; Co-Producer, Jaffe Cohen; Costumes, Jory Adam; Music, Frank Piazza; Casting, Eve Battaglia; Color; Rated R; 105 minutes; Release date: March 9, 2001. CAST: Michael Parducci (Alex Andero), Peter Jacobson (Elliot Springer), Judy Prescott (Gwen Colton), Kerr Smith (Joey Worcieukowski), Hoyt Richards (Jagger Stevens), John Fiore (Frank Andero), J. K. Simmons (Ray Tilman), Teresa De Priest (Lana), Jonathan Hogan (Bob), Bill Cohen (Norman Rizzolli), Rosemary De Angelis (Marie Andero), Marisa Redanty (Barbara), John DiResta (Bruno), Marion Quinn (Eileen), Stephen Singer (Rabbi Pinchas), Nicholas Kepros (Jack Springer), Jaffe Cohen (Comic Actor), David Drake (Michael), Bryan Batt (Carlos), Adoni Anastasse, Arthur Jolly (Villains), Cindy Guyer (Model Hostage), Jo Jo Lowe (Renee), Hillel Meltzer (Woody), Ali Marsh (Geraldine), Mike Arotsky (Harold the Weightlifter), Anderson Gabrych (Gay Bartender), William Severs (Father McWilliams), David Tumblety (Priest), Florence Anglin (Aunt Lois), Bobo Lewis (Cousin Rosalie), Andrew Polk (Gary Shapiro), Alicia Minschew (TV Actress), Julia Novack (Jennifer Andero), Elizabeth Muller (Zoe Springer), David Fillippi (Taxi Driver), David Juskow (Woody's Voice)

Michael Parducci, Peter Jacobson in *Hit and Runaway*
© Lot 47 Films

Joy Bisco, Dante Basco in *The Debut* © 5 Card Productions

AMERICAN DESI

(EROS) Producers, Piyush Dinker Pandya, Gitesh Pandya, Deep Katdare; Executive Producer, Cyrus Koewing; Director/Screenplay, Piyush Dinker Pandya; Photography, Renato Falcão; Designer, Len Clayton; Music, Wig; Editor, Robert Tate; from American Desi Production, ABCD Productions; Color; Not rated; 100 minutes; Release date: March 16, 2001. CAST: Deep Katdare (Krishns Reddy), Ronobir Lahiri (Jagit Singh), Rizwan Manji (Salim Ali Khan), Kal Penn (Ajay Pandya), Purva Bedi (Nina Shah), Sunita Param (Farah Saaed), Anil Kumar (Rakesh Patel), Aladdin (Gautam Rao), Eric Axen (Eric Berger), Ami Skukla (Priya), Sunil Malhotra (Hemant), Sanjit De Silva (Chandu), Laura Lockwood (Sheila)

THE DEBUT

(CELESTIAL PICTURES) Producer, Lisa Onodera; Executive Producer/ Director, Gene Cajayon; Screenplay, Gene Cajayon, John Manal Castro; Photography, Hisham Abed; Editor, Kenn Kashima; Music, Wendell Yuponce; Music Supervisor, Kormann Roque; Line Producer, Pia Clemente; Associate Producers, John Manal Castro, Lu Cien Hioe, Patricio Ginelsa, Jr.; a 5 Card Productions presentation in association with National Asian American Telecommunications Association, GMA Network Films, Visual Communications; FotoKem color; Not rated; 90 minutes; Release date: March 16, 2001. CAST: Dante Basco (Ben Mercado), Darion Basco (Augusto), Dion Basco (Rommel), Derek Basco (Edwin Mercado), Eddie Garcia (Lolo Carlos), Tirso Cruz III (Roland Mercado), Gina Alajar (Gina Mercado), Fe de Los Reyes (Alice), Ernie Zarate (Tito Lenny), Bernadette Balagtas (Rose Mercado), Joy Bisco (Annabelle Manalo), Gigi Floresca, Alisha Floresca, Leslye Maninang (Premiere), Conrad Cimarra (Nestor), DJ Icy Ice, DJ E-man, Kayamanan Ng Lahi (Themselves), Jayson Schaal (Doug), Mindy Spence (Jennifer), Nicole Hawkyard (Susie), Gina Honda (Tita Florie), Brian Card (Dave), Rowland Kerr (George), Brandon Martin (Rick), Emelita Moll (Tita Connie), Louie Gonzales (Tito Dante), Rawlins Apilado (Jun Mercado), Robbie Pagatpatan (DJ Robbie Rock), Blas Lorenzo (Car Guy), Arianna Basco (Car Girl), Abe Pagtama (Photographer), Gabe Pagtama (Videographer)

Jaime Gomez, Seidy Lopez in *Gabriela* © Power Point Films

GABRIELA

(POWER POINT FILMS) Producer/Director/Screenplay, Vincent Jay Miller; Executive Producers, Vincent Francillon, Seth Maxwell, Michael A. Miller, Jeff Silberman; Photography, Adrian Rudomin; Designers, Anne Cartegnie, Kathy Cook; Music, Craig Stuart Garfinkle, Leo Marchildon; Editors, John Hoffhines, Daniel H. Holland, Ray Pond; Casting, Gina Glatis; from Grindstone Pictures; Color; Rated R; 90 minutes; Release date: March 16, 2001. CAST: Jaime Gomez (Mike), Seidy Lopez (Gabriela), Zach Galligan (Pat), Troy Winbush (Douglas), Lupe Ontiveros (Grandma Josie), Stacy Haiduk (Ilona), Evelina Fernandez (Sofia), Frank Medrano (Manny), Sal Lopez, Danny De La Paz (Cops), Liz Torres (Julia), Lamont Bentley (Nick), Patrick Rowe (Gary), Gilbert Garcia (Transvestite), Teddy Lane Jr. (Rex), Jennifer Loto (Staci), Shashani Lombardo (Maria), Colette O'Connell (Ryan), Flora Burke (Ethyl), Patrick M. J. Finerty (Adrian), Anne Cartegnie (French Maid), Steve Valentine (Steven), Joe Rodriguez (Elegant Writer), Yeniffer Behrens (Jesica), Erika Garcia (Tania), Yesica Pineda (Magdalena)

Christopher Leibe,
Bert Kraemer in *Boys to
Men* © Jour de Fête Films

BOYS TO MEN

(JOUR DE FÊTE FILMS) *Crush:* Producer/Director/Screenplay, Phillip Bartell; Photography, Maida Sussman; Editor, Jonathan Knight; Music, Boris Worister; CAST: Ema A. Tuennerman (Tina), Brett Chukerman (Robbie), Weston Mueller (Tim), Rengin Altay (Brenda), Michael Zwiener (Bryan), Margaret Kustermann (Marge), Jack Rogers (Casey), Robert Carson (Lyle), Richard Blake (Jason Hewitt). *The Mountain King:* Producers, Amy Jelenko, Stephen Winter; Director/Screenplay, Duncan Tucker; Photography, Brian Przypek; Editor, Rodney Evans; Casting, Jordan Beswick; CAST: John Sloan, Paul Dawson. . . . *lost:* Producers, Dan Castle, Mike Thomas; Director/Screenplay, Dan Castle; Photography, John Matkowsky; CAST: Wayne Danner, Rick Eichelberger. *The Confession:* Producers, Grace Lee, Jonathan Wald; Director/Screenplay/Editor, Carl Pfirman; Photography, Patti Lee; Music, Barbara Cohen, David Long; CAST: Bert Kraemer (Joseph), Tom Fitzpatrick (Caesar), Christopher Liebe (Father Marcus); Color; Not rated; 75 minutes; Release date: March 16, 2001.

SAY IT ISN'T SO

(20TH CENTURY FOX) Producers, Bobby Farrelly, Bradley Thomas, Peter Farrelly; Director, J. B. Rogers; Screenplay, Peter Gaulke, Gerry Swallow; Photography, Mark Irwin; Designer, Sidney J. Bartholomew, Jr.; Editor, Larry Madaras; Co-Producer, Marc S. Fischer; Music, Mason Daring; Costumes, Lisa Jensen; Casting, Nancy Foy; a Conundrum Entertainment production; Dolby; Color; Rated R; 96 minutes; Release date: March 23, 2001. CAST: Chris Klein (Gilbert Noble), Heather Graham (Josephine Wingfield), Orlando Jones (Dig McCaffey), Sally Field (Valdine Wingfield), Richard Jenkins (Walter Wingfield), John Rothman (Larry Falwell), Jack Plotnick (Leon Pitofsky), Eddie Cibrian (Jack Mitchelson), Mark Pellegrino (Jimmy Mitchelson), Brent Hinkley (Streak), Henry Cho (Freddy), Richard Riehle (Sheriff Merle Hobbs), Brent Briscoe (Det. Vic Bloomfield), Ezra Buzzington (Stewart), Julie White (Ruthie Falwell), David L. Lander (Rev. Stillwater), Judith Maxie (Administrative Nurse), Lin Shaye (Nurse Bautista), Gigi Moran (Gate Agent), Barrow Davis (Angela), Joanne Wolfe (Ticket Agent), Rick Poltaruk (Man in Room), C. Ernst Harth (Mr. Campisi), Joyce Erickson, Alex Green, Mary McDonald (Old Ladies), Connor Widdows (Boy), Courtney Peldon (Cher Falwell), Matthew Peters (Buddy), Andrea Kinsky (Fat Ankles Amy), Annie O'Donnell (Delores), Stacey Goryl (Flight Attendant), Norman Armour, Daniel Boileau, Keith Dallas, E. W. Holden, Rain Draper (Hecklers), Sarah Silverman (Gina), Greg Kean (Front Desk Attendant), Reg Glass (Burly Guy), Alejandro Abellan, Martin Morales (Mexican Men), Dolores Drake (Mrs. Hartunian), Kate Robbins, Gina Stockdale (Elderly Women), Jackie Flynn (Rich Brown), Melanie Wood (Cook), Zahf Hajee (Asian Man), Jordan Weller (Benjy), 'r' Nelson Brown, Marcus Hondro, Pablo Coffey, Shawn Bordoff (Inmates), Mark Olea (Man in Alley), Dan Murphy (Mr. Murphy), Christopher R. Sumpton (Mr. Sumpton), Colin Foo (Mr. Chin), Austin Stark (Animal Shelter Guy), Alícia Calvo (Consuelo), Richard E. Coe (Barber), Michael Gradilone (Paramedic), Charlene Harns (Angry Trailer Park Woman), Floyd Faircrest (Indian Man)

Heather Graham, Chris Klein in *Say It Isn't So*
© Twentieth Century Fox

Jerry O'Connell in *Tomcats* © Revolution Studios

Tobias Schneebaum in *Keep The River on Your Right: A Modern Cannibal Tale* © IFC Films

FRIENDLY PERSUASION: IRANIAN CINEMA AFTER THE REVOLUTION

(COWBOY BOOKING) Producer/Director/Screenplay, Jamshced Akrami; Photography, Jamsheed Akrami, Shahram Assadi, Dan Nocera, Albert Xavier; Editors, Jamsheed Akrami, Dah Nankou; Music, Ahmad Pezhman; Narrator, Sara Nodjoums; from Jam-Hi Productions; Color; Not rated; 113 minutes; Release date: March 23, 2001. Documentary featuring Rakshan Bani Etemad, Bahram Bneizai, Ebrahim Hatamikia, Mahmoud Kalari, Niki Karimi, Abbas Kiarostami, Masud Kimiai, Majid Majidi, Mohsen Makhmalbaf, Dariush Mehrjui, Tahmineh Milani, Jafar Panahi, Richard Pena, Kamal Tabizi.

BUTTERFLY

(DOUG WOLENS PRODS.) Producer/Director/Photography, Doug Wolens; Editors, Zack Bennett, Doug Wolens; Associate Producers, Gary Schwartz, Claudia Kussano, Mike Wolens, Lois Wolens; Color; Not rated; 79 minutes; Release date: March 30, 2001. Documentary on Julia Butterfly Hill's two-year vigil spent 180 feet high on an ancient redwood tree to prevent it from being cut down. (Note: This film had its premiere on PBS in June 2000.)

TOMCATS

(COLUMBIA) Producers, Alan Riche, Tony Ludwig, Paul Kurta; Executive Producer, Todd Garner; Director/Screenplay, Gregory Poirier; Photography, Charles Minsky; Designer, Robb Wilson King; Costumes, Alix Friedberg; Music, David Kitay; Editor, Harry Keramidas; a Revolution Studios presentation of an Eagle Cover Entertainment production; Dolby; CFI color; Rated R; 95 minutes; Release date: March 30, 2001. CAST: Jerry O'Connell (Michael Delaney), Shannon Elizabeth (Natalie Parker), Jake Busey (Kyle Brenner), Horatio Sanz (Steve), Jaime Pressly (Tricia), Bernie Casey (Officer Hurley), David Ogden Stiers (Dr. Crawford), Travis Fine (Jan), Heather Stephens (Jill), Julia Schultz (Shelby), Scott Beehner (Max), Kam Heskin (Kimberly), J. Kenneth Campbell (Mr. MacDonald), Brandi Andres (Kelly), John Patrick White (Gary), Jason Allen (Otto), Josh Raisin (Dan), David St. James (Priest), Buck Kartalian (Grandfather MacDonald), Alexa Power (Grandmother MacDonald), Anthony Azizi (Sikh Elvis Chaplain), Marisa Parker (Maria), Lauren Moore (Janet), Damon Williams (Tony), Bryan Birge (Vegas Bartender), Amber Smith (Gorgeous Redhead), Philip Jon Schultz (Stick Man), Tommy Canary (Blackjack Dealer), Billy Hufsey (Pit Boss), Christopher Darga, Conrad Goode (Repo Men), Tracy Kay Wolfe (Golfing Girl), Soledad Alberti (Consuela), Nina Kaczorowski (Cheating Wife), Scott Lincoln (Homeless Man), Monica Serene Garnich (Barfing Girl), Amy Hanaiali'i Gilliom (Hawaiian Singer), Florence Stone Fevergeon (Lady in Library), Joan M. Blair (Moustache Lady), Marnie Crossen (Granny), Kinga Phillips (Steve's Nurse), Sandra Taylor (Nurse

Nancy), Katie Lohmann (Centerfold), Lucille M. Oliver (Nurse in Waste Storage), Bill Kohne (Orderly with Sticky Buns), Diana Terranova, Lisa Marie Waishes, Stephanie Chao, Nikita Ager (Girls in Michaael Dream), Doug Carfrae (French Maitre d'), Rachael Sterling (Cherry), Sara Ashlyn, Lisa Lopez, Jovanna Vitiello, Danielle Ciardi, Cinna Bunz-Bowie, Millicent Ally, Candice Beckman, Carrie Carroll, Jenifer Lynn Kinnear (Strippers), Jerry C. Banks (Male Stripper), Shelby Stockton (Mistaken Bride), Eric Gilliom (Mistaken Groom), Dakota Fanning (Little Girl in Park), Barry Sigismondi (Chasing Cop), Robin Kaye Shaw (Animal Rights Activist), Heather Ankeny (Mistaken Natalie), Joseph D. Reitman (Carrot Lover), Christian Whelan, Steve Fitchpatrick (Hollywood Blvd. Cops)

KEEP THE RIVER ON YOUR RIGHT: A MODERN CANNIBAL TALE

(IFC FILMS) Producers/Directors/Screenplay, David Shapiro; Executive Producers, Peter Broderick, Chris Vroom, Associate Producer, Mark Stolaroff; Photography, Jonathan Kovel; Editor, Tula Goenka; Music, Steve Bernstein; a Next Wave Films presentation of a Lifer Film in association with Stolen Car Productions; Dolby; Color; Rated R; 90 minutes; Release date: March 30, 2001. Documentary on Tobias Schneebaum, a seemingly mild-mannered New York art historian whose adventures have taken him into the heart of the Peruvian and Indonesian jungle where he was adopted into a tribe of cannibals.

ON HOSTILE GROUND

(COWBOY BOOKING) Producers, Liz Mermin, Jenny Raskin, Catherine Gund; Directors/Photography/Editors, Liz Mermin, Jenny Raskin; Music, Tom Verlaine, Tom Nishioka; Color; Not rated; 73 minutes; Release date: April 6, 2001. Documentary on the practical, legal, and emotional obstacles faced by three abortion providers, featuring Dr. Richard Stuntz, Susan Cahill, Dr. Morris Wortman.

BRIGHAM CITY

(ZION FILMS) Producer/Director/Screenplay, Richard Dutcher; Photography, Ken Glassing; Line Producer, David Greenlaw Sapp; Designer, Kee L. Miller; Costumes, Camile J. Morris; Editor, Michael Chaskes; Music, Sam Cardon; Casting, Jennifer Buster; Color; Not rated; 119 minutes; Release date: April 6, 2001. CAST: Richard Dutcher (Sheriff Wes Clayton), Matthew A. Brown (Deputy Terry Woodruff), Wilford Brimley (Stu Udall), Carrie Morgan (Peg), Jon Enos (Ed), Tayva Patch (Meredith Cole), Jeff Johnson (Garcia), Wendy Gardiner (April), Richard Clifford (Steve), Sterling Brimley (Glen), Jerry North (Ivan), Jack North (Max), Frank Gerrish (Ralph), Janice Power (Evelyn), Rick Macy (Ernie), Barta Heiner (Clara), Tim Hansen (McKay), Robert Nelson (Parker), Elisabeth Simmons (Jamie), Nick Whitaker (Spencer), Chris Clark (Ben), Christopher E. Kendrick (Mike Sommers), Emily Pearson (Kathleen), Madison Gordon (Sommers Girl #11), Bill Osborn (B. Markham), Kathryn Little (S. Markham), Haley Fife (Jenny Markham), Anne Sward (Carole), Bus Riley (Bob), Jayne Luke (Judy), Jeremy Elliott (Jack), Shannon Engemann (Sherry), Ivan Crosland (John), Shirley Bliss (Mae), Georgia Faux (Georgia), Oscar Rowland (Oscar, Old Man), Ali Seable (Rose), Ryan Shupe (Singer), Kent Richards (Red), Andres Orozco (Bill), Rolland Grubbe (Customer), J. Scott Bronson (Carpenter), Michelle Evans, Becky Christensen (Women), Drew Thueson (Husband), Logan Houston (Son), Teddy Carter, Ethan Dutcher (Boys), Kellen Jones, Ian Ferguson (Priests), Eric Peterson (Scott), Cathleen Mason (Townswoman), Owen Clark (Malachi), Jacque Gray (Caroline Merrill), Sydnie Carter (Red-Headed Girl), Peg Carter (Martha Sorenson)

Susan Cahill in *On Hostile Ground* © Cowboy

Richard Dutcher, Wilford Brimley in *Brigham City* © Zion Films

Carlos Santana in *All Access* © IMAX

ALL ACCESS

(IMAX) Producers, Jon Shapiro, Peter Shapiro; Executive Producers, Chris J. Ball, William Tyrer, Tisha Fein, Scooter Weintraub; Director, Martyn Atkins; Co-Producers, Kelly Knight, Alex Cornfeld; IMAX Directors of Photography, David Douglas, Reed Smoot, Rodney Taylor; Editor, William Bullen; Music Director, Peter Shapiro; an IMAX Corporation presentation in association with Newmarket of an Ideal Entertainment production, presented by Certs; Dolby; IMAX Panavision; CFI color; Not rated; 64 minutes; Release date: April 6, 2001. Concert documentary, featuring Sting, Cheb Mami, George Clinton & Parliament Funkadelic, Mary J. Blige, Kid Rock, Sheryl Crow, B. B. King, Trey Anastasio and the Roots, Macy Gray, Carlos Santana, Rob Thomas, Al Green, Dave Matthews Band, Moby.

MAU MAU SEX SEX

(7TH PLANET PICTURES) Producer/Director, Ted Bonnitt; Screenplay, Eddie Muller, Ted Bonnitt; Co-Producer, Eddie Muller; Executive Producer, Keith Robinson; Editors, Ted Bonnitt, Christopher Rowland, Eddie Muller; Color; Not rated; 80 minutes; Release date: April 6, 2001. Documentary on pioneering sexploitation filmmakers Dan Sonney and David Friedman.

Dan Sonney, Dave Friedman in *Mau Mau Sex Sex*
© 7th Planet Productions

JUST VISITING

(HOLLYWOOD PICTURES) Producers, Patrice Ledoux, Ricardo Mestres; Executive Producer, Richard Hashimoto; Director, Jean-Marie Gaubert; Screenplay, Christian Clavier, Jean-Marie Poire, John Hughes; Based on the film *Les Visiteurs* written by Jean-Marie Poire, Christian Clavier; Photography, Ueli Steiger; Designer, Doug Kraner; Visual Effects Supervisor, Igor Sekulic; Costumes, Penny Rose; Editor, Michael A. Stevenson; Music, John Powell; Casting, Billy Hopkins, Suzanne Smith, Kerry Barden; a Gaumont presentation; U.S.-French; Dolby; Technicolor; Rated PG-13; 87 minutes; Release date: April 6, 2001. CAST: Jean Reno (Thibault), Christina Applegate (Rosalind/Julia), Christian Clavier (Andre), Matt Ross (Hunter), Tara Reid (Angelique), Bridgette Wilson-Sampras (Amber), John Aylward (Byron), George Plimpton (Dr. Brady), Malcolm McDowell (Wizard), Matt Furlin, Chet Nichols, Martin Aistrope, Ellie Weingardt, Jordan Teplitz, Susan Murray, Michael Skewes, Frederick Husar (Barflies), Karen Vaccaro, Naomi Armstrong, Rebekah Louise Smith, Lisa Dodson, Thomas McElroy, Felipe Camacho, Ike Eichling, Anne Harris (Bystanders), Eric Aviles (Purse Snatcher), Sarah Badel (Queen), Bill Bailey (Thibault's Father), Tab Baker (Cabbie), Doug Barron (Reed Sikes), Clifford Barry (Museum Guard), Janette Bickerton (Screaming Peasant Woman), Kendra Torgan, Lucy Blair (Thibault's Sisters), William Bookston (Peasant), Roy Boutcher (Maitre d'), Richard Bremmer (King Henry), Richard Burton Brown (Irving the Drunk), Daniel Miller, Alexandra Caplan (Kids), Druann Carlson (Elevator Wife), Helen Caro (Screaming Woman), Lorenzo Clemons (Squad Chief), Paul Connell, Alan Kopischke (Crime Scene Cops), Laura Cox (Peasant Woman), William Dambra (Policeman), Oliver Ford Davies (Pit Rivers), Emily Deamer, Sophie Graham (Elevator Girls), Albena Dodeva (Nightclub Waitress), Madeline Fishman (Little Girl—Tammy), Marilyn Dodds Frank (Bag Lady), Jane Galloway Heitz (Dinah the Drunk), Matyelock Gibbs (Rosalind's Nurse), Ross Gibby (Museum Teacher), Chris Gillespie (Daughter at Restaurant), Robert Glenister (Earl of Warwick), Danny Goldring (Bartender), Brian Greene (Old Man with Hearing Aid), Valerie Griffiths (Hag), Molly Price, Amo Gulinello (Teachers), Crispin Harris (Archbishop), Darryl Henriques (Monk), Mike Houlihan (Little Boy's Father), Michelle Hurst (Pawnshop Broker), Rich Komenich (Sid the Drunk), Alexis Loret (Francois), Kevin McClarnon (Police Sgt.), Eric Meyers (Family Man), Larry Neumann, Jr. (Hot Dog Vendor), Steve Owen (Peasant Man), Donna Palmer (Museum Curator), Randall Paul (Bathroom Man), Suzanne Petri (Patsy the Drunk), Beau Sapsford (Little Boy in Elevator), Ric Sarabia (Priest), Adam Shaw (Kitchen Worker), Alan Shaw (Giant Sheriff), Whitney Sneed (Nightclub Woman), Robert Steinman (Cab Driver), Matthew Sussman (Chic Salesman), Kevin Theis (Cop O'Malley), Francesca Vetrano (Nancy the Drunk), Claire Welch (Thibault's Mother), Ruth Winblad (Old Woman), Carl Wright (Station Master), Cedric Young ("Miller"—Museum Guard), Anne Louise Zachry (Young Woman #2)

THE BODY

(TRISTAR) Producer, Rudy Cohen; Executive Producers, Mark Damon, Moshe Diamant; Director/Screenplay, Jonas McCord; Based on the novel by Richard Ben Sapir; Photography, Vilmos Zsigmond; Designer, Allan Starski; Costumes, Caroline Harris; Editor, Alain Jakubowicz; Music, Serge Colbert; Casting, Celestia Fox, Illana Diamant; a Diamant/Cohen production, presented by TriStar Pictures with MDP Worldwide and Helkon Media AG in association with Green Moon Productions; Dolby; Panavision; Color; Rated PG-13; 100 minutes; Release date: April 20, 2001. CAST: Antonio Banderas (Father Matt Gutierrez), Olivia Williams (Sharon Golban), John Shrapnel (Moshe Cohen), Derek Jacobi (Father Lavelle), Jason Flemyng (Father Walter Winstead), John Wood (Cardinal Pesci), Makhram J. Khoury (Nasir Hamid), Vernon Dobtcheff (Monsignor), Ian McNeice (Dr. Sproul), Muhamed Bakri (Abu Yusef), Yoav Dekelbaum (Avi), Sami Samir (Achmel), Jordan Licht (Dorene), Limor Goldstein (Galic), Ariel Horovitz (Reb Mecheal), Roi Horovitz (Zalman), Shai Sharabi (Street Urchin), Lillian Lax (Mrs. Kahn), Arye Elias (Hamied's Father), Sivan Shwartz (Mark), Gilad Bergman (Rani), Halima Abu Aguva (Jasmine)

HIDDEN WARS OF DESERT STORM

(FREE WILL PRODS.) Producers/Directors, Gerard Ungerman, Audrey Brophy; Photography, Gerard Ungerman; Music, Fritz Hede; Narrator, John Hurt; Color; Not rated; 64 minutes; Release date: April 20, 2001. Documentary exploring the unanswered questions about the Gulf War, featuring Gen. Norman Schwarzkopf, Ramsey Clark, Dennis Halliday, Scott Ritter.

FREDDY GOT FINGERED

(20TH CENTURY FOX) Producers, Larry Brezner, Lauren Lloyd, Howard Lapides; Executive Producer, Arnon Milchan; Director, Tom Green; Screenplay, Tom Green, Derek Harvie; Photography, Mark Irwin; Designer, Bob Ziembicki; Editor, Jacqueline Cambas; Co-Producer, Marc S. Fischer; Music, Mike Simpson; Casting, Nancy Mayor; a Regency Enterprises presentation of a New Regency/MBST Production; Dolby; Deluxe color; Rated R; 87 minutes; Release date: April 20, 2001. CAST: Tom Green (Gord Brody), Rip Torn (Jim Brody), Marisa Coughlan (Betty), Eddie Kaye Thomas (Freddy Brody), Harland Williams (Darren), Anthony Michael Hall (Mr. Davidson), Julie Hagerty (Julie Brody),

Jackson Davies (Mr. Malley), Connor Widdows (Andy Malloy), John R. Taylor, Bob Osborne (Farmers), Stephen E. Miller (Ernie), Charles Buettner (Rupert), Cliff Solomon (Big Bear), Fiona Hogan (Pregnant Woman), George Gordon (Doctor), Ronald Selmour (Security Guard, Studio), Drew Barrymore (Davidson's Receptionist), David Neale, Scott Heindl (Men in Restaurant), Wendy Chmelauskas (Woman in Restaurant), 'r' Nelson Brown (Larry, Truck Driver), Jorge Rodriguez, Henry O. Watson (Workers at Pulp Mill), Joe Flaherty (William), Allan Gray (Waiter), Laurie Murdoch (Bank Manager), Lorena Gale (Psychiatrist/Social Worker), Simon Longmore (Cop with Social Worker), Giacomo Baessato (Morose Kid), Mike Bullard (Policeman), Ralph Alderman (Locksmith), Eric Keenleyside (Foreman), Shaquille O'Neal (Shaquille), Darren Moore (Sandwich Customer), Rick Tae (Security Guard), Noel Fisher (Pimply Manager), Irene Karas (Cop at Fancy Restaurant), Ted Friend (Local Field Reporter), Balinder Johal, Kamaljeet Kler (Indian Women)

Olivia Williams, Antonio Banderas in *The Body* © Tin Star

Malcolm McDowell, Christina Applegate, Jean Reno in *Just Visiting* © Gaumont

Tom Green, Rip Torn in *Freddie Got Fingered*
© 20th Century Fox

THE BEST MAN IN GRASS CREEK

(HEARTLAND FILM) Producers, Mark Klitsie, John Newcombe; Director, John Newcombe; Screenplay, John Hines, John Newcombe; Photography, Wes Llewellyn; Music, Deborah Lurie; Editors, Scott Popies, Steve Waller; from Lovestruck Pictures; Color; Not rated; 86 minutes; Release date: April 20, 2001. CAST: Grace Phillips, John Newcombe, John Hines, Oksana Fedunyszyn, Michael Beattie, Tim Farmer, David Jeremiah, Al Leinonen, William Holmes, Mark McCracken, Megan Mullally

FREAKS, GLAM GODS AND ROCKSTARS

(RYANISLAND FILMS) Director, John T. Ryan; No other credits available; Color; Not rated; 74 minutes; Release date: April 20, 2001. Documentary on Manhattan's underground scene of punks, drag queens, glam rockers, and performance artists, featuring Bernard Scahel, *Bob*, Boob!, Brickbats, Flotilla DeBarge, Jackie Beat, Jayne County, Jimmy James, Justin Bond, Ken Feet, Kevin Aviance, Lee Chappell, Lunachicks, Lilly of the Valley, Mad Juana, Michael T., Miss Understood, Mistress Chaos, Nancy Boy: Donovan Leitch, Jason Nesmith; Patricia Field, Princess Zoraya, Rolando Cevallos, Sister Dimension, Sky Palkowitz, Starr, The "Lady" Bunny, Michael Musto, The Voluptuous Horror of Karen Black, Les Simpson, Toilet Boys, Ultra Nate, Velvet Mafia, Young & Fabulous

CROCODILE DUNDEE IN LOS ANGELES

(PARAMOUNT) Producers, Lance Hool, Paul Hogan; Executive Producers, Kathy Morgan, Steve Robbins, Jim Reeve; Director, Simon Wincer; Screenplay, Matthew Berry, Eric Abrams; Based on characters created by Paul Hogan; Photography, David Burr; Designer, Leslie Binns; Editor, Terry Blythe; Music, Basil Poledouris; Costumes, Marion Boyce; Casting, Lisa London, Catherine Stroud, Maura Fay, Ann Fay; a Lance Hool/Paul Hogan production in association with Guy Hands; Dolby; Color; Rated PG; 92 minutes; Release date: April 20, 2001. CAST: Paul Hogan (Mick Dundee), Linda Kozlowski (Sue Charleton), Jere Burns (Arnan Rothman), Jonathan Banks (Milos Drubnik), Alec Wilson (Jacko), Gerry Skilton (Nugget O'Cass), Steve Rackman (Donk), Serge Cockburn (Mikey Dundee), Aida Turturro (Jean Ferraro), Paul Rodriguez (Diego), Kaitlin Hopkins (Miss Mathis), David Clendinning (English Tourist), Duke Bannister (American Tourist), Betty Bobbitt (American Lady), Karen Crone (Barmaid Ida), Angela Campbell, Tiriel Mora (Tourist Couple), David Ngoombujarra (Arthur), Patrick Dargan (Troy), Matt Winston (Limo Driver), Morgan O'Neil (Matt), Clare Carey (Skater), Brian Turk, Vladimir McCrary, David Bickford (Drivers), Rhonda Aldrich (Passenger), Kevin Larosa (Chopper Pilot), Daryl Keith Roach, Joe Michael Burke, Jim Davidson (Cops), Hal Fishman, Marta Waller, Mike Tyson, George Hamilton (Themselves), Angelo Perez (Valet), Gerry Del Sol (Barman), Harvey Shain (Ponytail Guy), Keli Daniels (Didi), Lenny Citrano (Actor), Cara Michelle (Model), Matthew Kimbrough (Producer), Grant Piro (Guide), David Baldwin (Grumpy Guy), Gabriella Dilabio (Mrs. Grumpy), Alex Kuzelicki (Lethal Agent), Shanyn Asmar (Claire), John Billingsley (Barry), Jay Acavone (Eric), Gregg Donovan (Concierge), Chad Stephen Taylor (Juggler), Buddy Daniel Friedman (Pickpocket), Mark Kowalewycz, Ty Smith (Trench Coat Men), David Franklin (Assistant Director), Van Markell (Director), Gregory Wheeler (Classmate), Steven Grives (Evil Barron), Alan Zitner (Trainer), Carey Embry (Cowgirl), Mark Adair Rios, Rick Gonzalez (Gang Bangers), Kenneth Ransom (Phil), Nicholas Hammond (Curator), Slim De Grey (Minister), Peter Kent (Carl), Ray Anthony, Darko Tuskan, Ric Anderson, Keir Beck, Ron Vreeken, Nick McKinless, Nick Lawson (Thugs)

Linda Kozlowski, Paul Hogan in *Crocodile Dundee in Los Angeles* © Paramount Pictures

PIE IN THE SKY: THE BRIGID BERLIN STORY

(INDEPENDENT/FILM FORUM) Producers/Directors, Shelly Dunn Fremont, Vincent Fremont; Photography, Vic Losick; Associate Producer, Amy DiPasquale; Editor, Michael Levine; Music, Chris Stein; Color; Not rated; 75 minutes; Release date: April 25, 2001. Documentary on Andy Warhol performer/artist Brigid Berlin, featuring Brigid Berlin, Richard Bernstein, Larry Rivers, John Waters, Bob Colacello, Taylor Mead, Patricia Hearst.

A SENSIBLE OBSESSION

(HARVEST ENTERTAINMENT) Producer/Director/Screenplay/ Photography/Editor/Designer, George Jiha; Executive Producer, Joshua Mashiach; Costumes, Eduardo de la Vega; Music, Juan Salazar; Color; Not rated; 100 minutes; Release date: April 27, 2001. CAST: Mick Shane (Josh), Sylvie Hoffer (Violet), Todd Dylan (Sam), Michelle Russo (Rose), Mike Ellis (Josh's Dad), Patricia Dean (Josh's Mom), Mike Horton (Preacher), Greg Mlacker (Rock Throwing Boy), Virginia Jiha (Singer, Voice)

THE FORSAKEN

(SCREEN GEMS) Producers, Carol Kottenbrook, Scott Einbinder; Director/ Screenplay, J. S. Cardone; Photography, Steven Bernstein; Designer, Martina Buckley; Editor, Norman Buckley; Music, Johnny Lee Schell, Tim Jones; Music Supervisor, Alex Patsavas; Casting, Ferne Cassel; a Sandstorm Films production; Dolby; Color; Rated R; 90 minutes; Release date: April 27, 2001. CAST: Kerr Smith (Sean), Brendan Fehr (Nick), Izabella Miko (Megan), Phina Oruche (Cym), Simon Rex (Pen), Carrie Snodgress (Ina), Johnathon Schaech (Kit), Alexis Thorpe (Teddy), Luis Anaya (Orderly), Ed Anders (Patrolman), Elizabeth Barondes (Oats Diner Waitress), A. J. Buckley (Mike), Jessica R. Butts (Redhead), Sara Downing (Julie), Bert Emmett (Desk Clerk), F. J. Flynn (Hoot), Walter A. Johnson (Mose), Bryan Kirkwood (Merk), Jack Leal (Bus Driver), Jamie Marsh (Mitch), James O'Shea (Racer), Martha Parker (Nurse), Tony Pierce (Mechanic), Matt Reid (Dutton), Julia Schultz (Blonde), Ryan Shuck (Pride), Beth Ann Styne (Garage Woman), Marc Vann (Decker)

THE END OF THE ROAD

(JOINT PRODUCTIONS) Producers, Michael Dong, Douglas Hosdale, Brent Meeske; Director/Editor, Brent Meeske; Photography, Douglas Hosdale, Brent Meeske; Music, Jerry Garcia, Merl Saunders; a Slow Loris Films presentation; Color; Not rated; 97 minutes; Release date: April 27, 2001. Documentary on The Grateful Dead, featuring Mickey Hart, Bill Kreutzman, Phil Lesh, Babatunde Olatunji, Hugh Romney, Merl Saunders, Bob Weir.

Brigid Berlin in *Pie in the Sky*

Kerr Smith, Brendan Fehr in
The Forsaken © Screen Gems

Steve Railsback in *Ed Gein* © First Look

ED GEIN

(FIRST LOOK) formerly *In the Light of the Moon*; Producers, Michael Muscal, Hamish McAlpine; Executive Producers, Karen Nicholls, Steve Railsback; Director, Chuck Parello; Screenplay, Stephen Johnston; Photography, Vanja Cernjul; Designer, Mark Harper; Music, Robert McNaughton; Costumes, Niklas J. Palm; Makeup, Dan Striepeke; a Tartan Films presentation; Dolby; Color; Rated R; 89 minutes; Release date: May 4, 2001. CAST: Steve Railsback (Ed Gein), Carrie Snodgress (Augusta Gein), Carol Mansell (Collette Marshall), Sally Champlin (Mary Hogan), Steve Blackwood (Brian), Nancy Linehan Charles (Eleanor Adams), Bill Cross (George Gein), Travis McKenna (Ronnie), Jan Hoag (Judy Anderson), Brian Evers (Henry Gein), Pat Skipper (Sheriff Jim Stillwell), Craig Zimmerman (Pete Anderson), Nicholas Stojanovich (Dale), Dylan Kasch (Melvin), Tish Hicks (Leigh Cross), Lee McLaughlin (Phil Anderson), Bill Pirman (Dean Story), Tom Rainone (Butch), Dan Striepeke (Doctor), Heather Gunn (Georgeann), Ryan Thomas Brockington (Ed Gein—16 years old), Austin James Peck (Ed Gein—10 years old), Luke Rowland (Henry Gein—14 years old), Chad Halyard (Roger Johnson), Devin Alexander (Doris Wickstrom), Rick Simpson (Henry Gein—20 years old), Ben Caswell (Officer David Bell), Heather Gettings (Nazi Woman), Melissa Engle (June), Gladell Adelman (Virginia Boyd), Danny Keogh, Jim Kundig, Douglas Hunter (Hunters), Andrew Craig (Harris), Carole Raphaelle Davis (Rosemary)

ICE FROM THE SUN

(SUB ROSA STUDIOS) Producer, Jeremy Wallace; Executive Producer/Director/Screenplay/Editor, Eric Stanze; Designer, Tommy Biondo; a Wicked Pixel Cinema production; Color; Not rated; 120 minutes; Release date: May 4, 2001. CAST: D. J. Vivona (The Presence), Ramona Midgett (Alison), Angela Zimmerly (Dana), Todd Tevlin (Aaron), Jason Christ (Matt), Tommy Biondo (Keith), Jo Palermo (Buck), Tracey Hein (Pam), Jessica Wyman (The Vision), Charles Heuvelman (Twisted Priest), Alexander Crestwood (Drug Runner), Tony Bridges (Pill Pusher), Leslie A. Unterreiner (Vikki Tonatair), Michael Bradley (Steven), Jeremy Wallace (Hunt 'n' Peck), Rob Cope (Salt Hauler), Jerry Bates (Grave Digger), Dwight Karl Spurgin II (Papa Inbreed), Sandy Garrison (Woods Walker), Jeff Bergeron (Eye Boy), Shana Ko, Robert "Rupe" Daniel (People Pets), George Cousins (Voice of News Broadcaster), Eric Stanze (Voice of TV Program Host), David Berliner, Mark Wallace (Goons), Derek Christian Wallace (Senseless Guard), Mike "Scrub" Champion (Saw Boy), William Clifton (Chess Head), Lisa Morrison (Gun Girl), Paula Morhaus (Doll Mama), Jonny Bitch Esq (Jar Boy), Mandy Cousins (Bic Flicker), Larry O'Neal, Stephanie Strohman, John Fletcher, Nick Normal (Freak Show), Michael Bangert (The Bum), Mark W. Kettler, Jennifer Poirier-Wallace (Inbred Children)

THE YOUNG GIRL AND THE MONSOON

(ARTISTIC LICENSE) Executive Producers, Richard Mehrlich, Beverly Mehrlich; Director/Screenplay, James Ryan; Line Producer, Debi Zelko; Photography, Ben Wolf; Designer, Tina Manfredi; Music, David Carbonara; Editor, John David Allen; Casting, Jeff Block; Color; Not rated; 90 minutes; Release date: May 4, 2001. CAST: Terry Kinney (Hank), Ellen Muth (Constance), Mili Avital (Erin), Diane Venora (Giovanna), Tim Guinee (Jack), Domenick Lombardozzi (Frankie), Christine Mehrlich, Liana Ryan (Teenage Girls), Lee Wong (Waiter), Eugene Leong (Cook), James Ryan (Man on Street), Candyce Mason (Candy), Tina Flaherty (Tina von Gal), Patricia Francy, Connie Meehan, Richard Gibson, Daniela Bar-Illan, Richard Mehrlich, Beverly Mehrlich, Brian Flaherty (Socialites), Slavko Stimac (Milcho), Mark McKennon (Man in Coffin)

Ellen Muth in *The Young Girl* and the *Monsoon* © Artistic License Films

Jonathan LaPaglia, Vincent Pastore, Michael Rodrick in *Under Hellgate Bridge* © Cavo Pictures

UNDER HELLGATE BRIDGE

(CAVO PICTURES) Producers, Michael Sergio, Isil Bagdadi; Director/Screenplay, Michael Sergio; Executive Producers, Robert G. Dixon, Jr., Frank Marchello; Co-Executive Producers, Vivian Jang, Heinz Kluetmeier, David Anthony; Photography, Leland Krane; Music, Stephan Moccio; Editor, Stan Warnow; Casting, Michele Ortlip; a Fortune Films, Cavo Pictures & D3 Films presentation; Color; Rated R; 90 minutes; Release date: May 11, 2001. CAST: Michael Rodrick (Ryan), Jonathan LaPaglia (Vincent), Dominic Chianese (Father Nichols), Jordan Bayne (Carla), Brian Vincent (Eddie), Vincent Pastore (Mitch), Frank Vincent (Big Sal), Careena Melia (Doreen), Kristen Lee Kelly (Marsha), Frank Bongiorno (Mike), Alex Conlon (Tyler), Marie Barrientos (Teresa), Robert Capelli, Jr. (Ralph), Francesca Buccellato (Big Sal's Girlfriend)

THE TRUMPET OF THE SWAN

(TRISTAR) Producer, Lin Oliver; Executive Producer, Seldon O. Young; Directors, Richard Rich, Terry L. Noss; Screenplay, Judy Rothman Rofé; Based on the book by E. B. White; Co-Producer, Thomas J. Tobin; Music, Marcus Miller; Editor, Joseph L. Campana; a Rich-Crest Animation production of a Lin Oliver production; Dolby; Color; Rated G; 75 minutes; Release date: May 11, 2001. VOICE CAST: Jason Alexander (Father), Mary Steenburgen (Mother), Reese Witherspoon (Serena), Seth Green (Boyd), Carol Burnett (Mrs. Hammerbotham), Joe Mantegna (Monty), Dee Baker (Louie), Sam Gifaldi (Sam), Little Richard (Song Performer), Jeffrey Schoeny (Young Louie), Kath Soucie (Paramedic/Newscaster/Serena), Julie Nathanson (Felicity)

SORDID LIVES

(REGENT) Producers, Sharyn Lane, Victoria Alonso, Max CiVon; Director/Screenplay, Del Shores, based on his play; Photography, Max CiVon; Designer, Steve Cubine; Editor, Ed Marx; Costumes, Jim Echerd; Music, George S. Clinton; Produced in association with Daly/Harris & Davis Classics; Dolby; Color; Not rated; 111 minutes; Release date: May 11, 2001. CAST: Olivia Newton-John (Bitsy Mae Harling), Beau Bridges (G. W. Nethercott), Delta Burke (Noleta Nethercott), Bonnie Bedelia (Latrelle Williamson), Beth Grant (Sissy Hickey), Ann Walker (LaVonda Dupree), Kirk Geiger (Ty Williamson), Leslie Jordan (Brother Boy "Earl" Ingram), Newell Alexander (Wardell "Bubba" Owens), Rosemary Alexander (Dr. Eve Bolinger), Sarah Hunley (Juanita Bartlett), Earl H. Bullock (Odell Owens), Mitch Carter (Bumper), Sharron Alexis (Sara Kaufman), Mary-Margaret Lewis (Ethel), Lorna Scott (Vera Lisso), Dale Dickey (Glyndora), Robert L. Stephenson (Crazy Preacher Man), Carl Balton (Riley), Jane George (Crying Mental Patient), Sharyn Leavitt (Nurse Jackson), Andrew Hawkins (Jason), Beverly Nero (Theater Director), Gloria LeRoy (Peggy Ingram), Luisa Leschin (Leticia Bustamante), Terry Brannon (Tom Ed), Dona Hardy (Mrs. King, Organist), William Edward Phipps (Rev. Barnes)

Ann Walker, Delta Burke in *Sordid Lives*
© Regent Entertainment

Arye Gross, Tim DeKay in *Big Eden* © Jourde Fête

EVERYTHING MOVES ALONE

(HALE MANOR PRODS.) Producers, Mike Aransky, Philip Guerette, Thomas Edward Seymour; Co-Producer, Jennifer Gray; Director, Mike Aransky; Screenplay, Thomas Edward Seymour; Photography, Mike Aransky, Thomas Edward Seymour; Editors, Mike Aransky, Philip Guerette, Thomas Edward Seymour; Costumes, Jennifer Woymar; Music, Thomas Edward Seymour; Color; Not rated; 100 minutes; Release date: June 1, 2001. CAST: Philip Guerette (Scotch Leary), Thomas Edward Seymour (Anderson), Matt Ford (McDunley), Tina Angelillo (Diane), Mike Aransky (Rob Leary), Kelly Robinson (Mary), Erik Nivison (Josh), Chris Romine, Jennifer Roe (Lawyers), Jen Gorman (Woman in Car), Carmine Capobianco (Used Car Dealer), Jennifer Gray (Barbara J. Frost), James Abucewicz, Abbe Salamon (Deaf Customers), Tim Kulig (Town Drunk), Paul Nelson (Gas Station Attendant), Bruce Seymour (Policeman), Lisa Simlik (New Waitress), Jerry Hemphill (Bus Driver), Vera Hemphill (Bus Passenger), Craig Roel (White Trash Lenny), Matthew Ferelli, Monica Yontef, Mark Woocam, Don Ridgeway (Emma's Customers), Keith Thomassen (Drill Sergeant), Neil Thomassen, Mike Miglietta, Mark Miglietta, Drew Chaplinsky (Soldiers)

A PACKING SUBURBIA

(CINEMA ESPERANCA INTL. INC.) Producers, Steve J. Szklarski, Liz Soldo; Director/Screenplay/Editor, Designer/Costumes, Steve J. Szklarski; Executive Producer, Liz Soldo; Co-Producer/Casting, Donna McKenna; from Suburban Filmworks Inc.; Color; Not rated; 90 minutes; Release date: June 1, 2001. CAST: Thomas Brandise (James Maxwell), Mariana Carreno (Iris), Robert Alexander (Daryl), Aesha Waks (Celeste), Molly Castelloe (Mrs. Maxwell), Ed Kershen (Mr. Musso), Jason Jones (Alando), James Lawrence (Blade), Michael Brown (Bobby), Yvonne Mead (Mrs. Washington), Christine Nagy (News Reporter), Kevin O'Brien (Reggie), Eric Reyes (Jose), Brooke Lewis (Roselle), Carl Low (Nelson), Kenneth Wilson (Harold), Sam Melendez (Sammy), Joseph Minutello (Mr. Maxwell), Henry Marshal (Det. Cooper), Kal Cauthen (Det. Clark), John Fiske (Richard), Judy Prianti (Mrs. Romano), Andrea Frierson (Mrs. King), Johnny Giery (Greg Coleman), Susan Lupo (Gym Teacher), Kelly McKenna, Rick Giannino, Jamie Giannino, Nicole Giannino (Children)

BIG EDEN

(JOUR DE FÊTE FILMS) Producer, Jennifer Chaiken; Director/Screenplay, Thomas Bezucha; Photography, Rob Sweeney; Designer, Stephanie Carroll; Costumes, Sam Hamilton, Rene Holguin; Editor, Andrew London; Music, Joseph Conlan; Casting, David Bloch; a Chaiken Films presentation; Color; Not rated; 118 minutes; Release date: June 1, 2001. CAST: Arye Gross (Henry Hart), Eric Schweig (Pike Dexter), Tim DeKay (Dean Stewart), Louise Fletcher (Grace Cornwell), George Coe (Sam Hart), Nan Martin (Widow Thayer), O'Neal Compton (Jim Soams), Corinne Bohrer (Anna Rudolph), Veanne Cox (Mary Margaret Bishop), Douglas Sebern (John Cornwell), Parker Livingston (Andrew Stewart), Cody Wayne Meixner (Ben Stewart), Josie Adams (Becky Rudolph), Mark Twogood (Lloyd), Christopher Kendra (Bird), Steve Frye (Fulbright), Steven Brian Conard (Leon), Delbert High (Dick), Kenneth R. King (Wheeler), Dori Thompson (Jenny), Mary Cassidy (Carol), Dee Dee Van Zyl (Didi Soams), Tom Cordingley (Rev. Alston), Bekki Vallin, John Lystne (People at Church), Beau Holden (Douglas), Wayne Mansaw (Man at Piano), Christianne Brown, Cori Wolff, Alecia LaRue (Women in Car), Tenika Capouch, Morgan McCarthy, Sarah Dramstad, Amanda Upton

AUGGIE ROSE

(ROXIE) a.k.a. Beyond Suspicion; Producers, Matthew A. Rhodes, Dan Stone; Executive Producers, Mark McGarry, Elie Samaha, Jeremiah Samuels, Andrew Stevens; Director/Screenplay, Matthew Tabak; Photography, Adam Kimmel; Designer, Caroline Hanania; Costumes, Wendy Chuck; Editor, Brian Berdan; Music, Don Harper, Mark Mancina; Casting, Edye Belasco, Richard Pagano; from Franchise Pictures, Persistent Pictures; Dolby; Color; Not rated; 105 minutes; Release date: May 18, 2001. CAST: Jeff Goldblum (John C. Nolan), Anne Heche (Lucy Brown), Nancy Travis (Carol), Timothy Olyphant (Roy Mason), Joe Santos (Emanuel), Richard T. Jones (Officer Decker), Kim Coates (Auggie Rose), Paige Moss (Noreen), Jack Kehler (Oscar Weeks), J. E. Freeman (Pawn Shop Owner), Peter Siragusa (Tony), Nick Chinlund (Car Salesman), Max Perlich (Landlord), Douglas Roberts (Dr. Sachs), Randall Slavin (Robber), Vince Jolivette (Customer in Store), Tony Perez (Det. Cole), Hawthorne James (MacDoogal), Amy Hill (Employment Agency Rep), Tony Genaro (Romeo), Erich Anderson (Paul), Sydney Walsh (Suzanne), Gerald McCullouch (Mr. Lark), Adilah Barnes (Mailperson), Anthony DeSantis (Evidence Attendant), David S. Dunard (Desk Sgt.), Michael Chieffo (Mr. Williams), Tony Abatemarco (Maitre d'), Richard Pagano (Deli Owner #2), Joe Huertas, Tom Miller (Paramedics), Richard Gilbert-Hill (Officer Woods), Tanya Beilke (Waitress), Matthew Tabak (Customer at the End) (Note: This film had its U.S. premiere on cable television on March 18, 2001.)

(Schoolgirls), Nicholas Gilhool (Carl at Gallery), Caitlin Carter (Julie Bauer), John Dossett (John Bishop), Justin Fonda (Airline Attendant), Trish Walsh (Airport Security Woman), Brian Grossenbacher (Man in Bar), Amanda Caldwell, Doug Rommereim, Isaac Simpson, Jerry Fletcher (Choir Members), Maxine Rasmussen (Mrs. Stewart), Benny Reynolds (Mr. Stewart), William J. Adamo, Gregory Paul Johnson, James M. Barry, K. Mark Summers, Keith Clark, Brendan Magone (Eligible Men)

LET IT SNOW

(ARTISTIC LICENSE) Producer/Screenplay, Kipp Marcus; Director, Adam Marcus; Executive Producers, Donny Epstein, Yeeshai Gross; Photography, Ben Weinstein; Designer, Melissa Schrock; Costumes, Bobby Pearce; Editor, Joe Klotz; Line Producer, David Kramer; Casting, Marci Phillips; a Girl and Boy Productions presentation; Dolby; Color; Not rated; 90 minutes; Release date: June 8, 2001. CAST: Kipp Marcus (James Ellis), Alice Dylan (Sarah Milson), Bernadette Peters (Elise Ellis), Henry Simmons (Mitch Jennings), Larry Pine (Wendell Milson), Judith Malina (Grammy), Miriam Shor (Beth), Kristopher Scott Feidel (James—4 years old), Michael Ornstein (Lenny Ellis), Jean-Pierre Lamy (Strange Foreign Man), Wilfredo Medina (Jesus), Anders Hasselblad (Sven), Freeman (Muhammed), Jordan Siwek (James—10 years old), Season Oglesby (Betsy Clotworthy), Jordi Caballero (Jean-Claude), Debra Sullivan (Patricia Milson), Adam Marcus (Facist French Chef), Lou Carbonneau (Aspiring Chef), Sandra Prosper (Jenny), Ann Arvia (Bursar), David Deblinger (Psycho Boss), Kelly Saxon (Bride), Ken Krugman (Groom), Joel Robertson (Kitty-Cat Freak), Christina Ladysh (Crying Woman), Rob Campbell (Small Man), Krista Smith (Regan), Missi Pyle (Ily), Isabel Ruiz de la Prada (Eve), Ned Eisenberg (Carl), Peter Giles (Peter), Bill Migliore (Lonely Guy), Stephen Colbert (Happy Successful Guy), Joanna Bloomer (Sharon), Mary Birdsong (Sneakered Businesswoman), Joseph Siravo (Fredo Andolini), Deborah Langdon (Pat), Susan Lamy (Beverly), Nadya Ginsburg (Store Owner)

DIRTY COP, NO DONUT

(SUB ROSA STUDIOS) Producer/Director/Screenplay/Photography, Tim Ritter; Editor, Steve McNaughton; Music, R. M. Hoopes & Blue; Special Makeup Effects, Bill Cassinelli; Color; Not rated; 80 minutes; Release date: June 15, 2001. CAST: Joel D. Wynkoop (Officer Friendly), Bill Cassinelli (Tommy), Michael Hoffman, Jr. (Arresting Officer), Andrew Gulbrandsen (Abusive Husband), Lindsay Horgan (Abused Wife), Kathleen Ritter (Drunk Driver), Gertina Willemse (Prostitute)

Joel D. Wynkoop in *Dirty Cop, No Donut*
© Sub Rosa Studios

Kipp Marcus in *Let It Snow* © Artistic License

John Hartford in *Down From the Mountain* © Cowboy

DOWN FROM THE MOUNTAIN

(COWBOY BOOKING) Producers, Bob Neuwirth, Frazer Pennebaker; Executive Producers, T-Bone Burnett, Ethan Coen, Joel Coen; Directors, Nick Doob, Chris Hegedus, D. A. Pennebaker; Associate Producer, Rebecca Marshall; Filmed and Recorded by Joan Churchill, Jim Desmond, Nick Doob, Chris Hegedus, Bob Neuwirth, Jehane Noujaim, D. A. Pennebaker, John Paul Pennebaker; Editors, Nick Doob, D. A. Pennebaker; Color; Not rated; 98 minutes; Release date: June 15, 2001. Documentary on the American folk music featured in the film O Brother, Where Art Thou?, with The Cox Family, Fairfield Four, John Hartford, Emmylou Harris, Chris Thomas King, Alison Krauss and Union Station, Colin Linden, The Nashville Bluegrass Band, Tim Blake Nelson, The Peasall Sisters, Ralph Stanley, Gillian Welch and David Rawlings, The Whites, House Band, Terry Bulger, T-Bone Burnett, Ethan Coen, Joel Coen, Hairl Hensley, Holly Hunter.

LIFE & DEBT

(TUFF GONG PICTURES) Producer/Director, Stephanie Black; Photography, Malik Sayeed, Kyle Kibbe, Richard Lannaman, Alex Nepomniaschy; Narration written by Jamaica Kincaid, based on her book A Small Place; Narrator, Belinda Becker; Editor, John Mullen; Color; Not rated; 86 minutes; Release date: June 16, 2001. Documentary on the troubled state of Jamaica's economy.

W.I.S.O.R.

(COWBOY BOOKING) Producers, Michel Negroponte, Jane Weiner; Director/Photography, Michel Negroponte; Screenplay, Gabriel Morgan; Editor, Tom Cross; Music, Elephant Ears (Beo Morales, Carrie Giunta); Animation/Title Sequence, Lisa Crafts; Presented in association with Independent Television Service and ZDF/Arte; Color/black and white; Not rated; 75 minutes; Release date: June 22, 2001. Documentary on the creation of a Welding and Inspection Steam Operations Robot for use under the streets of New York; featuring the voices of Babi Floyd (Robot), George Bartenieff (Ancestral Voice), Gilbert Giles (Newscaster).

CHAIN CAMERA

(COWBOY BOOKING) Producers, Dody Dorn, Eddie Schmidt; Supervising Producer, Nancy Abraham; Executive Producers, Kirby Dick, Sheila Nevins; Director, Kirby Dick; Music, Blake Leyh; Editor, Matt Clarke; from Chain Camera Prods., Cinemax Reel Life; Color; Not rated; 90 minutes; Release date: June 22, 2001. Documentary in which ten students at John Marshall High School in Los Angeles filmed their lives; featuring Ethan Adaggio, Silva Arzunyan, Stephanie De La Garza, Leo Diaz, Timothy Docherty, Amy Hattemer, Cinammon Hunter, Mena Mulat, Victor Naranjo, Jesse Ramon, Manuel Ramirez, Lisa Reyes, Fernando Santillana, Suzana Sburlan, Rosemary To, Shannon Whitmore, Winfred Wilson.

LALEE'S KIN: THE LEGACY OF COTTON

(MAYSLES FILMS) Producers, Susan Fromke, John Hoffman; Executive Producer, Sheila Nevins; Co-Producer, Douglas Graves; Associate Producers, Charles Loxton, Can Parker, Susan Sloan; Directors, Deborah Dickson, Susan Fromke, Albert Maysles; Photography, Albert Maysles; Editor, Deborah Dickson; produced by HBO; Color; 88 minutes; Not rated; Release date: June 22, 2001. Documentary on the legacy of slavery and sharecropping in the Delta, featuring LaLee Wallace, Reggie Barnes.

W.I.S.O.R. © Cowboy

POOTIE TANG

(PARAMOUNT) Producers, David Gale, Ali LeRoi, Cotty Chubb, Chris Rock; Executive Producers, Michael Rotenberg, Dave Becky, Van Toffler, Sean Daniel; Director/Screenplay, Louis C. K.; Photography, Willy Kurant; Designer, Amy Silver; Costumes, Amanda Sanders; Editors, Doug Abel, David Lewis Smith; Co-Producers, Blair Breard, Louis C. K.; Music, QD3, Prince Paul; Casting, Brett Goldstein; Presented in association with MTV Films and Chris Rock Productions; an Alphaville/3 Arts Production in association with HBO Downtown Productions; Dolby; Deluxe color; Rated PG-13; 81 minutes; Release date: June 29, 2001. CAST: Lance Crouther (Pootie Tang), J.B. Smoove (Trucky), Jennifer Coolidge (Ireenie), Reg E. Cathey (Dirty Dee), Robert Vaughn (Dick Lecter), Wanda Sykes (Biggie Shorty), Chris Rock (J.B./Radio DJ/Pootie's Father), Mario Joyner (Lacey), Cathy Trien (Stacy), Dave Attell (Frank), Laura Kightlinger (Anchor Woman), Christopher Wynkoop (Sheriff), Rick Shapiro (Shakey), Qiana Drew, Lorria Richards (Singing Ladies), J. D. Williams (Froggy), Tara Jeffers (Solo Girl Singer), Cole Hawkins (Little Pootie), Andy Richter (Record Executive), Kristen Bell (Record Executive's Daughter), Ray Wills, Robert Trumbull (Board Directors), Jim Earl (Eddie), David Cross (Dennis), Chuck Jeffreys (Bad Bitty), Tammy Faye Starlight, Jodi Michelle Pynn (Dirty Dee Girls), Stacy Renae (Sidewalk Girl), Alem Brhan Sapp (Guitar Player), Joseph Dolphin, Todd Barry (Greasies), Keesha Sharp (Party Girl), Gregory Hahn (Prison Guard), John Glaser (Recording Engineer), William Stephenson (Fast Food Cook), Robin Montague (Screaming Woman), Devon Malik Beckford (Sweet Little Boy), Missy Elliott (Diva), Bryan Hearne (Little Trucky), Ebony Jo-Ann (Pootie's Mother), Michelle Robinson (Jilted Woman), Keenan Shimizu (Big Father), Linda Murrell (Burger Joint Reporter), Michael Broughton, Tony Rhune (Bad Bitty Goons), Andy Duppin, David Lomax (Dirty Dee Goons), Bob Colletti (Gorilla), Bob Costas (Himself)

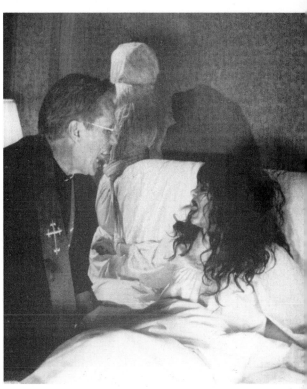

James Woods, Natasha Lyonne in *Scary Movie 2*
© Dimension Films

SCARY MOVIE 2

(DIMENSION) Producer, Eric L. Gold; Executive Producers, Bob Weinstein, Harvey Weinstein, Brad Weston, Peter Schwerin; Director, Keenen Ivory Wayans; Screenplay, Shawn Wayans, Marlon Wayans, Alyson Fouse, Greg Grabianski, Dave Polsky, Michael Anthony Snowden, Craig Wayans; Based on characters created by Shawn Wayans, Marlon Wayans, Buddy Johnson, Phil Beauman, Jason Friedberg, Aaron Seltzer; Co-Executive Producers, Shawn Wayans, Marlon Wayans, Lee R. Mayes, Tony Mark, Lisa Suzanne Blum, Rick Alvarez; Photography, Steven Bernstein; Designer, Cynthia Charette; Editors, Peter Teschner, Richard Pearson; Music Supervisor, Randy Spendlove; Casting, Juel Bestrop, Jeanne McCarthy, Christine Sheaks; a Wayans Bros. Entertainment Production in association with Gold-Miller, Brad Grey Pictures; Dolby; Deluxe color; Rated R; 82 minutes; Release date: July 4, 2001. CAST: Marlon Wayans (Shorty), Shawn Wayans (Ray), Anna Faris (Cindy), Regina Hall (Brenda), Tori Spelling (Alex), Kathleen Robertson (Theo), Andy Richter (Father Harris), Chris Masterson (Buddy), Chris Elliott (Hanson), Tim Curry (The Professor), David Cross (Dwight), Richard Moll (The Ghost), James Woods (Father McFeely), Natasha Lyonne (Megan), Antony Acker, Mark Barrett, Richard Bellos, Suzanne Bianqui, Natale Bosco, Joann Connor, Brad Fisher, Suzanne O'Donnell, Kristi Pearce, Donna Silverberg, Helene Strayer (Exorcist Partygoers), Veronica Cartwright (Mother), Lee R. Mayes (Hip Exorcist Partygoer), Robert Schimmel (Cab Driver), Cordelia Reinhard (Father Harris's Mother), James DeBello (Tommy), Vitamin C (Herself), Matthew Friedman (Bird Voice), Suli McCullough (Clown Voice), Jennifer Curran (Siren), Lester "Beetlejuice" Green (Shorty's Brain)

Chris Rock, J.B. Smoove, Lance Crouther, Mario Joyner in
Pootie Tang © Paramount Pictures

Walter Velasquez, Jamal Mackey in *Off the Hook*
© Dendrobium Films

WAITING

(MANAYUNK PICTURES) Producer, John Stefanic; Director/ Screenplay/Editor, Patrick Hasson; Co-Producer, Tim Kelly; Photography, Michael Pearlman; Designer, Christopher Jones; Costumes, Chante Brooks; Associate Producer, Will Keenan; Casting, Philadephia Casting; from No Head Films; Color; Not rated; 80 minutes; Release date: July 13, 2001. CAST: Will Keenan (Sean), Kerri Kennedy (Lily), Ron Jeremy (Seedy Father), Kurt Knobelsdorf (Trey), Hannah Dalton (Andrea), Lloyd Kaufman (Mr. Janyszek), Andi Rose (Mrs. Janyszek), Bill Robertson (Garrett), David Hallatt (Shamus), Mickey Goldhaber (Elsie), Casey McGinty (Mary Catherine), Harry Philabosian (Nick Broccoletti), Rocco Rosanio (Enrique "Sticky" Porrini), Rodney Grey (Jerry), Bobbi Martino (Kreg), Frank Ferrara (Michael), Don Allen (John), Aida Davis (Shelby), Eileen Marks (Bobbi), Christopher Thompson (Junior), Samuel Reynolds (Bo), Suzanne Smart (Dolly), Steve Lippe (Baby Poo Poo)

DOWNTOWN 81

(ZEITGEIST) a.k.a. *New York Beat Movie*; Producer, Maripol; Director, Edo Bertoglio; Screenplay/Co-Producer, Glenn O'Brien; Executive Producer, Michael Zilkha; Editor, Pamela French; Produced 1981; Color; Not rated; 73 minutes; Release date: July 13, 2001. Documentary looking at a day in the life of artist Jean Michel Basquiat, featuring Eszter Balint, Jean Michel Basquiat, Victor Bockris, Fab Five Reddie Brathwaite, Clem Burke, Marshall Chess, Diego Cortez, August Darnell, Jimmy Destri, Tav Falco, Bradley Field, Fab Five Freddy, Vincent Gallo, Patrick Geoffrois, Giorgio Gomelsky, Debbie Harry, Michael Holman, John Lurie, Compton Maddux, Steve Mass, David McDermott, Daniela Morera, Cookie Mueller, Coati Mundi, Glenn O'Brien, Amos Poe, "Lee" Georges Quinones, Danny Rosen, Lisa Rosen, Anna Schroeder, Walter Sterling, Chris Stein, Betsy Sussler, Marty Thau

OFF THE HOOK

(DENDROBIUM FILMS) Producers, Adam Watstein, Jennifer Lyne; Director/Screenplay, Adam Watstein; Co-Producers/Story, Walter Velasquez, Anthony Young; Photography, Peter Olsen; Music, Lord Finesse, Dinky Bingham, Pos-Neg; Editor, Ron Kalish; Color; Not rated; 103 minutes; Release date: July 6, 2001. CAST: Walter Velasquez (Himself), Jamal Mackey (Lorenzo), L. Vee Anduze (Lorenzo's Mother), Pamela Johnson (Narine), Kim Anthony (Delene), Anthony Young (Himself), Rene Alberta (Record Executive's Wife), Seanny Cash, Phanatic (Neighbors), Trevor David (Fry), Isaac Davis (Slick Teen), Jasmine Francis (Barbara), Aaron Francis (Lord), Austin Francis (Drug Buyer, Big), William Gee (Record Executive), Barbara J. Gibson (Print Shop Worker), Linwood Holder (Bud), Kash'Shay Jones (Little Girl), Oswald "Oz" Longsworth (Drug Dealer), John Nelson (Music Producer, Street), Mizan Nunes (Walter's Mother), Greg Prather (Sty), George Ratchford (Terry), Patreece Randall, Roslyn Tate (Girls at Office), Roland Sands (Charles), Ronald Smith (Music Producer), Nyrand Thomas (Shooter), Deion Velasquez (Little Boy), Antonio Washington (Shooter, Tall), Mitchell Washington (Terror)

INBRED REDNECKS

(SHADOWBOX ENTERPRISES) Producer/Director/Screenplay/ Music, Joshua P. Warren; Color; Not rated; 135 minutes; Release date: July 13, 2001. CAST: Steve Lewis (Monty), Brent Ponder (Billy Bob), Joshua P. Warren (Clovis)

JACKPOT

(SONY PICTURES CLASSICS) Producers/Screenplay, Mark Polish, Michael Polish; Director, Michael Polish; Executive Producers, James Egan, Marlise Karlin; Photography, M. David Mullen; Designer, Michele Montague; Costumes, Bic Owen; Music, Stuart Matthewman; Editor, Shawna Callahan; Dolby; HD 24P Widescreen; Color; Rated R; 96 minutes; Release date: July 27, 2001. CAST: Jon Gries (Sunny Holiday), Garrett Morris (Lester Irving), Adam Baldwin (Mel James), Patrick Bauchau (Santa Claus/Voice of Sevon), Crystal Bernard (Cheryl), Mac Davis (Sammy Bones), Anthony Edwards (Tracy), Daryl Hannah (Bobbi), Peggy Lipton (Janice), Rick Overton (Roland), Rosie O'Grady (Sweet Dreams), Larry W. Hunter (Mini-Mart Clerk), Suzanne Krull (Sneezy Waitress), Dig Wayne (Never My Love), Larry Pennell (Truck Driver), Toni Oswald (Truckstop Waitress), Tia Matza (Vicky), Camillia Clouse (Tangerine), Ashley Cohen, Kelly Cohen (Cheerleaders), David Cannizzaro, Allen Fawcett (Karaoke Jockeys), Ricky Trammell (Candy), Gil Gail, Joe Bays (State Troopers), Chip Godwin (Motel Clerk), Mark Polish (Sad Eyes)

RICHARD THE SECOND

(FARRELL MEDIA) Producer, Joseph Erickson; Executive Producers, Francis P. Rich, Philip Littlehale; Director/Screenplay, John Farrell; Associate Producers, Carol Ann Kando, Ted Arnott; Editor, George Mauro; Music, Liz A. Ficalora, Andrew M. Frazier; Color; Not rated; 93 minutes; Release date: July 27, 2001. CAST: Matte Osian (Richard), Kadina Delejalde (Isabel), Barry Smith (Bolingbroke), Ellen Zachos (Aumerle), Robert F. McCafferty (Northumberland), Daniel Maher (Bushy), Craig Alan Edwards (Green), Frank O'Donnell (Gaunt), David W. Frank (York), Tom Turbiville (Mowbray), Deb Snyder (Queen's Guard), Neil Tadken (Ross), Gary Brenner (Willoughby), Lisa Beth Kovetz (Scroop), Dai Kornberg (Herald), D. J. Kerzner (Gardener), Beth Goldman (Gaunt's Nurse), William Martin (The Keeper)

ALL OVER THE GUY

(LIONS GATE) Producers, Susan Dietz, Dan Bucatinsky, Donnie Land, Juan Mas; Executive Producers, Susan B. Landau, Don Roos; Director, Julie Davis; Screenplay, Dan Bucatinsky; Photography, Goran Pavicevic; Designer, Fanae Aaron; Costumes, Peter Mitchell; Music, Peter Stuart, Andrew Williams; Editors, Glenn Garland, Mary Morrissey; Casting, Patrick Rush, Sharon Klein; a Susan Dietz/Donnie Land production; Color; Rated R; 92 minutes; Release date: August 10, 2001. CAST: Dan Bucatinsky (Eli), Richard Ruccolo (Tom), Adam Goldberg (Brett), Sasha Alexander (Jackie Samantha Gold), Christina Ricci (Rayna), Lisa Kudrow (Marie), Doris Roberts (Esther), Tony Abatemarco (David), Joanna Kerns (Lydia), Andrea Martin (Ellen), Nicholas Surovy (Jim), Bev Land (Mitch), Michael Harris (Gary), Julie Claire (Lizz), Thea Mann (Donna), Nicole Tocantins (Rachael), Christian Gann (Stripper), Matthew Poage (Bartender), Ben Foreman (Young Eli), Sydney Foreman (Young Rayna), Blaise Garza (Young Tom), Caroline Hope Williams (Waitress)

THE TURNANDOT PROJECT

(ZEITGEIST) Producer, Margaret Smilov; Executive Producers, Walter Scheuer, Margaret Smilov; Director, Allan Miller; Photography, Tom Hurwitz; Music, Giacomo Puccini; Editors, Donald Klocek, Allan Miller; a co-production of Alternate Currents, EroArts Entertainment and The Four Oaks Foundation; Color; Not rated; 84 minutes; Release date: August 10, 2001. Documentary about the staging of Puccini's opera Turnandot in Beijing's Forbidden City in 1997, featuring Lando Bartolini, Barbara Hendricks, Zubin Mehta, Sharon Sweet, Zhang Yimou.

HAMLET

(COWBOY BOOKING) Producers, Mary Frances Budig, Jonathan Filley, Campbell Scott; Directors/Adaptation, Campbell Scott, Eric Simonson; Based on the play by William Shakespeare; Co-Producer, Margo Myers; Photography, Dan Gillham; Designer, Chris Shriver; Costumes, Michael Krass; Editor, Andy Keir; Music, Gary DeMichele; Associate Producer,

Adam Baldwin, Garrett Morris, Jon Gries in *Jackpot*
© Sony Pictures Entertainment

Adam Goldberg, Dan Bucatinsky in *All Over the Guy* © Lions Gate Films

Campbell Scott in *Hamlet* © Cowboy

Rebecca Morton; a Hallmark Entertainment presentation of a Spare Room production; Technicolor; Not rated; 178 minutes; Release date: August 17, 2001. CAST: Blair Brown (Gertrude), Roscoe Lee Browne (Polonius), Lisa Gay Hamilton (Ophelia), Campbell Scott (Hamlet), Jamey Sheridan (Claudius), Marcus Giamatti (Guildenstern), John Benjamin Hickey (Horatio), Byron Jennings (Ghost/Player King), Michael Imperioli (Rosencrantz), Denis O'Hare (Osric), Dan Moran (Grave Digger), Sam Robards (Fortinbras), Roger Guenveur Smith (Laertes), Bill Buell (Bernardo), David DeBesse (Francisco), John Campion (Marcellus), Lewis Arlt (Voltemand), Christopher Even Welch (Reynaldo), Leon Addison Brown (Third Player), Lynn Hawley (Player Queen), Matt Malloy (Captain), Robert Simonton (King's Attendant), Elisa Hurt (Queen's Attendant), Eric Simonson (Second Grave Digger), Peter McRobbie (Priest), Ryan Carey (British Ambassador), Clark Carmichael, Jillian Crane, Ramon de Ocampo (Players), Gary DeMichele (Pianist), Peck Allmond, Steve Berger (Musicians)

Jan Wiener in *Fighter* © First Run Features

Jake Gyllenhaal, Danny Trejo in *Bubble Boy*
© Touchstone Pictures

FIGHTER

(FIRST RUN) Producers, Amir Bar-Lev, Jonathan Crosby, Alex Mamlet; Executive Producer, Peter Broderick; Director/Screenplay/Editor, Amir Bar-Lev; Photography, David Collier, Gary Griffin, Jay Danner McDonald, Justin Schein; Music Supervisors, Jeff Daniel, Gillian Melris; a presentation of New Wave Films; Color; Not rated; 91 minutes; Release date: August 24, 2001. Documentary on two European Jews who lived through World War II, featuring Jan Weiner and Arnost Lustig.

CUPID'S MISTAKE

(PHAEDRA CINEMA) Producers, Young Man Kang, Gregory Hatanaka, Steve Shine; Director/Screenplay, Young Man Kang; Photography, Doo H. Lee; Editor, Bryan Kim; Music, Oliver Lyon; Color; Not rated; 70 minutes; Release date: August 24, 2001. CAST: Susan Petry (Susan), Toya Cho (Toya), Everado Gil (Gil), Ken Yasuda (Ken), Kingston Osagie (Kingston), Young Man Kang (Young)

BUBBLE BOY

(TOUCHSTONE) Producer, Beau Flynn; Executive Producer, Eric McLeod; Director, Blair Hayes; Screenplay, Cinco Paul, Ken Daurio; Photography, Jerzy Zielinski; Designer, Barry Robison; Costumes, Christopher Lawrence; Editor, Pamela Martin; Music, John Ottman; Music Supervisor, John Houlihan; Special Character Effects Designers and Creators, Alec Gillis, Tom Woodruff, Jr.; Dolby; Casting, John Papsidera; a Bandeira production; Dolby; Panavision; Technicolor; Rated PG-13; 84 minutes; Release date: August 24, 2001. CAST: Jake Gyllenhaal (Jimmy Livingston), Swoosie Kurtz (Mrs. Livingston), Marley Shelton (Chloe), Danny Trejo (Slim), John Carroll Lynch (Mr. Lvingston), Verne Troyer (Dr. Phreak), Dave Sheridan (Mark), Brian George (Pushpak), Patrick Cranshaw (Pappy/Pippy), Stephen Spinella (Chicken Man), Ever Carradine (Mark's Sister), Geoffrey Arend (Flipper Boy), Beetlejuice (Li'l Zip), Matthew McGrory (Human Sasquatch), Bonnie Morgan (Rubber Woman), Jason Sklar (Shlomo), Randy Sklar (Dawn), Fabio (Gil), Ping Wu (Emcee), Zach Galifianakis (Bus Stop Man), Boti Ann Bliss (Cashier), Pablo Schreiber, Brian Gattas, Cinco Paul, Ken Daurio, Malik Toure, Leo Fitzpatrick, J. P. Coe, R. J. Durell, Brian Friedman (Todds), Arden Myrin, Merle Kennedy, Shulie Cowen, Alicia Gilley, Mandy Moore (Lorraines), Mitch Holleman (Jimmy—4 years old), Alex Black (Jimmy—8 years old), Tony Black (Jimmy—10 years old), Robert Bailey, Jr., Oliver A. Kindred, Brandon Depaul (Neighborhood Boys), Steven Van Wormer (Mark's Friend), E. J. Callahan, Charlie Dell, Michael Loprete, Charles Noland, Emily Stewart, Pattie Tierce (Perris Townies), Gary Bullock (Perris Sheriff), Susan Hawk (Perris Waitress), Steven Lawrence (Ice Cream Boy), Raja Fenske (Indian Boy), Cleo King (Minister), Robert Lasardo (Skinny Biker), Jorge Cottini (Big Biker), Madajah McCullum O'Hearn (Red Hot), Stacy Keibler (Working Girl)

Jesse Bradford in *Speedway Junky* © Regent Entertainment

SPEEDWAY JUNKY

(REGENT ENTERTAINMENT) Producers, Rodney Omanoff, Randall Emmett, George Furla, Jeff Rice; Executive Producers, Gus Van Sant, Tony Cataldo, Cliff Brune; Director/Screenplay, Nickolas Perry; Photography, Steve Adcock; Designer, Candi Guterres; Music, Stan Ridgway; Editor, Craig A. Colton; Casting, Aaron Griffith; a Miracle Entertainment presentation of a Rodney Omanoff/Randall Emmett production; Dolby; Color; Rated R; 104 minutes; Release date: August 31, 2001. CAST: Jesse Bradford (Johnny), Jordan Brower (Eric), Jonathan Taylor Thomas (Steve), Daryl Hannah (Veronica), Brian Stark (Pez Boy), Justin Urich (Scooby), Erik Alexander Gavica (J. T.), Herbie Ade (Mickey), John Jett (Trish), Patsy Kensit (Donna), Nafisah Tahirah Sayyed (Oreo), Shevonne Durkin (Bridget), Warren G. (Brentley Shaw), Sam Menning (Homeless Man), Susan Gayle Clay (Melanie), Adrienne Frantz (Kelley), Milo Ventimigilia (Travis), Timothy McNeil (Russel), Tiffani-Amber Thiessen (Wilma Price), Faith McDevitt (Vera), Del Monroe (Old Timer), Steve Schirripa (Security Guard), Cynthia Palmer (Teller), Patrick Renna (Bud)

SOUL SURVIVORS

(ARTISAN) Producers, Neal H. Moritz, Stokley Chaffin; Executive Producers, Michele Weisler, Jonathan Shestack; Director/Screenplay, Steve Carpenter; Photography, Fred Murphy; Designer, Larry Fulton; Costumes, Denise Wingate; Music, Daniel Licht; Editors, Janice Hampton, Todd Ramsay; Special Effects, John Milinac; a Neal H. Moritz production; Dolby; Deluxe color; Rated PG-13; 84 minutes; Release date: September 7, 2001. CAST: Casey Affleck (Sean), Wes Bentley (Matt), Eliza Dushku (Annabel), Angela Featherstone (Raven), Melissa Sagemiller (Cassie), Luke Wilson (Father Jude), Allen Hamilton (Dr. Haverston), Ken Moreno (Hideous Dancer), Carl Paoli (Deathmask), Barbara Robertson (Margaret), Richard Pickren (Ben), Candace Kaye Kroslak (Cool Blonde), Ryan Kitley (Young Cop), Rick Snyder (Father McManus), Danny Goldberg, Scott Benjaminson (Campus Cops), T. J. Jagodowski (ER Doctor), Christine Mary Dunford (ER Nurse), Amy Farrington (ER Doctor, Midtown), Lily Mojekwu (ER Nurse, Midtown), Alex Schlegel,

Sam Schlegel (Jump Rope Twins), Michael Sassone (Minister), Lusia Strus (Stern Nurse), Adam Joyce (Student), Kelli Nonnemacher (Coed #1), Jaclyn Barker, Susan Wiltrakis (Halloween Children), Alberto J. Arias, Laurie Canning, Tina Cannon, Shannon Elliot, Nicholas Foote, James Gregg, Devert Hickman, Kelly Tonge Hill, Trisha Lee, Marcellina Marshall, Stephanie Martinez, Elaine McLaurin, Shana Montanez, Eddy Ocampo, Christopher Perricelli, Robyn M. Williams (Dancers)

Wes Bentley, Eliza Dushku in *Soul Survivors*
© Artisan Entertainment

Jordan Maldonado in Bounce: *Behind the Velvet Rope*
© Artistic License Films

BOUNCE: BEHIND THE VELVET ROPE

(ARTISTIC LICENSE) Producers, Steven Cantor, Daniel Laikind; Director/Screenplay, Steven Cantor; Music, Samantha Maloney; a Stick Figure production, from HBO; Color; Not rated; 77 minutes; Release date: September 7, 2001. Documentary on nightclub bouncers and doormen, featuring Jordan Maldonado, Alan Crosley, Mike and Frank DeMaio, Homer "Omar" Cook, Lenny "The Guv'nor" McLean, Terence "The Black Prince" Buckley.

NEW PORT SOUTH

(TOUCHSTONE) Producer, Billy Higgins; Executive Producer, John Hughes; Director, Kyle Cooper; Screenplay/Co-Producer, James Hughes; Photography, Juan Ruiz-Anchia; Designer, Maher Ahmad; Editor, Lawrence Jordan; Costumes, Melinda Eshelman; Music, Telefon Tel Aviv, Scott Herren, John Hughes III, Richard Devine; Casting, Billy Hopkins, Suzanne Smith, Kerry Barden; Distributed by Buena Vista; Dolby; Color; Rated PG-13; 95 minutes; Release date: September 7, 2001. CAST: Blake Shields (Maddox), Will Estes (Chris), Kevin Christy (Clip), Melissa George (Amanda), Brad Eric Johnson (Knox), Gabriel Mann (Wilson), Todd Field (Walsh), Nick Sandow (Armstrong), Raymond Barry (Edwards), Lawrence MacGowan (Lawson), Mike Shannon (Stanton), Rebekah Louise Smith (McAmmond), Janelle Snow (Foster), Chad Christ (Morehouse), Dahlia Salem (Kameron), Dennis Williams (Hatchet), Hal Dion (Reporter Garland), Angela Sue Egan (Kassidy #1), Martha Heather Egan (Kassidy #2), Nicholas Downard (Student, Gym), Michael Stahl David (Rossetti), Casey Zeman (Layton), Scott MacFarland (Angry Student), Stephnie Weir (Librarian), Rusty DeWees (School Janitor), Doug James (Anchor Man), Jenniffer Weigel (Anchor Woman), David Engel (Cafeteria Monitor), Jay Kiecolt Wahl (Keith), Marjorie Molitor (School Board Member)

KILL ME LATER

(7TH ART) Producers, Dana Lustig, Ram Bergman, Carole Curb Nemoy, Mike Nemoy; Executive Producer, Federico Pignatelli; Director, Dan Lustig; Screenplay, Annette Goliti Gutierrez; Story, Dana Lustig, Annette Goliti Gutierrez; Photography, David Ferrara; Designer, Tony Devenyi; Editor, Gabriel Wrye; Music, Tal Bergman, Renato Nero; Casting, Mary Margiotta, Karen Margiotta; a Curb Entertainment and Amazon Film Prods. presentation of a Bergman Lustig production; FotoKem color; Not rated; 105 minutes; Release date: September 7, 2001. CAST: Selma Blair (Shawn Holloway), Max Beesley (Charlie Anders), O'Neal Compton (Agent McGinley), Lochlyn Munro (Agent Reed), D. W. Moffett (Matthew Richmond), Brendan Fehr (Billy), Tom Heaton (Jason), David Adams (Ara), Alex Zahara (Officer Larry), Keegan Tracy (Keegan Connor Tracy), Pam Hyatt (Lucy), Stacy Fair (Elizabeth Richmond), Marcel Maillard (Lyle Holloway), Keith Gordey (Elevator Cop), Dana Lustig (Suzan Holloway), Sarah Chalke (Linda), Mecca Menard (Molly), Jillian Fargey, Roger Haskett (Bank Customers), Edward Diaz (Valet), Bethoe Shirkoff (Mrs. Sabatini), Juan Gómez, Octavio Carillo, Mario Valdez (Mariachis), Brett Kelly (Kid), Chris Wild (City Park Policeman), Jeffrey Seymour (Officer in Charge), Robert Marshall (Draftsman)

Blake Shields, Melissa George, Kevin Christy, Will Estes in *New Port South* © Touchstone Pictures

Rudolf Slansky in *A Trial in Prague* © Cinema Guild

A TRIAL IN PRAGUE

(CINEMA GUILD) Producers, Zuzana Justman, Jiri Jezek, Zuzana Cervenkova, David Charap; Director/Screenplay, Zuzana Justman; Photography, Miro Gabor, Marek Jicha; Editor, David Charap; Music, Peter Fish; a Pick Production; Color; Not rated; 83 minutes; Release date: September 14, 2001. Documentary on the 1952 trial of fourteen prominent Czechoslovakian communists tried for high treason and espionage.

HAIKU TUNNEL

(SONY PICTURES CLASSICS) Producers, Brian Benson, Jacob Kornbluth, Josh Kornbluth; Executive Producer, David R. Fuchs; Directors, Jacob Kornbluth, Josh Kornbluth; Screenplay, Josh Kornbluth, Jacob Kornbluth, John Bellucci; Photography, Don Matthew Smith; Designer, Chris Farmer; Editor, Robin Lee; Costumes, Chris Aysta; Music, Marco d'Ambrosio; Casting, Nancy Hayes; a Pandemonium production of a Hello Hooker Productions/Mike's Movies/B9 Films presentation; Dolby; Color; Rated R; 90 minutes; Release date: September 14, 2001. Josh Kornbluth (Himself), Warren Keith (Bob Shelby), Helen Shumaker (Marlina D'Amore), Amy Resnick (Mindy), Brian Thorstenson (Clifford), June Lomena (DaVonne), Harry Shearer (Orientation Leader), Joshua Raoul Brody (System Administrator), Sarah Overman (Julie Faustino), Leah Alperin, Jacob Kornbluth, Stephen Muller, Linda Norton (Temps), Joanna Evangelista (Caryl), Jennifer Laske (Helen the Ex-Girlfriend), Patricia Scanlon (Helen the Ex-Secretary), Joe Bellan (Jimmy the Mail Clerk), Michael X. Sommers (Crack Attorney), Jodean Lawrence (Denise the Receptionist), Adele Proom (Josh's Mom), Tracy O'Neal Heffernan (Lillian), Steve Klinger (Dashiell), Jessica Hird (Ann Dickerson), Margo Hall (Danielle), John Bellucci (Spastic Dancing Nerd), Brian Keith Russell (Security Guard), Baron Bruno (Tim Barnes), David Fine (Oldest Bike Messenger), Todd Hickey (Protester)

Helen Shumaker, Josh Kornbluth in *Haiku Tunnel*
© Sony Pictures Entertainment

CHILDREN UNDERGROUND

(HBO/CINEMAX) Producer/Director, Edet Belzberg; Executive Producer, Sheilah Kitt McKinnon; Co-Executive Producer, Michel Negroponte; Co-Producers, Jonathan Oppenheim, Alan Oxman; Photography, Wolfgang Held; Editor, Jonathan Oppenheim; HBO Executive Producer, Sheila Nevins; HBO Supervising Producer, Nancy Abraham; Music, Joel Goodman; Presented in association with Red Horse Inc. and Childhope International; Color; Not rated; 108 minutes; Release date: September 19, 2001. Documentary on the street children of Romania, featuring Mihai, Marian, Ana, Cristina, and Macarena.

IN SEARCH OF PEACE, PART 1, 1948–1967

(7TH ART) Producers, Rabbi Marvin Hier, Richard Trank; Director, Richard Trank; Screenplay, Richard Trank, Martin Gilbert, Rabbi Marvin Hier; Photography, Carl Bartels, Don Lenzer, Jeffrey Victor; Editors, Edgar

Mihai in *Children Underground* © HBO

Da Brat, Mariah Carey in *Glitter*
© Twentieth Century Fox/Columbia

Burcksen, Lorraine Salk; Music, Lee Holdridge; Color; Not rated; 113 minutes; Release date: September 21, 2001. Documentary on the first two decades of the state of Israel, featuring the voices of Michael Douglas (narrator), Edward Asner, Anne Bancroft, Richard Dreyfuss, Miriam Margolyes, Michael York.

GLITTER

(20TH CENTURY FOX/COLUMBIA) Producer, Laurence Mark; Director, Vondie Curtis Hall; Screenplay, Kate Lanier; Story, Cheryl L. West; Photography, Geoffrey Simpson; Designer, Dan Bishop; Costumes, Joseph G. Aulisi; Editor, Jeff Freeman; Music, Terence Blanchard; Music Supervisor, Robin Urdang; Additional Music, Jimmy Jam, Terry Lewis, Big Jim Wright; Casting, Victoria Thomas; a Maroon Entertainment Production in association with Laurence Mark Productions; Dolby; Super 35 Widescreen; Deluxe color; Rated PG-13; 104 minutes; Release date: September 21, 2001. CAST: Mariah Carey (Billie Frank), Max Beesley (Jonathan Dice), Da Brat (Louise), Tia Texada (Roxanne), Valarie Pettiford (Lillian Frank), Ann Magnuson (Kelly), Terrence Howard (Timothy Walker), Dorian Harewood (Guy Richardson), Grant Nickalls (Jack Bridges), Eric Benét (Rafael), Padma Lakshmi (Sylk), Don Ackerman (Peter), Ed Sahely (Francois), Carmen Wong (Rose), James Allodi (Video Director), Damon D'Olivera (Movie Producer), Mauricio Rodas (Chico), Marcia Bennett (Caseworker), Abdul Shawish (Iranian Cabbie), Chris Tessaro (Stage Manager), Isabel Gomes (Young Billie), Courtnie Beceiro (Young Roxanne), Lindsey Pickering (Young Louise), Kim Roberts (Mrs. Wilson), Bill Sage (Billie's Father), Tim Burd (Engineer), Brian Heighton, Matthew Olver, Colleen Bennett, JC Kenny, Claire Burton (Photographers), Jamia Eaton (Sheba), Emanuel Arruda (Martin), Kyle Thrash (Young Boy), Sonya Hensley (Homeless Woman), Derek Ritschel (Production Assistant), Kevin Keith (B-Boy), Novie Edwards (B-Girl), Dan Chameroy (Gary), Anthony Ashbee (Maitre d'), Tanya Kim (News Reporter), Jeni Anderson (Club Girl), Jose Arias (Manny), Michael Egan (Phone Booth Boy), Judi Mark (Demo Tape Woman), Kate McNeil (Karen Diana), Craig-Radioman (Radioman Street Bum), Neisha Folkes (Choreographer), Mark Mclean, Lionel Alston Williams, John T. Davis (Lillian's Band), Rich Brown, Richard Brown (Dice's Band), Dan Sutcliffe, Mike Jackson, Amy Todd, Michelle Carbery (Billie's Dancers), Craig Estrella, Carlos M. Morgan, Pharaoh Lambert, Andrew Craig, Joe Heslip, Simon Craig, Joel Joseph (Billie's Band), David Meinke, Martin Samuel, Rhett George, Louis Paquette (Music Video Dancers), Takeshi Yamamoto, Corrie Daniel, Paul Cantuba, Tony Thompson (Breakdancers)

GO TIGERS!

(IFC FILMS) Producers, Sidney Sherman, Kenneth A. Carlson; Executive Producer, Todd Robinson; Director/Screenplay, Kenneth A. Carlson; Photography, Curt Apduhan; Editor, Jeff Werner; Music, Randy Miller; Original Songs, Katrina Carlson, Ron Alan Cohen; Presented in association with Triple Play; Dolby; Color; Rated R; 102 minutes; Release date: September 21, 2001. Documentary on the dominance of football in the blue-collar town of Massillon, Ohio.

Go Tigers!
© IFC Films

ROCKY ROAD

(INTEGRATED PRODS.) Producer, Laura Caulfield; Co-Producer, Charles Arthur Berg; Director/Screenplay, Patrick Cunningham; Photography, David Trulli; Music, Vincent Callano; Editor, Adam P. Scott; Casting, Akua Campanella, Patrick Cunningham; Release date: September 21, 2001. CAST: Will Wallace (John Johnson), Nicole A. Smith (Talia Jones), Wolf Muser (Bill Johnson), Bob Wisdom (Michael Jones), Natasha Pearce (Tina Jones), Valeri Ross (Yvonne Jones), Bryan Handy (Dwayne Jones), Darryl Dismond (Rodney), James T. Locascio (Paul), Royce Herron (Jane Johnson), Michelle Merserau (Victoria), Reshidatu Foster (Debbie), Nina Womack (Edwina), J. R. Starr (Granddaddy James), Ravell Dameron (Grandma Edith), Sarah Scott Davis (Celia), Bernadette L. Clarke (Rene), Chris Brea, Geoff Cunningham (Paramedics), George Janeck (Byron), Daniel Southworth (James), Yolley DeBold (Cousin Sophie), Darryl Matthews (Gangster), Darrow Igus (Street Man), Alexa Motley (Fundraiser), Elizabeth Wilson (Grandma Louise), Laura A. Caulfield (Secretary), Dee Bryant (Policeman)

GOD, SEX & APPLE PIE

(CENTAUR PRODS.) Producers, Jerome Courshon, Paul Leaf; Executive Producers, Michelle James, Scott Vandiver, Phil Botana; Director, Paul Leaf; Screenplay, Jerome Courshon; Photography, Scott E. Steele; Designer, Colleen Devine; Costumes, Michelle Robinson; Editor, Karen Rasch; Music, John Boegehold; Presented in association with Brimstone Entertainment; Dolby; Color; Rated R; 97 minutes; Release date: September 21, 2001. CAST: Greg Wrangler (Tim), Penelope Crabtree (Bobbie), Mark Porro (Alex), Katy Kurtzman (Maggie), Jerome Courshon (Trent), Andrea Leithe (Debi), Steve Rifkin (Drew), Maria McCann (Tina), Phil Palisoul (Ron), Justina Denney (Cassandra), Lea Hastings (Morgan Tracer), Stephen Polk (Charles Blakely), Teresa Gilmore (Jonelle), Julie Rea (Ellen), Don Ridley (Fisherman)

SORORITY GIRLS' REVENGE

(IBEX PRODS.) Producer/Director/Screenplay, Keith Warn; Photography, Joel Deutsch; Designer, Ernest Hedge; Music, Abnormals; Editors, Chris Gosch, Encar Santos; FotoKem color; Rated R; 90 minutes; Release date: September 21, 2001. CAST: Stacy Oliver, Kevin Wortman, Kelly Kraegel, Tisha Brown, Nicole Holmes, Nikki Trexler, Keith Warn

MEGIDDO

(8X ENTERTAINMENT) Producers, Matthew Crouch, Lawrence Mortorff, Richard J. Cook; Executive Producer, Paul Crouch; Director, Brian Trenchard-Smith; Screenplay, John Fasano, Stephan Blinn; Photography, Bert Dunk; Designer, Charlie Daboub; Costumes, Shawn Holly Cookson; Co-Producers, Gary M. Bettman, Michael York; Music, Peter Bernstein; Editor, John Lafferty; Visual Effects, Rob Bredow; Casting, Jean Scoccimarro; a TBN Films presentation of a Gener8xion Entertainment production; Dolby; FotoKem color; Rated PG-13; 104 minutes; Release date: September 21, 2001. CAST: Michael York (Stone Alexander), Michael Biehn (David Alexander), Diane Venora (Gabriella Francini), R.

Penelope Crabtree, Greg Wrangler in *God, Sex & Apple Pie* © Centaur Productions

Lee Ermey (President Richard Benson), Udo Kier (The Guardian), Franco Nero (Gen. Francini), Jim Metzler (Breckenridge), Noah Huntley (Stone—21 years old), Michael Paul Chan (Chinese Premier), Gil Colon (Col. Rick Howard), David Hedison (Daniel Alexander), Elisa Scialpi (Gabriella—18 years old), Chad Michael Murray (David—16 years old), Eduardo Yanez (Gen. Garcia), Tony Amendola (Father Tirmaco), Forbes Riley (Dana Kincaid), Gavin Fink (Stone—6 years old)

Michael Biehn, Michael York in *Megiddo* © 8x Entertainment

Donnie Wahlberg, Robert Forster in *Diamond Men*
© Panorama Entertainment

DIAMOND MEN

(PANORAMA ENTERTAINMENT) Producer/Director/Screenplay, Daniel M. Cohen; Executive Producers, Robert E. Field, Robert Forster; Photography, John Huneck; Designer, Randal P. Earnest; Editor/Co-Producer, Rick Derby; Line Producer, Linda Lester; Music, Garrett Parks; a DMC Films in association with Sidekick Entertainment and Shiprock Productions; Dolby; Color; Not rated; 100 minutes; Release date: September 28, 2001. CAST: Robert Forster (Eddie Miller), Donnie Wahlberg (Bobby Walker), Bess Armstrong (Katie Harnish), Jasmine Guy (Tina), George Coe (Tip Rountree), Jeff Gendelman (Brad), Douglas Allen Johnson (John Lugwig), Kristen Minter (Cherry), Nikki Fritz (Fran), Shannah Laumeister (Amber), Kate Rimmer (Priscilla), Paul Price (Carl), Bruce Smirnoff (Executive), Kate Forster (Customer), Jana Ferner (Emily), Miriam Elizabeth Hyde (Sharon), Irving Simons (Jeweler), Glenn Phillips (Mick), Paul Hewitt (Fess), Leonard Kelly Young (Brennan), James Burns (Detective), Al Vicente (Cab Driver)

A.J. Buckley, Dante Basco, Ryan Browning, Derek Hamilton in *Extreme Days* © Provence Entretainment

Frank Rogala in *Won't Anybody Listen* © 7th Art

EXTREME DAYS

(PROVIDENCE) Producers, Cindy Bond, Betsy Chasse; Executive Producers, Howard Kazanjian, Craig C. Darian; Director, Eric Hannah; Screenplay, Eric Hannah, Craig Detweiler; Photography, Michael Wojciechowski; Designer, Dan Vivianco; Co-Producer, Alexander H. Gayner; Editor, Andrew Eisen; Music, Klaus Badelt; Line Producer, Scott Altomare; Casting, Heather Johnstone; a Truth Soul Armor presentation of a Norann Entertainment & Tricor Entertainment production; Dolby; Color; Rated PG; minutes; Release date: September 28, 2001. CAST: Dante Basco (Corey), Ryan Browning (Brian), A. J. Buckley (Will), Derek Hamilton (Matt), Cassidy Rae (Jessie), Chao Li Chi (Grandpa G), Virginia Montero (Grandma G), Dylan Bond (Young Brian), Scott Fisher (Young Will), Cameron Clark (Young Matt), Daniel Miranda (Young Corey), Ashlee Bond (Amanda), Jeff Enden (Baboo), John Rosenfeld (Monkey Wrench), Holly McClure (Flight Attendant), Sylva Cox (Waitress), Lee Ann Edwards (Mrs. Davidson), Josh Aver, Jesse Craig, Aaron Tosti, David Tosti (PAX217), Gregory Mark, Scott Hannah, Richard Brown, Scott Brinson (Karate Gang), Scott Lewis, Kory Lewis, Kelsy Lewis (Grandpa G Gang)

WON'T ANYBODY LISTEN

(7TH ART) Producer/Director, Dov Kelemer; Executive Producers, Frank Rogala, Vince Rogala; Photography, Richard King, Dominic Pereira; Editor, Richard King; a Gestating Pictures production with Integrated Entertainment; Release date: September 28, 2001. Documentary following the attempt of South California rock band NC-17 to make it in the music business, featuring Art Aviles, Robert Aviles, Roxanne Aviles, Lori Graves-Bartolini, Mark Billes, Hugo Burnham, Robin Canada, C. Tucker Cheadle, Keith Dean, Bob Diamond, Bruce Duff, Len Fagen, Lonn Friend, Danny Goodwin, Rich Heaton, Nina Heller, Chuck Hohn, Lance Hubp, Jeff Jampo, Tom Kidd, Chris Martin, Lena Michaels, Ron Perron, Doug Priestap, Frank Rogala, Rose Rogala, Vince Rogala, Billy Rose, Barry Squire, Katherine Turman, Jim Washburn.

Peter Johnson in *Chop Suey* © Zeitgeist

CHOP SUEY

(ZEITGEIST) Executive Producer, Nan Bush; Director, Bruce Weber; Screenplay, Bruce Weber, Maribeth Edwards; Photography, Lance Accord, Douglas Cooper, Jim Fealy; Editor, Angelo Corrao; Music, John Leftwich; Associate Producer, Leonard John Bruno; Dolby; Black and white/color; Not rated; 98 minutes; Release date: October 5, 2001. Photographer/filmmaker Bruce Weber's collage of his personal interests, made for model Peter Johnson; featuring Peter Johnson, Frances Faye, the Fletcher Family, the Gracie Family, Robert Mitchum, Teri Shepherd, Sir Wilfred Thesiger, Jan-Michael Vincent, Diana Vreeland, Hoots the Poodle.

GRATEFUL DAWG

(SONY CLASSICS) Producer/Director, Gillian Grisman; Executive Producers, Craig Miller, David Grisman; Editor, Josh Baron; Associate Producers, John Brittingham, Justin Kreutzmann, Pamela K; Dolby; Color; Rated PG-13; 81 minutes; Release date: October 5, 2001. Filmmaker Gillian Grisman's documentary on the friendship between Grateful Dead guitarist Jerry Garcia and her musician father David Grisman; featuring Jerry Garcia, David Grisman, Joe Craven, Jim Kerwin, Rob Bleetstein, Vassar Clements, Dave Dennison, Bela Fleck, Deborah Koons Garcia, John Goddard, Monroe Grisman, Pamela Grisman, Sam Grisman, Justin Kreutzmann, Dexter Johnson, Richard Loren, Ronnie McCoury, Craig Miller, Steve Parish, Peter Rowan, Eric Thompson, Lawrence Waltman.

Jerry Garcia, David Grisman in *Grateful Dawg* © Sony Pictures Entertainment

THE LEARNING CURVE

(MOTION PICTURE CORPORATION OF AMERICA) Producers, Oscar Delgado, Carey Westberg, Puntip Limrungroj; Executive Producers, Michael Hofstein, Daarek Szeto, Margaret M. Quitter; Director/Screenplay, Eric Schwab; Photography, Michael Hofstein; Designer, Nya Patrinos; Editor, Adam C. Frank; Music Supervisor, Ted Lowe; Casting, Susan Bluestein; Color; Rated R; 110 minutes; Release date: October 5, 2001. CAST: Carmine Giovinazzo (Paul Cleveland), Monet Mazur (Georgia), Vincent Ventresca (Marshal), Steven Bauer (York), Majandra Delfino (Ashley), Norbert Weisser (Usher), Tim Ransom (Steven), Rod Roesser (Norman), James Eckhouse (Mr. Stevens), Allan Wasserman (Lou), Harry Hutchinson (Barry), Dennis Blake (Hot Dog Server), Phil Nee (Businessman), Kei Rowan-Young (Sandy), Greg Lauren (Todd), Marisa Parker (Receptionist), Noeller Forbes (Secretary), Connie Blankenship (Assistant), Danny Strauss (Quentin), Helen Eigenberg (Cashier), Bayani Ison (Bouncer), Justine E. Boyriven (Hostess), Jarod Carey (Bartender), Stephen Burleigh (Councilman Sherman), Jack Laufer (Councilman Reynolds), Michael Horton (Councilman Nolan), Iheanyi Clemons, Ken Lawson (Beverly Hills Police), Richard Erdman (Ralph), Evan Mackenzie (Walter), Brian Simpson (Stretch), Chris Antonucci (Hip Friend), Mark Newman (Agent Newman), Rita Minor (Agent Minor), Carl Mueller, Marian Green, Phillip Tan (Federal Agents), Milana (Bennett), James McAuley (Policeman)

Carmine Giovinazzo, Vincent Ventresca, Monet Mazur in *The Learning Curve* © MoPic Corp. of America

Zena Grey, Alex D. Linz, Josh Peck in *Max Keeble's Big Move* © Disney Enterprises, Inc.

MAX KEEBLE'S BIG MOVE

(WALT DISNEY PICTURES) Producer, Mike Karz; Executive Producer, Guy Riedel; Director, Tim Hill; Screenplay, Jonathan Bernstein, Mark Blackwell, James Greer; Story, David Watts, Jonathan Bernstein, Mark Blackwell, James Greer; Co-Producers, Raymond C. Reed, Russell Hollander; Photography, Arthur Albert; Designer, Vincent Jefferds; Editors, Tony Lombardo, Peck Prior; Costumes, Susan Matheson; Music, Michael Wandmacher; Casting, Victoria Burrows, Scot Boland; a Kaz Entertainment production; Dolby; Technicolor; Rated PG; 86 minutes; Release date: October 5, 2001. CAST: Alex D. Linz (Max Keeble), Larry Miller (Jindraike), Jamie Kennedy (Evil Ice Cream Man), Zena Grey (Megan), Josh Peck (Robe), Nora Dunn (Lily Keeble), Robert Carradine (Don Keeble), Clifton Davis (Knebworth), Amy Hill (Mrs. Rangoon), Noel Fisher (Troy McGinty), Orlando Brown (Dobbs), Amber Valletta (Ms. Dingman), Justin Berfield (Caption Writer), Veronica Alicino (Mrs. Talia, Social Studies Teacher), Brooke Anne Smith (Jenna), Greg Lewis (Janitor), Chely Wright (Mrs. Styles, Homeroom Teacher), Jonathan Osser (Worried Kid), Cory Hodges (Yearbook Photographer), Kyle Sullivan (Techie Kid), Jordan Mahome (Marley), Myra (Chelsea), Sarah Rush (Ms. Lane, School Nurse), Chelsea Bond (Mrs. Didion, English Teacher), Shawn Pyfrom (Bus Prankster), Dennis Haskins (Mr. Kohls, Band Teacher), Teddy Lane, Jr. (P.E. Teacher), Martin Spanjers (Runty Band Member), Countess Vaughn (Officer Admin. Asst.), Bryan Matsuura, Andy Morrow (8th Graders), Adam Lamberg (8th Grader on Bike), Nick Albert (8th Grader in Gym), E. J. De La Pena (Pudgy 7th Grader), Marcus Toji (Food Fight Chess Player), Zachary Spound (Julius Klinghoffer), Alexandra Kaplan (Kelly Lloyd), Maximillian Kesmodel (Max—4 years old), Christian Boewe (Troy—6 years old), Jon Ryckman, Steve Provenzano, Joe Unitas (Slavs, Football Players), Lil' Romeo, Tony Hawk (Themselves), Marcus Hopson (Pizza Parlor Kid), Nicholas King (Skater Wannabe)

THE STRANGE CASE OF SEÑOR COMPUTER

(WORLD ARTISTS) Producer/Director/Screenplay/Editor/Designer, Tom Sawyer; Co-Producers, Adrienne Cox, Darlene Ford, Frenchy O'Brien; Music, Frenchy O'Brien; Photography, Marco Carpetta, Tom Sawyer; from Corrosive Liquid Productions; Black and white; Not rated; 91 minutes; Release date: October 5, 2001. CAST: Rick Ziegler (Charles O'Toole), Tom Sawyer (Voice of Señor Computer), Dr. Spencer Koerner (Lead Detective), Will Lewis, David Damico (Cops), Gladys Hans (Carlotta Sanchez), Lisa Goodman (Linda), Frenchy O'Brien (Delivery Person), Isaiah Jurado (Daniel Kim), Barbara Beneville (Marsha Spillane), Constance Tillotson (Ryan), Precious Chong (Spiritualist)

Cory McAbee in *The American Astronaut*
© Artistic License Films

STOCKPILE

(SEVENTH ART) Producer, Bruce Endie; Executive Producer, Bob Reid; Director/Screenplay, Stephen Trombley; Photography, Stephen McCarthy, Tomasz Mangierski; Editor, Peter Miller; Music, Rob Lane, Simon Whiteside; Narrator, Martin Sheen; a Worldview Pictures production for Discovery Channel in association with Evangelische Omroep (Netherlands) and DRS & TRS (Switzerland); U.S.-Netherlands-Swiss; Color; Not rated; 102 minutes; Release date: October 5, 2001. Documentary on the nuclear arms race between the United States and Russia, featuring Paul White, Vladislav N. Mokhor, Mike Burns, Radi I. Il'Kaev, Siegfried S. Hecker, Harold Agner, John Shaner, Vladimir I. Yuferev, George Vantiem, Hastings Smith, Merri Wood, Steve Younger, Yuri A. Romanov, Yuri A. Truner, Irv Lindemuth, Robert E. Reinovsky, Vladimir K. Chernychev, Ed Grothus.

THE AMERICAN ASTRONAUT

(ARTISTIC LICENSE) Producers, William Perkins, Joshua Taylor, Bobby Lurie; Director/Screenplay, Cory McAbee; Photography, W. Mott Hupfel III; Designer, Geoff Tuttle; Costumes, Dawn Weisberg; Editor, Pete Beaudreau; Co-Producer, Michael Krantz; Music, The Billy Nayer Show; Musical Director, Bobby Lurie; Casting, Ann Goulder; a BNS Production; Black and white; Not rated; 94 minutes; Release date: October 12, 2001. CAST: Cory McAbee (Samuel Curtis), Rocco Sisto (Professor Heiss), Gregory Russell Cook (The Boy), Annie Golden (Cloris), James Ransone (Bodysuit), Joshua Taylor (Blueberry Pirate), Tom Aldredge (Old Man), Peter McRobbie (Lee Vilensky), Bill Buell (Eddie), Mark Manley, Ned Sublette (Henchmen, Hey Boy!). Joseph McKenna (Doorman), Doug McKean (Silver Miner Jake), Melissa Wilder (Lady Venus)

JAILS, HOSPITALS & HIP-HOP

(KICKED DOWN PRODS.) Producers, Mark Benjamin, Garth Belcon; Executive Producers, William O'Neill, Michael Skolnik; Directors, Mark Benjamin, Danny Hoch; Screenplay, Danny Hoch; Photography, Mark Benjamin; Designer, David Ellis; Editor, Brian A. Kates; Co-Producer, Daniel Hank; Associate Producer, Blair Breard; Music, Mix Master Mike; Original Stage Direction & Development, Jo Bonney; Casting, Sue Crystal; Color; Rated R; 90 minutes; Release date: October 12, 2001. CAST: Danny Hoch (Danny/Brooks/Flip/Sam/Gabriel/Victor/Peter/Andy/Emcee Enuff), Lynn Schlansky-Hoch (Herself), Gina Brooke (Maritza), Pablo Herrera (American Tourist), Jeff Peters (Dave), Hector Arias, Jahaira Duarte, Jackie Garcia (Brooklyn Rappers), Doble Filo, Insinto, Obsesion, Primera Base (Cuban Reporters), Susan Blommaert (Dr. Lemmings), Bonz Malone (Sharif)

THE OPERATOR

(BLACK WOLF FILMS) Producer/Director/Screenplay, Jon Dichter; Executive Producer, Jay Barnet; Co-Producers, Douglas Bruce, Betty A. Buckley; Music, Victor Zupanc; Photography, Bert Guthrie; Designers, Bob Butcher, David Sewell McCann, Kara Sutherlin; Costumes, Kari Perkins; Editors, Michael Coleman, Darren Kloomok; Casting, Elizabeth Hayden-Passero, Jeffrey Passero; from Operator Films L.L.C.; Dolby; Color; Rated R; 102 minutes; Release date: October 12, 2001. CAST: Michael Laurence (Gary Wheelan), Jacqueline Kim (The Operator), Brion James (Vernon Woods), Stephen Tobolowsky (Doc), Christa Miller (Janice Wheelan), John Beasley (Rev. James), Frances Bay (Mrs. Sloan), Lori Heuring (Christie), Paul Heckman (Lawyer)

THINGS BEHIND THE SUN

(COWBOY BOOKING) Producers, Daniel Hassid, Doug Mankoff, Robin Alper; Director, Allison Anders; Screenplay, Allison Anders, Kurt

Voss; Executive Producers, Gary Barkin, Peter Wetherell, Marla Grossman, Joseph Rice; Co-Producer, Rick Dallago; Photography, Terry Stacey; Designer, Jeffrey Scott Taylor; Costumes, Jody Felz; Editor, Chris Figler; Music, Sonic Youth; Casting, Mark Bennett, Hopkins Smith and Barden; Echo Lake Productions; Color; Rated R; 117 minutes; Release date:

Jacqueline Kim in *The Operator* © Black Wolf Film

Don Cheadle, Kim Dickens in *Things Behind the Sun*
© Cowboy

October 12, 2001. CAST: Kim Dickens (Sherry), Gabriel Mann (Owen Richardson), Alison Folland (Lulu), Elizabeth Peña (Carmen), Patsy Kensit (Denise), CCH Pounder (Judge), Shawn Reaves (Tex), Brittany Finamore (Young Sherry), Owen Butler (Young Owen), Justin DePrume (Young Dan), Joshua Leonard (Todd), Jade Gordon (Samantha), Kadu Lennox (Jeremy), Kai Lennox (Colin), Eric Stoltz (Dan), Rosanna Arquette (Pete), Don Cheadle (Chuck), Tom Caffrey (Alex), Alexander Sommer (Randy), Jonathan Osteen (Sonny), Marty Stonerock (AA Speaker), Bill Cordell (AA Secretary), Aria Alpert (Violet), Hal Dion (Public Defender), Talia Osteen (Kathy), Jessica Howell (Jamie), Ruben Anders (Carlos), Jessie Gelaznick (Intern), J. Mascis (Erik), Jeffrey McDonald (Martin), Steve McDonald (Fred), Stephanie Stern (Truck Stop Girl), Rob Sullivan (Bystander) (This film premiered on Showtime cable in August 2001.

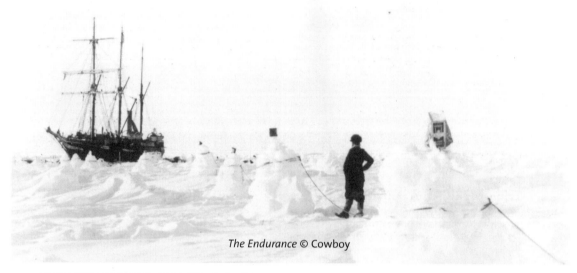

The Endurance © Cowboy

THE ENDURANCE: SHACKLETON'S LEGENDARY ANTARCTIC ADVENTURE

(COWBOY PICTURES) Producer/Director, George Butler; Screenplay, Caroline Alexander, Joseph Dorman; Based on the book by Caroline Alexander; Co-Producer, Louise Rosen; Executive Producer for Nova, Paula Apsell; Executive Producers, Edward R. Pressman, Terrence Malick, L. Dennis Kozlowski, John Mack, Caroline Alexander, Mike Ryan; Photography, Sandi Sissel; Music, Michael Small; Director of Editing and of Still Photo Filming, Joshua Waletzky; Line Producer, Steven Stoke; Narrator, Liam Neeson; a Morgan Stanley presentation of a White Mountain Films/Nova co-production in association with Shackleton Schools, Channel 4, Telepool/Germany, SVT Sweden, Discovery International, the American Museum of Natural History, Zegrahm Expeditions and Outward Bound USA; Color; Rated G; 93 minutes; Release date: October 19, 2001. Documentary on Sir Ernest Shackleton's 1914–16 expedition to Antarctica.

DOG RUN

(ARROW) Producers, Jeffrey Feldman, Brian Marc, D. Ze'Ev Gilad; Executive Producers, Michael Chambers, Patrick Panzarella; Director, D. Ze'Ev Gilad; Screenplay/Editor, Brian Marc, D. Ze'Ev Gilad; Story/Concept, Brian Marc; Photography, Andrew T. Dunn; Designer, Maria Alindato; Music Supervisors, Jeffrey Twiss, Steve Patch; a C&P Productions presentation of a Zampion Production; Color; Not rated; 100 minutes; Release date: October 19, 2001. CAST: Brian Marc (Eddie), Craig Duplessis (Miles), Lisa Ristorucci (Tara), Elizabeth Horsburgh (Rachel), Gary Cunningham (Lee), Lisa Cork-Twiss (Roberta), Michele Santopietro (Stephanie), Michelle Fierro (Angela), Leon Hartman (Boy on Bus), Ian Reid McCulloch, Jennifer Norton (Rachel's Friends), Jacques Monrose (New Orleans Apt. Guy), Felicia Caplan (New Orleans Apt. Girl), Chris Jones (Roberta's Thug), Ross Giunta (Police Officer), Flip Brown (Mugging Victim), Ayelet Kaznelson (Club Bartender), Al Dilorenzo (Bus Driver), Peter Marquette (Boy's Father), Gary Kittrell (Junkie Mugger), Glenn "Spinner" Jones (Performance Artist), Rajav "Roger" Shillersh (Deli Owner), Duane T. Okubo (Hotel Clerk), Jeffrey Twiss (Club Drug Dealer), Jeffrey Zimberg (Club Doorman), Rachel Plutzer (Club Doorgirl), Jean Daniel Edwards, Lisa Rock, Sarah Huber (Prostitutes), Tracy Feldman (Cute Girl in Bar), Gertrude (Rachel's Cat)

Craig Duplessis, Brian Marc, Lisa Ristorucci in *Dog Run*
© Arrow Releasing Inc.

ONE WEEK

(FILM LIFE) Producers, Amber Washington, Phil James; Executive Producer, Phil James; Director, Carl Seaton; Screenplay, Carl Seaton, Kenny Young; Photography, Jeffery T. Brown; Designer, Danielle Tate; Music, Michael Bearden; from Griot Filmworks; Color; Rated R; 97 minutes; Release date: October 19, 2001. CAST: Kenny Young (Varon Thomas), Saadiqa Mohammad (Kiya Parker), Eric Lane (Tyco), Milauna Jemai (Tasha), Pam Mack (Ms. Watts), Gwen Carter (Big Ma), Cynthia Maddox (Mrs. Parker), Charles Moore (Mr. Parker), Malik Middleton (Hook), J. J. McCormick (Mr. Jones), James T. Alfred (Smitty), P. Francois Battiste (Krew Sports Manager), Rhonda Bedgood (Woman at Ressie's Door), Shayrn Grose (Receptionist), Don Adams (Deandre), Hadrian Hooks, Calvin Richardson (Security Guards), Phil White (Mr. Davis), Tina Jordan (Danielle), Tracy Jones (Danielle's Boyfriend), Eva D (Mrs. Minnie), Makeda Falconer (Stripper), Jesse Sanford (Singer), Phil James (Bartender), Dale Morris, Poncho (Cops), Reggie James, Joe Gibson (Paramedics), Derek Edwards (Detective)

DANCING AT THE BLUE IGUANA

(LIONS GATE) Producers, Etchie Stroh, Ram Bergman, Dana Lustig, Michael Radford, Sheila Kelley, Damian Jones, Graham Broadbent; Director, Michael Radford; Screenplay, Michael Radford, David Linter; Photography, Ericson Core; Designer, Martina Buckley; Costumes, Louise Frogley; Executive Producers, Samuel Hadida, Leslie Jean Porter, Willi Baer; Music, Tal Bergman, Renato Neto; Editor, Roberto Perpignani; Line Producer, Dave Pomier; Casting, Sharon Howard-Field; a Moonstone Entertainment presentation of a Bergman Lustig/Dragon/Gallery production; Dolby; Color; Rated R; 123 minutes; Release date: October 19, 2001. CAST: Charlotte Ayanna (Jessie), Daryl Hannah (Angel), Sheila Kelley (Stormy), Elias Koteas (Sully), Vladimir Mashkov (Sacha), Sandra Oh (Jasmine), Jennifer Tilly (Jo), Robert Wisdom (Eddie), Kristin Bauer (Nico), W. Earl Brown (Bobby), Chris Hogan (Dennis), Rodney Rowland (Charlie), David Amos (Dave), Carolyne Aycaguer (Sophie), R. C. Bates (Jimmy), Jesse Bradford (Jorge), Christina Cabot (Christina), Bill Chott (Angel's Regular), Maurice Compte (Drug Buyer), Jack Conley (Officer Pete Foster), Marta Cunningham (Yolanda), Gino Dentie (Celebrity), Pete Gardner (Jerry), Ruthanna Hopper (Desiree), Stephen Hornyak (Trucker), Kevin Hunt (DJ), Peggy Jo Jacobs (Sarah), Joel Hurt Jones, Isabelle Pasco, Vincent Ricotta (Customers), Jason Kravits (Gordon), Michael Loprete (Stormy's Regular), Ellyn Maybe (Fiona), Tenya Neilsen (Castle), Buckley Norris (Talking Man), Shannon Ransom (Bartender), Harper Roisman (Harry Goldberg), Ted Rooney (Assistant), Lobo Sebastian (Rough Looking Guy), Thomas Shelorke (Jo's Turned On Customer), Iqbal Theba (Clerk), John Thomas (Poetry Man)

WHITE HOTEL

(SUB ROSA STUDIOS) Producers/Directors/Screenplay/Photography, Dianne Griffin, Tobi Solvang; Editors, Tobi Solvang, Dianne Griffin, Pat Barber; Music, Various Artists; a Wake Up! Productions Film; Color; Not rated; 90 minutes; Release date: October 19, 2001. Documentary following an AIDS research team as it travels to Eritrea in East Africa, an area long off-limits to Western visitors.

A GALAXY FAR, FAR AWAY

(MORNING STAR PRODS.) Producers, Terry Tocantins, Biagio Messina, Joke Fincioen; Director/Screenplay/Executive Producer/Narrator, Tariq Jalil; Editor, Biagio Messina; Photography, Jeremy Ides; Music, John Dickson; Color; Not rated; 62 minutes; Release date: October 19, 2001. Documentary on the phenomenal popularity of the Star Wars films, featuring interviews with many fans including appearances by Joe Pesci, Meat Loaf, Christopher Vogler, Roger Corman, Jam Master Jedi.

HISTORY LESSONS

(FIRST RUN) Producer/Director/Photography/Editor, Barbara Hammer; Additional Photography, Carolyn McCartney, Ann T. Rossetti; Music, Eve Beglarian, Lisa Ben, Mikael Karlsson, Gretchen Phillips, Jean Paul Keenon; Archivsts, Ann Maguire, Szu Burgess, Bertrand Grimault, Barbara Hammer, Jenni Olson; Black and white/color; Not rated; 65 minutes; Release date: October 26, 2001. Documentary looking at depictions of lesbianism on film throughout the years; featuring archival footage as well as staged sequences with Carmelita Tropicana, Kaja Aman, Antonio Caputo, Denise Coles, Cambrea Ezell, Mildred Gerestanta, Coco Feliciano, Mo Fisher, Anna Hallberg, Barbara Lempel, Piper Macleod, Kathryn Thomas, Laura Marie Thompson, Sharon Jane Smith, Coco Fusco, Jane Fine, David Del Tredici.

Coco Fusco, Jane Fine in *History Lessons* © Firs Run Features

Charlotte Ayanna in *Dancing at the Blue Iguana* © Lions Gate Films

ON THE LINE

(MIRAMAX) Producers, Wendy Thorlakson, Rich Hull, Peter Abrams, Robert L. Levy; Executive Producers, Johnny Wright, Lance Bass, Andrew Panay, Bob Osher, Jeremy Kramer, Robbie Brenner; Director, Eric Bross; Screenplay, Eric Aronson, Paul Stanton; Co-Executive Producers, Louise Rosner, Greg Silverman; Co-Producers, Joe Anderson, Far Shariat; Photography, Michael Bernard; Designer, Andrew Jackness; Editor, Eric Sears; Music, Stewart Copeland; Music Supervisors, Randy Spendlove, Jonathan McHugh; Costumes, Margaret Mohr; Casting, Nancy Nayor; a Tapestry Films Production in association with Happy Place; Dolby; Deluxe color; Rated PG; 85 minutes; Release date: October 26, 2001. CAST: Lance Bass (Kevin), Joey Fatone (Rod), Emmanuelle Chriqui (Abbey), GQ (Eric), James Bulliard (Randy), Al Green, Ananda Lewis, Chyna, Brandi Williams, Sammy Sosa, Damon Buford, Eric Young (Themselves), Tamala Jones (Jackie), Richie Sambora (Mick Silver), Amanda Foreman (Julie), Dan Montgomery (Brady), Dave Foley (Higgins), Jerry Stiller (Nathan), David Fraser (Barrett), Jenny Parsons (Margie, Receptionist), Kristin Booth (Sam), Sandra Cladwell (Reebok Client #1), Romona Pringle (Kayla Sanders), Jonathan Watton (Paul), Jeanie Calleja (Tabatha), Tracy Dawson (Goth Girl), Sarah McDonald (Diner Waitress), Kelley Hazen (Woman at Wrigley), Howard E. Brechner (Guy at Wrigley), Alexandra Delory (Girl with Braces), Adrian Churchill (Guy at Bar), Allen Alvarado (Boy), Amanda Brydon (High-School Girl at Party), Steve Clark, Paul Puzzella (Band Members), Dov Tiefenbach (High-School Kid), Sean O'Neil (Puberty-Ravaged Kid), Chip Caray (Cubs TV Announcer)

PUNKS

(URBANWORLD) Producers, Tracey E. Edmonds, Michael McQuarn, Patrik-Ian Polk; Executive Producers, Kenneth "Babyface" Edmonds, Stacy Spikes; Director/Screenplay, Patrik-Ian Polk; Photography, Rory King; Designer, Liana Reid; Editor, Anne Misawa; Costumes, Linda Stokes; Casting, Doran Reed, Robi Reed-Humes; Tall Skinny Black Boy Productions/e2 Filmworks; Dolby; Color; Rated R; 91 minutes; Release date: November 2, 2001. CAST: Seth Gilliam (Marcus), Dwight Ewell (Hill), Rockmond Dunbar (Darby), Jazzmun (Chris/Crystal), Renoly Santiago (Dante), Loretta Devine (Health Counselor), Vanessa Williams (Jennifer), Devon Odessa (Felicity), Rudolf Martin (Gilbert), Jullian Dulce

Vida (Spike), Marc Avalon (Masseur), Kevin Aviance (Miss Smokie), Dustin Blair (Sexy White Guy), Rainbow Borden (Wild Guy #1/Jim), Rodney Chester (Alexis Carrington Colby Dexter), Lamar Damon (Roger), Julio Dolcevita (Spike), Shaun Earl (Monique Jeanville), Nayib Estefan (Wild Guy #2/Mark), Ryan Findlay (Steve, Sexy Guy), Michael Holden (Mr. Geiger, Concierge), Walter E. Hong (Double Rainbow Proprietor), Ron Kochevar (Par), Andre McClain (Chris's Boyfriend), Brian-Paul Mendoza (Bath House Attendant), D-Taylor Murphy (Jo Jo), Jason Olive (Lucas), Phina Oruche, Gregory Keith (Super Model), Rhonda Ray (Bartender), Phillip Rhys (Rodney), Red Savage (Dominique Devereaux), Scott L. Schwartz (Convict), Thea Vidale (Nurse)

Seth Gilliam, Rockmond Dunbar in *Punks*
© Urbanworld Films

GQ, James Buillard, Lance Bass, Joey Fatone in *On the Line* © Miramax Films

THE ANNIHILATION OF FISH

(REGENT) Producers, Kris Dodge, Paul Heller, William Lawrence Fabrizio, Eric Mitchell, John Remark; Director, Charles Burnett; Screenplay, Anthony C. Winkler; Photography, John Ndiaga Demps, Rick Robinson; Designer, Nina Ruscio; Costumes, Christine Peters; Editor, Nancy Richardson; Music, Laura Karpman; a Paul Heller production in association with American Sterling Productions; Color; Rated R; 108; Release date: November 2, 2001. CAST: Lynn Redgrave (Poinsettia), James Earl Jones (Fish), Margot Kidder (Mrs. Muldroone), Ronald F. Hoiseck (Reno Minister), Tommy Redmond Hicks

EVERYTHING PUT TOGETHER

(VITAGRAPH FILMS) Producer, Sean Furst; Executive Producer, Adam Forgash; Director, Marc Foster; Screenplay, Catherine Lloyd Burns, Adam Forgash, Marc Forster; Photography, Roberto Schaefer; Designer, Paul Jackson; Editor, Matt Chesse; Music, Thomas Koppel; Dolby; Color; Not rated; 87 minutes; Release date: November 2, 2001. CAST: Radha Mitchell (Angie), Megan Mullally (Barbie), Justin Louis (Russ), Catherine Lloyd Burns (Judith), Alan Ruck (Kessel), Michele Hicks (April), Matt Malloy (Dr. Reiner), Jacqueline Heinze (Jean), Courtney Watkins (H20 Instructor), Mark Boone Junior (Bill), Blake Rossi (Michael), Stephanie Schneider (Party Videographer), Vince Vieluf (Jim), John P. Hunter (Hearse Driver), Kevin Ratliffe (Simon), Arly Jover (Nurse), Pamela Gordon, Octavia L. Spencer (Nurses), Jennie Vaughn (Cashier), Jonathan Slavin (Photo Clerk), Thomas Prisco (Doctor A), Martha Mendoza (Marie), Tom McCleister (Dr. Miller), Garvin Funches (Orderly), Pam Monroe (Loni), Scott Vance (Priest), Henry King, Oliver King (Barbie's Twins), Amy Carlson (Jane), Dakota Leopardi (Justin), Rob Swanson (Man in Park), Roland LaGarde (Mailman), Shelly Desai (Storage Man), Paul Hayes (Dr. Spiegel), Judy Geeson (Angie's Mother)

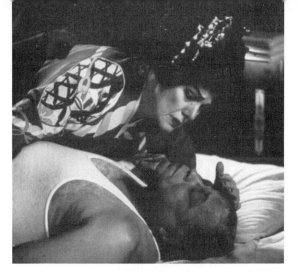

Lynn Redgrave, James Earl Jones in *The Annihilation of Fish* © Regent Entertainment

CITIZEN TOXIE: THE TOXIC AVENGER IV

(TROMA) Producers, Lloyd Kaufman, Michael Herz; Executive Producers, Ken Squire, Andrew Learner, James Coleman, Weston Quasha; Director, Lloyd Kaufman; Screenplay, Trent Haaga, Patrick Cassidy, Gabriel Friedman, Lloyd Kaufman; Photography, Brendan Flynt; Designer, Alison Grossman; Editor, Gabriel Friedman; Music, Wes Nagy; Creature Effects, Tim Considine; a Lloyd Kaufman and Michael Herz production; Dolby; Color; Not rated; 108 minutes; Release date: November 2, 2001. CAST: David Mattey, Heidi Sjursen, Clyde Lewis, Debbie Rochon, Ron Jeremy, Paul Krymse, Dan Snow, Trent Haaga, Hank the Angry Dwarf, Joseph Isaac Fleishmaker

Justin Louis, Radha Mitchell in *Everything Put Together* © Vitagraph Films

John Leguizamo in *King of the Jungle*
© Urbanworld Films

KING OF THE JUNGLE

(URBANWORLD) Producers, Robert S. Potter, Scott Macaulay, Robin O'Hara; Executive Producers, John Leguizamo, Jay Rifkin, Hans Zimmer, Stacy Spikes; Director/Screenplay, Seth Zvi Rosenfeld; Photography, Fortunato Procopio; Designer, Deana Sydney; Costumes, Richard Owings; Music, Harry Gregson-Williams; Editor, Kate Sanford; a Bombo Sports & Entertainment presentation of a Forensic Films/Media Ventures production; DuArt color; Rated R; 86 minutes; Release date: November 9, 2001. CAST: John Leguizamo (Seymour), Rosie Perez (Joanne), Julie Carmen (Mona), Cliff Gorman (Jack), Michael Rapaport (Francis), Marisa Tomei (Det. Costello), Justin Pierce (Lil' Mafsa), Annabella Sciorra (Mermaid), Judy Reyes (Lydia Morreto), Richie Perez (Pucho), Blaze (Dead-Eye), Rafael Nunez, Malcolm Barrett (Basketball Kids), Raymond Vincente (Colon), Yan Ming (Fat Ming), Rosario Dawson (Veronica), Seth Zvi Rosenfeld (Herbie), Raujit Chowdhry (Mr. Sith), William Prael (Officer with Sith), Scott Cohen (Officer Norman Turner), Jason Andrews (Turner's Partner), Jerry Dean (Rober), Eddie Hands (Dum Dum's Friend), Sixto Ramos (Det. Lemons), Carmen Serrano (Woman on Street), Bill Cwikowski (Freddy), Rebecca Cohen Alport (Pregnant Poet)

Laura Linney, Rob Morrow in *Maze* © Andora Pictures

Erin O'Hara, Greg Walloch, Michael Lucas in
Keeping It Real © Avatar Films

I REMEMBER ME

(ZEITGEIST) Producer/Director/Screenplay, Kim A. Snyder; Co-Producer, Sam Counter; Photography, Sam Counter, Lee Daniel, Don Lenzer; Editor, Paula Heredia; Coordinating Producer, Heidi Zecher; Color; Not rated; 74 minutes; Release date: November 9, 2001. Documentary on Chronic Fatigue Syndrome.

MAZE

(ANDORA PICTURES) Producers, Paul Colichman, Mark R. Harris, Stephen P. Jarchow, Rob Morrow; Executive Producers, Phyllis Carlyle, Joseph Pierson, David Forrest, Beau Rogers; Director, Rob Morrow; Screenplay/Story, Rob Morrow, Bradley White; Photography, Wolfgang Held; Designer, Kalina Ivanov; Costumes, Melissa Toth; Editor, Gary Levy; Music, Bobby Previte; Casting, Sheila Jaffe, Georgianne Walken; a Blockbuster & Starz! Pictures presentation in association with KBK Entertainment & Andora Pictures International of a Regent Entertainment/Bits and Pieces Picture Company/Goldheart Production in association with Cypress Films, Inc. & Carlyle Productions; Dolby; Color; Rated R; 97 minutes; Release date: November 9, 2001. CAST: Rob Morrow (Lyle Maze), Laura Linney (Callie), Craig Sheffer (Mike), Rose Gregorio (Helen), Robert Hogan (Lyle's Father), Gia Carides (Julianne), Betsy Aidem (Lydia), Keenan Shimizu (Korean Market Employee), Matthew Storff (Young Lyle), Sheila Zane (Lenna), Lenny Flaherty (Drunk), Susan Shacter (Photographer), Wally Dunn (Bartender), Billy Strong (Italian Restaurant Patron), Nick Terno (Waiter), Ken Leung (Dr. Mikao), Frank Pugliese (Scott), Brian Greene (Plat Techtonics Man), Merrill Holtzman (Male Nurse), Kathleen Goldpaugh (Birth Nurse), Alla (Fashion Model), Mary Kelsey (Pregnant Woman) (This movie had its premiere on Starz! cable network in 2001.)

KEEPING IT REAL: THE ADVENTURES OF GREG WALLOCH

(AVATAR FILMS) Producers/Screenplay, Eli Kabillio, Greg Walloch; Based on the show White Disabled Talent by Greg Walloch; Executive Producers, TC Rice, Lorna Thomas; Director, Eli Kabillio; Photography, David Sperling, Neil Smith, David Goldsmith; Designer, Niamh Byrne; Music, Melanie Rock, Greg Talenfeld, Martin Trum; Editor, Egon Kirincic; a Mad Dog Films Inc. Production; Color; Not rated; 83 minutes; Release date: November 9, 2001. A part-documentary, -concert film, -comedy based on the life of disabled gay man Greg Walloch; featuring Stephen Baldwin, Paul Borghese, Anne Meara, Michael Musto, Deborah Yates.

Dr. Dre, George Wallace, Snoop Dogg in *The Wash*
© Lions Gate Films

SNIDE AND PREJUDICE

(VINE INTERNATIONAL) Line Producer, Rodney Greene; Director/Producer/Screenplay, Philippe Mora; Photography, J. B. Letchinger; Casting, Felicia Fasano; Bombastic Pictures, Focusfilm Entertainment; Color; Not rated; 90 minutes; Release date: November 9, 2001. CAST: Rene Auberjonois (Dr. Sam Cohen), Joseph Bottoms (Himmler), Sam Bottoms (Schaub), Claudia Christian (Renate Muller), Richard Edson (Hess), Mick Fleetwood (Pablo Picasso), Brion James (Goehring), J. D. Johnson (Sheffield), Angus MacFadyen (Michael Davidson/Adolf Hilter), Brian McDermott (Hindenberg), Richard Moll (Von Ludendorf), Mena Suvari (Geli), Jesse Grey Walken (Christ), T. C. Warner (Tessa Percival/Eva Braun), Michael Zelniker (Goebbels), Mickey Cottrell, Brad Wilson, Jenny Dubasso, Armin Shimerman

THE WASH

(LIONS GATE) Producers, DJ Pooh, Phillip Atwell, Kip Konwiser; Executive Producers, Dr. Dre, Snoop Dogg; Director/Screenplay, DJ Pooh; Co-Producer, Jeremiah Samuels; Photography, Keith Smith; Designer, Albert Cuellar; Costumes, Tracey White; Music, Camara Kambon; Editor, Jack Hofstra; Casting, Monica R. Cooper; a Lithium Entertainment production; Dolby; Color; Rated R; 96 minutes; Release date: November 14, 2001. CAST: Dr. Dre (Sean), Snoop Dogg (Dee Loc), George Wallace (Mr. Washington), Angell Conwell (Antoinette), Tommy "Tiny" Lister, Jr. (Bear), Bruce Bruce (DeWayne), Alex Thomas (Jimmy), Shawn Fonteno (Face), Lamont Bentley (C-Money), Shari Watson (Vickey), Arif S. Kinchen (Lil' Dee), Demetrius Navarro (Juan), John Basinger (Mickey), Rashaan Nall (Ronald), Alvin Joiner (Wayne), DJ Pooh (Slim), Frank Chavez (Officer Hoppy), Julio R. Gonzales (Julio G.), Ricardo Brown (Maniac), Jeris Poindexter (Mr. Francis), Marcia Wright (Sharon), Pierre (Mark), Jude S. Walko (Window Man), Derek Thompson (Old Man), Isley (Karen), Tommy Chong (Dee's Connection), Pauly Shore (Man in Trunk), Anthony Albano (Mafia Tony), Shaquille O'Neal (Norman)

BOMBAY EUNUCH

(GIDALYA PICTURES) Producer, Alexandra Shiva; Directors, Alexandra Shiva, Sean MacDonald, Michelle Gucovsky; Photography, Ajay Narohna, Bimal Biswas; Editor, Penelope Falk; Music, John M. Davis; HD Video; Color; Not rated; 71 minutes; Release date: November 16, 2001. Documentary about a group of castrati living in the squalor of Bombay.

Bombay Eunuch © Gidalya Pictures

Michael Cunio in *The Fluffer* © First Run Features/TLA

THE FLUFFER

(FIRST RUN FEATURES/TLA RELEASING) Producers, John Sylla, Victoria Robinson; Executive Producer, Rose Kuo; Directors, Richard Glatzer, Wash West; Screenplay, Wash West; Line Producer, Pat Scanlon; Photography, Mark Putnam; Designer, Devorah Herbert; Costumes, Gitte Meldgaard; Editor, John Binninger; Music, The Bowling Green, John Vaughn; Casting, Elizabeth Jereski; a Fluff and Fold production; Color; Not rated; 94 minutes; Release date: November 16, 2001. CAST: Scott Gurney (Johnny Rebel), Michael Cunio (Sean McGinnis), Roxanne Day (Babylon), Taylor Negron (Tony Brooks), Richard Riehle (Sam Martins), Tim Bagley (Alan Dieser), Adina Porter (Silver), Ruben Madera (Hector), Josh Holland (Brian), Mickey Cottrell (Aunt at Bar, Ralph Shifflett), Guinevere Turner (Video Store Clerk), Robert Walden (Chad Cox), Deborah Harry (Marcella), Heather Shannon Ryan (L.A. Actress), David Pevsner (Casting Man), Gale Van Cott (Casting Woman), Sharon McCormick (Sean's Mama), Andy Zeffer (Rick Daniels), Penn Badgley (Young Sean), Stephen Michael Pace (Jeb Gordon), Zach Richards, Derek Cameron, John Sylla Rex, Chad Donovan, Thomas Lloyd, Chi Chi LaRue, Karen Dior, Bradley Picklesheimer, Louis Re, Jay Lyons, Chris Green, Ron Jeremy, Cole Tucker (Themselves), Squishy (Stacia), Jim Steel (Bartender), Ke (Endowed Go-Go Boy), Lori Alan (Harmony), Christopher Carroll (Businessman at Legg's), Rob Rumsey (Twinkie in a Sling), Johanna Went (Abortion Protester), Judith Benezra (Policewoman), Trev Broudy (TV Reporter), Franklin Hernandez (Mexican Boy)

THE SIMIAN LINE

(GABRIEL FILM GROUP) Producers, Linda Yellen, Robert Renfield; Executive Producers, Montel Williams, Daniel Bennett, Michael Escott; Director, Linda Yellen; Screenplay, Gisela Bernice; Story, Linda Yellen, Michael Leeds; Photography, David Bridges; Designer, Henry Dunn; Costumes, Tim Chappel; Music, Patrick Seymour; Co-Producers, Jordan Walker-Pearlman, Judith Zarin; Editor, Bob Jorissen; an S.L. Production in association with DaWa Movies; Color; Rated R; 106 minutes; Release date: November 16, 2001. CAST: Harry Connick, Jr. (Rick), Cindy Crawford (Sandra), Tyne Daly (Arnita), William Hurt (Edward), Monica Keena (Marta), Samantha Mathis (Mae), Lynn Redgrave (Katharine), Jamey Sheridan (Paul), Eric Stoltz (Sam), Dylan Bruno (Billy), Jeremy Zelig (Jimmy)

OUT COLD

(TOUCHSTONE) Producers, Lee R. Mayes, Michael Aguilar, Jonathan Glickman; Executive Producers, Lauren Shuler Donner, Gary Barber, Roger Birnbaum; Directors, The Malloys (Emmett Malloy, Brendan Malloy); Screenplay, Jon Zack; Photography, Richard Crudo; Designer, Michael Bolton; Costumes, Carla Hetland; Editor, Jeffrey Wolf; Music, Michael Andrews; Casting, Sarah Halley Finn, Randi Hiller; Stunts, J. J. Makaro; a Spyglass Entertainment presentation of a Donnners' Company production, a Barber/Birnbaum production; Dolby; Technicolor; Rated PG-13; 89 minutes; Release date: November 21, 2001. CAST: Jason

Harry Connick, Jr., Lynn Redgrave in *The Simian Line*
© Gabriel Film Group

London (Rick Rambis), Lee Majors (Jack Majors), Willie Garson (Ted Muntz), Zach Galifianakis (Luke), David Koechner (Stumpy), Flex Alexander (Anthony), A. J. Cook (Jenny), David Denman (Lance), Caroline Dhavernas (Anna), Derek Hamilton (Pig Pen), Thomas Lennon (Eric), Victoria Silvstedt (Inga), Lewis Arquette (Papa Muntz), Todd Richards (Barry), Rio Tahara (Tetsuo), Brett Kelly (Kid at Barbeque, Toby), Lee R. Mayes (Whitey), Alexis Glabus, Nicole Amos, Fawnia Mondey, Holly Eglington, Odessa Munroe, Christine Caux, Janette Wu, Kendall Saunders, Karen Robertson (Solid Gold Dancers), Danny Hagge (Stewart), Adam Harrington (Team Snownook Leader), Rob "Sluggo" Boyce, Scott Heindl (Snownook Guys), Rheta Hutton (Nurse), Jane Sowerby (Powder Room Woman), Peter Kawasaki, Art Irazawa (Japanese Businessmen), Wren Robertz (Snownook Bouncer), Amy Baldwin (Hot Tourist Chick), Lisa Marie Caruk (Other Tourist Chick), Ted Stryker (Tourist Dude in Lineup), Jack Hody Johnson, Adam Topol, Merlo Podlewski (Jack Johnson and Band), Tara Dakides, Devun Walsh, Javas Lehn, Sean Johnson (Themselves), Steve Kahan (Powder Room Bartender)

TEXAS RANGERS

(DIMENSION) Producers, Alan Greisman, Frank Price; Executive Producers, Bob Weinstein, Harvey Weinstein, Cary Granat, Larry Levinson; Director, Steve Miner; Screenplay, Scott Busby, Martin Copeland; Photography, Daryn Okada; Designer, Herbert Pinter; Music, Trevor Rabin; a Price Entertainment/Greisman Production in association with Larry Levinson Productions, Inc.; Distributed by Miramax Films; Dolby; Panavision; Color; Rated PG-13; 90 minutes; Release date: November 30, 2001. CAST: James Van Der Beek (Lincoln Rogers Dunnison), Dylan McDermott (Leander McNelly), Ashton Kutcher (George Durham), Robert Patrick (Sgt. John Armstrong), Randy Travis (Frank Bones), Usher Raymond (Randolph Douglas Scipio), Alfred Molina (John King Fisher), Jon Abrahams (Berry Smith), Tom Skerritt (Richard Dukes), Rachael Leigh Cook (Caroline Dukes), Leonor Varela (Perdita), Marco Leonardi (Jesus Sandoval), Matt Keeslar (Suh Suh Sam), Vincent Spano (Ed Simms), Bob Bancroft (Auctioneer), Stephen Bridgewater (Older Ranger), Jordan Brower (Jake Dunnison), Anthony Crivello (Ringmaster), Oded Fehr (Pete Marsele), Derek S. Flores (Leary), Breon Gorman (Mrs. Dunnison), Eric Johnson (Rollins), Matthew Kennedy (Ranch Hand Steve), Brad Loree (Outlaw #3), Brian Martell (Jean-Pierre Marsele), Gordon Michaels (Mariachi Guard), David Millbern (Marshal), Billy Morton (Abajo), Kate Newby (Henrietta Dukes), William Prael (Cale Dukes), Joe Renteria (Gen. Cortinas), A. Alexandra Sanford (Fischer's Prostitute), Jim Shield (Baldum), Joe Spano (Mr. Dunnison), Jesse G. Thompson (Purdy Dukes), Gareth Williams (Vigilante Vic)

Jason London, A.J. Cook in *Out Cold*
© Spyglass Entertainment Group

ABCD

(EROS/LAXMI) Producers, Krutin Patel, Naju Patel; Executive Producer, Madhur Jaffrey; Director/Story, Krutin Patel; Screenplay, Krutin Patel, James McManus; Photography, Milton Kam; Designer, Deborah Schreier; Costumes, Naju Patel; Editor, Ravi Subramanian; Music, Deirdre Broderick; Casting, Glenn Fisher; Color; Not rated; 105 minutes; Release date: November 30, 2001. CAST: Madhur Jaffrey (Anju), Faran Tahir (Raj), Sheetal Sheth (Nina), Aasif Mandvi (Ashok), David Ari (Brian), Jennifer Dorr White (Julia), Adriane Forlana Erdos (Tejal), Rex Young (Sam), Gil Grail (Mark), Bob Bonnet (Cop), Alexander Lasky (Gordon), David Mann (Tony), Janan Raouf (Jennifer), Vince Byrne, Sr. (MacKenzie), Nick Cochrane (Asha), Rashmi Sheth (Shailesh), Susham Bedi (Sona), M. N. Ahmed (Depak), Jessica Lyon (Cindy), Glenn Fisher (Maitre d'), Ismail Bashey (News Vendor), Ralph Amiano (Cashier), Kelly J. Montgomery (Linda), Ami Shukla (Shermila), Nayan Padrai (Prakash), Bipin Bhai (Priest), Naju Patel (Sharmil's Friend), Rahael Elias (Sharmila's Mother), Satish Patel (Sharmila's Father), Clarke Johnson (Minister), Mervin Crook (Samuel), Nancy Johnson (Nancy)

Ashton Kutcher, Usher Raymond, James Van Der Beek in *Texas Rangers* © Dimension Films

Janeane Garofalo, Jerry Stiller in *The Independent*
© Arrow Releasing

THE INDEPENDENT

(ARROW) Producer, Mike Wilkins; Executive Producer, Jerry Weintraub; Director, Stephen Kessler; Screenplay, Mike Wilkins, Stephen Kessler; Co-Executive Producer, Lesa Lakin Richardson; Co-Producer, Jack Ziga; Photography, Amir Hamed; Designer, Russell Christian; Costumes, Yoona Kwak; Editor, Chris Franklin; Music, Ben Vaughn; Casting, Nicole Arbusto, Joy Dickson; Color; Rated R; 95 minutes; Release date: November 30, 2001. CAST: Jerry Stiller (Morty Fineman), Janeane Garofalo (Paloma Fineman), Max Perlich (Ivan), Ted Demme, Roger Corman, Ron Howard, Karen Black, Peter Bogdanovich, Fred Williamson, Nick Cassavetes (Themselves), Paul Logan (Son), Stacy Fuson (Daughter), Herb Marcus (Old Man/Mr. Witz), Julie Strain (Ms. Kevorkian), Stephen Kessler (Steve), Mike Wilkins (Mike), Ethan Embry (Bert), Kimo Wills (Rob), Phil Proctor (Rob's Dad), Melinda Peterson (Rob's Mom), Louisa Moritz (Sally, Receptionist), Priscilla Taylor (Iris), Greg Behrendt (Redneck), Victoria Silvstedt (Blossom), Devon DeMaria (Violet), Clanton Williams, Joseph Dubow (Businessmen), Danielle Ciardi (Daisy), Lisa McCullough (Leather Girl), Jimmy Briscoe (Morty's Actor Friend), Gary Friedkin (Surfer Guy), Debbie Lee Carrington (Surfer Girl), Susie Rossitto (Morty's Actress Friend), Eric Schaefer (R. F. Fineman), Roy Kerry (Beardo), David Stifel (Hairface), Dennis McCullen (President), S. A. Griffin (Slate), Omer Mohamed (Mr. Singh), Maria Cina (Newscaster), Jennifer Elise Cox (Telluride Booth Girl), Billy Burke (Dwayne), Penelope Pumpkins, Fantasia, Brittany Andrews (Actresses), Amy Stiller (Dr. Rosaria McClesh), Gina Jackson (Foxy Chocolate Robot), John Finnegan (Guard), Larry Hankin (William Henry Ellis), Andy Dick (Maitre d'), Joanne Richter (Tula), Jeff Schoeny (Boy), Ben Stiller (Cop), Ancel Cook (Peter Worth), John Lydon (Baruce), Ginger Lynn Allen (Mayor Kitty Storm), Dr. Michael Robbins (Orthodontist), Ken Michelman (Prosecutor), Dana Gould (Victim), Rob Ingersoll (Christ), Ramon Sison (Mr. Ramos), Jade Herrera (Blue Sky), Anne Meara (Rita), Fred Dryer (Jean-Claude), Richard Paul (Jeffries), Sam Anderson (Ed), Bill Gerber (Dennis), Laura Kightlinger (Dian), Risa Mickenberg (Desk Clerk), Jay Johnson (Soldier), Joseph Griffo (Beach Guy), Bob Odenkirk (Figure), Melissa Daniels (Lover), Owen Bush (VFW Old Man), Aki Aleong (Mr. Ko), Maria Ford (Poster Model)

PORN STAR: THE LEGEND OF RON JEREMY

(MAELSTROM) Producers, Kirt Eftekhar, Scott J. Gill; Executive Producer, Tim Goldberg; Director/Editor, Scott J. Gill; Photography, Ralph King; Associate Producer, Sean Skelton; Music, Carvin Knowles; Dolby; Color; Not rated; 79 minutes; Release date: November 30, 2001. Documentary on well-endowed porno actor Ron Jeremy.

FINAL

(COWBOY) Producers, Gary Winick, Alexis Alexanian, Mary Frances Budig, Steve Dunn, Campbell Scott; Executive Producers, Jonathan Sehring, Caroline Kaplan, John Sloss; Director, Campbell Scott; Screenplay, Bruce McIntosh; Photography, Dan Gillham; Designer, Chris Shriver; Costumes, Toni Fusco; Music, Guy Davis; Executive Music Producer, Alex Steyermark; Editor, Andy Keir; Casting, Ellen Lewis, Marcia Debonis; The Independent Film Channel Productions presentation of an InDigEnt production in association with Spare Room Productions; Color; Not rated; 111 minutes; Release date: December 7, 2001. CAST: Denis Leary (Bill), Hope Davis (Ann), J. C. MacKenzie (Todd), Jim Gaffigan (Dayton), Jim Hornyak (Orderly), Maureen Anderman (Supervisor), Marin Hinkle (Sherry), Madison Arnold (Bill's Father), Caroline Kava (Bill's Mother), Mary Diveny (Murse), Janet Hovious (Doctor), Nadine Delallo (Ward Nurse), Bruce McIntosh (Edward), Steve Dunn (Larry), Anthony Pettine (Coloring Patient), Eric Gearity (Puzzle Patient), John Brainard (VCR Patient), Lisa Leguillou (Bookstore Clerk), Danny Drohojowski (Todd's Son), Tina Benko (Blonde in Bar), Guy Davis (Singer), Hélène Cardona (ICU Nurse), Christina Kirk (Mary), Ezra Knight (Lawyer), Seth Barrish, Catherine Brophy (Staff Members), Earl Hindman (Official), Ben Wilson (Attendant), Nancy Wu (Dancing Nurse), Alexis Alexanian (Pushy Nurse), Jody Burke (Coroner)

Ron Jeremy in *Porn Star* © Maelstrom

KIDS WORLD

(BLUE STEEL RELEASING) Producers, Grant Bradley, Tom Taylor; Executive Producers, John Massam, Alex Krem, Devesh Chetty, Walter Josten, Wolfram Tichy; Director, Dale G. Bradley; Screenplay, Michael Lach; Photography, Neil Cervin; Designer, Mark Robbins; Music, Bruce Lynch; Editor, Douglas Braddock; Line Producer, Brian Walden; Associate Producer, Jozsef Fityus; Casting, Roe Baker; a Daybreak Pacific Films and VIF Productions presentation; Color; Rated PG; 93 minutes; Release date: December 7, 2001. CAST: Christopher Lloyd (Leo), Blake Foster (Ryan Mitchell), Michael Purms (Twinkie), Anton Tennet (Stu), Todd Emerson (Detloff), Olivia Tennet (Nicole Mitchell), Anna Wilson (Holly)

UPRISING

(BROOKLYN FILMS) Producers, Jon Avnet, Raffaella De Laurentiis, Jordan Kerner; Executive Producer, Bill Haber; Director, Jon Avnet; Screenplay, Jon Avnet, Paul Brickman; Photography, Denis Lenoir; Designer, Benjamin Fernandez; Costumes, George L. Little; Music, Maurice Jarre; Editor, Sabrina Plisco-Morris; Casting, Debi Manwiller, Rick Pagano, Eva Stefankovicova, Sheila Trezise; Color; Not rated; 163 minutes; Release date: December 7, 2001. CAST: Leelee Sobieski (Tosia Altman), Hank Azaria (Mordechai Anielewicz), David Schwimmer (Yitzak Zuckerman), Jon Voight (Major-General Jurgen Stroop), Donald Sutherland (Adam Czerniakow), Cary Elwes (Dr. Fritz Hippler), Stephen Moyer (Kazik Rodem), Sadie Frost (Zivia Lubetkin), Radha Mitchell (Mira Fruchner), Mili Avital (Devorah Barga), Alexandra Holden (Frania Beatus), John Ales (Marek Edelman), Andy Nyman (Calel Wasser), Eric Lively (Arie Wilner), Nora Brickman (Clara Linder), Jesper Christensen (Gen. Kruger), Melanie Claus (Fergie), Ben Crystal (Julian Wald), Iddo Goldberg (Zygmundt), Luke Moably (Zachariah Artenstein), Nadiv Molcho (Isaac Linder) (Note: This film had its U.S. premiere on television on Nov. 4, 2001.)

LOST IN THE PERSHING POINT HOTEL

(NORTHERN ARTS) Producers, Julia Jay Pierrepont III, Erin Chandler; Executive Producers, Michael Tiberi, Jimmy "Kimo" Ciotti; Director, Julia Jay Pierrepont III; Screenplay, Leslie Jordan; Photography, Sacha Sarchielli; Designer, Cecil Gentry; Costumes, Chantal Thomas; Editor, Ila von Hasperg; Music, Dan Gilboy; Casting, Lisa Pantone, James Pantone; Dolby; Color; Not rated; 107 minutes; Release date: December 7, 2001. CAST: Leslie Jordan (Storyteller), Erin Chandler (Miss Make Do), Mark Pellegrino (Tripper), John Ritter (Christian Therapist), Marilu Henner (Mother), Michelle Phillips (DeeDee Westbrooks), Sheryl Lee Ralph (Nurse Talley-Mae), Kathy Kinney (Redneck Nurse), Carlos Gomez (Nico), Peter Mohawk (Contessa), Luke Eberl (Young Storyteller), Adam Wylie (Duane Striker), Jesse Petrick (Johnny Striker), Sean Moran (Big Tiny), Billy Butler (Irvin), Chad Gordon (Chicken Jimmy), Arthur Hiller (Street Evangelist), Karen Austin (PR Woman), Kris Kamm (Cotton Pine), Bobby McGee (T-Bone), Matt Flanders (Brandon), Ritch Schyder (Storyteller's Father), Badja Djola (Fast Eddie), John Fleck (Weird Guy), Patrick O'Neal (Angry Bartender), Stephanie Blake (Kayla, Stripper), Viveka Davis, Krista Metropolis, Cherise Leana Bangs (Debutantes), Newell Alexander (Preacher), Rosemary Alexander (Church Lady), Jimmy Bangley (Church Man), James Hampton (Pediatrician), Jane Abbott (Jean Jean), Essence (Lucinda), Donna Eskra (Starla), Lisa Smock (Pregnant Prostitute), Edward Ferry (Stairwell John), Vincent Castellanos (Toothpick Jorge), David Higlin (1990s Cabbie), Jeff Key (Wedding Photographer)

Denis Leary, Hope Davis in *Final* © Cowboy

Giovanni Andrade, Brent Fellows in *Eban & Charley*
© Picture This!

AS I WAS MOVING AHEAD OCCASIONALLY I SAW BRIEF GLIMPSES OF BEAUTY

(JONAS MEKAS PRODS.) Producer/Director/Screenplay/Photography/Editor, Jonas Mekas; Music, Auguste Varkalis; Color; Not rated; 288 minutes; Release date: December 12, 2001. Filmmaker Jonas Mekas's documentation of glimpses from his life over the past three decades.

EBAN AND CHARLEY

(PICTURE THIS!) Producer, Chris Monlux; Director/Screenplay, James Bolton; Photography, Judy Irola; Editor, Elizabeth Edwards; Music, Stephin Merritt; Color; Not rated; 86 minutes; Release date: December 14, 2001. CAST: Brent Fellows (Eban), Giovanni Andrade (Charley), Ellie Nicholson (Sunshine), Drew Zeller (Kevin), Pam Munter (Eban's Mother), Ron Upton (Eban's Father), Nolan V. Chard (Charley's Father)

LUSH

(i5 FILMS) Producers, Scott McGehee, Patrick Dollard; Executive Producers, Robert H. Nathan, Eileen Jones; Director/Screenplay, Mark Gibson; Photography, Caroline Champetier; Designer, Scott Plauche; Editor, Sarah Flack; Music, Barrett Martin; Co-Producer, Alicia Allain; Casting, Nicole Arbusto, Joy Dickson; Color; Not rated; 93 minutes; Release date: December 28, 2001. CAST: Campbell Scott (Lionel "Ex" Exley), Jared Harris (W. Firmin Carter), Laura Linney (Rachel Van Dyke), Laurel Holloman (Ash Van Dyke), Nick Offerman (Gerry), Kimo Wills (Pats), James R. Hall, Jr. (Buddha), Don Hood (Har), Joe Chrest (Greg), Michael Cahill (Brian), David Sellars (Conner), J. C. Sealy (Miss Billie), Anthony Marble (Brice), Layton Martens (Veteran Cop), Doug Barden (Detective), Marcus Lyle Brown (Rookie Cop), Chris Campbell (Carl), Phil Brady (Fuzzie), Sally Birdsong (Na-Non), Glen Paddie (Bob)

THE OTHER SIDE OF HEAVEN

(EXCEL ENTERTAINMENT) Producers, John Garbett, Gerald R. Molen; Executive Producer, Mitch Davis; Co-Producer, Tim Coddington; Director/Screenplay, Mitch Davis; Based on the book *In the Eye of the Storm* by John H. Groberg; Photography, Brian J. Breheny; Music, Kevin Kiner; Editor, Steven Ramirez; from 3Mark Entertainment, Molen/Garbett Productions; Dolby; Color; Rated PG; 113 minutes; Release date: Dec. 14, 2001. CAST: Christopher Gorham (John Groberg), Anne Hathaway (Jean Sabin), Joe Folau (Feki), Miriama Smith (Lavania), Whetu Fala (Asi), Alvin Fitisemanu (Tomasi), Peter Sa'ena Brown (Kuli), Apii McKinley (Noli), John Sumner (President Stone), Nathaniel Lees, Paki Cherrington, Pua Magasiva, John Paekau, Glynis Paraha

Christopher Gorham in *The Other Side of Heaven*
© Excel Entertainment

PROMISING NEW ACTORS
OF 2001

Hayden Christensen
(*Life as a House*)

Aunjanue Ellis
(*The Caveman's Valentine*)

Scarlett Johansson
(*An American Rhapsody, Ghost World,
The Man Who Wasn't There*)

Jay Hernandez
(*Crazy/Beautiful*)

Justin Long
(*Jeepers Creepers*)

Jena Malone
(*Donnie Darko, Life as a House*)

Audrey Tautou
(*Amélie, Happenstance*)

Dominic Monaghan
(*The Lord of the Rings: The Fellowship of the Ring*)

Mos Def
(*Monster's Ball*)

Emma Watson
(*Harry Potter and The Sorcerer's Stone*)

Naomi Watts
(*Mulholland Dr.*)

Daniel Radcliffe
(*Harry Potter and The Sorcerer's Stone,*
The Tailor of Panama)

ACADEMY AWARD WINNER
FOR BEST PICTURE OF 2001

Russell Crowe, Ed Harris

Russell Crowe

Russell Crowe, Christopher Plummer, Jennifer Connelly

A BEAUTIFUL MIND

(UNIVERSAL/DREAMWORKS) Producer, Brian Grazer; Executive Producers, Karen Kehela, Todd Hallowell; Director, Ron Howard; Screenplay, Akiva Goldsman; Based on the book by Sylvia Nasar; Photography, Roger Deakins; Designer, Wynn Thomas; Costumes, Rita Ryack; Editors, Mike Hill, Dan Hanley; Music, James Horner; Co-Producer, Maureen Peyrot; Casting, Jane Jenkins, Janet Hirshenson; an Imagine Entertainment presentation of a Brian Grazer production; Dolby; Deluxe color; Rated PG-13; 134 minutes; Release date: December 21, 2001

CAST

John Forbes Nash, Jr.	Russell Crowe
William Parcher	Ed Harris
Alicia Larde Nash	Jennifer Connelly
Dr. Rosen	Christopher Plummer
Charles Herman	Paul Bettany
Sol	Adam Goldberg
Hansen	Josh Lucas
Marcee	Vivien Cardone
Bender	Anthony Rapp
Ainsley	Jason Gray-Stanford
Helinger	Judd Hirsch
Thomas King	Austin Pendleton
Professor Horner	Victor Steinbach
Becky	Tanya Clarke
Captain	Thomas F. Walsh
General	Jesse Doran
Analyst	Kent Cassella
MIT Student	Patrick Blindauer
Photographer	John Blaylock
Governor	Roy Thinnes
Young Man	Anthony Easton
Harvard Administrator	Cheryl Howard
White-Haired Patron	Rance Howard
Code-Red Nurse	JJ Chaback
Adjunct	Darius Stone
Princeton Professor	Josh Pais
Toby	Alex Toma
Joyce	Valentina Cardinalli
Young Professor	Teagle F. Bougere
Bar Co-ed	Jill M. Simon
Josh Nash, Jr. (13 years old)	David B. Allen
Josh Nash, Jr. (20 years old)	Michael Esper
Girl at Bar	Catharina Eva Burkley
Blonde in Bar	Amy Walz

Insulin Treatment Nurses .... Kathleen Fellegara, Betsy Klompus and Tracey Toomey, Jennifer Weedon, Yvonne Thomas, Holly Pitrago (Brunettes), Isadore Rosenfeld, Thomas C. Allen, Dave Bayer, Brian Keith Lewis, Tom McNutt, Will Dunham, Glenn Roberts, Ed Jupp (Pen Ceremony Professors), Christopher Stockton, Gregory Dress, Carla Occhiogrosso, Matt Samson, Lyena Nomura (Princeton Students), Stelio Savante, Logan McCall, Bob Broder (Technicians)

John Nash, an eccentric but brilliant mathematician, is recruited to work as a code breaker during the Cold War, only to find his work hampered when he is diagnosed with paranoid schizophrenia.

2001 Academy Award-winner for Best Picture, Director, Supporting Actress (Jennifer Connelly), and Adapted Screenplay. This film received additional Oscar nominations for actor (Russell Crowe), editing, original score, and makeup.

© Universal Studios

Russell Crowe

Russell Crowe, Paul Bettany

Anthony Rapp, Adam Goldberg, Jennifer Connelly

Russell Crowe, Jennifer Connelly

DENZEL WASHINGTON

in *Training Day* © Warner Bros.

ACADEMY AWARD FOR BEST ACTOR OF 2001

HALLE BERRY

in *Monster's Ball* © Lions Gate Films

ACADEMY AWARD FOR BEST ACTRESS OF 2001

JIM BROADBENT

in *Iris* © Miramax Films

ACADEMY AWARD FOR BEST SUPPORTING ACTOR OF 2001

JENNIFER CONNELLY

in *A Beautiful Mind* © Universal Studios

ACADEMY AWARD FOR BEST SUPPORTING ACTRESS OF 2001

ACADEMY AWARD NOMINEES
FOR BEST ACTOR

Russell Crowe in *A Beautiful Mind*

Sean Penn in *I Am Sam*

Will Smith in *Ali*

Tom Wilkinson in *In The Bedroom*

ACADEMY AWARD NOMINEES
FOR BEST ACTRESS

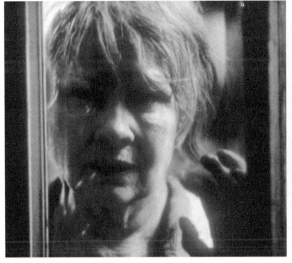

Judi Dench in *Iris*

Nicole Kidman in *Moulin Rouge!*

Sissy Spacek in *In The Bedroom*

Renée Zellweger in *Bridget Jones's Diary*

ACADEMY AWARD NOMINEES
FOR BEST SUPPORTING ACTOR

Ethan Hawke in *Training Day*

Ben Kingsley in *Sexy Beast*

Ian McKellen in *The Lord of the Rings:
The Fellowship of the Ring*

Jon Voight in *Ali*

ACADEMY AWARD NOMINEES
FOR BEST SUPPORTING ACTRESS

Helen Mirren in *Gosford Park*

Maggie Smith in *Gosford Park*

Marisa Tomei in *In The Bedroom*

Kate Winslet in *Iris*

ACADEMY AWARD WINNER
FOR BEST FOREIGN LANGUAGE FILM

Rene Bitorajac, Branko Djuric

Rene Bitorajac

NO MAN'S LAND

(UNITED ARTISTS) Producers, Frédérique Dumas-Zajdela, Marc Baschet, Cedomir Kilar; Co-Producers, Marco Müller, Marion Hänsel, Cat Villiers, Judy Counihan, Dunja Klemenc, Igor Pedicek; Director/Screenplay, Danis Tanovic; Photography, Walther Vanden Ende; Designer, Dusko Milavec; Costumes, Zvonka Makuc; Music, Danis Tanovic; Editor, Francesca Calvelli A.M.C.; a Noé Productions production in co-production with Fabrica Cinema (Italy), Man's Films (Belgium), and with Counihan Villiers Productions (United Kingdom), Studio Maj/Casablanca (Slovenia) in collaboration with the Centre du Cinema et de l'Audiovisuel de la Communauté Française de Belgique and the Télédistributeurs Wallons and Le Fonds Slovène du Cinéma; French-Italian-Belgian-British-Slovenian; Dolby; Color; Rated R; 97 minutes; U.S. release date: December 7, 2001

CAST

Ciki	Branko Djuric
Nino	Rene Bitorajac
Cera	Filip Sovagovic
Marchand	Georges Siatidis
Dubois	Serge-Henri Valcke
Michel	Sacha Kremer
Pierre	Alain Eloy
Old Serbian Soldier	Mustafa Nadarevic
Serbian Officer	Bogdan Diklic
Colonel Soft	Simon Callow
Jane Livingstone	Katrin Cartlidge
Martha	Tanja Ribic
Démineur	Branko Zavrsan
Bosnian Guide	Djuro Utjesanovic
Bosnian Officer	Mirza Tanovic

and Boro Stjepanovic, Almir Kurt, Ratko Ristic, Peter Sedmak, Aleksandar Petrovic (Bosnian Soldiers), Boris Cindric (Miralem), Danijel Smon (Serbian Officer 2), Peter Prikratki, Marinko Prga, Darjan Gorela, Srecko Dzumber (Serbian Soldiers), Primoz Ranik (Cameraman), Jure Plesec (Mark), Gordon Wilson (John), Maëlys De Rudder (Olivia), Alan Fairairn (Bill), Michel Obenga, Rok Strehovec (UNPROFOR Soldiers), Zvone Hribar, Ales Valic, Fred M. Liss, Franc Jakob Rac (Journalists), Predrag Brestovac (Rambo), Tadej Troha (Young Bosnian Soldier), Primoz Petrovsek (Serbian Lieutenant, Barricade), Janez Habic (Serbian Soldier, Barricade), Matej Bizjak (Boy Accordionist), Uros Tatomir (Serbian Sergeant), Matej Recer (Bosnian Officer, Barricade), Matija Bulatovic, Uros Furst (Bosnian Soldiers, Barricade)

A Bosnian and Serbian soldier are stuck in a trench between enemy lines with a wounded soldier, who is lying on a spring-loaded bomb set to explode if he moves.

Katrin Cartlidge, George Siantidis, Simon Callow

Branko Djuric, Rene Bitorajac

Katrin Cartlidge, Georges Siatidis

Branko Djuric, Rene Bitorajac

Rene Bitorajac, Branko Djuric

Katrin Cartlidge

TOP BOX OFFICE FILMS
OF 2001

1. Harry Potter and the Sorcerer's Stone (WB)....................$317,560,000
2. The Lord of the Rings: The Fellowship of the Ring (NL).......$312,970,000
3. Shrek (DW)...$267,670,000
4. Monsters, Inc. (BV)..$255,160,000
5. Rush Hour 2 (NL)...$225,170,000
6. The Mummy Returns (Univ)......................................$201,900,000
7. Pearl Harbor (BV)...$198,500,000
8. Ocean's Eleven (WB)...$183,260,000
9. Jurassic Park III (Univ)...$180,190,000
10. Planet of the Apes (20th)......................................$180,100,000

Milo Thatch in *Atlantis, The Lost Empire*
© Walt Disney Pictures

Daniel Radcliffe in *Harry Potter and The Sorcerer's Stone*
© Warner Bros.

11. A Beautiful Mind (Univ/DW) $170,710,000
12. Hannibal (MGM/Univ)...$165,100,000
13. The Fast and the Furious (Univ) $144,450,000
14. American Pie 2 (Univ)..$144,100,000
15. Lara Croft: Tomb Raider (Par) $131,170,000
16. Spy Kids (Mir) $112,720,000
17. Dr. Dolittle 2 (20th)...$111,910,000
18. Black Hawk Down (Col)..$108,270,000
19. The Princess Diaries (BV)..$108,250,000
20. Vanilla Sky (Par) $100,540,000
21. The Others (Mir)..$96,530,000
22. Legally Blonde (MGM)..$96,450,000
23. America's Sweethearts (Col) $93,520,000
24. Cats & Dogs (WB)..$93,270,000
25. Save the Last Dance (Par) $91,100,000

26. Atlantis: The Lost Empire (BV)......................................$83,920,000
27. Jimmy Neutron: Boy Genius (Par) $80,930,000
28. AI: Artificial Intelligence (WB)....................................$78,580,000
29. Training Day (WB)..$76,190,000
30. Along Came a Spider (Par) $74,100,000
31. Bridget Jones's Diary (Mir/Univ)...................................$71,550,000
32. The Score (Par) $70,990,000
33. Shallow Hal (20th)...$70,770,000
34. Scary Movie 2 (Mir)..$70,310,000
35. Swordfish (WB)..$69,670,000
36. The Mexican (DW)..$66,850,000
37. Down to Earth (Par)..$64,150,000
38. Spy Game (Univ)..$62,370,000
39. The Wedding Planner (Col)..$60,410,000
40. Behind Enemy Lines (20th) $58,770,000

Renée Zellweger in
Bridget Jones's Diary
© Miramax Films

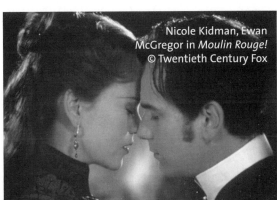

Nicole Kidman, Ewan
McGregor in *Moulin Rouge!*
© Twentieth Century Fox

41. Ali (Col) $58,120,000
42. Moulin Rouge! (20th)..$57,230,000
43. Rat Race (Par) $56,620,000
44. A Knight's Tale (Col) $55,790,000
45. The Animal (Col)...$55,690,000
46. Don't Say a Word (20th)..$54,940,000
47. The Royal Tenenbaums (BV) $52,310,000
48. Blow (NL)...$51,880,000
49. Exit Wounds (WB)..$51,470,000
50. Enemy at the Gates (Par)...$50,880,000

51. K-PAX (Univ) $50,340,000
52. Serendipity (Mir) $50,300,000
53. Kate & Leopold (Mir) $47,100,000
54. Zoolander (Par) $45,140,000
55. Domestic Disturbance (Par) $45,100,000
56. The One (Col) $43,910,000
57. Thirteen Ghosts (WB/Col)..............................$41,770,000
58. Bandits (MGM) $41,480,000
59. Gosford Park (USA Films)..............................$41,280,000

Justin Long, Gina Philips in *Jeepers Creepers*
© United Artists Films

Meg Ryan, Hugh Jackman in *Kate & Leopold*
© Miramax Films

60. I Am Sam (NL) $40,270,000
61. Hardball (Par) $40,230,000
62. Heartbreakers (MGM) $40,150,000
63. Evolution (DW/Col) $38,350,000
64. Not Another Teen Movie (Col) $37,890,000
65. Jeepers Creepers (UA) $37,830,000
66. Kiss of the Dragon (20th)...............................$36,770,000
67. Recess: School's Out (BV) $36,600,000
68. In the Bedroom (Mir)......................................$35,880,000
69. Black Knight (20th)...$33,370,000
70. See Spot Run (WB) $33,240,000
71. Amélie (Mir) $33,180,000
72. Driven (WB)..$32,590,000
73. What's the Worst That Could Happen? (MGM)............$32,130,000
74. Final Fantasy (Col)..$32,100,000
75. From Hell (20th) $31,560,000

76. Monster's Ball (Lions Gate) $31,260,000
77. How High (Univ) $31,160,000
78. Jay and Silent Bob Strike Back (Mir)...............$30,100,000
79. Riding in Cars With Boys (Col) $29,790,000
80. Double Take (BV)..$29,550,000
81. Baby Boy (Col) $28,360,000
82. The Majestic (WB) $27,800,000
83. The Brothers (Screen Gems) $27,410,000
84. Someone Like You (20th) $27,180,000
85. The Musketeer (Univ) $27,100,000
86. Joe Dirt (Col)..$26,970,000
87. Crocodile Dundee in Los Angeles (Par) $25,540,000
88. Captain Corelli's Mandolin (Univ) $25,500,000
89. Memento (Newmarket) $25,440,000
90. Sweet November (WB)......................................$25,180,000

Drew Barrymore, Steve Zahn, Cody Arens in *Riding in
Cars With Boys* © Columbia Pictures

91. 15 Minutes (New Line) $24,410,000
92. Angel Eyes (WB) $24,100,000
93. Hearts in Atlantis (WB)...................................$23,950,000
94. Corky Romano (BV) $23,940,000
95. Heist (WB) $23,410,000
96. Kingdom Come (Fox Search) $23,100,000
97. Joe Somebody (20th) $22,670,000
98. Joy Ride (20th) $21,950,000
99. Two Can Play That Game (Screen Gems).........$21,770,000
100. Valentine (WB)...$20,360,000

Milla Jovovich, Ben Stiller, Will Ferrell in *Zoolander*
© Paramount Pictures

FOREIGN FILMS
RELEASED IN THE US IN 2001

THE PERSONALS

(FIRST RUN FEATURES) Producer, Hsu Li-kong; Executive Producer, Hsu Li-kong, Chiu Shun-Ching; Director, Chen Kuo-fu; Screenplay, Chen Kuo-fu, Chen Shih-che; Story, Chen Yu-hui; Photography, Ho Nan-hong; Art Director, Wang Yi-bai; Editor, Chang Dar-lung; from Zoom Hunt Int. Productions Co. Ltd., Central Motion Picture Corporation; Taiwan, 2000; Dolby; Color; Not rated; 104 minutes; U.S. release date: January 12, 2001

CAST

Du Jiazhen ....Rene Liu
and Chin Shih-chieh, Chen Chao-jung, Wu Bai, Gu Bao-ming, Niu Chen-zer, Shih Yi-nan, Teddy Lo, Sisy Chen, Pu Hseueh-liang

A successful young eye doctor places a personal ad in the newspaper in order to land a husband and meets up with each of the men who respond.

© First Run Features

Rene Liu (right)

Bibiana Beglau, Alexander Beyer

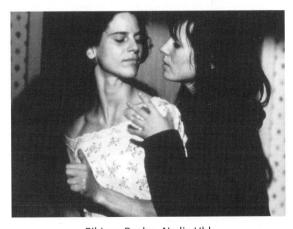

Bibiana Beglau, Nadja Uhl

THE LEGEND OF RITA

(KINO) Producers, Arthur Hofer, Emmo Lempert; Director, Volker Schlöndorff; Screenplay, Wolfgang Kohlhaase, Volker Schlöndorff; Photography, Andreas Höfer, BVK; Art Director, Susanne Hopf; Editor, Peter Przygodda; Costumes, Anne-Gret Oehme; a Babelsberg Film Produktion in association with Mitteldeutsches Filmkontor and MDR; German, 1999; Dolby; Color; Not rated; 101 minutes; U.S. release date: January 24, 2001

CAST

Rita ....Bibiana Beglau
Erwin Hull ....Martin Wuttke
Tatjana ....Nadja Uhl
Andi ....Harald Schrott
Jochen ....Alexander Beyer
Friederike ....Jenny Schily
Klatte ....Mario Irrek
Gerngross ....Thomas Arnold
Anna...Franca Kastein
The General ....Dietrich Körner
Milchgesicht ....Richard Kropf

Rita, a former West German terrorist, hides out in East Germany, assuming a new identity among the working class until her past catches up with her.

© Kino International

FAITHLESS

(GOLDWYN) Producer, Kaj Larsen; Executive Producer, Maria Curman; Director, Liv Ullmann; Screenplay, Ingmar Bergman; Photography, Jörgen Persson FSF; Art Director, Göran Wassberg; Costumes, Inger E Pehrsson; Editor, Sylvia Ingemarsson; an SVT Drama production in collaboration with AB Svensk Filmindustri, NRK, Yle, Classic SRL, RAI and ZDF, with the support of the Swedish Film Institute, Film Commissioner Mats Aréhn and Nordic Film and TV Fund; Presented in association with Fireworks Pictures; Swedish, 2000; Dolby; Color; Rated R; 142 minutes; US release date: January 26, 2001

CAST

Marianne Vogler ....Lena Endre
Bergman ....Erland Josephson
David ....Krister Henriksson
Markus Vogler ....Thomas Hanzon
Isabelle ....Michelle Gylemo
Margareta ....Juni Dahr
Martin Goldman ....Philip Zanden
Petra Holst ....Therese Brunnander
Anna Berg ....Marie Richardson
Eva ....Stina Ekblad
Johan ....Johan Rabaeus
Axel ....Jan-Olof Strandberg
Gustav ....Björn Granath
Martha ....Gertrud Stenung

Marianne, an actress married to an orchestra conductor, finds herself involved in an affair with a family friend, a reckless, gloomy film director.

© Goldwyn/Fireworks

Alana De Roma, Rachel Griffiths

Krister Henriksson, Lena Endre

AMY

(WORLD WIDE) Producers, Nadia Tass, David Parker; Director, Nadia Tass; Screenplay/Photography, David Parker; Co-Producer, Phil Jones; Designer, Jon Dowding; Editor, Bill Murphy; Costumes, Christiana Plitzco; Music, Phillip Judd; Australian, 1998; Color; Rated PG-13; 103 minutes; US release date: February 2, 2001

CAST

Tanya Rammus...Rachel Griffiths
Amy Enker...Alana De Roma
Robert Buchanan..Ben Mendelsohn
Will Enker...Nick Barker
Sarah Trendle..Kerry Armstrong
Zac Trendle...Jeremy Trigatti
Bill Trendle ....William Zappa
Luke Lassiter...Torquil Neilson
Wayne Lassiter ....Sullivan Stapleton
Mrs Mullins..Mary Ward
Anny Buchanan ....Susie Porter
Dr Urquhart..Frank Gallacher
Susan Hammnett ....Jan Friedl
Brian Cosgrove ....Malcolm Kennard
Maurice Reitman ....Jeremy Kewley
Franco Rammus ....Osvaldo Maione

A little girl who has retreated into silence following her father's death is encouraged to communicate through music by her mother and by a young musician who lives next door.

© Beyond Films Ltd.

Tony Leung Chiu-wai, Maggie Cheung   Maggie Cheung, Tony Leung Chiu-wai

IN THE MOOD FOR LOVE

(USA FILMS) Producer/Director/Screenplay, Wong Kar-Wai; Executive Producer, Chan Ye-Cheng; Associate Producer, Jacky Pang Yee-Wah; Photography, Christopher Doyle, Mark Li Ping-Bin; Designer/Costumes, William Chang Suk-Ping; Music, Michael Galasso; a Block 2 Pictures, Inc and Paradis Films presentation of a Jet Tone Films production; Hong Kong-French, 2000; Dolby; Color; Rated PG; 97 minutes; US release date: February 2, 2001

CAST

Chow Mo-wan ....Tony Leung Chiu-wai
Su Li-zhen ....Maggie Cheung
Mrs Suen..Rebecca Pan
Mr Ho ....Lai Chin
Ah Pong ....Siu Ping-lam
The Amah...Chin Tsi-ang
and Man-Lei Chan, Kan-wah Koo, Hsien Yu, Po-chun Chow

In 1962 Hong Kong, a journalist and a secretary, living next door to one another, discover that their spouses are having an affair, leading them to spend a great deal of time together while trying not to act on their growing feelings for one another.

© USA Films

Tony Leung Chiu-wai, Maggie Cheung

Fernando Ramallo, Jordi Vilches

NICO AND DANI
(KRÁMPACK)

(**AVATAR**) Producers, Marta Esteban, Gerardo Herrero; Director, Cesc Gay; Screenplay, Cesc Gay, Tomás Aragay; Based on the play *Krámpack* by Jordi Sánchez; Photography, Andreu Rebés; Music, Riqui Sabatés, Joan Díaz, Jordi Prats; Editor, Frank Gutiérrez; a Messidor Films production; Spanish, 2000; Dolby; Color; Not rated; 90 minutes; US release date: February 2, 2001

CAST

Dani	Fernando Ramallo
Nico	Jordi Vilches
Elena	Marieta Orozco
Berta	Esther Nubiola
Julián	Chisco Amado
Sonia	Ana Gracia
Marianne	Myriam Mézières
Dani's Mother	Muntsa Alcañiz
Dani's Father	Jesús Garay
Mario	Pau Durá
Camarero	Eduardo González
Chica	Gaelle Poulavec
Arturo	Mingo Ràfols
Manu	Eloi Yebra

During a summer on the Mediterranean coast, 17-year-old Dani's sexual experimentation with his best friend Nico brings him to the realization that he is attracted to men.

© Avatar Films

Fernando Ramallo, Jordi Vilches

Jordi Vilches, Fernando Ramallo

Bud Cort, Jimmy Smits, Jeremy Davies

THE MILLION DOLLAR HOTEL

(LIONS GATE) Producers, Deepak Nayar, Bono, Nicholas Klein, Bruce Davey, Wim Wenders; Executive Producer, Ulrich Felsberg; Director, Wim Wenders; Screenplay, Nicholas Klein; Story, Bono, Nicholas Klein; Photography, Phedon Papamichael; Designers, Robert D Freed, Arabella A Serrell; Music, Jon Hassell, Bono, Daniel Lanois, Brian Eno; Costumes, Nancy Steiner; Casting, Heidi Levitt, Monika Mikkelsen; an Icon Entertainment International presentation of a Road Movies production in association with Icon Productions and Kintop Pictures; German-US, 2000; Dolby; Panavision; Color; Rated R; 122 minutes; US release date: February 2, 2001

CAST

Tom Tom	Jeremy Davies
Eloise	Milla Jovovich
Detective Skinner	Mel Gibson
Geronimo	Jimmy Smits
Dixie	Peter Stormare
Vivien	Amanda Plummer
Jessica	Gloria Stuart
Hector	Tom Bower
Charley Best	Donal Logue
Shorty	Bud Cort
Terence Scopey	Julian Sands
Izzy Goldkiss	Tim Roth
Stix	Conrad Roberts
Stanley Goldkiss	Harris Yulin
Jean Swift	Charlayne Woodard
Marlene	Ellen Cleghorne

and Richard Edson (Joe), Tito Larriva (Jesu), Jon Hassell (Hollow), Justin Lafoe (Marlene's Son), Ezra Buzzington (Reporter), David Stifel (Screamer for Jesus), Winston J. Rochas (Waiter), Frederique Van Der Wal (Diamond Woman), Roger Stoneburner, Erik Rondell (Punks), Bono (Man in Hotel Lobby)

As childlike Tom Tom jumps from the roof of a shabby LA hotel, he narrates the events that led to this situation, starting when Detective Skinner arrived at the establishment to question its many oddball inhabitants concerning the death of resident Izzy Goldkiss.

THE TASTE OF OTHERS

(OFFLINE) Producers, Christian Bérard, Charles Gassot; Executive Producer, Jacques Hinstin; Director, Agnès Jaoui; Screenplay, Agnès Jaoui, Jean-Pierre Bacri; Photography, Laurent Dailland; Designer, François Emmanuelli; Line Producer, Daniel Chevalier; Editor, Hervé De Luze; Costumes, Jackie Stephens-Budin; Casting, Brigitte Moidon; Presented in association with Miramax Films, Sagittarius Films; French, 2000; Dolby; Super 35 Widescreen; Color; Not rated; 112 minutes; US release date: February 9, 2001

CAST

Clara	Anne Alvaro
Castella	Jean-Pierre Bacri
Beatrice	Brigitte Catillon
Deschamps	Alain Chabat
Manie	Agnès Jaoui
Moreno	Gerard Lanvin
Valerie	Anne Le Ny
Angelique	Christiane Millet
Antoine	Wladimir Yordanoff
Weber	Xavier de Guillebon
Benoît	Raphael Dufour
Fred	Bob Zarembar

and Sam Karmann (The Director), Marie-Agnes Brigot (The Secretary), Robert Bacri (Castella's Father), Desir Carre (Passerby), Celine Arnaud (Virginie), Reginald Huguenin (Titus), Jean-Marc Talbot (Antiochus), Jean-François Levistre (Arsace), Didier Mahieu (Hedda's Husband), Stanislas de la Tousche (The Judge)

Castella, a married man obsessed with Clara, an actress he has seen in a play, is delighted to discover that she is his new English instructor.

Jean-Pierre Bacri, Anne Alvaro

Regina Casé, Luiz Carlos Vasconcelos

Lima Duarte

ME YOU THEM

(SONY PICTURES CLASSICS) Producers, Andrucha Waddington, Flávio R Tambellini, Pedro B. de Hollanda, Leonardo M. de Barros; Director, Andrucha Waddington; Screenplay, Elena Soárez; Photography, Breno Silveira; Designer, Toni Vanzolini; Costumes, Claudia Kopke; Editor, Vicente Kubrusly; Music, Gilberto Gil; Line Producer, Mariza Figueiredo; Associate Producer, Flora Gil; a Conspiração Filmes, Columbia TriStar Filmes do Brasil presentation; Brazilian-Portuguese, 2000; Dolby; Color; Rated PG-13; 107 minutes; US release date: March 2, 2001

CAST

Darlene..Regina Casé
Osias Linares ....Lima Duarte
Zezinho ....Stênio Garcia
Ciro..Luís Carlos Vasconcelos
Raquel ....Nilda Spencer
Black Herdsman..Diogo Lopes
Darlene's Mother ....Helena Araújo
and Iami Rebouças (Young Woman at Ball), Lucien Paulo (Headman), Borges Cunha (Registry Employee), Plácido Alves Neto (Store Owner), D Dinorah (Osias's Mother), José Pascoal (Young Man at Ball), Zé Brocoió, Clésio Atanásio (Speakers), Fransico Alves Torres (Darlene's Brother), D Maria Isabel Borges, Maria do Roasio, D Luzia Gomes (Mourners), Tarjino Gondim e Banda (Band at São João Festival), Grupo Senhor do Bonfim (Forró Band #1, Darlene's Wedding), Sérgio do Forró e Banda (Forró Band #2), Herbert Medrado (Dimas—1 year old), Joanderson Cruz (Dimas—4 years old), Jocemar Damásio (Dimas—6 years old), Arielson Dos Santos (Baby Edinardo), Pablo Silva (Edinardo—1 year old), Jefferson Souza (Edinardo—4 years old), Vitor Da Conceição (Edinardo—6 years old), Lucas De Castro Silva (Baby Edinaldo), João Lucas De Barros Neto (Edinaldo—1 year old), Jonathan Dantas (Edinaldo—4 years old), Alessandro Dos Santos Ribeiro (Baby Edivaldi)

Years after Darlene had been abandoned at the altar while pregnant, she moves in with elderly Osias Linhares and becomes lovers with two other men while living in Osias's household.

LAST RESORT

(SHOOTING GALLERY) Producer, Ruth Caleb; Executive Producers, David M Thompson, Alex Holmes; Director/Screenplay, Pavel Pawlikwoski; Photography, Ryszard Lenczewski; Designer, Tom Bowyer; Editor, David Charap; Music, Max de Wardener, Rowan Oliver; Costumes, Julian Day; Casting, Chloe Emerson; from BBC Films; British; Dolby; Soho Images Color; Not rated; 73 minutes; US release date: February 23, 2001

CAST

Tanya ....Dina Korzun
Alfie ....Paddy Considine
Artiom..Artiom Strelnikov
Les ....Lindsey Honey
Immigration Officer ....Perry Benson
Katie..Katie Drinkwater
Frank..David Bean
and Adrian Scarborough, David Auker (Council Officials), Bruce Byron (Police Officer), Jim Trevelyan (Station Guard), Marcus Redwood (Cafe Owner), Zoe Sharpe (Gang Girl), Daniel Mobey (Danny)

Arriving with her young son in England, where she expects to meet her fiancé, a Russian woman is detained by immigration and taken to a holding area, where she and her child are befriended by an amusement park worker.

Paddy Considine, Artiom Strelnikov, Dina Korzun

Juliette Binoche

Emir Kusturica

THE WIDOW OF SAINT-PIERRE

(LIONS GATE) Producers, Gilles Legrand, Frédéric Brillion; Director, Patrice Leconte; Screenplay, Claude Faraldo; Adaptation, Patrice Leconte, Michel Duchaussoy, Philippe Magnan, Christian Charmetant, Philippe du Janerand; Photography, Eduardo Sarra; Editor, Joëlle Hache; Designer, Ivan Maussion; Costumes, Christian Gasc; Co-Producers, Denise Robert, Daniel Louis; Music, Pascal Esteve; Directors of Production, Frederic Blum, Paul Laine; an Epithete Films, Cinemaginaire, France 3 Cinema, France 2 Cinema production, with the participation of CNC Canal+, Telefilm Canada Sodec; French-Canadian, 2000; Dolby; Panavision; Color; Rated R; 108 minutes; US release date: March 2, 2001

CAST

Madame La (Pauline)	Juliette Binoche
The Captain (Jean)	Daniel Auteuil
Ariel Neel Auguste	Emir Kusturica
Judge Venot	Philippe Magnan
The Governor	Michel Duchaussoy
Supply and Secretariat Officer	Christian Charmetant
Customs Officer	Philippe Du Janerand
Louis Olivier	Reynald Bouchard
M Chevassus	Ghyslain Tremblay
Soldier Loic	Marc Béland
The Rear-Admiral	Yves Jacques
The Governor's Father	Maurice Chevit
La Malvilain	Catherine Lascault
The Proprietor	Dominique Quesnel
The Governor's Wife	Anne-Marie Philipe
President Venot's Wife	Isabelle Spade
The Governor's Children	Arianne Mallet, Julian Gutierrez
Adrienne	Sylvie Moreau

and Geneviève Cocke, Manon Gauthier (Washhouse Women), Marianne C Miron (Mme Chevassus), Jean-Paul Rouvray (The Priest), Michel Daigle (Father Coupard), Luc Guerin (Captain Dumontier), Niel Kroetsch (Captain of the Marie Galante), Sylvain Eluau (Captain Goelette), Raymond Cloutier (The Adjutant), Patrick Steltzer (The Brigadier), Patrick Caux (Young Soldier), Bernard Tanguay (The Orderly), Serge Christiaenssens (The Drummer), Martin Laroque (Town Crier), Boris Napes (Assessor), Yvon Roy (Granjean), Luc Proulx (Cafe Customer), Kendall Negro (The Child), Stefan Perrault (Oarsman), Sarah McKenna (Emilie)

On the island of Saint-Pierre, a man awaiting execution for accidentally killing someone during a drunken altercation is placed in custody of the French military commandant and his wife, who begins to question the justice of the death penalty.

Daniel Auteuil

Juliette Binoche, Daniel Auteuil

© Lions Gate Films

THE GLEANERS AND I

(ZEITGEIST) Director/Narrator, Agnès Varda; Photography, Stéphane Krausz, Didier Rouget, Didier Doussin, Pascal Sautelet, Agnès Varda; Music, Joanna Bruzdowicz; Editors, Agnès Varda, Laurent Pineau; Produced by Ciné Tamaris, with the help of Centre National de la Cinematographie, Procirep and Canal+; French, 2000; Color; Not rated; 82 minutes; US release date: March 7, 2001 A documentary–road-trip throughout France capturing images of gleaners, people who scavenge or pick up items left behind by others

© Zeitgeist Films

Rachel Griffiths, Natasha Richardson, Alan Rickman

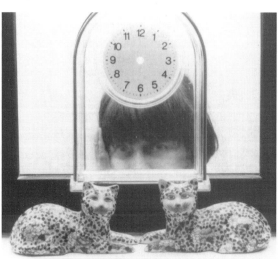

Agnès Varda

BLOW DRY

(MIRAMAX) Producers, Ruth Jackson, William Horberg, David Rubin; Executive Producers, Sydney Pollack, Meryl Poster, Julie Goldstein; Director, Paddy Breathnach; Screenplay, Simon Beaufoy, based on his screenplay *Never Better*; Photography, Cian De Buitléar; Designer, Sophie Becher; Costumes, Rosie Hackett; Co-Producer, Mark Cooper; Associate Producer, David Brown; Music, Patrick Doyle; Make-up and Hair Designer, Jenny Shircore; Casting, Gail Stevens; an Intermedia Films presentation of a Mirage Enterprises/West Eleven Production in association with IMF Productions; British-US; Dolby; Technicolor; Rated R; 90 minutes; US release date: March 7, 2001

CAST

Phil Allen ....Alan Rickman
Shelly ....Natasha Richardson
Sandra...Rachel Griffiths
Christina Robertson ....Rachael Leigh Cook
Brian Allen ....Josh Harnett
Ray Robertson..Bill Nighy
Tony ....Warren Clarke
Daisy...Rosemary Harris
Louis...Hugh Bonneville
Jasmine ....Heidi Klum
Vincent...Peter McDonald
Robert...Michael McElhatton
Noah ....David Bradley
Saul...Ben Crompton
and Anne Rye (Margaret, Farmer's Wife), Ray Emmet Brown (TJ), Oliver Ford Davies (Dr Hamilton), Elizabeth Woodcock (Sharon), Mark Benton (George, Journalist #1), Gordon Langford-Rowe (Stanley, Journalist #2), Johnny Leeze (Journalist), Stephen Graham (Photographer), Willie Ross (Louis's Volunteer), Jukka Hiltunen (Biker Volunteer), Paul Copley (Ken), Lorraine Balinska (Ebony), Peter Kay (Cyril the Barman), Janet Henfrey (Aerobics Teacher), Tony Barton, Philip Wright (Workmen), Margaret Blakemore (Receptionist)

Previous two-time winner of the British Hairdressing Championships, Phil Allen, finds himself facing some stiff competition from reigning champion Ray Robertson, his former rival.

© Miramax Films

Josh Hartnett, Rachael Leigh Cook

Peter McDonald, Flora Montgomery

SIMON MAGUS

(FIREWORKS) Producer, Robert Jones; Director/Screenplay, Ben Hopkins; Photography, Nic Knowland; Designer, Angela Davies; Costumes, Michelle Clapton; Line Producer, Anita Overland; Editor, Alan Levy; Music, Deborah Mollison; Casting, Susie Figgis; a FilmFour, Lucky Red, ARP and Hollywood Partners in association with the Arts Council of England presentation of a Jonescompany production; British-German-Italian-French, 1999; Dolby; Super 35 Widescreen; Deluxe color; Not rated; 106 minutes; US release date: March 9, 2001

CAST

Simon Magus	Noah Taylor
Dovid	Stuart Townsend
Maximilian Hase	Sean McGinley
Leah	Embeth Davidtz
Sarah	Amanda Ryan
Squire	Rutger Hauer
Sirius/Boris	Ian Holm
Bratislav	Terence Rigby
Buchholz	Toby Jones
Saul	Jim Dunk
Rebecca	Ursula Jones
Chaim	Cyril Shaps

and David De Keyser (Rabbi), Ken Dury (Priest), Tom Fisher (Thomas), Walter Sparrow (Benjamin), Jean Anderson (Roise), Katharine Schlesinger (Askha), Valerie Edmond (Eva), Kathryn Hunter (Grandmother), Maggie Steed (Muttchen), Mimi Potworowska (Angel), Barry Davis (Samuel the Cook), Frank Chersky (Feyder the Forester), Lawrence Werber (Zeidel the Carter), Hayley Carmichael (Rabbit Woman), Phil McKee (Railway Man), Brendan Charleson (Hireling 1), Nitzan Sharron (Joshua—21 years old), Joseph England (Elijah), Joel Freeman (Aaron), Nathan Grower (Anshel), Zoe Buckman (Beyle), Camilla Mars (Shifrah), Sam Davies (Joseph), Joshua Morris (Getsl), Jacob Morris (Simcha), Lexi Rose (Miryem), Elizabeth Margitta Miller (Rachel), Thomas Ingram (Gimpel), James Lewys Cox (Young Joshua), Linden Watts (Matthis), Isla Graham (Railway Man's Daughter)

In a small 19th-century European village, ruthless businessman Maximilian Hase, eager to bring his town into modern times by the building of a railroad station, enlists the help of outcast Simon Magus to help him plot against his rivals.

WHEN BRENDAN MET TRUDY

(SHOOTING GALLERY) Producer, Lynda Myles; Executive Producers, David M Thompson, Mike Phillips, Rod Stoneman, Claire Duignan; Director, Kieron J. Walsh; Screenplay/Co-Producer, Roddy Doyle; Photography, Ashley Rowe; Designer, Fiona Daly; Costumes, Consolata Boyle; Editor, Scott Thomas; Music, Richard Hartley; Casting, Leo Davis; a BBC Films, Bord Scannán na hÉireann/The Irish Film Board and Radio Telefís Éireann presentation of a Deadly Films 2 production of a Collins aVenue Film; British-Irish; Dolby; Color; Not rated; 95 minutes; US release date: March 9, 2001

CAST

Brendan	Peter McDonald
Trudy	Flora Montgomery
Mother	Marie Mullen
Nuala	Pauline McLynn
Niall	Don Wycherley
Edgar	Maynard Eziashi
Siobhan	Eileen Walsh
Headmaster	Barry Cassin
Judge	Niall O'Brien
Lynn	Rynagh O'Grady
Mary	Ali White

and Julie Hale, Christ McHallem (Choirsters), Jack Lynch (Conductor), Dr Stewart, Charlie Bird, Gabriel Byrne (Themselves), Robert O'Neill (Dylan), Eoin Manley (Cyril), George McMahon (James), Sean O'Flanagan (Eric), Pat Kinevane, Terry Byrne, Myles Horgan (Teachers), Anne Cassin (Newsreader), Harry Crosbie (Reporter), Luke Boyle (Flach), William O'Sullivan (Oisin), Jonathan White (Wig Man), Philip Judge (Garda Spokesman), Alicia O'Keeffe (Young Woman at Filmhaus), Kieron J Walsh (Young Man at Filmhaus), Berts Folan (School Caretaker), Kevin Sharkey (Celtic Cub), Robbie Doolin (Security Man), Keith McErlean, Martin Murphy, Frank O'Sullivan (Garda), Nuala Kelly, Triona McGarry, Jim Corry (Prison Officers), Ding Dong Denny O'Reilly and the Hairy Bowsies (Pub Band), Conor Evans (Doctor), Patricia Martin (Mrs O'Shaughnessy), Susan Murray, Gail Kainswarren (Wings Women), Amelia Crowley (Bookshop Babe), Robert Mack, James Mack, Coco Kenny, Francis Schurmann, Shauna Nugent (Brendan and Trudy's Children)

Brendan, a shy high-school teacher, meets Trudy, a free-spirited young woman who turns out to be a cat burglar.

Noah Taylor

Stuart Townsend, Embeth Davidtz

Sam Neill, Kevin Harrington, Tom Long

THE DISH

(WARNER BROS) Producers, Santo Cilauro, Tom Gleisner, Jane Kennedy, Rob Sitch, Michael Hirsch; Director, Rob Sitch; Screenplay, Santo Cilauro, Tom Gleisner, Jane Kennedy, Rob Sitch; Photography, Graeme Wood; Designer, Carrie Kennedy; Editor, Jill Bilcock; Music, Edmund Choi; Costumes, Kitty Stuckey; Line Producer, Debra Choate; Casting, Jane Kennedy, Yeskel Hicks; a Working Dog presentation in association with Distant Horizon; Australian, 2000; Dolby; Color; Rated PG-13; 102 minutes; US release date: March 14, 2001

CAST

Cliff Buxton	Sam Neill
Ross "Mitch" Mitchell	Kevin Harrington
Glenn Latham	Tom Long
Al Burnett	Patrick Warburton
May McIntyre	Genevieve Mooy
Rudi Kellerman	Taylor Kane
Prime Minister	Bille Brown
Mayor Bob McIntyre	Roy Billing
Len Purvis	Andrew S. Gilbert
Marie McIntyre	Lenka Kripac
Keith Morrison	Matthew Moore
Janine Kellerman	Eliza Szonert
US Ambassador	John McMartin
Billy McIntyre	Carl Snell
Cameron	Billy Mitchell
Miss Nolan	Roz Hammond
Damien	Christopher Robin-Street
Graeme	Luke Keltie
Melanie	Naomi Wright
Nicholas	Ben Wright-Smith

and Beverly Dunn (Secretary Voice-Over), Grant Thompson (Mr. Callen), Bernard Curry (Newspaper Reporter), Kerry Walker (Pearl), Denise Roberts (Bronwyn), Jeff Keogh (Ray), Jason Ritterman (Adrian Hobbs), Alexander Zent (Lead Guitarist), Rowan Macartney (Trumpet), Aidan Macartney (Trombone), Jarrod Factor (Drummer), Oliver McGill (Pianist), Marilyn O'Donnell (Melva), Jane Menelaus (Gwen), John Flaus (Ron), Neil Pigot (Journalist), Darren Davidson (Camera Person), Simon Donaldson (Sound Person), Frank Bennett (Barry Steele), Randall Berger (Ambassador's Aide), Charles "Bud" Tingwell (Reverend Loftus), Mal Walden (ABC Journalist Voice-Over), Rod McNeil (Radio Newsreader Voice-Over), Alister Paterson (ABC-TV Newsreader), Colette Mann (Betty the Bush Poet), Susan Ward (Print Journalist), Roger Crisp (Reporter)

At Australia's largest satellite dish, Cliff Buxton and his team are chosen to track the progress of Apollo 11 over the southern hemisphere.

© The Dish Film Productions PYY

Tom Long, Patrick Warburton, Sam Neill, Kevin Harrington

Tom Long

Kevin Harrington, Tom Long, Patrick Warburton, Sam Neill

Rachel Weisz, Jude Law

Joseph Fiennes, Jude Law

Ed Harris

ENEMY AT THE GATES

(PARAMOUNT) Producers, Jean-Jacques Annaud, John D Schofield; Executive Producers, Alain Godard, Alisa Tager; Director, Jean-Jacques Annaud; Screenplay, Alain Godard, Jean-Jacques Annaud; Photography, Robert Fraisse; Designer, Wolf Kroeger; Costumes, Janty Yates; Supervising Sound Editor, Eddy Joseph, MPSE; Visual Effects Supervisor, Peter Chiang; Casting, John and Ros Hubbard, Annette Borgman; a Mandalay Pictures presentation of a Repérage production, co-produced by MP Film Management DOS Productions GmbH & Co KG (Germany), Swanford Films Limited (United Kingdom), and Little Bird Limited (Ireland); German-British-Irish; Dolby; Panavision; Deluxe color; Rated R; 131 minutes; US release date: March 16, 2001

CAST

Danilov	Joseph Fiennes
Vassili Zaitsev	Jude Law
Tania Chernova	Rachel Weisz
Nikita Kruschev	Bob Hoskins
Major Konig	Ed Harris
Koulikov	Ron Perlman
Mother Filipov	Eva Mattes
Sacha Filipov	Gabriel Marshall-Thomson
General von Paulus	Matthias Habich
Ludmilla	Sophie Rois
Volody	Ivan Shvetloff
Anton	Mario Bandi
Red Army General	Hans Martin Stier
German Noncom	Clemans Schick
Grandfather	Mikhail Matveyev
Young Vassili	Alexander Schwan
Comrade in Train	Lenn Kudrjawizki
Fat Colonel	Hendrik Arnst
Aide de Camp	Claudius Freyer
Blond Captain	Dietmar Nieder
Captain with Lighter	Bernd Lambrecht
Stubborn Feldwebel	Jim Dowdall
Politruk/Sniper	Maxim Kovalevski
Russian Noncom	Gennadi Vengerov
Political Officer	Dan van Husen
Sweating Officer	Peter Silbereison
Stammering Officer	Markus Majowski
Spotter	Robert Stadlober
Corpse Robber	Gotthard Lange
Russian Typist	Anna Böttcher
Paulus's Aide de Camp	Holger Handtke
Stealing Photographer	Marc Bischoff
Russian Captain at Headquarters	Mark Zak
Russian Lieutenant	Thomas Petruo
Comrade in Shelter	Dimitri Alexandrov
Pravda Interviewer	David Pagel
Izvestija Interviewer	Galina Dobberstein
Krasnaja Zvezda Interviewer	Igor Rozinskij
Russian Reporter	Sergwei Tokarev
Footsoldier	Tom Wlaschia
Woman Plucking Eyebrows	Marischka Schubarth
Woman Officer	Natalja Bondar
Athletic Sniper	Dana Cebulla

and Piotr Papierz, Jarek Wozniak, Genia Makarov, Werner Dahn, Birol Ünel, Grigori Kofmann, Alexej Nesterov, Vladimir Vilanov (Politruks), Alexeji Volodin (Junior Politruk), Gennadi Tselbiansky (Senior Politruk), Andrej Kaminski (Russian Trench Officer), Michael Schenk (Russian Officer), Jury Cooper, Manfred Witt (Russian Noncoms), Arslan Kodirov (Tchechen Sniper), Axel Neumann (Gaunt German Prisoner), Morin Smolé, Inna Samian (Snipers), Arslan Kodirov (Sniper/Russian Officer), Keta Burowa (Female Russian Radio Operator)

During the bloody Battle of Stalingrad, the Russian people find a hero in sniper Vassili Zaitsev, prompting the Nazis to send their best sharpshooter to dispose of him.

Joseph Fiennes, Jude Law

Joseph Fiennes, Rachel Weisz

Jude Law

Jude Law

Jude Law, Bob Hoskins

Emilio Echevarría

AMORES PERROS

(LIONS GATE) Producer/Director, Alejandro González Iñárritu; Executive Producers, Martha Sosa, Francisco González Compeán; Screenplay, Guillermo Arriaga; Photography, Rodrigo Prieto; Designer, Brigitte Broch; Editors, Alejandro Gonzáles Iñárritu, Luis Carballar, Fernando Perez Unda; Music, Gustavo Santaolalla; Casting, Manuel Teil; an Altavista Films presentation of a Zeta Film and Altavista Films production; Mexican, 2000; Color; Rated R; 153 minutes; US release date: March 30, 2001

Gael García Bernal

CAST

El Chivo	Emilio Echevarría
Octavio	Gael García Bernal
Valeria	Goya Toledo
Daniel	Álvaro Guerrero
Susana	Vanessa Bauche
Luis	Jorge Salinas
Ramiro	Marco Peréz
Gustavo	Rodrigo Murray
Jorge	Humberto Busto
Mauricio	Gerardo Campbell
Aunt Luisa	Rosa María Bianchi
Susana's Mother	Dunia Saldívar
Octavio's Mother	Adriana Barraza
Leonardo	José Sefami
Maru	Lourdes Echevarría
Julieta	Laura Almela
Andres Salgado	Ricardo Dalmacci
Jarocho	Gustavo Sánchez Parra
Alvaro	Dagoberto Gama
El Chispas	Gustavo Muñoz
Javier	Carlo Bernal

and Rodrigo Obstab (El Jaibo), Heriberto Castillo (Stranger)

A car crash in Mexico City brings together three different people: teenager Octavio, model Valeria, and killer-for-hire El Chivo.

This film received an Oscar nomination for Foreign Language Film (2000).

© Lions Gate Films

Goya Toledo

Karma Wangel, Thilen Lhondup

HIMALAYA

(KINO) Producers, Jacques Perrin, Christophe Barratier; Executive Producer, Jean de Trégomain; Director, Eric Valli; Screenplay, Olivier Dazat; Based on a script by Eric Valli, Olivier Dazat, with the assistance of Jean-Claude Guillebaud, Louis Gardel, Nathalie Azoulai, Jacques Perrin; Photography, Eric Guichard AFC, Jean-Paul Meurisse; Art Directors, Jérôme Krowicki, Tenzing Norbu Lama; Editor, Marie-Josèphe Yoyotte; Music, Bruno Coulais; French-Swiss-British-Nepalese; 1999; Color; Not rated; 104 minutes; US release date: March 30, 2001

CAST

Tinle	Thilen Lhondup
Karma	Gurgon Kyap
Pema	Lhakpa Tsamchoe
Passang	Karma Wangel
Norbou	Karam Tenzing
Labrang	Labrang Tundup
Jampa	Jampa Kalsang Tamang
Rabkie	Tsering Dorjee
Tundup	Rapke Gurung
Tensing	Pemba Bika
Nene	Karma Chlewang
Chopga	Tenzen Charka

and Karma Chhuldim (Paljor), Karma Tenzing (Urgien), Yangzom (Dawa), Gyalsen Gurung (Chewan), Phuti Bika (Deld), Sangmo Gurung (Angmo), Karma Angbu Gurung (Karma's Father)

Believing Karma caused the death of his son, Himalayan chieftain Tinle refuses to allow him to lead a caravan, an edict Karma defies.

SHADOW MAGIC

(SONY PICTURES CLASSICS) Producer/Director, Ann Hu; Executive Producers, Charles Xue, Steve Chang, Chiu Shun-Ching, Han Sanping, Ulrich Felsberg, Eitan Hakami, Katia Milani; Screenplay, Huang Dan, Tang Louyi, Bob McAndrew, Kate Raisz, Ann Hu; Co-Producers, Sandra Schulberg, Zhang Xia, Cheng Zheng, Lee You-Ning; Photography, Nancy Schreiber; Deisgner, Wang Jixian; Editors, Keith Reamer, John Gilroy; Music, Zhang Lida; Costumes, Huang Bao Rong; a C & A Productions in association with Beijing Film Studio, China Film, Taiwan Central Motion Picture Corporation, Post Production Playground, Schulberg, Productions and Road Movies Vierte Produktionen presentation with the supporting of Filmstiftung Nordrhein-Westfalen GmbH; Chinese-German, 2000; Color; Rated PG; 115 minutes; US release date: April 6, 2001

CAST

Raymond Wallace	Jared Harris
Liu Jinglun	Xia Yu
Ling	Xing Yufei
Master Ren	Liu Peiqi
Madame Ren	Lu Liping
Old Liu	Wang Jingming
Lord Tan	Li Yusheng
Lao Chang	Zhang Yukui
Mi Hu	Chen Chuang
Fu Guan	Zheng Zhongwei
Jewelry Tower	Mu Qi
Widow Jiang	Fang Qingzhuo
Empress Ci Xi	Li Bin

In 1902 Peking, photographer Liu Jinglun is delighted by the arrival of silent movies, a new invention that visiting opera star Lord Tan believes will steal away his audience.

Xing Yufei, Xia Yu

Eric Bana

BEAUTIFUL CREATURES

(UNIVERSAL FOCUS) Producers, Alan J Wands, Simon Donald; Director, Bill Eagles; Screenplay, Simon Donald; Photography, James Welland; Designer, Andy Harris; Editor, Jon Gregory ACE; Costumes, Trisha Biggar; Casting, Nina Gold; a DNA Films in association with Universal Pictures International and The Arts Council of England presentation of a Snakeman production; British; Dolby; Technicolor; Rated R; 86 minutes; US release date: April 6, 2001

CAST

Petula	Rachel Weisz
Dorothy	Susan Lynch
Tony	Iain Glen
Ronnie McMinn	Maurice Roeves
Brian McMinn	Tom Mannion
Detective Inspector Hepburn	Alex Norton
Train Guard	Jake D'Arcy
Man in Lift	Paul Doonan
Man in Kiosk	Robin Laing
Sheena	Pauline Lynch
Man on Beach	John Murtagh

and Shane Cadzow (Small Boy on Beach), Juliet Cadzow (Mother on Beach), Stewart Preston (Duty Sergeant), Ron Donachie (Police Sergeant), Joel Strachan (Sgt Binnie), Stuart Hepburn (Policeman on Bridge), Ellie Haddington (Maureen), Paul Higgins (Aidan), Storm (Pluto)

Dorothy and Petula, two women who have suffered through bad relationships with men, concoct a plan to convince the police that Petula's boyfriend, Brian, has been kidnapped, when in fact Dorothy has accidentally killed him while defending Petula.

© Universal Pictures

CHOPPER

(FIRST LOOK) Producer, Michele Bennett; Executive Producers, Al Clark, Martin Fabinyi; Director/Screenplay, Andrew Dominik; Adapted from the books by Mark Brandon Read; Co-Producer, Michael Gudinski; Photography, Geoffrey Hall, Kevin Hayward; Designer, Paddy Reardon; Editor, Ken Sallows; Music, Mick Harvey; Costumes, Terry Ryan; Casting, Greg Apps; an Image Entertainment presentation in association with The Australian Film Finance Corporation and Mushroom Pictures of a Pariah Films production; Australian, 2000; Dolby; Color; Not rated; 93 minutes; US release date: April 11, 2001

CAST

Mark Brandon "Chopper" Read	Eric Bana
Jimmy Loughan	Simon Lyndon
Keithy George	David Field
Bluey	Dan Wyllie
Detective Downie	Bill Young
Neville Bartos	Vince Colosimo
Keith Read	Kenny Graham
Tanya	Kate Beahan

and Renee Brack (Television Interviewer), Gregory Pitt, Richard Sutherland, Andrew Dunn (Prison Officers), Gary Waddell (Kevin Darcy), Caleb Cluff (Detective Creswell), Hilton Henderson (Detective Wyatt), Fred Barker (Governor Beasley), Alan Close (Medical Officer #1), Mark Stratford (Classification Officer), Carl Price (Brunswick Court Judge), Brian Mannix (Ian James), Johnnie Targan (Paul the Bouncer), Robert Rabiah (Nick), Sam Houli (Robbo), Sarah Jane King (Glamour Queen), Serge Liistro (Sammy the Turk), Pam Western (Tanya's Mother), Peter Hardy (Detective Cooney), Skye Wansey (Mandy), Annalise Emtsis (Shazzy), Marcus Taylor (Jimmy's Mate), Ernie Gray (Crown Prosecutor), David Paterson (Morris Jeffrey), Fletcher Humphrys (Bucky), Terry Willesee (Current Affairs Show Host)

From his prison cell, Mark "Chopper" Read looks back on his attempts to make a name for himself in the criminal world.

© First Look Pictures

(Above) Iain Glen, Susan Lynch
(Below) Rachel Weisz, Susan Lynch

Nargess Mamizadeh, Maryiam Palvin Almani

Maryiam Palvin Almani

THE CIRCLE

(WINSTAR) Producer/Director/Original Idea/Editor, Jafar Panahi; Screenplay, Kambozia Patrovi; Photography, Bahram Badakhshani; Art Director, Iraj Raminfar; Associate Producer, Mohammad Atebbai; Line Producer, Morteza Motevali; a production of Jafar Panahi Film Productions (Iran), Mikado-Lumiere & Co (Italy); Iranian, 2000; Color; Not rated; 91 minutes; US release date: April 16, 2001

CAST

Arezou ....Maryiam Palvin Almani
Nargess...Nargess Mamizadeh
Pari..Fereshteh Sadr Orfani
Ticket Seller ....Monir Arab
Nurse ....Elham Saboktakin
Mother...Fatemeh Naghavi
Prostitute ....Mojhan Faramarzi
Solmaz...Solmaz Gholami

Several Iranian women find themselves on the run to escape the punishment their narrow-minded society enforces on their sex.

© Winstar Cinema

Nargess Mamizadeh, Fereshteh Sadr Orfani, Maryiam Parvin Almani

WITH A FRIEND LIKE HARRY...

(MIRAMAX ZOË) Producer, Michel Saint-Jean; Director, Dominik Moll; Screenplay, Dominik Moll, Gilles Marchand; Photography, Matthieu Poirot-Delpech; Art Director, Michel Barthélémy; Editor, Yannick Kergoat; Music, David Sinclair Whittaker; Casting, Antoinette Boulat; a Michel Saint-Jean presentation of a Diaphana Films, M6 Films Production with the participation of Canal+, M6, Du Centre National De La Cinematographie in association with La Sofica Sofinergie 5 with the support of La Procirep; French, 2000; Dolby; Super 35 Widescreen; Color; Rated R; 117 minutes; US release date: April 20, 2001

CAST

Michel	Laurent Lucas
Harry	Sergi Lopez
Claire	Mathilde Seigner
Plum	Sophie Guillemin
Michel's Mother	Liliane Rovere
Michel's Father	Dominique Rozan
Eric	Michel Fau
Jeanne	Victoire De Koster
Sarah	Laurie Caminita
Iris	Lorena Caminita

On the way to a vacation with his wife and kids, Michel meets a former schoolmate he can barely remember, Harry, who insists on joining the family's holiday getaway, becoming an increasingly menacing presence.

© Miramax Zoë

Sergi Lopez, Sophie Guillemin

Mathilde Seigner, Laurent Lucas

Sergi Lopez, Laurent Lucas

Sophie Guillemin

John Turturro, Stuart Wilson, Emily Watson

Emily Watson

Emily Watson, John Turturro

THE LUZHIN DEFENCE

(SONY CLASSICS) Producers, Caroline Wood, Stephen Evans, Louis Becker, Philippe Guez; Executive Producer, Jody Patton; Director, Marleen Gorris; Screenplay, Peter Berry; Based on the novel by Vladimir Nabokov; Co-Producers, Leo Pescarolo, Eric Robison; Photography, Bernard Lutic; Designer, Tony Burrough; Editor, Michaël Reichwein; Music, Alexandre Desplat; Costumes, Jany Temime; Casting, Celestia Fox; a Renaissance Films in association with Clear Blue Sky Production presentation of a Renaissance and ICE3 production in association with Lantia Cinema, Magic Media, and France 2 Cinéma; British-French, 2000; Dolby; Color; Rated PG-13; 106 minutes; US release date: April 20, 2001

CAST

Alexander Luzhin	John Turturro
Natalia	Emily Watson
Vera	Geraldine James
Valentinov	Stuart Wilson
Stassard	Christopher Thompson
Turati	Fabio Sartor
Ilya	Peter Blythe
Anna	Orla Brady
Luzhin's Father	Mark Tandy
Luzhin's Mother	Kelly Hunter
Young Luzhin	Alexander Hunting
Officials	Alfredo Pea, Fabio Pasquini
Santucci	Luigi Petrucci
Hotel Manager	Carlo Greco
Tailor	Massimo Sarchielli
Fascists	Luca Foggiano, Antonio Carli, David Ambrosi

Eccentric, tormented chess master Alexander Luzhin arrives at an Italian lakeside resort to participate in the greatest tournament of his career, and finds himself falling in love with an aristocratic Russian woman whose parents hope to marry her into wealth.

© Sony Pictures Entertainment

Uma Thurman, Nick Nolte

Uma Thurman, Jeremy Northam

THE GOLDEN BOWL

(**LIONS GATE**) Producer, Ismail Merchant; Executive Producers, Paul Bradley, Richard Hawley; Director, James Ivory; Screenplay, Ruth Prawer Jhabvala; Based on the novel by Henry James; Photography, Tony Pierce-Roberts; Designer, Andrew Sanders; Music, Richard Robbins; Editor, John David Allen; Costumes, John Bright; Casting, Celestia Fox; a Merchant Ivory Productions in association with TF1 International presentation; British; Dolby; Panavision; Color; Rated R; 130 minutes; US release date: April 27, 2001

CAST

Maggie Verver	Kate Beckinsale
Bob Assingham	James Fox
Fanny Assingham	Anjelica Huston
Adam Verver	Nick Nolte
Prince Amerigo	Jeremy Northam
Lady Casteldean	Madeleine Potter
Charlotte Stant	Uma Thurman
Duke's Older Son	Rossano Rubicondi
The Duchess	Marta Paola Richeldi
Duke's Younger Son	Francesco Giuffrida
The Duke	Mattia Sbragia
Shopkeeper	Peter Eyre
Lord Casteldean	Nicholas Day
Principino at Five Years	Daniel Byam Shaw
Mr Blint	Robin Hart
Lecturer	Nickolas Grace
Principino	Billy Monger

and Pauline Rainer (Nursemaid), Susan Gutfreund (Vivacious Guest), Arturo Venegas (Italian Ambassador), Raymond Green (Photographer), Anthony Bevan (Butler), Neville Phillips (Man Talking to Casteldean), Paul Bradley (Executioner), Lucy Freeman (Lucy Moncrief), Philip Tabor (William Davenport), Catherine Aldrich, Isabel de Pelet, Richard MacRory, Caroline Burnaby-Atkins (Guests at Fawns), Piers Gielgud (The Ballet Pasha), Antonia Franceschi (The Ballet First Queen), Philip Willingham (The Ballet Slave), William Dignon (The Ballet Little Prince), Ray Souza, Leanne Codrington, Amy Bailey, Michaela Burgess, Simon Humphrey, Michaela Burgess, Michela Meazza, Stephen Hughes, Tippi Maravala (Dancers)

Billionaire Adam Verver and his daughter Maggie both marry only to discover that their spouses are having an affair with one another.

© Lions Gate Films

Uma Thurman, Anjelica Huston, Jeremy Northam

Nick Nolte, Kate Beckinsale

Karen Bach, Raffaëla Anderson

Raffaëla Anderson

Karen Bach

BAISE-MOI
(RAPE ME)

(FILMFIX/REMSTAR) Producer, Philippe Godeau; Executive Producer, Dominique Chiron; Directors/Screenplay, Virginie Despentes, Coralie Trinh Thi; Based on the novel by Virginie Despentes; Photography, Benoît Chamaillard; Art Director, Irène Galitzine; Costumes, Magali Baret, Isabelle Fraysse; Editors, Aïlo Auguste-Judith, Francine Lemaitre; Music, Varou Jan; French, 2000; Color; Not rated; 77 minutes; US release date: April 27, 2001

CAST

Manu	Raffaëla Anderson
Nadine	Karen Lancaume/Karen Bach
Severine	Delphine MacCarty
Karla	Lisa Marshall
Alice	Estelle Isaac
Martin	H. P. G. (Hervé P. Gustave)
Architect	Marc Rioufol
Radouan	Ouassini Embarek

and Adama Niane (Boy with Billiards), Tewfik Saad (Server), Céline Beugnot (Blonde with Billiards), Christophe Claudi (Guy with Counter), Patrick Eudeline (Francis), Hacène Beddrouh (Lakim), Philippe Houillez, Steven Jhonsson, Ian Scott (Rapists), Gil Stuart (Nadine's Client), Karim Sabaddehine (Big Guy), Titof (Little Guy), Alexandre Milor (Receptionist, Hotel Francis), Marc Barrow (Receptionist, Seaside Hotel), Elodie Chérie (Lady Distributor), Rodolphe Antrim (The Local), Jean-Marc Minéo (Arms Seller), Gábor Rassov (Guy with Hood), Patrick Kodjo Topou, Simon Nahoum Karim Chala (Big Thugs), Jean-Louis Costes (Man in Sex Club), Nathalie Dune, Dany, Pascal Saint-James, Sébastien Barriot (BAP), Sylvain Cahen-Delabre, Didier Gardette, Jacques Sans (Dead Bodies)

Two angry women, one a victim of rape, the other a hardened prostitute, embark on a road trip full of destruction and vengeance aimed at the opposite sex.

Karen Bach

UNDER THE SAND

(WINSTAR) Producers, Olivier Delbosc, Marc Missonnier; Director, François Ozon; Screenplay, François Ozon, Emmanuèle Bernheim, Marina de Van, Marcia Romano; Photography, Jeanne Lapoirie, Antoine Heberlé; Editor, Laurence Bawedin; Music, Philippe Rombi; Costumes, Pascaline Chavanne; Casting, Antoinette Boulat; a Fidélité Productions presentation in co-production with Euro Space Inc, Haut et Court, Arte France Cinema with the participation of Canal+; French-Japanese, 2000; Dolby; Color; Not rated; 95 minutes; US release date: May 4, 2001

CAST

Marie Drillon	Charlotte Rampling
Jean Drillon	Bruno Cremer
Vincent	Jacques Nolot
Amanda	Alexandra Stewart
Gerard	Pierre Vernier
Suzanne	Andrée Tainsy

and Maya Gaugler (German Woman), Damien Abbou (Chief Lifeguard), David Portugais (Young Lifeguard), Pierre Soubestre (Policeman), Agathe Teyssier (In Charge of the Luxury Store), Laurence Martin (Apartment Seller), Jean-François Lapalus (Paris Doctor), Laurence Mercier (Paris Doctor's Secretary), Fabienne Luchetti (Pharmacist), Jo Doumerg (Taxi Driver), Michel Cordes (Superintendent), Maurice Antoni (The Landes Doctor), Patricia Couvillers (Evelyne), Patrick Grieco (José), Axelle Bossard (Student), Charlotte Gerbault (Nurse), Nicole Lartique (Morgue Attendant)

While on holiday, Marie's husband Jean suddenly disappears, forcing her to go on with her life alone, plunging her into a darker feeling of despair and loss than she is prepared for.

© Winstar Cinema

Charlotte Rampling, Jacques Nolot

(Above) Stuart Townsend, Kate Hudson
(Below) Stuart Townsend, Frances O'Connor

ABOUT ADAM

(MIRAMAX) Producers, Anna Devlin, Marina Hughes; Executive Producers, Harvey Weinstein, David M. Thompson, David Aukin, Trea Leventhal, Rod Stoneman; Director/Screenplay, Gerard Stembridge; Photography, Bruno de Keyzer; Designer, Fiona Daly; Editor, Mary Finlay; Music, Adrian Johnston; Costumes, Eimear Ni Mhaoldomhnaigh; Line Producer, Mary Alleguen; Casting, John & Ros Hubbard, Laura Rosenthal; a BBC Films presentation in association with Bord Scannán na hÉireann/The Irish Film Board, a Venus Production; British-Irish-US; Dolby; Color; Rated R; 105 minutes; US release date: May 9, 2001

CAST

Adam	Stuart Townsend
Laura Owens	Frances O'Connor
Alice Owens	Charlotte Bradley
Lucy Owens	Kate Hudson
David Owens	Alan Maher
Simon	Tommy Tiernan
Martin	Brendan Dempsey
Karen	Cathleen Bradley
Peggy Owens	Rosaleen Linehan
Professor McCormick	Roger Gregg
Customers	Stewart Roche, Aoife Maloney
Andy	Donal Beecher
Dympna	Kathy Downes
Dracula	Mark Smith

Believing she has found the man of her dreams, Lucy Owens brings Adam to meet her family, only to have her sisters fall for the charming young man.

© Miramax Films

Pilar Padilla, Adrien Brody

George Lopez

BREAD AND ROSES

(LIONS GATE) Producer, Rebecca O'Brien; Executive Producer, Ulrich Felsberg; Director, Ken Loach; Screenplay, Paul Laverty; Photography, Barry Ackroyd; Designer, Martin Johnson; Costumes, Michele Michel; Music, George Fenton; Editor, Jonathan Morris; Casting, Ronnie Yeskel, Richard Hicks; a Parallax Pictures, Road Movies Filmproduktion and Tornasol/Alta Films production with the participation of British Screen and BSkyB in association with Bac Films, BIM Distribuzione, Cin-Art and Film Co-Operative, Zurich, and in collaboration with FilmFour, WDR/Arte, La Sept-Arte, ARD/Degeto Film and Filmstiftung Nordrhein-Westfalen; British-German-Spanish-French; Dolby; Color; Rated R; 110 minutes; US release date: May 11, 2001

CAST

Maya ....Pilar Padilla
Sam ....Adrien Brody
Rosa ....Elpidia Carrillo
Perez ....George Lopez
Bert ....Jack McGee
Simona ....Monica Rivas
Luis ....Frank Dávila
Anna ....Lillian Hurst
Ben ....Mayron Payes
Berta ....Maria Orellana
Cynthia ....Melody Garrett
Dolores ....Gigi Jackman
Ella ....Beverly Reynolds
Juan ....Eloy Méndez
Maria ....Elena Antonenko
Olga ....Olga Gorelik
Oscar ....Jesús Pérez
and Alonso Chávez (Ruben), Estela Maeda (Teresa), José Jiménez (Freddy), Sherman Augustus (Ernest), Julian Orea, Javier Tores (Coyotes), Roscio Saenz (Emma), Blake Clark (Mr Griffin), Pepa Serna (Restaurateur), Tony Rizzoli (Personnel Manager), Tom Gilroy (Director of Campaigns), Neal Baer (Doctor), David Steinberg, Ted Baer (Lawyers), Terry Anzur (Reporter), Greg Montgomery (Supervising Policeman), Clement Blake (Gas Station Attendant), Tom Michael Bailey (Truck Driver), Richard Bravo (IMS Officer), Vanessa Angel, William Atherton, Lara Belmont, Cooper Campbell, Benicio Del Toro, Oded Fehr, Stuart Gordon, Rick Otto, Chris Penn, Ron Perlman, Tim Roth, Robin Tunney, Sam West, Stephanie Zimbalist (Themselves)

A spirited young Mexican woman, smuggled over the border to Los Angeles where she makes a living cleaning office buildings, is convinced by a union organizer to rally other janitors to fight for their rights.

© Lions Gate Films

Elpidia Carrillo, Pilar Padilla

Pilar Padilla

Jennifer Jason Leigh

Bruce Davison

Janet McTeer

Jennifer Jason Leigh, Romane Bohringer

THE KING IS ALIVE

(IFC FILMS) Producers, Patricia Krujer, Vibeke Windeløv; Executive Producers, William A Tyrer, Chris J Ball, David Linde, Peter Aalbaek Jensen; Director, Kristian Levring; Screenplay, Kristian Levring, Anders Thomas Jensen; Inspired by *King Lear* by William Shakespeare; Photography, Jens Schlosser; Editor, Nicholas Wayman Harris; Casting, Joyce Nettles, Mali Finn, Moonyeen Lee, Bruno Levi; a Newmarket and Good Machine International presentation of a Zentropa Entertainments production, in co-production with the Danish Broadcasting Corporation in collaboration with SVT Drama and supported by the Danish Film Institute and Nordic Film & TV Fund; Danish-US; Dolby; Color; Rated R; 108 minutes; US release date: May 11, 2001

CAST

Jack	Miles Anderson
Catherine	Romane Bohringer
Henry	David Bradley
Charles	David Calder
Ray	Bruce Davison
Ashley	Brion James
Kanana	Peter Kubheka
Moses	Vusi Kunene
Gina	Jennifer Jason Leigh
Liz	Janet McTeer
Paul	Chris Walker
Amanda	Lia Williams

A group of tourists, stranded in the middle of an African desert, decide to pass the time by staging a production of King Lear, a decision that only forces them to confront their tense situation.

© IFC Films

THE ROAD HOME

(SONY PICTURES CLASSICS) Producer, Zhao Yu; Executive Producer, Zhang Weiping; Director, Zhang Yimou; Screenplay, Bao Shi; Photography, Hou Yong; Designer, Cao Jiuping; Costumes, Dong Huamiao; Editor, Zhai Ru; Music, San Bao; a Columbia Pictures Film Production Asia presentation of a Guangxi Film Studios & Beijing New Picture Distribution Company production; Chinese, 1999; Dolby; Panavision; Color/Black & White; Rated G; 100 minutes; US release date: May 25, 2001

Zhang Ziyi, Zheng Hao

CAST

Zhao Di (Youth) ....Zhang Ziyi
Luio Yusheng...Sun Honglei
Luo Changyu...Zheng Hao
Zhao Di (Elderly)..Zhao Yuelin
Grandmother...Li Bin
Mayor (Elderly)..Chang Guifa
Mayor (Youth) ....Sung Wencheng
Carpenter Xia (Elderly)...Liu Qi
Carpenter Xia (Youth) ....Ji Bo
Crockery Repairman ....Zhang Zhongxi

Yusheng, returning to his hometown for his father's funeral, recalls the story of how his parents met.

© Sony Pictures Entertainment

Zhang Ziyi

Zhang Ziyi, Zheng Hao

Johnny Depp

Cate Blanchett, John Turturro

THE MAN WHO CRIED

(UNIVERSAL FOCUS) Producer, Christopher Sheppard; Executive Producers, Tim Bevan, Eric Fellner; Director/Screenplay, Sally Potter; Co-Producer, Simona Benzakein; Photography, Sacha Vierny ACE; Designer, Carlos Conti; Editor, Hervé Schneid; Costumes, Lindy Hemming; Music, Osvaldo Golijov; Line Producer, Linda Bruce; Casting, Irene Lamb, Mary Colquhoun; a Studio Canal presentation of a Working Title production in association with Adventure Pictures; British-French, 2000; Dolby; Color; Rated R; 97 minutes; US release date: May 25, 2001

CAST

Suzie	Christina Ricci
Lola	Cate Blanchett
Dante Dominio	John Turturro
Cesar	Johnny Depp
Felix Perlman	Harry Dean Stanton
Father	Oleg Yankovsky
Young Suzie	Claudia Lander-Duke
Grandmother	Hana Maria Pravda
Foster Mother	Diana Hoddinott
Foster Father	Richard Albrecht
Madame Goldstein	Miriam Karlin

and Danny Scheinman (Man in Suit), Anna Tzelniker (Mother of Man in Suit), Barry Davis, Thom Osborn, Frank Chersky, Daniel Hart, Peter Majer (Men in Village), Ayala Meir, Abraham Hassan, Lloyd Martin, Uri Meir, Sophie Richman, Theo Wishart (Children), Michael Mount, Harry Flinder (Boys in Cart), Danny Richman (Man in Cart), Victor Sobtchak (Man at Port), Sue Cleaver (Red Cross Woman), Clifford Barry (English Port Official), Paul Clayton (Second Official), Ornella Bryant, Sam Friend, Isabella Melling (Playground Bullies), Alan David (Welsh Teacher), Imogen Claire (Audition Mistress), Consuelo de Haviland (Party Hostess), Katia Labeque, Marielle Labeque (Pianists), George Yiasoumi (Reporter), Pablo Veron (Dancing Romany), Taraf de Haidouks (Romany Band), Odile Roire, Brigitte Boucher, Norah Krief, Helene Hardouin (Opera Chorus), Hugues Dalmagro, Cedric Gary (Romany Brothers), Saifi Ghoul (Romany Boy), Manfred Andrae (German Officer), Richard Sammel (German Officer Pianist), Ahmet Zirek (Father of Boy), Don Fellows (Joe), Joyce Springer (Refugee Worker), Cyril Shaps (Older Man in Sweatshop), Anna Korwin (Woman in Sweatshop), Mark Ivanir, Alfred Hoffman, Bernard Spear (Men in Sweatshop), Damien Puckler (Studio Assistant), David Baxt (Studio Lawyer), Katherine Hogarth (Father's New Wife), Patrick Clarke (Son), Bridget Clarke (Daughter), Chris Gillespie (Nurse)

Suzie, a Russian Jew, finds herself in Paris where she hopes to make enough money to join her father in America, a goal that becomes even more imperative when the Nazis begin their reign of terror.

© Universal Studios, Inc.

Christina Ricci

Christina Ricci, Johnny Depp, Cate Blanchett

BRIDE OF THE WIND

(PARAMOUNT CLASSICS) Producer, Lawrence Levy, Evzen Kolar; Executive Producers, Gerald Green, Frank Hübner; Director, Bruce Beresford; Screenplay, Marilyn Levy; Photography, Peter James ACS ASC; Designer, Herbert Pinter; Editor, Timothy Wellburn; Music, Stephen Endelman; Co-Producer, Norbert Blecha; Costumes, Shaun Harwood; Associate Producers, Steven Brown, Kirt Eftekhar; Casting, Joseph Middleton, Ari Raidel; a Total Film Group presentation of an Alma UK Ltd, Apollomedia, Firelight co-production, of a Kolar-Levy production; British-US; Dolby; Deluxe color; Rated R; 99 minutes; US release date: June 8, 2001

Jonathan Pryce

CAST

Alma Mahler	Sarah Wynter
Gustav Mahler	Jonathan Pryce
Oskar Kokoschka	Vincent Perez
Walter Gropius	Simon Verhoeven
Franz Werfel	Gregor Seberg
Anna Moll	Dagmar Schwarz
Karl Moll	Wolfgang Hübsch
Gustav Klimt	August Schmölzer
Bertha Zuckerkandl	Marion Rottenhofer

and Sophie Schweighofer (Anna Mahler—6 years old), Johannes Silberschneider (Alexander Zemlinsky), Daniele Dadieu (Justine Mahler), Brigitte Antonius (Frau Kokoschka), Johanna Mertinz (Frau Gropius), Erwin Ebenbauer (Dr Alfred Loos), Franziska Becker (Maria Mahler—3 years old), Sonia Madani (Maria Mahler—5 years old), Katrina Sztachovic (Anna Mahler—3 years old), Michaela Illetschko (Anna Mahler—13 years old), Renée Fleming (Frances Alda), Jean-Yves Thibaudet (Alda's Accompanist), Peter Gruber (Dr Blumenthal), Doris Pascher (Sophie Clemenceau), Robert Herzl (Arnold Schonberg), Werner Prinz (Archduke Franz Ferdinand), Patricia Hirschbichler (Duchess Sophie), Bernhard Bauer (Clarinetist), Gordon Catlin (Postman), Michael Rast (Stefan), Helen Zellweger (Helena), Sylvia Haider (Flora), Arthur Denberg (Kurt), Kathy Marothy (Nanny), Marianne Mendt, Angelika Rossaro (Alma's Maids), Heidelinde Theresina (Moll's Maid), Merab Ninidze (Russian Soldier), Josef Schutzhofer (Cavalry Sergeant), Mijou Kovacs, Anita Kolbert (Tobelbad Patients), Monika Mandl (Klimt's Model), Rich Cowan (Mute Waiter), Roby Lakatos, Ernest Bangó (Gypsy Ensemble)

Sarah Wynter

The story of Alma Mahler, who had love affairs with some of the most influential artists of their day, including composer Gustav Mahler, expressionist painter Oskar Kokoschka, architect Walter Gropius, and novelist Franz Werfel.

© Paramount Classics

Vincent Perez

Sarah Wynter, Gregor Seberg

Anna Siskova, Csongor Kassai

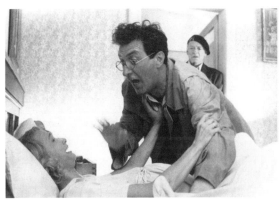

Anna Siskova, Boleslav Polivka

Boleslav Polivka

DIVIDED WE FALL

(SONY PICTURES CLASSICS) Producers, Ondrej Trojan, Pavel Borovan; Executive Producer, Ondrej Trojan; Director, Jan Hrebejk; Screenplay, Petr Jarchovsky, based on his novel; Photography, Jan Malir; Designer, Milan Bycek; Music, Ales Brenzina; Editor, Vladimir Barak; Costumes, Katarina Holla; a Total Helpart (THA) Film Company and Czech Television Production; Czech-German; Dolby; Color; Rated PG-13; 117 minutes; US release date: June 8, 2001

Boleslav Polivka, Richard Tesarik

CAST

Josef Cizek	Boleslav Polivka
Marie Cizek	Anna Siskova
Horst Prohaska	Jaroslav Dusek
David Wiener	Csongor Kassai
Doctor Fischer	Jiri Kodet
SS Officer	Vladimir Marek
Captain	Richard Tesarik
Frantisek Simacek	Jiri Pecha
Dr Albrecht Kepk	Martin Huba

In a small Czech town occupied by the German forces, Josef Cizek shelters a Jewish refugee then hopes to distract attention from this act by taking a job with a Nazi collaborator.

This film received an Oscar nomination as foreign-language film for 2000.

Anna Siskova, Jaroslav Dusek

Ben Kingsley, Ray Winstone

Ray Winstone, Alvaro Monje

SEXY BEAST

(FOX SEARCHLIGHT) Producer, Jeremy Thomas; Director, Jonathan Glazer; Screenplay, Louis Mellis, David Scinto; Photography, Ivan Bird; Designer, Jan Houllevigue; Co-Producer, Denise O'Dell; Associate Producers, Hercules Bellville, Peter Watson; Editors, John Scott, Sam Sneade; Music, Roque Baños, UNKLE with South; Costumes, Louise Stjernsward; Casting, Lucy Boulting; a Recorded Picture Company and FilmFour presentation in association with KanZaman SA, of a Jeremy Thomas production developed in association wtih Chronopolis Films; British; Dolby; Super 35 Widescreen; Deluxe color; Rated R; 91 minutes; US release date: June 13, 2001

Ben Kingsley

CAST

Gary "Gal" Dove ....Ray Winstone
Don Logan ....Ben Kingsley
Teddy Bass ....Ian McShane
Deedee ....Amanda Redman
Harry ....James Fox
Aitch ....Cavan Kendall
Jackie ....Julianne White
Enrique ....Alvaro Monje
Andy ....Robert Atiko
Air Hostess ....Nieves del Amo Oruet
Pilot ....Enrique Alemán Fabrega
Spanish Official ....Gerard Barray
Felipe's Friends ....José Ma Cano Ramos, José López Carrillo
Jean ....Desirée Erasmus
Policias ....José Lirola Ramos, Santiago Frías Muñoz,
        Pedro Zamora Hernández, Juan Manuel Martínez Cobos
Ginger Air Steward ....José Hernández
Maruja (Matronly Woman) ....Ana Maldonado Herreria
Jimmy ....Andy Lucas
and Antonio Fco Márquez (Steward), Dionisio Mesa (Felipe), Eddie O'Connell (Bruno), Terry Plummer (Mike), Manuel Sánchez Berlanga (Man on Plane), Frank Scinto (Pete), Darkie Smith (Stan), Rocky Taylor (Raymond), Chris Webb (Nicky)

Don Logan, a volatile and dangerous gangster, shows up at the Spanish villa of retired mobster Gal Dove to force Gal to participate in one final bank job.

This film received an Oscar nomination for supporting actor (Ben Kingsley).

© Twentieth Century Fox

Ray Winstone, Ben Kingsley

Benno Fürmann, Franka Potente

THE PRINCESS AND THE WARRIOR

(SONY PICTURES CLASSICS) Producers, Stefan Arndt, Maria Köpf; Director/Screenplay, Tom Tykwer; Photography, Frank Griebe; Designer, Ulli Hanisch; Costumes, Monika Jacobs; Editor, Mathilde Bonnefoy; Music, Tom Tykwer, Johnny Kilmek, Reinhold Heil; Casting, Filmcast; an X Filme, Creative Pool production; German, 2000; Dolby; Panavision; Color; Rated R; 130 minutes; US release date: June 22, 2001

CAST

Sissi (Simone) ....Franka Potente
Bodo..Benno Fürmann
Walter ....Joachim Kròl
Sissi's Mother..Marita Breuer
Schmatt..Jürgen Tarrach
Steini..Lars Rudolph
Otto..Melchior Beslon
Werner Dürr...Ludger Pistor
Bruno Kramer ....Steffen Schult
Dieter Strack..Rolf Dannemann
Paul Rummenhöller ....Gottfried Breitfuss
Ali Gören ....Susanne Bredehöft
Sigrun Mölke..Christa Fast
Maria ....Sybille Jacqueline Schedwill
and Sebastian Schipper, Armin Krug (Security Types), Jörg Reimers (Watchman), Natja Brunckhorst (Meike), Ali Nejat-uei (Ali Gören), Friederike Frerichs (Corinna), Stefanie Mühlhahn (Andrea), Irma Schmitt (Sandra), Max Urlacher (Holger), Thomas Gimbel (Markus), Alexander Wipprecht (Martin), Jan André Zinnschlag (Stefan), Sabina Riedel (Marita), Karl-Heinz Dickmann (Bank Clerk), Jana Schröder (Bank Trainee), Georg-Martin Bode (Bank Branch Manager), Georg Zurhelle (Postman), Peter Götz Korn (Birkenhof Porter), Marcel Segmüller (Rotzbalg), Michael Hanemann (Hartwich), Heiner Voigt (Priest), Eva Wolfertz (Meike's Mother), Ralf Knebel, Piet Paes (Filling Station Man), Jürgen Blumenthal (Lorry Driver), Ercan Sagnak, Winfried Walgenbach (Casualty Team), Manfred Götting, Tom Spiess (Schmatt Shop Customers), Axel Siefer (Casaulty Doctor), Eva Pilego (Casualty Nurse), Frank Dubowski (Casualty Male Nurse), Frank Plasberg (Aktuelle Stunde Newsreader), Ina Kiesewetter (Lokalzeit Newsreader), Dirk Brand (Pump Attendant), Thomas Wüpper (Policeman at Birkenhof), Frauke Jacob (Nurse at Birkenhof)

Following a horrific car accident, a shy nurse is rescued by a mysterious savior who turns out to be a crook on the run from the law.

© Sony Pictures Entertainment

Franka Potente

Franka Potente, Joachim Kròl

Benno Fürmann

Jérémie Elkaïm, Stéphane Rideau

Jérémie Elkaïm, Stéphane Rideau

COME UNDONE
(PRESQUE RIEN)

(PICTURE THIS! ENTERTAINMENT) aka Almost Nothing; Producers, Jean-Christophe Colson, Cecile Amillat, Christian Tison; Director, Sébastien Lifshitz; Screenplay, Stéphane Bouquet, Sébastien Lifshitz; Photography, Pascal Poucet; Designer, Roseanna Sacco; Costumes, Elisabeth Mehu; Music, Perry Blake; Associate Producers, Marion Hansel, Arlette Zylberberg; Editor, Yann Dedet; a Lancelot Films & Man's Films presentation in association with Arte France Cinema, RTBF (Television Belge), with the participation of Centre National de la Cinematographie, La Procirep, Canal+, Centre du Cinema et de L'Audiovisuel, and La Coummunaute Francaise de Belgique; French, 2000; Dolby; Color; Not rated; 94 minutes; US release date: June 27, 2001

Jérémie Elkaïm

CAST

Mathieu	Jérémie Elkaïm
Cédric	Stéphane Rideau
Annick	Marie Matheron
Mother	Dominique Reymond
Sarah	Laetitia Legrix
Pierre	Nils Ohlund
Psychiatrist	Réjane Kerdaffrec
Cédric Father	Guy Houssier
Pierre's Mother	Violeta Ferrer
Cafe Owner	Robert Darmel
Nurses	Marie-Claire Durand, Charline Levaque
Waffle Seller	Sarah Reviasse
Annick's Friend	Eric Savin
Club Bouncer	Gildas Chotard
Boy on the Beach	Maxence Rabrit

Mathieu, an 18-year-old boy on summer holiday with his family, finds himself falling in love with another boy.

Jérémie Elkaïm, Stéphane Rideau

Daniel Auteuil, Michèle Laroque

Gérard Depardieu, Daniel Auteuil

THE CLOSET
(LE PLACARD)

(MIRAMAX ZOË) Producer, Alain Poiré; Director/Screenplay, Francis Veber; Directors of Production, Philippe Desmoulins, Henri Brichetti; Photography, Luciano Tovoli; Editor, Georges Klotz; Art Director, Hugues Tissander; Music, Vladimir Cosma; Costumes, Jacqueline Bouchard; Casting, François Menidrey; Presented in association with Gaumont and Efve Films; a co-production of Gaumont/Efve Films/TF1 Films production; Dolby; Technovision; Color; Rated R; 87 minutes; US release date: June 27, 2001

Michel Aumont, Daniel Auteuil

CAST

Francois Pignon	Daniel Auteuil
Félix Santini	Gérard Depardieu
Guillaume	Thierry Lhermitte
Mlle Bertrand	Michèle Laroque
Belone	Michel Aumont
Kopel, Company Director	Jean Rochefort
Christine	Alexandra Vandernoot
Franck	Stanislas Crevillén
Mathieu	Edgar Givry
Victor	Thierry Ashanti
Ariane	Michèle Garcia
Alba	Laurent Gamelon
Ponce	Vincent Moscato
Martine	Irina Ninova
Suzanne	Marianne Groves
The Cop	Philippe Vieux
Moreau	Luq Hamet
Maitre D'Hotel	Eric Vanzetta
Wine Waiter	Michel Caccia
Photographer	Joel Demarty
Removal Man	Dominique Thomas

and Akihiro Nishida, Hiro Uchiyama, Yongsou Cho, Onochi Seietsu (Japanese Clients)

Francois Pignon, a dull employee at a condom factory, pretends to be gay in order to keep himself from being fired.

Daniel Auteuil

Thierry Lhermitte, Gérard Depardieu

Samantha Morton, Emily Woof, John Hannah, Linus Roache

PANDAEMONIUM

(USA FILMS) Producer, Nick O'Hagan; Executive Producers, David M Thompson, Mike Phillips, Tracey Scoffield; Co-Producer, Michael Kustow; Director, Julien Temple; Screenplay, Frank Cottrell Boyce; Photography, John Lynch; Designer, Laurence Dorman; Editor, Niven Howie; Costumes, Annie Symons; Line Producer, Jane Robertson; Hair & Makeup Designer, Liz Daxauer; Music, Dario Marianelli; Casting, Liora Reich; a BBC Films presentation of a Mariner Films production in association with The Arts Council of England and Moonstone Entertainment; Dolby; Color; Rated PG-13; 125 minutes; US release date: June 27, 2001

CAST

Samuel Coleridge ....Linus Roache
William Wordsworth ....John Hannah
Sara Coleridge ....Samantha Morton
Dorothy Wordsworth ....Emily Woof
Mary Wordsworth ....Emma Fielding
John Thelwall ....Andy Serkis
Robert Southey ....Samuel West
Walsh .... Michael N. Harbour
Tom Poole...William Scott-Masson
Dr. Gillman ....Clive Merrison
Humphry Davy ....Dexter Fletcher
and Guy Lankester (Lord Byron), Andrea Lowe (Edith Southey), Jacqueline Defferary (Miss Holland), Andy de la Tour (Andre Crosse), John Kane (Jones), Colin McCredie (Messenger), Glyn Owen (Fisherman), Peter Harkness (Journalist), Niall Vincent (Hartley Coleridge—4 years old), Jason & Miles Quick (Hartley Coleridge—18 months old), Eleanor Russell (Hartley Coleridge—2 months old), Juno Temple (Emma Southey), Leo Temple (Herbert Southey), Rowena Gaukroger (Edith Mae Southey)

A drama about the friendship, and ultimate betrayal, of two of the most celebrated poets at the turn of the 19th century, William Wordsworth and Samuel Taylor Coleridge.

EVERYBODY'S FAMOUS!

(MIRAMAX) Producers, Loret Meus, Dominique Deruddere; Director/Screenplay, Dominique Deruddere; Photography, Willy Stassen; Sets, Hubert Pouille; Music, Raymond van het Groenewoud; Editor, Ludo Troch; Costumes, Loret Meus; Co-Producers, Volkert Struycken, Errol Nayci, Pascal Judelewicz, Anne-Dominique Toussaint; Line Producer, Gérard Vercruysse; an Otomatic, Get Reel Productions, Les Films des Tournelles presentation; Belgian-French-Dutch, 2000; Dolby; Color; Rated R; 99 minutes; US release date: July 3, 2001

CAST

Jean Vereecken ....Josse De Pauw
Willy van Outreve ....Werner De Smedt
Marva Vereecken ....Eva Van Der Gucht
Debbie..Thekla Reuten
Michael Jansen ....Victor Löw
Chantal Vereecken ....Gert Portael
Gaby ....Ianka Fleerackers
Lies ....Alice Reys
Julio Iglesia Imitation ....Steve Ryckier
Freddy Mercury Imitation ....Olivier Ythier
Otis Redding Imitation..Hein Sienkiewicz
State Police Warrant Officer ....Jef Van Der Kuylen
Jim Poppe ....Matthias Sercu
Rik de Visser ....Wim Opbroeck
Georges ....Marc Van Eeghem
Greet ....Sylke Aerts
and Heidi Verheyden, Viko Cockx, Frank Iwens, Mario Despiegeleer, Jan Van Der Kuylen, Christophe Vercouillie, Gunter Van Den Bergh, Wouter Talon, Michel Van Herck (State Police Officers), Caroline Rottier (Hair Stylist), Lut Hannes (Friend), George Arrendell (Dave), Hilt Devos (Woman on Talk Show), Sylvia Claes (Announcer), Christian Nolens, Miriam Thys, Bert Vannieuwenhuyse (Newscasters), Filip Peeters (State Police Officer), Tanja Cloeck (Singer in Restroom), Carl Ridders (Producer), Sien Eggers (Neighbor), Siegred Vincke (Teacher), Francois Beukelaers (NTO Director), Damiaan Deschrijver (State Police Spokesperson), Dominiek Vansteertegem (DJ), Hugo Van Den Bremt (Yup Host), Marc Didden (Talk Show Director), Jan Roos ("Song Organ" Director), Ivo Kuyl (Pharmacist), Christophe Stienlet (VJ), Alain Van Goethem ("Green Room" Singers), Annick Vandercruyssen ("Lonesome Zorra" Sound Mixer), Silvia Anglade (Spanish Newscaster), Mieke Verdin (Psychiatrist), Guy Dermul, Max Thijsen (Hosts)

A blue-collar worker, intent on seeing his far-from-talented daughter make it as a singer, kidnaps a popular vocalist in hopes of attaining his goal.

Eva Van Der Gucht

Jet Li

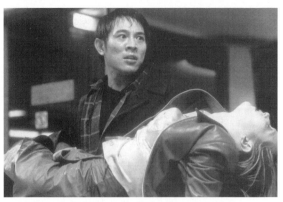

Jet Li, Bridget Fonda

Bridget Fonda

KISS OF THE DRAGON

(20TH CENTURY FOX) Producers, Luc Besson, Jet Li, Steven Chasman, Happy Walters; Director, Chris Nahon; Screenplay, Luc Besson, Robert Mark Kamen; Story, Jet Li; Photography, Thierry Arbogast AFC; Designer, Jacques Bufnoir; Editor, Marco Cave; Action Director, Cory Yuen; Music, Craig Armstrong; Co-Producer, Bernard Grenet; Stunts, Philippe Guegan, Pascal Guegan; a Europa Corp production in association with Quality Growth International Ltd; French-US; Dolby; Technovision; Color; Rated R; 97 minutes; US release date: July 6, 2001

CAST

Liu Jian	Jet Li
Jessica	Bridget Fonda
Richard	Tchéky Karyo
Aja	Laurence Ashley
Uncle Tai	Burt Kwouk
Twins	Cyril Raffaelli, Didier Azoulay
Max	John Forgeham
Lupo	Max Ryan
Lupo's Assistant	Colin Prince
Pluto	Vincent Glo
Mister Big	Ric Young
Minister Tang	Vincent Wong
Chen	Kentaro
Aides	Stefano Sao Nelet, Peter Lee
Isabel	Isabelle Duhauvelle

A top government agent comes to Paris to assist a police official only to find himself betrayed by the man, accused of a murder he didn't commit and on the run from the law.

Tchéky Karyo

Mischa Barton, Piper Perabo, Jessica Paré

LOST AND DELIRIOUS

(LIONS GATE) Producers, Lorraine Richard, Louis-Philippe Rochon, Greg Dummett; Director, Léa Pool; Screenplay, Judith Thompson; Based on the novel *The Wives of Bath* by Susan Swan; Photography, Pierre Gill; Designer, Serge Bureau; Costumes, Aline Gilmore; Editor, Gaëtan Huot; Music, Yves Chamberland; Casting, Gail Carr, Lucie Robitaille, Lina Todd; a Cité-Amérique/Dummett Films production; Canadian; Dolby; Color; Not rated; 103 minutes; US release date: July 6, 2001

CAST

Pauline Oster	Piper Perabo
Victoria Moller	Jessica Paré
Mary "Mouse" Bradford	Mischa Barton
Faye Vaughn	Jackie Burroughs
Joseph Menzies	Graham Greene
Eleanor Bannet	Mimi Kuzyk
Jake	Luke Kirby
Kara	Caroline Dhavernas
Cordelia	Amy Stewart
Morley Bradford	Noel Burton

and Emily Van Camp (Allison), Alan Fawcett (Bruce), Peter Oldring (Phil), Grace Lynn Kung (Lauren), Stephen Mwinga (John), Lydia Zadel (Monica), Felicia Schulman (Sal Bedford), Gabrielle Boni, Sheena Bernett, Meaghan Rath, Melissa Pirrera (Allison's Friends), David Dean (Boy of RAB), Jonathan Eliot (Tim), Phong Doan Huy (Fencing Teacher), Catherine Florent (Pauline's Fencing Opponent), Sophie Barsanti, Genevieve LaVallee, Myrtho Ouellette (Flutists)

Mouse Bradford becomes close friends with her two senior roommates at college until those girls are caught in a compromising position, tearing their relationship apart.

© Lions Gate Entertainment

JUMP TOMORROW

(IFC) Producer, Nicola Usborne; Executive Producers, Tim Perell, Paul Webster; Director/Screenplay, Joel Hopkins; Co-Producer, Jake Myers; Photography, Patrick Cady; Designer, John Paino; Costumes, Sarah J Holden; Associate Producers, Howard Gertler, Gill Holland; Editor, Susan Littenberg; Music, John Kimbrough; Casting, Ali Farrell; a Eureka Pictures/Jorge Productions, Inc production for FilmFour; British-US; Dolby; Technicolor; Rated PG; 96 minutes; US release date: July 6, 2001

CAST

George	Tunde Adebimpe
Gerard	Hippolyte Girardot
Alicia	Natalia Verbeke
Consuelo	Patricia Mauceri
George's Uncle	Isiah Whitlock, Jr
Heather Leather	Kaili Vernoff
Old Man	Gene Ruffini
Sophie	Abiola Wendy Abrams
Other Student in Class	Amy Sedaris
Priest	Deen Badarou
Nathan	James Wilby

and Murielle Arden (Claudette), Cherie Jimenez (Maria), Raul A Reyes (Co-Worker), Alan Gryfe (Teacher), Arthur Anderson (Jeweler), Leisa Heintzelman (Airport Official), William Barry (Compere), Carole Bayeux (PVC Girl), Anthony Genco (Boy at Falls), Charles Temo (Border Guard)

George, a shy man scheduled to marry a Nigerian woman his family has selected for him, finds himself questioning his destiny when he meets Alicia, a beautiful Spanish girl who is also heading for an uncertain marriage.

© IFC Films

Hippolyte Girardot, Tunde Adebimpe

Claude Maki, Beat Takeshi, Omar Epps

Beat Takeshi

Wanda-Lee Evans, Omar Epps, Tatyana M. Ali

Beat Takeshi, Joy Nakagawa

BROTHER

(SONY PICTURES CLASSICS) Producers, Masayuki Mori, Jeremy Thomas; Director/Screenplay/Editor, Takeshi Kitano; Line Producer, Shinji Komiya; Associate Producer, Peter Watson; Co-Producers, Takio Yoshida, Ann Carli; Photography, Katsumi Yanagijima; Designer, Norihiro Isoda; Costumes, Yohji Yamamoto; Music, Joe Hisaishi; Casting, Takefumi Yoshikawa, Robi Reed; a Recorded Picture Company and Office Kitano presentation in association with FilmFour and Bac Films; Japanese-British-French-U.S., 2000; Dolby; Color; Rated R; 107 minutes; US release date: July 20, 2001

CAST

Yamamoto..Beat Takeshi
Denny ....Omar Epps
Ken ....Claude Maki
Shirase ....Masaya Kato
Kato...Susumu Terajima
Jay ....Royale Watkins
Mo ....Lombardo Boyar
Harada ....Ren Ohsugi
Ishihara ....Ryo Ishibashi
Sugimoto...James Shigeta
Latifa...Tatyana M. Ali
Chief of Police...Makolo Ohtake
Hanaoka ....Koen Okumura
Hisamatsu..Naomasa Musaka
and Rino Katase (Night Club Madame), Tetsuya Watari (Jinseikai Boss), Ren Murakami (Minamino), Joy Nakagawa (Marina), Wanda-Lee Evans (Denny's Mother), Tony Colitti (Roberto), Koyo Into (Nishida), Alan Garcia (Bellboy), Antwon Tanner (Colin), Joseph Ragno (Mafia Ross Rossi), Nynno Ali (Oscar), Paul Feddersen (Limo Driver), Dan Gunther (Killer Waiter), Robert Covarrubias, Anthony Vatsula (Mexican Mafia Officers), Al Vicente, Luis Angel (Victor's Henchmen), Brad "The Animal" Lesley (Moose), Lobo Sebastian (Yamamoto Bodyguard), Tomas Chavez (Victor's Driver), Don Sato (Sushi Bar Owner), Hideo Kimura (Sushi Bar Part-Timer), Yayoi Otani (Sushi Bar Waitress), Tuesday Night (Prostitute), Yuji Hasegawa (Whorehouse Customer), Chuma Hunter-Gault (Sly), Kool Mo Dee (Jack), Peter Spellos (Taxi Driver), Amaury Nolasco (Victor), Jack Ong, Mike Wu (Chinese Bosses), Tad Horino (Coffee Shop Owner), Alvin Ing (Doctor), Herschel Sparber (Geppetti's Bodyguard), John Aprea (Mafia Boss Geppetti), Christopher Dergregorian, Manny Perez (Mexican Mafia Hitmen), Eddie Garcia (Mexican Mafia Henchman), Rainbow Borden, Manny Gavino, Hiroshi Otaguro, Darryl M Bell (Yamamoto's Henchmen), Eiji Inoue (Shirase's Henchman), Akira Kaneda (Mafia Hitman), Geoff Meed (Rossi's Bodyguard), Shoken Kunimoto (Ohyama), Shuhei Saga (Matsumoto)

A Japanese yakuza, forced to leave Tokyo, ends up in Los Angeles where he finds himself reverting to his violent ways, forming a gang, and taking over a major drug operation.

© Sony Pictures Entertainment

Bruno Ganz

BREAD AND TULIPS

(FIRST LOOK PICTURES) Producer, Daniele Maggioini; Director, Silvio Soldini; Screenplay/Story, Doriana Leondeff, Silvio Soldini; Photography, Luca Bigazzi; Art Director, Paola Bizzarri; Costumes, Silvia Nebiolo; Editor, Carlotta Cristiani; Music, Giovanni Venosta; Casting, Jorgelina Depetris; a co-production of Amka Films, Instituto Luce, Monogatari, Rai Cinemafiction, Televisione Svizzera Italian (TSI); Italian-Swiss, 2000; Dolby; Cinecitta color; Rated PG-13; 114 minutes; US release date: July 27, 2001

CAST

Rosalba Barletta	Licia Maglietta
Fernando Girasoli	Bruno Ganz
Constantino	Giuseppe Battiston
Grazia	Marina Massironi
Mimmo Barletta	Antonio Catania
Fermo	Felice Andreasi
Ketty	Vitalba Andrea
Adele	Tatiana Lepore
Eliseo	Ludovico Paladin
Nic	Tiziano Cucchiarelli
Salvo	Matteo Febo
Constantino's Mother	Silvana Bosi
Man at the Station	Manrico Gammarota
Goran	Massimiliano Speziani
Man in Car	Fausto Russo Alesi
Ballad Singer	Don Backy
Tour Guide	Nunzio Daniele

and Pierantio Micciarelli (Salesman), Daniela Piperno (Woman in Car), Lina Bernardi (Nancy), Antonia Miccoli (Sami), Mauro Marino (Lello), Paola Brolati (Florist Customer), Giselda Volodi (Pensione Housekeeper)

An unhappy housewife, accidentally left behind while on holiday, makes her way to Venice where she decides to stay on and take a job in a florist shop, finding all the joys that had been absent from her routine life.

© First Look Pictures

Licia Maglietta

Licia Maglietta, Bruno Ganz

Marina Massironi, Antonio Catania

Natasha Little, Clive Owen

David Kelly, Clive Owen

GREENFINGERS

(SAMUEL GOLDWYN) Producers, Travis Swords, Daniel J Victor, Trudie Styler; Executive Producer, Daniel J Victor; Director/Screenplay, Joel Hershman; Photography, John Daly BSC; Designer, Tim Hutchinson; Costumes, Frances Tempest; Music, Guy Dagul; Editor, Justin Krish; Casting, Michelle Guish; a Fireworks Pictures and Samuel Goldwyn Films and Boneyard Entertainment presentation in association with Xingu Films and Travis Swords Productions; British; Dolby; Color; Rated R; 91 minutes; US release date: July 27, 2001

CAST

Colin Briggs	Clive Owen
Georgina Woodhouse	Helen Mirren
Fergus Wilk	David Kelly
Governor Hodge	Warren Clarke
Tony	Danny Dyer
Raw	Adam Fogerty
Jimmy	Paterson Joseph
Primrose Woodhouse	Natasha Little
Dudley	Peter Guinness
Holly	Lucy Punch
Susan Hodge	Sally Edwards
Nigel	Donald Douglas
Laurence	Kevin McMonagle
Sarah	Julie Saunders
John	Jordan Maxwell

and David Lyon (Home Secretary), Jan Chappell (Peggy Tortworth), Timothy Carlton (Hampton Court Official), Sudha Bhuchar, Ian East, Paul Ridley (Prison Board Officials), Brenda Cowling (Book Shop Customer), Charles De'Ath (Julian), Trevor Bowen (Royal Horticultural Society President), Lindsay Swan (Royal Horticultural Society Publicist), Cate Fowler (Nurse), Chris Barnes (Reporter), Emily Stott (Interviewer), Elwyn A David (Bodybuilder), James Wooley (Parole Judge)

Two inmates find meaning in their lives when the flowers they have planted impress the governor so much that he allows them to cultivate the prison's first official garden.

© Fireworks/Goldwyn

Helen Mirren

Clive Owen

Helena Bergström

Helena Bergström, Rolf Lassgård

Rolf Lassgård, Helena Bergström

UNDER THE SUN

(SHADOW DISTRIBUTION) Producer/Director, Colin Nutley; Screenplay, Colin Nutley, Johanna Hald, David Neal; Based on the short story *The Little Farm* by H E Bates; Photography, Jens Fischer; Music, Paddy Maloney; Editor, Perry Schaffer; Costumes, Camilla Thulin; Produced by Sweetwater in cooperation with Svensk Filmindustri, SVT Goteborg/Drama, Film I Vast and Nordisk Film and TV-Fond; Swedish, 1998; Dolby; CinemaScope; Color; Not rated; 118 minutes; US release date: August 3, 2001

CAST

Olof	Rolf Lassgård
Ellen	Helena Bergström
Erik	Johan Widerberg
Newspaper Receptionist	Gunilla Röör
Preacher	Jonas Falk
Lena	Linda Ulvaeus

and Bergljót Arnadóttir (Shop Assistant), Per Sandberg (Undertaker)

In rural 1956 Sweden, an illiterate, isolated farmer advertises for a housekeeper and gets a response from the beautiful, worldly Ellen.

© Shadow Distribution

Johan Widerberg, Helena Bergström

Lena Headey

AUDITION

(VITAGRAPH) Producers, Akemi Suyama, Satoshi Hukushima; Executive Producer, Toyoyuki Yokohama; Director, Takashi Miike; Screenplay, Daisuke Tengan; Story, Ryû Murakami; Photography, Hideo Yamamoto; Designer, Tatsuo Ozeki; Editor, Yasushi Shimamura; Music, Kôji Endô; Japanese, 1999; Color; Not rated; 115 minutes; US release date: August 8, 2001

CAST

Shigeharu Aoyama	Ryô Ishibashi
Asami Yamazaki	Eihi Shiina
Shigehiko Aoyama	Tetsu Sawaki
Yasuhisa Yoshikawa	Jun Kunimura
Old Man in Wheelchair	Renji Ishibashi
Ryôko Aoyama	Miyuki Matsuda

and Toshie Negishi (Rie), Ren Osugi (Shibata), Shigeru Saiki (Toastmaster), Ken Mitsuishi (Director), Yuriko Hirooka (Michiyo Yanagida), Fumiyo Kohinata (TV Station Presenter), Misato Nakamura (Misuzu Takagi), Yuuto Arima (Shigeharu as a Child), Ayaka Izumi (Asami as a Child)

Widower Aoyama holds auditions for a non-existent movie in hopes of finding a bride. After choosing the seemingly demure Asami, he is shocked when their relationship takes an unexpected turn.

© Vitagraph

ABERDEEN

(FIRST RUN FEATURES) Producer, Petter J Borgli; Executive Producer, Tom Remlov; Director, Hans Petter Moland; Screenplay, Kristin Amundsen, Hans Petter Moland; Story, Lars Bill Lundholm; Photography, Philip Øgaard; Designer, Janusz Sosnowski; Costumes, Anne Pedersen; Music, Zbigniew Preisner; Editor, Sophie Hesselberg; Co-Producers, Kastro Khatib, John McGrath; Casting, Jeremy Zimmerman; from Filmfabriken Baltic Sea AB (Sweden), Freeway Films (UK), and Norsk Film A/S (Norway); British-Norwegian-Swedish, 2000; Dolby; Color; Not rated; 106 minutes; American release date: August 10, 2001

CAST

Tomas	Stellan Skarsgård
Kaisa	Lena Headey
Clive	Ian Hart
Helen	Charlotte Rampling
Nurse	Louise Goodall
Perkins	Jason Hetherington

Helen convinces her daughter to journey to Norway under the pretense of bringing her estranged alcoholic father to Scotland for rehab.

© First Run Features

Ryô Ishibashi, Jun Kunimura

Eihi Shiina

Alakina Mann, Nicole Kidman, James Bentley

Nicole Kidman (Above and Below)

THE OTHERS

(MIRAMAX) Producers, Fernando Bovaira, José Luis Cuerda, Sunmin Park; Executive Producers, Tom Cruise, Paula Wagner, Bob Weinstein, Harvey Weinstein, Rick Schwartz; Director/Screenplay/Music, Alejandro Amenábar; Photography, Javier Aguirresarobe AEC; Designer, Benjamín Fernández; Costumes, Sonia Grande; Casting, Jina Jay; a Cruise-Wagner Productions/Sogecine/Las Producciones Del Escorpión production; Spanish-US; Dolby; Deluxe color; Rated PG-13; 101 minutes; US release date: August 10, 2001

CAST

Grace Stewart	Nicole Kidman
Mrs. Mills	Fionnula Flanagan
Charles Stewart	Christopher Eccleston
Anne Stewart	Alakina Mann
Nicholas	James Bentley
Mr Tuttle	Eric Sykes
Lydia	Elaine Cassidy
Old Lady	Renée Asherson
Assistants	Gordon Reid, Ricardo López
Mr Marlish	Keith Allen
Mrs Marlish	Michelle Fairley
Victor	Alexander Vince
Gardene	Aldo Grilo

During the final days of World War II, Grace, who protects her two young children from extreme exposure to the light by shutting them up in her Victorian mansion, begins to sense the eerie presence of intruders in the house.

© Dimension Films

269

Julia Blake, Charles Tingwell

Kristine Van Pellicom, Kenny Aernouts
© Fireworks Pictures

INNOCENCE

(FIREWORKS/CINEVAULT) Producers, Paul Cox, Mark Patterson; Executive Producer, William T Marshall; Director/Screenplay, Paul Cox; Photography, Tony Clark ASC; Designer, Tony Cronin; Music, Paul Grabowsky; Associate Producer, Willem Thijssen; Editor, Simon Whitington; a Strand/New Oz Productions/Showtime Australia in association with the South Australian Film Corporation, Film Victoria, a division of Cinemedia, with HET Fonds Film in Vlaanderen and the International Film Festival Ghent and Illumination Films in association with Cinété presentation; Australian; Dolby; Color; Not rated; 95 minutes; US release date: August 17, 2001

CAST

Claire	Julia Blake
Andreas	Charles Tingwell
John	Terry Norris
David	Robert Menzies
Monique	Marta Dusseldorp
Young Claire	Kristine Van Pellicom
Young Andreas	Kenny Aernouts
Minister	Chris Haywood
Gerald	Norman Kaye
Sally	Joey Kennedy
Maudie	Liz Windsor

Fifty years after their brief but passionate love affair in post-war Belgium, music teacher Andreas Borg discovers that Claire still lives in the same town as he does, prompting him to contact her.

MAYBE BABY

(USA FILMS) Producer, Phil McIntyre; Executive Producers, Ernst Goldschmidt, David M Thompson; Director/Screenplay, Ben Elton; Associate Producer, Lucy Ansbro; Line Producer, Mary Richards; Photography, Roger Lanser ACS; Designer, Jim Clay; Editor, Peter Hollywood; Costumes, Anna Sheppard; Music, Colin Towns; Song: Maybe Baby by Charles Hardin, Norman Petty/performed by Paul McCartney; Casting, Mary Selway; a Pandora and BBC Films presentation of a Phil McIntyre production; British; Dolby; Deluxe color; Rated R; 93 minutes; US release date: August 24, 2001

CAST

Sam Bell	Hugh Laurie
Lucy Bell	Joely Richardson
George	Adrian Lester
Carl Phipps	James Purefoy
Ewan Proclaimer	Tom Hollander
Sheila	Joanna Lumley
Joanna	Rachael Stirling
Nigel	Matthew Macfadyen
Mr James	Rowan Atkinson
Charlene	Dawn French
Druscilla	Emma Thompson

and Yasmin Bannerman (Melinda), Dave Thompson (Dave the Comedian/Mrs Furblob), Stephen Simms (Trevor), John Brenner (Kit), Jaz Wilson (Baby Cuthbert), Guy Barrett, Delia Bhujoo, Abbey Careford, Marina Fiorato (Nigel's Posse), Richard Leaf (Justin Cocker), Lidija Zovkic (Petra), Connor Pearce (Boy on Bike in Park), Henrietta Garden (Mother in Park), Richard Sandells (Man Wrestling for Cab), Emma Cooke, Shelley Conn (Nurses), Stephanie Bartczak, Chris Belgrave, Catriona Pearson, Judith Shekoni (Ewan's Posse), Paul Ready (Student Doctor), Paul Tripp (Mr Furblob), Gemma Aston (Roz), Lisa Palfrey (Jan), Serena Evans (Dr Cooper), Katisha Kenyon, Anneli Harrison, Caroline Hayes (Commerical Girls), Elizabeth Woodcock (Tilda), John Lightbody (Hospital Administrator), Mina Anwar (Yasmin), Junix Nocian (Chinese Practitioner), John Fortune (Acupuncturist), Sally Reeve (Masseuse), Kelly Reilly (Nimnh), Emma Buckley (IVF Surgeon), Karen Bryson (Actor Playing Doctor), Bill & Ben (William the Dog)

A successful married couple tries every method imaginable to have a baby.

© USA Films

Joely Richardson, Hugh Laurie

Michael Nyqvist, Lisa Lindgren

Ola Norell

Jessica Liedberg, Lisa Lindgren

TOGETHER

(IFC FILMS) Producer, Lars Jönsson; Director/Screenplay, Lukas Moodysson; Photography, Ulf Brantås; Art Director, Carl Johan de Geer; Costumes, Mette Möller; Editors, Michal Leszczylowski SFK, Fredrik Abrahamsen; Casting, Imor Hermann; Produced by Memfis Film in co-production with Zentropa Entertainments, Film i Väst, SVT Drama Göteborg, Keyfilms Roma, Nordisk Film & TV-Fond; Swedish-Danish, 2000; Dolby; Color; Not rated; 107 minutes; US release date: August 24, 2001

CAST

Elisabeth	Lisa Lindgren
Rolf	Michael Nyqvist
Eva	Emma Samuelsson
Stefan	Sam Kessel
Goran	Gustaf Hammarsten
Lena	Anja Lundqvist
Anna	Jessica Liedberg
Lasse	Ola Norell
Tet	Axel Zuber
Klas	Shanti Roney
Erik	Olle Sarri
Signe	Cecilia Frode
Sigvard	Lars Frode
Mane	Emil Moodysson
Fredrik	Henrik Lundstrom
Margit	Therese Brunnander
Ragnar	Claes Hartelius
Birger	Sten Ljunggren

Elisabeth, a housewife tired of her husband's abusive behavior, takes her two young children and moves into a commune.

© IFC Films

Ola Norell, Shanti Roney

Michael Nyqvist, Lisa Lindgren

Tillsammans' Members

Giorgio Maiocchi

THE IRON LADIES

(STRAND) Producer, Visute Poolvoralaks; Co-Producers, Chatchavarian Klainak, Prasert Wiwatananonpong, Chanajai Tonsaithong; Director, Yongyoot Thongkongtoon; Screenplay, Visuthichai Boonyakarinjana, Jira Maligool, Yongyoot Thongkongtoon; Photography, Jira Maligool; Art Director, Narucha Vijitvarit; Costumes, Ekkawsit Meeprasertkul; Music, Wild at Heart; Editor, Sunit Assavinikul; a Tai Entertainment presentation; Thai, 2000; Dolby; Color; Not rated; 105 minutes; US release date: September 7, 2001

CAST

Jung	Chaichan Nimpoonsawas
Mon	Sahaparp Virakamin
Nong	Giorgio Maiocchi
Pia	Gokgorn Benjathikul
Chai	Jessdaporn Pholdee
Wit	Ekachai Buranapanit
Coach Bee	Siridhana Hongsophon
April	Phromsit Sittichumroenkhun
May	Suttipong Sittichumroenkhun
June	Anucha Chatkaew
Man	Suraphan Chaupaknam
Muk	Sujira Arunpipat
Chat	Pakorn Vipatawat

and Pairote Jaisinga (Jung's Father), Wiyada Umarin (Jung's Mother), Saneh Srisuwan (Sheriff), Umnuay Sirichan (Coach Bee's Father), Siriwan Suridej (Seller), Prawin Pattanaphong (Coach Chatree). Patcharapon Hitanant (Street Vendor), Sudjai Sunthornwipat (Grandma on Train), Damrong Puttaran, Sanya Kunakorn (TV Hosts), Weeraprawat Wonguapan (Wit's Father), Piatip Kumwong (Witt's Mother), Sukanya Raiwint (Juli), Komsan Meesombat (Referee), Suraphon Chonwilai (Wedding Photographer), Anupon Puwapoonphon (Northern Dialect MC), Samruay Saengtubtim (Nan Province Coach), Kritt Uttaseri, Wasan Utamayothin (TV Hosts), Kroi Samkao, Boonyod Sukthinthai (Referees), Theerachai Preukpiman (Coach), Kittipat Chainuwat (Kitti).

The true story of how a male volleyball team, consisting mostly of homosexuals, transvestites, and transsexuals, won the 1996 National Championships.

A MATTER OF TASTE

(ATTITUDE FILMS/TLA RELEASING) Producers, Catherine Dussart, Chantal Perrin; Director, Bernard Rapp; Screenplay, Gilles Taurand, Bernard Rapp; Based on the novel *Affairs de Gout* by Philippe Balland; Photography, Gérard de Battista; Designer, François Comtet; Costumes, Martine Rapin; Music, Jean-Philippe Goude; Editor, Juliette Welfling; Casting, Gérard Moulévrier; French, 2000; Dolby; Color; Not rated; 90 minutes; US release date: September 7, 2001

CAST

Frédéric Delamont	Bernard Giraudeau
Nicolas Rivière	Jean-Pierre Lorit
Béatrice	Florence Thomassin
René Rousset	Charles Berling
Magistrate	Jean-Pierre Léaud
Flavert	Artus de Penguern
Doctor Rossignon	Laurent Spielvogel
Caroline	Elisabeth Macocco
Doctor Ferrières	Anne-Marie Philipe
Nathalie	Delphine Zingg
Marco	David D'ingeo
Félix	Frédéric de Goldfiem

Frédéric Delamont, a wealthy, eccentric businessman, hires handsome waiter Nicolas to be his food taster, resulting in an increasingly unsettling relationship between the two, as Delamont becomes more demanding and obsessive.

Florence Thomassin, Jean-Pierre Lorit

Bernard Giraudeau, Jean-Pierre Lorit

Germàn Jaramillo

OUR LADY OF THE ASSASSINS

(PARAMOUNT CLASSICS) Producers, Margaret Menegoz, Barbet Schroeder; Director, Barbet Schroeder; Screenplay, Fernando Vallejo, based on his novel *La Virgen de los Sicarios*; Photography, Rodrigo Lalinde; Designer/Costumes, Monica Marulanda; Editor, Elsa Vasquez; Music, Jorge Arriagada; Casting, Marlin Franco, Margarita Florez, Ana Isabel Velasquez; a co-production of Les Films du Losange/Le Studio Canal+; French; Dolby; Color; Rated R; 100 minutes; US release date: September 7, 2001

CAST

Fernando	Germàn Jaramillo
Alexis	Anderson Ballesteros
Wilmar	Juan David Restrepo
Alfonso	Manuel Busquets
Child Sniffing Glue	Wilmar Agudelo
4X4 Thief	Juan Carlos Alvarez
Taxi Driver—Santo Domingo	Jairo Alzate
Waitress	Zulma Arango
Alexis's Mother	Cenobia Cano

and José Luis Bedoya (Taxi Sabaneta #1), Eduardo Carvajal (Taxi Driver Clinic), Olga Lucía Collazos (Pregnant Woman), Jorge A Correa (Dead Man), Phanor Delgado (Taxi Driver with Machette), Albeiro Lopera (Punk), Wilson Lòpez (Taxi Driver Sabaneta #2), Alexander Molina, Juan Tejada (Alexis's Brothers), Anibal Moncada (Don Anibal), Jaime Osorio (Forensic Pathologist), Carlos Ordòñez (Old Fool), Teyler Pérez (4X4 Youth), Edwin Porras, Ohn Mario Restrepo (Bad Guys), Gustavo Restrepo (Wounded Man), Carlos A Danita (Wounded Man's Friend), Nicolàs Franco, Juan Fdo Leòn (Hired Assassins), Hector Galàn (Tango Singer), Rubi Henao (Beggar), John Jaramillo (Child Beggar), Carlos Zapata (Motel Receptionist), Serafin Zapata (Clown), Martha Libia Zuluaga (Dead Punk Waitress)

Fernando, a wearied and cynical Colombian writer, returns to his home town of Medellín where he witnesses the devastation and crime that has become the norm to the population, including his younger lover, Alexis, who believes it is his duty to dispose of the underbelly of society.

© Paramount Classics

Anderson Ballesteros

Anderson Ballesteros, Germàn Jaramillo

Claire Hackett, Anthony Borrows, Ian Hart

LIAM

(LIONS GATE) Producers, Colin McKeown, Martin Tempia; Executive Producers, David M Thompson, Tessa Ross, Sally Hibbin; Co-Producer, Ulrich Felsberg; Director, Stephen Frears; Screenplay, Jimmy McGovern; Photography, Andrew Dunn; Designer, Stephen Fineren; Costumes, Alex Caulfield; Editor, Kristina Hetherington; Music, John Murphy; Casting, Pippa Hall, Leo Davis; a BBC Films presentation of a Liam Films production in co-production with Road Movies and in association with MIDA, Diaphana, BIM, WDR/Arte, ARD/Degeto Film; British-German-Italian; Dolby; Color; Rated R; 90 minutes; US release date: September 21, 2001

Anthony Borrows

CAST

Dad Tom Sullivan	Ian Hart
Mum Sullivan	Claire Hackett
Mrs. Abernathy	Anne Reid
Liam Sullivan	Anthony Borrows
Con Sullivan	David Hart
Teresa Sullivan	Megan Burns
Father Ryan	Russell Dixon
Auntie Aggie	Julia Deakin
Uncle Tom	Andrew Schofield
Lizzie	Bernadette Shortt
Lizzie's Husband	David Carey
Mr. Samuels	David Knopov
Mrs. Samuels	Jane Gurnett
Jane Samuels	Gema Loveday
David	Martin Hancock
Nunny	Sylvie Gatrill
Nunny's Husband	Chris Darwin
Lofty	James Foy
Pawnbroker	Arnold Brown

and Billy Moocho (Clubman), Stephen Walters (Black Shirt), Bryan Reagan (Gaffer), Sean Styles (Big Micky), Sean McKee (Little Micky), George Maudsley (Man at Political Rally)

A young boy, growing up in poverty in 1930 Liverpool, sees his desperate father join a group of fascists after he has convinced himself that the Jews are responsible for him losing his job at the shipyard.

© Lions Gate Films

Anthony Borrows, Megan Burns

(Above) Hélène De Fougerolles, Sergio Castellitto
(Below) Jeanne Balibar

BORN ROMANTIC

(UNITED ARTISTS) Producer, Michele Camarda; Executive Producers, David M Thompson, Alistair MacLean-Clark, Melvyn Singer; Director/Screenplay, David Kane; Photography, Robert Alazraki AFC; Designer, Sarah Greenwood; Costumes, Jill Taylor; Editor, Michael Parker; Music, Simon Boswell; Choreographers, Jose Ordonez Fernandes De Souza, Rodolpho Fournier; Casting, Jina Jay; a BBC Films and Harvest Pictures presentation of a Kismet Film Company production; British; Dolby; Deluxe color; Rated R; 96 minutes; US release date: September 28, 2001

CAST

Frankie..Craig Ferguson
Second Cab Driver ....Ian Hart
Mo..Jane Horrocks
Jimmy..Adrian Lester
Jocelyn ....Catherine McCormack
Eddie ....Jimi Mistry
Fergus ....David Morrissey
Eleanor..Olivia Williams
and Paddy Considine (Ray), Kenneth Cranham (Barney), Louise Delamere (Maria), Jose Ordonez Fernandes De Souza (Souza), Tony Maudsley (Turnkey), Hermione Norris (Carolanne), Sally Phillips (Suzy), Mel Raido (Brian), Martin Savage (Wayne), Jessica Stevenson (Libby), John Thomson (1st Driver), Ashley Walters (Lee), Victoria Willing (Frankie's Barmaid), Vanessa Samson, Alison Allen, Philip Langlais Garcia, Maria Legaspi, Sarah Davis, Rodolfo Fournier, Delena Dunster, Ernesto Estryou, Roisin Ahearne, Leonel Gamboa, Yamile Berral, Bill Williams, Homero Gonzalez, Stacey Dore, Cherryl Hancock, Ashwin Musiban, Gordon Haynes (Salsa Club Dancers), Simon Boswell, Jeff Clyne, Harry Dixon, Jimmy Hastings, Lew Hooper, George Patterson, Peter Strange, Eddie Taylor (Frankie's Band)

Three single London men searching for love find themselves pursuing seemingly unsuitable women.

© United Artists Films, Inc.

VA SAVOIR
(WHO KNOWS?)

(SONY PICTURES CLASSICS) Producer, Martine Marignac; Director, Jacques Rivette; Screenplay, Pascal Bonitzer, Christine Laurent, Jacques Rivette; Dialogue, Pascal Bonitzer, Christine Laurent, Jacques Rivette; Photography, William Lubtchansky; Designer, Manu de Chauvigny; Editor, Nicole Lubtchansky; Associate Producer, Maurice Tinchant; Costumes, Laurence Struz, Christine Laurent; a Pierre Grise Productions presentation; a co-production of Pierre Grise Productions, France 2 Cinema VM Productions (France), Mikado (Italy), Kinowelt (Germany), with the participation of Canal+, Cofimage 12, Gimages 4, Centre National de la Cinematographie with the support of Eurimages and La Procirep; French-Italian-German; Dolby; Color; Rated PG-13; 150 minutes; US release date: September 29, 2001

CAST

Camille Renard ....Jeanne Balibar
Ugo Bassani ....Sergio Castellitto
Sonia...Marianne Basler
Pierre Mauduit ....Jacques Bonnaffé
Dominique "Do" Desprez.....................................Hélène de Fougerolles
Arthur Delamarche ....Bruno Todeschini
Madame Desprez, Do's Mother.............................Catherine Rouvel
Autograph Librarian ....Claude Berri

CAST OF
As You Desire Me
(Come tu mi vuoi)

Salter ....Attilio Cucari
Greta (Mop) ....Bettina Kee
Bruno ....Arturo Armone Caruso
Lena..Luciana Castellucci
Salesio ....Emanuele Vacca
Ines...Valeria Cavalli
Silvio...Fausto Maria Sciarappa
The Madwoman ....Paola Andrea
and Enrico Marassi, Cesare Panzera Capitani, Roberto Manieri, Constantino Raimondi (Four Young Men), Christiana Visentin (Pamina), Fosco Perinti (Administrator), Walter Zoon (Doctor)

French actress Camille Renard returns to Paris after a three-year absence to participate in an Italian company's production of As You Desire Me, *directed by her lover, Ugo, who becomes obsessed with finding the lost manuscript of a play by Italian playwright Goldoni.*

© Sony Pictures Entertainment

David Morrissey, Jimi Mistry, Craig Ferguson

MULHOLLAND DR.

(UNIVERSAL) Producers, Mary Sweeney, Alain Sarde, Neal Edelstein, Michael Polaire, Tony Krantz; Executive Producer, Pierre Edelman; Director/Screenplay, David Lynch; Photography, Peter Fleming; Designer, Jack Fisk; Editor, Mary Sweeney; Costumes, Amy Stofsky; Music, Angelo Badalamenti; a co-production of Les Films Alain Sarde, Studio Canal, Picture Factory; French-US; Dolby; Color; Rated R; 146 minutes; US release date: October 8, 2001

CAST

Adam Kesher	Justin Theroux
Betty Elms/Diane Selwyn	Naomi Watts
Rita/Camilla Rhodes	Laura Elena Harring
Coco Lenoix	Ann Miller
Vincenzo Castigliane	Dan Hedaya
Joe	Mark Pellegrino
Detective Domgaard	Brent Briscoe
Detective Harry McKnight	Robert Forster
Cynthia	Katharine Towne
Louise Bonner	Lee Grant
Limo Driver	Scott Wulff
Gene	Billy Ray Cyrus
Jimmy Katz	Chad Everett
Linney James	Rita Taggart
Wally Brown	James Karen
Lorraine	Lori Heuring
Luigi Castigliane	Angelo Badalamenti
Billy	Michael Des Barres
Mr Darby	Marcus Graham
Waitress at Winkies	Melissa Crider
Ray Hott	Robert Katims
Irene	Jeanne Bates
Irene's Companion	Dan Birnbaum
Aunt Ruth	Maya Bond
Dan	Patrick Fischler
Herb	Michael Cooke
Bum	Bonnie Aarons
Mr Roque	Michael J. Anderson
Roque's Manservant	Joseph Kearney
Back of Head Man	Enrique Buelna
Hairy-Armed Man	Richard Mead
Cab Driver at LAX	Sean E. Markland
Valet Attendant	Daniel Rey
Robert Smith	David Schroeder
Espresso Man	Tom Morris
Camilla Rhodes	Melissa George
Castigliane Limo Driver	Matt Gallini
Ed	Vincent Castellanos

and Diane Nelson (Heavy-Set Woman), Charlie Croughwell (Vacuum Man), Rena Riffel (Laney), Tad Horino (Taka), Tony Longo (Kenny), Geno Silva (Cookie), Lafayette Montgomery (Cowboy), Kate Forster (Martha Johnson), Wayne Grace (Bob Booker), Michele Hicks (Nicki), Lisa Ferguson (Julia Chadwick/Dancer), William Ostrander (1st Assistant Director), Elizabeth Lackey (Carol), Brian Beacock, Blake Lindsley, Adrien Curry, Tyrah M Lindsey (Backup Singers), Michael Weatherred (Hank, Assistant Director), Michael Fairman (Jason), Johanna Stein (Woman in #12), Richard Green (The Magician), Conte Candoli (Trumpet Player), Cori Glazer (Blue-Haired Lady), Rebekah Del Rio (Herself), Lyssie Powell (Blonde in Bed), Scott Coffey (Wilkins), Kimberly Clever, Joshua Collazo, David Frutos, Peter Loggins, Theresa Salazar, Thea Samuels, Christian Thompson (Dancers)

A naive aspiring actress arrives in Hollywood where she meets up with an amnesiac who has just escaped death, leading the two of them into a hellish and puzzling adventure.

This film received an Oscar nomination for director.

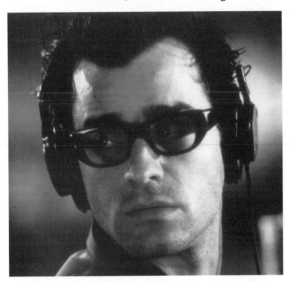

Naomi Watts, Laura Elena Harring

Justin Theroux

Ann Miller, Naomi Watts

Anaïs Reboux, Roxane Mesquida

Anaïs Reboux, Roxane Mesquida

Anaïs Reboux

Libero De Rienzo, Roxane Mesquida

FAT GIRL

(COWBOY PICTURES) Director/Screenplay, Catherine Breillat; Photography, Yorgos Arvanitis AFC; Art Directors, Francois Renaud Labarthe, Yann Richard, Cecilia Blom, Fabienne David, Christophe Graziani, Fabrice Heraud, Gerald Lemaire, Jean-Luc Molle; Costumes, Catherine Meillan; Editors, Pascale Chavance, Gwenola Heaulme, Frederic Barbe; Casting, Michael Weill; a Jean-François Lepetit presentation of a Flach Film-CB Films Production, Immagine & Cinema-Urbania Pictures, with the participation of Canal+ and the Centre National de la Cinématographie; French-Italian; Color; Not rated; 83 minutes; US release date: October 10, 2001

CAST

Anaïs	Anaïs Reboux
Elena	Roxane Mesquida
Fernando	Libero De Rienzo
Mother	Arsinée Khanjian
Father	Romain Goupil
Fernando's Mother	Laura Betti
The Killer	Albert Goldberg

and Odette Barriere, Ann Matthijsse, Pierre Renverseau, Jean-Marc Boulanger (Friends at Residence), Frederick Bodin (Waiter), Michel Guillemin (Janitor), Josette Cathalan (Saleswoman), Claude Sese (Police Officer), Marc Samuel (Inspector)

While on vacation with her family, Anaïs, an introverted overweight girl, finds herself jealous of her gorgeous sister's sexual dalliance with a young Italian.

Libero De Rienzo, Roxane Mesquida

Yu Rong Guang

IRON MONKEY

(MIRAMAX) Producer, Tsui Hark; Executive Producers, Raymond Chow, Wang Ying Hsiang; Director, Yuen Wo Ping; Screenplay, Tsui Hark, Elsa Tang, Lau Tai Mok; Co-Producer, Raymond Lee; Photography, Arthur Wong, Tam Chi Wai; Designer, Ringo Cheung; Costumes, Bo Bo Ng; Music, James L Venable; Editors, Angie Lam, Chan Chi Wai; Martial Arts Choreographers, Yuen Cheung Yan, Yuen Shun Yi, Ku Huen Chiu; a Media Asia, Golden Harvest and Quentin Tarantino presentation of an LS Pictures Ltd Film Work Shop Production; Hong Kong, 1993; Dolby; Color; Rated PG-13; 85 minutes; US release date: October 12, 2001

CAST

Dr Yang (Iron Monkey)	Yu Rong Guang
Wong Kei-Ying	Donnie Yen
Miss Orchid	Jean Wang
Wong Fei Hong	Tsang Sze Man
Chief Fox	Yuen Shun Yi
Governor	James Wong
Royal Minister	Yen Yee Kwan
Virgin Assassin	Lee Fai
Scarred Assassin	Hau Yin Chung
Governor's Favorite Wife	Cheung Fung Nay

and Chun Kwai Bo, Chan Siu Wah, Yip Choi Nam, Ko Man Dick (Monks)

In 19th-century eastern China, an evil governor attempts to increase food prices during a famine, prompting a mysterious fighter known as the Iron Monkey to try to save his village from this oppression.

© Miramax Films

INTIMACY

(EMPIRE) Producers, Jacques Hinstin, Patrick Cassavetti; Executive Producer, Charles Gassot; Director, Patrice Chereau; Screenplay, Patrice Chereau, Anne-Louise Trividic; Based on the stories *Intimacy* and *Night Light* by Hanif Kureishi; Photography, Eric Gautier; Designer, Hayden Griffin; Costumes, Caroline De Vivaise; Line Producer, Lesley Stewart; Music, Eric Neveux; Editor, Francois Gedigier; Casting, Karen Lindsay-Stewart; Studio Canal; French; Dolby; CinemaScope; Color; Not rated; 119 minutes; US release date: October 17, 2001

CAST

Jay	Mark Rylance
Claire	Kerry Fox
Andy	Timothy Spall
Victor	Alastair Galbraith
Ian	Philippe Calvario
Betty	Marianne Faithfull
Susan	Susannah Harker
Pam	Rebecca Palmer
Dave	Fraser Ayres

and Michael Fitzgerald, Robert Addie (Bar Owners), Deborah McLaren (Theatre Course Student), Greg Sheffield, Vinnie Hunter (Jay's Children), Joe Prospero (Claire's Son), Siân Reeves (Claire's Neighbor at Audition), Paola Dionisotti (Amanda in *The Glass Menagerie*), Marcello Walton (Tom in *The Glass Menagerie*), Christian Malcolm (Jim in *The Glass Menagerie*), Katie Campbell, Roderic Culver, Jonathan Emmett, Gideon Gent, Alison Lintott, Xavier Loira, Kate Orr, Clare Wayland

A man and woman meet every week to have sex, trying not to become emotionally attached, a vow they find hard to keep.

© Empire Pictures

(Above) Kerry Fox, Mark Rylance
(Below) Mark Rylance, Kerry Fox

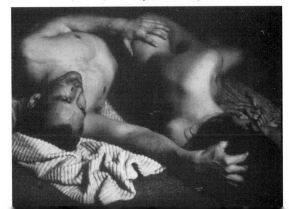

Mark (right)

BURNT MONEY
(PLATA QUEMADA)

(STRAND) Producer, Oscar Kramer; Director, Marcelo Piñeyro; Screenplay, Marcelo Figueras; Photography, Alfredo Mayo; Designers, Jorge Ferrari, Juan Mario Roust; Editor, Juan Carlos Macias; Music, Osvaldo Montes; a Cabezas, Mandarin, Taxi Films SA production; Argentine, 2000; Dolby; Color; Not rated; 125 minutes; US release date: October 19, 2001

CAST

Angel	Eduardo Noriega
Nene	Leonardo Sbaraglia
Cuervo	Pablo Echarri
Giselle	Leticia Brédice
Fontana	Ricardo Bartis
Vivi	Dolores Fonzi
Nando	Carlos Roffé
Tabaré	Daniel Valenzuela
Losardo	Héctor Alterio
Realtor	Claudio Rissi
Florian Reyes	Luis Zembosky
Carlos Tulian	Harry Havilio
Parisi	Roberto Vallejo
Cantante Cabaret	Adriana Varela

A pair of gay lovers, dubbed "The Twins" by the police, become noted criminals of the Buenos Aires underworld until a botched heist forces them to escape to Uruguay.

© Strand Releasing

TREMBLING BEFORE G-D

(NEW YORKER) Producers, Sandi Simcha DuBowski, Marc Smolowitz; Co-Producers, James Velaise, Philippa Kowarsky; Director, Sandi Simcha DuBowski; Creative Collaboration, Susan Korda; Editors, Susan Korda, Johanna Prenner; Music, John Zorn; Photography, Various; Music Supervisors, Carole Sue Baker, Jon L Fine; Pretty Pictures (Paris), Cinephil Ltd (Tel Aviv); Israeli-French; Color; Not rated; 84 minutes; US release date: October 24, 2001 Documentary on gay Hasidic and Orthodox Jews who practice Judaism despite their religion's condemnation of homosexuality.

© New Yorker Films

Eduardo Noriega

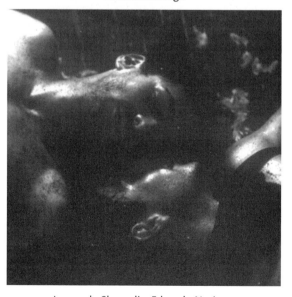

Leonardo Sbaraglia, Eduardo Noriega

Ariane Ascaride, Gérard Meylan

Ariane Ascaride

THE TOWN IS QUIET

(NEW YORKER) Director, Robert Guédiguian; Screenplay, Jean-Louis Milesi, Robert Guédiguian; Photography, Bernard Cavalié; Designer, Michel Vandestien; Editor, Bernard Sasia; Costumes, Catherine Keller; Director of Production, Malek Hamzaoui; a co-production of Agat & CIE/Diaphana with the participation of Canal+; French; Dolby; Color; Not rated; 132 minutes; US release date: October 26, 2001

CAST

Michèle	Ariane Ascaride
Fiona	Julie-Marie Parmentier
Claude	Pierre Banderet
Gérard	Gérard Meylan
Paul	Jean-Pierre Darroussin
Paul's Father	Jacques Boudet
Paul's Mother	Pascale Roberts
Viviane Froment	Christine Brücher
Yves Froment	Jacques Pieiller
Abderamane	Alexandre Ogou
Momo, Abderamane's Brother	Amar Toulé
Farid	Farid Ziane
Ameline	Véronique Balme
SarkisJulien	Sevan Papazian

and Danielle Stefan (The Prostitute), Patrick Bonnel (The Post Office Worker), Yann Trégouët (The Young Woman Who Provokes Gérard), Frédérique Bonnal (The Woman From the "National Preference"), Jacques Germain (Mr "National Preference"), Alain Lenglet (The Piano Mover), Emilie Angélini, Margaux Tartour, Noé Tellier (The Three Babies)

The lives of several Marseilles inhabitants overlap and influence one another, including a fishmonger and her heroin-addicted daughter, a dockworker-turned-cabbie, a bartender who deals drugs, and a young North African ex-con.

© New Yorker Films

Julie-Marie Parmentier, Ariane Ascaride

Alexandre Ogou, Christine Brücher

Audrey Tautou

Eric Savin, Lysiane Meis

© Lot 47 Films

Frédéric Bouraly, Franck Bussi

HAPPENSTANCE

(LOT 47) Producers, Anne-Dominique Toussaint, Pascal Judelewicz; Director/Screenplay, Laurent Firode; Executive Producer, Franck Landron; Photography, Jean-Rene Duveau; Music, Peter Chase; Costumes, Najat Kas; Editor, Didier Ranz; Casting, Stephane Gaillard; a co-production of Les Films des Tournelles and Les Films en Hiver; French; Dolby; Color; Not rated; 90 minutes; US release date: November 2, 2001

CAST

Younes ....Faudel
Irene ....Audrey Tautou
Richard ....Eric Slavin
Luc ....Eric Feldman
Stephanie ....Irene Ismailoff
Elsa ....Lysiane Meis
Marie ....Nathalie Besancon
Bobby ....Frederique Bouraly
and Franck Bussi (The Boy from the Filosophic Cafe), Marina Tome (Julie), Antoine Coesens (The Clochard), Said Serrari (The Pickpocket), Lily Boulogne (Luc's Mother), Gilbert Robin (The Destiny Man), Manu Layotte (Cailluox's Lanceurs), Husky Kihal (The Magazine Owner), Nor-eddin Abboud (The SAV Salesman), Louison Roblin (Irene's Neighbor), Felicite Wouassi (The Vigilant), Manuela Gourary (Elsa's Mother), Mathieu Ducrez (Franck), Abdessamada Chahidi (The Clandestine Moroccan), Sylvie Herbert (The Nurse), Michel Baladi (The Waiter From the Coffee Shop), Louise Vincent (The Gitane), Charlotte Maury-Sentier (The Horoscope Woman), Edith Le Merdy (The Subway Passenger), Oleg Imbert, Ludmila Imbert (The Russian Tourists), Francois Chattot (Marc), Pierre Bellemare (Taxi Driver)

A group of seemingly unconnected individuals becomes instrumental in reuniting two people who have interacted on the Metro and accidentally separated.

Faudel

Audrey Tautou in *Amélie*

Audrey Tautou in *Amélie*

Audrey Tautou in *Amélie*

Mathieu Kassovitz, Audrey Tautou in *Amélie*

Audrey Tautou in *Amélie*

AMÉLIE

(MIRAMAX ZOË) Producer, Claudie Ossard; Director, Jean Pierre Jeunet; Screenplay, Guillaume Laurant, Jean Pierre Jeunet; Dialogue, Guillaume Laurant; Photography, Bruno Delbonnel; Sets, Aline Bonetto; Costumes, Madeline Fontaine; Music, Yann Tiersen; Editor, Herve Schneid ACE; Visual Effects, Alain Carsoux, Duboi; Casting, Pierre Jacques Benichou; Presented in association with Claudie Ossard and UGC; a Victoires Productions, Tapioca Films, France 3 Cinema, MMC Independent Gmbh co-production in collaboration with the Sofica Sofinergie 5 and the support of the Filmstiftung with the participation of Canal+; French; Dolby; Technovision; Color; Rated R; 120 minutes; US release date: November 2, 2001

Audrey Tautou

CAST

Amélie Poulain	Audrey Tautou
Nino Quicampoix	Mathieu Kassovitz
Raphael Poulain (Amélie's Father)	Rufus
Madeleine Wallace (Concierge)	Yolande Moreau
Hipolito (The Writer)	Artus de Penguern
Collignon (The Grocer)	Urbain Cancellier
Joseph	Dominique Pinon
Bretodeau (The Box Man)	Maurice Benichou
Eva (The Strip Teaser)	Claude Perron
Old Man Collignon	Michel Robin
Georgette	Isabelle Nanty
Suzanne	Claire Maurier
Gina	Clotilde Mollet
Dufayel	Serge Merlin
Lucien	Jamel Debbouze
Amandine Poulain	Lorella Cravotta
Philomene	Armelle
Amélie, 8 years old	Flora Guiet
Nino as a Child	Amaury Babault
The Blind Man	Jean Darie
The Photo Booth Man	Ticky Holgado
The Stranger	Marc Amyot
The Screaming Neighbor	Dominique Bettenfeld
Eugene Koler	Eugène Berthier

Audrey Tautou

and Andrée Damant (Mrs. Collignon), Franckie Pain (The Newsstand Woman), Marion Pressburger (Credits Helper), Charles-Roger Bour (The Urinal Man), Luc Palun (Amandine's Grocer), Fabienne Chaudat (Woman in Coma), Jacques Viala (The Customer Who Humiliates His Friend), Fabien Behar (The Humiliated Customer), Jonathan Joss (The Humiliated Customer's Son), Jean-Pierre Becker (The Bum), Theirry Gibault (The Endive Client), François Bercovici (His Buddy), Guillaume Viry (The Vagrant), Valérie Zarrouk (Dominique Bredoteau Woman), Kevin Fernandes (Bretodeau as a Child), Marie-Laure Descouraux (The Dead Man's Concierge), Sophie Tellier (Aunt Josette), Gérald Weingand (The Teacher), François Viaur (The Bar Owner), Paule Dare (His Employee), Myriam Labbe (The Tobacco Buyer), Robert Gendreu (Cafe Patron), Julianne Kovacs (Grocer's Client), Philippe Paimblanc (Train Ticket Taker), Mady and Monette Malroux (The Twins), Valériane de Villeneuve (The Laughing Woman), Isis Peyrade (Samantha) Raymonde Heudeline (Phantom Train Cashier), Christiane Bopp (Woman by the Merry-Go-Round), Thierry Arfeuilleres (Statue Man), Jerry Lucas (The Sacré-Couer Boy), Patrick Paroux (The Street Prompter), Francois Aubineau (The Concierge's Postman), Philippe Beautier (Poulain's Postman), Régis Iacono (Felix L'Herbier); Off-Screen Voices: Frank-Oliver Bonnet (Palace Video), Alain Floret (The Concierge's Husband), Jean-Pol Brissart (The Postman), Jacques Thebault (Voice-Over), André Dussollier (Voice)

A waitress decides to transform the lives of her neighbors by doing anonymous deeds for them, while forsaking her own chance at happiness.

This film received Oscar nominations for foreign-language film, cinematography, original screenplay, and art direction.

Mathieu Kassovitz

Iñigo Garcés

Irene Visedo

Marisa Paredes, Eduardo Noriega

THE DEVIL'S BACKBONE

(SONY CLASSICS) Executive Producers, Augstín Almodóvar, Berta Navarro; Director, Guillermo Del Toro; Screenplay, Guillermo Del Toro, Antonio Trashorras, David Muñoz; Co-Producer, Rosa Bosch; Photography, Guillermo Navarro; Director of Production, Esther García; Art Director, Cesar Macarrón; Costumes, José Vico; Editor, Luis De La Madrid; Music, Javier Navarrete; Associate Producer, Michel Ruben; Digital Special Effects, Telson; Special Effects Makeup, DDT—David Martín; a Pedro and Augustín Almodóvar presentation, an El Deseo, SA, Tequila Gang and Anhelo Producciones co-production; Spanish; Dolby; Color; Rated R; 108 minutes; US release date: November 21, 2001

CAST

Jacinto ....Eduardo Noriega
Carmen ....Marisa Paredes
Cásares ....Federico Luppi
Jaime...Iñigo Garcés
Carlos..Fernando Tielve
and Irene Visedo (Conchita), Berta Ojea (Alma), Paco Maestre (El Puerco), José Manuel Lorenzo (Marcelo), Junio Valverde (Santi), Victor Barroso, Javier Gonzalez, Daniel Esparza, Adrián Lamana (Boys)

At an isolated school during the last days of the Spanish Civil War, ten-year old Carlos becomes aware of the ghost of a former student who was brutally murdered.

Victor Barroso, Javier Gonzalez, Daniel Esparza, Iñigo Garcés, Fernando Tielve, Adrián Lamana

THE WAY WE LAUGHED

(NEW YORKER) Producers, Vittorio and Rita Cecchi Gori (Tiger CinCa srl); Executive Producer, Mario Conte (Pacific Pictures); Director/Screenplay, Gianni Amelio; Photography, Luca Bigazzi; Designer, Giancarlo Basili; Costumes, Gianna Gissi; Editor, Simona Paggi; Music, Franco Piersanti; Casting, Nicola Conticello, Lorella Chiapatti; a Tiger CinCa srl and Pacific Pictures production; Italian, 1998; Dolby; Color; Not rated; 124 minutes; US release date: November 21, 2001

CAST

Arrivals

Pietro ....Francesco Guiffrida
Giovanni ....Enrico Lo Verso
The Father of the Family from Foggia...........................Guiliano Spadaro
His Wife...Patrizia Marino
His Son ....Giuseppe Sangari
His Daughter ....Francesca Monchiero
and Calogero Caruana, Roberto Marzo, Davide Negro, Giorgio Pittau, Pasqualino Vona, Giuseppe Zarbano (Giovanni's Friends), Salvatore Refano (The Old Sicilian), Giorgia Scuderi (Assuntina), Maria Terranova (Giovanni's Aunt), Antonio Trigilla (Giovanni's Uncle), Michele Trigilla (Giovanni's Cousin), Alessandro Bretti (The Young Cousin)

Deceptions

Rosario..Claudio Contartese
Girl at the Bar ....Barbara Braga
Sardinian Lance Corporal..Giovanni Leoni
Corporal's Assistant ....Luigi Mauro
Neapolitan Janitor ....Edoardo Ciciriello
and Aldo Rendina (The Dance Teacher), Sabrina Rubino (The Dancer/The Maid), Rosaria Danze (Lucia)

Money

Giovanni's Assistant ....Vittorio Rondella
The Boy from Lecce ....Antonio Madaro
Alessandra, the Student...Erika Doria
Mrs Verusio..Iolanda Donnini
Carmelo, the Mason ....Massimo Greco
The Train Thief ....Emanuele Aquilino
and Aldo Boarino (The Thief), Rosina Borgi (The Thief's Wife), Paolo Sansalone (The Boy in Public Baths), Bruno Casetta (The Restaurant's Waiter)

Letters

Female Student ....Irene Vistarini
Male Student ....Fabrizio Nicastro
The Janitor from Turin...Renato Liprandi
and Domenico Ragusa (Simone, the Guard), Francesco Guzzo (Man in the Bar)

Enrico Lo Verso, Francesco Giuffrida

Enrico Lo Verso

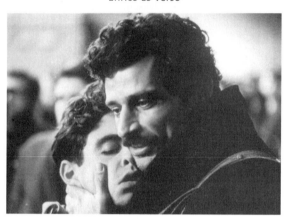

Francesco Giuffrida, Enrico Lo Verso

Blood

The Exam Professors...........................Antonio Prestipino, Corrado Borsa,
Pierfranco Ghisleni
Rosini, the Teacher ....Paolo Sena
Director of the Cooperative...Domenico Mungo
The Unemployed Calabrian..Valerio Contartese
and Marco Testa (The Singer at the Feast), Davide Pecetto (The Accordion Player), Mirella Ferrera (The Engaged Woman), Giuseppe D'Angelo (Giovanni's Assistant), Giannicola Resta (Young Thug)

Families

Ada..Simonetta Benozzo
Pelaia, the Educator...Fabrizio Gifuni
Battista, the Father..Pietro Paglietti
The Mother..Rosanna Rovere
Brother-in-Law ....Nanni Tormen
Sister-in-Law ....Ileana Spalla
The Grandson ....Gianluigi Marcone
and Luisella Tamietto, Tiziana Catalano (The Aunt), Clara Droetto (The Aunt)

In a story that takes place on six different days during a six-year span, illiterate Sicilian immigrant Giovanni encourages his younger brother to get a diploma and become a teacher so that he may have the rewards of knowledge.

© New Yorker Films

Javier Bardem, Jordi Mollá

SECOND SKIN (SEGUNDA PIEL)

(MENEMSHA) Producer, Andrés Vicente Gómez; Director, Gerardo Vera; Screenplay, Andrés González Sinde; Photography, Júlio Madurga; Art Director, Ana Alvargonzález; Costumes, Macarena Soto; Music, Roque Baños; Editor, Nicholas Wentworth; Associate Producer, Marco Gómez; Produced by Antena 3 Television, Lolafilms S.A., Via Digital; Spanish, 1999; Color; Not rated; 110 minutes; American release date: November 30, 2001

CAST

Diego	Javier Bardem
Alberto Garcia	Jordi Mollà
Elena	Ariadna Gil
Eva	Cecilia Roth
Rafael	Gil Albala
Adrian	Adrian Sac
Maria Elena	Mercedes Sampietro
Ana Mari	Cristina Espinosa
Neus	Pilar Castro
Oriol	Ramiro Alonso
Engineer	Silvia Espigado
Nurse	Carmen Grey
Tomasa	Ángela Rosal
Aitor	Luis B. Santiago
Luis	Christian Queipo
Ivan	Ivan Mateo

Diego, a doctor, falls in love with Alberto Garcia, a married man with a child, leading to an affair that has profound repercussions for all parties involved including Alberto's wife.

CODE UNKNOWN

(LEISURE TIME FEATURES/KIMSTIM) Producers, Alain Sarde, Marin Karmitz; Executive Producer, Yvon Crenn; Director/Screenplay, Michael Haneke; Photography, Jürgen Jürges; Designer, Manu de Chauvigny; Costumes, Francoise Clavel; Editors, Karin Hartusch, Andreas Prochaska; Casting, Kris Portier Debellair; French-German-Romanian, 2000; Dolby; Color; Not rated; 117 minutes; US release date: November 30, 2001

CAST

Anne	Juliette Binoche
Georges	Thierry Neuvic
Le Paysan	Sepp Bierbichler
Jean	Alexandre Hamidi
Amadou	Ona Lu Yenke
Maria	Luminata Gheorghiu
Aminate	Maimouna Hélène Diarra
The Father	Djibril Kouyaté
Irina	Crenguta Hariton Stoica

and Bob Nicolaescu (Dragos), Bruno Todeschini (Pierre), Paulus Manker (Perrin), Didier Flamand (The Director), Walid Afkir (The Young Arab), Maurice Bénichou (The Old Arab), Carlo Brandt (Henry), Philippe Demarle (Paul), Marc Duret (The Policeman), Arsinée Khanjian (Francine), Florence Loiret (Amadou's Friend), Nathalie Richard (Mathilde), Andrée Tainsy (Mrs Becker), Jean-Yves Chatelais (Shop Owner), Laurent Suire (Policeman), Malick Bowens (Witch Doctor), Ioan Marian Boris (Nicu), Monica Popa (Nuta), Ada Navrot (Florica), Dominique Douret (David), Tsuyu Bridwell (David's Friend), Antoine Mathieu (Restaurant Waiter), Constantin Barbulescu (Mihai Popa), Domeke Meite (Demba)

Several Parisians, including an aspiring actress, a music teacher for deaf-mute children, and a beggar, find themselves linked in unexpected ways.

© Leisure Time Features

Juliette Binoche

Michael Caine, Bob Hoskins, Tom Courtenay,
David Hemmings

Helen Mirren, Bob Hoskins

David Hemmings

Tom Courtenay, Bob Hoskins

LAST ORDERS

(SONY CLASSICS) Producers, Fred Schepisi, Elisabeth Robinson; Executive Producers, Nik Powell, Rainer Mockert, Gary Smith, Chris Craib; Director/Screenplay, Fred Schepisi; Based upon the novel by Graham Swift; Photography, Brian Tufano BSC; Designer, Tim Harvey; Costumes, Jill Taylor; Music, Paul Grabowsky; Editor, Kate Williams; Casting, Patsy Pollock, Shaheen Baig; from MBP, Scala Productions, Winchester Films; British-German; Dolby; Digitalscope; Color; Rated R; 109 minutes; US release date: December 7, 2001

CAST

Jack	Michael Caine
Vic	Tom Courtenay
Lenny	David Hemmings
Ray	Bob Hoskins
Amy	Helen Mirren
Vince	Ray Winstone
Young Jack	J.J. Feild
Young Vic	Cameron Fitch
Young Lenny	Nolan Hemmings
Young Ray	Anatol Yusef
Young Amy	Kelly Reilly
Young Vince	Stephen McCole
Bernie	Georges Innes
June	Laura Morelli
Mandy	Sally Hurst
Carol	Denise Black

and Sue James (Pam), Meg Wynn Owen (Joan), Kitty Leigh (Young Carol), Alex Reid (Young Pam), Tracey Murphy (Young Joan), Claire Harman (Young Sally), John Baker (11-year-old Vince), Emma Deigman (10-year-old Sally), Tom Baker (7-year-old Vince), Laura Deigman (5-year-old Sally), Simon Oats (Andy), Patricia Valentine (Sue), Lois Winstone (Kath), Brian Osborne (Tally Man), Joanna Bacon (Woman Picker), Teresa Lloyd (Ray's Prostitute), Alan Taylor (Sideshow Man), Charlotte Atkinson (Rochester Barmaid), Dani Foreman (Woman in Bar), Bea Sewell (Fairfax Home Receptionist), Aislinn Sands (Nurse Kelly)

A group of friends, gathering to spread the ashes of one of them who has passed away, reminisce on their lives.

© Sony Pictures Entertainment

Denis Lavant, Chulpan Hamatova

IN JULY

(FILM PHILOS) Producers, Stephan Schubert, Ralph Schwingel; Director/Screenplay, Fatih Akin; Photography, Pierre Aim; Designer, Jurgen Schnell; Costumes, Helen Achtermann; Music, Ulrich Kodjo Wendt; Editor, Andrew Bird; Casting, Ingeborg Molitoris; Produced by Argos Filmcilik Turizm, Quality Pictures, Wuste Filmproduktion; German, 2000; Dolby; Color; Not rated; 99 minutes; US release date: December 7, 2001

CAST

Daniel Bannier ....Moritz Bleibtreu
Juli ....Christiane Paul
Isa ....Mehmet Kurtulus
Melek ....Idil Ünel
Leo...Jochen Nickel
Luna...Branka Katic
Club Doyen ....Birol Ünel
Marion...Sandra Borgmann
and Cem Akin (Turkish Border Guard), Fatih Akin (Romanian Border Guard), Dylan Gray (Hungarian Border Guard)

© Film Philos

Christiane Paul

Phillippe Clay

TUVALU

(INDICAN) Producer/Director, Veit Helmer; Screenplay, Michaela Beck, Veit Helmer; Executive Producers, Vladimir Andreev, George Balkanski; Photography, Emil Christov; Art Director, Alexander Manasse; Costumes, Boriana Mintcheva; Editor, Araksi Mouhibian; Music, Jürgen Knieper; a Veit Helmer-Filmproduktion from Borough Film, Bavarai Film International; German, 1999; Dolby; Cinemascope; Color; Rated R; 100 minutes; US release date: December 7, 2001

CAST

Anton ....Denis Lavant
Eva ....Chulpan Hamatova
Karl ....Philippe Clay
Gregor ....Terrence Gillespie
Inspector...E. J. Callahan
Gustav...Djoko Rosic
Martha ....,......Catalina Murgea
Policeman ....Todor Georgiev

Anton, a shy attendant in a crumbling bathhouse, falls in love with Eva, whose father has been killed by falling debris at the pool.

© Indican

Christiane Paul, Moritz Bleibtreu

Nelofer Pazira

KANDAHAR

(AVATAR) Producer/Director/Screenplay/Editor, Mohsen Makhmalbaf; Photography, Ebrahim Ghafori; Set Designer, Akbar Meshkini; Music, Mohamad Reza Darvishi; a Makhmalbaf Film House presentation produced by Makhmalbaf Film House (Iran) and Bac Films (France); Iranian-French; Color; Not rated; 85 minutes; US release date: December 14, 2001

CAST

Nafas..Nelofer Pazira
Tabib Sahid ....Hassan Tantaï
Khak ....Sadou Teymouri
Hayat ....Hoyatala Hakimi

Nafas, an exiled Afghan journalist, attempts to cross over the border back into her homeland to find her sister who is suffering under Taliban rule.

© Avatar Films

Zahra Bahrami

Afghan Women

BARAN
(RAIN)

(MIRAMAX) Producers, Majid Majidi, Fouad Nahas; Director/Screenplay, Majid Majidi; Photography, Mohammad Davudi; Designer, Behzad Kazzazi; Costumes, Behzad Kazzazi, Malek Jahan Khazai; Editor, Hassan Hassandust; Music, Ahmad Pejman; a Majid Majidi & Fouad Nahas production; Iranian; Dolby; Color; Rated PG; 94 minutes; US release date: December 7, 2001

CAST

Lateef...Hossein Abedini
Memar...Mohammad Reza Naji
Rahmat & Baran ....Zahra Bahrami
Soltan ....Hossein Rahimi
Najaf..Gholam Ali Bakhshi

Lateef, a conniving, lazy Iranian teen who works as a caretaker at construction site manned by Afghan refugees, becomes resentful when his job is given over to a new employee, Rahmat, less capable of handling the more taxing labor.

© Miramax Films

Hossein Abedini

Judi Dench, Jim Broadbent

IRIS

(MIRAMAX) Producers, Robert Fox, Scott Rudin; Executive Producers, Guy East, David M Thompson, Tom Hedley, Harvey Weinstein, Anthony Minghella, Sydney Pollack; Director, Richard Eyre; Screenplay, Richard Eyre, Charles Wood; Based on John Bayley's books *Iris: A Memoir* and *Elegy for Iris*; Line Producer, Michael Dreyer; Photography, Roger Pratt BSC; Designer, Gemma Jackson; Editor, Martin Walsh; Music, James Horner; Solo Violin, Joshua Bell; Costumes, Ruth Myers; Hair and Makeup Designer, Lisa Westcott; Casting, Celestia Fox; a BBC Films, Intermedia Films presentation of a Mirage Enterprises/Robert Fox/Scott Rudin Production; British-US; Dolby; Color; Rated R; 91 minutes; US release date: December 14, 2001.

CAST

Iris Murdoch	Judi Dench
John Bayley	Jim Broadbent
Young Iris Murdoch	Kate Winslet
Young John Bayley	Hugh Bonneville
Janet Stone	Penelope Wilton
Young Maurice	Samuel West
Old Maurice	Timothy West
Principal, Somerville College	Eleanor Bron
Hostess	Angela Morant
Check-out Girl	Siobhan Hayes
Young Janet Stone	Juliet Aubrey
BBC Presenter	Joan Bakewell
BBC PA	Nancy Carroll
Dr. Gudgeon	Kris Marshall
Neurologist	Tom Mannion
Postman	Derek Hutchinson
Phillida Stone	Saira Todd
Emma Stone	Juliet Howland

and Charlotte Arkwright (Young Phillida Stone), Harriet Arkwright (Young Emma Stone), Matilda Allsopp (Little Stone), Steve Edis (Pianist), Emma Handy (Policewoman), Stephen Marcus (Taxi Driver), Pauline McGlynn (Maureen), Gabrielle Reidy (Tricia)

The courtship of independent writer Iris Murdoch and John Bayley is contrasted with Iris's last years, when Alzheimer's disease began to destroy her mind

2001 Academy Award-winner for Best Supporting Actor (Jim Broadbent) This film received an additional Oscar nomination for actress (Judi Dench).

Kate Winslet

Judi Dench

Hugh Bonneville, Kate Winslet

Jim Broadbent, Judi Dench

Judi Dench

Jim Broadbent

Hugh Bonneville, John Bayley, Kate Winslet

Kate Winslet

Geoffrey Rush

Barbara Hershey

Anthony LaPaglia, Kerry Armstrong

Rachael Blake

Anthony LaPaglia

LANTANA

(LIONS GATE) Producer, Jan Chapman; Executive Producer, Rainer Mockert, Mikael Borglund; Director, Ray Lawrence; Screenplay, Andrew Bovell, based on his play Speaking in Tongues; Photography, Mandy Walker; Designer, Kim Buddee; Costumes, Margot Wilson; Music, Paul Kelly; Editor, Karl Sodersten; Line Producer, Catherine Jarman; Casting, Susie Maizels, Sarah Beardsall; an MBP, Australian Film Finance Corporation, Jan Chapman Films presentation; Australian; Dolby; Panavision; Color; Rated R; 121 minutes; US release date: December 14, 2001

CAST

Leon Zat	Anthony LaPaglia
John Knox	Geoffrey Rush
Dr Valerie Somers	Barbara Hershey
Sonja Zat	Kerry Armstrong
Jane O'May	Rachael Blake
Nik Daniels	Vince Colosimo
Michael	Russell Dykstra
Paula Daniels	Daniela Farinacci
Patrick Phelan	Peter Phelps
Claudia	Leah Purcell
Pete O'May	Glenn Robbins
Steve	Jon Bennett
Lisa	Melissa Marinez
Old Man in Pajamas	Owen McKenna
Sam Zat	Nicholas Cooper
Dylan Zat	Marc Dwyer

and Puven Panther (Drug Dealer), Lionel Tozer, Glen Suter (Police Officers), Natasha Guthrie (Young Girl), James Cullington (Man at Book Launch), Ashley Fitzgerald (Eleanor), Keira Wingate (Hannah Daniels), Angus Cripps, William Cripps (Harry), Kay Armstrong (Dance Partner), Jacomb Borra (Jacob), Ben Mortley (Jose), Gabriella Maselli (Sarah), Richard Morecroft (News Reader), Lani Tupu (Patrick's Lover), Lesley Hancock (Lover's Wife), Angus McGulgan (Lover's Child)

Police detective Leon Zat's investigation into the mysterious death of a woman reveals unexpected connections between a disparate group of people in Sydney, Australia.

© Lions Gate Films

Veronika Zilková, Little Otik

© Zeitgeist Films

LITTLE OTIK
(OTESÁNEK)

(ZEITGEIST) Producer, Jaromir Kallista; Director/Screenplay/Story, Jan Svankmajer; Artistic Directors, Eva Svankmajerová, Jan Svankmajer; Photography, Juraj Galvanek; Editor, Marie Zemanová; Animators, Bedrich Glaser, Martin Kublák; Produced with financial contributions from the State Fund of the Czech Republic for the Support and Promotion of Czech Cinematography, Czech Literary Fund Foundation, REN Corporation Ltd, Ceskyk Ltd (Tokyo); Czech Republic, 2000; Dolby; Color; Not rated; 127 minutes; US release date: December 19, 2001

CAST

Bozena Horakova ....Veronika Zilková
Karel Horak ....Jan Hartl
Mrs Stadlerova...Jaroslava Kretschmerová
Franisek Stadler...Pavel Novy
Alzbetka ....Kristina Adamcová
The Caretaker ....Dagmar Stribrna
Mr Zlabek ....Zdenek Kozak
Social Worker Bulankova...Jitka Smutna
The Policeman at the Station ....Jiri Labus

A couple, who have longed to have a baby without success, find a tree stump resembling a small child and decide to raise the inanimate object as their offspring.

BEHIND THE SUN

(MIRAMAX) Producer, Arthur Cohn; Executive Producers, Lillian Birnbaum, Mauricio A Ramos; Director, Walter Salles; Screenplay, Walter Salles, Sérgio Machado, Karim Aïnouz; Inspired by the novel *Broken April* by Ismail Kadaré; Photography, Walter Carvalho; Designer, Cassio Amarante; Costumes, Cao Albuquerque; Editor, Isabelle Rathery; Music, Antonio Pinto, Ed Cortes, Beto Villares; Associate Producers, Jean Labadie, Carole Scotta; Line Producer, Marcelo Torres; an Arthur Cohn production, a Videofilms-Haut and Court-Bac Films-Dan Valley AG co-production; Brazilian-French-Swiss; Dolby; Super 35 Widescreen; Color; Rated PG-13; 105 minutes; US release date: December 21, 2001

CAST

Father ....José Dumont
Tonho ....Rodrigo Santoro
Mother ....Rita Assemany
Salustiano...Luís Carlos Vasconcelos
Pacu..Ravi Ramos Lacerda
Clara ....Flavia Marco Antonio
Old Blind Man ....Everaldo de Souza Pontes
Mr Lourenço ....Othon Bastos
Inácio..Caio Junqueira
Widow ....Mariana Loureiro
Isaias...Servilio de Holanda
Matheus...Wagner Moura
Reginaldo...Gero Camilo
and Vinicius de Oliveira, Sôia Lira, Maria do Socorro Nobre (Ferreira Family)

A long-standing land dispute between two Brazilian families forces the middle son of the Breves clan to avenge his brother's death.

© Miramax FIlms

Rodrigo Santoro, Ravi Ramos Lacerda

Cate Blanchett

Michael Gambon, Billy Crudup

CHARLOTTE GRAY

(WARNER BROS) Producers, Sarah Curtis, Douglas Rae; Executive Producers, Paul Webster, Robert Bernstein, Hanno Huth; Co-Producers, Elinor Day, Catherine Kerr; Director, Gillian Armstrong; Screenplay, Jeremy Brock; Based on the novel by Sebastian Faulks; Photography, Dion Beebe; Designer, Joseph Bennett; Costumes, Janty Yates; Music, Stephen Warbeck; Editor, Nicholas Beauman; an Ecosse Films production and a Pod Film production, presented in association with FilmFour and Senator Film; British; Dolby; Technicolor; Rated PG-13; 121 minutes; US release date: December 28, 2001

CAST

Charlotte Gray (Dominique)	Cate Blanchett
Julien Levade	Billy Crudup
Levade	Michael Gambon
Peter Gregory	Rupert Penry Jones
Renech	Anton Lesser
Mirabel	Ron Cook
Richard Cannerly	James Fleet
Daisy	Abigail Cruttenden
Sally	Charlotte McDougall
Borowski	Robert Hands
Psychiatrist	Hugh Ross
Assault Course Instructor	Martin Oldfield
Mr Jackson	Nicholas Farrell
Morse Code Instructor	Mike Burnside
Gun Instructor	Damian Myerscough
Instructor	Miranda Bell
Agent	Angus Wright
Andre	Lewis Crutch
Jacob	Matthew Plato
Auguste	Charlie Condou

and Tom Goodman-Hill, Michael Fitzgerald (Businessmen at Party), Victoria Scarborough (Claire Monceau), David Birkin (Jean-Paul), John Pierce Jones (Monsieur Monceau), Louise Vincent (Madame Cariteau), Gillian Barge (Madame Galliot), Michael Mellinger (Old Man Roudil), Carole Barbier, Francoise Heraut, Severine Bouche (Housewives), Rosanna Lavelle (Sophie the Telephonist), John Hug (Bartender), Helen McCrory (Francoise), John Benfield (Loque), Robert Shannon (Bernard), John Bennett (Gerard), Mathias Jung (German Sergeant), Jean-Pierre Roane (Mayor), Jack Shepherd (Pichon), Erich Redman (German Corporal), Wolf Kahler (Oberlieutenant Lindermann), Maurice Yeoman (German Soldier), Robin Pearce (Gendarme Claude), Amy Marston (Pregnant Mother)

During World War II, Charlotte Gray agrees to become a secret agent for Britain in hopes of finding her lover whose plane has been shot down over France.

Cate Blanchett

Lewis Crutch, Matthew Plato, Billy Crudup

DARK BLUE WORLD

(SONY CLASSICS) Producers, Eric Abraham, Jan Sverak; Co-Producers, Werner Koenig, Domenico Proccaci; Director, Jan Sverak; Screenplay, Zdenek Sverak; Photography, Vladimir Smutny; Designer, Jan Vlasak; Costumes, Vera Mirova; Editor, Alois Fisarek; Music, Ondrej Soukup; Visual Effects Designer, Milos Kohout; Casting, Sona Tichackova, Doreen Jones; a Portobello Pictures, Biograf, Jan Sverak Film in co-production with Helkon Media, Phoenix Film Investments, Fandango and Czech Television with the support of Eurimages and the Czech Film Fund; Czech-British; Dolby; Widescreen; Color; Rated R; 119 minutes; US release date: December 28, 2001

Kryštof Hàdek, Ondřej Vetchy

CAST

Frantisek Slama	Ondrej Vetchy
Karel Vojtisek	Krystof Hadek
Susan	Tara Fitzgerald
Wing-Commander Bentley	Charles Dance
Machaty	Oldrich Kaiser
Mrtvy	David Novotny
Hanicka	Linda Rybova
Kanka	Jaromir Dulava
Tom Tom	Lukas Kantor
Sysel	Radim Fiala
Gregora	Juraj Bernath
Houf	Miroslav Taborsky
Doctor Blaschke	Hans-Jorg Assmann
German Officer Hesse	Thure Riefenstein
English Teacher	Anna Massey
Major Skokan	Viktor Preiss

and John Warnaby (RAF Instructor), Caroline Holdaway (Mrs Brett), Timothy Otis, William McEnchroe, Jeff Tyler (Radio Operators), Cestmir Randa (Pavlata—Armorer), Sophie Wilcox (WAAF Jane), Charlotte Fairman (WAAF Sally), Rhian Heppleston, Lucy Fillery, Amy Huck (WAAFs), Jeremy Swift (Private Pierce), William S Masson (Susan's Husband), Ashley Clish (Beth—4 years old), Lexie Peel (David—7 years old), Gemma Scrimgeour (Girl—10 years old), Blaise Colangelo (Twin—Ann), Sienna Colangelo (Twin—Mary), Noel Le Bon (Telephone Operator), Jan Dvorak (Bustik—Prison Guard), Petr Burian (Vrba Vlastik), Joseph John Comer (English Mechanic), John Norton (Rear Gunner Captain), Jiri Labus (Pub Landlord), Daniela Kolarova (Pecharova), Anna Vesela (Jeannette), Frantisek Vyskocil, Martin Dostal (German Motorcyclists), David Fisher (Telephonist)

Tara Fitzgerald, Ondřej Vetchy

Escaping to England after the Nazis invade Czechoslovakia, a fighter pilot and his young protégé become flyers for their adopted country, only to find themselves falling in love with the same woman.

Kryštof Hàdek

Ondřej Vetchy, Charles Dance

Raymond Kojitski in *Terrorists in Retirement* © Zek Prods.

TERRORISTS IN RETIREMENT

(ZEK PRODS.) Director, Mosco Boucault; Photography, Jean Orjollet; Editor, Christiane Leherissey; Music, Jean Schwarz; Narrators, Simone Signoret, Gerard Desarthe; French, 1984; Color; Not rated; 84 minutes; U.S. release date: January 10, 2001. Documentary about the French Resistance in Nazi-occupied Paris.

A MONKEY'S TALE

(PROVIDENCE) Producers, Gerd Hecker, Patrick Moine, Steve Walsh; Director, Jean-François Laguionie; Screenplay, Norman Hudis, Jean-François Laguionie; Artistic Director, Zoltan Szilagyi Varga; Music, Alexandre Desplat; Editor, Soazic Veillon; Animation Directors, Ginger Gibbons, Henri Heidsieck; French, 1999; Color; Not rated; 76 minutes; U.S. release date: January 26, 2001. VOICE CAST: Matt Hill (Kom), John Hurt (Sebastian), Michael York (The King), Rik Mayall (Gerard the Gormless), Sally Ann Marsh (Gina), Michael Gambon (Master Martin), Shirley Ann Field (The Governess), French Tickner (Korkonak), Diana Quick (Princess Ida), William Vanderpuye (Lionel), Paul Dobson (Gavin), Janyse Jaud (Kom's Mother), Peter Elliott (Monkey Cries)

Lou Doillon, Maud Forget in *Bad Company*
© Menemsha

Jonny Lee Miller in *Love, Honour & Obey*
© Keystone Releasing

FALLEN ANGELS PARADISE

(ARTMATTAN PRODS.) Producer, Al Batrik; Director, Ossama Fawzi; Screenplay, Moustafa Zekri; Based on a novel by George Amado; Photography, Tarek Telmessani; Editor, Khaled Merhi; Music, Fathi Salama; Set Designer, Nehad Bahgat; an Art Production; Egyptian, 2000; Dolby; Color; Not rated; 100 minutes; U.S. release date: February 1, 2001. CAST: Mahmoud Hemida (Tabl), Lebleba (Hobba), Caroline Khalil (Salwa), Safwa (Shawkia), Amr Waked (Nonna), Serri Al Nagar (Adel), Salah Fahmi (Boussy), Saeed Al Saleh (George), Menha Al Batrawi (The Wife), Menha Zeytoun (The Aunt), Maged Kedwani (Atef), Kamal Soleiman (Abou Rasha), Raafat Ragi (Halim), Geena (The Girl Driver), Mohammad Dardiry (The Doctor), Tamer Habib (The Dentist)

BAD COMPANY

(FLACH PYRAMIDE/MENEMSHA) Producers, Philippe Godeau, Alain Sarde; Director, Jean-Pierre Ameris; Screenplay, Alain Layrac; Photography, Yves Vandermeeren; Editor, Martine Giordano; French, 1999; Color; Not rated; 98 minutes; U.S. release date: February 7, 2001. CAST: Maud Forget (Delphine), Lou Doillon (Olivia), Robinson Stevenin (Laurent), Maxime Mansion (Alain), Delphine Rich (Claire), François Berleand (Rene), Micheline Presle (Mamie)

LOVE, HONOUR & OBEY

(KEYSTONE) Producers/Directors/Screenplay, Dominic Anciano, Ray Burdis; Executive Producers, David M. Thompson, Jane Tranter, Jim Beach; Photography, John Ward; Designer, Nick Burnell; Costumes, Ali Brown; Line Producer, Mark Hudson; Editor, Rachel Meyrick; Song: Force of Nature written and performed by Noel Gallagher; Casting, Geraldine Geraghty; a BBC Films presentation of a Fugitive production; British, 2000; Dolby; Color; Rated R; 95 minutes; U.S. release date:

February 9, 2001. CAST: Sadie Frost (Sadie), Jonny Lee Miller (Jonny), Jude Law (Jude), Sean Pertwee (Sean), Kathy Burke (Kathy), Denise Van Outen (Maureen), Rhys Ifans (Matthew), Dominic Anciano (Dominic), Ray Burdis (Ray), John Beckett (John), Trevor H. Laird (Trevor), William Scully (Bill), Perry Benson (Perry "Fat Alan"), Mark Burdis (Mark), Laila Morse (Laila), Sam Smart, Rory Muir, Dane Keenan, Ryan Moore, Calum Callaghan, Eddie Cooper, Ricky Grover, Hugh Sachs, Mario Renzullo, Damien Anciano, Tom Shirley, Nancy-Jane Maun, Nula Conwell, Sky Burdis, Andy Denyer, David Gillespie, Derek Avery, Enoch Frost, Alan Fordham, John Davis, Phytos Neophytou, Eamonn Tully, Culver Greenidge, Mo Kahn, Jerry Mulcahy, Rick English, Cliff Tarr, Danny Sullivan, Louise Strachan, Megan Strachan, John Brooks, Ayiko, Lisa Moorish, Lucy Bowen, Dr. David Lomas

JOURNEY TO THE SUN

(CINEMA VILLAGE FEATURES) Producer, Behrooz Hashemian; Executive Producer, Ezel Akay; Director/Screenplay, Yesim Ustaoglu; Photography, Jacek Petrycki; Art Director, Natali Yeres; Editor, Nicolas Gaster; Music, Vlatko Stefanovski; an IFR Production, in collaboration with the Film Company Amsterdam, Media Res, Berlin, Fabrica & ZDF/Arte; Turkish-German-Dutch; Dolby; Color; Not rated; 104 minutes; U.S. release date: February 9, 2001. CAST: Newroz Baz (Mehmet), Nazmi Quirix (Berzan), Mizgin Kapazan (Arzu), Nigar Aktar (Laundromat Owner), Iskender Bagcilar (Police Interrogator), Ara Guler (Mehmet's Boss)

SIGNS & WONDERS

(STRAND) Producer, Marin Karmitz; Executive Producers, Nick Wechsler, Jed Alpert; Director, Jonathan Nossiter; Screenplay, James Lasdun, Jonathan Nossiter; Story, James Lasdun; Photography, Yorgos Arvanitis; Costumes, Kathryn Nixon; Music, Adrian Utley; Line Producer, Yvon Crenn; Editor, Madeleine Gavin; an MK2 production, presented in association with Idefixe Productions, Industry Entertainment, Sunshine Amalgamedia & GoatWorks Films; French, 2000; Dolby; Color; Not rated; 108 minutes; U.S. release date: February 9, 2001. CAST: Stellan Skarsgård (Alec Fenton), Charlotte Rampling (Marjorie Fenton), Deborah Kara Unger (Katherine), Dimitris Katalifos (Andreas), Ashley Remy (Siri), Michael Cook (Marcus), Dave Simonds (Kent), Arto Apartian (Police Interpreter), Alexandros Mylonas (Police Captain), Dimitris Kamberidis (Sotiris), Steven Goldstein (American Businessman)

Deborah Kara Unger, Stellan Skarsgård in
Signs & Wonders © Strand Releasing

THE PRICE OF MILK

(LOT 47) Producer, Fiona Copland; Executive Producer, Tim Sanders; Director/Screenplay, Harry Sinclair; Photography, Leon Narbey; Designer/Costumes, Kristy Cameron; Editor, Cushla Dillon; a John Swimmer presentation in association with The New Zealand Film Commission; New Zealand; Dolby; Widescreen; Color; Rated PG-13; 87 minutes; U.S. release date: February 14, 2001. CAST: Danielle Cormack (Lucinda), Karl Urban (Rob), Willa O'Neill (Drosophilia), Michael Lawrence (Bernie), Rangi Motu (Auntie)

Karl Urban, Danielle Cormack in *The Price of Milk*
© Lot 47 Films

Houari Djerir, Akhenhaton in *The Magnet* © Two Boots

YOM YOM

(KINO) Producers, Eyal Shiray, Laurent Truchot; Executive Producer, Ilan Moscovitch; Director, Amos Gitai; Screenplay, Jacky Cukier, Amos Gitai; Photography, Renato Berta; Editors, Nili Richter, Ruben Kornfeld; Art Director, Thierry François; Music, Philippe Eidel; an Agav Films and Cinema Factory production, in association with Canal+, Intereurop, Mikadoo, M.P. Productions, Telad, Arte, and Rai Due; Israeli-French-Italian, 1998; Dolby; Color; Not rated; 105 minutes; U.S. release date: February 16, 2001. CAST: Moshe Ivgi (Moshe), Hanna Maron (Hanna), Juliano Mer (Jules), Dalit Kahan (Didi), Yussef Abu Warda (Yussef), Nataly Atiya (Grisha), Anne Petit-Lagrange (The Doctor), Shmuel Calderon (Shmul), Gassan Abass (Nadim), Keren Mor (Mimi)

IN CHINA THEY EAT DOGS

(ENTERTECH) Producer, Steen Herdel; Executive Producer, Michael Brask; Director/Editor, Lasse Spang Olsen; Screenplay, Anders Thomas Jensen; Photography, Morten Søborg; Music, George Keller; from ScanBox, TiMe Filmverleih; Danish-German, 1999; Color; Not rated; 91 minutes; U.S. release date: February 16, 2001. CAST: Kim Bodnia (Harald), Dejan Cukic (Arvid), Nikolaj Lie Kaas (Martin), Tomas Villurn

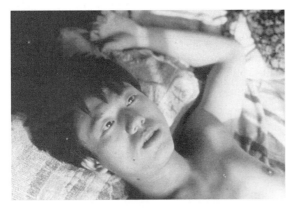

Shi Yu in *So Close to Paradise* © Cinema Village Features

Jensen (Peter), Peter Gantzler (Franz), Trine Dyrholm (Hanne), Line Kruse (Astrid), Brian Patterson (Vuk), Søren Sætter-Lassen (Jenning), Lester Wiese (Richard), Jesper Christensen (Bartender), Lasse Lunderskov (Jørgen), Preben Harris (Erling), Slavko Labovic (Ratko), Anne Britt Mathiaseen (Gunna), Martin Spang Olsen (Preben), Niels Brinch (Interviewer)

THE KITE

(PHAEDRA) Director, Gil Portes; Screenplay, Butch Dalisay, Gil Portes; No other credits available; Philippine, 1999; Color; Not rated; 85 minutes; U.S. release date: February 22, 2001. CAST: Ricky Davao (Homer), Lester Llannsong (Rex), Jennifer Sevilla (Anita)

THE MAGNET

(INDEPENDENT/TWO BOOTS) Producer, Richard Grandpierre; Executive Producer, Why Not Productions; Directors/Screenplay, Kamel Saleh, Akhenaton; Photography, Denis Rouden; Music, Bruno Coulais, Akhenaton; Editor, Fabrice Sallinié; a co-production of Le Studio Canal+, La Société 361, with the participation of the Centre National de la Cinematographie; French, 2000; Color; Not rated; 100 minutes; U.S. release date: March 9, 2001. CAST: Kamel Saleh (Cahuete), Houari Djerir (Houari), Brahim Aimad (Bra-Bra), Sofiane Madjid Mammeri (Christian), Kamel Ferrat (Fouad), Titoff (Santino), Akhenaton (Sauveur), Malek Brahimi (Kakou), Georges Neri, Bernard Fischetti, Raymond La Science, Loule Bilione, José Tygat, Elie du Mas (The Mafiosi), Khalil Mohamed (Kader), Virginie Gallo (Nathalie), Nadège Mignien (Beatrice), Bérangère Topart (Sylvie), Ahamed Abdou (Jackson), Jerome-Jérôme Esposito (The Informer), Diana Hamidovich (Diana), Samira Berriche (Linda), Hanane Mohim (Soraya), Nadéra Mouthoub (Sandra), Farida Bessa, Linda Tortoza (Flirt Girls), Samir Mohamed, Dadou (Little Boys)

SO CLOSE TO PARADISE

(CINEMA VILLAGE FEATURES) Producer, Han Sanping; Director, Wang Xiaoshuai; Executive Producers, Zhang Gonggu, Li Xiaogeng; Creators, Tian Zhuangzhuang, Li Buo; Screenplay, Wang Xiaoshuai, Pang Ming; Photography, Yang Tao; Editors, Liu Fang, Yang Hong Yu; Art

Venus Seye, Sosie Pathé in *Faat-Kine* © New Yorker Films

Director, Cheng Guangming; Music, Liu Lin; a co-production of the Beijing Film Studio and Beijing Goldenplate Film TV & Art Production Co. in association with Beijing Pegase Cultural Communication Centre; Chinese, 1998; Dolby; Color; Not rated; 90 minutes; U.S. release date: March 9, 2001. CAST: Wang Tong (Ruan Hong), Shi Yu (Dong Zi), Guo Tao (Gao Ping), Wu Tao (Su Wu)

FAAT-KINE

(NEW YORKER) Producer, Wongue Mbengue; Director/Screenplay, Ousmane Sembene; Photography, Dominique Gentil; Editor, Kahena Attia Riveill; Music, Yandé Codou Sène; Senegalese, 2000; Color; Not rated; 118 minutes; U.S. release date: March 28, 2001. CAST: Venus Seye (Faat-Kine), Mame Ndoumbé Diop (Maamy, Her Mother), Tabara Ndiaye (Amy Kasse), Awa Sène Sarr (Mada), Ndiagne Dia (Djip, Her Son), Mariama Balde (Aby, Her Daughter), Sosie Pathé

SMELL OF CAMPHOR, FRAGRANCE OF JASMINE

(NEW YORKER) Producer, Morteza Shayesteh; Executive Producer, Fazlollah Yousefpour; Director/Screenplay, Bahman Farmanara; Photography, Mahmoud Kalari; Art Director, Zilla Mehrjouii; Music, Ahmad Pejman; Iranian; Color; Not rated; 93 minutes; U.S. release date: April 6, 2001. CAST: Bahman Farmanara (Bahman Farjami), Roya Nonahali (Woman Hitchhiker), Reza Kianian (Dr. Arasteh, The Attorney), Valiyollah Shirandami (Homayouni, The Actor), Hossein Kasbian (Abdollah, The Servant), Firouz Behjat Mohammadi (Memorial Sign Rental), Parivash Nazarieh (Farzaneh), Mantaj Nojoomi (Bahman's Sister)

POKÉMON THE MOVIE 3

(WARNER BROS.) Producers, Norman J. Grossfeld, Choji Yoshikawa, Yukako Matsusako, Takemoto Mori; Executive Producers, Masakazu Kubo, Takashi Kawaguchi, Alfred R. Kahn; Directors, Kunihiko Yuyama, Michael Haigney; Screenplay, Takeshi Shudo, Hideki Sonoda; American Adaptation, Michael Haigney, Norman J. Grossfeld; Based on characters created by Satoshi Tajiri; Photography, Hisao Shirai; Art Director, Katsuyoshi Kanemura; Editors, Jay Film, Toshio Henmi, Yutaka Ito;

Music, Ralph Schuckett; Animation Supervisor, Yoichi Kotabe; a 4Kids Entertainment production; Japanese; Dolby; Color; U.S. release date: April 6, 2001. VOICE CAST: Veronica Taylor (Ash Ketchum/Mrs. Delia Ketchum), Eric Stuart (Brock/James), Rachael Lillis (Misty/Jessie), Maddie Blaustein (Meowth), Ikoue Ôtani (Pikachu), Stan Hart (Professor Oak), Ken Gates, Dan Green, Amy Birnbaum, Lisa Ortiz, Kathy Pilon, Peter R. Bird, Kayzie Rogers, Ed Paul, Tara Jayne, Lee Quick, Roger Kay (Additional Voices)

(Above) Bahman Farmanara in *Smell of Camphor, Fragrance of Jasmine* © New Yorker Films
(Below) Ash, Pikachu, Misty in *Pokémon The Movie 3* © Pikachu Projects

Agathe de La Boulaye, Claire Keim in *The Girl*
© Artistic License Films

Aidan Gillen in *The Low Down* © Shooting Gallery

THE DAY I BECAME A WOMAN

(SHOOTING GALLERY) Producer, Mohsen Makhmalbaf; Director, Marzieh Meshkini; Screenplay, Mohsen Makhmalbaf, Marzieh Meshkini; Photography, Mohamad Ahmadi, Ebrahim Ghafori; Art Director, Akbar Meshkini; Editors, Mezsaam Makhmalbaf, Shahrzad Pouya; Music, Ahmad Reza Darvish; a Makhmalbaf Production; Iranian, 2000; Color; Not rated; 78 minutes; U.S. release date: April 6, 2001. CAST: Fatemeh Cherag Akhar (Hava), Hassan Nebhan (Hassan), Shahr Banou Sisizadeh (Mother), Ameneh Passand (Grandmother), Shabhnam Toloui (Ahoo), Sirous Kahvarinegad (Husband), Mahram Zeinal Zadeh (Osmann), Norieh Mahigiran (Rival Cyclist), Azizeh Segidhi (Hoora), Badr Iravani (Young Boy)

The Charcoal People © Cimena Guild

THE GIRL

(ARTISTIC LICENSE) Producer, Dolly Hall; Executive Producers, Sue Delisle, Gil Donaldson; Director, Sande Zeig; Screenplay, Sande Zeig, Monique Wittig; Story, Monique Wittig; Co-Producer/Casting, Claude Martin; Photography, George Lechaptois; Designer, Phillipe Renucci; Editors, Geraldine Peroni; Music, Richard Robbins; a Dolly Hall production in association with Method Films; French, 1999; Color; Not rated; 84 minutes; U.S. release date: April 20, 2001. CAST: Claire Keim (The Girl), Agathe de la Boulaye (The Narrator), Cyril Lecomte (The Man), Sandra N'Kake (Bu Savé), Ronald Guttman (Bartender), Cyrille Hertel (Bodyguard), Pascal Cervo (Hotel Clerk), Franck Prevost (Piano Player)

THE CHARCOAL PEOPLE

(CINEMA GUILD) Producer/Screenplay, José Padilha; Director, Nigel Noble; Co-Producers, Marcos Prado, Jozine Resende; Photography, Flávio Zangrandi; Editor, Ann Collins; from Les Zazen Producoes; Brazilian; Color; Not rated; 72 minutes; U.S. release date: April 20, 2001. Documentary on Brazilian migrant workers.

THE LOW DOWN

(SHOOTING GALLERY) Producers, Sally Llewellyn, John Stewart; Director/Screenplay, Jamie Thraves; Photography, Igor Jadue-Lillo; Designer, Lucy Reeves; Costumes, Julie Jones; Music, Nick Currie, Fred Thomas; Editor, Lucia Zuccehtti; Casting, Amanda Tabak; a production of Bozie, British Screen, Channel Four Films, Oil Factory, and Sleeper Films; British; Color; Not rated; 96 minutes; U.S. release date: April 20, 2001. CAST: Aiden Gillen (Frank), Kate Ashfield (Ruby), Dean Lennox Kelly (Mike), Tobias Menzies (John), Rupert Procter (Terry), Samantha Power (Lisa), Deanna Smiles (Susan), Maggie Lloyd Williams (Jean), Agnieszka Liggett (Anna), Adam Buxton (Adam), Joe Cornish (Joe), Paula Hamilton (Cashpoint Woman), Alicya Eyo (Paul Girl), Dorian Lough (Squash Player), Clint Dyer (Nathan), Rachel Issac (Nicola), Elliot Levey (Peter), Martin Freeman (Solomon), Liz Liew (Vera), Michael Hodgson, Michael McKell, Alex Palmer (Pubman), Vass Anderson (Landlord), Anthony Warren, Paul Dungworth, Barry Dobbin (Street Corner Men)

RAT

(UNIVERSAL FOCUS) Producers, Steve Barron, Alison Owen; Director, Steve Barron; Screenplay, Wesley Burrowes; Photography, Brendan Galvin; Designer, Mark Geraghty; Costumes, Siobhan Barron; Music, Pete Briquette, Bob Geldof; Editor, David Yardley; Casting, Nina Gold; from United International Pictures; British-Irish, 2000; Dolby; Color; Rated PG; 88 minutes; U.S. release date: April 27, 2001. CAST: Imelda Staunton (Conchita Flynn), Pete Postlethwaite (Hubert Flynn), Frank Kelly (Uncle Matt), David Wilmot (Phelim Spratt), Andrew Lovern (Pius Flynn), Kerry Condon (Marietta Flynn), Hubert (Hubert the Rat), Veronica Duffy (Daisy), Ed Byrne (Randolph), Niall Toibin (Father Geraldo), Alfie (Mickey the Dog), Peter Caffrey (Mick the Barman), Rita Hamill (Estate Woman), Roxanna Williams (Hopscotch Child), Geoffrey Palmer (The Doctor), Stanley Townsend (Newsreader), Simon Delaney (Bookies Manager), Niall O'Brien, John O'Toole (Men in Bookies), Jer O'Leary, Mick Nolan (Men in Pub), Gavin Dowdall, Jamie McCormack, Keith O'Brien, Sian Napper, Aaron Joseph-Galvin (Kids), Pat Kinevane (Mr. Reilly), Mark Doherty (Barrister), Arthur Riordan (Sergeant), Michael Hayes (Young Garda), Billie Traynor, Mary Moynihan, Margaret Twomey (Women Shopping), Keith Moran, Aaron Moran, John Farrell, Shane Moran (Buskers)

NORA

(ANDORA PICTURES) Producers, Bradley Adams, Damon Bryant, Tracey Seaward, Tiernan MacBride; Executive Producers, Guy Collins, Rod Stoneman, Tony Miller; Director, Pat Murphy; Screenplay, Pat Murphy, Gerard Stembridge; Based on the biography by Brenda Maddox; Photography, Jean François Robin; Designer, Alan MacDonald; Editor, Pia Di Ciaula; Music, Stanislas Syrewicz; Costumes, Consolata Boyle; Casting, Nuala Moiselle, Frank Moiselle, Shaila Rubin; a Natural Nylon Entertainment in association with IAC Holdings/Volta Films/Road Movies Vierte Produktionen/Gam Film/Metropolitan Films production; British-Irish-German-Italian, 1999; Dolby; Deluxe color; Not rated; 107 minutes; U.S. release date: May 4, 2001. CAST: Ewan McGregor (James Joyce), Susan Lynch (Nora Barnacle), Peter McDonald (Stanislas Joyce), Roberto Citran (Roberto Prezioso), Andrew Scott (Michael Bodkin),

Susan Lynch, Ewan McGregor in *Nora* © Andora Pictures

Vincent McCabe (Uncle Tommy), Veronica Duffy (Annie Barnacle), Aedin Moloney (Eva Joyce), Pauline McLynn (Miss Kennedy), Neili Conroy, Sile Nugent (Maids), Daragh Kelly (Cosgrave), Alan Devine (Gogarty), Paul Hickey (Curran), Kate O'Toole (Miss Delahunty), Martin Murphy (George Russell), Karl Scully (John McCormack), Frances Burke (Old Woman), Monica Scattini (Amalia Globonik), Adrian McCourt (Eyers), Ignazio Oliva (Alessandro Francini Bruni), Stefania Montorsi (Clothilde Francini Bruni), Franco Trevisi (Tullio Sylvestri), Eamonn Hunt (George Roberts), Manuel Bragato (Baby Giorgio), Liam McCourt, Odin O'Sullivan (Giorgio, 2 years old), Dylan Mooney (Giorgio, 4 years old), Ben Harding (Giorgio, 6 years old), Robin Mooney (Lucia, 2 years old), Lauren Mulhall (Lucia, 4 years old)

Imelda Staunton in *Rat* © Universal Pictures International

TIME AND TIDE

(TRISTAR) Producer/Executive Producer/Director, Tsui Hark; Screenplay, Koan Hui, Tsui Hark; Photography, Ko Chiu Lam, Herman Yau; Editor, Marco Mak; Music, Tommy Wai; Line Producer, Ng Kam Chiu; a Columbia Pictures Film Production Asia presentation of a Film Workshop Company Limited production; Hong Kong; Dolby; Color; Rated R; 113 minutes; U.S. release date: May 4, 2001. CAST: Nicholas Tse (Tyler), Wu Bai (Jack), Anthony Wong (Uncle Ji), Joventino Couto Remotigue (Miguel), Candy Lo (Ah Hui), Cathy Chui (Ah Jo)

PAVILION OF WOMEN

(UNIVERSAL FOCUS) Producer, Luo Yan; Executive Producer, Hugo Shong; Co-Producer, Simon Edery; Director, Yim Ho; Screenplay, Luo Yan, Paul R. Collins; Based on the novel by Pearl S. Buck; Photography, Poon Hang Sang; Designer, James Leung; Editors, Duncan Burns, Claudia Finkle; Music, Conrad Pope; a Luo Yan production, a co-production with Beijing Film Studio in association with the China Film Co-Production Corporation; Chinese; Dolby; Color; Rated R; 119 minutes; U.S. release date: May 4, 2001. CAST: Willem Dafoe (Father Andre), Luo Yan (Madame Wu), Shek Sau (Mr. Wu), John Cho (Fengmo), Yi Ding (Chiuming), Koh Chieng Mun (Ying), Anita Loo (Old Lady), Amy Hill (Madame Kang), Kate McGregor-Stewart (Sister Shirley), Liu Jia Dong (Mr. Lang), Chen Shu (Head Servant), Poon Hang Sang (Fat Cook), Wang Li (Kang Lin Yi), Xu You Jin (Matchmaker), Gu Ding Yuan (Mayor), Zhao Pei Ying (Midwife), Mao Xiao Dong (Liangmo), Huang Lan (Meng), Sun Yang, Yu En Ti, Yan Huai Bo (Fengmo's Friends), Zhang Kang (Boldman), Jin Ge (Loud Mouth), Yang Rong (Kang's Maid), John Dunn (Kang's Doorman), Miu Yan Lei, Sun Li, Gun Xin-Qi, Guao Xuan Ming (Wu's Relatives), Yang Ge (Head of Police), Song Min Qi (Orphanage Woman), Zhang Lei, Gu Ying, Irene Zhen (Kang's Wives), Jin Ying Chun (Bride Carrier), Zauang Zhi Fang (Masseur), Pu Hong Kui (Land Steward), Hong Zi Yuan (Wu's Doorman), Zhu Shou Gen (Accountant), Linq Yim (Policeman), Zhuang Cun (KMT General), Chen Yin, Liu Hui Dong (Japanese Generals), Chen Yu Feng (Japanese Soldiers), Cao Xu Bai, Gu En Hao (Kang's Children), Cai Yue (Duck Kid), Mo Chen Hao, Qi Lin Hui, Dong Xu Chao, Yang Xi, Zhang Zhao, Ye De Jie, Jiang Yi Fei, Xu Ding, Xue Tian Yun, Huang Yin Yuan, Zhang Jian Wen, Liu Meng Shi, Zeng Ling Yuan (Orphans)

Koji Yakusho, Masaru Miyazaki, Aoi Miyazaki in *Eureka*
© Shooting Gallery

EUREKA

(SHOOTING GALLERY) Producer, Takenori Sento; Director/Screenplay/Editor, Shinji Aoyama; Co-Producer, Philippe Avril; Photography, Masaki Tamura; Designer, Takeshi Shimizu; Music, Shinji Aoyama, Isao Yamada; a co-production of Dentsu, Imagica Corp., J Works, Les Films de L'Observatoire, Suncent Cinema Works, Tokyo Theaters Co.; Japanese, 2000; Black and white; Not rated; 217 minutes; U.S. release date: May 4, 2001. CAST: Koji Yakusho (Makoto Sawai), Aoi Miyazaki (Kozue Tamura), Masaru Miyazaki (Naoki Tamura), Yoichiro Saito (Akihiko), Sayuri Kokusho (Yumiko), Ken Mitsuishi (Shigeo), Gô Rijû (Busjack Man), Yutaka Matsushige (Matsuoka), Sansei Shiomi (Yoshiyuki Sawai), Kimie Shingyoji (Mother), Machiko Ono (Mikiko)

Cathy Chui,
Nicholas Tse in
Time and Tide
© Tri Star
Pictures

Princess Margaret, Lord Glenconner in *The Man Who Bought Mustique* © First Run Features

THE MAN WHO BOUGHT MUSTIQUE

(FIRST RUN FEATURES) Producer, Vikram Jayanti; Executive Producer, Andre Singer; Director, Joseph Bullman; Editor, Sally Hilton; Photography, Ian Liggett, Peter Cannon, David Smith; Music, Dario Marianelli; British, 2000; Color; Not rated; 78 minutes; U.S. release date: May 9, 2001. Documentary follows Colin Tennant as he returns to Mustique, the Caribbean island he once owned.

FAST FOOD, FAST WOMEN

(LOT 47) Producers, Avram Ludwig, Hengameh Panahi; Director/ Screenplay, Amos Kollek; Photography, Jean-Marc Fabre; Designer, Stacey Tanner; Music, David Carbonara; Editor, Sheri Bylander; Costumes, Pascal Gosset; Casting, Caroline Sinclair; a Lumen Films presentation of a BIM Distribuzione, Lumen Films, Pandora Film, Paradis Films and Dryly Films production; French-Italian-U.S., 2000; Dolby; Color; Not rated; 96 minutes; U.S. release date: May 18, 2001. CAST: Anna Thomson (Bella), Jamie Harris (Bruno), Louise Lasser (Emily), Lonette McKee (Sherry-Lynn), Robert Modica (Paul), Victor Argo (Seymour), Angelica Torn (Vitka), Austin Pendleton (George), Valerie Geffner (Wanda), Mark Margolis (Graham), Judith Roberts (Bella's Mother), Salem Ludwig (Leo), Loulou Katz (Betsy), Irma St. Paul (Mugging Victim), Joe Davieau (Jasper), Lynn Cohen (Jesse), Ellee Panahi (Shawn)

STRANGE FITS OF PASSION

(LEISURE TIME FEATURES) Producer, Lucy Maclaren; Executive Producers, Tim White, Carole Sklan, Bryce Menzies, Ian Fairweather, Roslyn Walker; Director/Screenplay, Elisa McCredie; Photography, James Grant; Designer, Macgregor Knox; Editors, Chris Branagan, Ken Sallows; Music, Cezary Skubiszewski; Costumes, Kerri Mazzocco; Casting, Alison Telford; from Meridian Films, presented by ABC-TV Arena Film, Victoria; Australian, 2000; Color; Not rated; 83 minutes; U.S. release date: May 18, 2001. CAST: Michela Noonan (She), Mitchell Butel (Jimmy), Samuel Johnson (Josh), Steve Adams (Pablo), Anni Finsterer (Judy), Boyana Novakovic (Jaya), Rob Carlton (Blackson), Jack Finsterer (Francis), Nathan Page (Simon), Barry Dickins (Mr. Selditt), Jodie J. Hill (Penny), Luke Anderson (Lachlan), James Liotta (James), Howard Stanley (Jimmy's Father), Judith Roberts (Jimmy's Mother), Donni Frizzell (Boy at Bar), Sim Gray (Girl at Bar), Glenn Burns (Barman), Tommy Dysart (Taxi Driver), Tom Healey, James Wardlaw (Supermarket Men), Elizabeth Welch (Store Detective), Bradley Hulme (Slick Businessman), Genevieve Mooris (Church Woman), Maud Davey (Woman in Gay Bookshop), David Lih (Christian Boy), Paul Bongiovanni, Libby Stone (Nurses), Andrea Swifte (Doctor), Johanna Hanley, Michael Isaacs (Hot Dog Customers), David Schofield (Jaya's New Man), Jeremy Engelman (Simon's Other Man), Nick Barker (Boy in Hot Dog Shop), Natasha Lyne (Beautiful Young Girl), Eric Kowalewski (Mason, Soap Opera), Constance Lansberg (Charity, Soap Opera), Davage Thomas, Dave Morris, Justin "Juddy" Dwyer (Live Pussies)

Angelica Torn, Robert Modica in *Fast Food, Fast Women*
© Lot 47 Films

Michela Noonan in *Strange Fits of Passion*
© Leisure Time Features

Iliès Sefraoui, Stéphanie Touly in *Petits Freres* © First Run Features

PETITS FRERES ("LITTLE FELLAS")

(FIRST RUN FEATURES) Producer, Marin Karmitz; Director/ Screenplay, Jacques Doillon; Photography, Manuel Teran; Music, Oxmo Puccino; Editor, Camille Cotte; Casting, Lola Doillon, Emmanuelle Gaborit, Stéphane Foenkinos; a co-production of MK2 Productions-France 3 Cinema; French, 1999; Dolby; Color; Not rated; 92 minutes; U.S. release date: May 18, 2001. CAST: Stéphanie Touly (Talia), Iliès Sefraoui (Iliès), Mustapha Goumane (Mous), Nassim Izem (Nassim), Rachid Mansouri (Rachid), Dembo Goumane (Dembo), Sabrina Mansar (Sabrina), Gérald Dantsoff (Talia's Stepfather), Simone Zouari Sayada (Talia's Mother), Myriam Goumane (Myriam), Goundo Goumane (Goundo), Halimatou Goumane (Halimatou), Fedora Saidi (Talia's Kid Sister), Ludmilla Saidi (Ludmilla), Mohamed Fekiri (Momo), Karim Ferdjallah (Karim), Anthony Schmit (Anthony), David Estevez (David), Max Saint Jean (Lieutenant Leroy), Philippe Guyral (Police Inspector)

NO ONE SLEEPS

(GALERIA ALASKA PRODS.) Producer/Director/Screenplay, Jochen Hick; Photography, Tom Harting, Michael Maley; Designers, Craig T. Copher, Bernard Homann; Editor, Helga Scharf; Music, James Hardway; Costumes, Maria Rivera; German, 2000; Dolby; Color; Rated R; 108 minutes; U.S. release date: May 25, 2001. CAST: Kenn Lyon (Jon), Irit Levi (Louise Tolliver), Robert A. Bustamante (Fast Food Guy), Kalene Parker (Maureen Finley), Randy Wendelin (Sgt. Flinter), David Rice (Presidio Victim), Michael Lovaglia (Sascha), Earl Kingston (Prof. Witkins), Patricia Miller (Student), Lisa Kang (Dr. Givens), Jim Thalman (Jeffrey Russo), Richard Conti (Dr. Richard Burroughs), Karl Fischer (Nurse from AIDS Project), Brian Yates (Volunteer at AIDS Project), Lino Antonio Lezama-Aguilar (Boy with Cross), Brian A. Vouglas (Doorman at Sacrifice), Aaron Place (Clown Boy), Cody Bayne (Cowboy), Jon Gale (Man in Harness), Ron Athey (Performer at Club), Paradox Pollack (Victim #2), Jason Mannino (Ron), John M. Stevens (Doorman at Safe Sex Club), Curtiss Craig (Man in Safe Sex Club), Ed Burke (Stefan's Father), Paul C. Moffett (Mail Box Clerk), Steve Casavant (Verona Maid), Peter Hadres (Agent Morgan), Joe Wilson (Carlos), James Marks (Boy from Porn Arcade), William Brogan (Headquarters Boy), Charles Shaw Robinson (Tom), Jeffrey J. Davis (Beggar), Dolores Moloney (Hospital Receptionist), Gene Thompson (Doctor), Verona Paul Arthur (Hotel Clerk), Joseph Blosk (Police Officer at Headquarters), Gary Wayne Farris (Headquarters Victim), Michael Gaffrey (Confessing Sexaholic), Heather Plakke (Burroughs's Receptionist), Scott Walker (TV Cameraman), Robert K. Hedrick, Jr. (Senator Michael Atwood), Sherry Al-Mufti (Atwood's Wife), Benjamin McGee (Receptionist at Sir Francis Drake Hotel), Alberto Rosas (Bellboy), John Swenson (Opera Singer), Glorinda Marie (Mexican Woman), Jimbei Suzuki (Officer Brown), Michal Gizinski (Officer Burton), Antonio Ferrelli (Stefan's New Boyfriend)

ENLIGHTENMENT GUARANTEED

(CAPITOL ENTERTAINMENT) Producer, Franz X. Gernstl; Executive Producer, Louis Saul; Director, Doris Dörrie; Screenplay, Doris Dörrie, Ruth Stadler; Photography, Hans Karl Hu; Art Director, Ruth Stadler; Editors, Inez Regnier, Anne Sinwell; from Megaherz TV Fernsehproduktion GmbH; German, 2000; Dolby; Color; Not rated; 109

minutes; U.S. release date: June 1, 2001. CAST: Uwe Ochsenknecht (Uwe), Gustav-Peter Wohler (Gustav), Petra Zieser (Petra), Ulrike Kriener (Ulrike), Anica Dobra (Anica), Heiner Lauterbach (Heiner), Franz X. Gernstl, Gisela Gernstl (Ehepaar), Jimmy Ochsenknecht (Jimmy), Wilson Ochsenknecht (Wilson), Leopold Zieser (Leopold), Emilia Zieser (Emilia), Pierre Sanoussi-Bliss (Ulrikes Liebhaber), Imaseki (Sumo-Ringer)

A REAL YOUNG GIRL

(CINEMA VILLAGE FEATURES) Producer, André Génovès; Director/Screenplay/Designer, Catherine Breillat; Based on the novel by Andé Génovès; Photography, Pierre Fattori; Music, Mort Shuman; Editor, Annie Charrier; from Artédis, C.B. Films S.A., and Centre National de La Cinematographie; French, 1976; Color; Not rated; 94 minutes; U.S. release date: June 1, 2001. CAST: Charlotte Alexandria (Alice), Hiram Keller (Jim), Rita Maiden (Mother), Bruno Balp (Father), Georges Guéret (Martial), Shirley Stoler (Shopkeeper)

A LOVE DIVIDED

(CINEMA GUILD) Producers, Alan Moloney, Tim Palmer, Gerry Gregg; Executive Producers, David Blake Knox, Barbara McKissack, Rod Stoneman; Director, Sydney Macartney; Screenplay, Stuart Hepburn; Photography, Cedric Culliton; Designer, Alan Farquharson; Costumes, Allison Byrne; Editor, Ray Roantree; Music, Fiachra Trench; Casting, Nuala Moiselle; a Parallel Films production; Irish-British; Dolby; Color; Not rated; 98 minutes; U.S. release date: June 1, 2001. CAST: Liam Cunningham (Sean Cloney), Orla Brady (Sheila Kelly Cloney), Tony Doyle (Father Stafford), Peter Caffrey (Andy Bailey), John Kavanagh (Bishop Staunton), Brian McGrath (Fred Kelly), Jim Norton (Rev. Fischer), Ali White (Dorothy Kelly), Garrett Keogh (Jimmy Kennedy), Ian McElhinney (Rev. Hamilton), Rynagh O'Grady (Minnie Kennedy), Ger Ryan (Anna Walsh), Sarah Bolger (Eileen Cloney), Nicole Bohan (Mary Cloney), Joe Gallagher (Alec Auld), Doreen Keogh (Lucy Knipe), Peter Gowen (Patrick Pelly), Helen Norton (Katie Anderson), Melissa Bolger (Rebecca Auld), Grace Bolger (Rebecca's Sister), Emma Walsh (Molly Kennedy), Alvin Reid (William Auld), Eleanor Methven (Georgia Simpson), Brendan Conroy (The Drunk), Brian de Salvo (The Judge), Alan Barry (Ambrose), David Wilmot (Ted Nealan), Martin O'Malley (Reporter), Eileen Pollock (Helen Pottinger), Mark Mulholland (Mr. Pottinger), Peter Vollebregt (Callum), Gemma Hayes (Scottish Singer), Oliver O'Donohue (Papal)

FAREWELL, HOME SWEET HOME

(INDEPENDENT) Producer, Martine Marignac; Director/Screenplay, Otar Ioseliani; Photography, William Lubtchansky; Designer, Emmanuel de Chauvigny; Music, Nicholas Zourabichvili; Editors, Otar Ioseliani, Eva Lenkiewicz; French-Swiss-Italian, 1999; Color; Not rated; 118 minutes; U.S. release date: June 1, 2001. CAST: Nico Tarielashvili (Son), Lily Lavina (Mother), Philippe Bas (Moto Driver), Stephanie Hainque (Girl at Bar), Mirabelle Kirkland (Maid), Amiran Amiranashvili (Hobo), Joachim Salinger (Beggar), Emmanuel de Chauvigny (Lover), Otar Ioseliani (Father), Narda Blanchet (Old Lady)

Orla Brady, Liam Cunningham in *A Love Divided*
© Cinema Guild

THE WIDE BLUE ROAD

(MILESTONE) Producer, Maleno Malenotti; Director, Gillo Pontecorvo; Screenplay, Franco Solinas, Ennio De Concini, Gillo Pontecorvo; Based on the novella Squarciò by Franco Solinas; Photography, Mario Montuori; Music, Carlo Franci; Editor, Eraldo Da Roma; Costumes, Lucia Mirisola; from G.E.S.I. Cinematografica (Roma), Play-Art (Paris), Eichberg Film (Monaco), Triglav Film (Lubiana); Italian, 1957; Superscope; Ferraniacolor; Not rated; 90 minutes; U.S. release date: June 6, 2001. CAST: Yves Montand (Squarciò), Alida Valli (Rosetta), Francisco Rabal (Salvatore), Umberto Spadaro (Gaspare, 1st Coast Guard Officer), Peter Carsten (Riva, 2nd Coast Guard Officer), Federica Ranchi (Diana), Mario Girotti (Renato), Ronaldino Bonacchi (Bore), Giancarlo Soblone (Tonino)

Alida Valli, Yves Montand in *The Wide Blue Road*
© Milestone Film

Sho Aikawa in
Dead or Alive
© Viz Films

DEAD OR ALIVE

(VIZ FILMS) Producers, Katsumi Ono, Makoto Okada; Executive Producers, Mitsuru Kurosawa, Tsutomu Tsuchikawa; Director, Takashi Miike; Screenplay, Ichiro Ryu; Photography, Hideo Yamamoto; Art Director, Akira Ishige; Music, Kouri Endou; Editor, Taiji Shimamura; a Daiei Co./Toei Video Co. production; Japanese, 2000; Color; Not rated; 104 minutes; U.S. release date: June 8, 2001. CAST: Riki Takeuchi (Ryuichi), Sho Aikawa (Detective Jojima), Renji Ishibashi (Aoki), Hitoshi Ozawa (Satake), Shingo Tsurumi (Tsin), Kaoru Sugita (Mrs. Jojima)

WHATEVER HAPPENED TO HAROLD SMITH?

(USA FILMS) Producers, David Brown, Ruth Jackson; Executive Producers, Guy East, Nigel Sinclair; Director, Peter Hewitt; Screenplay, Ben Steiner; Photography, David Tattersall; Designer, Gemma Jackson; Costumes, Marie France; Music, Harry Gregson-Williams; Editor, Martin Walsh; Casting, Nina Gold; a co-production of the Arts Council of England, Intermedia Films, October Films, and West Eleven Films; British, 2000; Dolby; Color; Rated R; 95 minutes; U.S. release date: June 8, 2001. CAST: Tom Courtenay (Harold Smith), Michael Legge (Vince Smith), Laura Fraser (Joanna Robinson), Stephen Fry (Dr. Peter Robinson), Charlotte Roberts (Lucy Robinson), Amanda Root (Margaret Robinson), Lulu (Irene Smith), David Thewlis (Nesbit), Charlie Hunnam (Daz), Matthew Rhys (Ray Smith), James Corden (Walter), Rosemary Leach (Harold's Mother), Charles Simon (Oobie), Mark Williams (Roland Thornton), John Higgins (The Reverend Anthony Cooper), Keith Chegwin (Hugh Pimm), Jeremy Child (Dr. Bannister), Patrick Monckton (Peter Pringle), Andy Rashleigh (Sgt. Higgins), Iain Rogerson (North Now Presenter), Rebecca Hill, Janita Appa (Disco Girls), Dave Cooke (Boyfriend), Richenda Carey (Mary Blackcottage), Janus Stark (The Clique), Gizz Butt (Clique Lead Singer), Andrew Pincham (Clique Drummer), Swapan Nandi (Clique Bass Player), Matt Biffa (Clique Manager), Angela Rippon, John Craven, Alan Wicker, Jan Leeming (Themselves), David Law, Charlie Wathen, Sharon Holland (Harold Smith Followers), Jim Barclay, Simon Holmes, Peter Speedwell, Simon Scott (Journalists), Robert Curbishley, Jonah Russell, Ian Kirkby (Policemen), Anna Keaveney (Woman in Street), Dick Ward (Man in Street), John Harrison (Bus Driver)

THE ADVENTURES OF FELIX

(WINSTAR) Producer, Philippe Martin; Directors/Screenplay, Olivier Ducastel, Jacques Martineau; Photography, Matthieu Poirot-Delpech; Designer, Louis Soubrier; Costumes, Juliette Chanaud; Editor, Sabine Mamou; Songs performed by Blossom Dearie; a co-production of ARTE France Cinema and Pyramide Productions, in association with Gimages 2, with the participation of Canal+ and the Centre National de la Cinematographie; French, 2000; Dolby; Widescreen; Color; Not rated; 95 minutes; U.S. release date: June 15, 2001. CAST: Sami Bouajila (Felix), Patachou (Mathilde), Ariane Ascaride (Isabelle), Pierre-Loup Rajot (Daniel), Charly Sergue (Jules), Maurice Bénichou (Fisherman), Philippe Garziano (Railroader), Didier Mahieu (Friend/Unionist), Aliette Langloff-Colas (Unemployment Secretary), Christiane Millet (Woman on Bitherapy), Arno Feffer (Man on Pentatherapy), Clément Dupré (Teenager with Kite), Clément Révérend (Laurent, the Assailant), Daniel Lesur (Bar Owner), Antoine Marneur (Salesman), Lisa Guez (Little Girl), Jean-Stéphan Havert (Dancer at Zizy Folies), Jean-Michel Colon (Zizy

Tom Courtenay in
Whatever Happened to Harold Smith? © USA Films

Sami Bouajila, Charly Sergue in *The Adventures of Felix* © Winstar Cinema

Folies Owner), Virginie Blanc (Louise), Florian Rollez (Nicolas), Adrien Auzias (Antoine), Gilles Barba (Driver in Car Accident), Pascal Billon (Antoine's Father)

RUSSIAN DOLL

(LOT 47) Producers, Allanah Zitserman, Hugo Weaving; Executive Producer, Bruno Charlesworth; Director, Stavros Kazantzidis; Screenplay, Stavros Kazantzidis, Allanah Zitserman; Photography, Justin Brickle; Editor, Andrew MacNeil; Designer, Elizabeth Mary Moore; Casting, Sandra Wolfson; a co-production of Beyond Films, Screen Artists, and the Australian Film Finance Corp.; Australian; Dolby; Color; Rated R; 90 minutes; U.S. release date: June 15, 2001. CAST: Hugo Weaving (Harvey), Natalia Novikova (Katia), David Wenham (Ethan), Rebecca Frith (Miriam), Sacha Horler (Liza), Helen Dallimore (Alison)

SAUDADE DO FUTURO

(LATERIT PRODS.) Producers, Marie-Clémence Blanc-Paes, César Paes; Director, César Paes; Screenplay, Marie-Clémence Blanc-Paes, César Paes; Photography, Michel Berck, César Paes; Music, Fabio Freire, Thomas

Natalia Novikova, Hugo Weaving in *Russian Doll*
© Lot 47 FIlms

Rohrer; Editor, Agnès Contensou; Brazilian-French-Belgian, 2000; Color; Not rated; 92 minutes; U.S. release date: June 20, 2001. Documentary, featuring Luiza Erundina, Fabio Freire, Ezequias Lira, Thomas Rohrer.

JIN-ROH: THE WOLF BRIGADE

(VIZ/TIDEPOINT) Producers, Satoshi Kanuma, Toshifumi Yoshida; Director, Hiroyuki Okiura; Screenplay/Creator, Mamoru Oshii; Music, Hajime Mizoguchi; Key Animation Supervisor, Tetsuya Nishio; English Adaptation Producers, Bandai Entertainment and Viz Communications; English Script, Kevin McKeown, Robert Chomiack; Voice Director, Karl Willems; Casting, InterPacific Productions and Randi Riediger; Japanese, 1999, Color, Not rated, 102 minutes, U.S. release date: June 22, 2001. VOICE CAST: Michael Dobson (Kazuki Fuse), Moneca Stori (Kei Amemiya), Doug Abrahams (Hachiroh Tohbe), Colin Murdock (Atsushi Henmi), Dale Wilson (Bunmei Muroto), Michael Kopsa (Hajime Handa), Ron Halder (Shiroh Tatsumi), French Tickner (Isao Aniya), Maggie Blue O'Hara (Nanmi Agawa)

Saudade Do Futuro © Laterit Prods.

Ian Hart in *Strictly Sinatra* © Universal Studios

LUMUMBA

(ZEITGEIST) Executive Producer, Jacques Bidou; Director, Raoul Peck; Screenplay, Raoul Peck, Pascal Bonitzer; Photography, Bernard Lutic; Art Director, Andrew Fosny; Costumes, Charlotte David; Editor, Jacques Comets; Music, Jean-Claude Petit; Casting, Sylvie Brocheré; a JBA Productions (France), Entre Chine et Loup (Belgium), Essential Filmproduktion (Germany), Velvet S.A. (Haiti), Arte France Cinema, RTBF (Belgian Television), ARTE ZDF, Liberator Productions, FMB Films, SFP Cinema and Canal+, VRT, Cofimage 10; French-Belgian-Haitian-German, 2000; Dolby; Color; Not rated; 115 minutes; U.S. release date: June 27, 2001. CAST: Eriq Ebouaney (Patrice Lumumba), Alex Descas (Joseph Mobutu), Maka Kotto (Joseph Kasa Vubu), Théophile Moussa Sowié (Maurice Mpolo), Dieudonné Kabongo Bashila (Godefroid Munungo), Pascal Nzonzi (Moise Tshombe), André Debaar (Walter J. Ganshof Van der Meersch), Cheik Doukouré (Joseph Okito), Oumar Diop Makena (Thomas Kanza), Mariam Kaba (Pauline Lumumba), Rudi Delhem (General Emile Janssens)

THE CRIMSON RIVERS

(TRISTAR) Producer, Alain Goldman; Director, Mathieu Kassovitz; Screenplay, Jean-Christophe Grangé, Mathieu Kassovitz; Based on the novel *Red Blood Rivers* by Jean-Christophe Grangé; Photography, Thierry Arbogast; Designer, Thierry Flamand; Editor, Maryline Monthieux; Music, Bruno Coulais; a production Gaumont-Legende Enterprises-TF1 Films Production with the participation of Canal+; French, 2000; Dolby; Panavision; Color; Rated R; 106 minutes; U.S. release date: June 27, 2001. CAST: Jean Reno (Pierre Niemans), Vincent Cassel (Max Kerkerian), Nadia Farès (Fanny Ferreira), Jean-Pierre Cassel (Dr. Bernard Chernezé), Karim Belkhadra (Capt. Dahmane), Didier Flamand (The Rector), Laurent Avare (Rémy Caillois), Francine Berge (The Headmistress), Dominique Bettenfeld (The Idea Policeman), Tonio Descanvelle, Olivier Rousset (Policemen, Sarzac), Robert Gendreu (The Cemetery Warden), Alain Guerillot (Skinhead Cafe Owner), Nicolas Koretzky (Computer Cop), Laurent Lafitte (The Rector's Son), Francois Levantal (The Lawyer), Françoise Loreau (Sister at the Convent), Olivier Morel (Philippe Sertys), Philippe Nahon (Man at Motorway Services), Christophe Bernard, Nicky Naude (Skinheads), Alexis Robin (Child), Christophe Rossignon (The Bridge Break Policeman), Dominique Sanda (Sister Andrée), Vincent Schimenti (Policeman), Sami Zitouni, Slim Zitouni (Youths at Sarzac Estate)

STRICTLY SINATRA

(UNIVERSAL FOCUS) a.k.a. *Cocozza's Way*; Producer, Ruth Kenley-Letts; Executive Producers, Duncan Kenworthy, Andrew Macdonald; Director/Screenplay, Peter Capaldi; Photography, Stephen Blackman; Designer, Martyn John; Costumes, Kate Carin; Music, Stanislas Syrewicz; a co-production of the Arts Council of England, DNA Films, and Saracen Street; British; Dolby; Technicolor; Rated R; 97 minutes; U.S. release date: June 22, 2001. CAST: Ian Hart (Toni Cocozza), Kelly Macdonald (Irene), Alun Armstrong (Bill), Brian Cox (Chisholm), Tommy Flanagan (Michelangelo), Iain Cuthbertson (Connolly), Una McLean (Dainty), Jimmy Chisholm (Kenny), Jimmy Yuill (Rod Edmunds), Richard E. Grant, Jimmy Tarbuck (Themselves), Stewart Ennis (Doorman), Paul Dennan (Nicol), Anne Lacey (Coat Check Girl), Alex Howden (Kojak), Douglas Badie (Hard Man), Jamie Murphy (Drowned Rat), Brian McDermott (Youth in Supermarket), Alex McAvoy (Aldo), Pauline Lockhart ("Big T" Assistant), Billy McColl (John the Watchman), Iain Fraser (Joe the Bartender), Callum Beaton (Boy on Stairs)

Nadia Ferès, Jean Reno in *The Crimson Rivers* © Tristar Pictures

UNDER THE FLUTTERING MILITARY FLAG

(INDEPENDENT/SCREENING ROOM) Producers, Seishi Matsumaru, Eigasha Shinsei, Shohei Tokizane; Director, Kinji Fukasaku; Screenplay, Kinji Fukasaku, Norio Osada, Kaneto Shindô; Based on the novel by Shoji Yuki; Photography, Hiroshi Segawa; Music, Hiroshi Hayashi; Editor, Keiichi Uraoka; Japanese, 1972; Color; Not rated; 96 minutes; U.S. release date: July 6, 2001. CAST: Sachiko Hidari, Tetsuro Tamba, Noboru Mitani, Sanae Nakahara, Kanemon Nakamura

THE VERTICAL RAY OF THE SUN

(SONY PICTURES CLASSICS) Producer, Christophe Rossignon; Executive Producer, Benoit Jaubert; Director/Screenplay, Tran Anh Hung; Photography, Mark Lee Ping-Bin; Art Director, Benoît Barouh; Costumes, Susan Lu; Editor, Mario Battistel; Music, Ton That Tiet; Produced by Lazennec in association with Studio Canal+, Arte France Cinema; French-Vietnamese; Dolby; Color; Rated PG-13; 112 minutes; U.S. release date: July 6, 2001. CAST: Tran Nu Yên-Khé (Liên), Nguyen Nhu Quynh (Suong), Lê Khanh (Khanh), Ngô Quang Hai (Hai), Tran Manh Cuong (Kiên), Chu Ngoc Hung (Quôc), Le Tuan Anh (Tuân), Lê Van Lôc (Lôc)

ADANGGAMAN

(NEW YORKER) Producer, Tiziana Soudani; Director, Roger Gnoan M'Bala; Screenplay, Roger Gnoan M'Bala, Jean-Marie Adlaffi, Bertin Akaffou; Photography, Mohammed Soudani; Art Director, Jean-Baptiste Lerro; Costumes, Aïssatou Traoré; Editor, Monica Goux; Music, Lokua Kanza; a co-production of Abyssa Film, Amka Films, Canal+ Horizon, Direction de la Cinematographie Nationale, Fabrica, IMTM Films, Renardes Productions, Televisione Svizzera Italiana (TSI); French-Italian-Swiss-Ivory Coast-Burkina Faso; Dolby; Color; Not rated; 90 minutes; U.S. release date: July 11, 2001. CAST: Rasmane Ouedraogo (Adanggman), Albertine N'Guessan (Mo Akassi), Ziablé Honoré Goore (Ossei), Mylene-Perside Boti Kouame (Naka), Bintou Bakayoko (Ehua), Nicole Suzis Menyeng (Adjo), Mireille André Boti (Mawa), Tie Dijian Patrick (Kanga), Lou Nadege Blagone (Safo Aboua), Anastasie Tode Bohi (The Castanet Girl), Didier Grandidier (Bangalajan), Mylène-Perside Boti Kouame (Naka), Étienne Goheti Bi Gore (Poro), Zie Soro (Sory)

101 Reykjavik © Menemsha Entertainment

101 REYKJAVIK

(MENEMSHA ENTERTAINMENT) Producers, Ingvar Thordarson, Baltasar Kormakur; Director/Screenplay, Baltasar Kormakur; Based on the novel by Hallgrimur Helgason; Photography, Peter Steuger; Designer, Arni Pall Johannsson; Costumes, Thorunn Sveinsdottir, Sigridur Gudjonsdottir; from Zentropa Prods., Filmhuset, Liberator, Troik Entertainment; Icelandic-Danish-Norweigan-French-German, 2000; Dolby; Color; Not rated; 93 minutes; U.S. release date: July 25, 2001. CAST: Victoria Abril (Lola Milagros), Hilmir Snaer Gudnason (Hlynur), Hanna Maria Karlsdottir (Berglind), Thrudur Vihjalmsdottir (Hofi), Baltasar Kormakur (Throstur), Olafur Darri Olafsson (Marri), Throstur Leo Gunnarsson (Brusi), Eyvindur Erlendsson (Hafsteinn), Halldora Bjornsdottir (Elsa), Hilmar Jonsson (Maggi), Johann Sigurdarson (Pall), Edda Heidrun Backman (Pall's Wife), Gudmundur Ingi Thorvaldsson (Ellert)

Tran Nu Yën-Khé, Ngö Quang Hai in *The Vertical Ray of The Sun* © Sony Pictures Entertainment

Susie Porter, Kelly McGillis in *The Monkey's Mask*
© Strand Releasing

Dennis Hopper, Matthew Modine in *The Blackout*
© Trimark

THE MONKEY'S MASK

(STRAND) Producers, Robert Connolly, John Maynard; Director, Samantha Lang; Screenplay, Annie Kennedy; Based on the novel in poetry by Dorothy Porter; Co-Producer, Domenico Procacci; Photography, Garry Philips; Designer, Michael Philips; Costumes, Emily Seresin; Editor, Dany Cooper; Casting, Ann Robinson, Leo Davis; an Arenafilm Pty Ltd./Australian Film Finance Corporation/New South Wales Film and Television Office; Australian; Dolby; Color; Not rated; 91 minutes; U.S. release date: July 27, 2001. CAST: Susie Porter (Jill Fitzpatrick), Kelly McGillis (Diana), Marton Csokas (Nick), Deborah Mailman (Lou), Abbie Cornish (Mickey), Jean-Pierre Mignon (Tony Brach), Caroline Gillmer (Barbara Brach), Brendan Cowell (Hayden), Bojana Novakovic (Tianna), John Noble (Mr. Norris), Linden Wilkinson (Mrs. Norris), Jim Holt (Bill McDonald), Annie Jones (Evelyn McDonald), Chris Haywood (Dad Fitzgerald), John Batchelor (Steve), William Zappa (Det. Sgt. Wesley), Charlotte Rose Regan (Cerebral Girl), Johnny Lee (Tai Chi Instructor), Sara Nunn (Comforting Policewoman), Brian Wood (Brian the Poet), Amanda Herbert, Cassandra McGann (Strippers), Robert Choy, Sky Tse (Asian Fishermen), Billy Mitchell (Stan), Kathryn Hartman (Policewoman)

CURE

(COWBOY BOOKING) Producers, Tetsuya Ikeda, Satoshi Kanno, Tsutomu Tsuchikawa, Atsuyuki Shimoda; Director/Screenplay, Kiyoshi Kurosawa; Executive Producer, Hiroyuki Kato; Photography, Takusho Kikumura; Designer, Tomoyuki Maruo; Music, Gary Shiya; Editor, Kan Suzuki; a Code Red and Daiei Co. Ltd. presentation; Japanese, 1997; Color; Not rated; 111 minutes; U.S. release date: July 27, 2001. CAST: Koji Yakusho (Ken-ichi Takabe), Tsuyoshi Ujiki (Makoto Sakuma), Anna Nakagawa (Fumie Takabe), Masato Hagiwara (Kunio Mamiya), Yoriko Douguchi (Dr. Miyajima), Yukijiro Hotaru (Inchiro Kuwano), Denden (Oida), Ren Osugi (Fujiwara)

THE BLACKOUT

(TRIMARK) Producers, Edward R. Pressman, Clayton Townsend; Executive Producers, Alessandro Camon, Mark Damon; Director, Abel Ferrara; Screenplay, Abel Ferrara, Marla Hanson, Christ Zois; Photography, Ken Kelsch; Designer, Richard Hoover; Costumes, Melinda Eshelman; Editor, Anthony Redman; Casting, Lori Eastside; a co-production of CIPA, Les Films Number One, MDP Worldwide; French-U.S., 1997; Dolby; Color; Not rated; 98 minutes; U.S. release date: August 3, 2001. CAST: Matthew Modine (Matty), Claudia Schiffer (Susan), Dennis Hopper (Mickey Wayne), Beatrice Dalle (Annie 1), Sarah Lassez (Annie 2), Steven Bauer, Laura Bailey, Nancy Ferrara, Andy Fiscella, Vincent Lamberti (Mickey's Studio Actors), Victoria Duffy (Script Girl), Nicholas De Cegli (Miami Dealer), Daphne Duplaix, Mercy Lopez (Fly Girls), Lori Eastside (That Girl), Shareef Malnik (Gold Carder), Peter Cannold (Movie Investor) (Note: This film had its U.S. premiere on cable television in 2000.)

Koji Yakusho (right) in *Cure* © Cowboy Booking

Aylin Yay in *Thomas in Love* © IFC Films

THOMAS IN LOVE

(IFC FILMS) Producer, Diana Elbaum; Co-Producers, Jacques Bidou, Arlette Zylberberg; Director, Pierre Paul Renders; Screenplay, Philippe Blasband; Photography, Virginie Saint Martin; Art Director, Pierre Gerbaux; Costumes, Anne Fournier; Editor, Ewin Ryckaert; Music, Igor Sterpin; a co-production of JBA Productions, RTBF (Belgian Television); French-Belgian; Dolby; Color; Not rated; 97 minutes; U.S. release date: August 3, 2001. CAST: Benoît Verhaert (Thomas), Aylin Yay (Eva), Magali Pinglault (Melodie), Micheline Hardy (Nathalie, the Mother), Alexandre von Sivers (Insurance Agent), Frédéric Topart (Psychologist), Serge Larivière (Receptionist), Eric Kasongo (Ken)

BROOKLYN BABYLON

(ARTISAN) Producers, Henri M. Kessler, Ezra Swerdlow; Executive Producers, Alex Gibney, David Peipers, John Sloss; Associate Producers, Bonz Malone, Lisa West; Director, Marc Levin; Screenplay, Marc Levin, Bonz Malone, Pam Widener; Photography, Mark Benjamin; Designer, Andrea Stanley; Editor, Emir Lewis; Casting, Brett Goldstein; a co-production of Bac Films, Le Studio Canal+, Off Line Entertainment Group; French-U.S., 2000; Dolby; Color; Rated R; 89 minutes; U.S. release date: August 17, 2001. CAST: Tariq Trotter (Solomon), Karen Goberman (Sara), Bonz Malone (Scratch), David Vadim (Judah), Rahzel (Narrator), Earl Contasti (Ras Don), Carol Woods (Cislyn), Slick Rick (Buddah), Mad Cobra (Key Bouncer), Camille Cruse (Cindy), Ahmir Thompson, James "Mala" Gray, Leonard "Hub" Hubbard, Kyle "Scratch" Jones (Members of the Lions), Mina Bern (Nann), Joanne Baron (Aunt Rose), Daniel Serafini-Sauli (Abe), Steve "Simcha" Gottlieb (Sara's Father), Spragga Benz, Yossi Piamenta (Themselves)

Jalil Nazari (center), Mahmoud Behraznia in *Djomeh*
© New Yorker Films

DJOMEH

(NEW YORKER) Producer, Ahmad Moussazadeh; Director/Screenplay/Editor, Hassan Yektapanah; Co-Producer, Mehran Haguigui; Photography, Ali Loghmani; Iranian; Color; Not rated; 94 minutes; U.S. release date: September 5, 2001. CAST: Jalil Nazari (Djomeh), Mahmoud Behraznia (Agha Mohmoud), Rashid Akbari (Habib), Mahbobeh Khalili (Setareh)

VENGO

(COWBOY BOOKING) Director/Screenplay, Tony Gatlif; Adaptation and Dialogues, Tony Gatlif, David Trueba; Photography, Thierry Pouget; Editor, Pauline Dairou; Casting, Héléna Odier, Carmen Sanz, Matilde Rubio; a Code Red and Princes Films presentation; French-Spanish, 2000; Color; Not rated; 90 minutes; U.S. release date: September 7, 2001. CAST: Antonio Canales (Caco), Orestes Villasan Rodriguez (Diego), Antonio Perez Dechent (Primo Alejandro), Bobote (Primo Antonio), Juan Luis Corrientes (Primo Tres), Fernando Guerrero Rebollo (Fernando Caravaca), Francisco Chavero Rios (Francisco Caravaca), Jose Ramirez El Cheli, Juan-Luis Barrios Llorente, Jesus Maria Ventura (Primos Caravaca), El Moror (Pepe Sardina), Manuel Vega Salazar (Anselmo), Maria Faraco (La Catalana), Natasha Mayghine (Alma), Maria Altea Maya (La Coneja)

Vengo © Cowboy Booking

Mouna Noureddine, Sabah Bouzouita in
The Season of Men © Cowboy Booking

Han Suk-kyu, Shim Eun-ha in *Tell Me Something*
© Kino International

TELL ME SOMETHING

(KINO) Producers, Koo Bon-han, Chang Youn-hyun; Executive Producer, Choi Gwi-duk; Director, Chang Youn-Hyun; Screenplay, Chang Youn-hyun, Kong Su-chang, In Eun-Ah, Shim Hae-weon, Kim Eun-jung; Story, Koo Bon-han; Photography, Kim Sung-bok; Editor, Kim Sang-bum; Art Director, Chung Ku-ho; Music, Cho Young-ook, Bang Joon-suk; a Koo & C Film production in association with Cinema Service & Kookmin Venture Capital; South Korean, 2000; Dolby; Color; Not rated; 116 minutes; U.S. release date: September 14, 2001. CAST: Han Suk-kyu (Detective Cho), Shim Eun-ha (Su-Yeon Chae), Chang Hang-sun (Detective Oh), Yum Jung-ah (Sung-min)

VAMPIRE HUNTER D: BLOODLUST

(URBAN VISION) Producers, Mataichiro Yamamoto, Masao Maruyama, Takayuki Nagasawa; Director/Screenplay, Yoshiaki Kawajiri; Based on a novel by Hideyuki Kikuchi; Based on character illustrations by Yoshitaka Amano; Conceptual Designer, Yasushi Nirasawa; Mechanical Designer, Ken Koike; Art Director, Yuji Ikehata; from Madhouse Animation Studios; a Mata Yamamoto production from Filmlink International; Japanese, 2000; Dolby; Color; Rated R; 105 minutes; U.S. release date: September 21, 2001. VOICE CAST: Andrew Philpot (D), Pamela Segall (Leila), John Rafter Lee (Meier Link), Wendee Lee (Charlotte), Mike McShane (Left Hand), Julia Fletcher (Carmila), Matt McKenzie (Borgoff), John DiMaggio (Nolt/Sheriff/Mashira/John Elbourne), Alex Fernandez (Kyle), Jack Fletcher (Grove), John Hostetter (Polk), Dwight Schultz (Benge/Old Man of Barbarois), John Demita (Alan Elbourne/Priest), Mary Elizabeth McGlynn (Caroline), Debi Derryberry (Young Girl)

THE SEASON OF MEN

(COWBOY BOOKING) Producers, Margaret Menegoz, Mohamed Tlatli; Director/Screenplay, Moufida Tlatli; Adaptation & Dialogue, Nouri Bouzid; Photography, Chedli Chaouachi; Costumes, Nadia Anane, Naama Mejri; Editor, Isabelle Devinck; Music, Anouar Brahem; a co-production of Les Films Du Losange, Maghrebfilms Carthage and Arte France Cinema; Tunisian-French; Dolby; Color; Not rated; 124 minutes; U.S. release date: September 28, 2001. CAST: Rabiaa Ben Abdallah (Aïcha), Sabah Bouzouita (Zeineb), Ghania Ben Ali (Meriem), Hend Sabri (Emna), Ezzedine Gannoun (Saïd), Mouna Noureddine (Ommi), Azza Baaziz (Meriem's Child), Lilia Falkat (Emna's Child), Adel Hergal (Aziz), Houyem Rassaa (Zohra), Kaouther Bel Haj Ali (Fatma)

D in *Vampire Hunter D: Bloodlust* © Urban Vision

LA CIÉNAGA

(COWBOY BOOKING) Producer, Lita Stantic; Director/Screenplay, Lucrecia Martel; Co-Producers, Diego Guebel, Ana Aizenberg, Mario Pergolini; Photography, Hugo Colace; Art Director, Graciela Oderigo; Editor, Santiago Ricci; an Orfeo Films International presentation of a 4K Films Production; Argentine, 2000; Color; Not rated; 103 minutes; U.S. release date: October 3, 2001. CAST: Martín Adjemian (Gregorio), Diego Baenas (Joaquín), Leonora Balcarce (Verónica), Silvia Bayle (Mercedes), Sofia Bertolotto (Momi), Juan Cruz Bordeu (José), Graciela Borges (Mecha), Noelia Bravo Herrera (Agustina), Maria Micol Ellero (Mariana), Andrea Lopez (Isabel), Sebastián Montagna (Luciano), Mercedes Moran (Tali), Daniel Valenzuela (Rafael), Franco Veneranda (Martín), Fabio Villafañe (Perro)

THE HIDDEN HALF

(ARTA FILM) Producers, Tahmineh Milani, Mohammad Nikbin; Director/Screenplay, Tahmineh Milani; Photography, Mahmoud Kalari; Designer, Iraj Raminfar; Music, Amir Moini; Editor, Bahram Dehghani; Produced by the Iranian Film Society; Iranian; Color; Not rated; 103 minutes; U.S. release date: October 5, 2001. CAST: Niki Marimi (Fereshteh), Mohammad Nikbin (Khosro), Atila Pesiani (Husband), Soghra Abissi, Akbar Moazezi, Afarin Obeisi

Werckmeister Harmonies © Menemsha Entertainment

Silvia Bayle, Juan Cruz Bordeu in *La Ciénaga*
© Cowboy Booking

WERCKMEISTER HARMONIES

(MENEMSHA ENTERTAINMENT) Producers, Franz Goëss, Paul Saadoun, Miklós Szita, Joachim von Vietinghoff; Director, Béla Tarr; Screenplay, László Krasznahorkai, Béla Tarr; Additional Dialogue, Péter Dobai, Gyuri Dósa Kiss, György Fehér; Based on the novel The Melancholy of Resistance by László Krasznahorkai; Photography, Miklós Gurbán, Erwin Lanzensberger, Gábor Medvigy, Emil Novak, Rob Tregenza, Patrick de Ranter; Costumes, János Breckl; Music, Mihály Vig; Editor, Ágnes Hranitzky; German-French-Hungarian, 2000; Stereo; Black and white; 145 minutes; U.S. release date: October 10, 2001. CAST: Lars Rudolph (János Valuska), Peter Fitz (György Eszter), Hanna Schygulla (Tünde Eszter), Éva Almássy Albert (Aunt Piri), Irén Szajki (Mrs. Harrer), Alfréd Járai (Lajos Harrer), György Barkó (Mr. Nadabán), Lajos Dobák (Mr. Volent), András Fekete (Mr. Árgyelán), János Derzsi (Man in the Broad-Cloth Coat), Djoko Rosic (Man in Western Boots), Tamás Wichmann (Man in the Sailor Cap), Matuas Drafi (Man in the Fur Cap), Ferenc Kállai (Director), Mihály Kormos (Factotum), Putyi Horváth (Porter), Péter Dobai (Chief Constable), Kati Lázár (Sorter), László Fe-Lugossy (Housepainter), Gyula Pauer (Mr. Hagelmayer), Barna Mihók (Coachman), Viktor Lois (Loader), Béla Máriáss (Mr. Mádai), Sandor Bese (The Prince)

Yehuda Lerner in *Sobibor: October 14, 1943, 4 P.M.*
© New Yorker Films

SOBIBOR: OCTOBER 14, 1943, 4 P.M.

(NEW YORKER) Director, Claude Lanzmann; Photography, Caroline Champetier, Dominique Chapuis; Editors, Chantal Hymans, Sabine Marnou; a co-production of Why Not Productions-Les Films Aleph-France 2 Cinema, with the participation of Canal+ and France Television Images; French; DTS Stereo; Color; Not rated; 95 minutes; U.S. release date: October 12, 2001. Documentary on the only successful uprising ever staged by Jewish prisoners at an extermination camp against the Nazis, featuring Yehuda Lerner.

YANA'S FRIENDS

(FRIENDS OF FILM) Producers, Marek Rozenbaum, Moshe Levinson, Uri Sabag, Einat Bikel; Director, Arik Kaplun; Screenplay, Arik Kaplun, Simeon Vinokur; Photography, Valentin Belonogov; Art Director, Ariel Roshko; Music, Avi Binyamin; Israeli; Color; Not rated; 90 minutes; U.S. release date: October 12, 2001. CAST: Evelyne Kaplun (Yana), Nir Levi (Eli), Shmil Ben-Ari (Yuri), Moscu Alcalay (Yitzhak), Dalia Friedland (Rosa), Vladimir Friedman (Alik), Israel Demidov (Fima), Lena Sachanova (Mila), Jenya Fleischer (Edik), Eviatar Lazar (Daniel), Lucy Dubinchik (Yuri's Daughter)

Nir Levi, Evelyne Kaplun in *Yana's Friends* © Friends of Film

Berlin Babylon © S.U.M.O. Film

SPRIGGAN

(ADV FILMS) Director, Hirotsuge Kawasaki; Screenplay, Yasutaka Itô; General Supervisor, Katsuhiro Ôtomo; Character Designer/Animation Director, Hisashi Eguchi; CGI Director, Akiko Saito; Japanese, 1998; Dolby; Color; Rated R; 90 minutes; U.S. release date: October 12, 2001. VOICE CAST: Chris Patton (Yu Ominae), Kevin Corn (Gen. MacDougall), Ted Pfister (Dr. Meisel), Andy McAvin (Jean-Jacques Mondo), Kelly Manison (Margaret), Mike Kleinhenz (Fattman), Spike Spencer (Little Boy), John Paul Shepard (Yamamoto), John Swasey (Mr. Smith), Brett Weaver (Classmate A), Jason Douglas, Tiffany Grant, Adam Taylor (Additional Voices)

BERLIN BABYLON

(S.U.M.O. FILM) Producers, Hubertus Siegert, E.N. Wilsdorf, Boris Wilsdorf; Director/Screenplay, Hubertus Siegert; Photography, Ralf K. Dobrick, Thomas Plenert; Music, Einstürzende Neubauten; a co-production of S.U.M.O. Film Hubertus Siegert and Philip Gröning Filmproduktion; German, 2000; Dolby; Color; Not rated; 88 minutes; U.S. release date: October 17, 2001. Documentary about the building campaign of various international companies eager to establish themselves in Berlin following the fall of the Berlin Wall in 1989.

COOL & CRAZY

(FIRST RUN FEATURES) Producer, Tom Remlov; Director, Knut Erik Jensen; Line Producer, Jan-Erik Gammleng; Photography, Svein Krøvel, Aslaug Holm; Editor, Aslaug Holm; a Norsk Film AS co-production with Barentsfilm AS and Giraff Film AB; Norweigan; Color; Not rated; U.S. release date: October 19, 2001. Documentary on the Berlevåg Male Choir, featuring Odd Marino Frantzen (Conductor), Einar F. L. Strand, Arne Wensel, Kåre Wensel, Arne Blomsø, Leif Roger Ananiassen, Eirik Daldorff, Odd-Arne Olsen, Eirik Nilsen, Nils Grønberg (1st Tenor), Reidar Strand, Ragnar Rotnes, Randulf Antonsen, Ole Jonny Larsen, Einar Kristian Straumsne (2nd Tenor), Alf Håkon Pedersen, Harald Wensel, Kolbjørn Svendsen, Karl Ananiassen, Bjarne Mathisen, Tommy Bergersen, Oddvar Hansen, Einar Sætervoll, Terje Håkon Blickfeldt (1st Bass), Arne Nygård, Ken-Hugo Jensen, Trygg Lund, Kai Olav Jakobsen, Hilmar Wensel, Brynjar Langås (2nd Bass).

Berlevåg Male Choir in *Cool & Crazy* © First Run Features

BETTER THAN SEX

(GOLDWYN/FIREWORKS) Producers, Bruna Papandera, Frank Cox; Executive Producer, Marc Bonduel; Director/Screenplay, Jonathan Teplitzky; Photography, Garry Phillips; Designer, Tara Kamath; Costumes, Kelly May; Music, David Hirschfelder; Editor, Shawn Seet; Casting, Nicki Barrett; The New South Wales Film & Television Office, France Television Distribution, Meercat & NewVision Films presentation of a Better Than production; Australian-French, 2000; Dolby; Color; Not rated; 84 minutes; U.S. release date: October 24, 2001. CAST: David Wenham (Josh), Susie Porter (Cin), Catherine McClements (Sam), Kris McQuade (Taxi Driver), Simon Bossell (Tim), Imelda Corcoran (Carole), Dina Gillespie (Girl "B"), Emily Saunders (Girl "C"), Laura Keneally (Girl "D"), Leah Vandenberg (Girl "E"), Tammy MacIntosh (Girl "F"), Mark Priestley (Guy "A"), Tamblyn Lord (Guy "B"), Jason Clarke (Guy "C"), Jason Chong (Guy "D"), Tim Richards (Guy "E"), Harry Bragg (Old Man), Pauline Anderson (Old Woman)

MY VOYAGE TO ITALY
(Il Mio Viaggio in Italia)

(MIRAMAX) Producers, Barbara De Fina, Giuliana Del Punta, Bruno Restuccia; Executive Producers, Giorgio Armani, Riccardo Tozzi; Director, Martin Scorsese; Screenplay, Suso Cecchi D'Amico, Raffaele Donato, Kent Jones, Martin Scorsese; Editor, Thelma Schoonmaker; Associate Producer, Caterina D'Amico; Co-Executive Producer, Raffaele Donato; a Mediatrade presentation in association with Cappa Productions; a Mediatrade production in conjunction with Paso Doble Film; Italian-U.S.; Dolby; Color; Rated PG-13; 243 minutes; U.S. release date: October 24, 2001. Documentary hosted by director Martin Scorsese as he explores Italian movie history.

(Above) Susie Porter, David Wenham in *Better Than Sex* © Goldman-Fireworks
(Below) Martin Scorsese in *My Voyage to Italy* © Miramax Films

Pisek Intrakanchit in *Bangkok Dangerous*
© First Look Features

BANGKOK DANGEROUS

(FIRST LOOK FEATURES) Producer, Nonzee Nimibutr; Executive Producers, Pracha Maleenont, Brian L. Marcar, Adirek Wattaleela; Directors/Screenplay/Editors, Oxide Pang, Danny Pang; Photography, Decha Srimantra; Designer, Wut Chaoslip; Music, Orange Music; Thailand, 1999; Dolby; Color; Not rated; 105 minutes; American release date: October 19, 2001. CAST: Pawalit Mongkolpisit (Kong), Premsinee Ratanasopha (Fon), Patharawarin Timkul (Aom), Pisek Intrakanchit (Jo)

GINGER SNAPS

(TVA INTERNATIONAL) Producers, Steve Hoban, Karen Lee Hall; Executive Producers, Noah Segal, Alicia Reilly-Larson, Daniel Lyon; Director, John Fawcett; Screenplay, Karen Walton; Story, Karen Walton, John Fawcett; Photography, Thom Best; Designer, Todd Cherniawsky; Editor, Brett Sullivan; Costumes, Lea Carlson; Special Make-up and Creature Effects, Paul Jones; Music, Michael Shields; Casting, Robin D. Cook, Linda Philips-Palo, Robert McGee; a Copper Heat Entertainment/Water Pictures in association with Lions Gate Films and Unapix Entertainment presentation; Canadian; Dolby; Color; Not rated; 108 minutes; American release date: October 26, 2001. CAST: Emily Perkins (Brigitte Fitzgerald), Katharine Isabelle (Ginger Fitzgerald), Kris Lemche (Sam), Mimi Rogers (Pamela Fitzgerald), Jesse Moss (Jason), Danielle Hampton (Trina Sinclair), John Bourgeois (Henry Fitzgerald), Peter Keleghan (Mr. Wayne), Christopher Redman (Ben), Jimmy MacInnis (Tim), Lindsey Leese (Nurse Ferry), Nick Nolan (Creature & Gingerwolf), Wendii Fulford (Ms. Sykes), Ann Baggley (Mother), Graeme Robertson, Maxwell Robertson (Toddlers), Pak-Kong Ho (Janitor), Bryon Bully (Hockey Kid), Steven Taylor (Puppy Kid), Lucy Lawless (Announcer on School's PA System)

OUCH!

(NEW YORKER) Producers, Martine Marignac, Maurice Tinchant; Director/Screenplay, Sophie Fillieres; Photography, Christophe Pollock; Designer, Antoine Platteau; Editor, Valerie Loiseleux; Music, Michel Portal; Pierre Grise Productions; French, 2000; Dolby; Color; Not rated; 106 minutes; U.S. release date: October 26, 2001. CAST: André Dussollier (Robert), Hélène Fillieres (Aie), Emmanuelle Devos (Claire), Anne Le Ny (Marie), Gisèle Casadesus (Robert's Mother), Lucien Pascal (Robert's Father), Lucienne Hamon (Aie's Mother), Alain Rimoux (Aie's Father), Jean-Baptiste Malartre (David), Olivier Cruveiller (Francois)

HIGH HEELS AND LOW LIFES

(TOUCHSTONE) Producers, Uri Fruchtmann, Barnaby Thompson; Director, Mel Smith; Screenplay/Associate Producer, Kim Fuller; Story, Kim Fuller, Georgia Pritchett; Co-Producer, Nicky Kentish Barnes; Photography, Steven Chivers; Designer, Michael Pickwood; Costumes, Jany Temime; Editor, Christopher Blunden; Music, Charlie Mole; Casting, Kate Rhodes James, Deborah Aquila; a Fragile Films production, Distributed by Buena Vista; Dolby; Color; Rated R; 86 minutes; U.S.

Emily Perkins (right) in *Ginger Snaps* © TVA International

release date: October 26, 2001. CAST: Minnie Driver (Shannon), Mary McCormack (Frances), Kevin McNally (Mason), Michael Gambon (Kerrigan), Danny Dyer (Danny), Mark Williams (Tremaine), Kevin Eldon (McGill), Len Collin (Barry Tarson), Julian Wadham (Chief Inspector Rogers), Darren Boyd (Ray), Simon Scardifield (Tony), Jane Partridge (Receptionist), Jason Griffiths, Ben Lemel, Sophie Millet (Paramedics), Ranjit Krishnamma (Doctor), Mark Meadows (Romantic Actor), Ben Walden (Bloodied Actor), Mike Attwell (Duty Sergeant), Danny Babington (Suspect), John Sessions (Director), Paul Bown (Barman), James Cameron (Reporter), James Garbutt (Mr. Winters), Eve Slickie (Patient), Patrick Baladi (Car Driver), Barry Ewart (Busybody), Tom Ellis (Uniformed Officer), Ben Farrow (Julian), Junior Simpson (Mickey), Darren Tighe (Clubber), Kier Charles (Young Guy), Stewart Wright (Officer), Hugh Bonneville (Farmer), James Taylor (Ticket Collector), Liam Noble (Delivery Man)

MYSTERIOUS OBJECT AT NOON

(INDEPENDENT/ANTHOLOGY FILM ARCHIVES) Producers, Gridthiya Gaweewong, Mingmongkol Sonakul; Director, Apichatpong Weerasethakul; Photography, Prasong Klinborrom, Apichatpong Weerasethakul; Editors Tony Morias, Peter Jones; Story, Villagers of Thailand; Thailand, 2000; Black and white; Not rated; 85 minutes; U.S. release date: November 1, 2001. Part-fiction, part-documentary depiction of the lives of several inhabitants of Bangkok, Thailand, featuring Somsri Pinyopol, Duangjai Hiransri, To Hanudomlapr, Kannikar Narong, Kongkiert Komsiri, Mee Madmoon, Chakree Duangklao, Jaruwan Techasatiern, Somsri Pinyopol, Jarunee Jandang, Deaw, Jack of Ayuddhaya.

Minnie Driver, Mary McCormack in
High Heels and Low Lifes © Touchstone Pictures

Shah Rukh Khan in *Asoka* © Overseas Film Group

ASOKA

(ARCLIGHTZ) Executive Producer, Sanjiv Chawla; Director/Photography, Santosh Sivan; Screenplay, Saket Chaudhary, Santosh Sivan; Editor, Shreekar Prasad; Art Director, Sabu Cyril; Music, Sandeep Chowta; Indian; Color; Not rated; 169 minutes; U.S. release date: November 2, 2001. CAST: Shah Rukh Khan (Asoka), Kareena Kapoor (Kaurwaki), Danny Denzongpa (Virat), Ajit (Susima), Rahul Dev (Bheema), Hrishita Bhatt (Devi), Umesh Mehra (Chandragupta), Gerson Da Cuhna (Bindusara), Subhashini (Dharma), Suraj Balaje (Arya), Johnny Lever, Raghuvir Yadav, Suresh Menon (Magadha Soldiers), Rani Rajlaxmi (Bar Girl), Gayatri Jayaraman (Dancer), Shilpa R. Mehta (Queen), Shweta Menon (Nandaneshwari), Shabir Massani (Giri), Vinit Sharma (Sugatra), Vivek Sharma (Sugidha), Usha Jerajani (Nanny), N. Shyam Sunder (Radhagupta), C. L. Gurnani (Pandit), Mithilesh Chaturvedi (Kalinga Minister), P. Mantu Mohaputra (Kalinga Minister's Goon), Madhu (Vitasoka), Karan Dewani (Young Asoka), Jitendra Shriamali (Milkman), Shampa (Milkman's Wife), Rajendra Mehra (Village Head), Anu Ansari (Headman's Daughter), Master Hardik (Headman's Grandsom), Anjan Ghosh (Magadha General), Vijay Kumar, Bahadur (Buddhist Monks), Arvind Ayer (Assassin in the River), Ashok Mapara (Assassin in the Monastery), Samir Sarkar (Messenger), S. Krishna, Milind Vereker (Thugs), Balakrishna (Arya's Father), Sanghamitra Jena (Arya's Mother), Bomie E. Dotiwala (Devi's Father), Bunty (Groom), Col. Suresh Rege (Groom's Father), Chetan Motiwala (Announcer), Mangilal (Arya's Caretaker), Monika Kale (Flower Girl)

Isaach de Bankolé in *Otomo* © ArtMattan

Béatrice Dalle, Alex Descas in *Trouble Every Day*
© Lot 47 Films

OTOMO

(ARTMATTAN) Producers, Thomas Lechner, Claudia Tronnier, Irene von Alberti; Director, Frieder Schlaich; Screenplay, Frieder Schlaich, Klaus Pohl; Photography, Volker Tittel; Designer, Anne Schlaich; Editor, Magdolna Rokob; Costumes, Henrike Luz; Produced by Filmgalerie 451, Zweites Deutsches Fernsehen; German, 1999; Color; Not rated; 85 minutes; U.S. release date: November 2, 2001. CAST: Isaach de Bankolé (Frederic Omoto), Hanno Friedrich (Heinz), Barnaby Metschurat (Rolf), Lara Kugler (Simone), Eva Mattes (Gisela), Siegrid Burkholder, Gottfried Breitfuss, Traute Hoess, Stefan Moos, Katja Schmidt-Ohen, Hansjuergen Gerth

THE PRINCE OF LIGHT: THE LEGEND OF RAMAYANA

(SHOWCASE ENTERTAINMENT) Producers, Krishna Shah, Yugo Sata; Executive Producer, Atsushi Matsuo; Director, Yugo Sako; Screenplay, Krishna Shah, Yugo Sako; Based on The Ramayana by Valmiki; Animation Director, Kazuyuki Koyabayashi, for WRS Motion Picture and Video Lab; Art Director, Hajime Matsuoka; Editors, Makato Arai, Wayne Schmidt; Music, Vanraj Bhatia, Alan Howarth; a Showcase Entertainment and Krishna Shah presentation of a Nippon Ramayana & MRI Inc. production; Japanese-Indian-U.S.; Dolby; Color; Rated PG; 96 minutes; U.S. release date: November 9, 2001. VOICE CAST: Bryan Cranston, Edie Mirman, Tom Wyner, Richard Cansino, Michael Sorich, Mike L. Reynolds, Tony Pope, Mari Devon, Simon Prescott, Barbera Goodson, Kirk Thornton, Steve Bulen, Eddie Friarson, Jeff Winkless, Catherine Battisone, Michael McConnohie

JUNG (WAR) IN THE LAND OF THE MUJAHEDDIN

(KAROUSEL FILMS) Directors, Fabrizio Lazzaretti, Alberto Vendemmiati; Line Producer/Editor, Giuseppe Petitto; Photography, Fabrizio Lazzaretti; Music, Mario Crispi; a Human Rights Watch International Film Festival presentation; Italian, 2000; Color; Not rated; 114 minutes; U.S. release date: November 23, 2001. Documentary on Dr. Gino Strada and his efforts to build a hospital near the front lines in northern Afghanistan.

TROUBLE EVERY DAY

(LOT 47) Producers, Georges Benayoun, Jean-Michel Rey, Philippe Liégeois; Director, Claire Denis; Screenplay, Jean-Pol Fargeau, Claire Denis; Photography, Agnes Godard; Designer, Arnaud de Moléron; Editor, Nelly Quettier; Music, Tindersticks; Casting, Nicolas Lublin, James Calleri; a Messaouda Films, Rezo Prods., Arte France Cinema, Dacia Films Kinetique Inc. production with the participation of Canal+, Arte/ZDF, Rezo Films; French; Dolby; Color; Not rated; 102 minutes; U.S. release date: November 30, 2001. CAST: Vincent Gallo (Shane

Jung (War) in the Land of the Mujaheddin
© Karousel Films

Brown), Tricia Vessey (June Brown), Béatrice Dalle (Core), Alex Descas (Leo Semeneau), Florence Loiret-Caille (Christelle), Nicolas Duvauchelle (Erwan), Jose Garcia (Choart), Hélène Lapiower (Malecot), Marilu Marini (Friessen), Aurore Clément (Jeanne), Raphaël Neal (Ludo), Bakary Sangare (Night Watchman), Lionel Goldstein (Receptionist), Céline Samie (Woman in Brasserie), Arnaud Churin (Truck Driver), Slimane Brahimi (Christelle's Friend), Alice Houri (Young Girl in Metro), Véra Chidyvar (Woman in Metro), Nelly Zargarian, Rosa Nikolic, Csilla Lukacs-Molnar (Chambermaids), Lacrita Massix (Air Hostess), Myriam Theodoresco, Alexandre Uzureau de Martynoff (Couple), Laure Guerard (Woman in High Heels), Albert Szpiro (Community Clinic Boss)

B-52

(BITOMSKY) Producers, Albert Schwinges, Hartmut Bitomsky; Director/Screenplay, Hartmut Bitomsky, from an idea by Ben Nicholson; Photography, Volker Langhoff, Hugo Kroiss; Editor, Theo Bromin; German-U.S.-Swiss; Not rated; 122 minutes; U.S. release date: December 5, 2001. Documentary on the history of the powerful warplane, the B-52.

PRINCESA

(STRAND) Producer, Rebecca O'Brien; Director, Henrique Goldman; Screenplay, Henrique Goldman, Ellis Freeman; Based on the book by Fernanda Farias de Albuquerque; Photography, Guillermo Escalon; Costumes, Nivea Sibulka; Editor, Kerry Kohler; Music, Giovanni Venosta; a co-production of Bac Films, British Screen, Filmstiftung Nordrhein-Westfalen, Manga Films SL, Parallax Pictures Ltd., Road Movies Filmproduktion, Telepiu, Westdeutscher Rundfunk; French-Italian-German-British-Brazilian; Dolby; Color; Not rated; 96 minutes; U.S. release date: December 7, 2001. CAST: Ingrid de Souza (Fernanda), Cesare Bocci (Gianni), Lulu Pecorari (Karin), Biba Lerhue (Charlo), Sonia Morgan (Fofao), Mauro Pirovano (Fabrizio), Alessandra Acciai (Lidia)

Marco Polo in *Marco Polo: Return to Xanadu*
© Tooniversal Company

MARCO POLO: RETURN TO XANADU

(THE TOONIVERSAL COMPANY) Producers, Igor Meglic, Chris Holter, Ron Merk; Director, Ron Merk; Screenplay, Chris Holter, Ron Merk, Sheldon Moldoff; Associate Producer, Yan Luo; Production Designers/Animation Directors, Jaroslav Baran, Arne Wong; an Afanti International Animation Corporation, Interline s.r.o., Druzba Film Associates Ltd. presentation; Chinese-Slovakian-Korean-Canadaian-U.S.; Dolby; Eastmancolor; Rated G; 82 minutes; U.S. release date: December 21, 2001. VOICE CAST: Nicholas Gonzalez (Young Marco), John Matthew (Delicate Dinosaur/Marco Polo), Elea Bartling (Princess Ming-Yu), Tony Pope (Foo-Ling/Reginald the Seagull/Babu), Michael Kostroff (Kubla Khan/Lo Fat), John C. Hyke (Malgor), Robert Kramer (Grandpa/The Helmsman), Paul Ainsley (Wong Wei), Alan Altshuld (Pangu), Terry Wood, Joe Pizzulo, Steve Lively (Singers)

Ingrid de Souza, Cesare Bocci in *Princesa*
© Strand Releasing

F. Murray Abraham

Adam Arkin

Anne Bancroft

Antonio Banderas

BIOGRAPHICAL DATA

AAMES, WILLIE (William Upton): Los Angeles, July 15, 1960.
AARON, CAROLINE: Richmond, VA, Aug. 7, 1954. Catholic U.
ABBOTT, DIAHNNE: NYC, 1945.
ABBOTT, JOHN: London, England, June 5, 1905.
ABRAHAM, F. MURRAY: Pittsburgh, PA, Oct. 24, 1939. U TX.
ACKLAND, JOSS: London, Feb. 29, 1928.
ADAMS, BROOKE: NYC, Feb. 8, 1949. Dalton.
ADAMS, CATLIN: Los Angeles, Oct. 11, 1950.
ADAMS, DON: NYC, Apr. 13, 1926.
ADAMS, EDIE (Elizabeth Edith Enke): Kingston, PA, Apr. 16, 1927. Juilliard, Columbia.
ADAMS, JOEY LAUREN: Little Rock, AR, Jan. 6, 1971.
ADAMS, JULIE (Betty May): Waterloo, IA, Oct. 17, 1926. Little Rock, Jr. College.
ADAMS, MASON: NYC, Feb. 26, 1919. U WI.
ADAMS, MAUD (Maud Wikstrom): Lulea, Sweden, Feb. 12, 1945.
ADJANI, ISABELLE: Germany, June 27, 1955.
AFFLECK, BEN: Berkeley, CA, Aug. 15, 1972.
AFFLECK, CASEY: Falmouth, MA, Aug. 12, 1975.
AGAR, JOHN: Chicago, IL, Jan. 31, 1921.
AGUTTER, JENNY: Taunton, England, Dec. 20, 1952.
AIELLO, DANNY: NYC, June 20, 1933.
AIMEE, ANOUK (Dreyfus): Paris, France, Apr. 27, 1934. Bauer-Therond.
AKERS, KAREN: NYC, Oct. 13, 1945, Hunter College.
ALBERGHETTI, ANNA MARIA: Pesaro, Italy, May 15, 1936.
ALBERT, EDDIE (Eddie Albert Heimberger): Rock Island, IL, Apr. 22, 1908. U MN.
ALBERT, EDWARD: Los Angeles, Feb. 20, 1951. UCLA.
ALBRIGHT, LOLA: Akron, OH, July 20, 1925.
ALDA, ALAN: NYC, Jan. 28, 1936. Fordham.
ALEANDRO, NORMA: Buenos Aires, Argentina, Dec. 6, 1936.
ALEJANDRO, MIGUEL: NYC, Feb. 21, 1958.
ALEXANDER, JANE (Quigley): Boston, MA, Oct. 28, 1939. Sarah Lawrence.

ALEXANDER, JASON (Jay Greenspan): Newark, NJ, Sept. 23, 1959. Boston U.
ALICE, MARY: Indianola, MS, Dec. 3, 1941.
ALLEN, DEBBIE (Deborah): Houston, TX, Jan. 16, 1950. Howard U.
ALLEN, JOAN: Rochelle, IL, Aug. 20, 1956. E IL U.
ALLEN, KAREN: Carrollton, IL, Oct. 5, 1951. U MD.
ALLEN, NANCY: NYC, June 24, 1950.
ALLEN, TIM: Denver, CO, June 13, 1953. W. MI. U.
ALLEN, WOODY (Allan Stewart Konigsberg): Brooklyn, NY, Dec. 1, 1935.
ALLEY, KIRSTIE: Wichita, KS, Jan. 12, 1955.
ALLYSON, JUNE (Ella Geisman): Westchester, NY, Oct. 7, 1917.
ALONSO, MARIA CONCHITA: Cuba, June 29, 1957.
ALT, CAROL: Queens, NY, Dec. 1, 1960. Hofstra.
ALVARADO, TRINI: NYC, Jan. 10, 1967.
AMIS, SUZY: Oklahoma City, OK, Jan. 5, 1958. Actors Studio.
AMOS, JOHN: Newark, NJ, Dec. 27, 1940. CO U.
ANDERSON, GILLIAN: Chicago, IL, Aug. 9, 1968. DePaul.
ANDERSON, KEVIN: Waukeegan, IL, Jan. 13, 1960.
ANDERSON, LONI: St. Paul, MN, Aug. 5, 1946.
ANDERSON, MELISSA SUE: Berkeley, CA, Sept. 26, 1962.
ANDERSON, MELODY: Edmonton, Canada, 1955. Carlton.
ANDERSON, MICHAEL, JR.: London, England, Aug. 6, 1943.
ANDERSON, RICHARD DEAN: Minneapolis, MN, Jan. 23, 1950.
ANDERSSON, BIBI: Stockholm, Sweden, Nov. 11, 1935. Royal Dramatic Sch.
ANDES, KEITH: Ocean City, NJ, July 12, 1920. Temple, Oxford.
ANDRESS, URSULA: Bern, Switzerland, Mar. 19, 1936.
ANDREWS, ANTHONY: London, England, Dec. 1, 1948.
ANDREWS, JULIE (Julia Elizabeth Wells): Surrey, England, Oct. 1, 1935.
ANGLIM, PHILIP: San Francisco, CA, Feb. 11, 1953.
ANISTON, JENNIFER: Sherman Oaks, CA, Feb. 11, 1969.
ANN-MARGRET (Olsson): Valsjobyn, Sweden, Apr. 28, 1941. Northwestern.

ANSARA, MICHAEL: Lowell, MA, Apr. 15, 1922. Pasadena Playhouse.

ANSPACH, SUSAN: NYC, Nov. 23, 1945.

ANTHONY, LYSETTE: London, England, 1963.

ANTHONY, TONY: Clarksburg, WV, Oct. 16, 1937. Carnegie Tech.

ANTON, SUSAN: Yucaipa, CA, Oct. 12, 1950. Bemardino College.

ANTONELLI, LAURA: Pola, Italy, Nov. 28, 1941.

ANWAR, GABRIELLE: Lalehaam, England, Feb. 4, 1970

APPLEGATE, CHRISTINA: Hollywood, CA, Nov. 25, 1972.

ARCHER, ANNE: Los Angeles, Aug. 25, 1947.

ARCHER, JOHN (Ralph Bowman): Osceola, NB, May 8, 1915. USC.

ARDANT, FANNY: Monte Carlo. Mar 22, 1949

ARKIN, ADAM: Brooklyn, NY, Aug. 19, 1956.

ARKIN, ALAN: NYC, Mar. 26, 1934. LACC.

ARMSTRONG, BESS: Baltimore, MD, Dec. 11, 1953.

ARNAZ, DESI, JR.: Los Angeles, Jan. 19, 1953.

ARNAZ, LUCIE: Hollywood, CA, July 17, 1951.

ARNESS, JAMES (Aurness): Minneapolis, MN, May 26, 1923. Beloit College.

ARQUETTE, DAVID: Winchester, VA, Sept. 8, 1971.

ARQUETTE, PATRICIA: NYC, Apr. 8, 1968.

ARQUETTE, ROSANNA: NYC, Aug. 10, 1959.

ARTHUR, BEATRICE (Frankel): NYC, May 13, 1924. New School.

ASHER, JANE: London, England, Apr. 5, 1946.

ASHLEY, ELIZABETH (Elizabeth Ann Cole): Ocala, FL, Aug. 30, 1939.

ASHTON, JOHN: Springfield, MA, Feb. 22, 1948. USC.

ASNER, EDWARD: Kansas City, KS, Nov. 15, 1929.

ASSANTE, ARMAND: NYC, Oct. 4, 1949. AADA.

ASTIN, JOHN: Baltimore, MD, Mar. 30, 1930. U MN.

ASTIN, MacKENZIE: Los Angeles, May 12, 1973.

ASTIN, SEAN: Santa Monica, CA, Feb. 25, 1971.

ATHERTON, WILLIAM: Orange, CT, July 30, 1947. Carnegie Tech.

ATKINS, CHRISTOPHER: Rye, NY, Feb. 21, 1961.

ATKINS, EILEEN: London, England, June 16, 1934.

ATKINSON, ROWAN: England, Jan. 6, 1955. Oxford.

ATTENBOROUGH, RICHARD: Cambridge, England, Aug. 29, 1923. RADA.

AUBERJONOIS, RENE: NYC, June 1, 1940. Carnegie Tech.

AUDRAN, STEPHANE: Versailles, France, Nov. 8, 1932.

AUGER, CLAUDINE: Paris, France, Apr. 26, 1942. Dramatic Cons.

AULIN, EWA: Stockholm, Sweden, Feb. 14, 1950.

AUTEUIL, DANIEL: Alger, Algeria, Jan. 24, 1950.

AVALON, FRANKIE (Francis Thomas Avallone): Philadelphia, PA, Sept. 18, 1939.

AYKROYD, DAN: Ottawa, Canada, July 1, 1952.

AZARIA, HANK: Forest Hills, NY, Apr. 25, 1964. AADA, Tufts.

AZNAVOUR, CHARLES (Varenagh Aznourian): Paris, France, May 22, 1924.

AZZARA, CANDICE: Brooklyn, NY, May 18, 1947.

BACH, CATHERINE: Warren, OH, Mar. 1, 1954.

BACALL, LAUREN (Betty Perske): NYC, Sept. 16, 1924. AADA.

BACH, BARBARA: Queens, NY, Aug. 27, 1946.

BACKER, BRIAN: NYC, Dec. 5, 1956. Neighborhood Playhouse.

BACON, KEVIN: Philadelphia, PA, July 8, 1958.

BAIN, BARBARA: Chicago, IL, Sept. 13, 1934. U IL.

BAIO, SCOTT: Brooklyn, NY, Sept. 22, 1961.

BAKER, BLANCHE: NYC, Dec. 20, 1956.

BAKER, CARROLL: Johnstown, PA, May 28, 1931. St. Petersburg, Jr. College.

BAKER, DIANE: Hollywood, CA, Feb. 25, 1938. USC.

BAKER, JOE DON: Groesbeck, TX, Feb.12, 1936.

BAKER, KATHY: Midland, TX, June 8, 1950. UC Berkley.

BAKULA, SCOTT: St. Louis, MO, Oct. 9, 1955. Kansas U.

BALABAN, BOB: Chicago, IL, Aug. 16, 1945. Colgate.

BALDWIN, ADAM: Chicago, IL, Feb. 27, 1962.

BALDWIN, ALEC: Massapequa, NY, Apr. 3, 1958. NYU.

BALDWIN, DANIEL: Massapequa, NY, Oct. 5, 1960.

BALDWIN, STEPHEN: Massapequa, NY, 1966.

BALDWIN, WILLIAM: Massapequa, NY, Feb. 21, 1963.

BALE, CHRISTIAN: Pembrokeshire, West Wales, Jan. 30, 1974.

BALK, FAIRUZA: Point Reyes, CA, May 21, 1974.

BALLARD, KAYE: Cleveland, OH, Nov. 20, 1926.

BANCROFT, ANNE (Anna Maria Italiano): Bronx, NY, Sept. 17, 1931. AADA.

BANDERAS, ANTONIO: Malaga, Spain, Aug. 10, 1960.

BANERJEE, VICTOR: Calcutta, India, Oct. 15, 1946.

BANES, LISA: Chagrin Falls, OH, July 9, 1955. Juilliard.

BARANSKI, CHRISTINE: Buffalo, NY, May 2, 1952. Juilliard.

BARBEAU, ADRIENNE: Sacramento, CA, June 11, 1945. Foothill College.

BARDEM, JAVIER: Gran Canaria, Spain, May 1, 1969.

BARDOT, BRIGITTE: Paris, France, Sept. 28, 1934.

BARKIN, ELLEN: Bronx, NY, Apr. 16, 1954. Hunter College.

BARNES, CHRISTOPHER DANIEL: Portland, ME, Nov. 7, 1972.

BARR, JEAN-MARC: San Diego, CA, Sept. 1960.

BARRAULT, JEAN-LOUIS: Vesinet, France, Sept. 8, 1910.

BARRAULT, MARIE-CHRISTINE: Paris, France, Mar. 21, 1944.

BARREN, KEITH: Mexborough, England, Aug. 8, 1936. Sheffield Playhouse.

BARRETT, MAJEL (Hudec): Columbus, OH, Feb. 23, 1939. Western Reserve.

BARRIE, BARBARA: Chicago, IL, May 23, 1931.

BARRY, GENE (Eugene Klass): NYC, June 14, 1919.

BARRY, NEILL: NYC, Nov. 29, 1965.

BARRYMORE, DREW: Los Angeles, Feb. 22, 1975.

BARRYMORE, JOHN DREW: Beverly Hills, CA, June 4, 1932. St. John's Military Academy.

BARYSHNIKOV, MIKHAIL: Riga, Latvia, Jan. 27, 1948.

BASINGER, KIM: Athens, GA, Dec. 8, 1953. Neighborhood Playhouse.

BASSETT, ANGELA: NYC, Aug. 16, 1958.

BATEMAN, JASON: Rye, NY, Jan. 14, 1969.

BATEMAN, JUSTINE: Rye, NY, Feb. 19, 1966.

BATES, ALAN: Allestree, Derbyshire, England, Feb. 17, 1934. RADA.

BATES, JEANNE: San Francisco, CA, May 21, 1918. RADA.

BATES, KATHY: Memphis, TN, June 28, 1948. S. Methodist U.

BAUER, STEVEN (Steven Rocky Echevarria): Havana, Cuba, Dec. 2, 1956. U Miami.

BAXTER, KEITH: South Wales, England, Apr. 29, 1933. RADA.

BAXTER, MEREDITH: Los Angeles, June 21, 1947. Interlochen Academy.

BAYE, NATHALIE: Mainevile, France, July 6, 1948.

BEACH, ADAM: Winnipeg, Manitoba, Canada, Nov. 11, 1972.

BEACHAM, STEPHANIE: Casablanca, Morocco, Feb. 28, 1947.

BEALS, JENNIFER: Chicago, IL, Dec. 19, 1963.

BEAN, ORSON (Dallas Burrows): Burlington, VT, July 22, 1928.
BEAN, SEAN: Sheffield, Yorkshire, England, Apr. 17, 1958.
BEART, EMMANUELLE: Gassin, France, Aug. 14, 1965.
BEATTY, NED: Louisville, KY, July 6, 1937.
BEATTY, WARREN: Richmond, VA, Mar. 30, 1937.
BECK, JOHN: Chicago, IL, Jan. 28, 1943.
BECK, MICHAEL: Memphis, TN, Feb. 4, 1949. Millsap College.
BECKINSALE, KATE: England, July 26, 1974.
BEDELIA, BONNIE: NYC, Mar. 25, 1946. Hunter College.
BEGLEY, ED, JR.: NYC, Sept. 16, 1949.
BELAFONTE, HARRY: NYC, Mar. 1, 1927.
BEL GEDDES, BARBARA: NYC, Oct. 31, 1922.
BELL, TOM: Liverpool, England, 1932.
BELLER, KATHLEEN: NYC, Feb. 10, 1957.
BELLWOOD, PAMELA (King): Scarsdale, NY, June 26, 1951.
BELMONDO, JEAN PAUL: Paris, France, Apr. 9, 1933.
BELUSHI, JAMES: Chicago, IL, June 15, 1954.
BELZER, RICHARD: Bridgeport, CT, Aug. 4, 1944.
BENEDICT, DIRK (Niewoehner): White Sulphur Springs, MT, March 1, 1945. Whitman College.
BENEDICT, PAUL: Silver City, NM, Sept. 17, 1938.
BENIGNI, ROBERTO: Tuscany, Italy, Oct. 27, 1952.
BENING, ANNETTE: Topeka, KS, May 29, 1958. SF St. U.
BENJAMIN, RICHARD: NYC, May 22, 1938. Northwestern.
BENNENT, DAVID: Lausanne, Switzerland, Sept. 9, 1966.
BENNETT, ALAN: Leeds, England, May 9, 1934. Oxford.
BENNETT, BRUCE (Herman Brix): Tacoma, WA, May 19, 1909. U WA.
BENNETT, HYWEL: Garnant, So. Wales, Apr. 8, 1944.
BENSON, ROBBY: Dallas, TX, Jan. 21, 1957.
BENTLEY, WES: Jonesboro, AR, Sept. 4, 1978.
BERENGER, TOM: Chicago, IL, May 31, 1950. U MO.
BERENSON, MARISA: NYC, Feb. 15, 1947.
BERG, PETER: NYC, March 11, 1964. Malcalester College.
BERGEN, CANDICE: Los Angeles, May 9, 1946. U PA.
BERGEN, POLLY: Knoxville, TN, July 14, 1930. Compton, Jr. College.
BERGER, HELMUT: Salzburg, Austria, May 29, 1942.
BERGER, SENTA: Vienna, Austria, May 13, 1941. Vienna Sch. of Acting.
BERGER, WILLIAM: Austria, Jan. 20, 1928. Columbia.
BERGERAC, JACQUES: Biarritz, France, May 26, 1927. Paris U.
BERGIN, PATRICK: Dublin, Ireland, Feb. 4, 1951.
BERKLEY, ELIZABETH: Detroit, MI, July 28, 1972.
BERKOFF, STEVEN: London, England, Aug. 3, 1937.
BERLE, MILTON (Berlinger): NYC, July 12, 1908.
BERLIN, JEANNIE: Los Angeles, Nov. 1, 1949.
BERLINGER, WARREN: Brooklyn, NY, Aug. 31, 1937. Columbia.
BERNHARD, SANDRA: Flint, MI, June 6, 1955.
BERNSEN, CORBIN: Los Angeles, Sept. 7, 1954. UCLA.
BERRI, CLAUDE (Langmann): Paris, France, July 1, 1934.
BERRIDGE, ELIZABETH: Westchester, NY, May 2, 1962. Strasberg Inst.
BERRY, HALLE: Cleveland, OH, Aug. 14, 1968.
BERRY, KEN: Moline, IL, Nov. 3, 1933.
BERTINELLI, VALERIE: Wilmington, DE, Apr. 23, 1960.
BEST, JAMES: Corydon, IN, July 26, 1926.
BETTGER, LYLE: Philadelphia, PA, Feb. 13, 1915. AADA.
BEY, TURHAN: Vienna, Austria, Mar. 30, 1921.

BEYMER, RICHARD: Avoca, IA, Feb. 21, 1939.
BIALIK, MAYIM: San Diego, CA, Dec. 12, 1975.
BIEHN, MICHAEL: Anniston, AL, July 31, 1956.
BIGGERSTAFF, SEAN: Glasgow, Scotland, Mar. 15, 1983.
BIGGS, JASON: Pompton Plains, NJ, May 12, 1978.
BIKEL, THEODORE: Vienna, Austria, May 2, 1924. RADA.
BILLINGSLEY, PETER: NYC, Apr. 16, 1972.
BINOCHE, JULIETTE: Paris, France, Mar. 9, 1964.
BIRCH, THORA: Los Angeles, Mar. 11, 1982.
BIRKIN, JANE: London, England, Dec. 14, 1947
BIRNEY, DAVID: Washington, DC, Apr. 23, 1939. Dartmouth, UCLA.
BIRNEY, REED: Alexandria, VA, Sept. 11, 1954. Boston U.
BISHOP, JOEY (Joseph Abraham Gotllieb): Bronx, NY, Feb. 3, 1918.
BISHOP, JULIE (Jacqueline Wells): Denver, CO, Aug. 30, 1917. Westlake School.
BISSET, JACQUELINE: Waybridge, England, Sept. 13, 1944.
BLACK, KAREN (Ziegler): Park Ridge, IL, July 1, 1942. Northwestern.
BLACK, JACK: Edmonton, Alberta, Canada, Apr. 7, 1969.
BLACK, LUCAS: Danville, AL, Nov. 29, 1982.
BLACKMAN, HONOR: London, England, Aug. 22, 1926.
BLADES, RUBEN: Panama City, Panama, July 16, 1948. Harvard.
BLAIR, BETSY (Betsy Boger): NYC, Dec. 11, 1923.
BLAIR, JANET (Martha Jane Lafferty): Blair, PA, Apr. 23, 1921.
BLAIR, LINDA: Westport, CT, Jan. 22, 1959.
BLAIR, SELMA: Southfield, MI, June 23, 1972.
BLAKE, ROBERT (Michael Gubitosi): Nutley, NJ, Sept. 18, 1933.
BLAKELY, SUSAN: Frankfurt, Germany, Sept. 7, 1950. U TX.
BLAKLEY, RONEE: Stanley, ID, 1946. Stanford U.
BLANCHETT, CATE: Melbourne, Australia, May 14, 1969.
BLETHYN, BRENDA: Ramsgate, Kent, England, Feb. 20, 1946.
BLOOM, CLAIRE: London, England, Feb. 15, 1931. Badminton School.
BLOOM, VERNA: Lynn, MA, Aug. 7, 1939. Boston U.
BLOUNT, LISA: Fayettville, AK, July 1, 1957. U AK.
BLUM, MARK: Newark, NJ, May 14, 1950. U MN.
BLYTH, ANN: Mt. Kisco, NY, Aug. 16, 1928. New Waybum Dramatic School.
BOCHNER, HART: Toronto, Canada, Oct. 3, 1956. U San Diego.
BOCHNER, LLOYD: Toronto, Canada, July 29, 1924.
BOGOSIAN, ERIC: Woburn, MA, Apr. 24, 1953. Oberlin College.
BOHRINGER, RICHARD: Paris, France, Jan. 16, 1941.
BOLKAN, FLORINDA (Florinda Soares Bulcao): Ceara, Brazil, Feb. 15, 1941.
BOLOGNA, JOSEPH: Brooklyn, NY, Dec. 30, 1938. Brown.
BOND, DEREK: Glasgow, Scotland, Jan. 26, 1920. Askes School.
BONET, LISA: San Francisco, CA, Nov. 16, 1967.
BONHAM-CARTER, HELENA: London, England, May 26, 1966.
BOONE, PAT: Jacksonville, FL, June 1, 1934. Columbia.
BOOTHE, JAMES: Croydon, England, Dec. 19, 1930.
BOOTHE, POWERS: Snyder, TX, June 1, 1949. S. Methodist U.
BORGNINE, ERNEST (Borgnino): Hamden, CT, Jan. 24, 1917. Randall School.
BOSCO, PHILIP: Jersey City, NJ, Sept. 26, 1930. Catholic U.
BOSLEY, TOM: Chicago, IL, Oct. 1, 1927. DePaul U.
BOSTWICK, BARRY: San Mateo, CA, Feb. 24, 1945. NYU.
BOTTOMS, JOSEPH: Santa Barbara, CA, Aug. 30, 1954.
BOTTOMS, SAM: Santa Barbara, CA, Oct. 17, 1955.

Ned Beatty

David Bowie

Josh Brolin

Eleanor Bron

BOTTOMS, TIMOTHY: Santa Barbara, CA, Aug. 30, 1951.

BOULTING, INGRID: Transvaal, South Africa, 1947.

BOUTSIKARIS, DENNIS: Newark, NJ, Dec. 21, 1952. Catholic U.

BOWIE, DAVID (David Robert Jones): Brixton, South London, England, Jan. 8, 1947.

BOWKER, JUDI: Shawford, England, Apr. 6, 1954.

BOXLEITNER, BRUCE: Elgin, IL, May 12, 1950.

BOYLE, LARA FLYNN: Davenport, IA, Mar. 24, 1970.

BOYLE, PETER: Philadelphia, PA, Oct. 18, 1933. LaSalle College.

BRACCO, LORRAINE: Brooklyn, NY, 1955.

BRACKEN, EDDIE: NYC, Feb. 7, 1920. Professional Children's School.

BRAEDEN, ERIC (Hans Gudegast): Kiel, Germany, Apr. 3, 1942.

BRAGA, SONIA: Maringa, Brazil, June 8, 1950.

BRANAGH, KENNETH: Belfast, Northern Ireland, Dec. 10, 1960.

BRANDAUER, KLAUS MARIA: Altaussee, Austria, June 22, 1944.

BRANDIS, JONATHAN: CT, Apr. 13, 1976.

BRANDO, JOCELYN: San Francisco, Nov. 18, 1919. Lake Forest College, AADA.

BRANDO, MARLON: Omaha, NB, Apr. 3, 1924. New School.

BRANDON, CLARK: NYC, Dec. 13, 1958.

BRANDON, MICHAEL (Feldman): Brooklyn, NY, Apr. 20, 1945.

BRANTLEY, BETSY: Rutherfordton, NC, Sept. 20, 1955. London Central Sch. of Drama.

BRATT, BENJAMIN: San Francisco, CA, Dec. 16, 1963.

BRENNAN, EILEEN: Los Angeles, Sept. 3, 1935. AADA.

BRENNEMAN, AMY: Glastonbury, CT, June 22, 1964.

BRIALY, JEAN-CLAUDE: Aumale, Algeria, 1933. Strasbourg Cons.

BRIDGES, BEAU: Los Angeles, Dec. 9, 1941. UCLA.

BRIDGES, JEFF: Los Angeles, Dec. 4, 1949.

BRIMLEY, WILFORD: Salt Lake City, UT, Sept. 27, 1934.

BRINKLEY, CHRISTIE: Malibu, CA, Feb. 2, 1954.

BRITT, MAY (Maybritt Wilkins): Sweden, Mar. 22, 1936.

BRITTANY, MORGAN (Suzanne Cupito): Los Angeles, Dec. 5, 1950.

BRITTON, TONY: Birmingham, England, June 9, 1924.

BROADBENT, JIM: Lincoln, England, May 24, 1959.

BRODERICK, MATTHEW: NYC, Mar. 21, 1962.

BRODY, ADRIEN: NYC, Dec. 23, 1976.

BROLIN, JAMES: Los Angeles, July 18, 1940. UCLA.

BROLIN, JOSH: Los Angeles, Feb. 12, 1968.

BROMFIELD, JOHN (Farron Bromfield): South Bend, IN, June 11, 1922. St. Mary's College.

BRON, ELEANOR: Stanmore, England, Mar. 14, 1934.

BRONSON, CHARLES (Buchinsky): Ehrenfield, PA, Nov. 3, 1920.

BROOKES, JACQUELINE: Montclair, NJ, July 24, 1930. RADA.

BROOKS, ALBERT (Einstein): Los Angeles, July 22, 1947.

BROOKS, MEL (Melvyn Kaminski): Brooklyn, NY, June 28, 1926.

BROSNAN, PIERCE: County Meath, Ireland, May 16, 1952.

BROWN, BLAIR: Washington, DC, Apr. 23, 1947. Pine Manor.

BROWN, BRYAN: Panania, Australia, June 23, 1947.

BROWN, GARY (Christian Brando): Hollywood, CA, 1958.

BROWN, GEORGE STANFORD: Havana, Cuba, June 24, 1943. AMDA.

BROWN, JAMES: Desdemona, TX, Mar. 22, 1920. Baylor U.

BROWN, JIM: St. Simons Island, NY, Feb. 17, 1935. Syracuse U.

BROWNE, LESLIE: NYC, 1958.

BROWNE, ROSCOE LEE: Woodbury, NJ, May 2, 1925.

BUCHHOLZ, HORST: Berlin, Germany, Dec. 4, 1933. Ludwig Dramatic School.

BUCKLEY, BETTY: Big Spring, TX, July 3, 1947. TX CU.

BUJOLD, GENEVIEVE: Montreal, Canada, July 1, 1942.

BULLOCK, SANDRA: Arlington, VA, July 26, 1964.

BURGHOFF, GARY: Bristol, CT, May 24, 1943.

BURGI, RICHARD: Montclair, NJ, July 30, 1958.

BURKE, PAUL: New Orleans, LA, July 21, 1926. Pasadena Playhouse.

BURNETT, CAROL: San Antonio, TX, Apr. 26, 1933. UCLA.

BURNS, CATHERINE: NYC, Sept. 25, 1945. AADA.

BURNS, EDWARD: Valley Stream, NY, Jan. 28, 1969.

BURROWS, DARREN E.: Winfield, KS, Sept. 12, 1966.

BURROWS, SAFFRON: London, England, 1973.

BURSTYN, ELLEN (Edna Rae Gillhooly): Detroit, MI, Dec. 7, 1932.

BURTON, LeVAR: Los Angeles, Feb. 16, 1958. UCLA.

BUSCEMI, STEVE: Brooklyn, NY, Dec. 13, 1957.

BUSEY, GARY: Goose Creek, TX, June 29, 1944.

BUSFIELD, TIMOTHY: Lansing, MI, June 12, 1957. E. Tenn. St. U.

BUTTONS, RED (Aaron Chwatt): NYC, Feb. 5, 1919.

BUZZI, RUTH: Westerly, RI, July 24, 1936. Pasadena Playhouse.

BYGRAVES, MAX: London, England, Oct. 16, 1922. St. Joseph's School.

BYRNE, DAVID: Dumbarton, Scotland, May 14, 1952.

BYRNE, GABRIEL: Dublin, Ireland, May 12, 1950.

BYRNES, EDD: NYC, July 30, 1933.

Dean Cain   Michael Caine   Neve Campbell   Jim Carrey

CAAN, JAMES: Bronx, NY, Mar. 26,1939.

CAESAR, SID: Yonkers, NY, Sept. 8, 1922.

CAGE, NICOLAS (Coppola): Long Beach, CA, Jan.7, 1964.

CAIN, DEAN (Dean Tanaka): Mt. Clemens, MI, July 31, 1966.

CAINE, MICHAEL (Maurice Micklewhite): London, England, Mar. 14, 1933.

CAINE, SHAKIRA (Baksh): Guyana, Feb. 23, 1947. Indian Trust College.

CALLAN, MICHAEL (Martin Calinieff): Philadelphia, PA, Nov. 22, 1935.

CALLOW, SIMON: London, England, June 15, 1949. Queens U.

CALVERT, PHYLLIS: London, England, Feb. 18, 1917. Margaret Morris School.

CAMERON, KIRK: Panorama City, CA, Oct. 12, 1970.

CAMP, COLLEEN: San Francisco, CA, 1953.

CAMPBELL, BILL: Chicago, IL, July 7, 1959.

CAMPBELL, GLEN: Delight, AR, Apr. 22, 1935.

CAMPBELL, NEVE: Guelph, Ontario, Canada, Oct. 3, 1973.

CAMPBELL, TISHA: Oklahoma City, OK, Oct. 13, 1968.

CANALE, GIANNA MARIA: Reggio Calabria, Italy, Sept. 12, 1927.

CANNON, DYAN (Samille Diane Friesen): Tacoma, WA, Jan. 4, 1937.

CAPERS, VIRGINIA: Sumter, SC, Sept. 25, 1925. Juilliard.

CAPSHAW, KATE: Ft. Worth, TX, Nov. 3, 1953. U MO.

CARA, IRENE: NYC, Mar. 18, 1958.

CARDINALE, CLAUDIA: Tunis, N. Africa. Apr. 15, 1939. College Paul Cambon.

CAREY, HARRY, JR.: Saugus, CA, May 16, 1921. Black Fox Military Academy.

CAREY, PHILIP: Hackensack, NJ, July 15, 1925. U Miami.

CARIOU, LEN: Winnipeg, Manitoba, Canada, Sept. 30, 1939.

CARLIN, GEORGE: NYC, May 12, 1938.

CARLYLE, ROBERT: Glasgow, Scotland, Apr. 14, 1961.

CARMEN, JULIE: Mt. Vernon, NY, Apr. 4, 1954.

CARMICHAEL, IAN: Hull, England, June 18, 1920. Scarborough College.

CARNE, JUDY (Joyce Botterill): Northampton, England, 1939. Bush-Davis Theatre School.

CARNEY, ART: Mt. Vernon, NY, Nov. 4, 1918.

CARON, LESLIE: Paris, France, July 1, 1931. National Conservatory, Paris.

CARPENTER, CARLETON: Bennington, VT, July 10, 1926. Northwestern.

CARRADINE, DAVID: Hollywood, CA, Dec. 8, 1936. SF St. U.

CARRADINE, KEITH: San Mateo, CA, Aug. 8, 1950. CO St. U.

CARRADINE, ROBERT: San Mateo, CA, Mar. 24, 1954.

CARREL, DANY: Tourane, Indochina, Sept. 20, 1936. Marseilles Cons.

CARRERA, BARBARA: Managua, Nicaragua, Dec. 31, 1945.

CARRERE, TIA (Althea Janairo): Honolulu, HI, Jan. 2, 1965.

CARREY, JIM: Jacksons Point, Ontario, Canada, Jan. 17, 1962.

CARRIERE, MATHIEU: Hannover, West Germany, Aug. 2, 1950.

CARROLL, DIAHANN (Johnson): NYC, July 17, 1935. NYU.

CARROLL, PAT: Shreveport, LA, May 5, 1927. Catholic U.

CARSON, JOHN DAVID: California, Mar. 6, 1952. Valley College.

CARSON, JOHNNY: Corning, IA, Oct. 23, 1925. U NE.

CARSTEN, PETER (Ransenthaler): Weissenberg, Bavaria, Apr. 30, 1929. Munich Akademie.

CARTER, NELL: Birmingham, AL, Sept. 13, 1948.

CARTLIDGE, KATRIN: London, England, 1961.

CARTWRIGHT, VERONICA: Bristol, England, Apr 20, 1949.

CARUSO, DAVID: Forest Hills, NY, Jan. 7, 1956.

CARVEY, DANA: Missoula, MT, Apr. 2, 1955. SF St. College.

CASELLA, MAX: Washington D.C, June 6, 1967.

CASEY, BERNIE: Wyco, WV, June 8, 1939.

CASSAVETES, NICK: NYC, 1959, Syracuse U, AADA.

CASSEL, JEAN-PIERRE: Paris, France, Oct. 27, 1932.

CASSEL, SEYMOUR: Detroit, MI, Jan. 22, 1935.

CASSIDY, DAVID: NYC, Apr. 12, 1950.

CASSIDY, JOANNA: Camden, NJ, Aug. 2, 1944. Syracuse U.

CASSIDY, PATRICK: Los Angeles, Jan. 4, 1961.

CATES, PHOEBE: NYC, July 16, 1962.

CATTRALL, KIM: Liverpool, England, Aug. 21, 1956. AADA.

CAULFIELD, MAXWELL: Glasgow, Scotland, Nov. 23, 1959.

CAVANI, LILIANA: Bologna, Italy, Jan. 12, 1937. U Bologna.

CAVETT, DICK: Gibbon, NE, Nov. 19, 1936.

CAVIEZEL, JIM: Mt. Vernon, WA, Sept. 26, 1968.

CHAKIRIS, GEORGE: Norwood, OH, Sept. 16, 1933.

CHAMBERLAIN, RICHARD: Beverly Hills, CA, March 31, 1935. Pomona.

CHAMPION, MARGE (Marjorie Belcher): Los Angeles, Sept. 2, 1923.

CHAN, JACKIE: Hong Kong, China, Apr. 7, 1954

CHANNING, CAROL: Seattle, WA, Jan. 31, 1921. Bennington.

CHANNING, STOCKARD (Susan Stockard): NYC, Feb. 13, 1944. Radcliffe.

CHAPIN, MILES: NYC, Dec. 6, 1954. HB Studio.

CHAPLIN, BEN: London, England, July 31, 1970.

CHAPLIN, GERALDINE: Santa Monica, CA, July 31, 1944. Royal Ballet.

CHAPLIN, SYDNEY: Los Angeles, Mar. 31, 1926. Lawrenceville.

CHARISSE, CYD (Tula Ellice Finklea): Amarillo, TX, Mar. 3, 1922. Hollywood Professional School.

CHARLES, JOSH: Baltimore, MD, Sept. 15, 1971.

CHARLES, WALTER: East Strousburg, PA, Apr. 4, 1945. Boston U.

CHASE, CHEVY (Cornelius Crane Chase): NYC, Oct. 8, 1943.

CHAVES, RICHARD: Jacksonville, FL, Oct. 9, 1951. Occidental College.

CHAYKIN, MAURY: Canada, July 27, 1954.

CHEADLE, DON: Kansas City, MO, Nov. 29, 1964.

CHEN, JOAN (Chen Chung): Shanghai, China, Apr. 26, 1961. Cal. St. U.

CHER (Cherilyn Sarkisian): El Centro, CA, May 20, 1946.

CHILES, LOIS: Alice, TX, Apr. 15, 1947.

CHONG, RAE DAWN: Vancouver, Canada, Feb. 28, 1962.

CHONG, THOMAS: Edmonton, Alberta, Canada, May 24, 1938.

CHRISTIAN, LINDA (Blanca Rosa Welter): Tampico, Mexico, Nov. 13, 1923.

CHRISTIE, JULIE: Chukua, Assam, India, Apr. 14, 1941.

CHRISTOPHER, DENNIS (Carrelli): Philadelphia, PA, Dec. 2, 1955. Temple U.

CHRISTOPHER, JORDAN: Youngstown, OH, Oct. 23, 1940. Kent State.

CILENTO, DIANE: Queensland, Australia, Oct. 5, 1933. AADA.

CLAPTON, ERIC: London, England, Mar. 30, 1945.

CLARK, CANDY: Norman, OK, June 20, 1947.

CLARK, DICK: Mt. Vernon, NY, Nov. 30, 1929. Syracuse U.

CLARK, MATT: Washington, DC, Nov. 25, 1936.

CLARK, PETULA: Epsom, England, Nov. 15, 1932.

CLARK, SUSAN: Sarnid, Ont., Canada, Mar. 8, 1943. RADA.

CLAY, ANDREW DICE (Andrew Silverstein): Brooklyn, NY, Sept. 29, 1957. Kingsborough College.

CLAYBURGH, JILL: NYC, Apr. 30, 1944. Sarah Lawrence.

CLEESE, JOHN: Weston-Super-Mare, England, Oct. 27, 1939. Cambridge.

CLOONEY, ROSEMARY: Maysville, KY, May 23, 1928.

CLOSE, GLENN: Greenwich, CT, Mar. 19, 1947. William & Mary College.

COBURN, JAMES: Laurel, NB, Aug. 31, 1928. LACC.

CODY, KATHLEEN: Bronx, NY, Oct. 30, 1953.

COFFEY, SCOTT: HI, May 1, 1967.

COLE, GEORGE: London, England, Apr. 22, 1925.

COLEMAN, GARY: Zion, IL, Feb. 8, 1968.

COLEMAN, DABNEY: Austin, TX, Jan. 3, 1932.

COLEMAN, JACK: Easton, PA, Feb. 21, 1958. Duke U.

COLIN, MARGARET: NYC, May 26, 1957.

COLLET, CHRISTOPHER: NYC, Mar. 13, 1968. Strasberg Inst.

COLLETTE, TONI: Sydney, Australia, Nov. 1, 1972.

COLLINS, JOAN: London, May 21, 1933. Francis Holland School.

COLLINS, PAULINE: Devon, England, Sept. 3, 1940.

COLLINS, STEPHEN: Des Moines, IA, Oct. 1, 1947. Amherst.

Jim Caviezel   Billy Connolly

COLON, MIRIAM: Ponce, PR., 1945. U PR.

COLTRANE, ROBBIE: Ruthergien, Scotland, Mar. 30, 1950.

COMBS, SEAN "Puffy," "P. Diddy": NYC, Nov. 4, 1969.

COMER, ANJANETTE: Dawson, TX, Aug. 7, 1942. Baylor, Tex. U.

CONANT, OLIVER: NYC, Nov. 15, 1955. Dalton.

CONAWAY, JEFF: NYC, Oct. 5, 1950. NYU.

CONNELLY, JENNIFER: NYC, Dec. 12, 1970

CONNERY, SEAN: Edinburgh, Scotland, Aug. 25, 1930.

CONNERY, JASON: London, England, Jan. 11, 1963.

CONNICK, HARRY, JR.: New Orleans, LA, Sept. 11, 1967.

CONNOLLY, BILLY: Glasgow, Scotland, Nov. 24, 1942.

CONNORS, MIKE (Krekor Ohanian): Fresno, CA, Aug. 15, 1925. UCLA.

CONRAD, ROBERT (Conrad Robert Falk): Chicago, IL, Mar. 1, 1935. Northwestern.

CONSTANTINE, MICHAEL: Reading, PA, May 22, 1927.

CONTI, TOM: Paisley, Scotland, Nov. 22, 1941.

CONVERSE, FRANK: St. Louis, MO, May 22, 1938. Carnegie Tech.

CONWAY, GARY: Boston, MA, Feb. 4, 1936.

CONWAY, KEVIN: NYC, May 29, 1942.

CONWAY, TIM (Thomas Daniel): Willoughby, OH, Dec. 15, 1933. Bowling Green St.

COOGAN, KEITH (Keith Mitchell Franklin): Palm Springs, CA, Jan. 13, 1970.

COOK, RACHAEL LEIGH: Minneapolis, MN, Oct. 4, 1979.

COOPER, BEN: Hartford, CT, Sept. 30, 1930. Columbia.

COOPER, CHRIS: Kansas City, MO, July 9, 1951. U MO.

COOPER, JACKIE: Los Angeles, Sept. 15, 1921.

COPELAND, JOAN: NYC, June 1, 1922. Brooklyn College, RADA.

CORBETT, GRETCHEN: Portland, OR, Aug. 13, 1947. Carnegie Tech.

CORBIN, BARRY: Dawson County, TX, Oct. 16, 1940. Texas Tech. U.

CORCORAN, DONNA: Quincy, MA, Sept. 29, 1942.

CORD, ALEX (Viespi): Floral Park, NY, Aug. 3, 1931. NYU, Actors Studio.

CORDAY, MARA (Marilyn Watts): Santa Monica, CA, Jan. 3, 1932.

COREY, JEFF: NYC, Aug. 10, 1914. Fagin School.

CORNTHWAITE, ROBERT: St. Helens, OR, Apr. 28, 1917. USC.

CORRI, ADRIENNE: Glasgow, Scotland, Nov. 13, 1933. RADA.

CORT, BUD (Walter Edward Cox): New Rochelle, NY, Mar. 29, 1950. NYU.

| Billy Crystal | John Cusack | Joan Cusack | Hope Davis |

CORTESA, VALENTINA: Milan, Italy, Jan. 1, 1924.

COSBY, BILL: Philadelphia, PA, July 12, 1937. Temple U.

COSTER, NICOLAS: London, England, Dec. 3, 1934. Neighborhood Playhouse.

COSTNER, KEVIN: Lynwood, CA, Jan. 18, 1955. Cal St. U.

COURTENAY, TOM: Hull, England, Feb. 25, 1937. RADA.

COURTLAND, JEROME: Knoxville, TN, Dec. 27, 1926.

COX, BRIAN: Dundee, Scotland, June 1, 1946. LAMDA.

COX, COURTENEY: Birmingham, AL, June 15, 1964.

COX, RONNY: Cloudcroft, NM, Aug. 23, 1938.

COYOTE, PETER (Cohon)**:** NYC, Oct. 10, 1941.

CRAIG, MICHAEL: Poona, India, Jan. 27, 1929.

CRAIN, JEANNE: Barstow, CA, May 25, 1925.

CRAVEN, GEMMA: Dublin, Ireland, June 1, 1950.

CRAWFORD, MICHAEL (Dumbel-Smith)**:** Salisbury, England, Jan. 19, 1942.

CREMER, BRUNO: Paris, France, 1929.

CRENNA, RICHARD: Los Angeles, Nov. 30, 1926. USC.

CRISTAL, LINDA (Victoria Moya)**:** Buenos Aires, Argentina, Feb. 25, 1934.

CROMWELL, JAMES: Los Angeles, CA, Jan. 27, 1940.

CRONYN, HUME (Blake)**:** Ontario, Canada, July 18, 1911.

CROSBY, DENISE: Hollywood, CA, Nov. 24, 1957.

CROSBY, HARRY: Los Angeles, Aug. 8, 1958.

CROSBY, MARY FRANCES: Los Angeles, Sept. 14, 1959.

CROSS, BEN: London, England, Dec. 16, 1947. RADA.

CROSS, MURPHY (Mary Jane)**:** Laurelton, MD, June 22, 1950.

CROUSE, LINDSAY: NYC, May 12, 1948. Radcliffe.

CROWE, RUSSELL: New Zealand, Apr. 7, 1964.

CROWLEY, PAT: Olyphant, PA, Sept. 17, 1932.

CRUDUP, BILLY: Manhasset, NY, July 8, 1968. UNC/Chapel Hill.

CRUISE, TOM (T. C. Mapother, IV)**:** July 3, 1962, Syracuse, NY.

CRUZ, PENELOPE (P.C. Sanchez)**:** Madrid, Spain, Apr. 28, 1974.

CRYER, JON: NYC, Apr. 16, 1965, RADA.

CRYSTAL, BILLY: Long Beach, NY, Mar. 14, 1947. Marshall U.

CULKIN, KIERAN: NYC, Sept. 30, 1982.

CULKIN, MACAULAY: NYC, Aug. 26, 1980.

CULLUM, JOHN: Knoxville, TN, Mar. 2, 1930. U TN.

CULLUM, JOHN DAVID: NYC, Mar. 1, 1966.

CULP, ROBERT: Oakland, CA, Aug. 16, 1930. U WA.

CUMMING, ALAN: Perthshire, Scotland, Jan. 27, 1965.

CUMMINGS, CONSTANCE: Seattle, WA, May 15, 1910.

CUMMINGS, QUINN: Hollywood, CA, Aug. 13, 1967.

CUMMINS, PEGGY: Prestatyn, North Wales, Dec. 18, 1926. Alexandra School.

CURRY, TIM: Cheshire, England, Apr. 19, 1946. Birmingham U.

CURTIN, JANE: Cambridge, MA, Sept. 6, 1947.

CURTIS, JAMIE LEE: Los Angeles, CA, Nov. 22, 1958.

CURTIS, KEENE: Salt Lake City, UT, Feb. 15, 1925. U UT.

CURTIS, TONY (Bernard Schwartz)**:** NYC, June 3, 1924.

CUSACK, JOAN: Evanston, IL, Oct. 11, 1962.

CUSACK, JOHN: Chicago, IL, June 28, 1966.

CUSACK, SINEAD: Dalkey, Ireland, Feb. 18, 1948.

DAFOE, WILLEM: Appleton, WI, July 22, 1955.

DAHL, ARLENE: Minneapolis, Aug. 11, 1928. U MN.

DALE, JIM: Rothwell, England, Aug. 15, 1935.

DALLESANDRO, JOE: Pensacola, FL, Dec. 31, 1948.

DALTON, TIMOTHY: Colwyn Bay, Wales, Mar. 21, 1946. RADA.

DALTREY, ROGER: London, England, Mar. 1, 1944.

DALY, TIM: NYC, Mar. 1, 1956. Bennington College.

DALY, TYNE: Madison, WI, Feb. 21, 1947. AMDA.

DAMON, MATT: Cambridge, MA, Oct. 8, 1970.

DAMONE, VIC (Vito Farinola)**:** Brooklyn, NY, June 12, 1928.

DANCE, CHARLES: Plymouth, England, Oct. 10, 1946.

DANES, CLAIRE: NYC, Apr. 12, 1979.

D'ANGELO, BEVERLY: Columbus, OH, Nov. 15, 1953.

DANGERFIELD, RODNEY (Jacob Cohen)**:** Babylon, NY, Nov. 22, 1921.

DANIELS, JEFF: Athens, GA, Feb. 19, 1955. E MI St.

DANIELS, WILLIAM: Brooklyn, NY, Mar. 31, 1927. Northwestern.

DANNER, BLYTHE: Philadelphia, PA, Feb. 3, 1944. Bard College.

DANNING, SYBIL (Sybille Johanna Danninger)**:** Vienna, Austria, May 4, 1949.

DANSON, TED: San Diego, CA, Dec. 29, 1947. Stanford, Carnegie Tech.

DANTE, MICHAEL (Ralph Vitti)**:** Stamford, CT, 1935. U Miami.

DANZA, TONY: Brooklyn, NY, Apr. 21, 1951. U Dubuque.

D'ARBANVILLE-QUINN, PATTI: NYC, 1951.

DARBY, KIM (Deborah Zerby)**:** North Hollywood, CA, July 8, 1948.

DARCEL, DENISE (Denise Billecard)**:** Paris, France, Sept. 8, 1925. U Dijon.

DARREN, JAMES: Philadelphia, PA, June 8, 1936. Stella Adler School.

Catherine Deneuve

Gérard Depardieu

Johnny Depp

Angie Dickinson

DARRIEUX, DANIELLE: Bordeaux, France, May 1, 1917. Lycee LaTour.

DAVENPORT, NIGEL: Cambridge, England, May 23, 1928. Trinity College.

DAVID, KEITH: NYC, June 4, 1954. Juilliard.

DAVIDOVICH, LOLITA: Toronto, Ontario, Canada, July 15, 1961.

DAVIDSON, JAYE: Riverside, CA, 1968.

DAVIDSON, JOHN: Pittsburgh, PA, Dec. 13, 1941. Denison U.

DAVIES, JEREMY (Boring): Rockford, IA, Oct. 28, 1969.

DAVIS, CLIFTON: Chicago, IL, Oct. 4, 1945. Oakwood College.

DAVIS, GEENA: Wareham, MA, Jan. 21, 1957.

DAVIS, HOPE: Tenafly, NJ, 1967.

DAVIS, JUDY: Perth, Australia, Apr. 23, 1955.

DAVIS, MAC: Lubbock, TX, Jan. 21,1942.

DAVIS, NANCY (Anne Frances Robbins): NYC, July 6, 1921. Smith College.

DAVIS, OSSIE: Cogdell, GA, Dec. 18, 1917. Howard U.

DAVIS, SAMMI: Kidderminster, Worcestershire, England, June 21, 1964.

DAVISON, BRUCE: Philadelphia, PA, June 28, 1946.

DAWBER, PAM: Detroit, MI, Oct. 18, 1954.

DAY, DORIS (Doris Kappelhoff): Cincinnati, Apr. 3, 1924.

DAY, LARAINE (Johnson): Roosevelt, UT, Oct. 13, 1917.

DAY LEWIS, DANIEL: London, England, Apr. 29, 1957. Bristol Old Vic.

DAYAN, ASSI: Israel, Nov. 23, 1945. U Jerusalem.

DEAKINS, LUCY: NYC, 1971.

DEAN, JIMMY: Plainview, TX, Aug. 10, 1928.

DEAN, LOREN: Las Vegas, NV, July 31, 1969.

DeCARLO, YVONNE (Peggy Yvonne Middleton): Vancouver, BC, Canada, Sept. 1, 1922. Vancouver School of Drama.

DEE, FRANCES: Los Angeles, Nov. 26, 1907. Chicago U.

DEE, JOEY (Joseph Di Nicola): Passaic, NJ, June 11, 1940. Patterson State College.

DEE, RUBY: Cleveland, OH, Oct. 27, 1924. Hunter College.

DEE, SANDRA (Alexandra Zuck): Bayonne, NJ, Apr. 23, 1942.

DeGENERES, ELLEN: New Orleans, LA, Jan. 26, 1958.

DeHAVEN, GLORIA: Los Angeles, July 23, 1923.

DeHAVILLAND, OLIVIA: Tokyo, Japan, July 1, 1916. Notre Dame Convent School.

DELAIR, SUZY (Suzanne Delaire): Paris, France, Dec. 31, 1916.

DELANY, DANA: NYC, March 13, 1956. Wesleyan U.

DELPY, JULIE: Paris, France, Dec, 21, 1969.

DELON, ALAIN: Sceaux, France, Nov. 8, 1935.

DELORME, DANIELE: Paris, France, Oct. 9, 1926. Sorbonne.

DEL TORO, BENICIO: Santurce, Puerto Rico, Feb. 19, 1967.

DeLUISE, DOM: Brooklyn, NY, Aug. 1, 1933. Tufts College.

DeLUISE, PETER: NYC, Nov. 6, 1966.

DEMONGEOT, MYLENE: Nice, France, Sept. 29, 1938.

DeMORNAY, REBECCA: Los Angeles, Aug. 29, 1962. Strasberg Inst.

DEMPSEY, PATRICK: Lewiston, ME, Jan. 13, 1966.

DeMUNN, JEFFREY: Buffalo, NY, Apr. 25, 1947. Union College.

DENCH, JUDI: York, England, Dec. 9, 1934.

DENEUVE, CATHERINE: Paris, France, Oct. 22, 1943.

De NIRO, ROBERT: NYC, Aug. 17, 1943. Stella Adler.

DENNEHY, BRIAN: Bridgeport, CT, Jul. 9, 1938. Columbia.

DENVER, BOB: New Rochelle, NY, Jan. 9, 1935.

DEPARDIEU, GERARD: Chateauroux, France, Dec. 27, 1948.

DEPP, JOHNNY: Owensboro, KY, June 9, 1963.

DEREK, BO (Mary Cathleen Collins): Long Beach, CA, Nov. 20, 1956.

DERN, BRUCE: Chicago, IL, June 4, 1936. UPA.

DERN, LAURA: Los Angeles, Feb. 10, 1967.

DeSALVO, ANNE: Philadelphia, PA, Apr. 3, 1949.

DEVANE, WILLIAM: Albany, NY, Sept. 5, 1939.

DeVITO, DANNY: Asbury Park, NJ, Nov. 17, 1944.

DEY, SUSAN: Pekin, IL, Dec. 10, 1953.

DeYOUNG, CLIFF: Los Angeles, Feb. 12, 1945. Cal. St. U.

DIAMOND, NEIL: NYC, Jan. 24, 1941. NYU.

DIAZ, CAMERON: Long Beach, CA, Aug. 30, 1972.

DiCAPRIO, LEONARDO: Hollywood, CA, Nov.11, 1974.

DICKINSON, ANGIE (Angeline Brown): Kulm, ND, Sept. 30, 1932. Glendale College.

DIESEL, VIN: NYC, July 18, 1967.

DIGGS, TAYE (Scott Diggs): Rochester, NY, 1972.

DILLER, PHYLLIS (Driver): Lima, OH, July 17, 1917. Bluffton College.

DILLMAN, BRADFORD: San Francisco, CA, Apr. 14, 1930. Yale.

DILLON, KEVIN: Mamaroneck, NY, Aug. 19, 1965.

DILLON, MATT: Larchmont, NY, Feb. 18, 1964. AADA.

DILLON, MELINDA: Hope, AR, Oct. 13, 1939. Goodman Theatre School.

DIXON, DONNA: Alexandria, VA, July 20, 1957.

DOBSON, KEVIN: NYC, Mar. 18, 1944.

DOBSON, TAMARA: Baltimore, MD, May 14, 1947. MD Inst. of Art.

DOHERTY, SHANNEN: Memphis, TN, Apr. 12, 1971.

DOLAN, MICHAEL: Oklahoma City, OK, June 21, 1965.

DONAT, PETER: Nova Scotia, Canada, Jan. 20, 1928. Yale.

DONNELLY, DONAL: Bradford, England, July 6, 1931.

D'ONOFRIO, VINCENT: Brooklyn, NY, June 30, 1959.

DONOHOE, AMANDA: London, England, June 29 1962.

DONOVAN, MARTIN: Reseda, CA, Aug. 19, 1957.

DONOVAN, TATE: NYC, Sept. 25, 1963.

DOOHAN, JAMES: Vancouver, BC, Mar. 3, 1920. Neighborhood Playhouse.

DOOLEY, PAUL: Parkersburg, WV, Feb. 22, 1928. U WV.

DORFF, STEPHEN: CA, July 29, 1973.

DOUG, DOUG E. (Douglas Bourne): Brooklyn, NY, Jan. 7, 1970.

DOUGLAS, DONNA (Dorothy Bourgeois): Baywood, LA, Sept. 26, 1935.

DOUGLAS, ILLEANA: MA, July 25, 1965.

DOUGLAS, KIRK (Issur Danielovitch): Amsterdam, NY, Dec. 9, 1916. St. Lawrence U.

DOUGLAS, MICHAEL: New Brunswick, NJ, Sept. 25, 1944. U CA.

DOUGLASS, ROBYN: Sendai, Japan, June 21, 1953. UC Davis.

DOURIF, BRAD: Huntington, WV, Mar. 18, 1950. Marshall U.

DOWN, LESLEY-ANN: London, England, Mar. 17, 1954.

DOWNEY, ROBERT, JR.: NYC, Apr. 4, 1965.

DRAKE, BETSY: Paris, France, Sept. 11, 1923.

DRESCHER, FRAN: Queens, NY, Sept. 30, 1957.

DREW, ELLEN (formerly Terry Ray): Kansas City, MO, Nov. 23, 1915.

DREYFUSS, RICHARD: Brooklyn, NY, Oct. 19, 1947.

DRILLINGER, BRIAN: Brooklyn, NY, June 27, 1960. SUNY/Purchase.

DRIVER, MINNIE (Amelia Driver): London, England, Jan. 31, 1971.

DUCHOVNY, DAVID: NYC, Aug. 7, 1960. Yale.

DUDIKOFF, MICHAEL: Torrance, CA, Oct. 8, 1954.

DUGAN, DENNIS: Wheaton, IL, Sept. 5, 1946.

DUKAKIS, OLYMPIA: Lowell, MA, June 20, 1931.

DUKE, BILL: Poughkeepsie, NY, Feb. 26, 1943. NYU.

DUKE, PATTY (Anna Marie): NYC, Dec. 14, 1946.

DULLEA, KEIR: Cleveland, NJ, May 30, 1936. SF St. College.

DUNAWAY, FAYE: Bascom, FL, Jan. 14, 1941, Fla. U.

DUNCAN, SANDY: Henderson, TX, Feb. 20, 1946. Len Morris College.

DUNNE, GRIFFIN: NYC, June 8, 1955. Neighborhood Playhouse.

DUNST, KIRSTEN: Point Pleasant, NJ, Apr. 30, 1982.

DUPEREY, ANNY: Paris, France, 1947.

DURBIN, DEANNA (Edna): Winnipeg, Manitoba, Canada, Dec. 4, 1921.

DURNING, CHARLES: Highland Falls, NY, Feb. 28, 1923. NYU.

DUSHKU, ELIZA: Boston, MA, Dec. 30, 1980.

DUSSOLLIER, ANDRE: Annecy, France, Feb. 17, 1946.

DUTTON, CHARLES: Baltimore, MD, Jan. 30, 1951. Yale.

DUVALL, ROBERT: San Diego, CA, Jan. 5, 1931. Principia College.

DUVALL, SHELLEY: Houston, TX, July 7, 1949.

DYSART, RICHARD: Brighton, ME, Mar. 30, 1929.

DZUNDZA, GEORGE: Rosenheim, Germany, July 19, 1945.

EASTON, ROBERT: Milwaukee, WI, Nov. 23, 1930. U TX.

EASTWOOD, CLINT: San Francisco, CA, May 31, 1930. LACC.

EATON, SHIRLEY: London, England, 1937. Aida Foster School.

EBSEN, BUDDY (Christian, Jr.): Belleville, IL, Apr. 2, 1910. U FL.

ECKEMYR, AGNETA: Karlsborg, Sweden, July 2. Actors Studio.

EDELMAN, GREGG: Chicago, IL, Sept. 12, 1958. Northwestern.

EDEN, BARBARA (Huffman): Tucson, AZ, Aug. 23, 1934.

EDWARDS, ANTHONY: Santa Barbara, CA, July 19, 1962. RADA.

EDWARDS, LUKE: Nevada City, CA, Mar. 24, 1980.

EGGAR, SAMANTHA: London, England, Mar. 5, 1939.

EICHHORN, LISA: Reading, PA, Feb. 4, 1952. Queens Ont. U, RADA.

EIKENBERRY, JILL: New Haven, CT, Jan. 21, 1947.

EILBER, JANET: Detroit, MI, July 27, 1951. Juilliard.

EKBERG, ANITA: Malmo, Sweden, Sept. 29, 1931.

EKLAND, BRITT: Stockholm, Sweden, Oct. 6, 1942.

ELDARD, RON: Long Island, NY, Feb. 20, 1965.

ELFMAN, JENNA (Jennifer Mary Batula): Los Angeles, Sept. 30, 1971.

ELIZONDO, HECTOR: NYC, Dec. 22, 1936.

ELLIOTT, ALISON: San Francisco, CA, 1969.

ELLIOTT, CHRIS: NYC, May 31, 1960.

ELLIOTT, PATRICIA: Gunnison, CO, July 21, 1942. U CO.

ELLIOTT, SAM: Sacramento, CA, Aug. 9, 1944. U OR.

ELWES, CARY: London, England, Oct. 26, 1962.

ELY, RON (Ronald Pierce): Hereford, TX, June 21, 1938.

EMBRY, ETHAN (Ethan Randall): Huntington Beach, CA, June 13, 1978.

ENGLUND, ROBERT: Glendale, CA, June 6, 1949.

ERBE, KATHRYN: Newton, MA, July 2, 1966.

ERDMAN, RICHARD: Enid, OK, June 1, 1925.

ERICSON, JOHN: Dusseldorf, Germany, Sept. 25, 1926. AADA.

ERMEY, R. LEE (Ronald): Emporia, KS, Mar. 24, 1944

ESMOND, CARL (Willy Eichberger): Vienna, Austria, June 14, 1906. U Vienna.

ESPOSITO, GIANCARLO: Copenhagen, Denmark, Apr. 26, 1958.

ESTEVEZ, EMILIO: NYC, May 12, 1962.

ESTRADA, ERIK: NYC, Mar. 16, 1949.

EVANS, JOSH: NYC, Jan. 16, 1971.

EVANS, LINDA (Evanstad): Hartford, CT, Nov. 18, 1942.

EVERETT, CHAD (Ray Cramton): South Bend, IN, June 11, 1936.

EVERETT, RUPERT: Norfolk, England, 1959.

EVIGAN, GREG: South Amboy, NJ, Oct. 14, 1953.

FABARES, SHELLEY: Los Angeles, Jan. 19, 1944.

FABIAN (Fabian Forte): Philadelphia, Feb. 6, 1943.

FABRAY, NANETTE (Ruby Nanette Fabares): San Diego, Oct. 27, 1920.

FAHEY, JEFF: Olean, NY, Nov. 29, 1956.

FAIRCHILD, MORGAN (Patsy McClenny): Dallas, TX, Feb. 3, 1950. UCLA.

FALK, PETER: NYC, Sept. 16, 1927. New School.

FARENTINO, JAMES: Brooklyn, NY, Feb. 24, 1938. AADA.

FARGAS, ANTONIO: Bronx, NY, Aug. 14, 1946.

FARINA, DENNIS: Chicago, IL, Feb. 29, 1944.

FARINA, SANDY (Sandra Feldman): Newark, NJ, 1955.

FARR, FELICIA: Westchester, NY, Oct. 4. 1932. Penn St. College.

FARRELL, COLIN: Castleknock, Ireland, Mar. 31, 1976.

FARROW, MIA (Maria): Los Angeles, Feb. 9, 1945.

FAULKNER, GRAHAM: London, England, Sept. 26, 1947. Webber-Douglas.

| Rupert Everett | Colin Farrell | Jon Favreau | Harrison Ford |

FAVREAU, JON: Queens, NY, Oct. 16, 1966.

FAWCETT, FARRAH: Corpus Christie, TX, Feb. 2, 1947. TX U.

FEINSTEIN, ALAN: NYC, Sept. 8, 1941.

FELDMAN, COREY: Encino, CA, July 16, 1971.

FELDON, BARBARA (Hall): Pittsburgh, Mar. 12, 1941. Carnegie Tech.

FELDSHUH, TOVAH: NYC, Dec. 27, 1953, Sarah Lawrence College.

FELLOWS, EDITH: Boston, MA, May 20, 1923.

FENN, SHERILYN: Detroit, MI, Feb. 1, 1965.

FERRELL, CONCHATA: Charleston, WV, Mar. 28, 1943. Marshall U.

FERRELL, WILL: Irvine, CA, July 16, 1968.

FERRER, MEL: Elbeton, NJ, Aug. 25, 1912. Princeton.

FERRER, MIGUEL: Santa Monica, CA, Feb. 7, 1954.

FERRIS, BARBARA: London, England, 1943.

FIEDLER, JOHN: Plateville, WI, Feb. 3, 1925.

FIELD, SALLY: Pasadena, CA, Nov. 6, 1946.

FIELD, SHIRLEY ANNE: London, England, June 27, 1938.

FIELD, TODD (William Todd Field): Pomona, CA, Feb. 24, 1964.

FIENNES, JOSEPH: Salisbury, Wiltshire, England, May 27, 1970.

FIENNES, RALPH: Suffolk, England, Dec. 22, 1962. RADA.

FIERSTEIN, HARVEY: Brooklyn, NY, June 6, 1954. Pratt Inst.

FINCH, JON: Caterham, England, Mar. 2, 1941.

FINLAY, FRANK: Farnworth, England, Aug. 6, 1926.

FINNEY, ALBERT: Salford, Lancashire, England, May 9, 1936. RADA.

FIORENTINO, LINDA: Philadelphia, PA, Mar. 9, 1960.

FIRTH, COLIN: Grayshott, Hampshire, England, Sept. 10, 1960.

FIRTH, PETER: Bradford, England, Oct. 27, 1953.

FISHBURNE, LAURENCE: Augusta, GA, July 30, 1961.

FISHER, CARRIE: Los Angeles, CA, Oct. 21, 1956. London Central School of Drama.

FISHER, EDDIE: Philadelphia, PA, Aug. 10, 1928.

FISHER, FRANCES: Orange, TX, 1952.

FITZGERALD, TARA: London, England, Sept. 17, 1968.

FITZGERALD, GERALDINE: Dublin, Ireland, Nov. 24, 1914. Dublin Art School.

FLAGG, FANNIE: Birmingham, AL, Sept. 21, 1944. U AL.

FLANAGAN, FIONNULA: Dublin, Ireland, Dec. 10, 1941.

FLANNERY, SUSAN: Jersey City, NJ, July 31, 1943.

FLEMING, RHONDA (Marilyn Louis): Los Angeles, Aug. 10, 1922.

FLEMYNG, ROBERT: Liverpool, England, Jan. 3, 1912. Haileybury College.

FLETCHER, LOUISE: Birmingham, AL, July 22 1934.

FLOCKHART, CALISTA: Stockton, IL, Nov. 11, Rutgers.

FOCH, NINA: Leyden, Holland, Apr. 20, 1924.

FOLEY, DAVE: Toronto, Canada, Jan. 4, 1963.

FOLLOWS, MEGAN: Toronto, Canada, Mar. 14, 1968.

FONDA, BRIDGET: Los Angeles, Jan. 27, 1964.

FONDA, JANE: NYC, Dec. 21, 1937. Vassar.

FONDA, PETER: NYC, Feb. 23, 1939. U Omaha.

FONTAINE, JOAN: Tokyo, Japan, Oct. 22, 1917.

FOOTE, HALLIE: NYC, 1953. UNH.

FORD, GLENN (Gwyllyn Samuel Newton Ford): Quebec, Canada, May 1, 1916.

FORD, HARRISON: Chicago, IL, July 13, 1942. Ripon College.

FOREST, MARK (Lou Degni): Brooklyn, NY, Jan. 1933.

FORLANI, CLAIRE: London, England, July 1, 1972.

FORREST, FREDERIC: Waxahachie, TX, Dec. 23, 1936.

FORREST, STEVE: Huntsville, TX, Sept. 29, 1924. UCLA.

FORSLUND, CONNIE: San Diego, CA, June 19, 1950. NYU.

FORSTER, ROBERT (Foster, Jr.): Rochester, NY, July 13, 1941. Rochester U.

FORSYTHE, JOHN (Freund): Penn's Grove, NJ, Jan. 29, 1918.

FORSYTHE, WILLIAM: Brooklyn, NY, June 7, 1955

FOSSEY, BRIGITTE: Tourcoing, France, Mar. 11, 1947.

FOSTER, JODIE (Ariane Munker): Bronx, NY, Nov. 19, 1962. Yale.

FOSTER, BEN: Boston, MA, Oct. 29, 1980.

FOSTER, MEG: Reading, PA, May 14, 1948.

FOX, EDWARD: London, England, Apr. 13, 1937. RADA.

FOX, JAMES: London, England, May 19, 1939.

FOX, MICHAEL J.: Vancouver, BC, Canada, June 9, 1961.

FOX, VIVICA A.: Indianapolis, IN, July 30, 1964.

FOXWORTH, ROBERT: Houston, TX, Nov. 1, 1941. Carnegie Tech.

Brendan Fraser   Cuba Gooding, Jr.   Heather Graham   Bruce Greenwood

FRAIN, JAMES: Leeds, England, 1969.

FRAKES, JONATHAN: Bethlehem, PA, Aug. 19, 1952. Harvard.

FRANCIOSA, ANTHONY (Papaleo)**:** NYC, Oct. 25, 1928.

FRANCIS, ANNE: Ossining, NY, Sept. 16, 1932.

FRANCIS, ARLENE (Arlene Kazanjian)**:** Boston, MA, Oct. 20, 1908. Finch School.

FRANCIS, CONNIE (Constance Franconero)**:** Newark, NJ, Dec. 12, 1938.

FRANCKS, DON: Vancouver, BC, Canada, Feb. 28, 1932.

FRANKLIN, PAMELA: Tokyo, Japan, Feb. 4, 1950.

FRANZ, ARTHUR: Perth Amboy, NJ, Feb. 29, 1920. Blue Ridge College.

FRANZ, DENNIS: Chicago, IL, Oct. 28, 1944.

FRASER, BRENDAN: Indianapolis, IN, Dec. 3, 1968.

FRAZIER, SHEILA: NYC, Nov. 13, 1948.

FRECHETTE, PETER: Warwick, RI, Oct. 1956. URI.

FREEMAN, AL, JR.: San Antonio, TX, Mar. 21, 1934. CCLA.

FREEMAN, MONA: Baltimore, MD, June 9, 1926.

FREEMAN, MORGAN: Memphis, TN, June 1, 1937. LACC.

FREWER, MATT: Washington, DC, Jan. 4, 1958, Old Vic.

FRICKER, BRENDA: Dublin, Ireland, Feb. 17, 1945.

FRIELS, COLIN: Glasgow, Scotland, Sept. 25, 1952.

FRY, STEPHEN: Hampstead, London, Eng., Aug. 24, 1957.

FULLER, PENNY: Durham, NC, 1940. Northwestern.

FUNICELLO, ANNETTE: Utica, NY, Oct. 22, 1942.

FURLONG, EDWARD: Glendale, CA, Aug. 2, 1977.

FURNEAUX, YVONNE: Lille, France, 1928. Oxford U.

GABLE, JOHN CLARK: Los Angeles, Mar. 20, 1961. Santa Monica College.

GABOR, ZSA ZSA (Sari Gabor)**:** Budapest, Hungary, Feb. 6, 1918.

GAIL, MAX: Derfoil, MI, Apr. 5, 1943.

GAINES, BOYD: Atlanta, GA, May 11, 1953. Juilliard.

GALECKI, JOHNNY: Bree, Belgium, Apr. 30, 1975.

GALLAGHER, PETER: NYC, Aug. 19, 1955. Tufts.

GALLIGAN, ZACH: NYC, Feb. 14, 1963. Columbia.

GALLO, VINCENT: Buffalo, NY, Apr. 11, 1961.

GAM, RITA: Pittsburgh, PA, Apr. 2, 1928.

GAMBLE, MASON: Chicago, IL, Jan. 16, 1986.

GAMBON, MICHAEL: Dublin, Ireland, Oct. 19, 1940.

GANDOLFINI, JAMES: Westwood, NJ, Sept. 18, 1961.

GANZ, BRUNO: Zurich, Switzerland, Mar. 22, 1941.

GARBER, VICTOR: Montreal, Canada, Mar. 16, 1949.

GARCIA, ADAM: Wahroonga, New So. Wales, Australia, June 1, 1973.

GARCIA, ANDY: Havana, Cuba, Apr. 12, 1956. FL Inst.

GARFIELD, ALLEN (Allen Goorwitz)**:** Newark, NJ, Nov. 22, 1939. Actors Studio.

GARFUNKEL, ART: NYC, Nov. 5, 1941.

GARLAND, BEVERLY: Santa Cruz, CA, Oct. 17, 1926. Glendale College.

GARNER, JAMES (James Baumgarner)**:** Norman, OK, Apr. 7, 1928. OK U.

GAROFALO, JANEANE: Newton, NJ, Sept. 28, 1964.

GARR, TERI: Lakewood, OH, Dec. 11, 1949.

GARRETT, BETTY: St. Joseph, MO, May 23, 1919. Annie Wright Seminary.

GARRISON, SEAN: NYC, Oct. 19, 1937.

GARY, LORRAINE: NYC, Aug. 16, 1937.

GAVIN, JOHN: Los Angeles, Apr. 8, 1935. Stanford.

GAYLORD, MITCH: Van Nuys, CA, Mar. 10, 1961. UCLA.

GAYNOR, MITZI (Francesca Marlene Von Gerber)**:** Chicago, IL, Sept. 4, 1930.

GAZZARA, BEN: NYC, Aug. 28, 1930. Actors Studio.

GEARY, ANTHONY: Coalsville, UT, May 29, 1947. U UT.

GEDRICK, JASON: Chicago, IL, Feb. 7, 1965. Drake.

GEESON, JUDY: Arundel, England, Sept. 10, 1948. Corona.

GELLAR, SARAH MICHELLE: NYC, Apr. 14, 1977.

GEOFFREYS, STEPHEN (Miller)**:** Cincinnati, OH, Nov. 22, 1959. NYU.

GEORGE, SUSAN: West London, England, July 26, 1950.

GERARD, GIL: Little Rock, AR, Jan. 23, 1940.

GERE, RICHARD: Philadelphia, PA, Aug. 29, 1949. U MA.

GERROLL, DANIEL: London, England, Oct. 16, 1951. Central.

GERSHON, GINA: Los Angeles, June 10, 1962.

GERTZ, JAMI: Chicago, IL, Oct. 28, 1965.

GETTY, BALTHAZAR: Los Angeles, Jan. 22, 1975.

GETTY, ESTELLE: NYC, July 25, 1923. New School.

GHOLSON, JULIE: Birmingham, AL, June 4, 1958.

GHOSTLEY, ALICE: Eve, MO, Aug. 14, 1926. OK U.

GIANNINI, GIANCARLO: Spezia, Italy, Aug. 1, 1942. Rome Academy of Drama.

GIBB, CYNTHIA: Bennington, VT, Dec. 14, 1963.
GIBSON, HENRY: Germantown, PA, Sept. 21, 1935.
GIBSON, MEL: Peekskill, NY, Jan. 3, 1956. NIDA.
GIBSON, THOMAS: Charleston, SC, July 3, 1962.
GIFT, ROLAND: Birmingham, England, May 28 1962.
GILBERT, MELISSA: Los Angeles, May 8, 1964.
GILES, NANCY: NYC, July 17, 1960, Oberlin College.
GILLETTE, ANITA: Baltimore, MD, Aug. 16, 1938.
GILLIAM, TERRY: Minneapolis, MN, Nov. 22, 1940.
GILLIS, ANN (Alma O'Connor): Little Rock, AR, Feb. 12, 1927.
GINTY, ROBERT: NYC, Nov. 14, 1948. Yale.
GIRARDOT, ANNIE: Paris, France, Oct. 25, 1931.
GISH, ANNABETH: Albuquerque, NM, Mar. 13, 1971. Duke.
GIVENS, ROBIN: NYC, Nov. 27, 1964.
GLASER, PAUL MICHAEL: Boston, MA, Mar. 25, 1943. Boston U.
GLASS, RON: Evansville, IN, July 10, 1945.
GLEASON, JOANNA: Winnipeg, Manitoba, Canada, June 2, 1950. UCLA.
GLEASON, PAUL: Jersey City, NJ, May 4, 1944.
GLENN, SCOTT: Pittsburgh, PA, Jan. 26, 1942. William and Mary College.
GLOVER, CRISPIN: NYC, Sept 20, 1964.
GLOVER, DANNY: San Francisco, CA, July 22, 1947. SF St. College.
GLOVER, JOHN: Kingston, NY, Aug. 7, 1944.
GLYNN, CARLIN: Cleveland, Oh, Feb. 19, 1940. Actors Studio.
GOLDBERG, WHOOPI (Caryn Johnson): NYC, Nov. 13, 1949.
GOLDBLUM, JEFF: Pittsburgh, PA, Oct. 22, 1952. Neighborhood Playhouse.
GOLDEN, ANNIE: Brooklyn, NY, Oct. 19, 1951.
GOLDSTEIN, JENETTE: Beverly Hills, CA, 1960.
GOLDTHWAIT, BOB: Syracuse, NY, May 1, 1962.
GOLDWYN, TONY: Los Angeles, May 20, 1960. LAMDA.
GOLINO, VALERIA: Naples, Italy, Oct. 22, 1966.
GONZALEZ, CORDELIA: San Juan, PR, Aug. 11, 1958. U PR.
GONZALES-GONZALEZ, PEDRO: Aguilares, TX, Dec. 21, 1926.
GOODALL, CAROLINE: London, England, Nov. 13, 1959. Bristol U.
GOODING, CUBA, JR.: Bronx, N.Y., Jan. 2, 1968.
GOODMAN, DODY: Columbus, OH, Oct. 28, 1915.
GOODMAN, JOHN: St. Louis, MO, June 20, 1952.
GORDON, KEITH: NYC, Feb. 3, 1961.
GORDON-LEVITT, JOSEPH: Los Angeles, Feb. 17, 1981.
GORMAN, CLIFF: Jamaica, NY, Oct. 13, 1936. NYU.
GORSHIN, FRANK: Pittsburgh, PA, Apr. 5, 1933.
GORTNER, MARJOE: Long Beach, CA, Jan. 14, 1944.
GOSSETT, LOUIS, JR.: Brooklyn, NY, May 27, 1936. NYU.
GOULD, ELLIOTT (Goldstein): Brooklyn, NY, Aug. 29, 1938. Columbia.
GOULD, HAROLD: Schenectady, NY, Dec. 10, 1923. Cornell.
GOULD, JASON: NYC, Dec. 29, 1966.
GOULET, ROBERT: Lawrence, MA, Nov. 26, 1933. Edmonton.
GRAF, DAVID: Lancaster, OH, Apr. 16, 1950. OH St. U.
GRAFF, TODD: NYC, Oct. 22, 1959. SUNY/ Purchase.
GRAHAM, HEATHER: Milwaukee, WI, Jan. 29, 1970.
GRANGER, FARLEY: San Jose, CA, July 1, 1925.
GRANT, DAVID MARSHALL: Westport, CT, June 21, 1955. Yale.
GRANT, HUGH: London, England, Sept. 9, 1960. Oxford.
GRANT, KATHRYN (Olive Grandstaff): Houston, TX, Nov. 25, 1933. UCLA.

Rachel Griffiths   Ioan Gruffudd

GRANT, LEE: NYC, Oct. 31, 1927. Juilliard.
GRANT, RICHARD E: Mbabane, Swaziland, May 5, 1957. Cape Town U.
GRAVES, PETER (Aurness): Minneapolis, Mar. 18, 1926. U MN.
GRAVES, RUPERT: Weston-Super-Mare, England, June 30, 1963.
GRAY, COLEEN (Doris Jensen): Staplehurst, NB, Oct. 23, 1922. Hamline.
GRAY, LINDA: Santa Monica, CA, Sept. 12, 1940.
GRAY, SPALDING: Barrington, RI, June 5, 1941.
GRAYSON, KATHRYN (Zelma Hedrick): Winston-Salem, NC, Feb. 9, 1922.
GREEN, KERRI: Fort Lee, NJ, Jan. 14, 1967. Vassar.
GREEN, SETH: Philadelphia, PA, Feb. 8, 1974.
GREENE, ELLEN: NYC, Feb. 22, 1950. Ryder College.
GREENE, GRAHAM: Six Nations Reserve, Ontario, Canada, June 22, 1952
GREENWOOD, BRUCE: Quebec, Canada, Aug. 12, 1956.
GREER, MICHAEL: Galesburg, IL, Apr. 20, 1943.
GREIST, KIM: Stamford, CT, May 12, 1958.
GREY, JENNIFER: NYC, Mar. 26, 1960.
GREY, JOEL (Katz): Cleveland, OH, Apr. 11, 1932.
GREY, VIRGINIA: Los Angeles, Mar. 22, 1917.
GRIECO, RICHARD: Watertown, NY, Mar. 23, 1965.
GRIEM, HELMUT: Hamburg, Germany, Apr. 6, 1932. Hamburg U.
GRIER, DAVID ALAN: Detroit, MI, June 30, 1955. Yale.
GRIER, PAM: Winston-Salem, NC, May 26, 1949.
GRIFFITH, ANDY: Mt. Airy, NC, June 1, 1926. UNC.
GRIFFITH, MELANIE: NYC, Aug. 9, 1957. Pierce Col.
GRIFFITH, THOMAS IAN: Hartford, CT, Mar. 18, 1962.
GRIFFITHS, RACHEL: Melbourne, Australia, 1968.
GRIFFITHS, RICHARD: Tornaby-on-Tees, England, July 31, 1947.
GRIMES, GARY: San Francisco, CA, June 2, 1955.
GRIMES, SCOTT: Lowell, MA, July 9, 1971.
GRIMES, TAMMY: Lynn, MA, Jan. 30, 1934. Stephens College.
GRIZZARD, GEORGE: Roanoke Rapids, NC, Apr. 1, 1928. U NC.
GRODIN, CHARLES: Pittsburgh, PA, Apr. 21, 1935.
GROH, DAVID: NYC, May 21, 1939. Brown U. LAMDA.
GROSS, MARY: Chicago, IL, Mar. 25, 1953.
GROSS, MICHAEL: Chicago, IL, June 21, 1947.
GRUFFUDD, IOAN: Cardiff, Wales, Oct. 6, 1973.
GUEST, CHRISTOPHER: NYC, Feb. 5, 1948.

GUEST, LANCE: Saratoga, CA, July 21, 1960. UCLA.

GUILLAUME, ROBERT (Williams): St. Louis, MO, Nov. 30, 1937.

GULAGER, CLU: Holdenville, OK, Nov. 16 1928.

GUTTENBERG, STEVE: Massapequa, NY, Aug. 24, 1958. UCLA.

GUY, JASMINE: Boston, MA, Mar. 10, 1964.

HAAS, LUKAS: West Hollywood, CA, Apr. 16, 1976.

HACK, SHELLEY: Greenwich, CT, July 6, 1952.

HACKETT, BUDDY (Leonard Hacker): Brooklyn, NY, Aug. 31, 1924.

HACKMAN, GENE: San Bernardino, CA, Jan. 30, 1930.

HAGERTY, JULIE: Cincinnati, OH, June 15, 1955. Juilliard.

HAGMAN, LARRY (Hageman): Weatherford, TX, Sept. 21, 1931. Bard.

HAID, CHARLES: San Francisco, CA, June 2, 1943. Carnegie Tech.

HAIM, COREY: Toronto, Canada, Dec. 23, 1972.

HALE, BARBARA: DeKalb, IL, Apr. 18, 1922. Chicago Academy of Fine Arts.

HALEY, JACKIE EARLE: Northridge, CA, July 14, 1961.

HALL, ALBERT: Boothton, AL, Nov. 10, 1937. Columbia.

HALL, ANTHONY MICHAEL: Boston, MA, Apr. 14, 1968.

HALL, ARSENIO: Cleveland, OH, Feb. 12, 1959.

HAMEL, VERONICA: Philadelphia, PA, Nov. 20, 1943.

HAMILL, MARK: Oakland, CA, Sept. 25, 1952. LACC.

HAMILTON, CARRIE: NYC, Dec. 5, 1963.

HAMILTON, GEORGE: Memphis, TN, Aug. 12, 1939. Hackley.

HAMILTON, LINDA: Salisbury, MD, Sept. 26, 1956.

HAMLIN, HARRY: Pasadena, CA, Oct. 30, 1951.

HAMPSHIRE, SUSAN: London, England, May 12, 1941.

HAMPTON, JAMES: Oklahoma City, OK, July 9, 1936. N TX St. U.

HAN, MAGGIE: Providence, RI, 1959.

HANDLER, EVAN: NYC, Jan. 10, 1961. Juilliard.

HANKS, TOM: Concord, CA, Jul. 9, 1956. Cal. St. U.

HANNAH, DARYL: Chicago, IL, Dec. 3, 1960. UCLA.

HANNAH, PAGE: Chicago, IL, Apr. 13, 1964.

HARDEN, MARCIA GAY: LaJolla, CA, Aug. 14, 1959.

HARDIN, TY (Orison Whipple Hungerford, II): NYC, June 1, 1930.

HAREWOOD, DORIAN: Dayton, OH, Aug. 6, 1950. U Cincinnati

HARMON, MARK: Los Angeles, Sept. 2, 1951. UCLA.

HARPER, JESSICA: Chicago, IL, Oct. 10, 1949.

HARPER, TESS: Mammoth Spring, AK, 1952. SW MO St.

HARPER, VALERIE: Suffern, NY, Aug. 22, 1940.

HARRELSON, WOODY: Midland, TX, July 23, 1961. Hanover College.

HARRINGTON, PAT: NYC, Aug. 13, 1929. Fordham.

HARRIS, BARBARA (Sandra Markowitz): Evanston, IL, July 25, 1935.

HARRIS, ED: Tenafly, NJ, Nov. 28, 1950. Columbia.

HARRIS, JULIE: Grosse Point, MI, Dec. 2, 1925. Yale Drama School.

HARRIS, MEL (Mary Ellen): Bethlehem, PA, 1957. Columbia.

HARRIS, RICHARD: Limerick, Ireland, Oct. 1, 1930. London Academy.

HARRIS, ROSEMARY: Ashby, England, Sept. 19, 1930. RADA.

HARRISON, GREGORY: Catalina Island, CA, May 31, 1950. Actors Studio.

HARRISON, NOEL: London, England, Jan. 29, 1936.

HARROLD, KATHRYN: Tazewell, VA, Aug. 2, 1950. Mills College.

HARRY, DEBORAH: Miami, IL, July 1, 1945.

HART, ROXANNE: Trenton, NJ, 1952, Princeton.

HART, IAN: Liverpool, England, 1964.

HARTLEY, MARIETTE: NYC, June 21, 1941.

HARTMAN, DAVID: Pawtucket, RI, May 19, 1935. Duke.

HASSETT, MARILYN: Los Angeles, Dec. 17, 1947.

HATCHER, TERI: Sunnyvale, CA, Dec. 8, 1964.

HATOSY, SHAWN: Fredrick, MD, Dec. 29, 1975.

HAUER, RUTGER: Amsterdam, Holland, Jan. 23, 1944.

HAVER, JUNE: Rock Island, IL, June 10, 1926.

HAUSER, COLE: Santa Barbara, CA, Mar. 22, 1975.

HASUER, WINGS (Gerald Dwight Hauser): Hollywood, CA, Dec. 12, 1947.

HAVOC, JUNE (Hovick): Seattle, WA, Nov. 8, 1916.

HAWKE, ETHAN: Austin, TX, Nov. 6, 1970.

HAWN, GOLDIE: Washington, DC, Nov. 21, 1945.

HAYEK, SALMA: Coatzacoalcos, Veracruz, Mexico, Sept. 2, 1968.

HAYES, ISAAC: Covington, TN, Aug. 20, 1942.

HAYS, ROBERT: Bethesda, MD, July 24, 1947, SD St. College.

HEADLY, GLENNE: New London, CT, Mar. 13, 1955. Amherst.

HEALD, ANTHONY: New Rochelle, NY, Aug. 25, 1944. MI St. U.

HEARD, JOHN: Washington, DC, Mar. 7, 1946. Clark.

HEATHERTON, JOEY: NYC, Sept. 14, 1944.

HECHE, ANNE: Aurora, OH, May 25, 1969.

HEDAYA, DAN: Brooklyn, NY, July 24, 1940.

HEDISON, DAVID: Providence, RI, May 20, 1929. Brown.

HEDREN, TIPPI (Natalie): Lafayette, MN, Jan. 19, 1931.

HEGYES, ROBERT: Metuchen, NJ, May 7, 1951.

HELMOND, KATHERINE: Galveston, TX, July 5, 1934.

HEMINGWAY, MARIEL: Ketchum, ID, Nov. 22, 1961.

HEMMINGS, DAVID: Guilford, England, Nov. 18, 1941.

HEMSLEY, SHERMAN: Philadelphia, PA, Feb. 1, 1938.

HENDERSON, FLORENCE: Dale, IN, Feb. 14, 1934.

HENDRY, GLORIA: Jacksonville, FL, 1949.

HENNER, MARILU: Chicago, IL, Apr. 6, 1952.

HENRIKSEN, LANCE: NYC, May 5, 1940.

HENRY, BUCK (Henry Zuckerman): NYC, Dec. 9, 1930. Dartmouth.

HENRY, JUSTIN: Rye, NY, May 25, 1971.

HENSTRIDGE, NATASHA: Springdale, Newfoundland, Canada, Aug. 15, 1974.

HEPBURN, KATHARINE: Hartford, CT, May 12, 1907. Bryn Mawr.

HERRMANN, EDWARD: Washington, DC, July 21, 1943. Bucknell, LAMDA.

HERSHEY, BARBARA (Herzstein): Hollywood, CA, Feb. 5, 1948.

HESSEMAN. HOWARD: Lebanon, OR, Feb. 27, 1940.

HESTON, CHARLTON: Evanston, IL, Oct. 4, 1922. Northwestern.

HEWITT, JENNIFER LOVE: Waco, TX, Feb. 21, 1979.

HEWITT, MARTIN: Claremont, CA, Feb. 19, 1958. AADA.

HEYWOOD, ANNE (Violet Pretty): Birmingham, England, Dec. 11, 1932.

HICKMAN, DARRYL: Hollywood, CA, July 28, 1933. Loyola.

HICKMAN, DWAYNE: Los Angeles, May 18, 1934. Loyola.

HICKS, CATHERINE: NYC, Aug. 6, 1951. Notre Dame.

HIGGINS, ANTHONY (Corlan): Cork City, Ireland, May 9, 1947. Birmingham Sch. of Dramatic Arts.

HIGGINS, MICHAEL: Brooklyn, NY, Jan. 20, 1926. Am. Th. Wing.

Marcia Gay Harden Ed Harris Shawn Hatosy Dan Hedaya

HILL, ARTHUR: Saskatchewan, Canada, Aug. 1, 1922. U Brit. College.

HILL, BERNARD: Manchester, England, Dec. 17, 1944.

HILL, STEVEN: Seattle, WA, Feb. 24, 1922. U WA.

HILL, TERRENCE (Mario Girotti): Venice, Italy, Mar. 29, 1941. U Rome.

HILLER, WENDY: Bramhall, Cheshire, England, Aug. 15, 1912. Winceby House School.

HILLERMAN, JOHN: Denison, TX, Dec. 20, 1932.

HINES, GREGORY: NYC, Feb.14, 1946.

HINGLE, PAT: Denver, CO, July 19, 1923. TX U.

HIRSCH, JUDD: NYC, Mar. 15, 1935. AADA.

HOBEL, MARA: NYC, June 18, 1971.

HODGE, PATRICIA: Lincolnshire, England, Sept. 29, 1946. LAMDA.

HOFFMAN, DUSTIN: Los Angeles, Aug. 8, 1937. Pasadena Playhouse.

HOFFMAN, PHILIP SEYMOUR: Fairport, NY, July 23, 1967.

HOGAN, JONATHAN: Chicago, IL, June 13, 1951.

HOGAN, PAUL: Lightning Ridge, Australia, Oct. 8, 1939.

HOLBROOK, HAL (Harold): Cleveland, OH, Feb. 17, 1925. Denison.

HOLLIMAN, EARL: Tennesas Swamp, Delhi, LA, Sept. 11, 1928. UCLA.

HOLM, CELESTE: NYC, Apr. 29, 1919.

HOLM, IAN: Ilford, Essex, England, Sept. 12, 1931. RADA.

HOLMES, KATIE: Toledo, OH, Dec. 18, 1978.

HOMEIER, SKIP (George Vincent Homeier): Chicago, IL, Oct. 5, 1930. UCLA.

HOOKS, ROBERT: Washington, DC, Apr. 18, 1937. Temple.

HOPE, BOB (Leslie Townes Hope): London, England, May 26, 1903.

HOPKINS, ANTHONY: Port Talbot, So. Wales, Dec. 31, 1937. RADA.

HOPPER, DENNIS: Dodge City, KS, May 17, 1936.

HORNE, LENA: Brooklyn, NY, June 30, 1917.

HORROCKS, JANE: Rossendale Valley, England, Jan. 18, 1964.

HORSLEY, LEE: Muleshoe, TX, May 15, 1955.

HORTON, ROBERT: Los Angeles, July 29, 1924. UCLA.

HOSKINS, BOB: Bury St. Edmunds, England, Oct. 26, 1942.

HOUGHTON, KATHARINE: Hartford, CT, Mar. 10, 1945. Sarah Lawrence.

HOUSER, JERRY: Los Angeles, July 14, 1952. Valley Jr. College.

HOWARD, ARLISS: Independence, MO, 1955. Columbia College.

HOWARD, KEN: El Centro, CA, Mar. 28, 1944. Yale.

HOWARD, RON: Duncan, OK, Mar. 1, 1954. USC.

HOWARD, RONALD: Norwood, England, Apr. 7, 1918. Jesus College.

HOWELL, C. THOMAS: Los Angeles, Dec. 7, 1966.

HOWELLS, URSULA: London, England, Sept. 17, 1922.

HOWES, SALLY ANN: London, England, July 20, 1930.

HOWLAND, BETH: Boston, MA, May 28, 1941.

HUBLEY, SEASON: NYC, May 14, 1951.

HUDDLESTON, DAVID: Vinton, VA, Sept. 17, 1930.

HUDSON, ERNIE: Benton Harbor, MI, Dec. 17, 1945.

HUDSON, KATE: Los Angeles, Apr. 19, 1979.

HUGHES, BARNARD: Bedford Hills, NY, July 16, 1915. Manhattan College.

HUGHES, KATHLEEN (Betty von Gerkan): Hollywood, CA, Nov. 14, 1928. UCLA.

HULCE, TOM: Plymouth, MI, Dec. 6, 1953. NC Sch. of Arts.

HUNNICUT, GAYLE: Ft. Worth, TX, Feb. 6, 1943. UCLA.

HUNT, HELEN: Los Angeles, June 15, 1963.

HUNT, LINDA: Morristown, NJ, Apr. 1945. Goodman Theatre.

HUNT, MARSHA: Chicago, IL, Oct. 17, 1917.

HUNTER, HOLLY: Atlanta, GA, Mar. 20, 1958. Carnegie-Mellon.

HUNTER, KIM (Janet Cole): Detroit, Nov. 12, 1922.

HUNTER, TAB (Arthur Gelien): NYC, July 11, 1931.

HUPPERT, ISABELLE: Paris, France, Mar. 16, 1955.

HURLEY, ELIZABETH: Hampshire, England, June 10, 1965.

HURT, JOHN: Lincolnshire, England, Jan. 22, 1940.

HURT, MARY BETH (Supinger): Marshalltown, IA, Sept. 26, 1948. NYU.

HURT, WILLIAM: Washington, DC, Mar. 20, 1950. Tufts, Juilliard.

HUSSEY, RUTH: Providence, RI, Oct. 30, 1917. U MI.

HUSTON, ANJELICA: Santa Monica, CA, July 9, 1951.

HUTTON, BETTY (Betty Thornberg): Battle Creek, MI, Feb. 26, 1921.

HUTTON, LAUREN (Mary): Charleston, SC, Nov. 17, 1943. Newcomb College.

HUTTON, TIMOTHY: Malibu, CA, Aug. 16, 1960.

HYER, MARTHA: Fort Worth, TX, Aug. 10, 1924. Northwestern.

Janet Jackson

Samuel L. Jackson

Lainie Kazan

Nastassja Kinski

ICE CUBE (O'Shea Jackson): Los Angeles, June 15, 1969.

IDLE, ERIC: South Shields, Durham, England, Mar. 29, 1943. Cambridge.

INGELS, MARTY: Brooklyn, NY, Mar. 9, 1936.

IRELAND, KATHY: Santa Barbara, CA, Mar. 8, 1963.

IRONS, JEREMY: Cowes, England, Sept. 19, 1948. Old Vic.

IRONSIDE, MICHAEL: Toronto, Canada, Feb. 12, 1950.

IRVING, AMY: Palo Alto, CA, Sept. 10, 1953. LADA.

IRWIN, BILL: Santa Monica, CA, Apr. 11, 1950.

ISAAK, CHRIS: Stockton, CA, June 26, 1956. U Pacific.

IVANEK, ZELJKO: Lujubljana, Yugoslavia, Aug. 15, 1957. Yale, LAMDA.

IVEY, JUDITH: El Paso, TX, Sept. 4, 1951.

IZZARD, EDDIE: Aden, Yemen, Feb. 7, 1962.

JACKSON, ANNE: Alleghany, PA, Sept. 3, 1926. Neighborhood Playhouse.

JACKSON, GLENDA: Hoylake, Cheshire, England, May 9, 1936. RADA.

JACKSON, JANET: Gary, IN, May 16, 1966.

JACKSON, KATE: Birmingham, AL, Oct. 29, 1948. AADA.

JACKSON, MICHAEL: Gary, IN, Aug. 29, 1958.

JACKSON, SAMUEL L.: Atlanta, GA, Dec. 21, 1948.

JACKSON, VICTORIA: Miami, FL, Aug. 2, 1958.

JACOBI, DEREK: Leytonstone, London, England, Oct. 22, 1938. Cambridge.

JACOBI, LOU: Toronto, Canada, Dec. 28, 1913.

JACOBS, LAWRENCE-HILTON: Virgin Islands, Sept. 14, 1953.

JACOBY, SCOTT: Chicago, IL, Nov. 19, 1956.

JAGGER, MICK: Dartford, Kent, England, July 26, 1943.

JAMES, CLIFTON: NYC, May 29, 1921. OR U.

JANNEY, ALLISON: Dayton, OH, Nov. 20, 1960. RADA.

JARMAN, CLAUDE, JR.: Nashville, TN, Sept. 27, 1934.

JASON, RICK: NYC, May 21, 1926. AADA.

JEAN, GLORIA (Gloria Jean Schoonover): Buffalo, NY, Apr. 14, 1927.

JEFFREYS, ANNE (Carmichael): Goldsboro, NC, Jan. 26, 1923. Anderson College.

JEFFRIES, LIONEL: London, June 10, 1926. RADA.

JERGENS, ADELE: Brooklyn, NY, Nov. 26, 1922.

JETER, MICHAEL: Lawrenceburg, TN, Aug. 26, 1952. Memphis St. U.

JILLIAN, ANN (Nauseda): Cambridge, MA, Jan. 29, 1951.

JOHANSEN, DAVID: Staten Island, NY, Jan. 9, 1950.

JOHN, ELTON (Reginald Dwight): Middlesex, England, Mar. 25, 1947. RAM.

JOHNS, GLYNIS: Durban, S. Africa, Oct. 5, 1923.

JOHNSON, DON: Galena, MO, Dec. 15, 1950. U KS.

JOHNSON, PAGE: Welch, WV, Aug. 25, 1930. Ithaca.

JOHNSON, RAFER: Hillsboro, TX, Aug. 18, 1935. UCLA.

JOHNSON, RICHARD: Essex, England, July 30, 1927. RADA.

JOHNSON, ROBIN: Brooklyn, NY, May 29, 1964.

JOHNSON, VAN: Newport, RI, Aug. 28, 1916.

JOLIE, ANGELINA (Angelina Jolie Voight): Los Angeles, June 4, 1975.

JONES, CHRISTOPHER: Jackson, TN, Aug. 18, 1941. Actors Studio.

JONES, DEAN: Decatur, AL, Jan. 25, 1931. Actors Studio.

JONES, GRACE: Spanishtown, Jamaica, May 19, 1952.

JONES, JACK: Bel-Air, CA, Jan. 14, 1938.

JONES, JAMES EARL: Arkabutla, MS, Jan. 17, 1931. U Mich.

JONES, JEFFREY: Buffalo, NY, Sept. 28, 1947. LAMDA.

JONES, JENNIFER (Phyllis Isley): Tulsa, OK, Mar. 2, 1919. AADA.

JONES, L.Q. (Justice Ellis McQueen): Aug 19, 1927.

JONES, ORLANDO: Mobile, AL, Apr. 10, 1968.

JONES, SAM J.: Chicago, IL, Aug. 12, 1954.

JONES, SHIRLEY: Smithton, PA, March 31, 1934.

JONES, TERRY: Colwyn Bay, Wales, Feb. 1, 1942.

JONES, TOMMY LEE: San Saba, TX, Sept. 15, 1946. Harvard.

JOURDAN, LOUIS: Marseilles, France, June 19, 1920.

JOVOVICH, MILLA: Kiev, Ukraine, Dec. 17, 1975.

JOY, ROBERT: Montreal, Canada, Aug. 17, 1951. Oxford.

JUDD, ASHLEY: Los Angeles, Apr. 19, 1968.

JURADO, KATY (Maria Christina Jurado Garcia): Guadalajara, Mex., Jan. 16, 1927.

KACZMAREK, JANE: Milwaukee, WI, Dec. 21, 1955.

KANE, CAROL: Cleveland, OH, June 18, 1952.

KAPLAN, MARVIN: Brooklyn, NY, Jan. 24, 1924.

KAPOOR, SHASHI: Calcutta, India, Mar. 18, 1938.

KAPRISKY, VALERIE (Cheres): Paris, France, Aug. 19, 1962.

KARRAS, ALEX: Gary, IN, July 15, 1935.

KARTHEISER, VINCENT: Minneapolis, MN, May 5, 1979.

KASSOVITZ, MATHIEU: Paris, France, Aug. 3, 1967.

KATT, WILLIAM: Los Angeles, Feb. 16, 1955.

KATTAN, CHRIS: Mt. Baldy, CA, Oct. 19, 1970.

KAUFMANN, CHRISTINE: Lansdorf, Graz, Austria, Jan. 11, 1945.

KAVNER, JULIE: Burbank, CA, Sept. 7, 1951. UCLA.

KAZAN, LAINIE (Levine): Brooklyn, NY, May 15, 1942.

KAZURINSKY, TIM: Johnstown, PA, March 3, 1950.

KEACH, STACY: Savannah, GA, June 2, 1941. U CA, Yale.

KEATON, DIANE (Hall): Los Angeles, Jan. 5, 1946. Neighborhood Playhouse.

KEATON, MICHAEL: Coraopolis, PA, Sept. 9, 1951. Kent State.

KEEGAN, ANDREW: Los Angeles, Jan. 29, 1979.

KEEL, HOWARD (Harold Leek): Gillespie, IL, Apr. 13, 1919.

KEENER, CATHERINE: Miami, FL, 1960.

KEESLAR, MATT: Grand Rapids, MI, 1972.

KEITEL, HARVEY: Brooklyn, NY, May 13, 1939.

KEITH, DAVID: Knoxville, TN, May 8, 1954. U TN.

KELLER, MARTHE: Basel, Switzerland, 1945. Munich Stanislavsky Sch.

KELLERMAN, SALLY: Long Beach, CA, June 2, 1936. Actors Studio West.

KELLY, MOIRA: Queens, NY, Mar. 6, 1968.

KEMP, JEREMY (Wacker): Chesterfield, England, Feb. 3, 1935. Central Sch.

KENNEDY, GEORGE: NYC, Feb. 18, 1925.

KENNEDY, LEON ISAAC: Cleveland, OH, 1949.

KENSIT, PATSY: London, England, Mar. 4, 1968.

KERR, DEBORAH: Helensburg, Scotland, Sept. 30, 1921. Smale Ballet Sch.

KERR, JOHN: NYC, Nov. 15, 1931. Harvard, Columbia.

KERWIN, BRIAN: Chicago, IL, Oct. 25, 1949.

KEYES, EVELYN: Port Arthur, TX, Nov. 20, 1919.

KIDDER, MARGOT: Yellow Knife, Canada, Oct. 17, 1948. U BC.

KIDMAN, NICOLE: Hawaii, June 20, 1967.

KIEL, RICHARD: Detroit, MI, Sept. 13, 1939.

KIER, UDO: Koeln, Germany, Oct. 14, 1944.

KILMER, VAL: Los Angeles, Dec. 31, 1959. Juilliard.

KINCAID, ARON (Norman Neale Williams, III): Los Angeles, June 15, 1943. UCLA.

KING, ALAN (Irwin Kniberg): Brooklyn, NY, Dec. 26, 1927.

KING, PERRY: Alliance, OH, Apr. 30, 1948. Yale.

KINGSLEY, BEN (Krishna Bhanji): Snaiton, Yorkshire, England, Dec. 31, 1943.

KINNEAR, GREG: Logansport, IN, June 17, 1963.

KINSKI, NASTASSJA: Berlin, Germany, Jan. 24, 1960.

KIRBY, BRUNO: NYC, Apr. 28, 1949.

KIRK, TOMMY: Louisville, KY, Dec.10 1941.

KIRKLAND, SALLY: NYC, Oct. 31, 1944. Actors Studio.

KITT, EARTHA: North, SC, Jan. 26, 1928.

KLEIN, CHRIS: Hinsdale, IL, March 14, 1979.

KLEIN, ROBERT: NYC, Feb. 8, 1942. Alfred U.

KLINE, KEVIN: St. Louis, MO, Oct. 24, 1947. Juilliard.

KLUGMAN, JACK: Philadelphia, PA, Apr. 27, 1922. Carnegie Tech.

KNIGHT, MICHAEL E.: Princeton, NJ, May 7, 1959.

KNIGHT, SHIRLEY: Goessel, KS, July 5, 1937. Wichita U.

KNOX, ELYSE: Hartford, CT, Dec. 14, 1917. Traphagen School.

KOENIG, WALTER: Chicago, IL, Sept. 14, 1936. UCLA.

KOHNER, SUSAN: Los Angeles, Nov. 11, 1936. U CA.

KORMAN, HARVEY: Chicago, IL, Feb. 15, 1927. Goodman.

KORSMO, CHARLIE: Minneapolis, MN, July, 1978.

Lisa Kudrow   Anthony LaPaglia

KOTEAS, ELIAS: Montreal, Quebec, Canada, 1961. AADA.

KOTTO, YAPHET: NYC, Nov. 15, 1937.

KOZAK, HARLEY JANE: Wilkes-Barre, PA, Jan. 28, 1957. NYU.

KRABBE, JEROEN: Amsterdam, The Netherlands, Dec. 5, 1944.

KREUGER, KURT: St. Moritz, Switzerland, July 23, 1917. U London.

KRIGE, ALICE: Upington, South Africa, June 28, 1955.

KRISTEL, SYLVIA: Amsterdam, The Netherlands, Sept. 28, 1952.

KRISTOFFERSON, KRIS: Brownsville, TX, June 22, 1936. Pomona College.

KRUGER, HARDY: Berlin, Germany, April 12, 1928.

KRUMHOLTZ, DAVID: NYC, May 15, 1978.

KUDROW, LISA: Encino, CA, July 30, 1963.

KURTZ, SWOOSIE: Omaha, NE, Sept. 6, 1944.

KUTCHER, ASHTON (Christopher A. K.): Cedar Rapids, IA, Feb. 7, 1978.

KWAN, NANCY: Hong Kong, May 19, 1939. Royal Ballet.

LaBELLE, PATTI: Philadelphia, PA, May 24, 1944.

LACY, JERRY: Sioux City, IA, Mar. 27, 1936. LACC.

LADD, CHERYL (Stoppelmoor): Huron, SD. July 12, 1951.

LADD, DIANE (Ladner): Meridian, MS, Nov. 29, 1932. Tulane.

LAHTI, CHRISTINE: Detroit, MI, Apr. 4, 1950. U MI.

LAKE, RICKI: NYC, Sept. 21, 1968.

LAMAS, LORENZO: Los Angeles, Jan. 28, 1958.

LAMBERT, CHRISTOPHER: NYC, Mar. 29, 1958.

LANDAU, MARTIN: Brooklyn, NY, June 20, 1931. Actors Studio.

LANDRUM, TERI: Enid, OK, 1960.

LANE, ABBE: Brooklyn, NY, Dec. 14, 1935.

LANE, DIANE: NYC, Jan. 22, 1963.

LANE, NATHAN: Jersey City, NJ, Feb. 3, 1956.

LANG, STEPHEN: NYC, July 11, 1952. Swarthmore College.

LANGE, HOPE: Redding Ridge, CT, Nov. 28, 1931. Reed College.

LANGE, JESSICA: Cloquet, MN, Apr. 20, 1949. U MN.

LANGELLA, FRANK: Bayonne, NJ, Jan. 1, 1940. Syracuse U.

LANSBURY, ANGELA: London, Oct. 16, 1925. London Academy of Music.

LaPAGLIA, ANTHONY: Adelaide, Australia. Jan 31, 1959.

LARROQUETTE, JOHN: New Orleans, LA, Nov. 25, 1947.

LASSER, LOUISE: NYC, Apr. 11, 1939. Brandeis.

LATIFAH, QUEEN (Dana Owens): East Orange, NJ, 1970.

LAUGHLIN, JOHN: Memphis, TN, Apr. 3.

Cyndi Lauper   Jude Law   Robert Sean Leonard   Patti LuPone

LAUGHLIN, TOM: Minneapolis, MN, 1938.

LAUPER, CYNDI: Queens, NY, June 20, 1953.

LAURE, CAROLE: Montreal, Canada, Aug. 5, 1951.

LAURIE, HUGH: Oxford, England, June 11, 1959.

LAURIE, PIPER (Rosetta Jacobs): Detroit, MI, Jan. 22, 1932.

LAUTER, ED: Long Beach, NY, Oct. 30, 1940.

LAVIN, LINDA: Portland, ME, Oct. 15 1939.

LAW, JOHN PHILLIP: Hollywood, CA, Sept. 7, 1937. Neighborhood Playhouse, U HI.

LAW, JUDE: Lewisham, England, Dec. 29, 1972.

LAWRENCE, BARBARA: Carnegie, OK, Feb. 24, 1930. UCLA.

LAWRENCE, CAROL (Laraia): Melrose Park, IL, Sept. 5, 1935.

LAWRENCE, MARTIN: Frankfurt, Germany, Apr. 16, 1965.

LAWRENCE, VICKI: Inglewood, CA, Mar. 26, 1949.

LAWSON, LEIGH: Atherston, England, July 21, 1945. RADA.

LEACHMAN, CLORIS: Des Moines, IA, Apr. 30, 1930. Northwestern.

LEARY, DENIS: Boston, MA, Aug. 18, 1957.

LEAUD, JEAN-PIERRE: Paris, France, May 5, 1944.

LeBLANC, MATT: Newton, MA, July 25, 1967.

LEDGER, HEATH: Perth, Australia, Apr. 4, 1979.

LEE, CHRISTOPHER: London, England, May 27, 1922. Wellington College.

LEE, JASON: CA, Apr. 25, 1970.

LEE, MARK: Sydney, Australia, 1958.

LEE, MICHELE (Dusiak): Los Angeles, June 24, 1942. LACC.

LEE, PEGGY (Norma Delores Egstrom): Jamestown, ND, May 26, 1920.

LEE, SHERYL: Augsburg, Germany, Apr. 22, 1967.

LEE, SPIKE (Shelton Lee): Atlanta, GA, Mar. 20, 1957.

LEGROS, JAMES: Minneapolis, MN, Apr. 27, 1962.

LEGUIZAMO, JOHN: Colombia. July 22, 1965. NYU.

LEIBMAN, RON: NYC, Oct. 1l, 1937. Ohio Wesleyan.

LEIGH, JANET (Jeanette Helen Morrison): Merced, CA, July 6, 1926. College of Pacific.

LEIGH, JENNIFER JASON: Los Angeles, Feb. 5, 1962.

LeMAT, PAUL: Rahway, NJ, Sept. 22, 1945.

LEMMON, CHRIS: Los Angeles, Jan. 22, 1954.

LENO, JAY: New Rochelle, NY, Apr. 28, 1950. Emerson College.

LENZ, KAY: Los Angeles, Mar. 4, 1953.

LENZ, RICK: Springfield, IL, Nov. 21, 1939. U MI.

LEONARD, ROBERT SEAN: Westwood, NJ, Feb. 28, 1969.

LEONI, TÉA (Elizabeth Tea Pantaleoni): NYC, Feb. 25, 1966.

LERNER, MICHAEL: Brooklyn, NY, June 22, 1941.

LESLIE, JOAN (Joan Brodell): Detroit, Jan. 26, 1925. St. Benedict's.

LESTER, MARK: Oxford, England, July 11, 1958.

LETO, JARED: Bossier City, LA, Dec. 26, 1971.

LEVELS, CALVIN: Cleveland, OH, Sept. 30, 1954. CCC.

LEVIN, RACHEL: NYC, 1954. Goddard College.

LEVINE, JERRY: New Brunswick, NJ, Mar. 12, 1957, Boston U.

LEVY, EUGENE: Hamilton, Canada, Dec. 17, 1946. McMaster.

LEWIS, CHARLOTTE: London, Aug.7, 1967.

LEWIS, GEOFFREY: San Diego, CA, Jan. 1, 1935.

LEWIS, JERRY (Joseph Levitch): Newark, NJ, Mar. 16, 1926.

LEWIS, JULIETTE: Los Angeles, June 21, 1973.

LI, JET: Beijing, China, Apr. 26, 1963.

LIGON, TOM: New Orleans, LA, Sept. 10, 1945.

LILLARD, MATTHEW: Lansing, MI, Jan. 24, 1970.

LINCOLN, ABBEY (Anna Marie Woolridge): Chicago, IL, Aug. 6, 1930.

LINDEN, HAL: Bronx, NY, Mar. 20, 1931. CCNY.

LINDO, DELROY: London, England, Nov. 18, 1952.

LINDSAY, ROBERT: Ilketson, Derbyshire, England, Dec. 13, 1951, RADA.

LINN-BAKER, MARK: St. Louis, MO, June 17, 1954. Yale.

LINNEY, LAURA: NYC, Feb. 5, 1964.

LIOTTA, RAY: Newark, NJ, Dec. 18, 1955. U Miami.

LISI, VIRNA: Rome, Italy, Nov. 8, 1937.

LITHGOW, JOHN: Rochester, NY, Oct. 19, 1945. Harvard.

LIU, LUCY: Queens, NY, Dec. 2, 1967.

LL COOL J (James Todd Smith): Queens, NY, Jan. 14, 1968.

LLOYD, CHRISTOPHER: Stamford, CT, Oct. 22, 1938.

LLOYD, EMILY: London, England, Sept. 29, 1970.

LOCKE, SONDRA: Shelbyville, TN, May, 28, 1947.

LOCKHART, JUNE: NYC, June 25, 1925. Westlake School.

LOCKWOOD, GARY: Van Nuys, CA, Feb. 21, 1937.

LOGGIA, ROBERT: Staten Island, NY, Jan. 3, 1930. U MO.

LOLLOBRIGIDA, GINA: Subiaco, Italy, July 4, 1927. Rome Academy of Fine Arts.

LOM, HERBERT: Prague, Czechoslovakia, Jan. 9, 1917. Prague U.

LOMEZ, CELINE: Montreal, Canada, May 11, 1953.

LONE, JOHN: Hong Kong, China, Oct 13, 1952. AADA.

LONG, NIA: Brooklyn, NY, Oct. 30, 1970.

LONG, SHELLEY: Ft. Wayne, IN, Aug. 23, 1949. Northwestern.

LOPEZ, JENNIFER: Bronx, NY, July 24, 1970.

LOPEZ, PERRY: NYC, July 22, 1931. NYU.

LORDS, TRACY (Nora Louise Kuzma): Steubenville, OH, May 7, 1968.

LOREN, SOPHIA (Sophia Scicolone): Rome, Italy, Sept. 20, 1934.

LOUIS-DREYFUS, JULIA: NYC, Jan. 13, 1961.

LOUISE, TINA (Blacker): NYC, Feb. 11, 1934, Miami U.

LOVE, COURTNEY (Love Michelle Harrison): San Francisco, CA, July 9, 1965.

LOVETT, LYLE: Klein, TX, Nov. 1, 1957.

LOVITZ, JON: Tarzana, CA, July 21, 1957.

LOWE, CHAD: Dayton, OH, Jan. 15, 1968.

LOWE, ROB: Charlottesville, VA, Mar. 17, 1964.

LOWITSCH, KLAUS: Berlin, Germany, Apr. 8, 1936, Vienna Academy.

LUCAS, LISA: Arizona, 1961.

LUCKINBILL, LAURENCE: Fort Smith, AK, Nov. 21, 1934.

LUFT, LORNA: Los Angeles, Nov. 21, 1952.

LULU (Marie Lawrie): Glasgow, Scotland, Nov. 3, 1948.

LUNA, BARBARA: NYC, Mar. 2, 1939.

LUNDGREN, DOLPH: Stockolm, Sweden, Nov. 3, 1959. Royal Inst.

LuPONE, PATTI: Northport, NY, Apr. 21, 1949, Juilliard.

LYDON, JAMES: Harrington Park, NJ, May 30, 1923.

LYNCH, KELLY: Minneapolis, MN, Jan. 31, 1959.

LYNLEY, CAROL (Jones): NYC, Feb. 13, 1942.

LYON, SUE: Davenport, IA, July 10, 1946.

LYONNE, NATASHA (Braunstein): NYC, Apr. 4, 1979.

MacARTHUR, JAMES: Los Angeles, Dec. 8, 1937. Harvard.

MACCHIO, RALPH: Huntington, NY, Nov. 4, 1961.

MacCORKINDALE, SIMON: Cambridge, England, Feb. 12, 1953.

MACDONALD, KELLY: Glasgow, Scotland, Feb. 23, 1976.

MacDOWELL, ANDIE (Rose Anderson MacDowell): Gaffney, SC, Apr. 21, 1958.

MacFADYEN, ANGUS: Scotland, Oct. 21, 1963.

MacGINNIS, NIALL: Dublin, Ireland, Mar. 29, 1913. Dublin U.

MacGRAW, ALI: NYC, Apr. 1, 1938. Wellesley.

MacLACHLAN, KYLE: Yakima, WA, Feb. 22, 1959. U WA.

MacLAINE, SHIRLEY (Beaty): Richmond, VA, Apr. 24, 1934.

MacLEOD, GAVIN: Mt. Kisco, NY, Feb. 28, 1931.

MacNAUGHTON, ROBERT: NYC, Dec. 19, 1966.

MACNEE, PATRICK: London, England, Feb. 1922.

MacNICOL, PETER: Dallas, TX, Apr. 10, 1954. U MN.

MacPHERSON, ELLE: Sydney, Australia, 1965.

MacVITTIE, BRUCE: Providence, RI, Oct. 14, 1956. Boston U.

MACY, WILLIAM H. (W. H.): Miami, FL, Mar. 13, 1950. Goddard College.

MADIGAN, AMY: Chicago, IL, Sept. 11, 1950. Marquette.

MADONNA (Madonna Louise Veronica Cicone): Bay City, MI, Aug. 16, 1958. U MI.

MADSEN, MICHAEL: Chicago, IL, Sept. 25, 1958.

MADSEN, VIRGINIA: Winnetka, IL, Sept. 11, 1963.

MAGNUSON, ANN: Charleston, WV, Jan. 4, 1956.

MAGUIRE, TOBEY: Santa Monica, CA, June 27, 1975.

MAHARIS, GEORGE: Queens, NY, Sept. 1, 1928. Actors Studio.

MAHONEY, JOHN: Manchester, England, June 20, 1940, WU Ill.

MAILER, STEPHEN: NYC, Mar. 10, 1966. NYU.

MAJORS, LEE: Wyandotte, MI, Apr. 23, 1940. E KY St. College.

Natasha Lyonne   William H. Macy

MAKEPEACE, CHRIS: Toronto, Canada, Apr. 22, 1964.

MAKO (Mako Iwamatsu): Kobe, Japan, Dec. 10, 1933. Pratt Inst.

MALDEN, KARL (Malden Sekulovich): Gary, IN, Mar. 22, 1914.

MALKOVICH, JOHN: Christopher, IL, Dec. 9, 1953, IL St. U.

MALONE, DOROTHY: Chicago, IL, Jan. 30, 1925.

MANN, TERRENCE: KY, 1945. NC Sch. Arts.

MANOFF, DINAH: NYC, Jan. 25, 1958. Cal. Arts.

MANTEGNA, JOE: Chicago, IL, Nov. 13, 1947. Goodman Theatre.

MANZ, LINDA: NYC, 1961.

MARAIS, JEAN: Cherbourg, France, Dec. 11, 1913. St. Germain.

MARCEAU, SOPHIE (Maupu): Paris, France, Nov. 17, 1966.

MARCOVICCI, ANDREA: NYC, Nov. 18, 1948.

MARGULIES, JULIANNA: Spring Valley, NY, June 8, 1966.

MARIN, CHEECH (Richard): Los Angeles, July 13, 1946.

MARIN, JACQUES: Paris, France, Sept. 9, 1919. Conservatoire National.

MARINARO, ED: NYC, Mar. 31, 1950. Cornell.

MARS, KENNETH: Chicago, IL, 1936.

MARSDEN, JAMES: Stillwater, OK, Sept. 18, 1973.

MARSH, JEAN: London, England, July 1, 1934.

MARSHALL, KEN: NYC, 1953. Juilliard.

MARSHALL, PENNY: Bronx, NY, Oct. 15, 1942. U NM.

MARSHALL, WILLIAM: Gary, IN, Aug. 19, 1924. NYU.

MARTIN, ANDREA: Portland, ME, Jan. 15, 1947.

MARTIN, DICK: Battle Creek, MI Jan. 30, 1923.

MARTIN, GEORGE N.: NYC, Aug. 15, 1929.

MARTIN, MILLICENT: Romford, England, June 8, 1934.

MARTIN, PAMELA SUE: Westport, CT, Jan. 15, 1953.

MARTIN, STEVE: Waco, TX, Aug. 14, 1945. UCLA.

MARTIN, TONY (Alfred Norris): Oakland, CA, Dec. 25, 1913. St. Mary's College.

MASON, MARSHA: St. Louis, MO, Apr. 3, 1942. Webster College.

MASSEN, OSA: Copenhagen, Denmark, Jan. 13, 1916.

MASTERS, BEN: Corvallis, OR, May 6, 1947. U OR.

MASTERSON, MARY STUART: Los Angeles, June 28, 1966, NYU.

MASTERSON, PETER: Angleton, TX, June 1, 1934. Rice.

MASTRANTONIO, MARY ELIZABETH: Chicago, IL, Nov. 17, 1958. U IL.

MASUR, RICHARD: NYC, Nov. 20, 1948.

MATHESON, TIM: Glendale, CA, Dec. 31, 1947. Cal. St.

MATHIS, SAMANTHA: NYC, May 12, 1970.

MATLIN, MARLEE: Morton Grove, IL, Aug. 24, 1965.

MATTHEWS, BRIAN: Philadelphia, Jan. 24. 1953. St. Olaf.

MAY, ELAINE (Berlin): Philadelphia, PA, Apr. 21, 1932.

MAYO, VIRGINIA (Virginia Clara Jones): St. Louis, MO, Nov. 30, 1920.

MAYRON, MELANIE: Philadelphia, PA, Oct. 20, 1952. AADA.

MAZURSKY, PAUL: Brooklyn, NY, Apr. 25, 1930. Bklyn College.

MAZZELLO, JOSEPH: Rhinebeck, NY, Sept. 21, 1983.

McCALLUM, DAVID: Scotland, Sept. 19, 1933. Chapman College.

McCAMBRIDGE, MERCEDES: Jolliet, IL, Mar. 17, 1918. Mundelein College.

McCARTHY, ANDREW: NYC, Nov. 29, 1962, NYU.

McCARTHY, KEVIN: Seattle, WA, Feb. 15, 1914. MN U.

McCARTNEY, PAUL: Liverpool, England, June 18, 1942.

McCLANAHAN, RUE: Healdton, OK, Feb. 21, 1934.

McCLORY, SEAN: Dublin, Ireland, Mar. 8, 1924. U Galway.

McCLURE, MARC: San Mateo, CA, Mar. 31, 1957.

McCLURG, EDIE: Kansas City, MO, July 23, 1950.

McCORMACK, CATHERINE: Alton, Hampshire, Eng., Jan. 1, 1972.

McCOWEN, ALEC: Tunbridge Wells, England, May 26, 1925. RADA.

McCRANE, PAUL: Philadelphia, PA, Jan. 19. 1961.

McCRARY, DARIUS: Walnut, CA, May 1, 1976.

McDERMOTT, DYLAN: Waterbury, CT, Oct. 26, 1962. Neighborhood Playhouse.

McDONALD, CHRISTOPHER: NYC, 1955.

McDONNELL, MARY: Wilkes Barre, PA, Apr. 28, 1952.

McDORMAND, FRANCES: Illinois, June 23, 1957.

McDOWELL, MALCOLM (Taylor): Leeds, England, June 19, 1943. LAMDA.

McELHONE, NATASCHA (Natasha Taylor): London, England, Mar. 23, 1971.

McENERY, PETER: Walsall, England, Feb. 21, 1940.

McENTIRE, REBA: McAlester, OK, Mar. 28, 1955. Southeastern St. U.

McGAVIN, DARREN: Spokane, WA, May 7, 1922. College of Pacific.

McGILL, EVERETT: Miami Beach, FL, Oct. 21, 1945.

McGILLIS, KELLY: Newport Beach, CA, July 9, 1957. Juilliard.

McGINLEY, JOHN C.: NYC, Aug. 3, 1959. NYU.

McGOOHAN, PATRICK: NYC, Mar. 19, 1928.

McGOVERN, ELIZABETH: Evanston, IL. July 18, 1961. Juilliard.

McGOVERN, MAUREEN: Youngstown, OH, July 27, 1949.

McGREGOR, EWAN: Perth, Scotland, March 31, 1971

McGUIRE, BIFF: New Haven, CT, Oct. 25. 1926. MA St. Col.

McHATTIE, STEPHEN: Antigonish, NS, Feb. 3. Acadia U, AADA.

McKAY, GARDNER: NYC, June 10, 1932. Comell.

McKEAN, MICHAEL: NYC, Oct. 17, 1947.

McKEE, LONETTE: Detroit, MI, July 22, 1955.

McKELLEN, IAN: Burnley, England, May 25, 1939.

McKENNA, VIRGINIA: London, England, June 7, 1931.

McKEON, DOUG: Pompton Plains, NJ, June 10, 1966.

McKERN, LEO: Sydney, Australia, Mar. 16, 1920.

McKUEN, ROD: Oakland, CA, Apr. 29, 1933.

McLERIE, ALLYN ANN: Grand Mere, Canada, Dec. 1, 1926.

McMAHON, ED: Detroit, MI, Mar. 6, 1923.

McNAIR, BARBARA: Chicago, IL, Mar. 4, 1939. UCLA.

McNAMARA, WILLIAM: Dallas, TX, Mar. 31, 1965.

McNICHOL, KRISTY: Los Angeles, Sept. 11, 1962.

McQUEEN, ARMELIA: NC, Jan. 6, 1952. Bklyn Consv.

McQUEEN, CHAD: Los Angeles, Dec. 28, 1960. Actors Studio.

McRANEY, GERALD: Collins, MS, Aug. 19, 1948.

McSHANE, IAN: Blackburn, England, Sept. 29, 1942. RADA.

McTEER, JANET: York, England, 1961.

MEADOWS, JAYNE (Jayne Cotter): Wuchang, China, Sept. 27, 1924. St. Margaret's.

MEANEY, COLM: Dublin, Ireland, May 30, 1953.

MEARA, ANNE: Brooklyn, NY, Sept. 20, 1929.

MEAT LOAF (Marvin Lee Aday): Dallas, TX, Sept. 27, 1947.

MEDWIN, MICHAEL: London, England, 1925. Inst. Fischer.

MEKKA, EDDIE: Worcester, MA, June 14, 1952. Boston Cons.

MELATO, MARIANGELA: Milan, Italy, 1941. Milan Theatre Acad.

MEREDITH, LEE (Judi Lee Sauls): Oct. 22, 1947. AADA.

MERKERSON, S. EPATHA: Saganaw, MI, Nov. 28, 1952. Wayne St. U.

MERRILL, DINA (Nedinia Hutton): NYC, Dec. 29, 1925. AADA.

MESSING, DEBRA: Brooklyn, NY, Aug. 15, 1968.

METCALF, LAURIE: Edwardsville, IL, June 16, 1955. IL St. U.

METZLER, JIM: Oneonta, NY, June 23, 1955. Dartmouth.

MEYER, BRECKIN: Minneapolis, MN, May 7, 1974.

MICHELL, KEITH: Adelaide, Australia, Dec. 1, 1926.

MIDLER, BETTE: Honolulu, HI, Dec. 1, 1945.

MILANO, ALYSSA: Brooklyn, NY, Dec. 19, 1972.

MILES, JOANNA: Nice, France, Mar. 6, 1940.

MILES, SARAH: Ingatestone, England, Dec. 31, 1941. RADA.

MILES, SYLVIA: NYC, Sept. 9, 1934. Actors Studio.

MILES, VERA (Ralston): Boise City, OK, Aug. 23, 1929. UCLA.

MILLER, ANN (Lucille Ann Collier): Chireno, TX, Apr. 12, 1919. Lawler Professional School.

MILLER, BARRY: Los Angeles, Feb. 6, 1958.

MILLER, DICK: NYC, Dec. 25, 1928.

MILLER, JONNY LEE: Surrey, England, Nov. 15, 1972.

MILLER, LINDA: NYC, Sept. 16, 1942. Catholic U.

MILLER, PENELOPE ANN: Santa Monica, CA, Jan. 13, 1964.

MILLER, REBECCA: Roxbury, CT, 1962. Yale.

MILLS, DONNA: Chicago, IL, Dec. 11, 1945. U IL.

MILLS, HAYLEY: London, England, Apr. 18, 1946. Elmhurst School.

MILLS, JOHN: Suffolk, England, Feb. 22, 1908.

MILLS, JULIET: London, England, Nov. 21, 1941.

MILNER, MARTIN: Detroit, MI, Dec. 28, 1931.

MIMIEUX, YVETTE: Los Angeles, Jan. 8, 1941. Hollywood High.

MINNELLI, LIZA: Los Angeles, Mar. 19, l946.

MIOU-MIOU (Sylvette Henry): Paris, France, Feb. 22, 1950.

MIRREN, HELEN (Ilynea Mironoff): London, July 26, 1946.

MITCHELL, JAMES: Sacramento, CA, Feb. 29, 1920. LACC.

MITCHELL, JOHN CAMERON: El Paso, TX, Apr. 21, 1963. Northwestern.

MITCHUM, JAMES: Los Angeles, CA, May 8, 1941.

MODINE, MATTHEW: Loma Linda, CA, Mar. 22, 1959.

MOFFAT, DONALD: Plymouth, England, Dec. 26, 1930. RADA.

MOFFETT, D. W.: Highland Park, IL, Oct. 26, 1954. Stanford.

MOHR, JAY: NJ, Aug. 23, 1971.

MOKAE, ZAKES: Johannesburg, South Africa, Aug. 5, 1935. RADA.

Frances McDormand   Breckin Meyer   Demi Moore   Viggo Mortensen

MOLINA, ALFRED: London, England, May 24, 1953. Guildhall.
MOLL, RICHARD: Pasadena, CA, Jan. 13, 1943.
MONAGHAN, DOMINIC: Berlin, Germany, Dec. 8, 1976.
MONK, DEBRA: Middletown, OH, Feb. 27, 1949.
MONTALBAN, RICARDO: Mexico City, Mexico, Nov. 25, 1920.
MONTENEGRO, FERNADA (Arlete Pinheiro)**:** Rio de Janiero, Brazil, 1929.
MONTGOMERY, BELINDA: Winnipeg, Manitoba, Canada, July 23, 1950.
MOODY, RON: London, England, Jan. 8, 1924. London U.
MOOR, BILL: Toledo, OH, July 13, 1931. Northwestern.
MOORE, CONSTANCE: Sioux City, IA, Jan. 18, 1919.
MOORE, DEMI (Guines)**:** Roswell, NM, Nov. 11, 1962.
MOORE, DICK: Los Angeles, Sept. 12, 1925.
MOORE, DUDLEY: Dagenham, Essex, England, Apr. 19, 1935.
MOORE, JULIANNE (Julie Anne Smith)**:** Fayetteville, NC, Dec. 30, 1960.
MOORE, KIERON: County Cork, Ireland, 1925. St. Mary's College.
MOORE, MARY TYLER: Brooklyn, NY, Dec. 29, 1936.
MOORE, ROGER: London, England, Oct. 14, 1927. RADA.
MOORE, TERRY (Helen Koford)**:** Los Angeles, Jan. 7, 1929.
MORALES, ESAI: Brooklyn, NY, Oct. 1, 1962.
MORANIS, RICK: Toronto, Canada, Apr. 18, 1954.
MOREAU, JEANNE: Paris, France, Jan. 23, 1928.
MORENO, RITA (Rosita Alverio)**:** Humacao, PR, Dec. 11, 1931.
MORGAN, HARRY (HENRY) (Harry Bratsburg)**:** Detroit, MI, Apr. 10, 1915. U Chicago.
MORGAN, MICHELE (Simone Roussel)**:** Paris, France, Feb. 29, 1920. Paris Dramatic School.
MORIARTY, CATHY: Bronx, NY, Nov. 29, 1960.
MORIARTY, MICHAEL: Detroit, MI, Apr. 5, 1941. Dartmouth.
MORISON, PATRICIA: NYC, Mar. 19, 1915.
MORITA, NORIYUKI "PAT": Isleton, CA, June 28, 1932.
MORRIS, GARRETT: New Orleans, LA, Feb. 1, 1937.
MORRIS, HOWARD: NYC, Sept. 4, 1919. NYU.
MORROW, ROB: New Rochelle, NY, Sept. 21, 1962.
MORSE, DAVID: Hamilton, MA, Oct. 11, 1953.
MORSE, ROBERT: Newton, MA, May 18, 1931.
MORTENSEN, VIGGO: NYC, Oct. 20, 1958.
MORTON, JOE: NYC, Oct. 18, 1947. Hofstra.

MORTON, SAMANTHA: Nottingham, England, 1977.
MOSES, WILLIAM: Los Angeles, Nov. 17, 1959.
MOSS, CARRIE-ANNE: Vancouver, BC, Canada, Aug. 21, 1967.
MOSTEL, JOSH: NYC, Dec. 21, 1946. Brandeis U.
MOUCHET, CATHERINE: Paris, France, 1959. Ntl. Consv.
MUELLER-STAHL, ARMIN: Tilsit, East Prussia, Dec. 17, 1930.
MULDAUR, DIANA: NYC, Aug. 19, 1938. Sweet Briar College.
MULGREW, KATE: Dubuque, IA, Apr. 29, 1955. NYU.
MULHERN, MATT: Philadelphia, PA, July 21, 1960. Rutgers.
MULL, MARTIN: N. Ridgefield, OH, Aug. 18, 1941. RI Sch. of Design.
MULRONEY, DERMOT: Alexandria, VA, Oct. 31, 1963. Northwestern.
MUMY, BILL (Charles William Mumy, Jr.)**:** San Gabriel, CA, Feb. 1, 1954.
MURPHY, BRITTANY: Atlanta, GA, Nov. 10, 1977.
MURPHY, DONNA: Queens, NY, March 7, 1958.
MURPHY, EDDIE: Brooklyn, NY, Apr. 3, 1961.
MURPHY, MICHAEL: Los Angeles, May 5, 1938. U AZ.
MURRAY, BILL: Wilmette, IL, Sept. 21, 1950. Regis College.
MURRAY, DON: Hollywood, CA, July 31, 1929.
MUSANTE, TONY: Bridgeport, CT, June 30, 1936. Oberlin College.
MYERS, MIKE: Scarborough, Canada, May 25, 1963.
NABORS, JIM: Sylacauga, GA, June 12, 1932.
NADER, GEORGE: Pasadena, CA, Oct. 19, 1921. Occidental College.
NADER, MICHAEL: Los Angeles, 1945.
NAMATH, JOE: Beaver Falls, PA, May 31, 1943. U AL.
NAUGHTON, DAVID: Hartford, CT, Feb. 13, 1951.
NAUGHTON, JAMES: Middletown, CT, Dec. 6, 1945.
NEAL, PATRICIA: Packard, KY, Jan. 20, 1926. Northwestern.
NEESON, LIAM: Ballymena, Northern Ireland, June 7, 1952.
NEFF, HILDEGARDE (Hildegard Knef)**:** Ulm, Germany, Dec. 28, 1925. Berlin Art Acad.
NEILL, SAM: Northern Ireland, Sept. 14, 1947. U Canterbury.
NELL, NATHALIE: Paris, France, Oct. 1950.
NELLIGAN, KATE: London, Ontario, Canada, Mar. 16, 1951. U Toronto.
NELSON, BARRY (Robert Nielsen)**:** Oakland, CA, Apr. 16, 1920.
NELSON, CRAIG T.: Spokane, WA, Apr. 4, 1946.

Paul Newman   Clive Owen   Amanda Peet   Joaquin Phoenix

NELSON, DAVID: NYC, Oct. 24, 1936. USC.

NELSON, JUDD: Portland, ME, Nov. 28, 1959, Haverford College.

NELSON, LORI (Dixie Kay Nelson): Santa Fe, NM, Aug. 15, 1933.

NELSON, TRACY: Santa Monica, CA, Oct. 25, 1963.

NELSON, WILLIE: Abbott, TX, Apr. 30, 1933.

NEMEC, CORIN: Little Rock, AK, Nov. 5, 1971.

NERO, FRANCO (Francisco Spartanero): Parma, Italy, Nov. 23, 1941.

NESMITH, MICHAEL: Houston, TX, Dec. 30, 1942.

NETTLETON, LOIS: Oak Park, IL, 1931. Actors Studio.

NEUWIRTH, BEBE: Princeton, NJ, Dec. 31, 1958.

NEWHART, BOB: Chicago, IL, Sept. 5, 1929. Loyola.

NEWMAN, BARRY: Boston, MA, Nov. 7, 1938. Brandeis.

NEWMAN, LARAINE: Los Angeles, Mar. 2, 1952.

NEWMAN, NANETTE: Northampton, England, 1934.

NEWMAN, PAUL: Cleveland, OH, Jan. 26, 1925. Yale.

NEWMAR, JULIE (Newmeyer): Los Angeles, Aug. 16, 1933.

NEWTON, THANDIE: Zambia, 1972.

NEWTON-JOHN, OLIVIA: Cambridge, England, Sept. 26, 1948.

NGUYEN, DUSTIN: Saigon, Vietnam, Sept. 17, 1962.

NICHOLAS, DENISE: Detroit, MI, July 12, 1945.

NICHOLAS, PAUL: London, England, 1945.

NICHOLS, NICHELLE: Robbins, IL, Dec. 28, 1933.

NICHOLSON, JACK: Neptune, NJ, Apr. 22, 1937.

NICKERSON, DENISE: NYC, 1959.

NICOL, ALEX: Ossining, NY, Jan. 20, 1919. Actors Studio.

NIELSEN, BRIGITTE: Denmark, July 15, 1963.

NIELSEN, LESLIE: Regina, Saskatchewan. Canada, Feb. 11, 1926. Neighborhood Playhouse.

NIMOY, LEONARD: Boston, MA, Mar. 26, 1931. Boston College, Antioch College.

NIXON, CYNTHIA: NYC, Apr. 9, 1966. Columbia.

NOBLE, JAMES: Dallas, TX, Mar. 5, 1922, SMU.

NOIRET, PHILIPPE: Lille, France, Oct. 1, 1930.

NOLAN, KATHLEEN: St. Louis, MO, Sept. 27, 1933. Neighborhood Playhouse.

NOLTE, NICK: Omaha, NE, Feb. 8, 1940. Pasadena City College.

NORRIS, BRUCE: Houston, TX, May 16, 1960. Northwestern.

NORRIS, CHRISTOPHER: NYC, Oct. 7, 1943. Lincoln Square Academy

NORRIS, CHUCK (Carlos Ray): Ryan, OK, Mar. 10, 1940.

NORTH, HEATHER: Pasadena, CA, Dec. 13, 1950. Actors Workshop.

NORTH, SHEREE (Dawn Bethel): Los Angeles. Jan. 17, 1933. Hollywood High.

NORTHAM, JEREMY: Cambridge, England, Dec. 1, 1961.

NORTON, EDWARD: Boston, MA, Aug. 18, 1969.

NORTON, KEN: Jacksonville, IL, Aug. 9, 1945.

NOSEWORTHY, JACK: Lynn, MA, Dec. 21, 1969.

NOURI, MICHAEL: Washington, DC, Dec. 9, 1945.

NOVAK, KIM (Marilyn Novak): Chicago, IL, Feb. 13, 1933. LACC.

NOVELLO, DON: Ashtabula, OH, Jan. 1, 1943. U Dayton.

NUYEN, FRANCE (Vannga): Marseilles, France, July 31, 1939. Beaux Arts School.

O'BRIAN, HUGH (Hugh J. Krampe): Rochester, N,. Apr. 19, 1928. Cincinnati U.

O'BRIEN, CLAY: Ray, AZ, May 6, 1961.

O'BRIEN, MARGARET (Angela Maxine O'Brien): Los Angeles, Jan. 15, 1937.

O'CONNELL, JERRY (Jeremiah O'Connell): NYC, Feb. 17, 1974.

O'CONNOR, CARROLL: Bronx, NY, Aug. 2, 1924. Dublin National U.

O'CONNOR, DONALD: Chicago, IL, Aug. 28, 1925.

O'CONNOR, GLYNNIS: NYC, Nov. 19, 1955. NYSU.

O'DONNELL, CHRIS: Winetka, IL, June 27, 1970.

O'DONNELL, ROSIE: Commack, NY, March 21, 1961.

O'HARA, CATHERINE: Toronto, Canada, Mar. 4, 1954.

O'HARA, MAUREEN (Maureen Fitz-Simons): Dublin, Ireland, Aug. 17, 1920.

O'HERLIHY, DAN: Wexford, Ireland, May 1, 1919. National U.

O'KEEFE, MICHAEL: Larchmont, NY, Apr. 24, 1955. NYU, AADA.

OLDMAN, GARY: New Cross, South London, England, Mar. 21, 1958.

OLIN, KEN: Chicago, IL, July 30, 1954. U PA.

OLIN, LENA: Stockholm, Sweden, Mar. 22, 1955.

OLMOS, EDWARD JAMES: Los Angeles, Feb. 24, 1947. CSLA.

O'LOUGHLIN, GERALD S.: NYC, Dec. 23, 1921. U Rochester.

OLSON, JAMES: Evanston, IL, Oct. 8, 1930.

OLSON, NANCY: Milwaukee, WI, July 14, 1928. UCLA.

OLYPHANT, TIMOTHY: HI, May 20, 1968.
O'NEAL, GRIFFIN: Los Angeles, 1965.
O'NEAL, RON: Utica, NY, Sept. 1, 1937. OH St.
O'NEAL, RYAN: Los Angeles, Apr. 20, 1941.
O'NEAL, TATUM: Los Angeles, Nov. 5, 1963.
O'NEIL, TRICIA: Shreveport, LA, Mar. 11, 1945. Baylor.
O'NEILL, ED: Youngstown, OH, Apr. 12, 1946.
O'NEILL, JENNIFER: Rio de Janeiro, Brazil, Feb. 20, 1949. Neighborhood Playhouse.
ONTKEAN, MICHAEL: Vancouver, BC, Canada, Jan. 24, 1946.
O'QUINN, TERRY: Newbury, MI, July 15, 1952.
ORBACH, JERRY: Bronx, NY, Oct. 20, 1935.
ORMOND, JULIA: Epsom, England, Jan. 4, 1965.
O'SHEA, MILO: Dublin, Ireland, June 2, 1926.
OSMENT, HALEY JOEL: Los Angeles, Apr. 10, 1988.
O'TOOLE, ANNETTE (Toole): Houston, TX, Apr. 1, 1953. UCLA.
O'TOOLE, PETER: Connemara, Ireland, Aug. 2, 1932. RADA.
OVERALL, PARK: Nashville, TN, Mar. 15, 1957. Tusculum College.
OWEN, CLIVE: Coventry, England, 1965.
OZ, FRANK (Oznowicz): Hereford, England, May 25, 1944.
PACINO, AL: NYC, Apr. 25, 1940.
PACULA, JOANNA: Tamaszow Lubelski, Poland, Jan. 2, 1957. Polish Natl. Theatre Sch.
PAGET, DEBRA (Debralee Griffin): Denver, CO, Aug. 19, 1933.
PAIGE, JANIS (Donna Mae Jaden): Tacoma, WA, Sept. 16, 1922.
PALANCE, JACK (Walter Palanuik): Lattimer, PA, Feb. 18, 1920. U NC.
PALIN, MICHAEL: Sheffield, Yorkshire, England, May 5, 1943, Oxford.
PALMER, BETSY: East Chicago, IN, Nov. 1, 1926. DePaul.
PALMER, GREGG (Palmer Lee): San Francisco, Jan. 25, 1927. U UT.
PALMINTERI, CHAZZ (Calogero Lorenzo Palminteri): NYC, May 15, 1952.
PALTROW, GWYNETH: Los Angeles, Sept. 28, 1973.
PAMPANINI, SILVANA: Rome, Italy, Sept. 25, 1925.
PANEBIANCO, RICHARD: NYC, 1971.
PANKIN, STUART: Philadelphia, PA, Apr. 8, 1946.
PANTOLIANO, JOE: Jersey City, NJ, Sept. 12, 1954.
PAPAS, IRENE: Chiliomodion, Greece, Mar. 9, 1929.
PAQUIN, ANNA: Winnipeg, Manitoba, Canada, July, 24, 1982.
PARE, MICHAEL: Brooklyn, NY, Oct. 9, 1959.
PARKER, COREY: NYC, July 8, 1965. NYU.
PARKER, ELEANOR: Cedarville, OH, June 26, 1922. Pasadena Playhouse.
PARKER, FESS: Fort Worth, TX, Aug. 16, 1925. USC.
PARKER, JAMESON: Baltimore, MD, Nov. l8, 1947. Beloit College.
PARKER, JEAN (Mae Green): Deer Lodge, MT, Aug. 11, 1912.
PARKER, MARY-LOUISE: Ft. Jackson, SC, Aug. 2, 1964. Bard College.
PARKER, NATHANIEL: London, England, 1963.
PARKER, SARAH JESSICA: Nelsonville, OH, Mar. 25, 1965.
PARKER, SUZY (Cecelia Parker): San Antonio, TX, Oct. 28, 1933.
PARKER, TREY: Auburn, AL, May 30, 1972.
PARKINS, BARBARA: Vancouver, BC, Canada, May 22, 1943.
PARKS, MICHAEL: Corona, CA, Apr. 4, 1938.
PARSONS, ESTELLE: Lynn, MA, Nov. 20, 1927. Boston U.
PARTON, DOLLY: Sevierville, TN, Jan. 19, 1946.
PATINKIN, MANDY: Chicago, IL, Nov. 30, 1952. Juilliard.

PATRIC, JASON: NYC, June 17, 1966.
PATRICK, DENNIS: Philadelphia, PA, Mar. 14, 1918.
PATTERSON, LEE: Vancouver, BC, Canada, Mar. 31, 1929. Ontario College.
PATTON, WILL: Charleston, SC, June 14, 1954.
PAULIK, JOHAN: Prague, Czechoslovakia, 1975.
PAVAN, MARISA (Marisa Pierangeli): Cagliari, Sardinia, June 19, 1932. Torquado Tasso College.
PAXTON, BILL: Fort Worth, TX, May. 17, 1955.
PAYMER, DAVID: Long Island, NY, Aug. 30, 1954.
PAYS, AMANDA: Berkshire, England, June 6, 1959.
PEACH, MARY: Durban, South Africa, 1934.
PEARCE, GUY: Ely, England, Oct. 5, 1967.
PEARSON, BEATRICE: Dennison, TX, July 27, 1920.
PECK, GREGORY: La Jolla, CA, Apr. 5, 1916. U CA.
PEET, AMANDA: NYC, Jan. 11, 1972.
PEÑA, ELIZABETH: Cuba, Sept. 23, 1961.
PENDLETON, AUSTIN: Warren, OH, Mar. 27, 1940. Yale.
PENHALL, BRUCE: Balboa, CA, Aug. 17, 1960.
PENN, SEAN: Burbank, CA, Aug. 17, 1960.
PEREZ, JOSE: NYC, 1940.
PEREZ, ROSIE: Brooklyn, NY, Sept. 6, 1964.
PERKINS, ELIZABETH: Queens, NY, Nov. 18, 1960. Goodman School.
PERKINS, MILLIE: Passaic, NJ, May 12, 1938.
PERLMAN, RHEA: Brooklyn, NY, Mar. 31, 1948.
PERLMAN, RON: NYC, Apr. 13, 1950. U MN.
PERREAU, GIGI (Ghislaine): Los Angeles, Feb. 6, 1941.
PERRINE, VALERIE: Galveston, TX, Sept. 3, 1943. U AZ.
PERRY, LUKE (Coy Luther Perry, III): Fredricktown, OH, Oct. 11, 1966.
PESCI, JOE: Newark, NJ. Feb. 9, 1943.
PESCOW, DONNA: Brooklyn, NY, Mar. 24, 1954.
PETERS, BERNADETTE (Lazzara): Jamaica, NY, Feb. 28, 1948.
PETERS, BROCK: NYC, July 2, 1927. CCNY.
PETERSEN, PAUL: Glendale, CA, Sept. 23, 1945. Valley College.
PETERSEN, WILLIAM: Chicago, IL, Feb. 21, 1953.
PETERSON, CASSANDRA: Colorado Springs, CO, Sept. 17, 1951.
PETTET, JOANNA: London, England, Nov. 16, 1944. Neighborhood Playhouse.
PETTY, LORI: Chattanooga, TN, 1964.
PFEIFFER, MICHELLE: Santa Ana, CA, Apr. 29, 1958.
PHIFER, MEKHI: NYC, Dec. 12, 1975.
PHILLIPPE, RYAN (Matthew Phillippe): New Castle, DE, Sept. 10, 1975.
PHILLIPS, LOU DIAMOND: Phillipines, Feb. 17, 1962, U TX.
PHILLIPS, MacKENZIE: Alexandria, VA, Nov. 10, 1959.
PHILLIPS, MICHELLE (Holly Gilliam): Long Beach, CA, June 4, 1944.
PHILLIPS, SIAN: Bettws, Wales, May 14, 1934. U Wales.
PHOENIX, JOAQUIN: PR, Oct. 28, 1974.
PICARDO, ROBERT: Philadelphia, PA, Oct. 27, 1953. Yale.
PICERNI, PAUL: NYC, Dec. 1, 1922. Loyola.
PIDGEON, REBECCA: Cambridge, MA, 1963.
PIERCE, DAVID HYDE: Saratoga Springs, NY, Apr. 3, 1959.
PIGOTT-SMITH, TIM: Rugby, England, May 13, 1946.
PINCHOT, BRONSON: NYC, May 20, 1959. Yale.
PINE, PHILLIP: Hanford, CA, July 16, 1920. Actors' Lab.

PISCOPO, JOE: Passaic, NJ, June 17, 1951.

PISIER, MARIE-FRANCE: Vietnam, May 10, 1944. U Paris.

PITILLO, MARIA: Mahwah, NJ, 1965.

PITT, BRAD (William Bradley Pitt): Shawnee, OK, Dec. 18, 1963.

PIVEN, JEREMY: NYC, July 26, 1965.

PLACE, MARY KAY: Tulsa OK, Sept. 23, 1947. U Tulsa.

PLATT, OLIVER: Oct. 10, 1960.

PLAYTEN, ALICE: NYC, Aug. 28, 1947. NYU.

PLESHETTE, SUZANNE: NYC, Jan. 31, 1937. Syracuse U.

PLIMPTON, MARTHA: NYC, Nov. 16, 1970.

PLOWRIGHT, JOAN: Scunthorpe, Brigg, Lincolnshire, England, Oct. 28, 1929. Old Vic.

PLUMB, EVE: Burbank, CA, Apr. 29, 1958.

PLUMMER, AMANDA: NYC, Mar. 23, 1957. Middlebury College.

PLUMMER, CHRISTOPHER: Toronto, Canada, Dec. 13, 1927.

PODESTA, ROSSANA: Tripoli, Libya, June 20, 1934.

POITIER, SIDNEY: Miami, FL, Feb. 27, 1927.

POLANSKI, ROMAN: Paris, France, Aug. 18, 1933.

POLITO, JON: Philadelphia, PA, Dec. 29, 1950. Villanova.

POLITO, LINA: Naples, Italy, Aug. 11, 1954.

POLLACK, SYDNEY: South Bend, IN, July 1, 1934.

POLLAK, KEVIN: San Francisco, CA, Oct. 30, 1958.

POLLAN, TRACY: NYC, June 22, 1960.

POLLARD, MICHAEL J.: Passaic, NJ, May 30, 1939.

POLLEY, SARAH: Jan. 8, 1979.

PORTMAN, NATALIE; Jerusalem, Israel, June 9, 1981.

POSEY, PARKER: Baltimore, MD, Nov. 8, 1968.

POSTLETHWAITE, PETE: London, England, Feb. 7, 1945.

POTTER, MONICA: Cleveland, OH, June 30, 1971.

POTTS, ANNIE: Nashville, TN, Oct. 28, 1952. Stephens College.

POWELL, JANE (Suzanne Burce): Portland, OR, Apr. 1, 1928.

POWELL, ROBERT: Salford, England, June 1, 1944. Manchester U.

POWER, TARYN: Los Angeles, Sept. 13, 1953.

POWER, TYRONE, IV: Los Angeles, Jan. 22, 1959.

POWERS, MALA (Mary Ellen): San Francisco, CA, Dec. 29, 1921. UCLA.

POWERS, STEFANIE (Federkiewicz): Hollywood, CA, Oct. 12, 1942.

PRENTISS, PAULA (Paula Ragusa): San Antonio, TX, Mar. 4, 1939. Northwestern.

PRESLE, MICHELINE (Micheline Chassagne): Paris, France, Aug. 22, 1922. Rouleau Drama School.

PRESLEY, PRISCILLA: Brooklyn, NY, May 24, 1945.

PRESNELL, HARVE: Modesto, CA, Sept. 14, 1933. USC.

PRESTON, KELLY: Honolulu, HI, Oct. 13, 1962. USC.

PRESTON, WILLIAM: Columbia, PA, Aug. 26, 1921. PA St. U.

PRICE, LONNY: NYC, Mar. 9, 1959. Juilliard.

PRIESTLEY, JASON: Vancouver, BC, Canada, Aug, 28, 1969.

PRIMUS, BARRY: NYC, Feb. 16, 1938. CCNY.

PRINCE (P. Rogers Nelson): Minneapolis, MN, June 7, 1958.

PRINCIPAL, VICTORIA: Fukuoka, Japan, Jan. 3, 1945. Dade Jr. College.

PRINZE, FREDDIE, JR.: Los Angeles, March 8, 1976.

PROCHNOW, JURGEN: Berlin, Germany, June 10, 1941.

PROSKY, ROBERT: Philadelphia, PA, Dec. 13, 1930.

PROVAL, DAVID: Brooklyn, NY, May 20, 1942.

PROVINE, DOROTHY: Deadwood, SD, Jan. 20, 1937. U WA.

PRYCE, JONATHAN: Wales, UK, June 1, 1947, RADA.

PRYOR, RICHARD: Peoria, IL, Dec. 1, 1940.

PULLMAN, BILL: Delphi, NY, Dec. 17, 1954. SUNY/Oneonta, U MA.

PURCELL, LEE: Cherry Point, NC, June 15, 1947. Stephens.

PURDOM, EDMUND: Welwyn Garden City, England, Dec. 19, 1924. St. Ignatius College.

QUAID, DENNIS: Houston, TX, Apr. 9, 1954.

QUAID, RANDY: Houston, TX, Oct. 1, 1950. U Houston.

QUINLAN, KATHLEEN: Mill Valley, CA, Nov. 19, 1954.

QUINN, AIDAN: Chicago, IL, Mar. 8, 1959.

RADCLIFFE, DANIEL: London, England, July 23, 1989.

RAFFERTY, FRANCES: Sioux City, IA, June 16, 1922. UCLA.

RAFFIN, DEBORAH: Los Angeles, Mar. 13, 1953. Valley College.

RAGSDALE, WILLIAM: El Dorado, AK, Jan. 19, 1961. Hendrix College.

RAILSBACK, STEVE: Dallas, TX, 1948.

RAINER, LUISE: Vienna, Austria, Jan. 12, 1910.

RALSTON, VERA (Vera Helena Hruba): Prague, Czechoslovakia, July 12, 1919.

RAMIS, HAROLD: Chicago, IL, Nov. 21, 1944. Washington U.

RAMPLING, CHARLOTTE: Surmer, England, Feb. 5, 1946. U Madrid.

RAMSEY, LOGAN: Long Beach, CA, Mar. 21, 1921. St. Joseph.

RANDALL, TONY (Leonard Rosenberg): Tulsa, OK, Feb. 26, 1920. Northwestern.

RANDELL, RON: Sydney, Australia, Oct. 8, 1920. St. Mary's College.

RAPAPORT, MICHAEL: March 20, 1970.

RAPP, ANTHONY: Chicago, IL, Oct. 26, 1971.

RASCHE, DAVID: St. Louis, MO, Aug. 7, 1944.

REA, STEPHEN: Belfast, Northern Ireland, Oct. 31, 1949.

REAGAN, RONALD: Tampico, IL, Feb. 6, 1911. Eureka College.

REASON, REX: Berlin, Germany, Nov. 30, 1928. Pasadena Playhouse.

REDDY, HELEN: Melbourne, Australia, Oct. 25, 1942.

REDFORD, ROBERT: Santa Monica, CA, Aug. 18, 1937. AADA.

REDGRAVE, CORIN: London, England, July 16, 1939.

REDGRAVE, LYNN: London, England, Mar. 8, 1943.

REDGRAVE, VANESSA: London, England, Jan. 30, 1937.

REDMAN, JOYCE: County Mayo, Ireland, 1919. RADA.

REED, PAMELA: Tacoma, WA, Apr. 2, 1949.

REEMS, HARRY (Herbert Streicher): Bronx, NY, 1947. U Pittsburgh.

REES, ROGER: Aberystwyth, Wales, May 5, 1944.

REESE, DELLA: Detroit, MI, July 6, 1932.

REEVE, CHRISTOPHER: NYC, Sept. 25, 1952. Cornell, Juilliard.

REEVES, KEANU: Beiruit, Lebanon, Sept. 2, 1964.

REGEHR, DUNCAN: Lethbridge, Canada, Oct. 5, 1952.

REID, ELLIOTT: NYC, Jan. 16, 1920.

REID, TIM: Norfolk, VA, Dec, 19, 1944.

REILLY, CHARLES NELSON: NYC, Jan. 13, 1931. U CT.

REILLY, JOHN C.: Chicago, IL, May 24, 1965.

REINER, CARL: NYC, Mar. 20, 1922. Georgetown.

REINER, ROB: NYC, Mar. 6, 1947. UCLA.

Burt Reynolds   Christina Ricci   Cliff Robertson   Mimi Rogers

REINHOLD, JUDGE (Edward Ernest, Jr.): Wilmington, DE, May 21, 1957. NC Sch. of Arts.
REINKING, ANN: Seattle, WA, Nov. 10, 1949.
REISER, PAUL: NYC, Mar. 30, 1957.
REMAR, JAMES: Boston, MA, Dec. 31, 1953. Neighborhood Playhouse.
RENFRO, BRAD: Knoxville, TN, July 25, 1982.
RENO, JEAN (Juan Moreno): Casablanca, Morocco, July 30, 1948.
REUBENS, PAUL (Paul Reubenfeld): Peekskill, NY, Aug. 27, 1952.
REVILL, CLIVE: Wellington, New Zealand, Apr. 18, 1930.
REY, ANTONIA: Havana, Cuba, Oct. 12, 1927.
REYNOLDS, BURT: Waycross, GA, Feb. 11, 1935. FL. St. U.
REYNOLDS, DEBBIE (Mary Frances Reynolds): El Paso, TX, Apr. 1, 1932.
RHOADES, BARBARA: Poughkeepsie, NY, Mar. 23, 1947.
RHODES, CYNTHIA: Nashville, TN, Nov. 21, 1956.
RHYS-DAVIES, JOHN: Salisbury, England, May 5, 1944.
RHYS-MEYERS, JONATHAN: Cork, Ireland, July 27, 1977.
RIBISI, GIOVANNI: Los Angeles, Dec. 17, 1974.
RICCI, CHRISTINA: Santa Monica, CA, Feb. 12, 1980.
RICHARD, CLIFF (Harry Webb): India, Oct. 14, 1940.
RICHARDS, DENISE: Downers Grove, IL, Feb. 17, 1972.
RICHARDS, MICHAEL: Culver City, CA, July 14, 1949.
RICHARDSON, JOELY: London, England, Jan. 9, 1965.
RICHARDSON, MIRANDA: Southport, England, Mar. 3, 1958.
RICHARDSON, NATASHA: London, England, May 11, 1963.
RICKLES, DON: NYC, May 8, 1926. AADA.
RICKMAN, ALAN: Hammersmith, England, Feb. 21, 1946.
RIEGERT, PETER: NYC, Apr. 11, 1947. U Buffalo.
RIFKIN, RON: NYC, Oct. 31, 1939.
RIGG, DIANA: Doncaster, England, July 20, 1938. RADA.
RILEY, JOHN C.: Chicago, IL, May 24, 1965.
RINGWALD, MOLLY: Rosewood, CA, Feb. 16, 1968.
RITTER, JOHN: Burbank, CA, Sept. 17, 1948. USC.
RIVERS, JOAN (Molinsky): Brooklyn, NY, June 8, 1933.
ROACHE, LINUS: Manchester, England, 1964.
ROBARDS, SAM: NYC, Dec. 16, 1963.
ROBBINS, TIM: NYC, Oct. 16, 1958. UCLA.
ROBERTS, ERIC: Biloxi, MS, Apr. 18, 1956. RADA.

ROBERTS, JULIA: Atlanta, GA, Oct. 28, 1967.
ROBERTS, RALPH: Salisbury, NC, Aug. 17, 1922. UNC.
ROBERTS, TANYA (Leigh): Bronx, NY, Oct. 15, 1954.
ROBERTS, TONY: NYC, Oct. 22, 1939. Northwestern.
ROBERTSON, CLIFF: La Jolla, CA, Sept. 9, 1925. Antioch College.
ROBERTSON, DALE: Oklahoma City, OK, July 14, 1923.
ROBINSON, CHRIS: West Palm Beach, FL, Nov. 5, 1938. LACC.
ROBINSON, JAY: NYC, Apr. 14, 1930.
ROBINSON, ROGER: Seattle, WA, May 2, 1940. USC.
ROCHEFORT, JEAN: Paris, France, 1930.
ROCK, CHRIS: Brooklyn, NY, Feb. 7, 1966.
ROCKWELL, SAM: Daly City, CA, Nov. 5, 1968.
ROGERS, MIMI: Coral Gables, FL, Jan. 27, 1956.
ROGERS, WAYNE: Birmingham, AL, Apr. 7, 1933. Princeton.
RONSTADT, LINDA: Tucson, AZ, July 15, 1946.
ROOKER, MICHAEL: Jasper, AL, Apr. 6, 1955.
ROONEY, MICKEY (Joe Yule, Jr.): Brooklyn, NY, Sept. 23, 1920.
ROSE, REVA: Chicago, IL, July 30, 1940. Goodman.
ROSEANNE (Barr): Salt Lake City, UT, Nov. 3, 1952.
ROSS, DIANA: Detroit, MI, Mar. 26, 1944.
ROSS, JUSTIN: Brooklyn, NY, Dec. 15, 1954.
ROSS, KATHARINE: Hollywood, Jan. 29, 1943. Santa Rosa College.
ROSSELLINI, ISABELLA: Rome, Italy, June 18, 1952.
ROSSOVICH, RICK: Palo Alto, CA, Aug. 28, 1957.
ROTH, TIM: London, England, May 14, 1961.
ROUNDTREE, RICHARD: New Rochelle, NY, Sept. 7, 1942. Southern IL.
ROURKE, MICKEY (Philip Andre Rourke, Jr.): Schenectady, NY, Sept. 16, 1956.
ROWE, NICHOLAS: London, England, Nov. 22, 1966, Eton.
ROWLANDS, GENA: Cambria, WI, June 19, 1934.
RUBIN, ANDREW: New Bedford, MA, June 22, 1946. AADA.
RUBINEK, SAUL: Fohrenwold, Germany, July 2, 1948.
RUBINSTEIN, JOHN: Los Angeles, Dec. 8, 1946. UCLA.
RUCK, ALAN: Cleveland, OH, July 1, 1960.
RUCKER, BO: Tampa, FL, Aug. 17, 1948.
RUDD, PAUL S.: Boston, MA, May 15, 1940.
RUDD, PAUL: Passaic, NJ, Apr. 6, 1969.

Susan Sarandon   Diana Scarwid   Stellan Skarsgård   Christian Slater

RUDNER, RITA: Miami, FL, Sept. 17, 1955.

RUEHL, MERCEDES: Queens, NY, Feb. 28, 1948.

RULE, JANICE: Cincinnati, OH, Aug. 15, 1931.

RUPERT, MICHAEL: Denver, CO, Oct. 23, 1951. Pasadena Playhouse.

RUSH, BARBARA: Denver, CO, Jan. 4, 1927. U Calif.

RUSH, GEOFFREY: Toowoomba, Queensland, Australia, July 6, 1951. U Queensland.

RUSSELL, JANE: Bemidji, MI, June 21, 1921. Max Reinhardt Sch.

RUSSELL, KURT: Springfield, MA, Mar. 17, 1951.

RUSSELL, THERESA (Paup): San Diego, CA, Mar. 20, 1957.

RUSSO, JAMES: NYC, Apr. 23, 1953.

RUSSO, RENE: Burbank, CA, Feb. 17, 1954.

RUTHERFORD, ANN: Toronto, Canada, Nov. 2, 1920.

RYAN, JOHN P.: NYC, July 30, 1936. CCNY.

RYAN, MEG: Fairfield, CT, Nov. 19, 1961. NYU.

RYAN, TIM (Meineslschmidt): Staten Island, NY, 1958. Rutgers.

RYDER, WINONA (Horowitz): Winona, MN, Oct. 29, 1971.

SACCHI, ROBERT: Bronx, NY, 1941. NYU.

SÄGEBRECHT, MARIANNE: Starnberg, Bavaria, Aug. 27, 1945.

SAINT, EVA MARIE: Newark, NJ, July 4, 1924. Bowling Green St. U.

SAINT JAMES, SUSAN (Suzie Jane Miller): Los Angeles, Aug. 14, 1946. CT College.

ST. JOHN, BETTA: Hawthorne, CA, Nov. 26, 1929.

ST. JOHN, JILL (Jill Oppenheim): Los Angeles, Aug. 19, 1940.

SALA, JOHN: Los Angeles, Oct. 5, 1962.

SALDANA, THERESA: Brooklyn, NY, Aug. 20, 1954.

SALINGER, MATT: Windsor, VT, Feb. 13, 1960. Princeton, Columbia.

SALT, JENNIFER: Los Angeles, Sept. 4, 1944. Sarah Lawrence College.

SAMMS, EMMA: London, England, Aug. 28, 1960.

SAN GIACOMO, LAURA: Orange, NJ, Nov. 14, 1961.

SANDERS, JAY O.: Austin, TX, Apr. 16, 1953.

SANDLER, ADAM: Bronx, NY, Sept. 9, 1966. NYU.

SANDS, JULIAN: Yorkshire, England, Jan 15, 1958.

SANDS, TOMMY: Chicago, IL, Aug. 27, 1937.

SAN JUAN, OLGA: NYC, Mar. 16, 1927.

SARA, MIA (Sarapocciello): Brooklyn, NY, June 19, 1967.

SARANDON, CHRIS: Beckley, WV, July 24, 1942. U WV, Catholic U.

SARANDON, SUSAN (Tomalin): NYC, Oct. 4, 1946. Catholic U.

SARRAZIN, MICHAEL: Quebec City, Quebec, Canada, May 22, 1940.

SAVAGE, FRED: Highland Park, IL, July 9, 1976.

SAVAGE, JOHN (Youngs): Long Island, NY, Aug. 25, 1949. AADA.

SAVIOLA, CAMILLE: Bronx, NY, July 16, 1950.

SAVOY, TERESA ANN: London, England, July 18, 1955.

SAXON, JOHN (Carmen Orrico): Brooklyn, NY, Aug. 5, 1935.

SBARGE, RAPHAEL: NYC, Feb. 12, 1964.

SCACCHI, GRETA: Milan, Italy, Feb. 18, 1960.

SCALIA, JACK: Brooklyn, NY, Nov. 10, 1951.

SCARWID, DIANA: Savannah, GA, Aug. 27, 1955, AADA. Pace U.

SCHEIDER, ROY: Orange, NJ, Nov. 10, 1932. Franklin-Marshall.

SCHEINE, RAYNOR: Emporia, VA, Nov. 10. VA Commonwealth U.

SCHELL, MARIA: Vienna, Austria, Jan. 15, 1926.

SCHELL, MAXIMILIAN: Vienna, Austria, Dec. 8, 1930.

SCHLATTER, CHARLIE: Englewood, NJ, May 1, 1966. Ithaca College.

SCHNEIDER, JOHN: Mt. Kisco, NY, Apr. 8, 1960.

SCHNEIDER, MARIA: Paris, France, Mar. 27, 1952.

SCHREIBER, LIEV: San Francisco, CA, Oct. 4, 1967.

SCHRODER, RICK: Staten Island, NY, Apr. 13, 1970.

SCHUCK, JOHN: Boston, MA, Feb. 4, 1940.

SCHULTZ, DWIGHT: Milwaukee, WI, Nov. 10, 1938. Marquette.

SCHWARZENEGGER, ARNOLD: Austria, July 30, 1947.

SCHWARTZMAN, JASON: Los Angeles, June 26, 1980.

SCHWIMMER, DAVID: Queens, NY, Nov. 12, 1966.

SCHYGULLA, HANNA: Katlowitz, Germany, Dec. 25, 1943.

SCIORRA, ANNABELLA: NYC, Mar. 24, 1964.

SCOFIELD, PAUL: Hurstpierpoint, England, Jan. 21, 1922. London Mask Theatre Sch.

SCOGGINS, TRACY: Galveston, TX, Nov. 13, 1959.

SCOLARI, PETER: Scarsdale, NY, Sept. 12, 1956. NYCC.

SCOTT, CAMPBELL: South Salem, NY, July 19, 1962. Lawrence.

SCOTT, DEBRALEE: Elizabeth, NJ, Apr. 2, 1953

SCOTT, GORDON (Gordon M. Werschkul): Portland, OR, Aug. 3, 1927. Oregon U.

SCOTT, LIZABETH (Emma Matso): Scranton, PA, Sept. 29, 1922.

SCOTT, MARTHA: Jamesport, MO, Sept. 22, 1914. U MI.

SCOTT THOMAS, KRISTIN: Redruth, Cornwall, England, May 24, 1960.

SEAGAL, STEVEN: Detroit, MI, Apr. 10, 1951.

SEARS, HEATHER: London, England, Sept. 28, 1935.

SEDGWICK, KYRA: NYC, Aug. 19, 1965. USC.

SEGAL, GEORGE: NYC, Feb. 13, 1934. Columbia.

SELBY, DAVID: Morganstown, WV, Feb. 5, 1941. UWV.

SELLARS, ELIZABETH: Glasgow, Scotland, May 6, 1923.

SELLECK, TOM: Detroit, MI, Jan. 29, 1945. USC.

SERBEDZIJA, RADE: Bunic, Yugoslavia, July 27, 1946.

SERNAS, JACQUES: Lithuania, July 30, 1925.

SERRAULT, MICHEL: Brunoy, France. Jan. 24, 1928. Paris Cons.

SETH, ROSHAN: New Delhi, India. 1942.

SEWELL, RUFUS: Twickenham, England, Oct. 29, 1967.

SEYMOUR, JANE (Joyce Frankenberg): Hillingdon, England, Feb. 15, 1952.

SHALHOUB, TONY: Oct. 7, 1953.

SHARIF, OMAR (Michel Shalhoub): Alexandria, Egypt, Apr. 10, 1932. Victoria College.

SHANDLING, GARRY: Chicago, IL, Nov. 29, 1949.

SHATNER, WILLIAM: Montreal, Canada, Mar. 22, 1931. McGill.

SHAVER, HELEN: St. Thomas, Ontario, Canada, Feb. 24, 1951.

SHAW, FIONA: Cork, Ireland, July 10, 1955. RADA.

SHAW, STAN: Chicago, IL, 1952.

SHAWN, WALLACE: NYC, Nov. 12, 1943. Harvard.

SHEA, JOHN: North Conway, NH, Apr. 14, 1949. Bates, Yale.

SHEARER, HARRY: Los Angeles, Dec. 23, 1943. UCLA.

SHEARER, MOIRA: Dunfermline, Scotland, Jan. 17, 1926. London Theatre School.

SHEEDY, ALLY: NYC, June 13, 1962. USC.

SHEEN, CHARLIE (Carlos Irwin Estevez): Santa Monica, CA, Sept. 3, 1965.

SHEEN, MARTIN (Ramon Estevez): Dayton, OH, Aug. 3, 1940.

SHEFFER, CRAIG: York, PA, Apr. 23, 1960. E Stroudsberg U.

SHEFFIELD, JOHN: Pasadena, CA, Apr. 11, 1931. UCLA.

SHELLEY, CAROL: London, England, Aug. 16, 1939.

SHEPARD, SAM (Rogers): Ft. Sheridan, IL, Nov. 5, 1943.

SHEPHERD, CYBILL: Memphis, TN, Feb. 18, 1950. Hunter College, NYU.

SHER, ANTONY: England, June 14, 1949.

SHERIDAN, JAMEY: Pasadena, CA, July 12, 1951.

SHIELDS, BROOKE: NYC, May 31, 1965.

SHIRE, TALIA: Lake Success, NY, Apr. 25, 1946. Yale.

SHORT, MARTIN: Toronto, Canada, Mar. 26, 1950. McMaster.

SHUE, ELISABETH: S. Orange, NJ, Oct. 6, 1963. Harvard.

SIEMASZKO, CASEY: Chicago, IL, March 17, 1961.

SIKKING, JAMES B.: Los Angeles, Mar. 5, 1934.

SILVA, HENRY: Brooklyn, NY, 1928.

SILVER, RON: NYC, July 2, 1946. SUNY.

SILVERMAN, JONATHAN: Los Angeles, Aug. 5, 1966. USC.

SILVERSTONE, ALICIA: San Francisco, CA, Oct. 4, 1976.

SILVERSTONE, BEN: London, England, Apr. 9, 1979.

SIMMONS, JEAN: London, England, Jan. 31, 1929. Aida Foster School.

SIMON, PAUL: Newark. NJ, Nov. 5, 1942.

SIMON, SIMONE: Bethune, France, Apr. 23, 1910.

SIMPSON, O. J. (Orenthal James): San Francisco, CA, July 9, 1947. UCLA.

SINBAD (David Adkins): Benton Harbor, MI, Nov. 10, 1956.

SINCLAIR, JOHN (Gianluigi Loffredo): Rome, Italy, 1946.

Kerr Smith   Paul Sorvino

SINDEN, DONALD: Plymouth, England, Oct. 9, 1923. Webber-Douglas.

SINGER, LORI: Corpus Christi, TX, May 6, 1962. Juilliard.

SINISE, GARY: Chicago, IL, Mar. 17. 1955.

SIZEMORE, TOM: Detroit, MI, Sept. 29, 1964.

SKARSGÅRD, STELLAN: Gothenburg, Vastergotland, Sweden, June 13, 1951.

SKERRITT, TOM: Detroit, MI, Aug. 25, 1933. Wayne St. U.

SKYE, IONE (Leitch): London, England, Sept. 4, 1971.

SLATER, CHRISTIAN: NYC, Aug. 18, 1969.

SLATER, HELEN: NYC, Dec. 15, 1965.

SMITH, CHARLES MARTIN: Los Angeles, Oct. 30, 1953. Cal. St. U.

SMITH, JACLYN: Houston, TX, Oct. 26, 1947.

SMITH, JADA PINKETT: Baltimore, MD, Sept. 18, 1971.

SMITH, KERR: Exton, PA, Mar. 9, 1972.

SMITH, KEVIN: Red Bank, NJ, Aug. 2, 1970.

SMITH, KURTWOOD: New Lisbon, WI, July 3, 1942.

SMITH, LANE: Memphis, TN, Apr. 29, 1936.

SMITH, LEWIS: Chattanooga, TN, 1958. Actors Studio.

SMITH, LOIS: Topeka, KS, Nov. 3, 1930. U WA.

SMITH, MAGGIE: Ilford, England, Dec. 28, 1934.

SMITH, ROGER: South Gate, CA, Dec. 18, 1932. U AZ.

SMITH, WILL: Philadelphia, PA, Sept. 25, 1968.

SMITHERS, WILLIAM: Richmond, VA, July 10, 1927. Catholic U.

SMITS, JIMMY: Brooklyn, NY, July 9, 1955. Cornell.

SNIPES, WESLEY: NYC, July 31, 1963. SUNY/Purchase.

SNODGRESS, CARRIE: Chicago, IL, Oct. 27, 1946. UNI.

SOBIESKSI, LEELEE (Liliane Sobieski): NYC, June 10, 1982.

SOLOMON, BRUCE: NYC, 1944. U Miami, Wayne St. U.

SOMERS, SUZANNE (Mahoney): San Bruno, CA, Oct. 16, 1946. Lone Mt. College.

SOMMER, ELKE (Schletz): Berlin, Germany, Nov. 5, 1940.

SOMMER, JOSEF: Greifswald, Germany, June 26, 1934.

SORDI, ALBERTO: Rome, Italy, June 15, 1920.

SORVINO, MIRA: Tenafly, NJ, Sept. 28, 1967.

SORVINO, PAUL: NYC, Apr. 13, 1939. AMDA.

SOTO, TALISA (Miriam Soto): Brooklyn, NY, Mar. 27, 1967.

SOUL, DAVID: Chicago, IL, Aug. 28, 1943.

SPACEK, SISSY: Quitman, TX, Dec. 25, 1949. Actors Studio.

SPACEY, KEVIN: So. Orange, NJ, July 26, 1959. Juilliard.

SPADE, DAVID: Birmingham, MS, July 22, 1964.

SPADER, JAMES: Buzzards Bay, MA, Feb. 7, 1960.

SPANO, VINCENT: Brooklyn, NY, Oct. 18, 1962.

SPENSER, JEREMY: Ceylon, 1937.

SPINELLA, STEPHEN: Naples, Italy, Oct. 11, 1956. NYU.

SPRINGFIELD, RICK (Richard Spring Thorpe): Sydney, Australia, Aug. 23, 1949.

STACK, ROBERT: Los Angeles, Jan. 13, 1919. USC.

STADLEN, LEWIS J.: Brooklyn, NY, Mar. 7, 1947. Neighborhood Playhouse.

STAHL, NICK: Dallas, TX, Dec. 5, 1979.

STALLONE, FRANK: NYC, July 30, 1950.

STALLONE, SYLVESTER: NYC, July 6, 1946. U Miami.

STAMP, TERENCE: London, England, July 23, 1939.

STANG, ARNOLD: Chelsea, MA, Sept. 28, 1925.

STANTON, HARRY DEAN: Lexington, KY, July 14, 1926.

STAPLETON, JEAN: NYC, Jan. 19, 1923.

STAPLETON, MAUREEN: Troy, NY, June 21, 1925.

STARR, RINGO (Richard Starkey): Liverpool, England, July 7, 1940.

STEELE, BARBARA: England, Dec. 29, 1937.

STEELE, TOMMY: London, England, Dec. 17, 1936.

STEENBURGEN, MARY: Newport, AR, 1953. Neighborhood Playhouse.

STEIGER, ROD: Westhampton, NY, Apr. 14, 1925.

STERLING, JAN (Jane Sterling Adriance): NYC, Apr. 3, 1923. Fay Compton Sch.

STERLING, ROBERT (William Sterling Hart): Newcastle, PA, Nov. 13, 1917. U Pittsburgh.

STERN, DANIEL: Bethesda, MD, Aug. 28, 1957.

STERNHAGEN, FRANCES: Washington, DC, Jan. 13, 1932.

STEVENS, ANDREW: Memphis, TN, June 10, 1955.

STEVENS, CONNIE (Concetta Ann Ingolia): Brooklyn, NY, Aug. 8, 1938. Hollywood Professional School.

STEVENS, FISHER: Chicago, IL, Nov. 27, 1963. NYU.

STEVENS, STELLA (Estelle Eggleston): Hot Coffee, MS, Oct. 1, 1936.

STEVENSON, PARKER: Philadelphia, PA, June 4, 1953. Princeton.

STEWART, ALEXANDRA: Montreal, Quebec, Canada, June 10, 1939. Louvre.

STEWART, ELAINE (Elsy Steinberg): Montclair, NJ, May 31, 1929.

STEWART, FRENCH (Milton French Stewart): Albuquerque, NM, Feb. 20, 1964.

STEWART, JON (Jonathan Stewart Liebowitz): Trenton, NJ, Nov. 28, 1962.

STEWART, MARTHA (Martha Haworth): Bardwell, KY, Oct. 7, 1922.

STEWART, PATRICK: Mirfield, England, July 13, 1940.

STIERS, DAVID OGDEN: Peoria, IL, Oct. 31, 1942.

STILES, JULIA: NYC, Mar. 28, 1981.

STILLER, BEN: NYC, Nov. 30, 1965.

STILLER, JERRY: NYC, June 8, 1931.

STING (Gordon Matthew Sumner): Wallsend, England, Oct. 2, 1951.

STOCKWELL, DEAN: Hollywood, CA, Mar. 5, 1935.

STOCKWELL, JOHN (John Samuels, IV): Galveston, TX, Mar. 25, 1961. Harvard.

STOLTZ, ERIC: Whittier, CA, Sept. 30, 1961. USC.

STONE, DEE WALLACE (Deanna Bowers): Kansas City, MO, Dec. 14, 1948. U KS.

STORM, GALE (Josephine Cottle): Bloomington, TX, Apr. 5, 1922.

STOWE, MADELEINE: Eagle Rock, CA, Aug. 18, 1958.

STRASSMAN, MARCIA: NJ, Apr. 28, 1948.

STRATHAIRN, DAVID: San Francisco, CA, Jan. 26, 1949.

STRAUSS, PETER: NYC, Feb. 20, 1947.

STREEP, MERYL (Mary Louise): Summit, NJ, June 22, 1949. Vassar, Yale.

STREISAND, BARBRA: Brooklyn, NY, Apr. 24, 1942.

STRITCH, ELAINE: Detroit, MI, Feb. 2, 1925. Drama Workshop.

STROUD, DON: Honolulu, HI, Sept. 1, 1937.

STRUTHERS, SALLY: Portland, OR, July 28, 1948. Pasadena Playhouse.

STUDI, WES (Wesley Studie): Nofire Hollow, OK, Dec. 17, 1947.

SUMMER, DONNA (LaDonna Gaines): Boston, MA, Dec. 31, 1948.

SUTHERLAND, DONALD: St. John, New Brunswick, Canada, July 17, 1935. U Toronto.

SUTHERLAND, KIEFER: Los Angeles, Dec. 18, 1966.

SUVARI, MENA: Newport, RI, Feb. 9, 1979.

SVENSON, BO: Goreborg, Sweden, Feb. 13, 1941. UCLA.

SWANK, HILARY: Bellingham, WA, July 30, 1974.

SWAYZE, PATRICK: Houston, TX, Aug. 18, 1952.

SWEENEY, D. B. (Daniel Bernard Sweeney): Shoreham, NY, Nov. 14, 1961.

SWINTON, TILDA: London, England, Nov. 5, 1960.

SWIT, LORETTA: Passaic, NJ, Nov. 4, 1937. AADA.

SYLVESTER, WILLIAM: Oakland, CA, Jan. 31, 1922. RADA.

SYMONDS, ROBERT: Bistow, AK, Dec. 1, 1926. TX U.

SYMS, SYLVIA: London, England, June 1, 1934. Convent School.

SZARABAJKA, KEITH: Oak Park, IL, Dec. 2, 1952. U Chicago.

T, MR. (Lawrence Tero): Chicago, IL, May 21, 1952.

TABORI, KRISTOFFER (Siegel): Los Angeles, Aug. 4, 1952.

TAKEI, GEORGE: Los Angeles, Apr. 20, 1939. UCLA.

TALBOT, NITA: NYC, Aug. 8, 1930. Irvine Studio School.

TAMBLYN, RUSS: Los Angeles, Dec. 30, 1934.

TARANTINO, QUENTIN: Knoxville, TN, Mar. 27, 1963.

TATE, LARENZ: Chicago, IL, Sept. 8, 1975.

TAUTOU, AUDREY: Beaumont, France, Aug. 9, 1978.

TAYLOR, ELIZABETH: London, England, Feb. 27, 1932. Byron House School.

TAYLOR, LILI: Glencoe, IL, Feb. 20, 1967.

TAYLOR, NOAH: London, England, Sept. 4, 1969.

TAYLOR, RENEE: NYC, Mar. 19, 1935.

TAYLOR, ROD (Robert): Sydney, Australia, Jan. 11, 1929.

TAYLOR-YOUNG, LEIGH: Washington, DC, Jan. 25, 1945. Northwestern.

TEEFY, MAUREEN: Minneapolis, MN, 1954, Juilliard.

TEMPLE, SHIRLEY: Santa Monica, CA, Apr. 23, 1927.

TENNANT, VICTORIA: London, England, Sept. 30, 1950.

TERZIEFF, LAURENT: Paris, France, June 25, 1935.

TEWES, LAUREN: Braddock, PA, Oct. 26, 1954.

THACKER, RUSS: Washington, DC, June 23, 1946. Montgomery College.

THAXTER, PHYLLIS: Portland, ME, Nov. 20, 1921. St. Genevieve.

James Spader   Hilary Swank   Jennifer Tilly   Marisa Tomei

THELEN, JODI: St. Cloud, MN, 1963.

THERON, CHARLIZE: Benoni, South Africa, Aug. 7, 1975.

THEWLIS, DAVID: Blackpool, England, 1963.

THOMAS, HENRY: San Antonio, TX, Sept. 8, 1971.

THOMAS, JAY: New Orleans, LA, July 12, 1948.

THOMAS, JONATHAN TAYLOR (Weiss): Bethlehem, PA, Sept. 8, 1981.

THOMAS, MARLO (Margaret): Detroit, Nov. 21, 1938. USC.

THOMAS, PHILIP MICHAEL: Columbus, OH, May 26, 1949. Oakwood College.

THOMAS, RICHARD: NYC, June 13, 1951. Columbia.

THOMPSON, EMMA: London, England, Apr.15, 1959. Cambridge.

THOMPSON, FRED DALTON: Sheffield, AL, Aug. 19, 1942

THOMPSON, JACK (John Payne): Sydney, Australia, Aug. 31, 1940.

THOMPSON, LEA: Rochester, MN, May 31, 1961.

THOMPSON, REX: NYC, Dec. 14, 1942.

THOMPSON, SADA: Des Moines, IA, Sept. 27, 1929. Carnegie Tech.

THORNTON, BILLY BOB: Hot Spring, AR, Aug. 4, 1955.

THORSON, LINDA: Toronto, Canada, June 18, 1947. RADA.

THULIN, INGRID: Solleftea, Sweden, Jan. 27, 1929. Royal Drama Theatre.

THURMAN, UMA: Boston, MA, Apr. 29, 1970.

TICOTIN, RACHEL: Bronx, NY, Nov. 1, 1958.

TIERNEY, LAWRENCE: Brooklyn, NY, Mar. 15, 1919. Manhattan College.

TIFFIN, PAMELA (Wonso): Oklahoma City, OK, Oct. 13, 1942.

TIGHE, KEVIN: Los Angeles, Aug. 13, 1944.

TILLY, JENNIFER: Los Angeles, Sept. 16, 1958.

TILLY, MEG: Texada, Canada, Feb. 14, 1960.

TOBOLOWSKY, STEPHEN: Dallas, TX, May 30, 1951. So. Methodist U.

TODD, BEVERLY: Chicago, IL, July 1, 1946.

TODD, RICHARD: Dublin, Ireland, June 11, 1919. Shrewsbury School.

TOLKAN, JAMES: Calumet, MI, June 20, 1931.

TOMEI, MARISA: Brooklyn, NY, Dec. 4, 1964. NYU.

TOMLIN, LILY: Detroit, MI, Sept. 1, 1939. Wayne St. U.

TOPOL (Chaim Topol): Tel Aviv, Israel, Sept. 9, 1935.

TORN, RIP: Temple, TX, Feb. 6, 1931. U TX.

TORRES, LIZ: NYC, Sept. 27, 1947. NYU.

TOTTER, AUDREY: Joliet, IL, Dec. 20, 1918.

TOWSEND, ROBERT: Chicago, IL, Feb. 6, 1957.

TRAVANTI, DANIEL J.: Kenosha, WI, Mar. 7, 1940.

TRAVIS, NANCY: Queens, NY, Sept. 21, 1961.

TRAVOLTA, JOEY: Englewood, NJ, 1952.

TRAVOLTA, JOHN: Englewood, NJ, Feb. 18, 1954.

TREMAYNE, LES: London, England, Apr. 16, 1913. Northwestern, Columbia, UCLA.

TRINTIGNANT, JEAN-LOUIS: Pont-St. Esprit, France, Dec. 11, 1930. Dullin Balachova Drama School.

TRIPPLEHORN, JEANNE: Tulsa, OK, 1963.

TSOPEI, CORINNA: Athens, Greece, June 21, 1944.

TUBB, BARRY: Snyder, TX, 1963. Am. Cons. Th.

TUCCI, STANLEY: Katonah, NY, Jan. 11, 1960.

TUCKER, CHRIS: Decatur, GA, Aug. 31, 1972.

TUCKER, JONATHAN: Boston, MA, May 31, 1982.

TUCKER, MICHAEL: Baltimore, MD, Feb. 6, 1944.

TUNE, TOMMY: Wichita Falls, TX, Feb. 28, 1939.

TURNER, JANINE (Gauntt): Lincoln, NE, Dec. 6, 1963.

TURNER, KATHLEEN: Springfield, MO, June 19, 1954. U MD.

TURNER, TINA (Anna Mae Bullock): Nutbush, TN, Nov. 26, 1938.

TURTURRO, JOHN: Brooklyn, NY, Feb. 28, 1957. Yale.

TUSHINGHAM, RITA: Liverpool, England, Mar. 14, 1940.

TWIGGY (Lesley Hornby): London, England, Sept. 19, 1949.

TWOMEY, ANNE: Boston, MA, June 7, 1951. Temple U.

TYLER, BEVERLY (Beverly Jean Saul): Scranton, PA, July 5, 1928.

TYLER, LIV: Portland, ME, July 1, 1977.

TYRRELL, SUSAN: San Francisco, CA, 1946.

TYSON, CATHY: Liverpool, England, June 12, 1965. Royal Shake. Co.

TYSON, CICELY: NYC, Dec. 19, 1933. NYU.

UGGAMS, LESLIE: NYC, May 25, 1943. Juilliard.

ULLMAN, TRACEY: Slough, England, Dec. 30, 1959.

ULLMANN, LIV: Tokyo, Japan, Dec. 10, 1938. Webber-Douglas Academy.

ULRICH, SKEET (Bryan Ray Ulrich): NC, Jan. 20, 1969.

UMEKI, MIYOSHI: Otaru, Hokaido, Japan, Apr. 3, 1929.

UNDERWOOD, BLAIR: Tacoma, WA, Aug. 25, 1964. Carnegie-Mellon.

UNGER, DEBORAH KARA: Victoria, BC, Canada, 1966.

URICH, ROBERT: Toronto, Canada, Dec. 19, 1946.

USTINOV, PETER: London, England, Apr. 16, 1921. Westminster School.

VACCARO, BRENDA: Brooklyn, NY, Nov. 18, 1939. Neighborhood Playhouse.

VALANDREY, CHARLOTTE (Anne Charlone Pascal)**:** Paris, France, 1968.

VALLI, ALIDA: Pola, Italy, May 31, 1921. Academy of Drama.

VALLONE, RAF: Riogio, Italy, Feb. 17, 1916. Turin U.

VAN ARK, JOAN: NYC, June 16, 1943. Yale.

VAN DAMME, JEAN-CLAUDE (J-C Vorenberg)**:** Brussels, Belgium, Apr. 1, 1960.

VAN DE VEN, MONIQUE: The Netherlands, 1952.

VAN DER BEEK, JAMES: Cheshire, CT, March 8, 1977.

VAN DEVERE, TRISH (Patricia Dressel)**:** Englewood Cliffs, NJ, Mar. 9, 1945. Ohio Wesleyan.

VAN DIEN, CASPER: Ridgefield, NJ, Dec. 18, 1968.

VAN DOREN, MAMIE (Joan Lucile Olander)**:** Rowena SD, Feb. 6, 1933.

VAN DYKE, DICK: West Plains, MO, Dec. 13, 1925.

VANITY (Denise Katrina Smith)**:** Niagara, Ontario, Canada, Jan. 4, 1959.

VAN PALLANDT, NINA: Copenhagen, Denmark, July 15, 1932.

VAN PATTEN, DICK: NYC, Dec. 9, 1928.

VAN PATTEN, JOYCE: NYC, Mar. 9, 1934.

VAN PEEBLES, MARIO: NYC, Jan. 15, 1958. Columbia.

VAN PEEBLES, MELVIN: Chicago, IL, Aug. 21, 1932.

VANCE, COURTNEY B.: Detroit, MI, Mar. 12, 1960.

VAUGHN, ROBERT: NYC, Nov. 22, 1932. USC.

VAUGHN, VINCE: Minneapolis, MN, Mar. 28, 1970.

VEGA, ISELA: Mexico, 1940.

VELJOHNSON, REGINALD: NYC, Aug. 16, 1952.

VENNERA, CHICK: Herkimer, NY, Mar. 27, 1952. Pasadena Playhouse.

VENORA, DIANE: Hartford, CT, 1952. Juilliard.

VERNON, JOHN: Montreal, Quebec, Canada, Feb. 24, 1932.

VEREEN, BEN: Miami, FL, Oct. 10, 1946.

VICTOR, JAMES (Lincoln Rafael Peralta Diaz)**:** Santiago, Dominican Republic, July 27, 1939. Haaren HS/NYC.

VINCENT, JAN-MICHAEL: Denver, CO, July 15, 1944. Ventura.

ULTRA VIOLET (Isabelle Collin-Dufresne)**:** Grenoble, France, 1935.

VITALE, MILLY: Rome, Italy, July 16, 1928. Lycee Chateaubriand.

VOHS, JOAN: St. Albans, NY, July 30, 1931.

VOIGHT, JON: Yonkers, NY, Dec. 29, 1938. Catholic U.

VON BARGEN, DANIEL: Cincinnati, OH, June 5, 1950. Purdue.

VON DOHLEN, LENNY: Augusta, GA, Dec. 22, 1958. U TX.

VON SYDOW, MAX: Lund, Sweden, July 10, 1929. Royal Drama Theatre.

WAGNER, LINDSAY: Los Angeles, June 22. 1949.

WAGNER, NATASHA GREGSON: Los Angeles, Sept. 29, 1970.

WAGNER, ROBERT: Detroit, MI, Feb. 10, 1930.

WAHL, KEN: Chicago, IL, Feb. 14, 1953.

WAITE, GENEVIEVE: South Africa, 1949.

WAITE, RALPH: White Plains, NY, June 22, 1929. Yale.

WAITS, TOM: Pomona, CA, Dec. 7, 1949.

WALKEN, CHRISTOPHER: Astoria, NY, Mar. 31, 1943. Hofstra.

WALKER, CLINT: Hartfold, IL, May 30, 1927. USC.

WALKER, PAUL: Glendale, CA, Sept. 12, 1973.

WALLACH, ELI: Brooklyn, NY, Dec. 7, 1915. CCNY, U TX.

WALLACH, ROBERTA: NYC, Aug. 2, 1955.

WALLIS, SHANI: London, England, Apr. 5, 1941.

WALSH, M. EMMET: Ogdensburg, NY, Mar. 22, 1935. Clarkson College, AADA.

WALTER, JESSICA: Brooklyn, NY, Jan. 31, 1944. Neighborhood Playhouse.

WALTER, TRACEY: Jersey City, NJ, Nov. 25, 1942.

WALTERS, JULIE: London, England, Feb. 22, 1950.

WALTON, EMMA: London, England, Nov. 1962. Brown.

WANAMAKER, ZOË: NYC, May 13, 1949.

WARD, BURT (Gervis)**:** Los Angeles, July 6, 1945.

WARD, FRED: San Diego, CA, Dec. 30, 1942.

WARD, RACHEL: London, England, Sept. 12, 1957.

WARD, SELA: Meridian, MS, July 11, 1956.

WARD, SIMON: London, England, Oct. 19, 1941.

WARDEN, JACK (Lebzelter)**:** Newark, NJ, Sept. 18, 1920.

WARNER, DAVID: Manchester, England, July 29, 1941. RADA.

WARNER, MALCOLM-JAMAL: Jersey City, NJ, Aug. 18, 1970.

WARREN, JENNIFER: NYC, Aug. 12, 1941. U WI.

WARREN, LESLEY ANN: NYC, Aug. 16, 1946.

WARREN, MICHAEL: South Bend, IN, Mar. 5, 1946. UCLA.

WARRICK, RUTH: St. Joseph, MO, June 29, 1915. U MO.

WASHINGTON, DENZEL: Mt. Vernon, NY, Dec. 28, 1954. Fordham.

WASSON, CRAIG: Ontario, OR, Mar. 15, 1954. U OR.

WATERSTON, SAM: Cambridge, MA, Nov. 15, 1940. Yale.

WATLING, JACK: London, England, Jan. 13, 1923. Italia Conti School.

WATSON, EMILY: London, England, Jan. 14, 1967.

WATSON, EMMA: Oxford, England, Apr. 15, 1990.

WAYANS, DAMON: NYC, Sept. 4, 1960.

WAYANS, KEENEN, IVORY: NYC, June 8, 1958. Tuskegee Inst.

WAYNE, PATRICK: Los Angeles, July 15, 1939. Loyola.

WEATHERS, CARL: New Orleans, LA, Jan. 14, 1948. Long Beach CC.

WEAVER, DENNIS: Joplin, MO, June 4, 1924. U OK.

WEAVER, FRITZ: Pittsburgh, PA, Jan. 19, 1926.

WEAVER, SIGOURNEY (Susan)**:** NYC, Oct. 8, 1949. Stanford, Yale.

WEAVING, HUGO: Nigeria, Apr. 4, 1960. NIDA.

WEBER, STEVEN: Queens, NY, March 4, 1961.

WEDGEWORTH, ANN: Abilene, TX, Jan. 21, 1935. U TX.

WEISZ, RACHEL: London, England, Mar. 7, 1971.

WELCH, RAQUEL (Tejada)**:** Chicago, IL, Sept. 5, 1940.

WELD, TUESDAY (Susan)**:** NYC, Aug. 27, 1943. Hollywood Professional School.

WELDON, JOAN: San Francisco, CA, Aug. 5, 1933. SF Cons.

WELLER, PETER: Stevens Point, WI, June 24, 1947. Am. Th. Wing.

WENDT, GEORGE: Chicago, IL, Oct. 17, 1948.

WEST, ADAM (William Anderson)**:** Walla Walla, WA, Sept. 19, 1929.

WEST, SHANE: Baton Rouge, LA, June 10, 1978.

WETTIG, PATRICIA: Cincinatti, OH, Dec. 4, 1951. Temple.

WHALEY, FRANK: Syracuse, NY, July 20, 1963. SUNY/Albany.

WHALLEY-KILMER, JOANNE: Manchester, England, Aug. 25, 1964.

WHEATON, WIL: Burbank, CA, July 29, 1972.

WHITAKER, FOREST: Longview, TX, July 15, 1961.

WHITAKER, JOHNNY: Van Nuys, CA, Dec. 13, 1959.

WHITE, BETTY: Oak Park, IL, Jan. 17, 1922.

WHITE, CHARLES: Perth Amboy, NJ, Aug. 29, 1920. Rutgers.

WHITELAW, BILLIE: Coventry, England, June 6, 1932.

WHITMAN, STUART: San Francisco, CA, Feb. 1, 1929. CCLA.

WHITMORE, JAMES: White Plains, NY, Oct. 1, 1921. Yale.

WHITNEY, GRACE LEE: Detroit, MI, Apr. 1, 1930.

WHITTON, MARGARET: Philadelphia, PA, Nov, 30, 1950.

WIDDOES, KATHLEEN: Wilmington, DE, Mar. 21, 1939.

WIDMARK, RICHARD: Sunrise, MN, Dec. 26, 1914. Lake Forest.

WIEST, DIANNE: Kansas City, MO, Mar. 28, 1948. U MD.

WILBY, JAMES: Burma, Feb. 20, 1958.

WILCOX, COLIN: Highlands, NC, Feb. 4, 1937. U TN.

WILDER, GENE (Jerome Silberman): Milwaukee, WI, June 11, 1935. U IA.

WILKINSON, TOM: Leeds, England, 1948. U Kent.

WILLIAMS, BILLY DEE: NYC, Apr. 6, 1937.

WILLIAMS, CARA (Bernice Kamiat): Brooklyn, NY, June 29, 1925.

WILLIAMS, CINDY: Van Nuys, CA, Aug. 22, 1947. KACC.

WILLIAMS, CLARENCE, III: NYC, Aug. 21, 1939.

WILLIAMS, ESTHER: Los Angeles, Aug. 8, 1921.

WILLIAMS, JOBETH: Houston, TX, Dec 6, 1948. Brown.

WILLIAMS, MICHELLE: Kalispell, MT, Sept. 9, 1980.

WILLIAMS, PAUL: Omaha, NE, Sept. 19, 1940.

WILLIAMS, ROBIN: Chicago, IL, July 21, 1951. Juilliard.

WILLIAMS, TREAT (Richard): Rowayton, CT, Dec. 1, 1951.

WILLIAMS, VANESSA L.: Tarrytown, NY, Mar. 18, 1963.

WILLIAMSON, FRED: Gary, IN, Mar. 5, 1938. Northwestern.

WILLIAMSON, NICOL: Hamilton, Scotland, Sept. 14, 1938.

WILLIS, BRUCE: Penns Grove, NJ, Mar. 19, 1955.

WILLISON, WALTER: Monterey Park, CA, June 24, 1947.

WILSON, DEMOND: NYC, Oct. 13, 1946. Hunter College.

WILSON, ELIZABETH: Grand Rapids, MI, Apr. 4, 1925.

WILSON, LAMBERT: Paris, France, 1959.

WILSON, LUKE: Dallas, TX, Sept. 21, 1971.

WILSON, OWEN: Dallas, TX, Nov. 18, 1968.

WILSON, SCOTT: Atlanta, GA, 1942.

WINCOTT, JEFF: Toronto, Canada, May 8, 1957.

WINCOTT, MICHAEL: Toronto, Canada, Jan. 6, 1959. Juilliard.

WINDE, BEATRICE: Chicago, IL, Jan. 6.

WINDOM, WILLIAM: NYC, Sept. 28, 1923. Williams College.

WINFIELD, PAUL: Los Angeles, May 22, 1940. UCLA.

WINFREY, OPRAH: Kosciusko, MS, Jan. 29, 1954. TN St. U.

WINGER, DEBRA: Cleveland, OH, May 17, 1955. Cal. St.

WINKLER, HENRY: NYC, Oct. 30, 1945. Yale.

WINN, KITTY: Washington, DC, Feb, 21, 1944. Boston U.

WINNINGHAM, MARE: Phoenix, AZ, May 6, 1959.

WINSLET, KATE: Reading, England, Oct. 5, 1975.

WINSLOW, MICHAEL: Spokane, WA, Sept. 6, 1960.

WINTER, ALEX: London, England, July 17, 1965. NYU.

WINTERS, JONATHAN: Dayton, OH, Nov. 11, 1925. Kenyon College.

WINTERS, SHELLEY (Shirley Schrift): St. Louis, Aug. 18, 1922. Wayne St. U.

WITHERS, GOOGIE: Karachi, India, Mar. 12, 1917. Italia Conti.

WITHERS, JANE: Atlanta, GA, Apr. 12, 1926.

WITHERSPOON, REESE (Laura Jean Reese Witherspoon): Nashville, TN, Mar. 22, 1976.

WOLF, SCOTT: Newton, MA, June 4, 1968.

WONG, B.D.: San Francisco, CA, Oct. 24,1962.

WONG, RUSSELL: Troy, NY, Mar. 1, 1963. Santa Monica College.

WOOD, ELIJAH: Cedar Rapids, IA, Jan 28, 1981.

Diane Venora   Billy Dee Williams

WOODARD, ALFRE: Tulsa, OK, Nov. 2, 1953. Boston U.

WOODLAWN, HOLLY (Harold Ajzenberg): Juana Diaz, PR, 1947.

WOODS, JAMES: Vernal, UT, Apr. 18, 1947. MIT.

WOODWARD, EDWARD: Croyden, Surrey, England, June 1, 1930.

WOODWARD, JOANNE: Thomasville, GA, Feb. 27, 1930. Neighborhood Playhouse.

WORONOV, MARY: Brooklyn, NY, Dec. 8, 1946. Cornell.

WORTH, IRENE (Hattie Abrams): Nebraska, June 23, 1916. UCLA.

WRAY, FAY: Alberta, Canada, Sept. 15, 1907.

WRIGHT, AMY: Chicago, IL, Apr. 15, 1950.

WRIGHT, MAX: Detroit, MI, Aug. 2, 1943. Wayne St. U.

WRIGHT, ROBIN: Dallas, TX, Apr. 8, 1966.

WRIGHT, TERESA: NYC, Oct. 27, 1918.

WUHL, ROBERT: Union City, NJ, Oct. 9, 1951. U Houston.

WYATT, JANE: NYC, Aug. 10, 1910. Barnard College.

WYLE, NOAH: Los Angeles, June 2, 1971.

WYMAN, JANE (Sarah Jane Fulks): St. Joseph, MO, Jan. 4, 1914.

WYMORE, PATRICE: Miltonvale, KS, Dec. 17, 1926.

WYNN, MAY (Donna Lee Hickey): NYC, Jan. 8, 1930.

WYNTER, DANA (Dagmar): London, June 8. 1927. Rhodes U.

YORK, MICHAEL: Fulmer, England, Mar. 27, 1942. Oxford.

YORK, SUSANNAH: London, England, Jan. 9, 1941. RADA.

YOUNG, ALAN (Angus): North Shield, England, Nov. 19, 1919.

YOUNG, BURT: Queens, NY, Apr. 30, 1940.

YOUNG, CHRIS: Chambersburg, PA, Apr. 28, 1971.

YOUNG, SEAN: Louisville, KY, Nov. 20, 1959. Interlochen.

YULIN, HARRIS: Los Angeles, Nov. 5, 1937.

CHOW YUN-FAT: Lamma Island, Hong Kong, China, May 18, 1955.

ZACHARIAS, ANN: Stockholm, Sweden, 1956.

ZADORA, PIA: Hoboken, NJ, May 4, 1954.

ZELLWEGER, RENEE: Katy, TX, Apr. 25, 1969.

ZERBE, ANTHONY: Long Beach, CA, May 20, 1939.

ZETA-JONES, CATHERINE: Swansea, Wales, Sept. 25, 1969.

ZIMBALIST, EFREM, JR.: NYC, Nov.30, 1918. Yale.

ZUNIGA, DAPHNE: Berkeley, CA, Oct.28,1963. UCLA.

OBITUARIES
FOR 2001

LARRY ADLER, 87, Baltimore-born harmonica player-composer, died on Aug. 7, 2001 in London. In addition to his stage appearances he was seen performing in movies such as *The Singing Marine, The Big Broadcast of 1937, St. Martin's Lane (Sidewalks of London)*, and *Music for Millions*. Survived by his son, three daughters, two granddaughters, and two great-grandchildren.

SAMUEL Z. ARKOFF, 83, Iowa-born motion picture executive and producer who, together with his late partner James H. Nicholson, established American International Pictures, died on Sept. 16, 2001 in Burbank, CA. His studio output of "B" exploitation pictures that became a staple in drive-in theaters from the mid-1950s throughout the 1970s included titles such as *I Was a Teenage Werewolf, Invasion of the Saucer Men, I Was a Teenage Frankenstein, Attack of the Puppet People, Bucket of Blood, The Pit and the Pendulum, Beach Party, What's Up Tiger Lily?, The Wild Angels, Wild in the Streets, Bloody Mama, The Abominable Dr. Phibes, Black Caesar*, and *Blacula*. He is survived by his son, Louis Arkoff, and a daughter, Donna Roth, both of whom are producers; five grandchildren; and a great-grandson.

Pat Ast   Jean-Pierre Aumont

LEWIS ARQUETTE, 65, Chicago-born film and television character player, died of congestive heart failure on Feb. 10, 2001 in Los Angeles. The son of comedian Cliff Arquette (Charley Weaver), he appeared in movies such as *The China Syndrome, Big Business, Tango & Cash, The Linguini Incident, Sleep With Me, Twilight, Best in Show*, and *Little Nicky*. He is

survived by his brother, a sister, and five children, Rosanna, Richmond, Patricia, Alexis, and David Arquette, all of whom are actors.

PAT AST, 59, Brooklyn-born actress, died of natural causes at her home in West Hollywood, CA, on Oct. 2, 2001. She could be seen in movies such as *Heat* (1972), *The Duchess and the Dirtwater Fox, The World's Greatest Lover, Foul Play, The Incredible Shrinking Woman, The Pursuit of D. B. Cooper*, and *Reform School Girls*. No reported survivors.

Sandy Baron   Budd Boetticher

JEAN-PIERRE AUMONT (J-P Salomons), 90, Paris-born star of French and American films, died on Jan. 30, 2001 at his home in Saint-Tropez. His films include *Hotel du Nord, Flight Into Darkness, Assignment in Brittany, The Cross of Lorraine, Heartbeat, Song of Scheherazade, Sirens of Atlantis, The First Gentleman, Lili, Royal Affairs in Versailles, Charge of the Lancers, Hilda Crane, John Paul Jones, The Devil at 4 O'Clock, Five Miles to Midnight, Castle Keep, Day for Night, Mahogany, Cat and Mouse, Becoming Colette, Jefferson in Paris*, and *The Proprietor*. He is survived by his second wife, actress Marisa Pavan, their two sons, and his daughter from his marriage to actress Maria Montez.

SANDY BARON (Sanford Beresofsky), 64, Brooklyn-born comedian-actor died on Jan. 21, 2001 in Van Nuys, CA, after suffering for years from emphysema. Among the films he appeared in were *Targets, Sweet November* (1968), *If It's Tuesday This Must Be Belgium, The Out of Towners* (1970), *Straight*

Time, *Broadway Danny Rose*, *Birdy*, *Vamp*, *The Grifters*, and *The Hi-Lo Country*. He is survived by his sister.

JAMES BERNARD, 75, British composer-writer, who won the Academy Award for collaborating with Paul Dehn on the screenplay for *Seven Days to Noon*, died of unspecified causes on July 12, 2001 in London. As a composer at Hammer Studios he scored movies such as *The Quatermass Experiment* (*The Creeping Unknown*), *The Curse of Frankenstein*, *Dracula* (*Horror of Dracula*), *The Hound of the Baskervilles* (1959), *The Terror of the Tongs*, *These Are the Damned*, *She* (1965), *The Devil Rides Out*, and *Dracula Has Risen From the Grave*. Survived by a sister.

BUDD BOETTICHER (Oscar Boetticher, Jr.), 85, Chicago-born motion picture director, best known for low-budget westerns such as *Seminole* and *The Tall T*, died on Nov. 29, 2001 at his home in Ramona, CA. His other films include *Bullfighter and the Lady*, *The Cimarron Kid*, *Bronco Buster*, *Red Ball Express*, *Horizons West*, *City Beneath the Sea*, *The Man From the Alamo*, *East of Sumatra*, *The Magnificent Matador*, *Seven Men From Now*, *Decision at Sundown*, *Buchanan Rides Alone*, *Ride Lonesome*, *Comanche Station*, and *The Rise and Fall of Legs Diamond*. He is survived by his fourth wife.

ROY BOULTING, 87, British film director-producer-writer who collaborated with his twin brother John on several notable films in the 1950s and '60s, died of cancer on Nov. 5, 2001 in London. Among his films as producer were *Brighton Rock*, *Seven Days to Noon*, *The Magic Box*, *Private's Progress* (also writer), *I'm All Right Jack* (also co-writer), *Heaven's Above!* (also co-writer), and *Rotten to the Core*, while his credits as director include *High Treason* (also co-writer), *Run for the Sun* (also co-writer), *Carlton Browne of the F.O.* (*Man in a Cocked Hat*; also co-writer), *The Family Way* (also co-writer), and *There's a Girl in My Soup*. Survivors include his son from his marriage to actress Hayley Mills.

FOSTER BROOKS, 89, Kentucky-born comedian, known for his drunk act, died of natural causes at his home in Encino, CA, on Dec. 20, 2001. His handful of film appearances include *The Villain*, *Cracking Up* (*Smorgasbord*), and *Cannonball Run II*. Survived by his wife, two daughters, and three grandchildren.

JULES BUCK, 83, St. Louis-born cameraman-turned-producer died in Paris on July 19, 2001 of complications from Alzheimer's disease. With actor Peter O'Toole he formed Keep Films, resulting in the collaborations *Lord Jim*, *Great Catherine*, *The Ruling Class*, and *Under Milk Wood*. His other credits as producer include *Love Nest*, *Fixed Bayonets*, *The Day They Robbed the Bank of England*, and *Operation Snatch*. Survived by his daughter.

RALPH BURNS, 79, motion picture arranger-composer, who won Academy Awards for his work on the Bob Fosse films *Cabaret* and *All That Jazz*, died on Nov. 21, 2001 in Los Angeles of pneumonia and complications from a stroke. He also worked on such other movies as *Bananas*, *Mame*, *Lenny*, *New York New York*, *Annie*, *My Favorite Year*, *The Muppets Take Manhattan*, *Perfect*, *In the Mood*, and *Bert Rigby You're a Fool*. No immediate survivors.

Roy Boutling   Corinne Calvet

CORINNE CALVET (Corinne Dibois), 75, French screen and television actress died of a cerebral hemorrhage on June 23, 2001 in Los Angeles. After coming to the U.S. in 1949 she appeared in movies such as *Rope of Sand*, *When Willie Comes Marching Home*, *My Friend Irma Goes West*, *Quebec*, *On the Riviera*, *Peking Express*, *Sailor Beware*, *What Price Glory?* (1952), *Flight to Tangier*, *The Far Country*, *So This Is Paris*, *The Plunderers of Painted Flats*, *Bluebeard's Ten Honeymoons*, *Hemingway's Adventures of a Young Man*, and *Apache Uprising*. She is survived by a son.

JOHN CHAMBERS, 78, screen and television makeup artist, who won a special Academy Award in 1968 for his work on the film *Planet of the Apes*, died on Aug. 25, 2001 in Woodland Hills, CA. His other movies include *The List of Adrian Messenger* and *The Island of Dr. Moreau* (1977). No reported survivors.

Imogene Coca   Perry Como

IMOGENE COCA, 92, Philadelphia-born actress-comedian, best known for her Emmy Award-winning pairing opposite Sid Caesar on the television series "Your Show of Shows," died on June 2, 2001 at her home in Westport, CT. She appeared in such movies as *Under the Yum Yum Tree*, *Rabbit Test*, and *National Lampoon's Vacation*. No survivors.

CHARLOTTE COLEMAN, 33, British actress, best known for playing Hugh Grant's roommate in the 1994 comedy hit *Four Weddings and a Funeral*, died at her London home on Nov. 14, 2001 following an asthma attack. Survived by her father, mother, and sister.

PERRY COMO (Pierino Como), 88, Pittsburgh-born singer, who became one of the top recording artists of the 1950s with such songs as "Hot Diggity," "Don't Let the Stars Get in Your Eyes," "Round and Round," and "Catch a Falling Star," died in his sleep at his home in Jupiter, FL, on May 12, 2001. In addition to his long-running television series, he showed up in movies such as *Something for the Boys*, *Doll Face*, and *Words and Music*. He is survived by two sons, a daughter, thirteen grandchildren, and four great-grandchildren.

PEGGY CONVERSE, 95, Oregon-born screen, stage, and television actress, died on March 2, 2001 in her Los Angeles home. She could be seen in films such as *Girl of the Limberlost*, *The Brute Man*, *Day of the Bad Man*, *Father Is a Bachelor*, *Miss Sadie Thompson*, and *The Accidental Tourist*. She is survived by her daughter, actress-singer Melissa Converse, a son, three grandchildren, and three great-grandchildren.

ROSEMARY DeCAMP, 90, Arizona-born screen, stage, and television actress, died at her home in Torrance, CA, on Feb. 20, 2001. Following her 1941 debut in *Cheers for Miss Bishop* she appeared in such motion pictures as *Hold Back the Dawn*, *Yankee Doodle Dandy* (as James Cagney's mother), *Commandos Strike at Dawn*, *This Is the Army*, *The Merry Monahans*, *Pride of the Marines*, *Rhapsody in Blue*, *Week-End at the Waldorf*, *Blood on the Sun*, *Two Guys From Milwaukee*, *Nora Prentiss*, *Look for the Silver Lining*, *The Story of Seabiscuit*, *On Moonlight Bay*, *By the Light of the Silvery Moon*, *Many Rivers to Cross*, *Strategic Air Command*, and *13 Ghosts*. On television she appeared on the series "The Life of Riley" (she had appeared in a film version as well), "The Bob Cummings Show," and "That Girl." Survived by four daughters.

Rosemary DeCamp   Anthony Dexter

FRED DeCORDOVA, 90, New York City-born film and television producer-director, best known as the long-running producer of "The Tonight Show Starring Johnny Carson," died in Los Angeles, CA, on Sept. 15, 2001. His film credits as director include *Too Young to Know*, *That Way With Women*, *The Countess of Monte Cristo*, *Peggy*, *Bedtime for Bonzo*, *Katie Did It*, *Little Egypt*, *Here Come the Nelsons*, *Bonzo Goes to College*, *I'll Take Sweden*, and *Frankie and Johnny*. Survived by his wife.

ANTHONY DEXTER (Walter Reinhold Alfred Fleischmann), 82, Nebraska-born screen actor, best known for playing the title role in the 1952 film biography *Valentino*, died on Mar. 27, 2001, in Greeley, CO. His other movies included *The Brigand, Captain John Smith and Pocahontas, Fire Maidens From Outer Space, The Story of Mankind* (as Christopher Columbus), *The Parson and the Outlaw, 12 to the Moon*, and *Thoroughly Modern Millie*. He eventually left show business and became a teacher. No reported survivors.

Troy Donahue   Dale Evans

TROY DONAHUE (Merle Johnson, Jr.), 65, New York City-born screen and television actor, best known for starring in the 1959 romance *A Summer Place*, died of a heart attack in Los Angeles, on Sept. 2, 2001. Following his 1957 film debut in *Man Afraid*, he was seen in such pictures as *The Tarnished Angels, The Voice in the Mirror, Summer Love, Monster on the Campus, Imitation of Life* (1959), *The Crowded Sky, Parrish, Susan Slade, Rome Adventure, Palm Springs Weekend, A Distant Trumpet, My Blood Runs Cold, Blast Off!* (*Those Fantastic Flying Fools*), *Seizure, Cockfighter, The Godfather Part II, Omega Cop*, and *Cry-Baby*. One of his four wives was actress Suzanne Pleshette. Survived by his sister and two children.

DANILO DONATI, 75, Italian costume and set designer, who won Academy Awards for his costume designs for *Romeo and Juliet* and *Fellini's Casanova*, died at his home in Rome on Dec. 1, 2001. His other film credits include *The Gospel According to St. Matthew, Ginger and Fred*, and *Life Is Beautiful*. No reported survivors.

Gloria Foster   Arlene Francis

DALE EVANS (Frances Octavia Smith), 88, Texas-born film and television actress, who became famous for the many westerns she starred in opposite husband Roy Rogers, died on Feb. 7, 2001 at her home in Apple Valley, CA. A few years after her 1940 motion picture debut in *The East Side Kids*, she was hired by Republic Pictures. That company made her a leading lady in westerns, including her first with Rogers, *The Cowboy and the Senorita*, in 1944. They married in 1948, continuing to co-star in such features as *The Man From Oklahoma, Rainbow Over Texas, My Pal Trigger, Out California Way, Under Nevada Skies, Helldorado, Susanna Pass, Trigger Jr.*, and *Pals of the Golden West*, her last acting credit, in 1952. Rogers died in 1998.

A. D. FLOWERS, 84, special effects coordinator who won Academy Awards for his work on the films *Tora! Tora! Tora!* and *The Poseidon Adventure*, died on July 5, 2001 in Fullerton, CA. His other credits include *The Godfather, The Towering Inferno*, and *Apocalypse Now*. No reported survivors.

GLORIA FOSTER, 64, Chicago-born screen, stage, and television actress died from diabetes on Sept. 29, 2001 at her Manhattan home. She was seen in films such as *Nothing but a Man, The Angel Levine, Man and Boy, Leonard Part 6*, and *The Matrix*. No survivors.

ARLENE FRANCIS (Arlene Francis Kazanjian), 93, Boston-born screen, stage, and television actress, better known for appearing as a panelist on the quiz show "What's My Line?" for 25 years, died of complications of cancer and Alzheimer's disease in San Francisco on May 31, 2001. She was seen in films such as *All My Sons*, *One Two Three*, and *The Thrill of It All*. She is survived by her son from her marriage to actor Martin Gabel (who died in 1986).

KATHLEEN FREEMAN, 78, Chicago-born screen, stage, and television character actress, who played vocal coach Phoebe Dinsmore in the classic musical *Singin' in the Rain* and made eleven movies opposite Jerry Lewis, died of lung cancer on Aug. 23, 2001 in New York City. She was appearing in the Broadway musical *The Full Monty*, for which she received a Theatre World Award, at the time of her death. Her many other movies include *The Naked City*, *A Life of Her Own*, *A Place in the Sun*, *Love Is Better Than Ever*, *Wait Till the Sun Shines Nellie*, *The Bad and the Beautiful*, *Bonzo Goes to College*, *Three Ring Circus* (her first with Lewis), *The Far Country*, *Houseboat*, *The Fly*, *Don't Give Up the Ship*, *North to Alaska*, *The Ladies Man*, *The Errand Boy*, *The Nutty Professor* (1963), *The Disorderly Orderly*, *The Rounders*, *Point Blank*, *Support Your Local Sheriff!*, *Myra Breckinridge*, *The Blues Brothers*, *Dragnet* (1987), *In the Mood*, *Naked Gun 33 1/3: The Final Insult*, and *I'll Be Home for Christmas*. No reported survivors.

Kathleen Freeman   Jane Greer

RUTH GOETZ (Ruth Goodman), 93, Philadelphia-born writer, who collaborated with her husband Augustus Goetz on the 1947 play *The Heiress* and adapted it to the screen two years later, died in Englewood, NJ, on Oct. 12, 2001. The Goetzes also wrote screenplays such as *Carrie* (1952) and *Stage Struck*. Augustus died in 1957. She is survived by her daughter and a granddaughter.

SALLY GRACIE, 80, screen, stage, and television actress died on Aug. 13, 2001 at her home in Manhattan. Her films include *Patterns*, *Stage Struck*, *The Fugitive Kind*, *The Rain People*, and *Passed Away*. She was the first wife of actor Rod Steiger. She is survived by a son from her second marriage, a stepdaughter, a stepson, and six grandchildren.

JANE GREER (Bettejane Greer), 76, Washington-born screen and television actress, perhaps best known for her femme fatale role in the 1947 noir *Out of the Past*, died from complications of cancer on Aug. 24, 2001 in Los Angeles. A former big band singer, she was briefly married to crooner-actor Rudy Vallee, shortly before embarking on her film career, in 1945, with *Pan American*, billed under her real name. Her other credits included *Dick Tracy* (1945), *Sunset Pass*, *Sinbad the Sailor*, *They Won't Believe Me*, *The Big Steal*, *You're in the Navy Now* (*U.S.S. Teakettle*), *I Married a Communist*, *The Company She Keeps*, *The Prisoner of Zenda* (1952), *You for Me*, *The Clown*, *Down Among the Sheltering Palms*, *Run for the Sun*, *Man of a Thousand Faces*, *Where Love Has Gone*, *Billie*, *Against All Odds* (the 1984 remake of *Out of the Past*), *Just Between Friends*, and *Immediate Family*. Survived by three sons, a twin brother, and two grandchildren.

JACK GWILLIM, 91, British character player died on July 2, 2001 in Los Angeles. Among his many film appearances are *Solomon and Sheba*, *Flame Over India*, *Sink the Bismarck!*, *Circus of Horror*, *Lawrence of Arabia*, *Lisa* (*The Inspector*), *In Search of the Castaways*, *Jason and the Argonauts*, *A Boy Ten Feet Tall* (*Sammy Going South*), *A Man for All Seasons*, *Battle of Britain*, *Patton*, *Cromwell*, *Clash of the Titans*, and *The Monster Squad*. Survived by his wife, three children, two grandchildren, and a brother.

JACK HALEY, JR., 67, Los Angeles-born producer, director, and documentarian, best known for the 1974 tribute to MGM musicals *That's Entertainment!*, died of respiratory failure on Apr. 21, 2001 in Santa Monica, CA. His other films include *The Love Machine* and *That's Dancing!* On television he won an Emmy for directing the special "Movin' With Nancy." He was the son of actor Jack Haley and had been married in the 1970s to actress-singer Liza Minnelli. Survived by his sister.

Minister," the bulk of his film credits did not come until late in his life. His motion pictures include *Young Winston*, *The Hiding Place*, *History of the World Part 1*, *Gandhi*, *Turtle Diary*, *Demolition Man*, *Richard III* (as Clarence), *Twelfth Night* (as Malvolio), *Amistad*, *The Object of My Affection*, *Madeleine*, and *The Winslow Boy* (1999). He won a Tony Award for his performance in *Shadowlands*. Survived by his companion, Trevor Bentham.

Jack Haley, Jr.

George Harrison

Nigel Hawthorne

Eileen Heckart

GEORGE HARRISON, 58, Liverpool-born singer-song-writer-film producer-actor-guitarist, who helped revolutionize the rock music scene as one of the members of the Beatles, died of cancer in Los Angeles on Nov. 29, 2001. With the Beatles he performed his own compositions such as "Taxman," "While My Guitar Gently Weeps," "Here Comes the Sun," and "Something," and appeared with them in the films *A Hard Day's Night*, *Help!*, *Yellow Submarine*, and *Let It Be* (sharing the Academy Award for Best Music Score). As a solo performer, he went on to write and record such hit songs as "My Sweet Lord" and "All Those Years Ago." As a film producer and head of his own company, Handmade Films, he was responsible for such movies as *Life of Brian*, *Time Bandits*, *The Long Good Friday*, *Mona Lisa*, and *Withnail and I*. Survived by his second wife, their son, two brothers, and a sister.

NIGEL HAWTHORNE, 72, British screen, stage, and television actor, who received an Oscar nomination for his performance in *The Madness of King George*, died of a heart attack at his home in Baldock, Hertfordshire, England, on Dec. 26, 2001. Well-known in theater, and on television for his series "Yes,

EILEEN HECKART (Anna Eileen Heckart), 82, Columbus-born screen, stage, and television character actress, who won an Academy Award as Best Supporting Actress for repeating her stage role as the protective mother of a young blind man in *Butterflies Are Free*, died of cancer on Dec. 31, 2001 at her home in Norwalk, CT. In addition to her countless appearances on the New York stage, she was seen in such other films as *Miracle in the Rain*, *Somebody Up There Likes Me*, *The Bad Seed* (for which she received an Oscar nomination), *Hot Spell*, *Up the Down Staircase*, *No Way to Treat a Lady*, *The Hiding Place*, *Burnt Offerings*, *Heartbreak Ridge*, and *The First Wives Club*. In 2000 she was awarded a special Tony Award for her lifetime of work in the theater. She is survived by three sons, two half-sisters, and two grandchildren.

CHRISTOPHER HEWETT, 80, British screen, stage, and television character actor, who played the flamboyant director Roger DeBris in the classic comedy *The Producers*, died on Aug. 3, 2001 in Los Angeles. He appeared in only three other theatrical features: *Pool of London*, *The Lavender Hill Mob*, and *Ratboy*. On television he was best known for starring in the series "Mr. Belvedere." No reported survivors.

 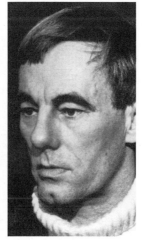

Christopher Hewett   Ken Hughes

KEN HUGHES, 79, Liverpool-born director-writer of such films as *Chitty Chitty Bang Bang* and *Cromwell*, died in Los Angeles on Apr. 28, 2001. He had been suffering from Alzheimer's disease. Among his other films as director and writer are *The House Across the Lake*, *The Trials of Oscar Wilde*, *Jazz Boat*, *The Small World of Sammy Lee*, *Arrivederci Baby! (Drop Dead Darling)*, and *Alfie Darling*. He is survived by his wife and a daughter.

EUGENE JACKSON, 84, Buffalo-born screen and television actor, who had appeared as "Pineapple" in six silent Our Gang shorts, died of a heart attack at his home in Compton, CA, on Oct. 26, 2001. He could also be seen in such feature films as *Cimarron* (1931), *Dixiana*, *Tumbling Tumbleweeds*, *Thoroughbreds Don't Cry*, *Arrest Bulldog Drummond*, *Reap the Wild Wind*, *Reveille With Beverly*, *Jeanne Eagles*, and *Cleopatra Jones*. He is survived by his wife, two daughters, and a son.

BURT KENNEDY, 78, Michigan-born director-writer of westerns such as *The War Wagon* and *Support Your Local Sheriff!*, died at his home in Sherman Oaks, CA, on Feb. 15, 2001. His other credits include *The Rounders*, *Welcome to Hard Times*, *The Good Guys and the Bad Guys*, *Dirty Dingus Magee*, *Hannie Caulder*, and *The Train Robbers*. Survived by his companion, Nancy Pendleton, two daughters, and five grandchildren.

STANLEY KRAMER, 87, New York City-born director-producer, noted for such socially conscious commercial entertainments as *The Defiant Ones*, *Judgment at Nuremberg*, and *Guess Who's Coming to Dinner* (each of which earned him dual Oscar nominations as producer and director), died of complications from pneumonia in Woodland Hills, CA, on Feb. 19, 2001. His films as a producer include *Champion*, *Home of the Brave*, *The Men*, *Cyrano de Bergerac* (1950), *Death of a Salesman*, *High Noon* (Oscar nomination), *The Member of the Wedding*, *The 5000 Fingers of Dr. T*, *The Wild One*, and *The Caine Mutiny* (Oscar nomination). He made his debut as director in 1955 with *Not as a Stranger*, followed by such titles (most of which found him also serving as producer) as *The Pride and the Passion*, *On the Beach*, *Inherit the Wind*, *It's a Mad Mad Mad Mad World*, *Ship of Fools* (Oscar nomination as producer), *The Secret of Santa Vittoria*, *Bless the Beasts and Children*, and his last, *The Runner Stumbles*, in 1979. In 1962 he was given the Irving G. Thalberg Award by the Academy of Motion Picture Arts and Sciences. Survived by his wife, a son, three daughters.

Stanley Kramer

Jack Lemmon

JACK LEMMON (John Uhler Lemmon 3rd), 76, Boston-born screen, stage, and television actor, who became one of America's most popular and beloved performers in his nearly 50-year career in movies, died on June 27, 2001 in Los Angeles of complications from cancer. Following work in theater and on live television, he made his motion picture debut in 1954 in *It Should Happen to You*. He went on to win Academy Awards for Best Supporting Actor for *Mister Roberts*, in 1955, and as Best Actor for *Save the Tiger*, in 1973. There were additional nominations for *Some Like It Hot, The Apartment, Days of Wine and Roses, The China Syndrome, Tribute,* and *Missing*. His other films are *Phffft, Three for the Show, My Sister Eileen* (1955), *You Can't Run Away from It, Fire Down Below, Operation Mad Ball, Cowboy, Bell Book and Candle, It Happened to Jane, The Wackiest Ship in the Army, Pepe, The Notorious Landlady, Irma La Duce, Under the Yum Yum Tree, Good Neighbor Sam, How to Murder Your Wife, The Great Race, The Fortune Cookie, Luv, The Odd Couple, The April Fools, The Out-of-Towners, Kotch* (which he also directed), *The War Between Men and Women, Avanti!, The Front Page* (1974), *The Prisoner of Second Avenue, Alex and the Gypsy, Airport '77, Buddy Buddy, Mass Appeal, Macaroni, That's Life!, Dad, JFK, The Player, Glengarry Glen Ross, Short Cuts, Grumpy Old Men, Grumpier Old Men, Getting Away With Murder, The Grass Harp, Hamlet* (1996), *My Fellow Americans, Out to Sea, The Odd Couple 2,* and *The Legend of Bagger Vance*. He was the recipient of such awards as the Kennedy Center Honors and the American Film Institute Life Achievement Award. Survived by his second wife, actress Felicia Farr; their daughter; a son from his first marriage, actor Chris Lemmon; and three grandchildren.

JAY LIVINGSTON, 86, Pennsylvania-born composer-lyricist who, with his collaborator Ray Evans, won Academy Awards for the songs "Buttons and Bows" (from *The Paleface*), "Mona Lisa" (from *Captain Carey, U.S.A.*), and "Que Sera Sera/Whatever Will Be Will Be" (from *The Man Who Knew Too Much*), died from pneumonia in Los Angeles on Oct. 17, 2001. He received additional nominations for "The Cat and the Canary" (from *Why Girls Leave Home*), "Tammy" (from *Tammy and the Bachelor*), "Almost in Your Arms" (from *Houseboat*), and the title song from *Dear Heart*. Two of his most famous songs were the title tune written for but not used in *To Each His Own,* and "Silver Bells," composed for *The Lemon Drop Kid*. He is survived by his second wife; his daughter; his brother, Alan Livingston, president of Capitol Records; a granddaughter; and three great-grandchildren.

TED MANN, 84, North Dakota-born theater entrepreneur and movie producer, died of complications from a stroke on Jan. 15, 2001, in Los Angeles. He ran the Mann Theatres company and, later, National General Theaters, before turning to film production with such films as *The Illustrated Man, Buster and Billie, Lifeguard, The Nude Bomb,* and *Krull*. He is survived by his wife, actress Rhonda Fleming, two daughters, a sister, and four grandchildren.

Dorothy McGuire

LAWRENCE B. MARCUS, 84, Utah-born screenwriter, who received an Oscar nomination in collaboration with Richard Rush for adapting the script for *The Stunt Man*, died in Los Angeles on Aug. 28, 2001 due to complications from Parkinson's disease. His other credits include *Petulia, Justine, Going Home,* and *Alex & the Gypsy*. Survived by his wife, son, sister, and a grandchild.

WHITMAN MAYO, 70, New York City-born screen and television character actor, best known for playing "Grady Wilson" on the series "Sanford and Son," died of a heart attack on May 22, 2001 in Atlanta, GA. He was seen in films such as *The Main Event, D.C. Cab, The Seventh Coin,* and *Boyz N the Hood.* No reported survivors.

DOROTHY McGUIRE, 83, Omaha-born screen, stage, and television actress, who starred in such notable films as *A Tree Grows in Brooklyn, Gentleman's Agreement* (for which she earned an Oscar nomination), and *Swiss Family Robinson,* died on Sept. 14, 2001 in Santa Monica, CA. She had broken her leg three weeks prior and had developed an arrhythmia. She came to Hollywood in 1943 to repeat her stage role in *Claudia,* and thereafter was seen in such movies as *The Enchanted Cottage, The Spiral Staircase* (1946), *Till the End of Time, Mr. 880, I Want You, Three Coins in the Fountain, Trial, Friendly Persuasion, Old Yeller, This Earth Is Mine, A Summer Place, The Dark at the Top of the Stairs, Summer Magic, The Greatest Story Ever Told,* and *Flight of the Doves.* She is survived by her daughter and a son.

JASON MILLER, 62, New York-born actor-playwright, who earned an Academy Award nomination for playing the title role in the 1973 horror hit *The Exorcist,* died of a heart attack on May 13, 2001 in Scranton, PA. He first came to prominence as the Pulitzer Prize-winning author of the Broadway success *That Championship Season,* which he later adapted into a film, also serving as director. His other movie credits as an actor include *The Nickel Ride, Twinkle Twinkle Killer Kane (The Ninth Configuration), Light of Day,* and *Rudy.* Survived by three sons, including actor Jason Patric, and a daughter.

JOHN MITCHUM, 82, Connecticut-born character actor, and younger brother of Robert Mitchum, died in Los Angeles on Nov. 28, 2001. Among his movie credits are *Flying Leathernecks, The Lusty Men, Johnny Rocco, El Dorado, Paint Your Wagon, Chisum, Dirty Harry, Magnum Force,* and *The Outlaw Josey Wales.* Survived by his wife, two daughters, and several grandchildren.

PAULINE MOORE, 87, Pennsylvania-born film actress died of amyotrophic lateral sclerosis on Dec. 7, 2001 in Sequim, WA. In addition to starring in the serial *King of the Texas Rangers,* she was seen in features such as *Love Is News, Heidi* (1937), *The Three Musketeers* (1939; as Constance), *Charlie Chan at Treasure Island, Young Mr. Lincoln,* and *Trail Blazers.* Survived by her two daughters and a son.

PEGGY MOUNT, 85, British character actress, best known to American audiences for playing Mrs. Bumble in the Oscar-winning musical *Oliver!,* died in London on Nov. 13, 2001. Her other films include *Panic in the Parlor (Sailor Beware), The Embezzler, Ladies Who Do, One Way Pendulum,* and *Hotel Paradiso.* No immediate survivors.

Jason Miller   Virginia O'Brien

PORTIA NELSON (Betty Mae Nelson), 80, Utah-born actress and nightclub singer, died at her home in Manhattan on March 6, 2001. In addition to appearing on Broadway in *The Golden Apple* and acting in the soap opera "All My Children," she was seen in movies such as *The Sound of Music* (as Sister Berthe). Survived by a brother.

VIRGINIA O'BRIEN, 81, Los Angeles-born screen and stage actress-singer, famous for her deadpan comical specialty numbers in several MGM musicals, died on Jan. 16, 2001 in Woodland Hills, CA. She made her film debut in 1940 in *Hullabaloo,* which was followed by such films as *The Big Store, Lady Be Good, Ship Ahoy, Panama Hattie, Du Barry Was a Lady, Thousands Cheer, Two Girls and a Sailor, Meet the People, Ziegfeld Follies, The Harvey Girls, The Show-Off, Till the Clouds Roll By, Francis in the Navy,* and *Gus.* She is survived by three daughters, a son, several grandchildren, and two great-grandchildren.

CARROLL O'CONNOR, 76, New York City-born screen, television, and stage actor, best known for his Emmy Award-winning characterization of Archie Bunker on the classic television series "All in the Family," died on June 21, 2001 in Culver City, CA, of a heart attack brought on by complications from diabetes. He was seen in such motion pictures as *Parrish, By Love Possessed, Lonely Are the Brave, Cleopatra* (1963), *In Harm's Way, Hawaii, Not With My Wife You Don't, What Did You Do in the War Daddy?, Waterhole #3, Point Blank, The Devil's Brigade, Marlowe, Law and Disorder,* and *Return to Me.* Survived by his wife.

JOHN PHILLIPS, 65, South Carolina-born singer-songwriter, a member of the 1960s pop group the Mamas and the Papas, died of heart failure on March 18, 2001 in Los Angeles. He wrote such hit songs as "Monday, Monday," "San Francisco," and "California Dreamin'." The Mamas and the Papas were seen in the concert documentary *Monterey Pop,* and Phillips supplied songs for the film *Brewster McCloud* and the hit "Kokomo," featured in *Cocktail.* Survived by his fourth wife; three daughters, actresses Mackenzie and Bijou Phillips and singer Chynna Phillips; two sons; and two stepdaughters.

including *The Plainsman* (1936), *Swing High Swing Low, Waikiki Wedding, The Buccaneer* (1938; he also directed the 1958 remake), *Union Pacific, Road to Singapore, The Ghost Breakers, City for Conquest, Blood and Sand* (1941), *They Died With Their Boots On, Larceny Inc., Road to Morocco, Irish Eyes Are Smiling, California, Sinbad the Sailor, The Brave Bulls, The World in His Arms, Against All Flags, Ride Vacquero!, Blowing Wild, Ulysses* (1954), *La Strada, Seven Cities of Gold, Man From Del Rio, The Hunchback of Notre Dame* (1957), *Wild Is the Wind* (Oscar nomination), *Hot Spell, Last Train From Gun Hill, Warlock, Portrait in Black, The Savage Innocents, The Guns of Navarone, Lawrence of Arabia, Requiem for a Heavyweight, Behold a Pale Horse, The Visit, Zorba the Greek* (receiving another Oscar nomination, for perhaps his most famous role), *High Wind in Jamaica, The Happening, The Shoes of the Fisherman, The Secret of Santa Vittoria, A Dream of Kings, A Walk in the Spring Rain, Flap, R.P.M., Across 110th Street, The Don Is Dead, The Greek Tycoon, The Passage, Lion of the Desert, Jungle Fever, Mobsters, Only the Lonely, Last Action Hero,* and *A Walk in the Clouds.* He is survived by his companion, Kathy Benvin, their two children, seven other sons, and three other daughters.

FRANCISCO RABAL, 75, Spanish film actor died of compensatory dilating emphysema during a flight between Montreal and Madrid on Aug. 29, 2001. His many credits include *The Wide Blue Road, Nazarin, The Witches* (1966), *Belle de Jour, Stay As You Are, The Holy Innocents, A Time of Destiny, Tie Me Up! Tie Me Down!,* and *Goya in Bordeaux.* Survived by his wife, a daughter, and a son.

ALAN RAFKIN, 73, New York City-born Emmy Award-winning television and motion picture director, died of heart disease on Aug. 6, 2001 in Los Angeles. Although he principally directed for television, he also helmed the movies *Ski Party, The Ghost and Mr. Chicken, Nobody's Perfect* (1968), *The Shakiest Gun in the West, Angel in My Pocket,* and *How to Frame a Figg.* No reported survivors.

Carroll O'Connor   Francisco Rabal

ANTHONY QUINN, 86, Mexican-born screen, stage, and television actor, who, during a career spanning more than 60 years, won Academy Awards for his performances in *Viva Zapata!* and *Lust for Life,* died of respiratory failure in Boston, MA, on June 3, 2001. After making his film debut in 1936 in *Parole,* he went on to appear in more than 100 motion pictures

Anthony Quinn

WALTER REED, 85, Washington-born character actor, died of kidney failure on Aug. 20, 2001 at his home in Santa Cruz, CA. His film appearances include *Mexican Spitfire's Elephant*, *Bombardier*, *Fighter Squadron*, *Return of the Bad Men*, *Young Man With a Horn*, *The Clown*, *Submarine Command*, *Horizons West*, *The High and the Mighty*, *Forever Female*, *The Horse Soldiers*, and *Where Love Has Gone*. Survived by his three children and a brother.

MICHAEL RITCHIE, 62, Wisconsin-born motion picture director of such films as *The Candidate*, *The Bad News Bears*, and *Semi-Tough*, died of complications from prostate cancer on Apr. 16, 2001 in Manhattan. Following some work in television, he made his theatrical directorial debut in 1969 with *Downhill Racer*, followed by such other pictures as *Smile*, *An Almost Perfect Affair*, *Divine Madness*, *The Survivors*, *Fletch*, *Wildcats*, *Diggstown*, *Cops and Robbersons*, and *The Fantasticks*. He is survived by his wife, a son, four daughters, two stepchildren, a brother, and a sister.

serving as producer as well) as *The Owl and the Pussycat*, *Play It Again Sam*, *The Last of Sheila*, *Funny Lady*, *The Sunshine Boys*, *The Seven Percent Solution*, *The Goodbye Girl*, *California Suite*, *Nijinsky*, *Pennies From Heaven* (1981), *Max Dugan Returns*, *Footloose*, *Protocol*, *The Secret of My Success*, *Steel Magnolias*, *My Blue Heaven*, *True Colors*, and *Boys on the Side*. He is survived by his sister, a niece, and a nephew.

HARRY SECOMBE, 79, British actor, comedian, and singer, best known as one of the stars (along with Peter Sellers and Spike Milligan) of Britain's pioneering humor series "The Goon Show," died of cancer on Apr. 11, 2001 in Guildford, England. In America he was perhaps most known by movie audiences for playing Mr. Bumble in the Oscar-winning *Oliver!*, in 1968. His other films include *Down Among the Z Men*, *Penny Points to Paradise*, *Davy*, *Jet Storm*, *The Bed Sitting Room*, *Song of Norway*, and *The Magnificent Seven Deadly Sins*. Survived by his wife of 53 years, four children, and five grandchildren.

Michael Ritchie

Herbert Ross

Harry Secombe

Kim Stanley

NORMAN RODWAY, 72, British actor and noted member of the Royal Shakespeare Company, died in Banbury, England on Mar. 13, 2001, following a stroke. He was seen in such motion pictures as *Chimes at Midnight*, *I'll Never Forget What's 'is Name*, *The Penthouse*, *Tai Pan*, *Mother Night*, and *The Empty Mirror*. Survived by his fourth wife and a daughter.

HERBERT ROSS, 74, Brooklyn-born choreographer-turned-film director, who earned dual Oscar nominations for helming and producing the 1977 film *The Turning Point*, died of heart failure on Oct. 9, 2001 in New York City. Following his stage work he came to Hollywood to choreograph the films *Inside Daisy Clover*, *Doctor Dolittle*, and *Funny Girl*. He became a film director starting in 1969 with the musical remake of *Goodbye Mr. Chips* and followed it with such other pictures (sometimes

ANTHONY SHAFFER, 75, British playwright, who won a Tony Award for *Sleuth*, which he later adapted into a film starring Laurence Olivier and Michael Caine, died of a heart attack on Nov. 6, 2001 in London. After his stage success he went on to write screenplays for such films as *Frenzy*, *The Wicker Man*, *Death on the Nile*, and *Absolution*. Survived by his third wife, actress Diane Cilento; his twin brother, writer Peter Shaffer; and two daughters from his second marriage.

ANN SOTHERN (Harriette Lake), 92, North Dakota-born screen and television actress, whose films ranged from "B's" like *Maisie* to "A" films like *A Letter to Three Wives*, died of heart failure at her home in Ketchum, ID, on March 15, 2001. Following her 1927 film debut in *Broadway Nights*, she was seen in such movies as *The Show of Shows, Broadway Thru a Keyhole, Kid Millions, Folies Bergere, My American Wife, Hell Ship Morgan, The Smartest Girl in Town, There Goes My Girl, Danger—Love at Work, Trade Winds, Joe and Ethel Turp Call on the President, Elsa Maxwell's Hotel for Women, Congo Maisie, Brother Orchid, Maisie Was a Lady, Lady Be Good, Panama Hattie, Cry Havoc, Thousands Cheer, Three Hearts for Julia, Undercover Maisie, Words and Music, Nancy Goes to Rio, The Blue Gardenia, Lady in a Cage, The Best Man* (1964), *Sylvia, The Killing Kind, Crazy Mama,* and *The Whales of August,* for which she received an Oscar nomination. Survived by her daughter, actress Tisha Sterling, from her marriage to actor Robert Sterling; a sister; and a granddaughter.

KIM STANLEY (Patricia Reid), 76, New Mexico-born screen, stage, and television actress, one of the leading Broadway stars of the 1950s, who appeared in the original productions of *Picnic* and *Bus Stop*, died in Santa Fe, NM, on Aug. 20, 2001 of uterine cancer. She appeared in only five motion pictures: *The Goddess, Seance on a Wet Afternoon* (Oscar nomination), *The Three Sisters, Frances* (Oscar nomination), and *The Right Stuff,* in addition to narrating *To Kill a Mockingbird.* She is survived by a son, two daughters, three grandchildren, and a brother.

Anthony Steel   Beatrice Straight

ANTHONY STEEL, 80, British screen and television actor, died on March 21, 2001 in London. Among his films are *The Mudlark, The Wooden Horse, Malta Story, Outpost in Malaya, Anzio,* and *The Mirror Crack'd.* Survived by a son and two daughters.

BEATRICE STRAIGHT, 86, New York-born screen, stage, and television actress, who won an Academy Award for playing William Holden's neglected wife in *Network*, died on Apr. 7, 2001 in North Ridge, CA. Principally a stage actress in productions such as *The Crucible* and *The Innocents*, she was seen in such films as *Phone Call From a Stranger, Patterns, The Nun's Story, Bloodline, The Formula, Endless Love, Poltergeist,* and *Power.* She is survived by two sons, two stepchildren, seven grandchildren, and three great-grandchildren.

Ann Sothern

DAVID SWIFT, 82, Minnesota-born director-writer responsible for films such as *Pollyanna* and *How to Succeed in Business Without Really Trying,* died of a heart attack in Santa Monica, CA, on Dec. 31, 2001. A former animator for Disney Studios, he went on to create the television series "Mr. Peepers" and then to direct and write other movies such as *The Parent Trap* (1961), *The Interns, Under the Yum Yum Tree, Good Neighbor Sam,* and *Candleshoe.* He is survived by his wife, two daughters, and two grandchildren.

RALPH TABAKIN, 79, Texas-born screen character actor, who received a tiny role in director Barry Levinson's 1982 film *Diner* and then went on to appear in all of his films up to *Liberty Heights,* in 1999, died of heart disease on May 13, 2001 in Rockville, MD. Other Levinson movies include *Young Sherlock Holmes, Good Morning Vietnam, Rain Man, Avalon, Bugsy, Disclosure,* and *Wag the Dog.* Survived by two daughters, two sisters, and a granddaughter.

Dorothy Tutin

Deborah Walley

RALPH THOMAS, 85, British film director, best known for helming *Doctor in the House* and several of its sequels, died in London on March 17, 2001. His other credits include *The Clouded Yellow, Appointment With Venus, The Wind Cannot Read, Conspiracy of Hearts, The Iron Petticoat, Campbell's Kingdom, A Tale of Two Cities* (1958), *The Thirty-Nine Steps* (1959), *Hot Enough for June,* and *Percy.* He is survived by his wife; his son, producer Jeremy Thomas; and a daughter.

HARRY TOWNES, 86, Alabama-born character actor, died at his home in Huntsville, AL, on May 23, 2001. Among his films are *The Mountain, Screaming Mimi, The Brother Karamazov, Sanctuary, Fitzwilly,* and *The Hawaiians.* In 1970 he became an Episcopalian minister. No reported survivors.

Ray Walston   Edward Winter

LARRY TUCKER, 67, Philadelphia-born writer-producer, who, in collaboration with Paul Mazursky, created the series "The Monkees" and earned an Oscar nomination for the script for *Bob & Carol & Ted & Alice,* died on Apr. 1, 2001 in Los Angeles due to complications from multiple sclerosis and cancer. He also worked with Mazursky on the films *I Love You Alice B. Toklas* and *Alice in Wonderland.* No reported survivors.

DOROTHY TUTIN, 71, London-born screen, stage, and television actress, who played Cecily in the 1952 film version of *The Importance of Being Earnest,* died of leukemia on Aug. 6, 2001 in London. Although principally a theater performer she was seen in other movies such as *The Beggar's Opera, A Tale of Two Cities* (1958), *Cromwell, Savage Messiah,* and *The Shooting Party.* She is survived by her husband, actor Derek Waring; a daughter; and a son.

DIANA VAN DER VLIS, 66, Toronto-born actress died from a pulmonary embolism on Oct. 22, 2001 in Missoula, MT. Her films include *The Girl in Black Stockings, X: The Man With the X-Ray Eyes, The Incident,* and *The Swimmer,* among others. Survived by her husband, a son, and a daughter.

DEBORAH WALLEY, 57, Connecticut-born screen, stage, and television actress, who appeared in such teen-oriented sixties fare as *Gidget Goes Hawaiian* and *Beach Blanket Bingo*, died of esophageal cancer on May 10, 2001 at her home in Sedona, AZ. Her other movie credits include *Bon Voyage!*, *Summer Magic*, *The Young Lovers*, *Sergeant Deadhead*, *Ski Party*, *Dr. Goldfoot and the Bikini Machine*, *It's a Bikini World*, and *Benji*. Survived by two sons.

RAY WALSTON, 86, New Orleans-born screen, stage, and television actor, best known for his star-making, Tony Award-winning performance as the Devil in the musical *Damn Yankees*, which he then recreated for film, died after a long battle with lupus on Jan. 1, 2001 at his home in Beverly Hills, CA. He was seen in such other films as *Kiss Them for Me*, *South Pacific*, *The Apartment*, *Portrait in Black*, *Tall Story*, *Who's Minding the Store?*, *Kiss Me Stupid*, *Caprice*, *Paint Your Wagon*, *The Sting*, *Silver Streak*, *Popeye*, *Fast Times at Ridgemont High*, *Johnny Dangerously*, *From the Hip*, *Popcorn*, *Of Mice and Men* (1992), and *My Favorite Martian* (based on the television series on which he had starred). Also on television he received an Emmy Award for "Picket Fences." He is survived by his wife, a daughter, and two grandchildren.

EDWARD WINTER, 63, California-born screen, stage, and television actor, died of Parkinson's disease on March 8, 2001 in Los Angeles. He was seen in movies such as *The Parallax View*, *A Change of Seasons*, *The Buddy System*, and *From the Hip*. No reported survivors.

VICTOR WONG, 74, San Francisco-born character actor who made his way from journalism to acting with the Asian-American Theatre Group, died of heart failure on Sept. 12, 2001 at his home near Locke, CA. His movies include *Dim Sum: A Little Bit of Heart*, *Year of the Dragon*, *Big Trouble in Little China*, *The Golden Child*, *The Last Emperor*, *Tremors*, *3 Ninjas*, *The Joy Luck Club*, *Jade*, and *Seven Years in Tibet*. Survived by his wife, two daughters, a brother, three sisters, and five grandchildren.

Victor Wong   Otis Young

OTIS YOUNG, 69, Providence-born screen and television actor, best known for appearing opposite Jack Nicholson in the 1973 film *The Last Detail*, died on October 11, 2001. His few other movie roles include *Don't Just Stand There*, *The Hollywood Knights*, and *Blood Beach*. He later served as a pastor and as a college professor. Survived by his wife and four children.

INDEX

Hale Manor Prods., 184
Haley, Brian, 54, 125
Haley, Jack, Jr., 356
Haley, Jackie Earle, 333
Haley, Michael, 154
Halfon, Lianne, 78
Hall, Albert, 156, 333
Hall, Alex, 53
Hall, Anthony Michael, 20, 96, 179, 333
Hall, Arsenio, 333
Hall, Barbara A., 78, 166
Hall, Carol E., 103
Hall, Dean, 117
Hall, Dolly, 92, 301
Hall, Geoffrey, 243
Hall, Jack, 146
Hall, James R., Jr., 210
Hall, Karen Lee, 317
Hall, Kristin, 64
Hall, Lowell, 20
Hall, Margo, 193
Hall, Nguyen, 36
Hall, Pippa, 275
Hall, Regina, 187
Hall, Vondie Curtis, 194
Hallatt, David, 188
Hallberg, Anna, 201
Hallett, Jack, 144
Halliday, Dennis, 179
Hallmark Entertainment, 190
Hallowell, Todd, 214
Hallström, Lasse, 159
Halpern, Alex, 170
Halsey, Richard, 38
Halyard, Chad, 182
Hamatova, Chulpan, 289
Hamburg, John, 107
Hamed, Amir, 208
Hamel, Veronica, 333
Hames, Frank, 168
Hamet, Luq, 260
Hamidi, Alexandre, 287
Hamidovich, Diana, 299
Hamill, Mark, 94, 333
Hamill, Rita, 302
Hamilton, Allen, 191
Hamilton, Carrie, 333
Hamilton, Derek, 196, 207
Hamilton, George, 180, 333
Hamilton, Linda, 333
Hamilton, Lisa Gay, 190
Hamilton, Paula, 301
Hamilton, Quancetia, 28
Hamilton, Sam, 184
Hamilton, Trinity, 8
Hamlet, 189–90
Hamlin, Diane E., 139
Hamlin, Harry, 333
Hamm, Sam, 18
Hammarsten, Gustaf, 271
Hammel, Thomas M., 119
Hammer, Barbara, 201
Hammond, Alexander, 123

Hammond, Michael, 18
Hammond, Nicholas, 180
Hammond, Roz, 238
Hamon, Lucienne, 317
Hampshire, Russ, 167
Hampshire, Susan, 333
Hampton, Danielle, 317
Hampton, James, 209, 333
Hampton, Janice, 191
Hamsher, Jane, 119
Hamzaoui, Malek, 281
Han, Maggie, 333
Han Sanping, 242, 299
Han Suk-gyu, 313
Hanan, Michael, 34
Hanania, Caroline, 43, 110, 184
Hancock, Cherryl, 276
Hancock, Lesley, 293
Hancock, Martin, 275
Handler, Evan, 333
Hands, Eddie, 204
Hands, Guy, 180
Hands, Robert, 295
Handtke, Holger, 239
Handy, Bryan, 195
Handy, Christal, 131
Handy, Emma, 291
Handy, James, 23
Handy, Scott, 46
Haneke, Michael, 287
Hanemann, Michael, 257
Hanft, Helen, 170
Hanisch, Ulli, 257
Hank, Daniel, 199
Hank the Angry Dwarf, 203
Hankin, Larry, 208
Hanks, Colin, 24
Hanks, Tom, 333
Hanley, Chris, 73
Hanley, Dan, 214
Hanley, Johanna, 304
Hanna-Barbera, 37
Hannah, Daryl, 188, 191, 201, 333
Hannah, Eric, 196
Hannah, John, 45, 261
Hannah, Page, 333
Hannah, Scott, 196
Hanner, Zach, 129, 136
Hannes, Lut, 261
Hannibal, 14–15, 227
Hannigan, Alyson, 88
Hannigan, Denis M., 16
Hannon, Mary Claire, 110
Hanover, Donna, 22, 32
Hans, Gladys, 198
Hansard, Bart, 64
Hänsel, Marion, 224, 258
Hansen, Oddvar, 315
Hansen, Tim, 177
Hanson, Jaclyn, 51
Hanson, Marla, 311
Hanudomlapr, To, 318
Hanzon, Thomas, 230

Happenstance, 212, 282
Happy Accidents, 96
Happy Place, 202
Harambasic, Melinda, 19
Harberts, Aaron, 171
Harbour, Michael N., 261
Hard Eight Pictures, 128
Hardacre, Richard, 170
Hardball, 103, 228
Hardball: A Season in the Projects, 103
Harden, Marcia Gay, 333–334
Hardik, Master, 318
Hardin, Charles, 270
Hardin, Kimberly R., 66
Hardin, Ty, 333
Harding, Ben, 302
Harding, Mike, 64
Harding, Phillip, 20
Hardin-Irmer, Patrick, 51
Hardouin, Helen, 253
Hardrict, Cory, 67
Hardway, James, 305
Hardwick, Gary, 28
Hardwicke, Catherine, 9, 146
Hardy, Dona, 183
Hardy, John, 143
Hardy, Jonathan, 51
Hardy, Micheline, 312
Hardy, Peter, 243
Hardy, Thomas, 165
Hardy, Tim, 90
Harel, Sharon, 160
Harelik, Mark, 75
Harewood, Dorian, 194, 333
Hargett, Hester, 38
Hargreaves, Sean, 120
Hark, Tsui, 279
Harker, Susannah, 279
Harker, Wiley, 12
Harkness, Peter, 261
Harlan, Jan, 69
Harlin, Lukas, 44
Harlin, Renny, 44
Harling, Laura, 160
Harlow, Shalom, 146, 169
Harlow, Trent, 51
Harman, Claire, 288
Harmon, Amanda Tascher, 131
Harmon, Mark, 168, 333
Harnett, Josh, 236
Harns, Charlene, 175
Harper, Derrick, 88
Harper, Don, 184
Harper, Hollie, 17
Harper, Jessica, 333
Harper, Leroy, 12
Harper, Mark, 182
Harper, Ron, 54
Harper, Shakira, 28
Harper, Tess, 333
Harper, Thomas Robinson, 62

Harper, Valerie, 333
Harrelson, Woody, 333
Harring, Laura Elena, 277
Harrington, Adam, 171, 207
Harrington, Alex, 51
Harrington, Desmond, 114, 118
Harrington, Kevin, 238
Harrington, Pat, 333
Harris, Andy, 243
Harris, Anne, 178
Harris, Barbara, 333
Harris, Caroline, 46, 179
Harris, Crispin, 178
Harris, Ed, 214, 239, 333–334
Harris, Emmylou, 186
Harris, George, 165
Harris, Harriet Sansom, 26, 128
Harris, J. Todd, 98
Harris, Jackie, 147
Harris, Jamie, 71, 105, 304
Harris, Jared, 210, 242
Harris, Jodi, 74
Harris, Julie, 173, 333
Harris, Lynn, 43, 122
Harris, Mark R., 204
Harris, Mel, 333
Harris, Michael, 189
Harris, Nicholas Wayman, 251
Harris, Nikki, 168
Harris, Preben, 299
Harris, Richard, 132–133, 333
Harris, Ricky, 120
Harris, Rosemary, 236, 333
Harris, Thomas, 14
Harrison, Anneli, 270
Harrison, Babo, 22
Harrison, George, 356
Harrison, Gregory, 333
Harrison, Joel, 173
Harrison, John, 307
Harrison, Linda, 82
Harrison, Matthew, 120
Harrison, Noel, 333
Harrison, Philip, 99
Harrison, Robert F., 146
Harrison, Simon, 119
Harrison, Todd, 146
Harrison, Troy, 51
Harrold, Jamie, 72
Harrold, Kathryn, 333
Harry, Debbie, 188
Harry, Deborah, 206, 333
Harry Potter and the Philosopher's Stone, 132
Harry Potter and the Sorcerer's Stone, 132–133, 213, 227
Hart, Daniel, 253
Hart, David, 275
Hart, Ian, 132, 268, 275–276, 309, 333

Hart, Mary, 152
Hart, Melissa Joan, 16
Hart, Mickey, 181
Hart, Nicole Taylor, 146
Hart, Oona, 146
Hart, Robin, 247
Hart, Roxanne, 333
Hart, Shannon, 139
Hart, Stan, 300
Hartelius, Claes, 271
Harter, Wayne, 19
Hartford, John, 186
Harth, C. Ernst, 120, 175
Harting, Tom, 305
Hartl, Jan, 294
Hartley, Les, 151
Hartley, Mariette, 333
Hartley, Richard, 237
Hartman, David, 333
Hartman, Kathryn, 311
Hartman, Leon, 200
Hartnett, Josh, 43, 54–55, 97, 164–165
Hartusch, Karin, 287
Hartwell, Jane, 48
Hartwick, Noah, 118
Harvest Entertainment, 181
Harvest Pictures, 276
Harvey, Erik Laray, 20, 121
Harvey, Megan Taylor, 39, 56
Harvey, Mick, 243
Harvey, Robert, 9
Harvey, Rupert, 120
Harvey, Terence, 119
Harvey, Tim, 288
Harvie, Derek, 179
Harwell, Bobby, 69
Harwell, Steve, 91
Harwood, Shaun, 254
Hasbrouk, Vivian, 64
Hasegawa, Yuji, 264
Hasenzahl, Will, 98
Hashemian, Behrooz, 298
Hashimoto, Richard, 178
Haskell, Colleen, 56
Haskett, Roger, 22, 192
Haskins, Dennis, 198
Haslinger, Paul, 67
Hassan, Abraham, 253
Hassandust, Hassan, 290
Hasselblad, Anders, 185
Hassell, Jon, 233
Hassett, Marilyn, 333
Hassid, Daniel, 199
Hasson, Patrick, 188
Hastings, Jimmy, 276
Hastings, Lea, 195
Hatamikia, Ebrahim, 176
Hatanaka, Gregory, 190
Hatcher, Teri, 30–31, 170, 333
Hatchett, Carol, 156
Hathaway, Anne, 83, 210
Hatosy, Shawn, 333–334

Hattemer, Amy, 186
Hau Yin Chung, 279
Hauer, Rutger, 237, 333
Hauff, Thomas, 170
Hauser, Cole, 333
Hauser, Wings, 333
Haut et Court, 249
Have a Heart Thru Art, 172
Haven, Annette, 167
Haven, James, 85
Haven, Jamie, 162
Havens, Steve, 31
Haver, June, 333
Havert, Jean-Stéphen, 307
Haviland, Consuelo de, 253
Havilio, Harry, 280
Havoc, June, 333
Hawk, Susan, 190
Hawk, Tony, 198
Hawke, Ethan, 108–109, 115, 128, 222, 333
Hawkins, John, 103
Hawkins, Andrew, 183
Hawkins, Cole, 158, 187
Hawkins, Dale, 172
Hawks, Sunny, 83
Hawkyard, Nicole, 174
Hawley, Lynn, 190
Hawley, Richard, 247
Hawn, Goldie, 43, 333
Hawthorne, Kim, 19, 22, 36
Hawthorne, Nigel, 356
Hay, Phil, 67
Hayashi, Hiroshi, 310
Hayden, Greg, 107
Hayden, Rony, 92
Hayden-Passero, Elizabeth, 199
Hayek, Salma, 333
Hayes, Blair, 190
Hayes, Caroline, 270
Hayes, Deryl, 91
Hayes, Gemma, 306
Hayes, Isaac, 64, 333
Hayes, Kevin, 9, 36
Hayes, Michael, 302
Hayes, Nancy, 193
Hayes, Paul, 91, 203
Hayes, Sean, 70
Hayes, Siobhan, 291
Hayes, Taylor, 64
Hayes, Terry, 119
Hayman, David, 33
Haynes, Gordon, 276
Hays, Robert, 333
Hays, Sanja Milkovic, 36, 65
Hayslip, Tom, 123
Hayward, Debra, 41, 90
Hayward, Kevin, 243
Haywood, Chris, 270, 311
Hazen, Kelley, 202
Hazzard, Larry, Sr., 156

HBO, 186, 192–193
HBO Downtown Productions, 187
HBO Theatrical, 173
HD Video, 205
Head Over Heels, 169
Headey, Lena, 268
Headly, Glenne, 56, 333
HeadQuarters, 144
Heald, Anthony, 333
Healey, Tim, 172
Healey, Tom, 304
Healy, Eamonn, 115
Healy, Pat, 54, 78
Heard, Brett, 44
Heard, John, 97, 333
Hearne, Bryan, 103, 187
Hearst, Patricia, 181
Heartbreakers, 29, 228
Heartland Film, 180
Hearts in Atlantis, 104, 228
Heath, Darrel, 99
Heatherton, Joey, 333
Heatley, Sparrow, 83
Heaton, Rich, 196
Heaton, Tom, 19, 192
Heaulme, Gwenola, 278
Heaven Can Wait, 17
Heberlé, Antoine, 249
Heche, Anne, 184, 333
Hecht, Albie, 152
Hecht, Paul, 17
Heckart, Eileen, 356
Hecker, Gerd, 297
Hecker, Siegfried S., 199
Heckman, Paul, 199
Hedaya, Dan, 277, 333–334
Hede, Fritz, 179
Hedge, Ernest, 195
Hedison, David, 195, 333
Hedley, Tom, 291
Hedren, Tippi, 333
Hedrick, Robert K., Jr., 305
Hedwig and the Angry Inch, 76–77
Hee, Dana, 57
Heffernan, Tracy O'Neal, 193
Hegedus, Chris, 47, 186
Hegedus, James, 48
Hegyes, Robert, 333
Heidsieck, Henri, 297
Heighton, Brian, 44, 194
Heigl, Katherine, 171
Heil, Reinhold, 257
Heiman, Jesse, 88
Heimann, Betsy, 146
Hein, Tracey, 182
Heindl, Scott, 36, 179, 207
Heiner, Barta, 177
Heinrichs, Rick, 82
Heintzelman, Leisa, 263
Heinze, Jacqueline, 203
Heist, 130, 228

Heitz, Jane Galloway, 178
Held, Wolfgang, 193, 204
Helfer, Ian, 81
Helfrich, Mark, 84
Helgason, Hallgrimur, 310
Helgeland, Brian, 46
Helkon Media AG, 179, 296
Helleny, Joel, 93
Heller Highway Productions, 120
Heller, Nina, 196
Heller, Paul, 203
Heller, Peter, 120
Hellman, Nina, 81
Hellman, Ocean, 36
Hello Hooker Productions, 193
Helmer, Veit, 289
Helmond, Katherine, 333
Helmsley, Sherman, 333
Helmuth, Mark, 173
Hemida, Mahmoud, 297
Hemingway, Mariel, 333
Hemming, Lindy, 63, 253
Hemmings, David, 135, 288, 333
Hemmings, Nolan, 288
Hemphill, Jerry, 184
Hemphill, Vera, 184
Henao, Rubi, 274
Henderson, Cathy, 170
Henderson, Duncan, 132
Henderson, Florence, 333
Henderson, Hilton, 243
Henderson, Judy, 101
Henderson, Shirley, 40–41
Hendricks, Barbara, 189
Hendricks, Bruce, 54
Hendricks, Daniel, 139
Hendry, Gloria, 333
Henfrey, Janet, 236
Henkels, Amy, 77
Henley, Barry Shabaka, 156
Henmi, Toshio, 300
Henner, Marilu, 209, 333
Hennessy, Jill, 28, 168
Henriksen, Lance, 333
Henriksson, Krister, 230
Henriques, Darryl, 178
Henry, Buck, 43, 92, 110, 333
Henry, Dilva, 112
Henry Gray & the Hurricanes, 172
Henry, Justin, 333
Hensen, Nathan, 115
Hensley, Hairl, 186
Hensley, Shuler, 32
Hensley, Sonya, 194
Henson, Elden, 97
Henson, Taraji P., 66
Henstridge, Natasha, 95, 333
Henter, Shawn, 10

Hentoff, Nat, 171
Hepburn, Katharine, 333
Hepburn, Stuart, 243, 306
Heppleston, Rhian, 296
Heraut, Francoise, 295
Herbert, Amanda, 311
Herbert, Devorah, 206
Herbert, Sylvie, 282
Herbstein, Julian, 47
Herdel, Steen, 299
Herdman, Josh, 132
Here Cames Mr. Jordan, 17
Heredia, Paula, 204
Herek, Stephen, 100
Hergal, Adel, 313
Heritage Film Group, 167
Herman, Darra, 56
Herman, Josh, 34
Herman, Paul, 23
Herman, Richard, 47
Herman, Susan, 47
Herman, Tia, 47
Herman, Tom, 47
Hermann, Imor, 271
Hernandez, Carlos, 73
Hernandez, Catherine, 24, 110
Hernandez, Franklin, 206
Hernandez, Jay, 67, 111, 211
Hernandez, Jorge R., 143
Hernández, José, 256
Hernandez, Juan, 105
Hernandez, Sandra, 8, 145
Herold, Kristen, 99
Herren, Scott, 192
Herrera, Emil, 154
Herrera, Jade, 95, 208
Herrera, Pablo, 199
Herrera, Randy, 8
Herrero, Gerardo, 232
Herring, Craig P., 64
Herring, Tony, 168
Herriot, Arthur W., 170
Herrmann, Edward, 9, 333
Herron, Royce, 195
Hershberger, Garrison, 168
Hershberger, Sally, 37
Hershey, Barbara, 293, 333
Hershman, Joel, 266
Hersi, Abdibashir Mohamed, 165
Herskovitz, Marshall, 166
Hertel, Cyrille, 301
Herz, Adam, 88
Herz, Michael, 203
Herzfeld, John, 23
Herzl, Robert, 254
Herzog, Tim, 56
Heskin, Kam, 82, 176
Heslip, Joe, 194
Hess, David, 156
Hesselberg, Sophie, 268
Hesseman, Howard, 333
Hession, Eddie, 90
Heston, Charlton, 43, 70, 82, 333

HET Fonds Film in Vlaanderen, 270
Heterington, Jason, 268
Hetherington, Kristina, 275
Hetland, Carla, 206
Heudeline, Raymonde, 284
Heuring, Lori, 199, 277
Heuvelman, Charles, 182
Hewett, Christopher, 357
Hewitt, Jennifer Love, 29, 333
Hewitt, Martin, 333
Hewitt, Paul, 196
Hewitt, Peter, 307
Hewtrey, Kay, 116
Heyday Films, 132
Heyman, David, 132
Heysen, Kerry, 104
Heywood, Anne, 333
Hibbin, Sally, 275
Hick, Jochen, 305
Hickey, John Benjamin, 58–59, 190
Hickey, Paul, 302
Hickey, Todd, 193
Hickman, Darryl, 333
Hickman, Devert, 191
Hickman, Dwayne, 333
Hicks, Catherine, 333
Hicks, Lara, 115
Hicks, Merritt, 94
Hicks, Michele, 203, 277
Hicks, Richard, 250
Hicks, Scott, 104
Hicks, Timothy Redmond, 203
Hicks, Tish, 182
Hicks, Yeskel, 238
Hidalgo, Mary, 126
Hidari, Sachiko, 310
Hidden Half, The, 314
Hidden Wars of Desert Storm, 179
Hier, Rabbi Marvin, 193
Higgins, Amy, 18
Higgins, Anthony, 333
Higgins, Billy, 192
Higgins, Bob, 47
Higgins, Douglas, 120
Higgins, John, 307
Higgins, John Michael, 125
Higgins, Michael, 333
Higgins, Paul, 243
High, Delbert, 184
High Heels and Low Lifes, 317–18
High, Joel, 162
Highsmith, Asio, 107
Higlin, David, 209
Hikawa, Dale, 83
Hilary-Lakin, Leigh, 13
Hild, Jim, 36
Hildebrandt, Jason, 165
Hilfiger, Tommy, 107

399

428